Microsoft®
Office 2013
ILLUSTRATED

First Course   Second Course   Third Course

Microsoft®
Office 2013
ILLUSTRATED

First Course | Second Course | **Third Course**

Cram/Friedrichsen/Wermers

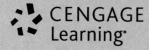
CENGAGE
Learning·

Australia • Brazil • Japan • Korea • Mexico • Singapore • Spain • United Kingdom • United States

CENGAGE
Learning®

Microsoft® Office 2013—Illustrated Third Course
Cram/Friedrichsen/Wermers

Senior Product Team Manager: Marjorie Hunt

Associate Product Manager: Amanda Lyons

Senior Content Developer: Christina Kling-Garrett

Content Developer: Kim Klasner

Product Assistant: Brandelynn Perry

Brand Manager: Elinor Gregory

Print Buyer: Fola Orekoya

Developmental Editors: Barbara Clemens,
 Pamela Conrad, Lisa Ruffolo

Senior Content Project Manager: Catherine G.
 DiMassa

Copyeditors: Karen Annett, Mark Goodin,
 Kathy Orrino

Proofreaders: Brandy Lilly, Lisa Weidenfeld,
 Vicki Zimmer

Indexer: Alexandra Nickerson

QA Manuscript Reviewers: John Freitas, Susan
 Pedicini, Danielle Shaw, Susan Whalen,
 Jeff Schwartz

Cover Designer: GEX Publishing Services

Cover Artist: Dimec/Shutterstock

Composition: GEX Publishing Services

For product information and technology assistance, contact us at
Cengage Learning Customer & Sales Support, 1-800-354-9706
For permission to use material from this text or product, submit all requests online at **www.cengage.com/permissions**
Further permissions questions can be emailed to
permissionrequest@cengage.com

Library of Congress Control Number: 2013945550

ISBN-13: 978-1-285-08246-2
ISBN-10: 1-285-08246-X

Cengage Learning
200 First Stamford Place, 4th Floor
Stamford, CT 06902
USA

Cengage Learning is a leading provider of customized learning solutions with office locations around the globe, including Singapore, the United Kingdom, Australia, Mexico, Brazil, and Japan. Locate your local office at:
www.cengage.com/global

Cengage Learning products are represented in Canada by
Nelson Education, Ltd.

For your course and learning solutions, visit **www.cengage.com**

Purchase any of our products at your local college store or at our preferred online store **www.cengagebrain.com**

Trademarks:
Some of the product names and company names used in this book have been used for identification purposes only and may be trademarks or
registered trademarks of their respective manufacturers and sellers.

Microsoft and the Windows logo are registered trademarks of Microsoft Corporation in the United States and/or other countries. Cengage Learning is an independent entity from Microsoft Corporation, and not affiliated with Microsoft in any manner.

Printed in the United States of America
1 2 3 4 5 6 7 19 18 17 16 15 14 13

Brief Contents

Contents

Word 2013

Access 2013

Preface

Welcome to *Microsoft Office 2013—Illustrated Third Course*. This book has a unique design: Each skill is presented on two facing pages, with steps on the left and screens on the right. The layout makes it easy to learn a skill without having to read a lot of text and flip pages to see an illustration.

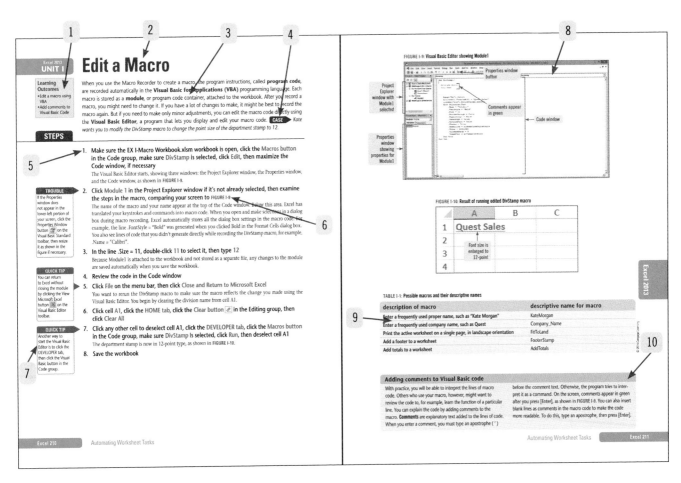

1   New! Learning Outcomes box lists measurable learning goals for which a student is accountable in that lesson.

2   Each two-page lesson focuses on a single skill.

3   Introduction briefly explains why the lesson skill is important.

4   A case scenario motivates the steps and puts learning in context.

5   Step-by-step instructions and brief explanations guide students through each hands-on lesson activity.

6   New! Figure references are now in red bold to help students refer back and forth between the steps and screenshots.

7   Tips and troubleshooting advice, right where you need it—next to the step itself.

8   New! Larger screen shots with green callouts now placed on top keep students on track as they complete steps.

9   Tables provide summaries of helpful information such as button references or keyboard shortcuts.

10 Clues to Use yellow boxes provide useful information related to the lesson skill.

This book is an ideal learning tool for a wide range of learners—the "rookies" will find the clean design easy to follow and focused with only essential information presented, and the "hotshots" will appreciate being able to move quickly through the lessons to find the information they need without reading a lot of text. The design also makes this book a great reference after the course is over! See the illustration on the left to learn more about the pedagogical and design elements of a typical lesson.

What's New in this Edition

- **Coverage** — This book is a continuation of *Microsoft Office 2013 Illustrated, Second Course*, covering advanced skills for using Word, Excel, and Access.

- **New! Learning Outcomes** — Each lesson displays a green Learning Outcomes box that lists skills-based or knowledge-based learning goals for which students are accountable. Each Learning Outcome maps to a variety of learning activities and assessments. (See the *New! Learning Outcomes* section on page xx for more information.)

- **New! Updated Design** — This edition features many new design Improvements to engage students — including larger lesson screenshots with green callouts placed on top, and a refreshed Unit Opener page.

- **New! Independent Challenge 4: Explore** — This new case-based assessment activity allows students to explore new skills and use creativity to solve a problem or create a project.

Assignments

This book includes a wide variety of high-quality assignments you can use for practice and assessment. Assignments include:

- **Concepts Review** — Multiple choice, matching, and screen identification questions.

- **Skills Review** — Step-by-step, hands-on review of every skill covered in the unit.

- **Independent Challenges 1-3** — Case projects requiring critical thinking and application of the unit skills. The Independent Challenges increase in difficulty. The first one in each unit provides the most hand-holding; the subsequent ones provide less guidance and require more critical thinking and independent problem solving.

- **Independent Challenge 4: Explore** — Case projects that let students explore new skills that are related to the core skills covered in the unit and are often more open ended, allowing students to use creativity to complete the assignment.

- **Visual Workshop** — Critical thinking exercises that require students to create a project by looking at a completed solution; they must apply the skills they've learned in the unit and use critical thinking skills to create the project from scratch.

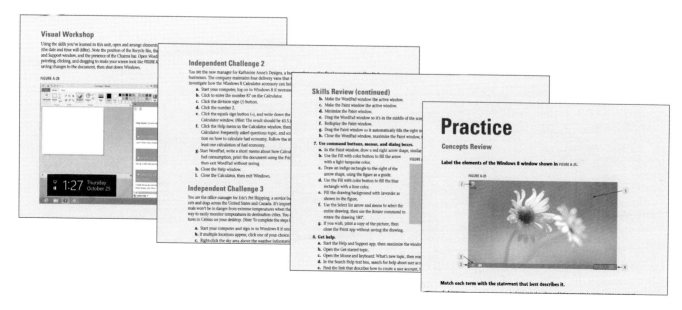

New! Learning Outcomes

Every 2-page lesson in this book now contains a green **Learning Outcomes box** that states the learning goals for that lesson.

- **What is a learning outcome?** A learning outcome states what a student is expected to know or be able to do after completing a lesson. Each learning outcome is skill-based or knowledge-based and is *measurable*. Learning outcomes map to learning activities and assessments.

- **How do students benefit from learning outcomes?** Learning outcomes tell students exactly what skills and knowledge they are *accountable* for learning in that lesson. This helps students study more efficiently and effectively and makes them more active learners.

- **How do instructors benefit from learning outcomes?** Learning outcomes provide clear, measurable, skills-based learning goals that map to various high-quality learning activities and assessments. A **Learning Outcomes Map**, available for each unit in this book, maps every learning outcome to the learning activities and assessments shown below.

Learning Outcomes Map to These Learning Activities:

1. **Book lessons:** Step-by-step tutorial on one skill presented in a two-page learning format
2. **SAM Training:** Short animations and hands-on practice activities in simulated environment

Learning Outcomes Map to These Assessments:

1. **End-of-Unit Exercises: Concepts Review** (screen identification, matching, multiple choice); **Skills Review** (hands-on review of each lesson); **Independent Challenges** (hands-on, case-based review of specific skills); **Visual Workshop** (activity that requires student to build a project by looking at a picture of the final solution).
2. **Exam View Test Banks:** Objective-based questions you can use for online or paper testing.
3. **SAM Assessment:** Performance-based assessment in a simulated environment.
4. **SAM Projects:** Auto-graded projects for Word, Excel, Access and PowerPoint that students create live in the application.
5. **Extra Independent Challenges:** Extra case-based exercises available in the Instructor Resources that cover various skills.

Learning Outcomes Map

A **Learning Outcomes Map**, contained in the Instructor Resources, provides a listing of learning activities and assessments for each learning outcome in the book.

	Concepts Review	Skills Review	IC1	IC2	IC3	IC4	VW	Cap1	Cap2	EIC1	EIC2	Test Bank	SAM Assessment	SAM Projects	SAM Training
Format with fonts															
Change font and font size		✓	✓	✓	✓	✓	✓	✓	✓			✓	✓	✓	✓
Change font color		✓	✓	✓	✓	✓	✓	✓	✓	✓		✓	✓		✓
Select entire document		✓	✓	✓			✓			✓	✓	✓			
Copy formats using the Format Painter															
Apply font styles and effects		✓	✓	✓			✓	✓	✓	✓		✓	✓	✓	✓
Add a shadow to text							✓			✓	✓	✓	✓	✓	✓
Change character spacing		✓		✓			✓		✓	✓	✓	✓			
Change line and paragraph spacing															
Add spacing under paragraphs		✓	✓	✓			✓	✓	✓		✓		✓	✓	
Change line spacing in paragraphs		✓				✓			✓	✓	✓	✓	✓	✓	✓
Apply styles to text		✓	✓	✓	✓			✓			✓	✓	✓	✓	✓
Align paragraphs															
Center text		✓	✓	✓	✓	✓	✓		✓	✓		✓	✓		✓
Justify text		✓						✓	✓	✓		✓	✓	✓	✓
Right-align text		✓				✓	✓		✓		✓		✓	✓	✓
Work with tabs															
Set tab stops and tab leaders		✓	✓	✓			✓	✓				✓	✓	✓	✓
Modify tabs	✓	✓	✓			✓	✓		✓	✓		✓	✓		✓
Use tabs to align text		✓	✓	✓	✓		✓					✓	✓		✓
Work with indents															
Indent a paragraph	✓	✓		✓											
Indent the first line		✓													

WHAT'S NEW FOR SAM 2013?

Get your students workplace ready with

The market-leading assessment and training solution for Microsoft Office

SAM 2013

Exciting New Features and Content

➤ Computer Concepts Trainings and Assessments *(shown on monitor)*

➤ Student Assignment Calendar

➤ All New SAM Projects

➤ Mac Hints

➤ More MindTap Readers

More Efficient Course Setup and Management Tools

➤ Individual Assignment Tool

➤ Video Playback of Student Clickpaths

➤ Express Assignment Creation Tool

Improved Grade Book and Reporting Tools

➤ Institutional Reporting

➤ Frequency Analysis Report

➤ Grade Book Enhancements

➤ Partial Credit Grading for Projects

SAM's active, hands-on environment helps students master Microsoft Office skills and computer concepts that are essential to academic and career success.

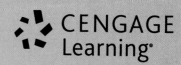

Instructor Resources

This book comes with a wide array of high-quality technology-based, teaching tools to help you teach and to help students learn. The following teaching tools are available for download at our Instructor Companion Site. Simply search for this text at *login.cengage.com*. An instructor login is required.

- **New! Learning Outcomes Map** — A detailed grid for each unit (in Excel format) shows the learning activities and assessments that map to each learning outcome in that unit.

- **Instructor's Manual** — Available as an electronic file, the Instructor's Manual includes lecture notes with teaching tips for each unit.

- **Sample Syllabus** — Prepare and customize your course easily using this sample course outline.

- **PowerPoint Presentations** — Each unit has a corresponding PowerPoint presentation covering the skills and topics in that unit that you can use in lectures, distribute to your students, or customize to suit your course.

- **Figure Files** — The figures in the text are provided on the Instructor Resources site to help you illustrate key topics or concepts. You can use these to create your own slide shows or learning tools.

- **Solution Files** — Solution Files are files that contain the finished project that students create or modify in the lessons or end-of-unit material.

- **Solutions Document** — This document outlines the solutions for the end-of-unit Concepts Review, Skills Review, Independent Challenges and Visual Workshops. An Annotated Solution File and Grading Rubric accompany each file and can be used together for efficient grading.

- **ExamView Test Banks** — ExamView is a powerful testing software package that allows you to create and administer printed, computer (LAN-based), and Internet exams. Our ExamView test banks include questions that correspond to the skills and concepts covered in this text, enabling students to generate detailed study guides that include page references for further review. The computer-based and Internet testing components allow students to take exams at their computers, and also save you time by grading each exam automatically.

Key Facts About Using This Book

Data Files are needed: To complete many of the lessons and end-of-unit assignments, students need to start from partially-completed Data Files, which help students learn more efficiently. By starting out with a Data File, students can focus on performing specific tasks without having to create a file from scratch. All Data Files are available as part of the Instructor Resources. Students can also download Data Files themselves for free at cengagebrain.com. (For detailed instructions, go to www.cengage.com/ct/studentdownload.)

System Requirements: This book was developed using Microsoft Office 2013 Professional running on Windows 8. Note that Windows 8 is not a requirement for the units on Microsoft Office; Office 2013 runs virtually the same on Windows 7 and Windows 8. Please see Important Notes for Windows 7 Users on the next page for more information.

Screen Resolution: This book was written and tested on computers with monitors set at a resolution of 1366 x 768. If your screen shows more or less information than the figures in this book, your monitor is probably set at a higher or lower resolution. If you don't see something on your screen, you might have to scroll down or up to see the object identified in the figure.

Tell Us What You Think!

We want to hear from you! Please email your questions, comments, and suggestions to the Illustrated Series team at: **illustratedseries@cengage.com**

Important Notes for Windows 7 Users

The screenshots in this book show Microsoft Office 2013 running on Windows 8. However, if you are using Microsoft Windows 7, you can still use this book because Office 2013 runs virtually the same on both platforms. There are only two differences that you will encounter if you are using Windows 7. Read this section to understand the differences.

Dialog boxes

If you are a Windows 7 user, dialog boxes shown in this book will look slightly different than what you see on your screen. Dialog boxes for Windows 7 have a light blue title bar, instead of a medium blue title bar. However, beyond this superficial difference in appearance, the options in the dialog boxes across platforms are the same. For instance, the screen shots below show the Font dialog box running on Windows 7 and the Font dialog box running on Windows 8.

FIGURE 1: Font dialog box in Windows 7

FIGURE 2: Font dialog box in Windows 8

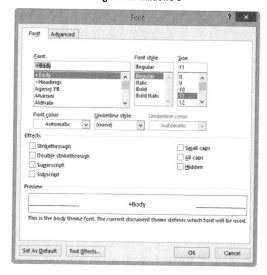

Alternate Steps for Starting an App in Windows 7

Nearly all of the steps in this book work exactly the same for Windows 7 users. However, starting an app (or program/application) requires different steps for Windows 7. The steps below show the Windows 7 steps for starting an app. (Note: Windows 7 alternate steps also appear in red Trouble boxes next to any step in the book that requires starting an app.)

Starting an app (or program/application) using Windows 7

1. Click the **Start button** on the taskbar to open the Start menu.
2. Click **All Programs**, then click the **Microsoft Office 2013 folder**. See Figure 3.
3. Click the app you want to use (such as **Excel 2013**)

FIGURE 3: Starting an app using Windows 7

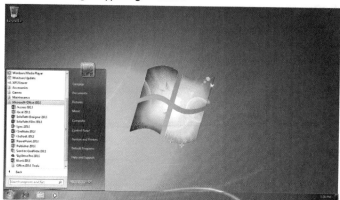

Acknowledgements

Author Acknowledgements

A big thank you to my developmental editor Pam Conrad for her patience, good humor, and insight! And, as always, everything I do is made possible by Gregg and Julia. They make everything worthwhile.

–**Carol Cram**

The Access portion is dedicated to my students, and all who are using this book to teach and learn about Access. Thank you. Also, thank you to all of the professionals who helped me create this book.

–**Lisa Friedrichsen**

Thanks to Barbara Clemens for her insightful contributions, invaluable feedback, great humor, and patience. Thanks also to Christina Kling-Garrett for her encouragement and support in guiding and managing this project.

–**Lynn Wermers**

Advisory Board Acknowledgements

We thank our Illustrated Advisory Board who gave us their opinions and guided our decisions as we developed this edition. They are as follows:

Merlin Amirtharaj, Stanly Community College

Londo Andrews, J. Sargeant Reynolds Community College

Rachelle Hall, Glendale Community College

Terri Helfand, Chaffey Community College

Sheryl Lenhart, Terra Community College

Dr. Jose Nieves, Lord Fairfax Community College

Develop Multipage Documents

CASE As a marketing assistant at the head office of Quest Specialty Travel in San Diego, you have been asked to edit and format a set of guidelines to help QST managers sponsor tour presentations, tour information sessions, and travel clubs. You start by working in Outline view to revise the structure for the guidelines, and then you use several advanced Word features to format the document for publication.

Unit Objectives

After completing this unit, you will be able to:

- Build a document in Outline view
- Work in Outline view
- Navigate a document
- Insert a table of contents
- Mark text for an index

- Generate an index
- Insert footers in multiple sections
- Insert headers in multiple sections
- Finalize a multipage document

Files You Will Need

WD I-1.docx	WD I-6.docx
WD I-2.docx	WD I-7.docx
WD I-3.docx	WD I-8.docx
WD I-4.docx	WD I-9.docx
WD I-5.docx	WD I-10.docx

Build a Document in Outline View

You work in Outline view to organize the headings and subheadings that identify topics and subtopics in multipage documents. In Outline view, each heading is assigned a level from 1 to 9, with Level 1 being the highest level and Level 9 being the lowest level. In addition, you can assign the Body Text level to each paragraph of text that appears below a document heading. Each level is formatted with one of Word's predefined styles. For example, Level 1 is formatted with the Heading 1 style, and the Body Text level is formatted with the Normal style. **CASE** ▶ *You work in Outline view to develop the structure of the Tour Presentation Guidelines.*

STEPS

1. **Start Word, create a new blank document, click the** VIEW **tab, then click the** Outline **button in the Views group**

   The document appears in Outline view. Notice that the OUTLINING tab is now active. **TABLE I-1** describes the buttons on the OUTLINING tab.

TROUBLE
If the headings do not appear blue and bold, click the Show Text Formatting check box in the Outline Tools group to select it.

2. **Type** Tour Presentation

   FIGURE I-1 shows the text in Outline view. By default, the text appears at the left margin and is designated as Level 1. By default, Level 1 text is formatted with the Heading 1 style. You will work more with styles in the next unit.

3. **Press [Enter], click the** Demote button ➔ **in the Outline Tools group to move to Level 2, then type** Presentation Structure

   The text is indented, designated as Level 2, and formatted with the Heading 2 style.

4. **Press [Enter], then click the** Demote to Body Text button ⇒ **in the Outline Tools group**

5. **Type the following text:** Three activities relate to the organization of a QST Tour Presentation: gather personnel, advertise the event, and arrange the physical space.

   The text is indented, designated as Body Text level, and formatted with the Normal style. Notice that both the Level 1 and Level 2 text are preceded by a plus symbol ⊕. This symbol indicates that the heading includes subtext, which could be another subheading or a paragraph of body text.

6. **Press [Enter], then click the** Promote to Heading 1 button ⇐ **in the Outline Tools group**

   The insertion point returns to the left margin and the Level 1 position.

7. **Type** Personnel**, press [Enter], then save the document as** WD I-Tour Presentation Outline **to the location where you store your Data Files**

   When you create a long document, you often enter all the headings and subheadings first to establish the overall structure of your document.

QUICK TIP
You can press [Tab] to move from a higher level to a lower level, and you can press [Shift][Tab] to move from a lower level to a higher level.

8. **Use the** Promote ⇐**,** Demote ➔**, and** Promote to Heading 1 ⇐ **buttons to complete the outline shown in** FIGURE I-2

9. **Place the insertion point after** Tour Presentation **at the top of the page, press [Enter], click** ⇒**, type** Prepared by **followed by your name, save the document, submit it to your instructor, then close it**

FIGURE I-1: Text in Outline view

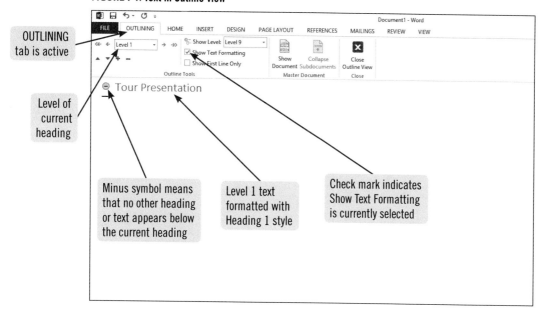

FIGURE I-2: Completed outline

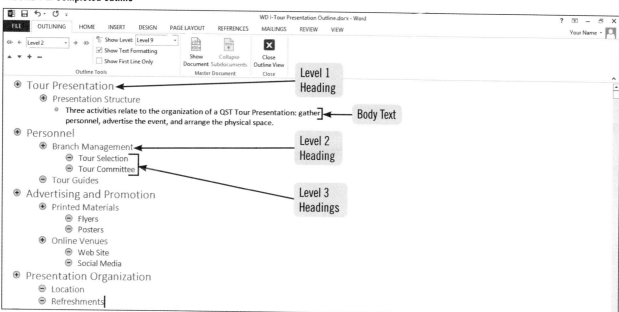

TABLE I-1: Frequently used outlining buttons in the Outline Tools group on the OUTLINING tab

button	use to	button	use to
≪	Promote text to Heading 1	▲	Move a heading and its text up one line
←	Promote text one level	▼	Move a heading and its text down one line
→	Demote text one level	＋	Expand text
≫	Demote to body text	－	Collapse text

Work in Outline View

In Outline view, you can promote and demote headings and subheadings and move or delete whole blocks of text. When you move a heading in Outline view, all of the text and subheadings under that heading move with the heading. You also can use the Collapse, Expand, and Show Level commands on the OUTLINING tab to view all or just some of the headings and subheadings. For example, you can choose to view just the headings assigned to Level 1 so that you can quickly evaluate the main topics of your document. **CASE** ▶ *You work in Outline view to develop a draft of the guidelines for running a tour presentation. In Outline view, each heading is formatted with a heading style based on its corresponding level.*

STEPS

1. **Open the file** WD I-1.docx **from the location where you store your Data Files, save the document as** WD I-Tour Presentation Guidelines, **scroll through the document to get a sense of its content, click the** VIEW tab, **then click** Outline **in the Views group**

   The document changes to Outline view, and the OUTLINING tab opens. The chart at the end of the document is not visible in Outline view.

2. **Click the** Show Level list arrow **in the Outline Tools group, then click** Level 1

   Only the headings assigned to Level 1 appear. All the headings assigned to Level 1 are formatted with the Heading 1 style. Notice that the title of the document Tour Presentation Guidelines does not appear because the title text is not formatted as Level 1.

3. **Click the** plus sign ⊕ **to the left of Printed Materials**

   The heading and all its subtext (which is hidden because the topic is collapsed) are selected.

4. **Press and hold** [Shift], **click the heading** Online Venues, **release** [Shift], **then click the** Demote button → **in the Outline Tools group**

   You use [Shift] to select several adjacent headings at once. The headings are demoted one level to Level 2, as shown in **FIGURE I-3**.

5. **Press** [Ctrl][A] **to select all the headings, then click the** Expand button ⊞ **in the Outline Tools group**

   The outline expands to show all the subheadings and body text associated with each of the selected headings along with the document title. You can also expand a single heading by selecting only that heading and then clicking the Expand button.

6. **Click the** plus sign ⊕ **next to Advertising and Promotion, click the** Collapse button ⊟ **in the Outline Tools group two times to collapse all the subheadings and text associated with the heading, then double-click** ⊕ **next to Personnel to collapse it**

   You can double-click headings to expand or collapse them, or you can use the Expand or Collapse buttons.

7. **Click the** Move Up button ▲ **in the Outline Tools group once, then double-click** ⊕ **next to Personnel**

   When you move a heading in Outline view, all subtext and text associated with the heading also move.

8. **Click the** Show Level list arrow, **select** Level 3, **double-click** ⊕ **next to Printed Materials under the Advertising and Promotion heading, click** ⊕ **next to Counter Items, then press** [Delete]

   The Counter Items heading and its associated subtext are deleted from the document. The revised outline is shown in **FIGURE I-4**.

9. **Click the** Show Level list arrow, **click** All Levels, **click the** Close Outline View button **in the Close group, then save the document**

FIGURE I-3: Headings demoted to Level 2

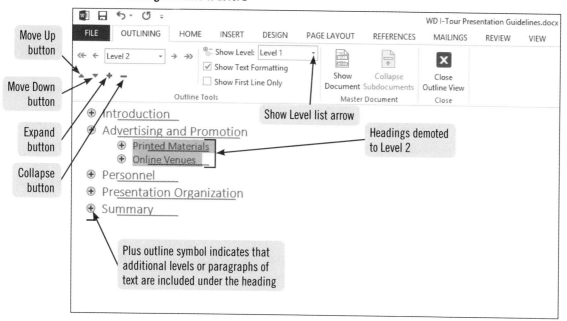

FIGURE I-4: Revised outline

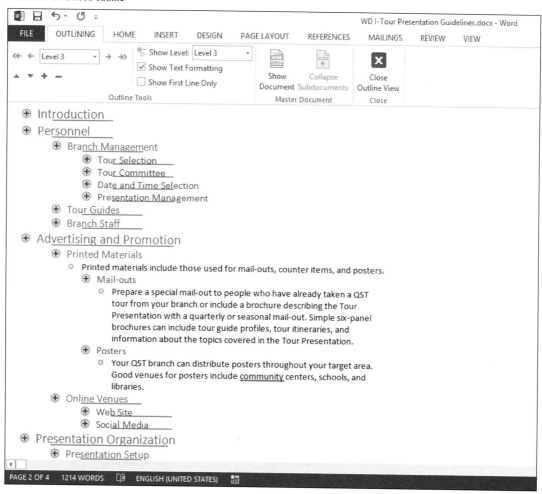

Navigate a Document

Learning Outcomes
- Collapse/expand headings: Print Layout view
- Move headings in the Navigation pane
- Create a cross-reference

After you develop the headings and subheadings that make up the structure of your document in Outline view, you work in Print Layout view to add more text. You can expand and collapse headings and subheadings in Print Layout view so you can quickly see the structure of your document. Finally, you can make adjustments to the document structure in the Navigation pane, which you open from Print Layout view. The **Navigation pane** opens along the left side of the document window and shows all the headings and subheadings in the document. You can click a heading in the Navigation pane to move directly to it, and you can drag and drop headings to change their order just like you do in Outline view. You can also view thumbnails of the document pages in the Navigation pane. In addition to using the Navigation pane to navigate a document, you can create cross-references in your document. A **cross-reference** is text that electronically refers the reader to another part of the document, such as a numbered paragraph, a heading, or a figure. **CASE** ▶ *You expand and collapse headings in Print Layout view, work in the Navigation pane to make further changes to the document and then add a cross-reference to a heading.*

STEPS

1. **Press [Ctrl][Home], click Introduction, move the mouse slightly to the left to show the ◢, then click ◢**

   The paragraph under the Introduction heading is hidden. You can click ▷ to expand the heading again so you read the text associated with it.

2. **Right-click Introduction, point to Expand/Collapse, then click Collapse All Headings**

   Only Level 1 headings are visible.

3. **Right-click Introduction, point to Expand/Collapse, then click Expand All Headings**

   All headings and their associated text are visible again.

TROUBLE
If the headings do not show, click HEADINGS at the top of the Navigation pane

4. **Click the VIEW tab, click the Navigation Pane check box in the Show group, then click Branch Staff in the Navigation pane**

   The Branch Staff subheading is selected in the Navigation pane, and the insertion point moves to the Branch Staff subheading in the document.

5. **Drag Branch Staff up so that it appears above Tour Guides as shown in FIGURE I-5**

   The order of the headings in the Navigation pane and in the document change.

6. **Click PAGES at the top of the Navigation pane, scroll up and click the page 1 thumbnail, then double-click summary in paragraph 2 of the Introduction to select it**

7. **Click the INSERT tab, click Cross-reference in the Links group, click the Reference type list arrow, then click Heading**

   The Cross-reference dialog box opens and all the headings and subheadings in the document are listed.

8. **Scroll to and click Summary as shown in FIGURE I-6**

   In the Cross-reference dialog box you can also create a cross-reference to a numbered item, a bookmark, a footnote or an endnote, an equation that has been created with the Equation Editor, a figure such as a chart, a picture, or a diagram, and a table.

9. **Click Insert, click Close, then insert a space after Summary**

   The word "Summary" is now a hyperlink to the Summary heading at the end of the document.

10. **Move the pointer over Summary to show the Click message, press and hold [Ctrl] to show 🖑, click Summary to move directly to the Summary heading, click ✖ to close the Navigation pane, then save the document**

FIGURE I-5: Changing the order of a subheading in the Navigation pane

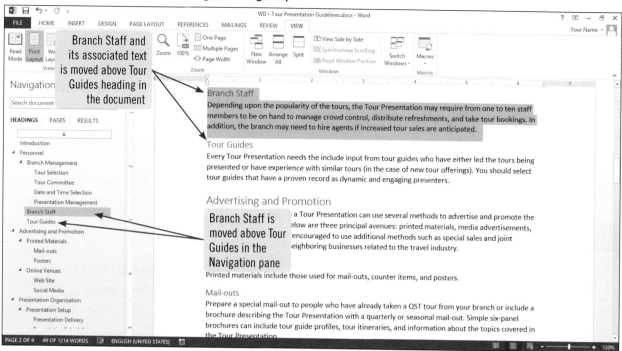

FIGURE I-6: Cross-reference dialog box

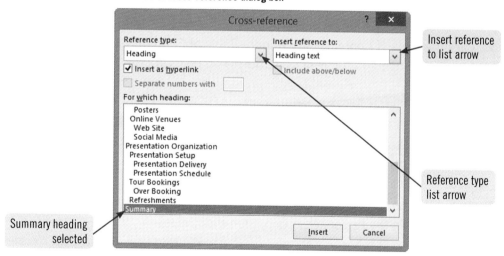

Using bookmarks

A **bookmark** identifies a location or a selection of text in a document. To create a bookmark, you first move the insertion point to the location in the text that you want to reference. This location can be a word, the beginning of a paragraph, or a heading. Click the INSERT tab, then click Bookmark in the Links group to open the Bookmark dialog box. In this dialog box, you type a name (which cannot contain spaces) for the bookmark, then click Add. To find a bookmark, press [Ctrl][G] to open the Find and Replace dialog box with the Go To tab active, click Bookmark in the Go to what list box, click the Enter bookmark name list arrow to see the list of bookmarks in the document, select the bookmark you require, click Go To, then close the Find and Replace dialog box. To delete a bookmark you no longer need, click Bookmark in the Links group, click the bookmark you want to remove, then click Delete in the Bookmark dialog box.

Insert a Table of Contents

Learning Outcomes
- Insert a table of contents
- Update a table of contents

Readers refer to a table of contents to obtain an overview of the topics and subtopics covered in a multipage document. When you generate a table of contents, Word searches for headings, sorts them by heading levels, and then displays the completed table of contents in the document. By default, a table of contents lists the top three heading levels in a document. Consequently, before you create a table of contents, you must ensure that all headings and subheadings are formatted with heading styles such as Heading 1, Heading 2, and Heading 3. When you work in Outline view, the correct heading styles are assigned automatically to text based on the outline level of the text. For example, the Heading 1 style is applied to Level 1 text, the Heading 2 style to Level 2 text, and so on. **CASE** ➤ *You are pleased with the content of the document and are now ready to create a new page that includes a table of contents. You use commands on the REFERENCES tab to generate a table of contents.*

STEPS

1. **Press [Ctrl][Home], click the** INSERT tab, **then click** Blank Page **in the Pages group**

2. **Press [Ctrl][Home], click the** HOME tab, **then click the** Clear All Formatting button 🅰❖ **in the Font group**

   The insertion point is positioned at the left margin where the table of contents will begin.

3. **Click the** REFERENCES tab, **then click the** Table of Contents button **in the Table of Contents group**

   A gallery of predefined styles for a table of contents opens.

4. **Click** Automatic Table 2 **as shown in** FIGURE 1-7, **then scroll up to see the table of contents**

   A table of contents that includes all the Level 1, 2, and 3 headings is inserted on page 1.

5. **Click the** Table of Contents button **in the Table of Contents group, click** Custom Table of Contents **to open the Table of Contents dialog box, click the** Formats list arrow, **then click** Formal

   The Table of Contents dialog box opens, as shown in **FIGURE I-8.**

6. **Click** OK, **click** Yes, **click the** VIEW tab, **click the** Navigation Pane check box **in the Show group to open the Navigation pane, then click** HEADINGS **at the top of the Navigation pane**

   In the Navigation pane, you can move quickly to a section of the document and delete it.

7. **Right-click the** Presentation Management subheading **below the Branch Management subheading in the Personnel section, then click** Delete

   The Presentation Management subheading and its related subtext are deleted from the document but the heading is not yet deleted from the table of contents.

8. **Scroll to the top of the table of contents, then click** Update Table

   The table of contents is updated. The Presentation Management subheading is no longer listed in the table of contents.

9. **Move the pointer over the heading** Online Venues, **press [Ctrl], click** Online Venues, **then save the document**

   The insertion point moves to the Online Venues heading in the document. The Navigation pane remains open.

FIGURE I-7: Inserting an automatic table of contents

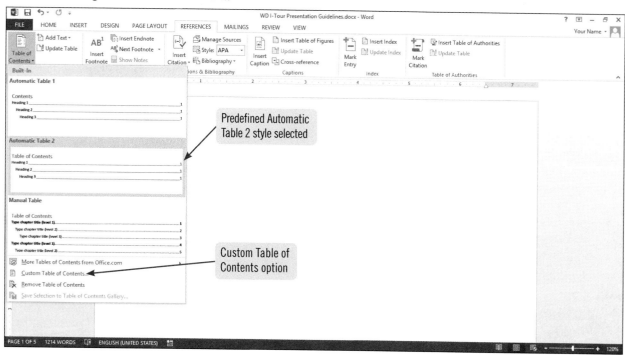

FIGURE I-8: Table of Contents dialog box

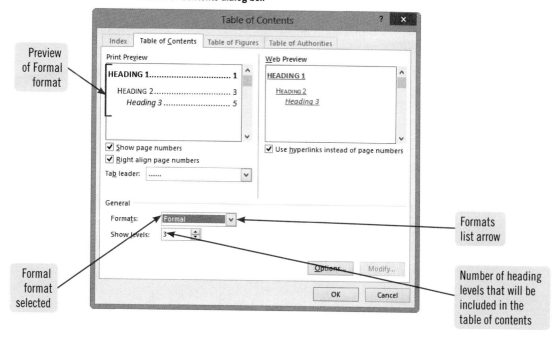

Mark Text for an Index

Learning Outcomes
• Mark index entries
• Search for text

An **index** lists many of the terms and topics included in a document, along with the pages on which they appear. An index can include main entries, subentries, and cross-references. **CASE** ▶ *To help readers quickly find main concepts in the document, you decide to generate an index. You get started by marking the terms that you want to include as main entries in the index.*

STEPS

1. **Press [Ctrl][Home], press [Ctrl], then click Introduction in the table of contents**

   The insertion point moves to the Introduction heading in the document.

2. **Click Personnel in the Navigation pane, select branch staff in the second line under the Personnel heading in the document, click the REFERENCES tab, then click the Mark Entry button in the Index group**

   The Mark Index Entry dialog box opens. By default, the selected text is entered in the Main entry text box and is treated as a main entry in the index.

3. **Click Mark All, click the Mark Index Entry dialog box title bar, then use your mouse to drag the dialog box down so you can see "branch staff" as shown in FIGURE I-9.**

   Notice the term "branch staff" is marked with the XE field code. **XE** stands for **Index Entry**. When you mark an entry for the index, the paragraph marks are turned on automatically so that you can see hidden codes such as paragraph marks, field codes, page breaks, and section breaks. These codes do not appear in the printed document. The Mark Index Entry dialog box remains open so that you can continue to mark text for inclusion in the index.

4. **Click anywhere in the document to deselect the current index entry, click RESULTS at the top of the Navigation pane, then type branch manager in the Search Document text box in the Navigation pane**

   Each occurrence of the term "branch manager" is shown in context and in bold in the Navigation pane, and each occurrence is highlighted in the document.

5. **Click the first instance of branch manager in the Navigation pane, then click the title bar of the Mark Index Entry dialog box**

   The text "branch manager" appears in the Main entry text box in the Mark Index Entry dialog box.

6. **Click Mark All**

   All instances of "branch manager" in the document are marked for inclusion in the index.

7. **Click anywhere in the document, type theme in the Search Document text box, click the result in the Navigation pane, click the title bar of the Mark Index Entry dialog box, then click Mark All**

QUICK TIP
Make sure you click in the document to deselect the currently selected text before you enter another search term.

8. **Follow the procedure in Step 7 to find and mark all instances of the following main entries: brochures, target market, Ron Dawson, and shopping cart**

9. **Click ✕ to close the Mark Index Entry dialog box, then scroll up until you see the document title (Tour Presentation Guidelines)**

   You see two entries marked for the index, as shown in **FIGURE I-10**. The other entries you marked are further down the document.

FIGURE I-9: Selected text in the Mark Index Entry dialog box

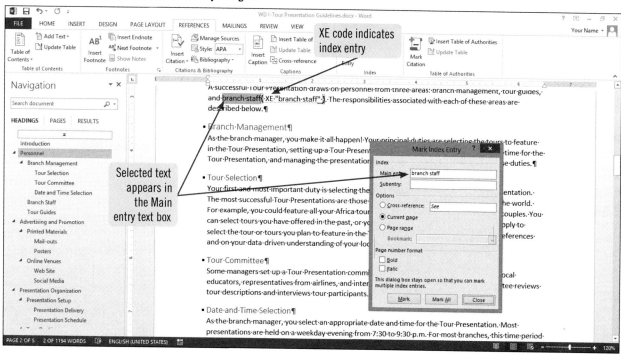

XE code indicates index entry

Selected text appears in the Main entry text box

FIGURE I-10: Index entries on the first page of the document

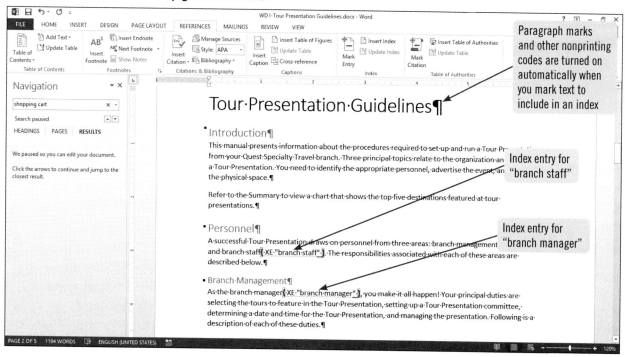

Paragraph marks and other nonprinting codes are turned on automatically when you mark text to include in an index

Index entry for "branch staff"

Index entry for "branch manager"

Generate an Index

Learning Outcomes
• Mark index subentries
• Insert a cross-reference in an index
• Generate an index

In addition to main entries, an index often includes subentries and cross-references. A **subentry** is text included under a main entry. For example, you could mark the text "shopping cart" as a subentry to appear under the main entry "Web site." A **cross-reference** in an index refers the reader to another entry in the index. For example, a cross-reference in an index might read, "lecture. *See* events." Once you have marked all the index entries, you select a design for the index, and then you generate it. If you make changes to the document, you can update the index just like you update a table of contents. **CASE** *You mark one subentry and one cross-reference for the index, create a new last page in the document, and then generate the index. You add one new main entry, and then update the index to reflect this change.*

STEPS

1. **Type** airlines **in the Search Document text box in the Navigation pane, click the entry that appears in the Navigation pane, then click** Mark Entry **in the Index group on the REFERENCES tab to open the Mark Index Entry dialog box**

   The search term "airlines" is already entered into the Mark Index Entry dialog box.

2. **Type** Tour Committee **in the Main entry text box, click in the** Subentry text box**, type** airline representatives **in the Subentry text box as shown in FIGURE I-11, then click** Mark

   The first and only instance of the text "airlines" is marked as a subentry renamed "airline representatives" that will appear following the Main entry, Tour Committee.

3. **Click anywhere in the document, type** laptops **in the Search Document text box, click the** Cross-reference option button **in the Mark Index Entry dialog box, click after** See**, type** bookings **as shown in FIGURE I-12, then click** Mark

   You need to also mark "bookings" so the Index lists the page number for "bookings."

TROUBLE
Drag the Mark Index Entry dialog box out of the way as needed to see the selected phrase.

4. **Click anywhere in the document, type** bookings **in the Search Document text box, click the entry in the Navigation pane that contains the phrase "bookings on the spot" (the fourth entry), double-click** bookings **in the phrase "bookings on the spot" in the document, click the** Mark Index Entry dialog box**, click** Mark**, then click** Close

   The term "laptops" is cross-referenced to the term "bookings" in the same paragraph. Now that you have marked entries for the index, you can generate the index at the end of the document.

5. **Press [Ctrl][End], press [Ctrl][Enter], type** Index**, press [Enter], select** Index**, click the HOME tab, apply** 18 pt**,** bold**, and** center alignment formatting**, then click at the left margin below Index**

6. **Click the REFERENCES tab, click** Insert Index **in the Index group, click the** Formats list arrow **in the Index dialog box, scroll down the list, click** Formal**, then click** OK

   Word has collected all the index entries, sorted them alphabetically, included the appropriate page numbers, and removed duplicate entries.

QUICK TIP
The refreshments entry that appears in the table of contents is not included because it appears before the entry you selected.

7. **Search for** refreshments**, click the** second instance **of "refreshments" (below Refreshments 4) in the search results in the Navigation pane, click the** Mark Entry button **in the Index Group, then click** Mark All

   The index now includes each instance of refreshments from the selected text to the end of the document.

8. **Close the dialog box and Navigation pane, scroll to the end of the document, right-click the index, click** Update Field**, click** Index **to deselect the index, then save the document**

   The updated index is shown in **FIGURE I-13**.

FIGURE I-11: Subentry in the Mark Index Entry dialog box

FIGURE I-12: Cross-reference in the Mark Index Entry dialog box

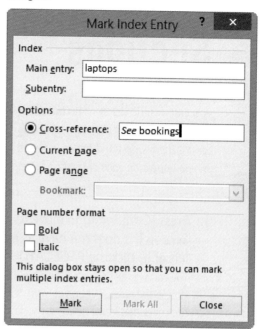

FIGURE I-13: Completed index

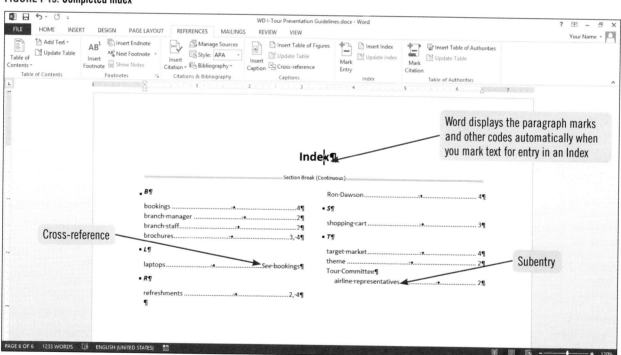

Learning Outcomes
- Insert sections
- Insert footers in sections

Insert Footers in Multiple Sections

Multipage documents often consist of two or more sections that you can format differently. For example, you can include different text in the footer for each section, and you can change how page numbers are formatted from section to section. **CASE** ▶ *You want to divide the report into two sections, and then format the headers and footers differently in each section. The diagram in* **FIGURE I-14** *explains how the footer should appear on each of the first three pages in the document.*

STEPS

1. **Press [Ctrl][Home] to move to the top of the document, right-click the** status bar, **click** Section **if it does not have a check mark next to it, scroll to the page break, click to the left of it, click the** PAGE LAYOUT tab, **then click** Breaks **in the Page Setup group**

   You can see the page break because the paragraph marks were turned on when you marked entries for inclusion in the index. When you work with sections, you should leave paragraph marks showing so you can see the codes that Word inserts for section breaks and page breaks.

2. **Click** Next Page **under Section Breaks, press [Delete] to remove the original page break, then press [Delete] to remove the extra blank line**

   The document is divided into two sections. Section 1 contains the Table of Contents and section 2 contains the rest of the document.

3. **Press [Ctrl][Home], click the** INSERT tab, **click the** Footer button **in the Header & Footer group, then click** Blank (Three Columns)

   The footer area opens showing the Blank (Three Columns) format.

4. **Click to the left of the placeholder text to select all three items, press [Delete], press [Tab] once, type** Page, **press [Spacebar], click the** Page Number button **in the Header & Footer group, point to** Current Position, **then click** Plain Number **(the top selection)**

   The current footer for the entire document contains the word Page and a page number.

5. **Click the** Page Number button, **click** Format Page Numbers, **click the** Number format list arrow, **click i, ii, iii, then click** OK

   The page number in the footer area of the table of contents page is formatted as i.

6. **Click** Next **in the Navigation group, then click the** Link to Previous button **in the Navigation group to deselect it**

   You deselect the Link to Previous button to make sure that the text you type into the footer appears only in the footer in section 2. You must deselect the Link to Previous button each time you want the header or footer in a section to be unique.

7. **Type your name, then press [Tab] once to move Page 2 to the right margin**

   By default, Word continues numbering the pages in section 2 based on the page numbers in section 1. The footer in section 2 starts with Page 2 because section 1 contains just one page. You want section 2 to start with Page 1 because the first page in section 2 is the first page of the report. Note also that the i, ii, iii format is not applied to the page number in section 2. Changes to page number formatting apply only to the section in which the change is made originally (in this case, section 1).

8. **Click the** Page Number button, **click** Format Page Numbers, **click the** Start at option button, **verify that 1 appears, click** OK, **then compare the footer to** FIGURE I-15

9. **Click the** Close Header and Footer button, **then save the document**

FIGURE I-14: Diagram of section formatting for footers

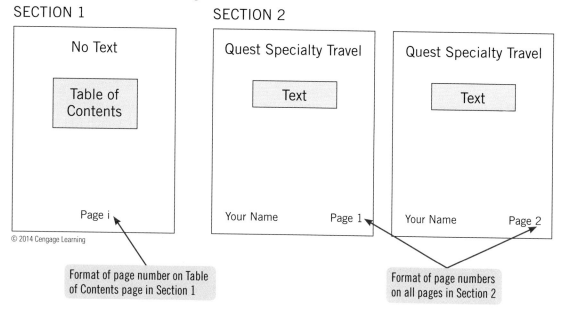

FIGURE I-15: Completed footer

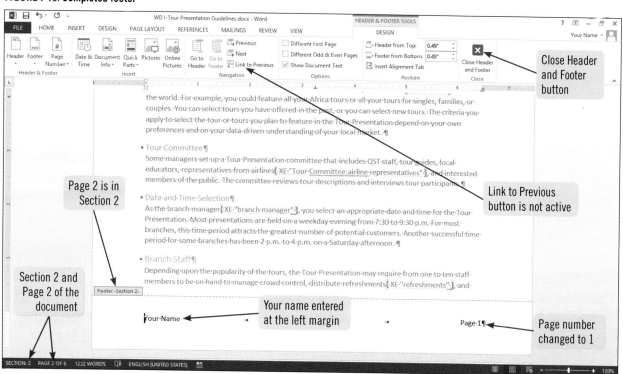

Using text flow options

You adjust text flow options to control how text in a multipage document breaks across pages. To change text flow options, you use the Paragraph dialog box. To open the Paragraph dialog box, click the launcher in the Paragraph group on the HOME tab, and then select the Line and Page Breaks tab. In the Pagination section, you can choose to select or deselect four text flow options.

For example, you select the Widow/Orphan control option to prevent the last line of a paragraph from printing at the top of a page (a widow) or the first line of a paragraph from printing at the bottom of a page (an orphan). By default, Widow/Orphan control is active. You can also select the Keep lines together check box to keep a paragraph from breaking across two pages.

Insert Headers in Multiple Sections

Learning Outcomes
• Insert headers in sections
• Add a cover page

When you divide your document into sections, you can modify the header to be different in each section. As you learned in the previous lesson, you must deselect the Link to Previous button when you want the text of a header (or footer) in a new section to be different from the header (or footer) in the previous section. **CASE** ▸ *The diagram in* **FIGURE I-16** *shows that text will appear in the header on every page in section 2. You do not want any text to appear in the header on the table of contents page (section 1). You modify the headers in the two sections of the document and then add a cover page.*

STEPS

1. **Press [Ctrl][Home] to move to the top of the document, then double-click in the blank area above Table of Contents**

   The header area opens. The Header -Section 1- identifier appears along with the HEADER & FOOTER TOOLS DESIGN tab. Refer to **FIGURE I-16**. Notice that you do not want text in the header in section 1.

2. **Click Next in the Navigation group, then click the Link to Previous button to deselect it**

   The identifier Header -Section 2- appears. You want text to appear on all the pages of section 2. You deselect the Link to Previous button so that the text you type appears only on this page and on subsequent pages.

3. **Type Quest Specialty Travel, select the text, then use the Mini toolbar to increase the font size to 14 pt, apply bold, and apply italic**

4. **Click the Close Header and Footer button, notice that the page number for the Introduction in the table of contents is page 2, scroll up to see the Table of Contents head, click the Table of Contents head, click Update Table, then click OK**

   The page numbers in the table of contents are updated.

5. **Press [Ctrl][End] to move to the Index page, right-click the index, then click Update Field**

   The page numbers in the index are updated.

6. **Press [Ctrl][Home], click the INSERT tab, click Cover Page in the Pages group, scroll to view the selections, then select the Semaphore style**

   Several placeholders called content controls are included on the cover page. Before you add text to the content controls you want to keep, you delete the ones you don't need.

7. **Click DATE at the top of the page to show the Publish Date content control handle, click the content control handle to select it (the handle turns blue gray and the text in the control is shaded with light blue), press [Delete], click the frame of the text box that remains, press [Delete], then scroll to and delete the Company Address content control but not the text box surrounding it**

8. **Enter text as shown in FIGURE I-17**

9. **Save the document**

FIGURE I-16: Diagram of section formatting for headers

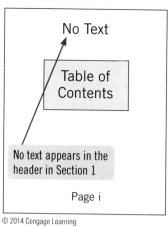
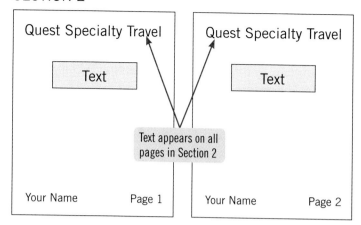

© 2014 Cengage Learning

FIGURE I-17: Text to type in cover page

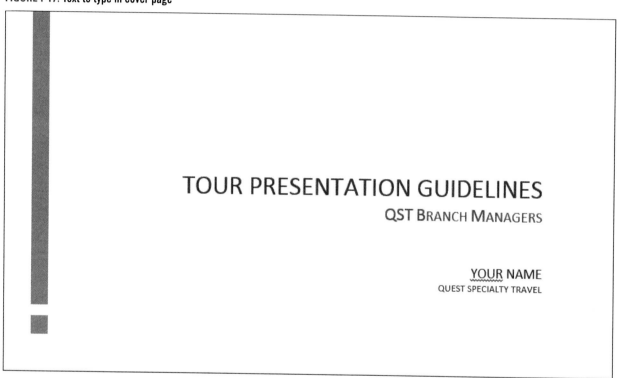

Understanding headers, footers, and sections

One reason you divide a document into sections is so that you can modify the page layout and the headers and footers differently in different sections. You can even modify the header and footer within a section because each section consists of two parts. The first part of a section is the first page, and the second part of the section is the remaining pages in the section. This section structure allows you to omit the header and footer on the first page of section 2, and then include the header and footer on all subsequent pages in section 2. To do this, place the insertion point in the section you want to modify, then click the Different First Page check box in the Options group to specify that you wish to include a different header and/or footer (or no header and footer at all) on the first page of a section. In addition, you can also choose to format odd and even pages in a document in different ways by clicking the Different Odd & Even Pages check box in the Options group. For example, you can choose to right-align the document title on odd-numbered pages and left-align the chapter indicator on even-numbered pages.

Finalize a Multipage Document

Learning
Outcomes
• Use Resume
Reading
• Customize a table
of contents

The Resume Reading feature takes you to the last location you were working on before you saved and closed a document. You can customize the table of contents so that readers can identify the document structure. By default, a table of contents shows only headings formatted with the Heading 1, Heading 2, or Heading 3 styles (Levels 1, 2, and 3 in Outline view). You can also include headings formatted with other styles, such as the Title style or a style you create. **CASE** ▶ *You use the Resume Reading feature, modify the headers and footers, and then customize the table of contents.*

STEPS

1. **Make sure you've saved the document, press [Ctrl][G], be sure Page in the Go to what area is selected, type 5, click Go To, click Close, close the document, open the document, then click the Welcome back! notice**

   The Resume Reading feature returns you to where you were working before saving and closing the document.

2. **Scroll up to view the page break below the chart, select the page break, click the PAGE LAYOUT tab, click Breaks, then click Next Page in the Section Breaks area**

3. **Open WD I-2.docx, press [Ctrl][A] to select all the text, press [Ctrl][C] to copy all the text, switch to the WD I-Tour Presentation Guidelines document, press [Ctrl][V], click the FILE tab, click Save As, then save the document as WD I-Tour Guidelines**

   The three pages of the Information Session Guidelines document appear in their own section.

   QUICK TIP
   Make sure you click the Link to Previous button before you modify the header text.

4. **Scroll up to the Table of Contents page, double-click in the header area for section 1, click Next, select Quest Specialty Travel, type Tour Presentation Guidelines, click Next, click the Link to Previous button in the Navigation group to deselect it, change the header text to Information Session Guidelines, then close the header**

5. **Scroll to the Index page, insert a Next Page section break to the left of Index, double-click in the header area, click the Link to Previous button, delete the header text, then close the header**

   The document now contains four sections, and you have modified the header text in sections 2, 3, and 4.

   QUICK TIP
   The title of each document is not included in the table of contents so you cannot easily see which headings belong to which documents.

6. **Scroll up to the table of contents page and click the table of contents, click Update Table, click the Update entire table option button, then click OK**

7. **Click the REFERENCES tab, click the Table of Contents button, click Custom Table of Contents, click Options, select 1 next to Heading 1, type 2, type 3 next to Heading 2, type 4 next to Heading 3 as shown in FIGURE I-18, scroll down to Title, type 1 in the TOC level text box, then click OK until you are returned to the document**

   The Information Session document starts at page 1 and you want page numbering to be consecutive.

8. **Press [Ctrl], click Information Session Guidelines in the table of contents, scroll to the footer (you'll see Page 1), double-click in the footer, click the Page Number button in the Header & Footer group, click Format Page Numbers, click the Continue from previous section option button, then click OK**

   QUICK TIP
   Submit files to your instructor as directed.

9. **Click Next in the Navigation group, click the Page Number button in the Header & Footer group, click Format Page Numbers, click the Continue from previous section option button, click OK, exit the footer area, update the table of contents for page numbers only, reduce the zoom to 90% and compare the revised table of contents to FIGURE I-19, then save and close all documents and exit Word**

FIGURE I-18: Table of Contents Options dialog box

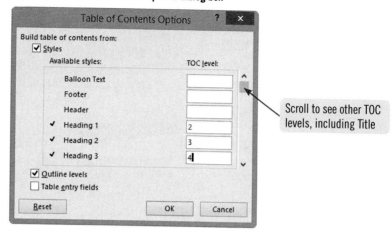

Scroll to see other TOC levels, including Title

FIGURE I-19: Revised table of contents

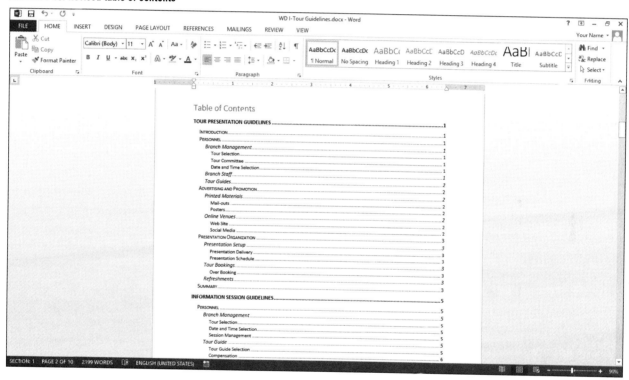

Using Advanced Print Options

With Word 2013, you can scale a document to fit a different paper size and you can choose to print pages from specific sections or a series of sections, even when the page numbering restarts in each section. To scale a document, click the FILE tab, click Print, click the 1 Page Per Sheet list arrow, then click Scale to Paper Size and view the list of paper sizes available. You can also choose to print a multiple-page document on fewer sheets; for example, you can print the document on two pages per sheet up to 16 pages per sheet. In the Print dialog box, you can also specify how to print the pages of a multiple-section document that uses different page numbering in each section. You need to enter both the page number and the section number for the range of pages you wish to print. The syntax required is: PageNumberSectionNumber-PageNumberSectionNumber which is shortened to p#s#-p#s#. For example, if you want to print from page 1 of section one to page 4 of section three, you enter p1s1-p4s3 in the Pages text box in the Settings area, and then click Print.

Develop Multipage Documents

Practice

Concepts Review

Label the numbered items on the OUTLINING tab shown in FIGURE I-20.

FIGURE I-20

Match each term with the statement that best describes it.

6. **Demote button**
7. **Table of Contents**
8. **Resume Reading**
9. **Footer**
10. **Cross-reference**
11. **Link to Previous button**
12. **Mark All**

a. Used to enter a lower-level heading in Outline view
b. Text that appears at the bottom of every page in a document or section
c. Text that electronically refers the reader to another part of the document
d. Click to designate each instance of a specific term for inclusion in an index
e. List of topics and subtopics usually with page numbers, and shown at the beginning of a document
f. Deselect to create a header or footer in one section that is different from the header or footer in a previous section
g. Feature that allows you to return to the last place you were working in a document before you saved and closed it

Select the best answer from the list of choices.

13. **On the OUTLINING tab, which button do you click to move directly to Level 1 from any other level?**
    a. ←
    b. →
    c. ≪
    d. ✛

14. **Which symbol in Outline view indicates that a heading includes subtext such as subheadings or paragraphs of text?**
    a. −
    b. ⊕
    c. ▲
    d. ✛

15. **Which of the following options do you select when you want to search for text from the Navigation pane?**
    a. HEADINGS
    b. RESULTS
    c. SEARCH
    d. FIND TEXT

16. **Which index entry appears subordinate to a main entry?**
    a. Cross-reference
    b. Next entry
    c. Mark place
    d. Subentry

17. **Which tab contains the commands used to create an index?**
    a. PAGE LAYOUT
    b. INSERT
    c. REVIEW
    d. REFERENCES

Skills Review

1. Build a document in Outline view.

a. Start Word, create a new blank document, then switch to Outline view from the VIEW tab.

b. Type **Introduction** followed by your name as a Level 1 heading, press [Enter], type **Partnership Conditions** as another Level 1 heading, then press [Enter].

c. Type the text shown in **FIGURE I-21** as body text under the Partnership Conditions heading.

d. Type **Background**, then use the Demote button to demote it to a Level 2 heading.

e. Use the Promote button to type the heading **Benefits** as a Level 2 heading, then complete the outline, as shown in **FIGURE I-21**.

FIGURE I-21

⊖ Introduction by Your Name
⊕ Partnership Conditions
　⊙ This section provides background information about Arcadia Training and discusses how the partnership could benefit both Markham Communications and Arcadia Training.
　⊖ Background
　⊖ Benefits
　⊖ Partnership Need
⊕ Products and Services
　⊖ Arcadia Training Services
　⊖ Markham Communications
　⊖ Package Opportunities
⊕ Financial Considerations
　⊖ Projected Revenues
　⊖ Financing Required
⊖ Conclusion

f. Save the document as **WD I-Partnership Outline** to the location where you store your Data Files, then close the document.

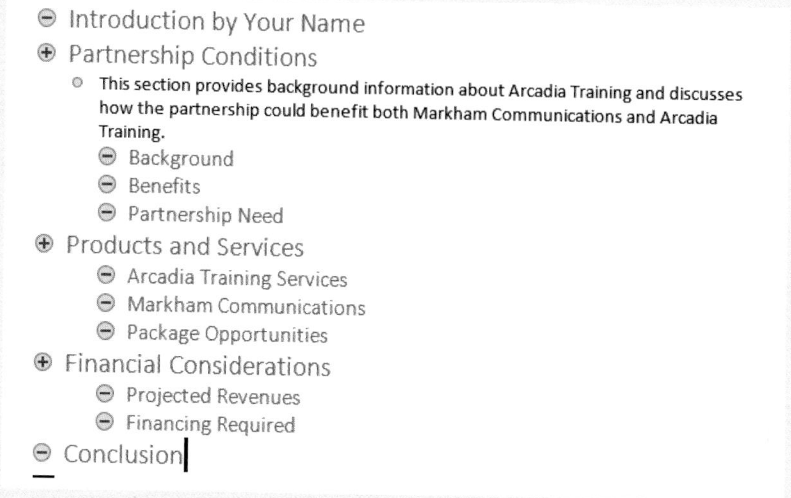

2. Work in Outline view.

a. Open the file WD I-3.docx from the location where you store your Data Files, save it as **WD I-Partnership Proposal**, switch to Outline view, then show all Level 1 headings.

b. Move the heading Products and Services above Financial Considerations.

c. Select the Partnership Conditions heading, expand the heading, collapse Benefits, collapse Partnership Need, then move Benefits and its subtext below Partnership Need and its subtext.

d. Collapse the Partnership Conditions section to show only the Level 1 heading.

e. Show all levels of the outline, close Outline view, then save the document.

3. Navigate a document.

a. In Print Layout view, collapse all the headings in the document.

b. Open the Navigation pane, navigate to Financing Required, expand the heading, then change "six months" to **year** in the last line of the paragraph below the Financing Required heading.

c. Expand all headings in Print Layout view.

d. Click the Package Opportunities heading in the Navigation pane, then use the Navigation pane to delete the heading and its subtext.

e. View the thumbnails of the document pages in the Navigation pane, click the first page, close the Navigation pane, scroll to the Benefits heading, then select the text "Projected Revenues" at the end of the paragraph.

f. Create a cross-reference from the text Projected Revenues to the Projected Revenues heading.

g. Test the cross-reference, then save the document.

4. Insert a table of contents.

a. Go to the top of the document.

b. Insert a page break, then return to the top of the document.

c. Insert the Automatic Table 2 predefined table of contents style.

d. Replace it with a custom table of contents using the Fancy format.

e. Use [Ctrl][click] to navigate to Partnership Need in the document, open the Navigation pane, view the document headings, then right-click and delete the Partnership Need heading from the Navigation pane.

f. Update the table of contents, then save the document.

Skills Review (continued)

5. Mark entries for an index.

   a. Show the RESULTS section of the Navigation pane, find the words **computer labs**, and mark all occurrences for inclusion in the index.

   b. Find and mark only the first instance of each of the following main entries: **Web page design, Networking, software training**, and **PowerPoint**. (*Hint:* Click Mark instead of Mark All.)

   c. Save the document.

6. Generate an index.

   a. Find **online publishing**, click in the Mark Index Entry dialog box, select online publishing in the Main entry text box, type **Markham Communications Products** as the Main entry and **online publishing** as the Subentry, then click Mark All.

   b. Repeat the process to insert **business writing seminars** as a subentry of Arcadia Training.

   c. Find the text **courses**, then create a cross-reference in the Mark Index Entry dialog box to **software training**. Note that you already have an index entry for software training.

   d. Close the Mark Index Entry dialog box and the Navigation pane.

   e. Insert a new page at the end of the document, type **Index** at the top of the page, and format it with bold and 18 pt and center alignment.

   f. Double-click below the index, clear any formatting so the insertion point appears at the left margin, then insert an index in the Fancy format.

   g. Find and mark all instances of **Seattle**, scroll to the index page, update the index so it includes the new entry, close the Mark Index Entry dialog box and the Navigation pane, then save the document.

7. Insert footers in multiple sections.

   a. At the top of the document, select the page break below the Table of Contents, replace it with a Next Page section break, then remove the page break and the extra blank line.

   b. On the table of contents page, insert a footer using the Blank (Three Columns) format.

   c. Delete the placeholders, type your name, press [Tab] twice, type **Page**, press [Spacebar], then insert a page number at the current position using the Plain Number format.

   d. Change the format of the page number to i, ii, iii.

   e. Go to the next section, then deselect the Link to Previous button.

   f. Format the page number to start at 1.

   g. Exit the footer area, scroll through the document to verify that the pages are numbered correctly, scroll to and update the page numbers in the table of contents, then save the document.

8. Insert headers in multiple sections.

   a. Move to the top of the document, then double-click to position the insertion point in the header area.

   b. Go to the next section, then deselect the Link to Previous button.

   c. Type **Markham Communications**, then apply bold and italic.

   d. Exit the header area, then scroll through the document to verify that the header text does not appear on the table of contents and that it does appear on all subsequent pages.

   e. Insert a cover page using the Whisp style, then delete the Date content control.

   f. Enter **Partnership Agreement Proposal** as the Document title, **Markham Communications** as the Document subtitle, and your name where indicated.

   g. Delete the Company Name content control.

   h. Save the document.

9. Finalize a multipage document.

   a. Go to the Index page, then save and close the document.

   b. Open the document, then use the Resume Reading feature to return to the last page of the document.

   c. Scroll up to the Page Break after the Conclusion, then replace the page break with a Next Page section break.

Skills Review (continued)

d. Open the file WD I-4.docx from the drive and folder where you store your Data Files, copy all the text, paste it into the Partnership Agreement Proposal document, then save the document as **WD I-Partnership Agreements**.

e. From the table of contents page, access the Header area, move to section 2, replace Markham Communications with **Arcadia Training**, move to section 3, click the Link to Previous button, then replace Arcadia Training with **Parallel Presenters**.

f. Exit the header, insert a Next Page section break before the index, and delete the page break and the extra blank line, open the header area in section 4 (the index page), then deselect the Link to Previous button and remove the header from the index page.

g. Check that the correct headers appear in each of the four sections, then update the table of contents page (select the Update entire table option).

h. Modify the table of contents options so that Heading 1 corresponds to TOC level 2 text, Heading 2 corresponds to TOC level 3 text, Heading 3 corresponds to TOC level 4 text, and Title text corresponds to TOC level 1 text.

i. Modify the footers in sections 3 and 4 so that the page numbering is continuous. You should see page 6 on the index page.

j. Update the index and table of contents pages, compare your document to the pages from the completed document shown in **FIGURE I-22**, save the document, submit all files to your instructor, close it, then exit Word.

FIGURE I-22

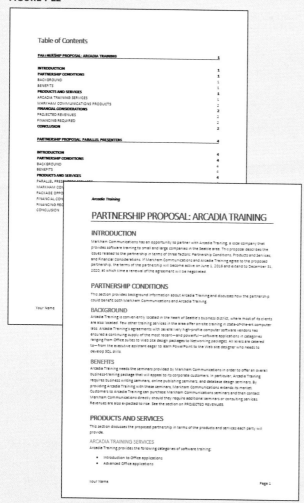

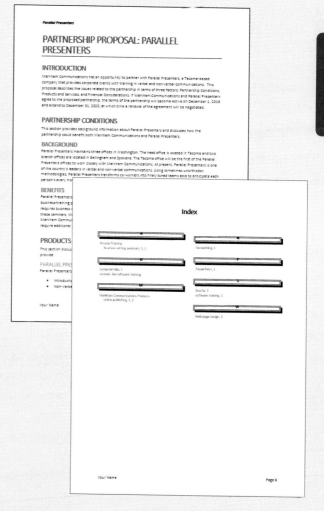

Independent Challenge 1

You work in the Finance Department of Holistic Fitness. Recently, the owners began selling franchises. Your supervisor asks you to format a report that details the development of these franchise operations.

a. Start Word, open the file WD I-5.docx from the drive and folder where you store your Data Files, then save it as **WD I-Holistic Fitness Franchises**.

b. In Outline view, organize the document as shown in the following table, starting with Introduction, followed by Scope of the Report, and then moving column by column. Text that you designate as headings will be formatted with the blue font color.

heading	level	heading	level	heading	level
Introduction	1	Maureen Knowles	2	Philadelphia Clientele	3
Scope of the Report	2	Franchise Locations	1	New York	2
Owner Information	1	Boston	2	New York Clientele	3
Don Green	2	Boston Clientele	3	Opening Schedules	2
Jorge Morales	2	Philadelphia	2		

© 2014 Cengage Learning

c. Show level 3, then switch the order of New York and its subtext so it follows Boston and its subtext.

d. In Print Layout view, collapse all the headings to show only Level 1 headings, then expand the headings again.

e. Show the Navigation pane, then move the Opening Schedules heading so it appears just below Franchise Locations.

f. Starting from the top of the document, find the text listed in column 1, and mark all instances of that text as Main entry or subentry for an index, based on the information in columns 2 and 3.

g. Find Best Fitness, then make it a main entry with a cross-reference to **Don Green**.

h. Insert a new page at the end of the document, type **Index** as the page title, format it with bold, a larger font size, and center alignment, then generate an index in the Modern format.

find this text	main entry	subentry
Boston	Location	Boston
New York	Location	New York
Philadelphia	Location	Philadelphia
Don Green	Owner	Don Green
Jorge Morales	Owner	Jorge Morales
Maureen Knowles	Owner	Maureen Knowles
marketing vice president	marketing vice president	
mall	mall	

© 2014 Cengage Learning

i. At the top of the document, insert a Next Page section break, then on the new first page, insert an automatic table of contents using the Automatic Table 1 style.

j. Add and format a header and footer so that the completed document appears as follows:

location	contents
Table of Contents page (section 1)	Footer containing your name at the left margin and Page i at the right margin
Page 1 and the following pages of the report (section 2)	Footer containing your name at the left margin and Page 1 at the right margin
Page 1 and the following pages of the report (section 2)	Header containing the text Holistic Fitness Franchises, centered, and bold

© 2014 Cengage Learning

k. Scroll through the document to ensure the headers and footers are correct, click the Index heading when you get to the Index page, then save and close the document.

l. Open the document and click the Resume Reading message to return to the Index page, update the index page, then scroll up and update the table of contents page.

m. Save the document, submit your file to your instructor, then close the document.

Independent Challenge 2

As the program assistant at Lakeview College in Minnesota, you are responsible for creating and formatting reports about programs at the college. You work in Outline view to create a report for a college program of your choice.

a. Start Word, create a new blank document, then save it as **WD I-Program Information Report**.

b. In Outline view, enter the headings and subheadings for the report as shown in the table starting with **Program Overview**, followed by **Career Opportunities**. You need to substitute appropriate course names for Course 1, Course 2, and so on. For example, courses in the first

heading	level	heading	level
Program Overview	1	[Enter name for Course 1]	3
Career Opportunities	2	[Enter name for Course 2]	3
Admission Requirements	2	Second Term	2
Program Content	1	[Enter name for Course 1]	3
First Term	2	[Enter name for Course 2]	3

© 2014 Cengage Learning

term of a business studies program could be **Introduction to Business, Marketing Basics**, and so on. You choose the program and courses you want to include in the report.

c. Enter one paragraph of appropriate body text for the following headings: Program Overview, Career Opportunities, and Admission Requirements, then enter short course descriptions for each of the four courses included in the document. For ideas, refer to college Web sites and catalogs. Collapse all the headings to Level 1.

d. In Print Layout view, add a cover page using the style of your choice. Include the name of the program as the title (for example, **Business Program**), the name of the college (**Lakeview College, Minnesota**) as the subtitle, and your name where indicated. Remove all other content controls. If the cover page style you choose does not include a content control for a subtitle, enter the information as text and format it attractively.

e. Insert a Next Page section break following the cover page, then insert a page break in the body of the report to spread the report over two pages if it does not already flow to two pages.

f. Format the cover page (section 1) with no header and no footer.

g. Go to the section 2 header and deselect the Different First Page check box in the Options group so that you see Header - Section 2 in the tab below the header area, not First Page Header - Section 2. Format the section 2 header with a right-aligned page number starting with Page 1 using the 1, 2, 3 format. Make sure you deselect Link to Previous.

h. Format the section 2 footer with the name of the program left-aligned in the footer and your name right-aligned. Make sure you deselect Link to Previous.

i. Insert a next page section break above the Program Overview heading.

j. Scroll up to the new blank page, then insert an automatic table of contents in either the Automatic Table 1 or Automatic Table 2 formats. Replace the table of contents with a custom table of contents that uses the format of your choice (for example, Classic, Fancy, etc.).

k. Customize the table of contents so that it includes only Heading 1 at TOC level 1 and Heading 3 at TOC level 2. None of the Heading 2 headings should appear in the revised table of contents.

l. Double click in the header area on the table of contents page, then delete Page 1.

m. Go to the next section (Section 3), click the Link to Previous button to deselect it, then insert Page 1 right-aligned. Be sure the page number starts at 1. Verify that the header appears on both pages of the section 3 header and that the footer appears on all pages except the cover page.

n. Update the table of contents, save the document, close it, then submit your file to your instructor.

Independent Challenge 3

Many businesses post job opportunities on their Web sites. You can learn a great deal about opportunities in a wide range of fields just by checking out the job postings on these Web sites. You decide to create a document that describes a selection of jobs available on an employment Web site of your choice.

a. Use your favorite search engine and the search phrase **job search** to find Web sites that post jobs online. Popular sites include jobs.com, workopolis.com, and monster.com.

b. On the Web site you chose, identify two job categories (e.g., Marketing and Web Page Development, or Accounting and Administration) and then find two jobs that appeal to you and that you may even wish to apply for. You can choose to search for jobs in your home town or in another location.

c. Create a new document in Word, then save it as **WD I-Online Job Opportunities**.

d. In Outline view, set up the document starting with the name of the employment Web site (e.g., monster.com), and followed by Job Category 1 as shown in the table. (*Note*: You need to enter specific text for headings such as **Marketing** for Job Category 1 and **Marketing Assistant** for Job Posting.)

heading	level
Name of Web Site	1
Job Category 1	2
Job Name	3
Summary of Job Posting	Body Text
Job Category 2	2
Job Name	3
Summary of Job Posting	Body Text

e. Complete the Word document with information you find on the Web site. Include a short description of each job you select, and list some of the job duties. You do not need to include the entire job posting. If you copy selected text from a Web site, make sure you clear the formatting so that the text in the document is formatted only with the Normal style. Edit any copied text so that only the most important information is included.

f. Divide the document into two pages so that each job posting appears on one page.

g. Above the first job posting, enter the following text: **Following is a description of two jobs that interest me. The first job is a[n] [name of job] and the second job is a[n] [name of job]. Information in this report was copied from the [Web site name or URL] Web site on [date]**. Make sure you substitute the job titles you've identified for [name of job], the name of the Web site name or its URL for the [Web site name or URL], and the date you created the report for [date].

h. Make each job title a cross-reference to the appropriate heading in your outline, then test the cross-references.

i. Insert a header that starts on page 1 and includes the text **Online Job Opportunities for** followed by your name, then include a page number on each page of the document in the footer.

j. Save the document and submit the file to your instructor, then close the document.

Independent Challenge 4: Explore

You work for an author who has just written a series of vignettes about her travels in France and Italy. The author hopes to publish the vignettes and accompanying illustrations in a book called *Lyric Journals*. She has written a short proposal that she plans to present to publishers. As her assistant, your job is to create a proposal that includes three of the vignettes, each with a unique header. You will further explore the features available in Outline view by using some of the tools available in the Master Document group.

a. Start Word, open WD I-6.docx, then save it as **WD I-Lyric Journals Proposal**. Keep the document open.

b. Open WD I-7.docx, save it as **WD I-Lyric Journals Lavender**, then close it.

c. Open WD I-8.docx, save it as **WD I-Lyric Journals Ocher**, then close it.

d. Open WD I-9.docx, save it as **WD I-Lyric Journals Roman Rain**, then close it.

e. From the WD I-Lyric Journals Proposal document, switch to Outline view, then promote the Lyric Journals Overview heading to Level 1.

f. Click at the end of the outline on the first blank line after the last sentence.

g. Click the Show Document button in the Master Document group.

h. Click the Insert button in the Master Document group, navigate to the location where you saved the files for this challenge, double-click WD I-Lyric Journals Lavender.

i. Repeat step h to insert WD I-Lyric Journals Ocher as a subdocument, then repeat step h once more to insert WD I-Lyric Journals Roman Rain as a subdocument. The master document now consists of introductory text and three subdocuments.

j. Click the Collapse Subdocuments button in the Master Document group, then click OK in response to the message. Scroll down as needed to see that each document is now a hyperlink.

k. Press the [Ctrl] key and click the hyperlink to the Lyric Journals Lavender document. View the document, then close it.

l. Click the Expand Subdocuments button, then close Outline view.

m. At the top of the document, add a next page section break, then at the top of the new blank page, insert one of the automatic table of contents.

n. Replace the table of contents with a custom table of contents that uses the Formal format.

o. Insert a footer at the bottom of the table of contents page that includes your name at the left margin and the page number formatted in lower case Roman numerals (i) at the right margin.

p. Go to section 2, deselect Link to Previous, then format the page numbers so they start at 1.

q. Create a header for each section as shown in the table below. Make sure you deselect Link to Previous each time you go to a new section. Enter the text for each header at the left margin and format it with italics. The document contains a total of seven sections and five pages. Note that extra sections are inserted when you insert subdocuments.

section	contains	header text
1	Table of Contents	no header
2	Overview	Lyric Journals Overview
3	Lavender	Lavender
5	Ocher	Ocher
7	Roman Rain	Roman Rain

© 2014 Cengage Learning

r. Update the table of contents, save the document, submit a copy of all four documents to your instructor, then close the document. Note that when you open the document again, the three subdocuments will appear as hyperlinks.

Visual Workshop

Open the file WD I-10.docx from the drive and folder where you store your Data Files, then save it as **WD I-Term Paper Outline**. Modify the outline so that it appears as shown in **FIGURE I-23**. You need to change the order of some sections. In Print Layout view, insert a next page section break at the beginning of the document, then generate a table of contents using the Automatic Table 2 format and the custom Distinctive format. Insert a page break before Social Networking Development in the text, create a footer in section 2 (remember to deselect Link to Previous) with your name at the left margin and a page number that starts with 1 at 0 right margin. Make sure no text appears in the footer in section 1. Update the table of contents so that it appears as shown in **FIGURE I-24**. Save and close the document, then submit the file to your instructor.

FIGURE I-23

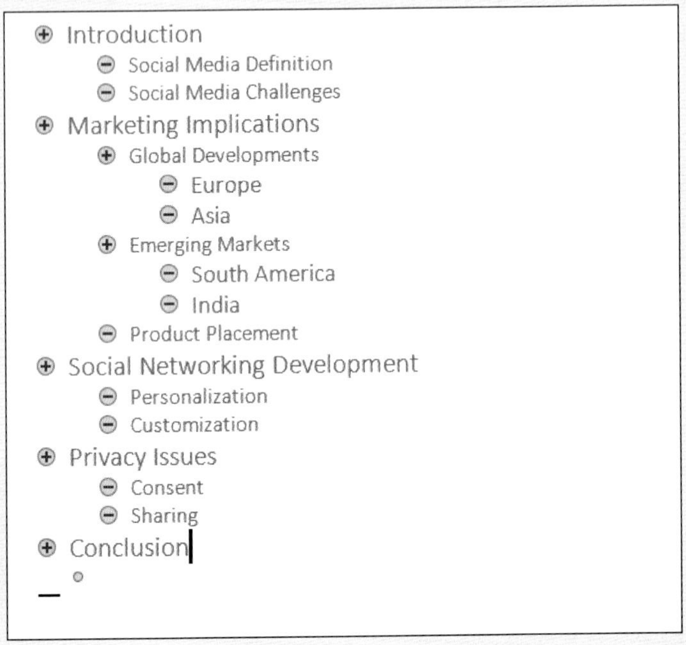

⊕ Introduction
  ⊖ Social Media Definition
  ⊖ Social Media Challenges
⊕ Marketing Implications
  ⊕ Global Developments
      ⊖ Europe
      ⊖ Asia
  ⊕ Emerging Markets
      ⊖ South America
      ⊖ India
  ⊖ Product Placement
⊕ Social Networking Development
  ⊖ Personalization
  ⊖ Customization
⊕ Privacy Issues
  ⊖ Consent
  ⊖ Sharing
⊕ Conclusion
  ○
—

FIGURE I-24

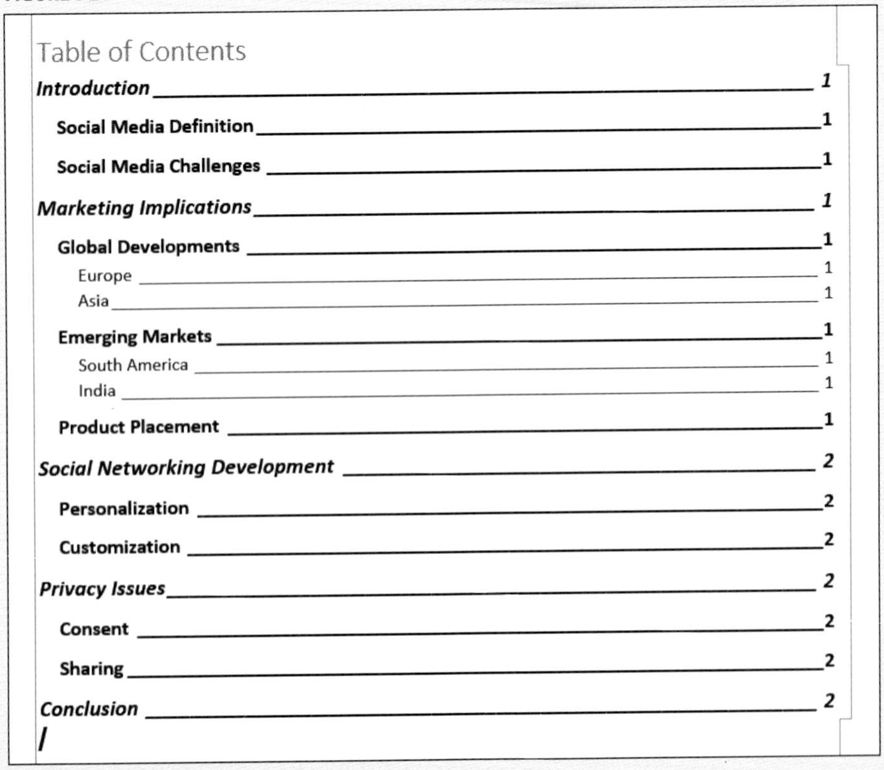

Table of Contents

Introduction _____ 1
  Social Media Definition _____ 1
  Social Media Challenges _____ 1
Marketing Implications _____ 1
  Global Developments _____ 1
    Europe _____ 1
    Asia _____ 1
  Emerging Markets _____ 1
    South America _____ 1
    India _____ 1
  Product Placement _____ 1
Social Networking Development _____ 2
  Personalization _____ 2
  Customization _____ 2
Privacy Issues _____ 2
  Consent _____ 2
  Sharing _____ 2
Conclusion _____ 2
/

Working with Styles and Templates

CASE ▶ As a special projects assistant at Quest Specialty Travel (QST) in San Diego, you've been asked to produce profiles of the top QST tour guides for distribution at the company's annual meeting. To save time, you modify styles in an existing profile, create new styles, and then develop a template on which to base each tour guide profile. This template includes a custom Style Set.

Unit Objectives

After completing this unit, you will be able to:

- Explore styles and templates
- Modify built-in styles
- Create paragraph styles
- Create character and linked styles
- Create list and table styles
- Create a Style Set
- Manage styles
- Create a template
- Modify and attach a template

Files You Will Need

WD J-1.docx	WD J-8.docx
WD J-2.docx	WD J-9.docx
WD J-3.docx	WD J-10.docx
WD J-4.docx	WD J-11.docx
WD J-5.docx	WD J-12.docx
WD J-6.docx	WD J-13.docx
WD J-7.docx	

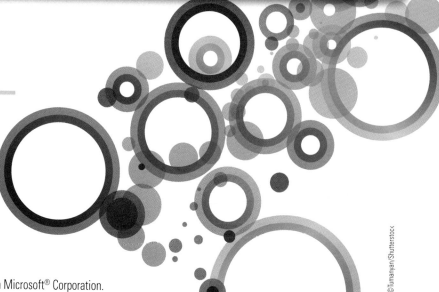

Explore Styles and Templates

Learning Outcomes
• Define why to use styles
• Identify style types
• Define why to use templates

You use styles and templates to automate document-formatting tasks and to ensure consistency among related documents. A **style** consists of formats such as font, font size, and alignment that you name and then save as one set. For example, the settings for a style called Main Head could be Arial font, 14-pt font size, bold, and a bottom border. Each time you apply the Main Head style to selected text, all format settings included in the style are applied. A **template** is a file that contains the basic structure of a document, such as the page layout, headers and footers, styles, graphic elements, and boilerplate text. **CASE** *You plan to use styles to format a tour guide profile and then create a template for a series of tour guide profiles. You start by familiarizing yourself with styles and templates.*

DETAILS

Information about how you can use styles and templates to help you format documents quickly and efficiently follows:

- You apply styles to selected text from the Styles gallery on the HOME tab. Using styles helps you save time in two ways. First, when you apply a style, you apply a set of formats all at once. Second, if you modify a style by changing one or more of the formats associated with that style, all text formatted with that style is updated automatically. For example, suppose you apply a style named "Section Head" to each section head in a document. If you then modify the formatting associated with the Section Head style, Word automatically updates all the text formatted with the Section Head style. As discussed in Unit I, default heading styles are applied automatically to headings and subheadings when you work in Outline view to create the structure of a document. For example, the Heading 1 style is applied to text associated with Level 1, the Heading 2 style is applied to text associated with Level 2, and so on. You can modify a default heading style or you can create a new heading style.

- In Word, you can choose from 17 built-in Style Sets on the DESIGN tab or you can create your own Style Set. Each **Style Set** contains **styles** for text elements such as headings, titles, subtitles, and lists. All of the styles associated with a Style Set are stored in the **Styles gallery.**

- Word includes five major style categories. A **paragraph style** includes font formats, such as font and font size, and paragraph formats, such as line spacing or tabs. You use a paragraph style when you want to format all of the text in a paragraph at once. A **character style** includes character formats only, such as font, font size, and font color. You use a character style to apply character format settings only to selected text within a paragraph. A **linked style** contains both a character style and a paragraph style. Either the character style or the paragraph style is applied depending on whether you click in a paragraph to select the entire paragraph or you select specific text. A **table style** specifies how you want both the table grid and the text in a table to appear. A **list style** allows you to format a series of lines with numbers or bullets and with selected font and paragraph formats. **FIGURE J-1** shows a document formatted with the five style types. These styles have been saved in a new Style Set called QST Profiles.

- Every document you create in Word is based on a template. Most of the time, this template is the **Normal template** because the Normal template is loaded automatically when you start a new document. The styles assigned to the Normal template, such as Normal, Title, Heading 1, Heading 2, and so on, are the styles you see in the Styles gallery on the HOME tab when you open a new document.

- Word includes a number of built-in templates. In addition, you can access a variety of templates online. You can also create a template that includes a custom Style Set. Finally, you can attach a template to an existing document and then apply the styles included with the template to text in the document.

Working with Styles and Templates

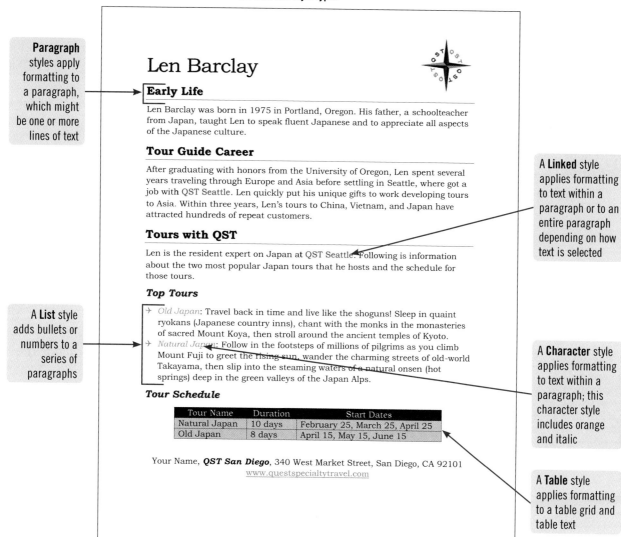

Paragraph styles apply formatting to a paragraph, which might be one or more lines of text

A **List** style adds bullets or numbers to a series of paragraphs

A **Linked** style applies formatting to text within a paragraph or to an entire paragraph depending on how text is selected

A **Character** style applies formatting to text within a paragraph; this character style includes orange and italic

A **Table** style applies formatting to a table grid and table text

Understanding Themes, Style Sets, and the Normal style

Style Sets are not the same as themes but they work with themes to provide you with an almost unlimited range of formatting options. A theme is a set of unified design elements including theme colors, theme fonts for body text and headings, and theme effects for graphics. When you apply a theme to a document, you can further modify the appearance of the text, colors, and graphics in the document by applying one of the 17 built-in Style Sets. You can then modify the appearance even further by changing the settings of the styles associated with the Style Set.

Text that you type into a blank document is formatted with the Normal style from the default Style Set associated with the Office 2013 theme until you specify otherwise. By default, text formatted with the Normal style uses the 11-point Calibri font and is left-aligned, with a line spacing of 1.08 within a paragraph and 8 pt After Paragraph spacing. When you select a new Style Set, the styles associated with that Style Set are applied to the document.

Modify Built-in Styles

Learning
Outcomes
• Modify a style
• Update a style

Word includes built-in styles, such as the Normal, Title, Heading 1, and Heading 2 styles, for each built-in Style Set. The styles associated with the active Style Set are displayed in the Styles gallery on the HOME tab. These styles along with other, less frequently used styles, can also be accessed from the Styles task pane. You can personalize documents by modifying any style. **CASE** ▸ *You modify the Normal style currently applied to all body text in a profile of Len Barclay, a tour guide from QST Seattle. You also modify the Heading 1 style and the Title style.*

STEPS

1. **Start Word, open the file** WD J-1.docx **from the location where you store your Data Files, save the file as** WD J-Profile of Len Barclay, **click in the paragraph below "Early Life," right-click** Normal **in the Styles gallery on the HOME tab, then click** Modify

   The Modify Style dialog box opens, as shown in **FIGURE J-2**.

2. **Click the** Font list arrow **in the Formatting area, scroll to and select** Bookman Old Style, **click the** Font Size list arrow, **click** 12, **then click** OK

   The Modify Style dialog box closes, and all body text in the document is modified automatically to match the new settings for the Normal style.

3. **Select the** Early Life **heading, then use the commands in the Font group to change the font to** Bookman Old Style **and the font color to** Green, Accent 6, Darker 50%

   You made changes to the character formatting for the selected text.

4. **Be sure the** Early Life **heading is still selected, click the** Borders list arrow ▦ ▾ **in the Paragraph group, click the** Bottom Border button, **click the** PAGE LAYOUT tab, **click the** Spacing Before text box **in the Paragraph group, type** 10, **click the** Spacing After text box, **type** 6, **then press** [Enter]

   You made changes to the paragraph formatting for the selected text.

5. **Click the** HOME tab, **right-click** Heading 1 **in the Styles gallery to open the menu shown in** FIGURE J-3, **then click** Update Heading 1 to Match Selection

   The Heading 1 style is updated to match the formatting options you applied to the Early Life heading. All headings in the text that are formatted with the Heading 1 style are updated to match the new Heading 1 style. Notice that the Heading 1 style in the Styles gallery shows a preview of the formatting associated with the Heading 1 style.

6. **Click the launcher** ▨ **in the Styles group to open the Styles task pane**

   By default, the **Styles task pane** lists a selection of the styles available in the active Style Set. The Styles task pane also includes options for creating new styles, using the Style Inspector, and managing styles.

7. **Select** Len Barclay **at the top of the page, point to** Title **in the Styles task pane, click the** list arrow **that appears, then click** Modify

8. **Change the font to** Bookman Old Style, **click the** Automatic list arrow, **select the** Green, Accent 6, Darker 50% color box, **then click** OK

   The selected text in the document and the preview of the Title style in the Styles gallery changes to show the new settings.

9. **Save the document**

   You have used three methods to modify the formatting attached to a style. You can modify the style using the Modify Styles dialog box, you can make changes to text associated with a style and then update the style to match the selected text, or you can modify a style from the Styles task pane. You generally use this last method when you need to modify a style that does not appear in the Styles gallery.

FIGURE J-2: Modify Style dialog box

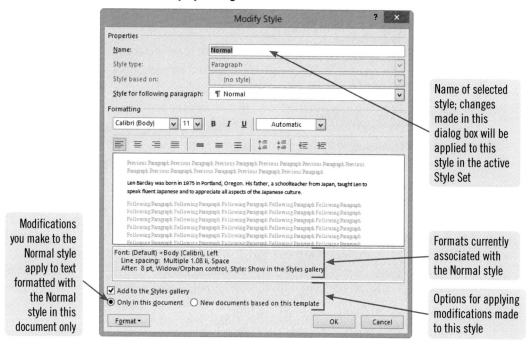

Name of selected style; changes made in this dialog box will be applied to this style in the active Style Set

Modifications you make to the Normal style apply to text formatted with the Normal style in this document only

Formats currently associated with the Normal style

Options for applying modifications made to this style

FIGURE J-3: Updating the Heading 1 style with new formats

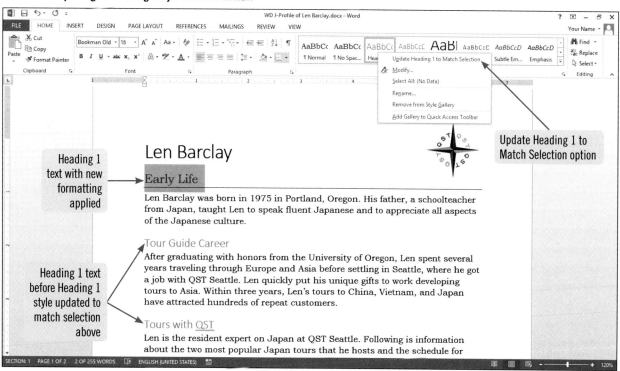

Update Heading 1 to Match Selection option

Heading 1 text with new formatting applied

Heading 1 text before Heading 1 style updated to match selection above

Create Paragraph Styles

**Learning
Outcomes**
• Create a
  paragraph style
• Apply a paragraph
  style

Instead of using the built-in styles, you can create your own styles. You can base a new style on an existing style or you can base it on no style. When you base a style on an existing style, both the formatting associated with the existing style and any new formatting you apply are associated with the new style. One type of style you can create is a paragraph style. A paragraph style is a combination of character and paragraph formats that you name and store as a set. You can create a paragraph style and then apply it to any paragraph. Any line of text followed by a hard return is considered a paragraph, even if the line consists of only one or two words. **CASE** ➤ *You create a new paragraph style called Guide Subtitle and apply it to two headings in the document.*

STEPS

1. **Scroll to and select the heading** Top Tours, **then click the** New Style button 📑 **at the bottom of the Styles task pane**

   The Create New Style from Formatting dialog box opens. You use this dialog box to enter a name for the new style, select a style type, and select the formatting options you want associated with the new style.

2. **Type** Guide Subtitle **in the Name text box**

   The Guide Subtitle style is based on the Normal style because the selected text is formatted with the Normal style. When you create a new style, you can base it on the style applied to the selected text if a style has been applied to that text, another style by selecting a style in the Style based on list box, or no preset style. You want the new style to also include the formatting associated with the Normal style so you leave Normal as the Style based on setting.

3. **Click** 12 **in the font size text box, type** 13, **click the** Italic button *I*, **click the** Automatic list arrow, **click the** Green, Accent 6, Darker 25% color box, **then click** OK

4. **Select the heading** Tour Schedule (you may need to scroll down), **then click** Guide Subtitle **in the Styles task pane**

   The new Guide Subtitle style is applied to two headings in the document.

5. **Click the** Show Preview check box **at the bottom of the Styles task pane to select it if it is not already selected**

   With the Show Preview option active, you can quickly see the formatting associated with each of the predefined styles and the new style you created.

6. **Move your mouse over** Guide Subtitle **in the Styles task pane to show the settings associated with the Guide Subtitle style**

   The Styles task pane and the document are shown in **FIGURE J-4**.

7. **Click** Options **at the bottom of the Styles task pane, then click the** Select styles to show list arrow

   The Style Pane Options dialog box appears as shown in **FIGURE J-5**. You can choose to show recommended styles (the default setting), all the styles associated with the Style Set, or just the styles currently in use.

8. **Click** In use, **then click** OK

   Only the styles currently applied to the document are displayed in the Styles task pane.

9. **Save the document**

FIGURE J-4: Formatting associated with Guide Subtitle style

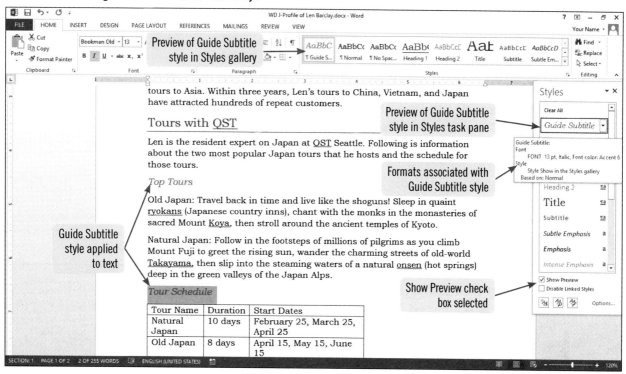

FIGURE J-5: Style Pane Options dialog box

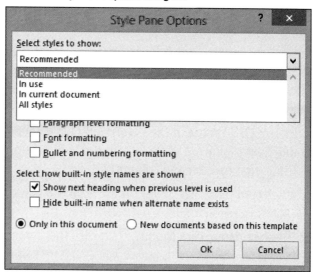

Revealing style formatting

Word includes two ways to quickly determine exactly what styles and formatting are applied to selected text. These methods are useful when you apply a style to text and not all the formatting changes you expect to be made are made. To find out why, use the Style Inspector to open the Reveal Formatting task pane. To open the Style Inspector, click the text formatted with the style, then click the Style Inspector button at the bottom of the Styles task pane. The **Style Inspector** lists the styles applied to the selected text and indicates if any extra formats were applied that are not included in the style. For example, another user could apply formatting such as bold and italic that is not included in the style. You can clear these formats by clicking one of the four buttons along the right side of the Style Inspector or by clicking Clear All to remove all extra formats. If you need to investigate even further, you can click the Reveal Formatting button at the bottom of the Style Inspector to open the Reveal Formatting task pane. The **Reveal Formatting task pane** lists exactly which formats are applied to the character, paragraph, and section of the selected text.

Learning Outcomes
- Create a character style
- Create a linked style

Create Character and Linked Styles

A character style includes character format settings—such as font, font size, bold, and italic—that you name and save as a style. You apply a character style to selected text within a paragraph. Any text in the paragraph that is not formatted with the character style is formatted with the currently applied paragraph style. A linked style includes both character formats and paragraph formats, just like a paragraph style. The difference is that you can apply the paragraph style associated with a linked style to an entire paragraph or you can apply the character style associated with the linked style to selected text within a paragraph. Linked styles are therefore very versatile. **CASE** *You create a character style called Tours to apply to each tour name and a linked style called QST to apply to each instance of QST Seattle.*

STEPS

1. **Select the text** Old Japan **in the section below Top Tours, press and hold** [Ctrl], **then select the text** Natural Japan **at the beginning of the next paragraph**

2. **Click the** New Style button **at the bottom of the Styles task pane, type** Tours **in the Name text box, click the** Style type list arrow, **then click** Character

3. **Select these character formatting settings: the** Bookman Old Style font, 12 pt, Italic, **and the** Green, Accent 6, Darker 25% font color, **click** OK, **then click away from the text to deselect it**

   The text you selected is formatted with the Tours character style.

4. **Select** Old Japan, **change the font color to** Orange, Accent 2, Darker 25%, **right-click** Tours **in the Styles task pane to open the menu shown in** FIGURE J-6, **then click** Update Tours to Match Selection

   Both of the phrases formatted with the Tours character style are updated.

5. **Scroll up and select** QST Seattle **in the paragraph below Tour Guide Career, click the** Text Effects and Typography list arrow **in the Font group, then select the** Fill – Blue, Accent 1, Shadow (first row, second column)

6. **Right-click the selected text, click** Styles **on the Mini toolbar, then click** Create a Style

   The Create New Style from Formatting dialog box opens.

7. **Type** QST **as the style name, click** Modify, **then click the** Center button

   In the Create New Style from Formatting dialog box, you see that the Linked (paragraph and character) style type is automatically assigned when you create a new style from selected text. The style you created includes character formatting (the text effect format) and paragraph formatting (center alignment).

8. **Click** OK, **click anywhere in the paragraph under Early Life, then click** QST **in the Styles task pane**

   The entire paragraph is formatted with the QST style, as shown in **FIGURE J-7**. Both the character formatting and the paragraph formatting associated with the QST linked style are applied to the paragraph, but only the character formatting associated with the QST linked style is applied to the QST Seattle text in the next paragraph.

9. **Click the** Undo button **on the Quick Access toolbar, scroll to the paragraph below the Tours with QST heading, select** QST Seattle **in the paragraph, click** QST **in the Styles task pane, then save the document**

FIGURE J-6: Updating the Tours character style

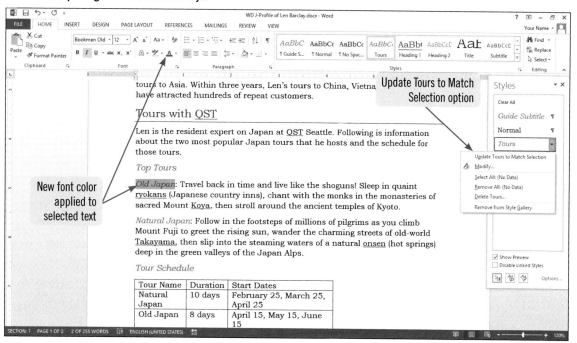

FIGURE J-7: QST linked style applied to a paragraph and to selected text

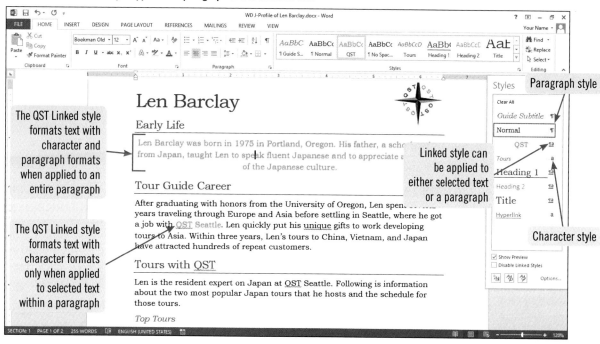

Identifying paragraph, character, and linked styles

Style types are identified in the Styles task pane by different symbols. Each paragraph style is marked with a paragraph symbol: ¶. You can apply a paragraph style just by clicking in any paragraph or line of text and selecting the style. The most commonly used predefined paragraph style is the Normal style. Each character style is marked with a character symbol: a. You apply a character style by clicking anywhere in a word or by selecting a phrase within a paragraph. Built-in character styles include Emphasis, Strong, and Book Title. Each linked style is marked with both a paragraph symbol and a character symbol: ¶a. You can click anywhere in a paragraph to apply the linked style to the entire paragraph, or you can select text and then apply only the character formats associated with the linked style to the selected text. Predefined linked styles include Heading 1, Title, and Quote.

Working with Styles and Templates

Create List and Table Styles

Learning Outcomes
• Create a list style
• Create a table style

A list style includes settings that format a series of paragraphs so they appear related in some way. For example, you can create a list style that adds bullet characters to paragraphs or sequential numbers to a list of items. A table style includes formatting settings for the table grid and the table text. **CASE** *You create a list style called Tour List with a special bullet character and a table style called Tour Schedule.*

STEPS

1. **Click to the left of** Old Japan **in the Top Tours section, click the** New Style button ⧆ **at the bottom of the Styles task pane, type** Tour List **as the style name, click the** Style type list arrow, **then click** List

   You can also click the Multilevel List button in the Paragraph group on the HOME tab, and then click Define New List Style to open the Define New List Style dialog box and create a new style.

2. **Click the** Bullets button ⧉, **click the** Symbol button Ω, **click the** Font list arrow, **scroll down and click** Wingdings, **double-click the number in the** Character code text box, **type 81, click OK, click the** Font Color list arrow, **then click** Blue, Accent 5

   The Create New Style from Formatting dialog box appears as shown in **FIGURE J-8**.

QUICK TIP
List styles are stored in the List Styles area of the Multilevel List gallery in the document, not in the Styles task pane.

3. **Click** OK, **click** Natural **in the phrase "Natural Japan", click the** Multilevel List button ⧉ **in the Paragraph group, move the mouse pointer over the style in the List Styles area and notice the ScreenTip reads** Tour List, **then click the** Tour List **style**

   The bullet character of a blue plane is added, the text is indented, and the spacing above the paragraph is removed. By default, Word removes spacing between paragraphs formatted with a list style, which is part of the List Paragraph style. When you create a list style, the List style type is based on the List Paragraph style.

4. **Scroll down and click in the table, click the** table move handle ⊞ **at the upper-left corner of the table to select the table, click the** New Style button ⧆, **type** Tour Schedule **in the Name text box, click the** Style type list arrow, **then click** Table

   The Create New Style from Formatting dialog box changes to show formatting options for a table.

5. **Refer to** FIGURE J-9: **select the** Bookman Old Style font, 12 pt font size, a 1 pt border width, black (Automatic) border color, **and** Green, Accent 6, Lighter 60% fill color, **then click the** All Borders button

QUICK TIP
Table styles are stored in the Table Styles gallery on the TABLE TOOLS DESIGN tab, not in the Styles task pane.

6. **Click the** Apply formatting to list arrow, **click** Header row, **change the font color to** white **and the fill color to** Green, Accent 6, Darker 50%, **click the** Align list arrow, **click the** Align Center button, **then click** OK

   The table is formatted with the new Tour Schedule table style, which includes a modified header row.

TROUBLE
If the table columns do not resize, resize each column manually.

7. **Double-click the** right edge **of the table so all text in each row fits on one line**

8. **Click the** TABLE TOOLS DESIGN tab, **right-click the currently selected table style (far-left selection), click** Modify Table Style, **click** Format **in the lower-left corner of the dialog box, click** Table Properties, **click the** Center button **in the Alignment area, click** OK, **then click** OK

   The table is centered as shown in **FIGURE J-10** and the center format is part of the table style.

9. **Click below the table to deselect it, then save the document**

FIGURE J-8: Create New Style from Formatting dialog box

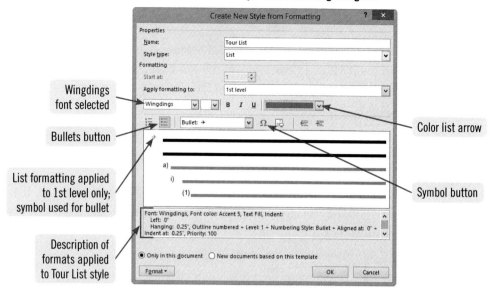

Wingdings font selected

Bullets button

List formatting applied to 1st level only; symbol used for bullet

Description of formats applied to Tour List style

Color list arrow

Symbol button

FIGURE J-9: Table formatting selections

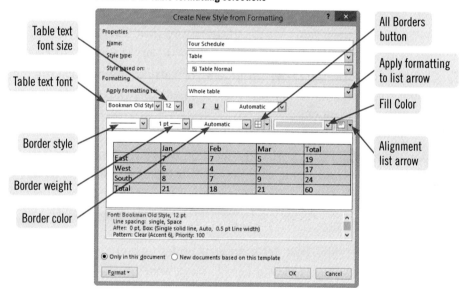

Table text font size

Table text font

Border style

Border weight

Border color

All Borders button

Apply formatting to list arrow

Fill Color

Alignment list arrow

FIGURE J-10: Tour List and Tour Schedule styles applied

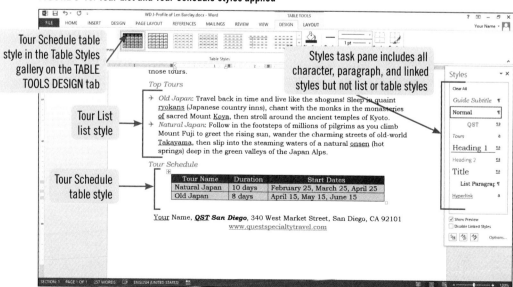

Tour Schedule table style in the Table Styles gallery on the TABLE TOOLS DESIGN tab

Tour List list style

Tour Schedule table style

Styles task pane includes all character, paragraph, and linked styles but not list or table styles

Word 2013

Create a Style Set

Once you have formatted a document with a selection of styles that includes both new and existing styles, you can save all the styles as a new Style Set. You can then apply the Style Set to format other documents. **CASE** ▶ *You create a new Style Set called QST Profiles, and then apply it to another profile.*

STEPS

1. **Press [Ctrl][Home] to move to the top of the document, click the DESIGN tab, then click the More button ⌄ in the Document Formatting group to open the gallery of Style Sets**

2. **Click Save as a New Style Set**

   The Save as a New Style Set dialog box opens to the default location where Style Sets are saved.

3. **Type QST Profiles in the File name text box, then click Save**

4. **Click the More button ⌄ to expand the gallery of Style Sets, move your mouse over the Style Set thumbnail that appears under Custom to show the name of the Style Set as shown in FIGURE J-11, then click the document to close the gallery**

   The QST Profiles Style Set is now one of the Style Sets you can use to format other documents.

5. **Click the Colors button in the Document Formatting group, move the mouse over the various color schemes to see how the document changes, scroll to and click Red Orange, then save the document**

   The color scheme for the document has changed.

6. **Open the file WD J-2.docx from the location where you store your Data Files, save it as WD J-Profile of Kayla Wong, click the DESIGN tab, then show the gallery of Style Sets**

   Kayla Wong's profile is currently formatted with one of the 17 built-in Style Sets. The Title style is applied to "Kayla Wong", and the Heading 1 style is applied to the "Early Life", "Tour Guide Career", and "Tours with QST" headings.

7. **Click the QST Profiles Style Set thumbnail under Custom**

   The QST Profiles Style Set is applied to the text in Kayla Wong's profile, and all the new styles you created in previous lessons, except the Tour List list style and the Tour Schedule table style, are available in the Styles gallery and the Styles task pane. Notice that the Red Orange color scheme you applied to Len Barclay's profile is not applied. Color schemes are not saved with a Style Set. You must reapply the color scheme.

8. **Click the Colors button in the Document Formatting group, then click Red Orange**

9. **Click the HOME tab, apply the Guide Subtitle and Tours styles from the Styles Gallery to the text as shown in FIGURE J-12, then save the document**

   You applied styles associated with the QST Profiles Style Set to document text. You will learn more about managing styles and applying the QST style, the Tour List style, and the Tour Schedule style in the next lesson.

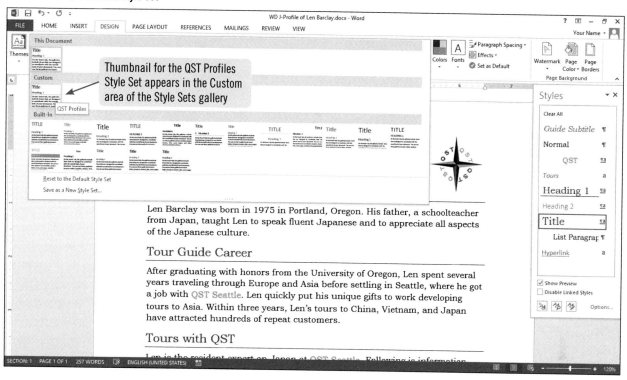

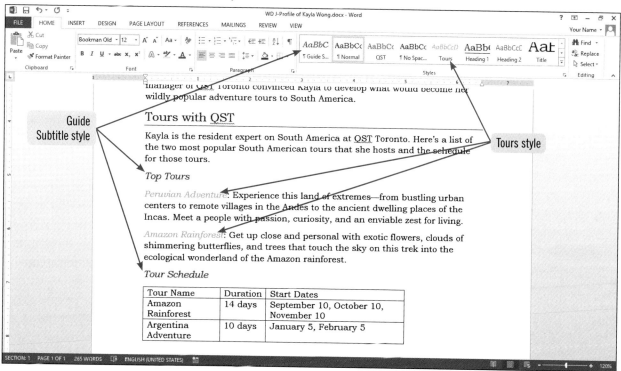

Working with Styles and Templates

Manage Styles

Learning Outcomes
• Find and replace styles
• Copy styles between documents

You can manage styles in many ways. For example, you can rename and delete styles, find and replace styles, and copy styles from one document to another document. After you create list and table styles, you must copy them from the source file (the document where you created the styles) to the target file (the document where you want to use the styles). **CASE** ▶ *You use Find and Replace to find each instance of QST Toronto and replace it with the same text formatted with the QST style, then copy the Tour List and the Tour Schedule styles from Len Barclay's profile (source file) to Kayla Wong's profile (target file).*

STEPS

1. Press [Ctrl][Home], click Replace in the Editing group on the HOME tab, type QST Toronto in the Find what text box, press [Tab], then type QST Toronto in the Replace with text box

   QUICK TIP
   Two versions of the QST style are listed in the Replace Style dialog box because the QST style is a linked style.

2. Click More, click Format, click Style, click QST Char, click OK, click Replace All, click OK, then click Close

   QST Toronto is formatted with the QST Char version of the QST linked style. Notice that only the character formats associated with the QST style were applied to QST Toronto.

3. Click the launcher ⌐ in the Styles group to open the Styles task pane, click the Manage Styles button 🖉 at the bottom of the Styles task pane, then click Import/Export to open the Organizer dialog box

   You copy styles from the document shown in the left side of the Organizer dialog box (the source file) to a new document that you open in the right side of the Organizer dialog box (the target file). By default, the target file is the Normal template.

   TROUBLE
   You do not see any Word documents listed because, by default, Word lists only templates.

4. Click Close File under the list box on the left, click Open File, then navigate to the location where you store your files

5. Click the All Word Templates list arrow, select All Word Documents as shown in FIGURE J-13, click WD J-Profile of Len Barclay.docx, then click Open

   The styles assigned to Len Barclay's profile appear in the list box on the left side. This document contains the Tour List and Tour Schedule styles.

6. Click Close File under the list box on the right, click Open File, navigate to the location where you store your files, show all Word documents, click WD J-Profile of Kayla Wong.docx, then click Open

7. Scroll the list of styles on the left side of the Organizer dialog box, click Tour List, press and hold [Ctrl], click Tour Schedule to select both styles (see FIGURE J-14), click Copy, then click Close

8. Select the two tour descriptions (from the heading Peruvian Adventure to the heading Amazon Rainforest), click the Multilevel List button ⊞▾ in the Paragraph group, then click the Tour List style shown under List Styles

   TROUBLE
   If your name forces the text to a second line, make adjustments as needed so the contact information appears on two lines.

9. Select the table, click the TABLE TOOLS DESIGN tab, click the Tour Schedule table style, adjust column widths as needed so no lines wrap, enter your name where indicated, then save and close the document

   The file WD J-Profile of Len Barclay is again the active document.

FIGURE J-13: Selecting Word Documents in the Open dialog box

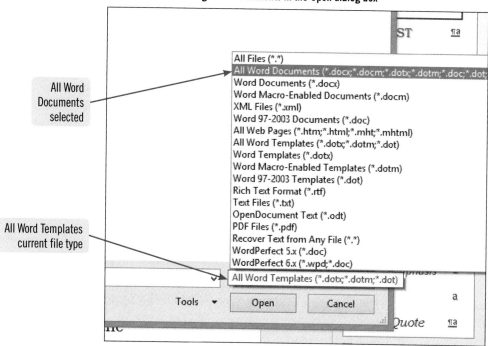

All Word Documents selected

All Word Templates current file type

FIGURE J-14: Managing styles using the Organizer dialog box

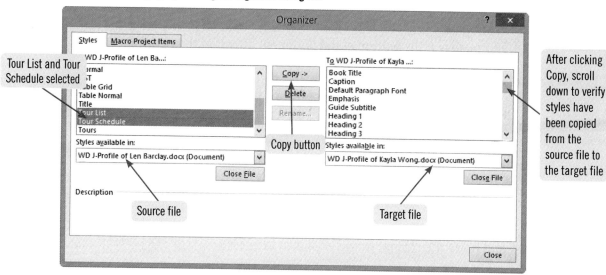

Tour List and Tour Schedule selected

Copy button

Source file

Target file

After clicking Copy, scroll down to verify styles have been copied from the source file to the target file

More ways to manage styles

To rename a style, right-click it in the Styles task pane, click Modify, type a new name, then press [Enter]. To delete a style, right-click the style, then click Delete [Style name]. The style is deleted from the Styles task pane, but it is not deleted from your computer. Click the Manage Styles button [icon] at the bottom of the Styles task pane, select the style to delete, click Delete, then click OK to close the Manage Styles dialog box.

Using Find and Replace to Format Text

You work in the Find and Replace dialog box to replace text formatted with one set of character formats such as bold and italic and replace it with the same or different text formatted with different formatting. Click More, enter the text to find, click Format and specify the formats attached to the text (for example, Font, Bold), click the Replace tab, enter the text to replace and click Format to specify the new formats, then click Replace All.

Working with Styles and Templates

Create a Template

Learning
Outcomes
• Create a template
• Create a
  document based
  on a template

A quick way to use all the styles contained in a document, including list and table styles, is to create a template. A template contains the basic structure of a document, including all the paragraph, character, linked, list, and table styles. You can create a template from an existing document, or you can create a template from scratch. Templates that you create are stored in the Custom Office Templates folder in your My Documents folder. **CASE** ▶ *You save the Len Barclay profile as a template, modify the template, and then open the template as a new document.*

STEPS

1. **Click the** FILE **tab, click** Save As, **click** Computer **in the list of Save As locations, then click** Browse

2. **Click the** Save as type list arrow, **then click** Word Template (*.dotx)
   When you select Word Template, the save location automatically changes to the Custom Office Templates folder in the My Documents folder on your computer.

3. **Select the** filename **in the File name text box, type** WD J-Profile Template, **then click** Save
   The file is saved as WD J-Profile Template.dotx to the Custom Office Templates folder in the My Documents folder on your computer. The .dotx filename extension identifies this file as a template file.

4. **Select** Len Barclay **at the top of the document, then type** [Enter Guide Name Here]

TROUBLE
If the plane bullet
symbol appears
when you delete text
under Top Tours,
click the HOME tab,
then click the Clear
All Formatting button
🖋 in the Font
group.

5. **As shown in** FIGURE J-15, **enter the** placeholder text, **be sure to leave the contact information at the bottom of the document as part of the template, click** FILE, **click** Close, **then click** Save
   Now that you have created a template, you can use it to create a new document that contains all the styles and formatting you want.

6. **Click the** FILE **tab, click** New, **then click** PERSONAL
   A document icon named WD-J Profile Template appears.

7. **Click the** WD J-Profile Template **icon**
   The template opens as a new document. You can enter text into this document and then save the document just as you would any document.

8. **Select the text** [Enter Guide Name Here], **type** Mark Lalonde, **then type text in the table and resize the column widths as shown in** FIGURE J-16

9. **Type your name where indicated, click the** FILE **tab, click** Save As, **navigate to the location where you store your files, save the document as** WD J-Profile of Mark Lalonde, **then close the document**

[Enter Guide Name Here]

Early Life

[Describe early life]

Tour Guide Career

[Describe tour guide's career]

Tours with QST

[Introduce two top tours and schedule]

Top Tours

[Describe top tours; format each tour name with the Tours style and format the list with the Tour List style]

Tour Schedule

Tour Name	Duration	Start Dates

Your Name, ***QST San Diego***, 340 West Market Street, San Diego, CA 92101
www.questspecialtytravel.com |

Tour Schedule

Tour Name	Duration	Start Dates
Dreams of Provence	10 days	May 15, June 15
Barging through Burgundy	7 days	July 1, August 1

Modify and Attach a Template

Learning
Outcomes
• Modify a template
• Attach a template

You can modify a template just as you would any Word document. All new documents you create from the modified template will use the new settings. All documents that you created before you modified the template are not changed unless you open the Templates and Add-ins dialog box and direct Word to update styles automatically. **CASE** ▸ *You modify the Guide Subtitle style in the Profile Template and then attach the revised template to a profile for Ally Stein. You then delete the QST Profiles Style Set.*

STEPS

1. Click the FILE tab, click Open, navigate to and open the Custom Office Templates folder in the Documents folder, click WD J-Profile Template.dotx, then click Open

2. Show the Styles task pane if it is not open, right-click Guide Subtitle in the Styles task pane, click Modify, apply Bold, change the font size to 14 pt, click OK, select Early Life, apply Bold, right-click Heading 1 in the Styles task pane, then click Update Heading 1 to Match Selection

   You need to resave the QST Profiles Style Set so that the new settings are available to new documents.

3. Click the DESIGN tab, click the More button ⊽ in the Document Formatting group, right-click the thumbnail under This Document, click Save, click QST Profiles.dotx, click Save, click Yes, then save and close the template

4. Open the file WD J-3.docx from the location where you store your Data Files, save the file as WD J-Profile of Ally Stein, click the DESIGN tab, apply the QST Profiles Style Set (under Custom in the Style Set gallery), then change the color scheme to Red Orange

5. Click the FILE tab, click Options, click Customize Ribbon, click the Developer check box in the list of Main Tabs as shown in FIGURE J-17 then click OK

   You use the DEVELOPER tab to work with advanced features such as attaching the Profile Template to Ally's profile and applying all the new styles you created to the document.

6. Click the DEVELOPER tab on the Ribbon, click Document Template in the Templates group, click Attach, navigate to the Custom Office Templates folder in the Documents folder, click WD J-Profile Template.dotx, click Open, click the Automatically update document styles check box, then click OK

   Now you can apply the styles associated with the WD J-Profile Template to Ally's profile.

7. Click the HOME tab, apply styles as shown in FIGURE J-18, be sure your name is on the document, then save and close the document

8. Create a new blank document, click the DESIGN tab, click the More button in the ⊽ Document Formatting group, right-click the thumbnail under Custom, click Delete, then click Yes

   You delete the QST Profiles Style Set from the list of Style Sets so only the default Style Sets appear for the next user of your computer system.

9. Click the FILE tab, click Options, click Customize Ribbon, click the Developer check box to deselect it, click OK, close the Styles task pane, exit Word, then submit all your files to your instructor

FIGURE J-17: Adding the DEVELOPER tab to the Ribbon

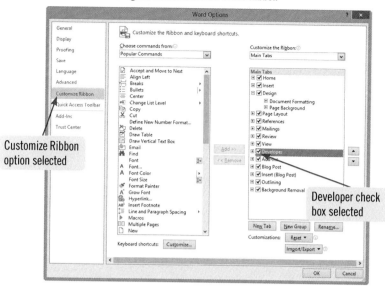

Customize Ribbon option selected

Developer check box selected

FIGURE J-18: Ally Stein's profile formatted with styles

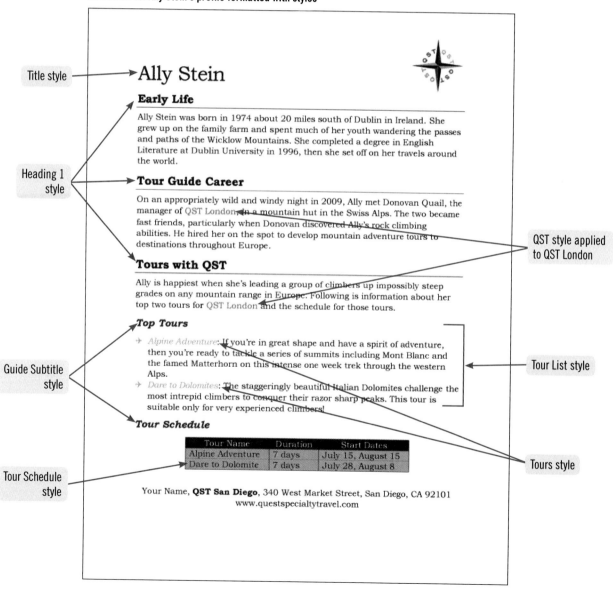

Title style

Heading 1 style

Guide Subtitle style

Tour Schedule style

QST style applied to QST London

Tour List style

Tours style

Practice

Concepts Review

Identify each of the items in FIGURE J-19.

FIGURE J-19

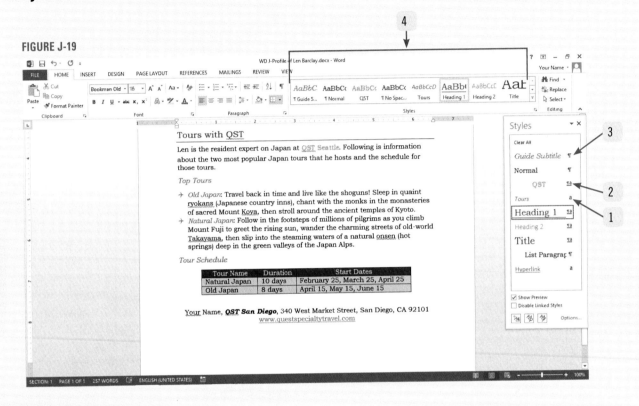

Match each term with the statement that best describes it.

5. Style Set

6. Organizer dialog box

7. Template

8. Style

9. Character style

a. Character formats that you name and store as a set

b. A file that contains the basic structure of a document in addition to selected styles; can be custom made

c. A collection of character, paragraph, and linked styles that is named and available to all documents

d. Used to copy styles from a source document to a target document

e. A collection of saved formats that is used to provide consistent formatting to related items, such as all Heading 1 text

Select the best answer from the list of choices.

10. **What is available in the Style Set gallery?**
    a. Themes associated with the current Style Set
    b. The DEVELOPER tab
    c. Colors associated with the current Style Set
    d. Styles associated with the current Style Set

11. **How do you modify a style?**
    a. Double-click the style in the Styles task pane.
    b. Right-click the style in the Styles gallery, then click Revise.
    c. Right-click the style in the Styles gallery, then click Modify.
    d. Click the style in the Styles task pane, then click New Style.

12. **Which of the following definitions best describes a paragraph style?**
    a. Format settings applied only to selected text within a paragraph
    b. Format settings applied to a table grid
    c. Format settings applied to all text in a paragraph
    d. Format settings applied to the structure of a document

13. **Which of the following style types is not saved with a Style Set?**
    a. Table style
    b. Paragraph style
    c. Linked style
    d. Character style

14. **Which dialog box do you use to copy styles from one document to another?**
    a. Reveal Formatting dialog box
    b. Organizer dialog box
    c. Styles dialog box
    d. Modify Styles dialog box

15. **What is the filename extension for a template?**
    a. .docx
    b. .RTF
    c. .dotx
    d. .dotm

16. **Which tab do you use to attach a template to an existing document?**
    a. INSERT
    b. REFERENCES
    c. DEVELOPER
    d. PAGE

Skills Review

1. **Modify built-in styles.**
   a. Start Word, open the file WD J-4.docx from the location where you store your Data Files, save it as **WD J-Jigsaws_Shaped**, then open the Styles task pane.
   b. Modify the Normal style by changing the font to Times New Roman and the font size to 12 pt.
   c. Select the Map Jigsaws heading, then change the font to Arial, the font size to 18 pt, and the font color to Orange, Accent 2, Darker 25%.
   d. Add a border line below the text.
   e. From the PAGE LAYOUT tab, change the Before spacing to 6 pt and the After spacing to 6 pt.
   f. Update the Heading 1 style so that it uses the new formats.
   g. Modify the Title style by changing the font to Arial and the color to Orange, Accent 2, Darker 50%, then save the document.

2. **Create paragraph styles.**
   a. Scroll to and select the heading "Marketing Plan," then create a new paragraph style called **Operations** that uses the Arial font, 14 pt, bold, and italic, and changes the font color to Gold, Accent 4, Darker 25%.
   b. Apply the Operations style to "Summary of New Products."
   c. From the Styles task pane, show only the styles currently in use in the document and make sure the Show Preview check box is selected.
   d. Save the document.

Skills Review (continued)

3. Create character and linked styles.

a. Select "France" under Map Jigsaws, then create a new character style named **Jigsaw Theme** that uses the Arial font, 12 pt, Italic, and the Orange, Accent 2, Darker 50% font color.

b. Apply the Jigsaw Theme style to "United States," "Grizzly Bear," and "Dolphin."

c. Select "Bit Part Puzzles" in the first paragraph, apply the Fill - Gold, Accent 4, Soft Bevel text effect, open the Create New Style from Formatting dialog box, name the style **Company**, and select the Linked style type, then select the option to right-align the paragraph.

d. Apply the Company style to the France paragraph, undo the application, then apply the Company style just to the text "Bit Part Puzzles" in the paragraph above the table.

e. Save the document.

4. Create list and table styles.

a. Click to the left of "France" under Map Jigsaws, then define a new list style called **Jigsaw List**. (*Hint:* Click the Multilevel List button in the Paragraph group on the HOME tab, then click Define New List Style.)

b. Change the list style to Bullet, open the Symbol dialog box, verify the Wingdings character set is active, type **216** in the Character code text box, then change the symbol color to Purple in the Standard Colors area.

c. Apply the Jigsaw List style to each paragraph that describes a jigsaw: United States, Grizzly Bear, and Dolphin. (*Hint:* You access the Jigsaw List style by clicking the Multilevel List button.)

d. Select the table at the bottom of the document, then create a new table style called **Jigsaw Table**.

e. Select Gold, Accent 4, Lighter 80% for the fill color, change the border style to 3/4 pt and the border color to Automatic, then apply All Borders to the table.

f. Format the header row with bold, the White font color, the Gold, Accent 4, Darker 50% fill color, and Center alignment, then apply the new table style to your table.

g. With the table selected, double-click between columns to reduce the column sizes.

h. From the TABLE TOOLS DESIGN tab, modify the style by changing the table properties so the table is centered between the left and right margins of the page, then save the document.

5. Create a Style Set.

a. From the DESIGN tab, save the current Style Set as **Jigsaws**, then view the Jigsaws Style Set in the Custom section of the Style Sets gallery.

b. Change the color scheme to Blue, then save the document.

c. Open the file WD J-5.docx from the location where you store your Data Files, then save it as **WD J-Jigsaws_3D**.

d. Apply the Jigsaws Style Set to the document, then apply the Blue color scheme.

e. Apply the Jigsaw Theme style to the four jigsaw titles (e.g., "Eiffel Tower, "Log Cabin," etc.).

f. Apply the Operations style to "Marketing Plan," and "Summary of New Products," then save the document.

6. Manage styles.

a. Position the insertion point at the beginning of the document, open the Replace dialog box, enter **Bit Part Puzzles** in the Find what text box, then enter **Bit Part Puzzles** in the Replace with text box.

b. Open the More options area, select the Style option on the Format menu, select the Company Char style, then replace both instances of Bit Part Puzzles with Bit Part Puzzles formatted with the Company Char style.

c. Open the Manage Styles dialog box from the Styles task pane, then click Import/Export to open the Organizer dialog box.

d. Close the file in the left pane of the Organizer dialog box, then open the file WD J-Jigsaws_Shaped.docx. Remember to navigate to the location where you save files and to change the Files of type to Word documents.

e. Close the file in the right pane of the Organizer dialog box, then open the file WD J-Jigsaws_3D.docx.

f. Copy the Jigsaw List and Jigsaw Table styles from the WD J-Jigsaws_Shaped document to the WD J-Jigsaws_3D document, then close the Organizer dialog box and return to the document.

g. In the file WD J-Jigsaws_3D.docx, apply the Jigsaw List style to each of the four jigsaw descriptions.

h. Select the table, use the TABLE TOOLS DESIGN tab to apply the Jigsaw Table style to the table, reduce the column widths, type your name where indicated at the end of the document, save the document, then close it.

7. Create a template.

   a. Save the current document (which should be WD J-Jigsaws_Shaped) as a template called **WD J-Jigsaw Descriptions.dotx** in the Custom Office Templates folder in the My Documents folder on your computer.

   b. Select "Shaped Jigsaws" at the top of the page, type **[Enter Category Here]**, then delete text and enter directions so the document appears as shown in **FIGURE J-20**. (*Hint:* If new text is formatted with a style you don't want associated with that text, such as the Company style, the Heading 1 style, or the Jigsaw Theme, select the formatted text and click the Clear All Formatting button in the Font group on the HOME tab.)

FIGURE J-20

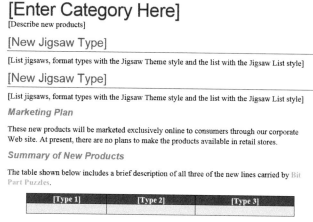

   c. Save and close the template.

   d. Create a new document based on the WD J-Jigsaw Descriptions template. Remember to show the list of PERSONAL templates.

   e. Replace the title of the document with the text **Brain Teaser Jigsaws**, save the document as **WD J-Jigsaws_Brain Teaser** to the location where you store your files, then close it.

8. Modify and attach a template.

   a. Open the template file WD J-Jigsaw Descriptions.dotx, then modify the Title style so that the font is Century Gothic. (*Note:* Be sure to open the template using the FILE and Open commands so you can work on the template document itself.)

   b. Modify the Jigsaw Theme style by changing the font to Georgia.

   c. Resave the Jigsaws Style Set, then save and close the template.

   d. Open the file WD J-6.docx from the location where your Data Files are located, save the file as **WD J-Jigsaws_Landscape**, then from the DESIGN tab, apply the Jigsaws Style Set and select the Blue color scheme.

   e. Show the DEVELOPER tab on the Ribbon, open the Templates and Add-ins dialog box, attach the WD J-Jigsaw Descriptions.dotx template from the Custom Office Templates folder, click the Automatically update document styles check box, then click OK.

   f. Apply styles from the Jigsaws Style Set that are associated with the WD J-Puzzle Descriptions template so that the WD J-Jigsaws_Landscape document resembles the other documents you have formatted for this Skills Review (*Hint:* Remember to apply the Title, Jigsaw Theme, Operations, Jigsaw List, and Jigsaw Table styles, and to apply the Company style to all three instances of "Bit Part Puzzles.")

   g. Enter your name where indicated, then save and close the document.

   h. In a new blank document in Word, from the DESIGN tab, delete the Jigsaws Style Set, then remove the DEVELOPER tab from the Ribbon and exit Word.

   i. Submit your files to your instructor.

Independent Challenge 1

You are the office manager of Green Solutions, a company that creates educational materials for courses and workshops in environmental studies. The annual company fitness day is coming soon, and you need to inform the employees about the date and time. You have already typed the text of the staff notice and included some formatting. Now you need to modify some of the styles, create new styles, create a new Style Set and copy a style to a new document, and then use the Style Set to format another staff notice about a different event.

   a. Start Word, open the file WD J-7.docx from the location where you store your Data Files, then save it as **WD J-Staff Notice of Fitness Day**.

Independent Challenge 1 (continued)

b. Modify and update styles as shown in **TABLE J-1**.

TABLE J-1

style name	changes
Title	Arial Black font; 22-pt font size; Green, Accent 6, Darker 50%
Heading 1	Arial Black font; 14-pt font size; Green, Accent 6, Darker 25%

© 2014 Cengage Learning

c. Apply the Heading 1 style to the three headings shown in ALL CAPS in the document.

d. Create a new paragraph style called **Event** that uses the Arial font, 20-pt font size, italic, and Blue, Accent 5, Darker 25%, then apply it to "Company Fitness Day."

e. Create a new character style called **Green** that uses the Arial font, 14-pt font size, italic, and Green, Accent 6, Darker 25%.

f. Find every instance of "Green Solutions" and replace it with Green Solutions formatted with the Green style.

g. Modify the Green style by changing the font size to 12 pt.

h. Create a table style called **Activities** using formats as shown in **TABLE J-2**, then apply the table style to the table in the document.

TABLE J-2

table area	changes
whole table	Fill - Green, Accent 6, Lighter 80%; 1 pt border lines
header row	Fill - Green, Accent 6, Darker 50%; White font color and bold

© 2014 Cengage Learning

i. Save the Style Set as **Staff Events**, change the color scheme to Red Violet, type your name where indicated, then save the document (and keep it open).

j. Open the file WD J-8.docx, save the document as **WD J-Staff Notice of Holiday Party**, apply the Staff Events Style Set, then change the color scheme to Red Violet.

k. Save the file, then open the Organizer dialog box from the Manage Styles dialog box. (*Hint:* Click Import/Export.)

l. In the Organizer dialog box, make WD J-Staff Notice of Fitness Day the source file and WD J-Staff Notice of Holiday Party the target file. Remember to select All Word Documents as the file type when opening the files.

m. Copy the Activities table style from the file WD J-Staff Notice of Fitness Day file to the WD J-Staff Notice of Holiday Party file, then close the Organizer dialog box.

n. Apply styles to selected headings and text in WD J-Staff Notice of Holiday Party to match the Staff Notice of Fitness Day document. (*Hint:* You need to apply the Event, Heading 1, and Green styles, as well as the Activities table style. Note that you can use Find and Replace to find every instance of "Green Solutions" and replace it with Green Solutions formatted with the Green character style.)

o. Type your name where indicated, then save the document.

p. Remove the Staff Events Style Set from the list of Style Sets, then submit the files to your instructor.

Independent Challenge 2

As the owner of the Sunrise Bistro, a vegetarian café in Sante Fe, you need to create two menus—one for spring and one for fall. You have already created an unformatted version of the spring menu and of the fall menu. Now you need to format text in the spring menu with styles, save the styles in a new Style Set called Menus, then use the Menus Style Set to format text in the fall version of the menu. You also need to work in the Organizer dialog box to copy the list and table styles you created for the spring menu to the fall version of the menu.

a. Start Word, open the file WD J-9.docx from the location where you store your Data Files, then save it as **WD J-Sunrise Bistro Spring Menu**. Apply the Slipstream color scheme.

b. Select the title (Sunrise Bistro Spring Menu), apply these formats: Bauhaus 93, 18 pt, a font color of Green, Accent 4, Darker 50%, and Center alignment, then create a new linked style called **Menu Title** based on these formats. (*Hint:* Right-click the formatted text, click the Styles button on the Mini toolbar, click Create a Style, type Menu Title, then click OK. You can verify that the style is a linked style by clicking Modify in the Create New Style from Formatting dialog box.)

Independent Challenge 2 (continued)

c. Select Appetizers, apply the formats Bauhaus 93, 14 pt, italic, a font color of Green, Accent 4, Darker 25%, then create a new linked style from the selection called **Menu Category**.

d. Apply the Menu Category style to each of the remaining main headings: Soups and Salads, Entrees, Desserts, and Opening Times.

e. Click to the left of Feta cheese (the first appetizer), then create a new list style called **Bistro Menu Item** that includes a bullet character from Wingdings symbol 123 (a stylized flower) that is colored Green, Accent 4, Darker 50%.

f. Click the Multilevel List button, right-click the new Bistro Menu Item style in the List Styles area, click Modify, then in the Modify Style dialog box, click Format (bottom left), click Numbering, click More (bottom left), click the Add tab stop at: check box, select the contents of the text box, type **5.5**, click OK, then click OK.

g. Apply the Bistro Menu Item list style (remember to click the Multilevel List button) to all the menu items in each category.

h. Save the styles in a Style Set called **Menus**.

i. Click anywhere in the table, then create a new table style called **Bistro Times** that fills the table cells with a light fill color of your choice and includes border lines, and then format the header row with the corresponding dark fill color of your choice and the white font color, bold, and centering.

j. Modify the Bistro Times table style so that the table is centered between the left and right margins of the page.

k. Type your name where indicated at the bottom of the document, then save the document and keep it open.

l. Open the file WD J-10.docx, save it as **WD J-Sunrise Bistro Fall Menu**, then apply the Menus Style Set.

m. Format the appropriate headings with the Menu Title and Menu Category styles. Note that the Bistro Menu Items list style and the Bistro Times table styles are not saved with the Menus Style Set. You need to copy them separately.

n. Change the color scheme to the color scheme of your choice. You do not need to select the same color scheme you applied to the summer menu.

o. Save the file, then open the Organizer dialog box from the Manage Styles dialog box.

p. In the Organizer dialog box, make WD J-Sunrise Bistro Spring Menu the source file and WD J-Sunrise Bistro Fall Menu the target file. Remember to select All Word Documents as the file type when opening the files.

q. Copy the Bistro Menu Item list style and the Bistro Times table style from the file WD J-Sunrise Bistro Spring Menu file to the WD J-Sunrise Bistro Fall Menu file, then close the Organizer dialog box.

r. In the Fall menu document, apply the Bistro Menu Item list style to the first appetizer (Harvest cheddar cheeses).

s. Click the Multilevel List button, right-click the Bistro Menu Item style, click Modify, then change the bullet symbol for the Menu Item style to Wingdings 124 (a dark flower symbol).

t. Apply the updated Bistro Menu Item list style to all the menu items, apply the Bistro Times table style to the table, type your name where indicated, then remove the Menus style from the list of Style Sets. (*Note:* You may need to modify the colors associated with the table style in order to match the color scheme you selected for this document.)

u. Save the documents, submit all files to your instructor, then close all files.

Independent Challenge 3

As a student in the business program at your local community college, you have volunteered to create a design for a bi-monthly class newsletter and another classmate has volunteered to write text for the first newsletter, which is to be distributed in November. First, you create a template for the newsletter, then you apply the template to the document containing the newsletter text.

a. Open the file WD J-11.docx, then save it as a template called **WD J-Newsletter Template.dotx** to the Custom Office Templates folder in the My Documents folder on your computer.

Independent Challenge 3 (continued)

b. Enter text and create styles as shown in **FIGURE J-21**. (*Hint:* Use the text in bold for the style names.)

FIGURE J-21

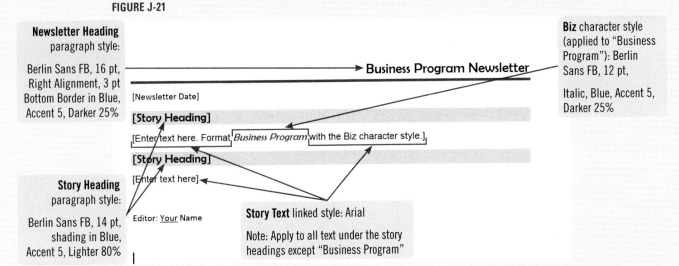

c. Save the Style Set as **Biz Program**.

d. Click to the left of the first [Story Heading], then create two columns from this point forward. (*Hint:* Click the PAGE LAYOUT tab, click the Columns button in the Page Setup group, click More Columns, then in the Columns dialog box, click Two in the Presets section, click the Apply to list arrow, select This point forward, then click OK.)

e. Type your name where indicated, then save and close the template.

f. Start a new document based on the WD J-Newsletter Template, type **November 2016** in place of [Newsletter Date], then type **Class Projects** in place of the first [Story Heading] and **Upcoming Events** in place of the next [Story Heading]. Make sure both headings are formatted with the Story Heading style and that the date is formatted with the Normal style.

g. Save the document as **WD J-Newsletter_November** to the location where you store your files, then close the document.

h. Open the file WD J-12.docx, save it as **WD J-Newsletter_December**, show the DEVELOPER tab on the Ribbon, attach the WD J-Newsletter Template.dotx to the document, apply the Biz Program Style Set via the DESIGN tab, then apply styles and formatting as follows: apply the Newsletter Heading style to the newsletter title, the Story Heading style to all four headings, the Story Text style to all paragraphs of text that are not headings (excluding the date and Editor: Your Name), and the Biz style to Business Program (*Hint:* Use the Find Next, not Replace All, Replace feature to replace three instances of Business Program in the story text (but not to Business Program in the Newsletter Heading.)

i. Apply the two-column format starting at the Class Projects heading. (*Note:* You need to apply the two-column format because options related to the structure of a document saved with a template are lost when you attach the template to an existing document.)

j. Modify the Story Text style so that the font size is 10 pt, then resave the Biz Program Style Set.

k. Click at the end of the document (following your name), click the PAGE LAYOUT tab, click Breaks, then click Continuous to balance the columns in the newsletter.

l. Save and close the document.

m. Open the file WD J-Newsletter Template.dotx (*Hint:* Be sure to open the template using the FILE menu. Do not double-click it.)

n. Apply the Biz Program Style Set again, modify the Newsletter Heading style so the font size is 20 pt. (*Hint:* Make sure you modify the style, not just the heading text.)

o. Resave the Biz Program Style Set.

p. Save and close the template.

Independent Challenge 3 (continued)

q. Open the file WD J-Newsletter_November.docx, attach the updated template and make sure styles automatically update, verify that Newsletter heading text is 20 pt and the story text is 10 pt, then save and close the document.

r. Open the file WD J-Newsletter_December.docx, then verify that the document is updated with the new styles.

s. Save the document, delete the Biz Program Style Set, remove the DEVELOPER tab from the Ribbon, close the document and exit Word, then submit all files to your instructor.

Independent Challenge 4: Explore

From the Microsoft Office Web site, you can access templates that you can use to create and then customize hundreds of different types of documents from calendars to business proposals to trip itineraries. You use keywords to search for a template, select and create it in Word and then modify it for your own purposes. You also explore more options in the Styles task pane. *(Note: To complete these steps your computer must be connected to the Internet.)*

a. Start Word, open a new blank document, click the FILE tab, click New, click in the Search text box, type **itinerary**, then click the Start searching button.

b. Select the template Business trip itinerary, click Create, then save the document as **WD J-Business Trip Itinerary.docx**.

c. Enter your name where indicated above the itinerary table.

d. Select and then delete the Phone number and Travel time columns in the itinerary table, then widen the Comments column so its right edge is even with the border line above the itinerary title.

e. Complete the itinerary table with the information shown in **FIGURE J-22**.

FIGURE J-22

Business Trip Itinerary | [Name]

Date	Depart from	Depart time	Destination	Arrival time	Destination address	Comments
May 2	Vancouver, BC	20:00	London, UK	13:00 (May 3)	Park Place Hotel	Meet with Paul M. for dinner
May 6	London, UK	10:00	Paris, France	14:35	Eiffel Tower Hotel	Train arrives at the Gare du Nord
May 12	Paris, France	9:00	Berlin, Germany	10:30	Aparthotel	Fly from Orly

f. Open the Styles task pane, then click the Style Inspector button at the bottom of the task pane.

g. Click to the left of Business Trip Itinerary and notice that the Style Inspector lists the Title style as the current paragraph formatting.

h. Click Date and notice that the Style Inspector lists the Normal style with the addition of Bold and the Background 1 color. You can use the Style Inspector to determine exactly what formatting is applied to selected text and then clear the formatting if you wish.

i. Click the Reveal Formatting button at the bottom of the Style Inspector and if necessary, move the Styles task pane so you can see the Reveal Formatting task pane that opens to the right of your screen. The Reveal Formatting task pane lists all the formatting applied to the document.

j. Scroll down the Reveal Formatting task pane to view all the settings. You can click the arrow to the right of any heading to see additional settings.

k. Click TABLE STYLE once under the Table heading to open the Table AutoFormat dialog box. In this dialog box you can quickly select a new built-in table style for the table.

l. Click List Table 4 - Accent 6 (green), then click OK to use the Reveal Formatting, Styles, and Style Inspector task panes to make two more modifications of your choice to the document.

m. Close the Reveal Formatting, Styles, and Style Inspector task panes.

n. Select a new color scheme of your choice, save and close the document, exit Word, then submit the file to your instructor.

Visual Workshop

Create a new document, then type the text and create the tables shown in **FIGURE J-23**. Save the file as **WD J-Price List_ Still Waters Spa**. Do not include any formatting. Select the Violet II color scheme, apply the Title style to the title, then modify the Title style so that it appears as shown in **FIGURE J-23**. Note that all the colors are variations of the Violet II color scheme, Plum, Accent 1, and the font style for the title and headings is Comic Sans MS font (or a similar font). Apply the Heading 1 style to the names of the price lists, then modify the Heading 1 style so that it appears as shown in **FIGURE J-23**. Create a new Style Set called **Prices**. Create a table style called **Price List** that formats each table as shown in **FIGURE J-23**, then modify the column widths as shown. (*Note:* You will not see the center alignment applied until after the column widths are adjusted.) Save the document. Open WD J-13.docx, save it as **WD J-Price List_Ultimate Spa**, apply the Prices Style Set, copy the Price List table style from WD J-Price List_Still Waters Spa to WD J-Price List_Ultimate Spa, then apply styles and modify column widths so the document resembles the document shown in **FIGURE J-23**. Apply the Green color scheme. Save and close the documents, then submit both files to your instructor.

FIGURE J-23

Still Waters Spa

Essential Oils Price List

Product #	Essential Oil	Price
3300	Basil	$6.50
3500	Clove	$8.00
4000	Ginger	$7.50
4500	Lavender	$6.00

Fragrance Oils Price List

Product #	Fragrance Oil	Price
5000	Blackberry	$7.00
7780	Green Tea	$7.50
7790	Magnolia	$7.00
7792	Plum	$8.00
7795	Vanilla	$7.50

Prepared by Your Name

Working with References

CASE ▶ As a special projects assistant at Quest Specialty Travel (QST) in San Diego, you compile reference materials containing background information about tour destinations. You use the AutoCorrect feature to insert text in an article for QST's Art Tour to Italy, then modify footnotes and citations, and add figure captions, a bibliography, and a table of figures. You also open a file saved as a Portable Document Format (PDF) file, edit it in Word, and add equations.

Unit Objectives

After completing this unit, you will be able to:

- Work with AutoCorrect
- Customize footnotes
- Use the Translate feature
- Modify citations and manage sources
- Add and modify captions
- Generate a bibliography and table of figures
- Work with PDF Files in Word
- Work with equations

Files You Will Need

WD K-1.docx	WD K-6.docx
WD K-2.pdf	WD K-7.docx
WD K-3.docx	WD K-8.docx
WD K-4.pdf	WD K-9.docx
WD K-5.docx	

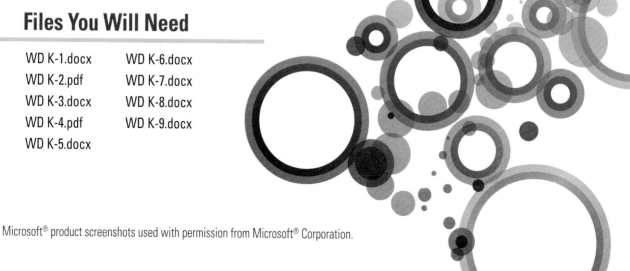

Work with AutoCorrect

Learning
Outcomes
• Create a new
  AutoCorrect entry
• Use keystrokes to
  insert a symbol
• Delete an
  AutoCorrect entry

The AutoCorrect feature is set up to automatically correct most typos and misspelled words. For example, if you type "teh" and press the Spacebar, the AutoCorrect feature inserts "the." The AutoCorrect feature also inserts symbols when you type certain character combinations. For example, if you type (r), the ® symbol appears. You can modify the list of AutoCorrect options, and you can create your own AutoCorrect entries. These entries can be a word, a phrase, or even a paragraph. You set up AutoCorrect to automatically enter the text you specify when you type a certain sequence of characters. For example, you could specify that "San Francisco, California" be entered each time you type "sfc" followed by a space. **CASE** *You need to enter the term "Renaissance" in multiple places in an article you are editing on the Renaissance artist Cellini. You decide to create an AutoCorrect entry that will insert "Renaissance" each time you type "ren." You also use AutoCorrect to insert symbols, view the AutoFormat settings, and delete an entry from the AutoCorrect list.*

STEPS

1. **Start Word, open the file WD K-1.docx from the drive and folder where you store your Data Files, save the file as WD K-Artist Article, click the FILE tab, click Options, then click Proofing**

   All the options related to how Word corrects and formats text appear in the Proofing section of the Word Options dialog box.

2. **Click AutoCorrect Options**

   The AutoCorrect: English (United States) dialog box opens. By default the AutoCorrect tab is active. In this dialog box, you can specify common tasks such as correcting TWo INitial CApitals, create new AutoCorrect entries, and see what keystrokes you can use to quickly enter common symbols such as the € or ®.

3. **Scroll through the AutoCorrect list to view the predefined pairs of symbols and words**

   Notice how many symbols you can create with simple keystrokes. The AutoCorrect list is used in all the programs in the Microsoft Office suite, which means that any word you add or delete from the AutoCorrect list in one program is also added or deleted from all other Office programs. On the AutoCorrect tab, you can create a new AutoCorrect entry.

   TROUBLE
   If the insertion point is not blinking in the Replace text box, click the Replace text box to make it active.

4. **Type ren in the Replace text box, press [TAB], type Renaissance as shown in FIGURE K-1, click Add, click OK, then click OK**

   When you create an AutoCorrect entry, you need to enter an abbreviation that is not a real word. For example, you should not create an AutoCorrect entry for "Antarctic" from "ant" because every time you type "ant" followed by a space, the word "Antarctic" will appear whether you want it to or not.

5. **Press [Ctrl][F] to open the Navigation pane, type rest of the world, click to the left of world in the document, type ren, then press [Spacebar]**

   The word "Renaissance" is inserted so the phrase is now "Renaissance world."

6. **Press [Ctrl][End] to move to the end of the document, then click in the blank table cell below Cost**

   QUICK TIP
   Use the AutoCorrect entry (e) to enter the € symbol each time.

7. **Type (e) to insert the symbol for the Euro currency, type 95.00, then enter €75.00 in the blank cell of the third row and €85.00 in the fourth row as shown in FIGURE K-2**

8. **Click the FILE tab, click Options, click Proofing, then click AutoCorrect Options**

   As a courtesy to others who might use the computer you are currently working on, you delete the "ren" Autocorrect entry. If you are the only user of your computer, you can leave the entry so it is available for future use.

9. **Type ren in the Replace text box, click Delete, click Close, click OK, then save the document**

   The "ren" AutoCorrect entry is deleted from Word and all other Office applications.

Working with References

FIGURE K-1: Creating a new AutoCorrect entry

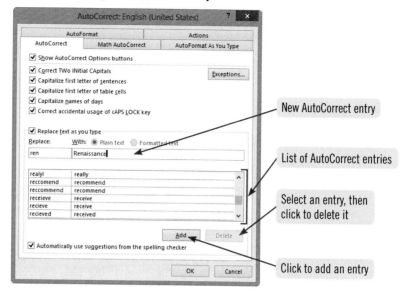

New AutoCorrect entry

List of AutoCorrect entries

Select an entry, then click to delete it

Click to add an entry

FIGURE K-2: Completed tour costs

Tour	Description	Cost
Private Tour of the Uffizi	Join a special after hours tour of the great Uffizi Gallery in Florence.	€95.00
The Gardens of Florence	Explore the great gardens of Florence, including the famous Boboli Gardens.	€75.00
Golden Artisans of Florence	Visit the workshops of three Florentine goldsmiths and marvel at their incredible skill.	€85.00

Symbol added automatically by Autocorrect when (e) typed

Accessing AutoFormat options in the AutoCorrect dialog box

Two tabs in the AutoCorrect dialog box relate to how Word formats text that you type. From the AutoFormat tab, you can view the list of formats that Word applies automatically to text. The AutoFormat As You Type tab shows some of the same options included in the AutoFormat tab along with some additional options, as shown in **FIGURE K-3**. Usually, you do not need to change the default options. However, if you do not want an option, you can click the check box next to the option to deselect it. For example, if you decide that you do not want Word to make an ordinal such as 1st into 1st, you can click the Ordinals (1st) with superscript check box to deselect it.

FIGURE K-3: Options available on the AutoFormat As You Type tab in the AutoCorrect dialog box

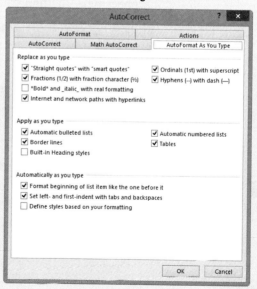

Working with References

Customize Footnotes

You use **footnotes** or **endnotes** to provide additional information or to acknowledge sources for text in a document. Footnotes appear at the bottom of the page on which the footnote reference appears and endnotes appear at the end of the document. Every footnote and endnote consists of a **note reference mark** and the corresponding note text. When you add, delete, or move a note, any additional notes in the document are renumbered or re-lettered automatically. You can customize footnotes by changing the number format, by adding a custom mark, or by modifying the numbering sequence. **CASE** *The footnotes in the current document use the A, B, C number format and are set to restart on every page. You change the number format of the footnotes to the 1, 2, 3 style and set the footnotes to number consecutively starting from "1." You then add a new footnote, and edit footnotes you inserted earlier.*

STEPS

1. **Increase the zoom to 140%, scroll to the top of the document and notice as you scroll that the footnotes on each page start with "A," click the REFERENCES tab, click the launcher ⌐ in the Footnotes group, click the Number format list arrow, then select the 1, 2, 3... Number format**

2. **Click the Numbering list arrow, click Continuous, verify Whole document appears next to Apply changes to, compare the Footnote and Endnote dialog box to FIGURE K-4, click Apply, then scroll to see the renumbered footnotes**
   The footnotes are numbered continuously through the document starting at "1".

3. **Type rigorous training in the Search document text box in the Navigation pane, then click after training in the document**
   The insertion point is positioned where you need to insert a new footnote.

4. **Click the Insert Footnote button in the Footnotes group, type Artists began training at an early age. They apprenticed with a master, as Cellini did when he was fifteen., then scroll down so you can see all four footnotes on the page**
   FIGURE K-5 shows the footnote area with the newly inserted footnote (footnote 2).

5. **Click in the line of text immediately above the footnote separator line, click the Next Footnote button in the Footnotes group to move to footnote 5, double-click 5 to move the insertion point to the footnote at the bottom of the page, click after the word Clement, press [Spacebar], type VII, then scroll up and click above the footnote separator**

6. **Press [Ctrl][G], click Footnote in the Go to what list, click in the Enter footnote number text box, type 1, click Go To, then click Close**
   The insertion point moves to the footnote 1 reference mark in the document.

7. **Press [Delete] two times to remove the footnote reference mark and its associated footnote text, then scroll down to see the newly labeled footnote 1, which is the footnote you inserted in step 4 (begins with "Artists began training...)**
   The original footnote reference mark 1 and its corresponding footnote are deleted, and the remaining footnote reference marks and their corresponding footnotes are renumbered starting with 1.

8. **Click any word in one of the footnotes at the bottom of a page, right-click, then click Style**
   The Style dialog box opens with Footnote Text already selected.

9. **Click Modify, click the Format button in the lower left of the dialog box, click Paragraph, reduce the After spacing to 6 pt, click the Line spacing list arrow, click Single, click OK, click OK, click Apply, then save the document**
   Text in all of the footnotes is now single spaced with 6 point After spacing.

FIGURE K-4: Footnote and Endnote dialog box

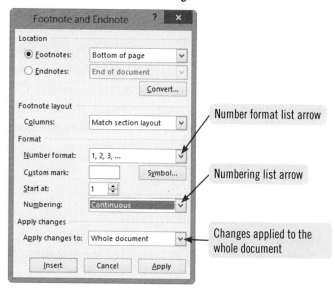

FIGURE K-5: Text for footnote 2

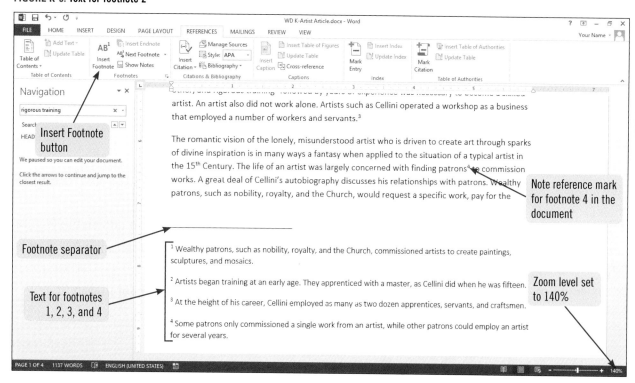

Inserting endnotes

Click the Insert Endnote button in the Footnotes group on the REFERENCES tab to insert a note reference mark for an endnote. When you click the Insert Endnote button, the insertion point moves to the end of your document so that you can enter text for the endnote in the same way you enter text for a footnote. You click above the endnote separator to return to the text of your document. You work in the Footnote and Endnote dialog box to modify options for endnotes.

Use the Translate Feature

Learning
Outcomes
• Translate selected
text
• Use the Mini
Translator

You can use the Translate feature on the REVIEW tab to translate single words or short passages of text into another language or from another language into English. You can also access Web-based translation services from Word when you need to translate longer documents that require a high degree of accuracy. Finally, you can use the Mini Translator to provide an instant translation of a single word or selected phrase by moving the pointer over the information you want translated. **CASE** ▸ *Some of the text in the article is written in Italian. You use the Translate feature to translate the text from Italian to English, and then you experiment with the Mini Translator feature.*

STEPS

1. **Press [Ctrl][Home] to move to the top of the document, click in the Search document text box in the Navigation pane, type** produce sculpture, **then select the text from Cellini to adornamenti at the end of the sentence (do not include the opening parenthesis)**

2. **Click the** REVIEW tab, **then click the** Translate button **in the Language group**

   Three translation options are listed.

3. **Click** Translate Selected Text **to open the Research task pane, verify that Italian (Italy) appears in the From text box, then if necessary, click the** To list arrow **and click** English (United States)

   A machine translation of the selected text appears in the Research task pane, as shown in **FIGURE K-6**. The translation is an approximation of the meaning and is not meant to be definitive.

4. **Close the Research task pane**

5. **Click the word** goldsmith **in the line above the Italian quote, click the** Translate button **in the Language group, then click** Choose Translation Language

   The Translation Language Options dialog box opens. You use this dialog box to set the options for translating the document or the options for the Mini Translator.

6. **Click the** Translate To: list arrow **in the Choose Mini Translator language area, select** Italian (Italy), **then click** OK

7. **Click the** Translate button, **then click** Mini Translator [Italian (Italy)] **to turn on this feature**

8. **Move the pointer over and then slightly above goldsmith to view the Online Bilingual Dictionary, then note that the Italian translation is "orefice" as shown in** FIGURE K-7

9. **Click the** Translate button **in the Language group, click** Mini Translator [Italian (Italy)] **to turn the feature off, then save the document**

FIGURE K-6: Translating text

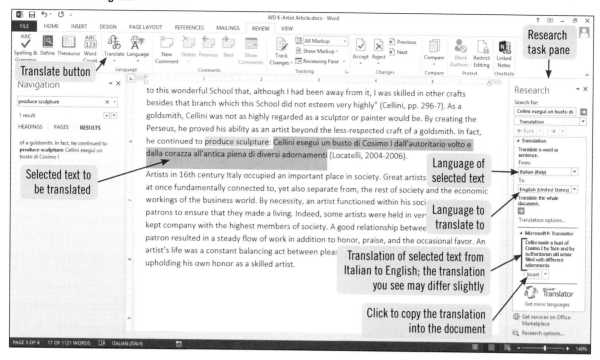

Translate button

Selected text to be translated

Language of selected text

Language to translate to

Translation of selected text from Italian to English; the translation you see may differ slightly

Click to copy the translation into the document

Research task pane

FIGURE K-7: Using the Mini Translator

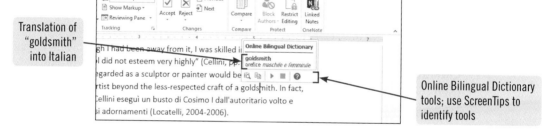

Translation of "goldsmith" into Italian

Online Bilingual Dictionary tools; use ScreenTips to identify tools

Exploring the Research task pane

The Research task pane provides you with a variety of options for finding information. You can open the Research task pane by clicking the Translate button in the Language group on the REVIEW tab, and then clicking Translate Selected Text. Once the Research task pane is open, you can change the settings so you can search for both translations and for information on a specific topic. To find information about a specific topic, you enter keywords into the Search for text box, then click the list arrow for the box under the Search for text box to show the list of services. For example, you can choose to search All Reference Books or All Research Sites, or you can select a specific resource under these broader categories. The services listed under the broader category of All Reference Books include dictionaries, thesauruses, and translation. The services listed under the broader category All Research Sites include various Internet research Web sites. **FIGURE K-8** shows the results when "Italy" is entered in the Search text box and All Research Sites is selected as the service. You can scroll through the list to find research sites that meet your needs.

FIGURE K-8: Options in the Research task pane

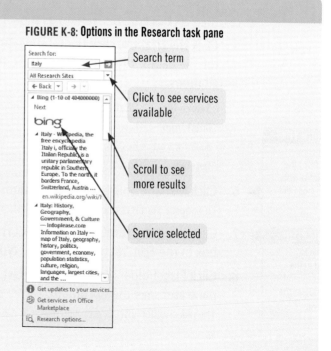

Search term

Click to see services available

Scroll to see more results

Service selected

Working with References

Modify Citations and Manage Sources

Learning Outcomes
• Insert a Placeholder
• Edit a citation
• Edit a source

The Citations & Bibliography group on the REFERENCES tab includes features to help you keep track of the resources you use to write research papers and articles. You can use the Manage Sources feature to help you enter and organize your sources. A **citation** is a short reference, usually including the author and page number, that gives credit to the source of a quote or other information included in a document. Citations are based on information you entered in the Create Source form. You can modify the contents of a citation you have inserted in a document, edit the source of the citation, and format a citation for specific guidelines such as MLA or APA. **CASE** *You have completed source forms for some sources and inserted associated citations into the artist article. The citations use the APA style. Now you need to include a placeholder citation, change the citation style, edit the citation content, and work in the Manage Sources dialog box to edit and delete sources.*

STEPS

1. Search for the text space of time, click to the right of the closing quotation mark, click the REFERENCES tab, click the Insert Citation button in the Citations & Bibliography group, click Add New Placeholder, then click OK to add the citation (Placeholder1)

QUICK TIP
The field selection handle is a tab on the left side of the content control.

2. Search for Adams, click Adams in the document, click the field selection handle to select the entire citation (the citation is shaded when it is selected), click the Style list arrow in the Citations & Bibliography group, then click MLA as shown in FIGURE K-9

   Consistent with the MLA style, the year is removed and the citation includes only the author's name.

3. Click the Citation Options list arrow, click Edit Citation, type 82 in the Pages text box, then click OK

   The citation now shows the author's name and page number reference.

4. Click outside the citation to deselect it, find the text space of time, click (Placeholder1), click the field selection handle to select the entire citation, click the Insert Citation button, then click Cellini, Benvenuto as shown in FIGURE K-10

5. Click the citation, click the Citation Options list arrow, click Edit Citation, type 324-325 for the pages, click OK, click outside the citation to deselect it, then edit the following citations:

Search for	Citation to edit	Page number to add
apart from	Lawrence	123
sculptor's art	Kostiuk	75
Locatelli	Locatelli	150

QUICK TIP
You can copy sources from the master list to your current document or vice versa.

6. Click Manage Sources in the Citations & Bibliography group

   The Source Manager dialog box opens as shown in FIGURE K-11.

QUICK TIP
The name is changed in the source entry and in the citation in the document.

7. Click the entry for Kostiuk in the Current List, click Edit, select Kostiuk in the Author text box in the Edit Source dialog box, type Kostuk, click OK, then click Yes if prompted

8. Click Placeholder1 in the Current List, click Delete, click Close, then close the Navigation pane and save the document

   The placeholder entry is removed and will not be included when you generate a bibliography in a later lesson.

FIGURE K-9: Changing the citation style

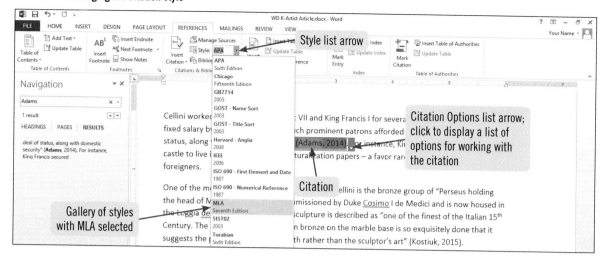

Style list arrow

Citation Options list arrow; click to display a list of options for working with the citation

Citation

Gallery of styles with MLA selected

FIGURE K-10: Selecting an existing source

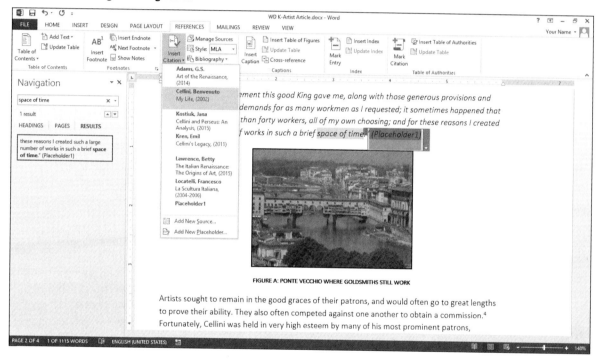

FIGURE A: PONTE VECCHIO WHERE GOLDSMITHS STILL WORK

FIGURE K-11: Source Manager dialog box

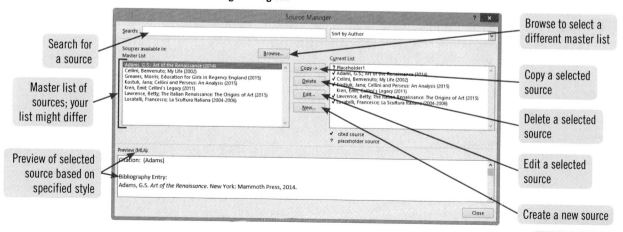

Search for a source

Master list of sources; your list might differ

Preview of selected source based on specified style

Browse to select a different master list

Copy a selected source

Delete a selected source

Edit a selected source

Create a new source

Working with References

Add and Modify Captions

A **caption** is text that is attached to a figure in Word and provides a title or a brief explanation of the figure. A **figure** is any object such as a chart, a picture, an equation, a table, or an embedded object. By default, captions are formatted with the Caption style. **CASE** ▶ *You add a caption to one of the pictures in the current document, edit a caption label, change the style applied to the captions, then remove the label from one of the captions and update the captions.*

STEPS

1. **Scroll through the document and note the captions on four of the five pictures, press [Ctrl][Home], then click the picture on page 1**

   This picture does not have a caption. You insert captions from the REFERENCES tab.

2. **Click Insert Caption in the Captions group, type a colon (:), press [Spacebar], then type Classic View of Florence (by default, the text appears in all caps as shown in FIGURE K-12)**

   In the Caption dialog box, you can choose to position the caption above the selected item or below the selected item (the default). You can also choose to exclude the caption number and you can select how you wish the captions to be numbered (for example, Figure A).

3. **Click Numbering, click the Format list arrow, click 1, 2, 3, ... if it is not already selected, click OK, click OK, then scroll to the next page to verify that the next picture is labeled Figure 2.**

   You can modify the appearance of a figure caption by modifying its style. When you modify the appearance of one caption, all other captions are also modified since each caption is formatted with the same style.

4. **Click WHERE in the Figure 2 caption, click the HOME tab, click the Bold button B, click the launcher in the Font group, click the Small caps check box to select it, then click OK**

   You've specified the settings you want applied to the Caption style. Now you need to update the Caption style.

5. **Right-click the formatted word, then click the Styles button on the Mini toolbar**

   The gallery of available styles opens. The Caption style is selected because you right-clicked text currently formatted with the Caption style.

6. **Right-click Caption in the gallery, click Update Caption to Match Selection as shown in FIGURE K-13, then scroll to verify that the updated style is applied to each of the figure captions**

7. **Scroll to and click the picture above FIGURE 3: DUOMO IN FLORENCE, press [Delete], select the caption text, press [Delete], then delete the extra blank line between the paragraphs**

   After you delete a caption, you need to update the numbering of the remaining captions

8. **Scroll to the Figure 4 picture, right click 4, click Update Field, scroll to the Figure 5 picture, right click 5, click Update Field to update the field to 4 as shown in FIGURE K-14, then save the document**

FIGURE K-12: Caption dialog box

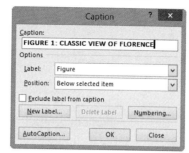

FIGURE K-13: Caption style selected

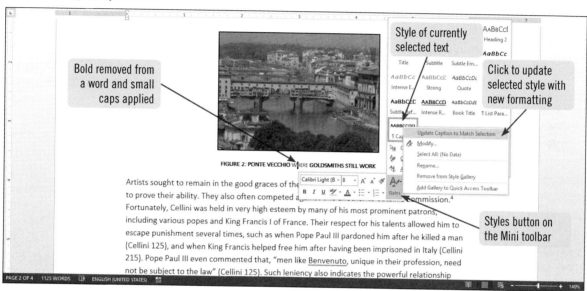

Bold removed from a word and small caps applied

Style of currently selected text

Click to update selected style with new formatting

Styles button on the Mini toolbar

FIGURE 2: PONTE VECCHIO WHERE GOLDSMITHS STILL WORK

Artists sought to remain in the good graces of the [...] to prove their ability. They also often competed a[...] [...] commission.[4] Fortunately, Cellini was held in very high esteem by many of his most prominent patrons, including various popes and King Francis I of France. Their respect for his talents allowed him to escape punishment several times, such as when Pope Paul III pardoned him after he killed a man (Cellini 125), and when King Francis helped free him after having been imprisoned in Italy (Cellini 215). Pope Paul III even commented that, "men like Benvenuto, unique in their profession, need not be subject to the law" (Cellini 125). Such leniency also indicates the powerful relationship

FIGURE K-14: Caption number updated

kept company with the highest members of society. A good relationship between an artist and his patron resulted in a steady flow of work in addition to honor, praise, and the occasional favor. An artist's life was a constant balancing act between pleasing patrons in order to keep in work, and upholding his own honor as a skilled artist.

Updated number in Figure caption

FIGURE 4: ROOFTOPS OF FLORENCE

Working with References

Generate a Bibliography and Table of Figures

Learning Outcomes
- Generate a bibliography
- Update a bibliography
- Generate a table of figures

You can document sources in a works cited list or a bibliography. A **works cited** page lists only the works that are included in citations in your document. A **bibliography** lists all the sources you used to gather information for the document. You can also include a **table of figures**, which is a list of all the figures with captions that are used in a document along with the page number on which each figure is found. **CASE** ▶ *You generate a bibliography and a table of figures.*

STEPS

1. **Press [Ctrl][End], press [Ctrl][Enter], click the REFERENCES tab, click the Bibliography button in the Citations & Bibliography group, click Bibliography, then scroll up to see the bibliography**

   A field containing the bibliography is inserted. When you choose one of the built-in options, Word automatically inserts a title (Bibliography or Works Cited).

2. **Note that a date appears at the end of each entry, click any entry, click the Style list arrow in the Citations & Bibliography group, then click APA**

   The bibliography is formatted according to APA guidelines. When you change the style for the bibliography, the style for the citations in the document is also changed.

3. **Click the Style list arrow, then click Chicago**

   The bibliography and the citations in the document are formatted according to the Chicago style.

4. **Click Manage Sources in the Citations & Bibliography group, then click the entry for Kren, Emil in the Current List**

   A check mark does not appear next to Emil Kren's name, indicating that this work was not cited in the article. You also did not use the source in your research so you can delete it from the bibliography.

5. **Click Delete, click Close, then click the Update Citations and Bibliography button on the Bibliography tab**

   The Kren entry is removed and the bibliography is updated as shown in **FIGURE K-15**.

6. **Press [Ctrl][Home], press [Ctrl][Enter], press [Ctrl][Home], type Table of Figures, click the HOME tab, then format Table of Figures using 24 pt, bold, and centering**

7. **Click after Figures, press [Enter], then click the Clear All Formatting button 🖋 in the Font group**

8. **Click the REFERENCES tab, click the Insert Table of Figures button in the Captions group, click the Formats list arrow, click Formal, then click OK**

   The list of figures included in the document is generated.

9. **Click the table of figures (it appears shaded), press and hold [Ctrl], click Figure 3, select the Figure 3 caption, press [Delete], click the picture, press [Delete], press [Delete] as needed to remove the extra blank lines, scroll to the Figure 4 caption, right click 4 in the figure caption, then click Update Field**

   The figure caption number is updated to reflect the deletion of Figure 3.

TROUBLE
If a blank page follows page 4, delete the paragraph mark on page 4 under the Optional Tours table.

10. **Press [Ctrl][Home], click in the table of figures, click Update Table in the Captions group, scroll to verify that the document is five pages long, then save the document**

    The table of figures now includes three figures as shown in **FIGURE K-16**.

FIGURE K-15: Updated bibliography using the Chicago format

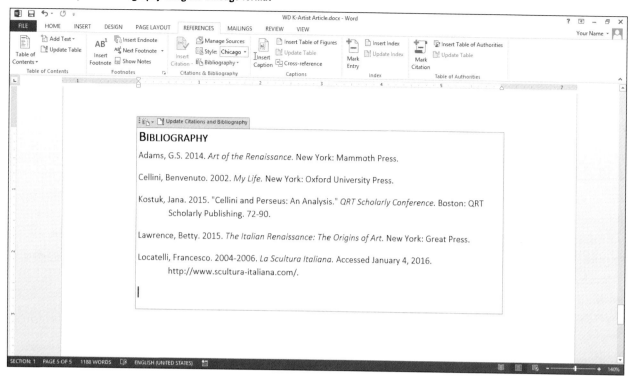

FIGURE K-16: Updated Table of Figures

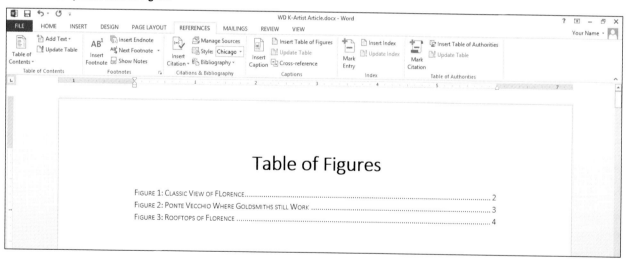

Table of Authorities

A table of authorities lists all the cases, statutes, rules, and other legal references included in a legal document, along with the page on which each reference appears. To create a table of authorities, click the REFERENCES tab, go to the first reference (called a citation) that you wish to include in the table of authorities, then click the Mark Citation button in the Table of Authorities group. After you have marked all the citations in the document, click the Insert Table of Authorities button in the Table of Authorities group to build the table of authorities. Word organizes and then displays each citation you marked by category.

Work with PDF Files in Word

Learning Outcomes
• Export a document to PDF
• Open and edit a PDF document

In Word 2013, you can open a file that has been saved as a Portable Document Format (PDF) file and edit the file in Word. If the original PDF document contains only text, the document will look almost identical in Word as it does in the original PDF, although the page to page correspondence may not be exact. If the PDF document includes graphics, some discrepancies between the original and the Word version may appear. **CASE** *You save the art article as a PDF file for distribution to clients. You then open and edit a short paper related to raising the price of the Renaissance Art Tour that a colleague has saved as a PDF document.*

STEPS

1. **Type your name where indicated in the footer, close the Footer area, then click the** Save button 🖫 **to save the file**

   After saving a copy of the Word document, you export it to a PDF file.

2. **Click the** FILE tab, **click** Export, **then click the** Create PDF/XPS button **shown in** FIGURE K-17

   The Publish as PDF or XPS dialog box opens.

3. **Click** Publish

   In a few moments, the document is saved as WD K-Artist Article.pdf and it opens in the Adobe Acrobat Reader window.

   QUICK TIP
   Click Zoom to Page Level if you don't see Fit Page.

4. **Maximize the window if it is not maximized, click the** Zoom list arrow **on the toolbar, click** Fit Page, **click the** down arrow **on the toolbar to move from page to page, click the** Close button ✕ **to exit Adobe Reader, click the** FILE tab **in Word, then click** Close

5. **Click the** FILE tab, **click** Open, **navigate to the location where you store your files, click** WD K-2.pdf, **then click** Open

   TROUBLE
   It may take up to a minute before the document is open and ready for editing.

6. **If the message shown in** FIGURE K-18 **appears, click** OK

7. **When the document opens in Word, scroll to page 2 and notice that "Your Name" appears at the top of the page**

   You want Your Name to appear in the footer. Sometimes text in a PDF document does not display correctly in Word.

8. **Select** Your Name, **press** [Backspace] **two times, click the** INSERT tab, **click** Footer **in the Header & Footer group, click** Blank, **type your name, then click the** Close Header and Footer button

9. **Click the** FILE tab, **click** Save As, **navigate to the location where you store your files, enter** WD K-Tour Price Increase **as the filename, then click** Save

   The document is saved as a Word document.

FIGURE K-17: Export tab in Backstage view

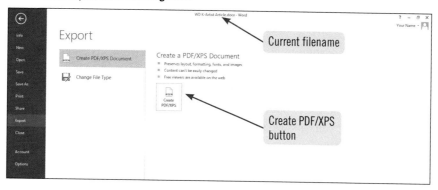

Current filename

Create PDF/XPS button

FIGURE K-18: Message box that can appear when opening a PDF file in Word

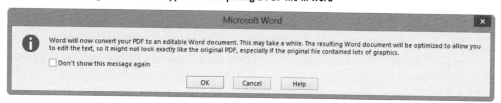

Opening non-native files directly in Word

By default, Microsoft Word saves files in one of its proprietary formats. The saved file is called a native Word file because it is saved in a file format that is native to Word, such as .docx for Word documents and .dotx for Word templates. A Word file may not be recognized by other software programs. Sometimes you may need to open a file in Word that is a non-native file—that is, a file created with a different software program. Depending on the program used to create the original file, you may not be able to open the non-native file in Word. For example, you will get an error message if you attempt to open an Excel or PowerPoint file in Word.

When you are working with a different program and you want to use the file in Word, you should save the file as a PDF file, as a txt, or as an rtf file. You can open and work on any of these three non-native file formats in Word. For example, you can save an Excel file as a PDF file, then open and work on the file in Word. **FIGURE K-19** shows how an Excel file appears after it is saved as a PDF file and then opened in Word.

FIGURE K-19: Excel file saved as PDF and opened in Word

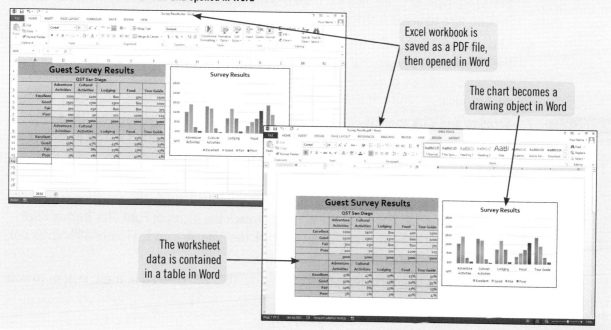

Excel workbook is saved as a PDF file, then opened in Word

The chart becomes a drawing object in Word

The worksheet data is contained in a table in Word

Word 2013

Work with Equations

Learning Outcomes
- Insert an equation
- Format an equation

You use the Equations feature to insert mathematical and scientific equations using commands on the EQUATION TOOLS DESIGN tab. You can also create your own equations that use a wide range of math structures including fractions, radicals, and integrals. When you select a structure, Word inserts a placeholder that you can then populate with symbols, values, or even text. If you write an equation that you want to use again, you can save the equation and then access it from a custom equation gallery. You can also use the Math AutoCorrect feature to type math symbols instead of selecting them from a gallery. For example, if you type \inc, Word inserts Δ, which is the increment symbol. **CASE** *The paper on raising the tour price uses the economic concept of elasticity to describe the result of raising the price tour from $2,400 to $3,000. The paper includes equations to express the economics concepts. You need to create one equation from scratch and then edit another equation.*

STEPS

1. **Scroll up and select the text [Equation 1 to be created] below the second paragraph, press [Delete], click the INSERT tab, then click Equation in the Symbols group**

   The EQUATION TOOLS DESIGN tab opens. This tab is divided into three groups: Tools, Symbols, and Structures. **TABLE K-1** describes the content of each group.

2. **Click the Fraction button in the Structures group to show a selection of fraction structures, click the first fraction structure in the top row, then increase the zoom to 180%**

   Increasing the zoom helps you see the components of the equation.

3. **Click in the top half of the fraction (the numerator)**

   The box is shaded to indicate it is selected.

4. **Click the More button ⊽ in the Symbols group to expand the Symbols gallery, click the Basic Math list arrow on the title bar, click Greek Letters, then click the Delta symbol (Δ) as shown in FIGURE K-20**

   You can select commonly used math symbols from eight galleries as follows: Basic Math, Greek Letters, Letter-Like Symbols, Operators, Arrows, Negated Relations, Scripts, and Geometry.

5. **Type Q, press [↓] to move to the bottom half of the fraction (the denominator), type Q, press [→], type an equal sign (=), then complete the equation as shown in FIGURE K-21, making sure to insert fraction structures as needed**

6. **Click the equation under the next paragraph and note that it has been imported from the PDF file as a picture, not as an equation**

   One of the challenges of opening a PDF document in Word is that graphics such as equations are not retained. Fortunately, the next two equations are correct; however, the last equation must be replaced.

7. **Scroll to and click the last equation in the document, press [Delete], click the INSERT tab, click Equation in the Symbols group, create the new equation shown in FIGURE K-22, then click away from the equation**

   You can format an equation by changing its font size and adding shading.

8. **Click the equation you just created, click the selection handle (the equation is shaded), click the HOME tab if it is not the active tab, click the Increase Font Size button until 14 appears, click the Shading list arrow, click the Blue, Accent 5, Lighter 40% color box, then click away from the equation**

9. **Save and close the document, then submit the files you created in these lessons to your instructor**

FIGURE K-20: Selecting a symbol

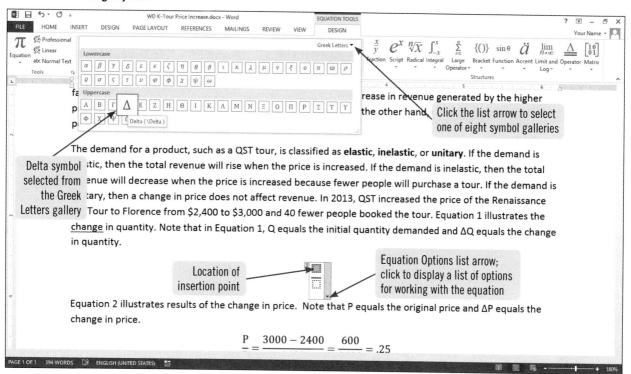

FIGURE K-21: Completed Equation 1

$$\frac{\Delta Q}{Q} = \frac{100-40}{100} = \frac{60}{100}$$

FIGURE K-22: Completed Equation 2

$$E = \frac{.6}{.25} = 2.4 > 1$$

TABLE K-1: Contents of the EQUATION TOOLS DESIGN tab

group	description
Tools	• Use the Equation button to select a built-in equation • Select the equation style: Professional, Linear, or Normal Text • Click the launcher ⌐ to access the Equation Options dialog box where you can specify equation settings and access the AutoCorrect list of symbols
Symbols	• Select commonly used mathematical symbols such as (±) and (∞) • Click the More button ▼ to show a gallery of symbols • Click the list arrow in the gallery to select the group for which you would like to see symbols
Structures	• Select common math structures, such as fractions and radicals • Click a structure button (such as the Fraction button) to select a specific format to insert in the equation for that structure

Working with References

Practice

Concepts Review

Label the numbered items shown in FIGURE K-23.

FIGURE K-23

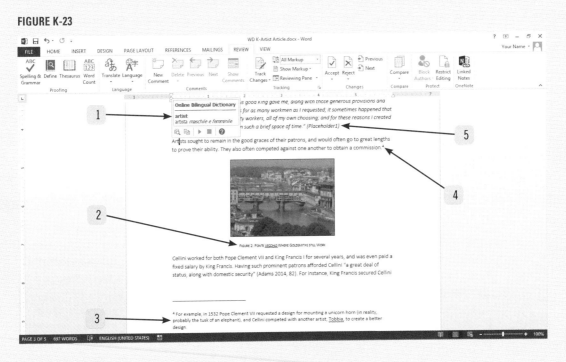

Match each term with the statement that best describes it.

6. Table of Figures
7. REVIEW
8. Footnote
9. Bibliography
10. Citation
11. MLA

a. List of references included in a document, such as an essay or report
b. Provides additional comments on information provided in the text
c. Tab that includes the Translate feature
d. Short reference that credits the source of a quote
e. List of objects, such as charts and pictures, included in a document
f. Example of a style applied to a bibliography and citations

Select the best answer from the list of choices.

12. **Which of the following activities is *not* available in the Manage Sources dialog box?**
    a. Copy a source to your document
    b. Add a source
    c. Change the source style
    d. Delete a source

13. **Which option in the Word Options dialog box do you choose to work with the AutoCorrect feature?**
    a. General
    b. Display
    c. Advanced
    d. Proofing

14. **How do you modify the style of a caption?**
    a. Right-click the caption, then click Style
    b. Edit the formats
    c. Right-click the caption, then click the Styles button on the Mini toolbar
    d. Click Styles in the Caption dialog box

Skills Review

1. Work with AutoCorrect.

a. Start Word, open the file WD K-3.docx from the drive and folder where you store your Data Files, then save the file as **WD K-History Term Paper**.

b. Open the Word Options dialog box, open Proofing, then open the AutoCorrect dialog box.

c. Verify that the AutoCorrect tab is the active tab, type **sc** in the Replace text box, type **Saint Cyr** in the With text box, click Add, then exit all dialog boxes.

d. Search for **xx**, use the AutoCorrect keystroke to replace xx with **Saint Cyr**, then adjust the spacing and punctuation as needed. (*Hint*: Select xx, type **sc**, and press [Spacebar] to enter the AutoCorrect text.)

e. Repeat the process in Step d to replace xx in the next sentence, then check both inserts and delete extra spaces as needed.

f. Double-click to the left of Your Name in the document footer, type **(c)** to insert the copyright symbol, then replace the "Your Name" placeholder with your name.

g. Delete the sc entry from the AutoCorrect dialog box.

2. Customize footnotes.

a. Change the Number format of the footnotes to the 1, 2, 3 number format and select the Continuous option for footnote numbering. Apply the formatting to the whole document.

b. Find the text "practical skills", then position the insertion point following the period after the word "skills."

c. Insert a footnote with the following text: **For example, training in textiles enabled girls to obtain employment in the factories**.

d. Go to footnote 1 and edit it by typing **In the eighteenth century**, before "English girls" at the beginning of the footnote, then click above the separator line.

e. Go to footnote reference mark **4** in the document text, then delete the footnote reference mark.

f. Scroll up to page 5, then modify the style of the footnote text in the footnote area by changing the font size to 9 pt, the After spacing to 6 pt, and the line spacing to 1.5.

g. Click above the separator line, then save the document.

3. Use the Translate feature.

a. Find the text **This French quote**, then select the text from L'enseignement charitable... to ... à la vie extérieure at the end of the sentence (do not include the period).

b. Use the Translate feature to view a translation of the selected text from French to English.

c. Read the English translation, which is an approximate translation of the text.

d. Close the Research task pane, click the word "schools" in the second line of the next paragraph, then turn on and use the Mini Translator to view the French translation of school (école). Remember to change the Translate to language to French.

e. Change the Mini Translator language to Spanish (Spain), turn on the Mini Translator, then move the pointer over the word "schools" and note the Spanish translation to escuela.

f. Turn off the Mini Translator, then save the document.

4. Modify citations and manage sources.

a. Find the text **popular education in England**, then after the ending quotation mark and before the period, insert a new citation placeholder.

b. Find the text **roles in society**, then edit the citation so that it includes 28 as the page number. Remember to click the citation to show the Citation Options list arrow.

c. Find the text **household activities**, then edit the citation so that it includes **93** as the page number.

d. Change the style to Chicago.

e. Find the text **Placeholder**, select the Placeholder1 citation, then replace the placeholder with a citation using the Phyllis Stock source. (*Note*: Be sure to select the citation using the field selection handle; do not edit the citation.)

f. Edit the citation so that it suppresses the year and displays page **70**. (*Hint*: Click the Year check box to suppress the year.)

g. Open the Source Manager dialog box, edit the entry for Wats so the name is **Watts**.

h. Delete the Placeholder 1 entry from the Source Manager dialog box, then close the dialog box.

5. Add and modify captions.

a. Scroll to the picture of the church on page 4, then add a caption with the text **Figure 3: Schools attached to convents and churches educated girls in France** that uses the A, B, C numbering format.

b. Scroll to the next picture and verify that the caption includes Figure D.

c. Modify the Caption style so that the font color is black and the font size is 11 pt.

d. Delete the first picture and caption in the document (the picture of the two girls).

e. Select all the text in the document, use F9 to update all the captions in the document, then verify that the figure letters have updated. (*Notes*: You may need to use the [Fn] key in conjunction with the [F9] key. If [F9] does not update all captions, scroll through the document and update each caption manually by right-clicking the caption and clicking Update Field.)

f. Save the document.

6. Generate a bibliography and table of figures.

a. Move to the end of the document, insert a page break, and clear any formatting.

b. Insert a bibliography, then scroll up to view it.

c. Change the style of the citations and bibliography to MLA.

d. Open the Source Manager dialog box, then change the entry for Darren Jonson to Darren Johnson.

e. Update the bibliography and confirm that Darren's last name is now Johnson. The completed bibliography appears as shown in **FIGURE K-24**.

FIGURE K-24

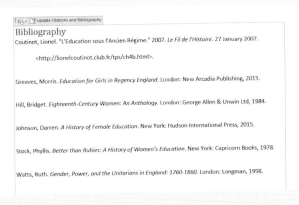

f. Go to the top of the document, insert a page break, type **Table of Figures** at the top of the document, then format it with 18 pt, bold, and center alignment.

g. Press [Enter] following "Table of Figures," clear the formatting, then generate a table of figures using the Distinctive format.

h. Use [Ctrl][Click] to go from the entry for Figure D to the figure in the document, then delete Figure D and its caption.

i. Update the table of figures, be sure your name is in the footer at the bottom of the page, then save the document.

7. Work with PDF files in Word.

a. Export the document to a PDF file, then publish the document.

b. Fit the document to the page, view the pages of the document, then close it. It will be saved as **WD K-History Term Paper.pdf**.

c. Open the file WD K-4.pdf in Word from the location where you store your Data Files.

d. Scroll to the top of page 2, then delete Your Name so the document fits on one page.

e. Insert your name in the footer.

f. Save the file as **WD K-Common Equations.docx**.

8. Work with equations.

a. Go to the [Equation 1] placeholder, then replace it with an equation content control.

b. Type **A =**, then select the pi symbol Π from the uppercase area of the Greek Letters gallery.

c. Click the Script button in the Structures group.

d. Select the first script structure, then type **r** in the large box, and **2** in the small box as shown in **FIGURE K-25**.

e. Select the [Pythagorean Theorem] placeholder near the end of the document, change the After Spacing to 0, delete the placeholder, then press [Enter] so the insertion point appears on a new line. (*Note*: Spacing is often adjusted when a PDF file is opened in Word which means that you frequently need to modify spacing before you can work with the text in Word.)

FIGURE K-25

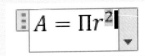

$$A = \Pi r^2$$

Skills Review (continued)

f. Insert an equation content control and create the new equation shown in **FIGURE K-26**. (*Hint*: Use the same Script structures three times to create the formula. Be sure to use the arrow keys to move off the Script structure.)

g. Format the new equation by increasing its font size to 14 pt, shading it with Green, Accent 6, Lighter 80%, and centering it. (*Hint*: Remember to select the equation content control before applying the shading.)

FIGURE K-26

$$a^2 + b^2 = c^2$$

h. Save and close the document, then submit all the files you created for this skills review to your instructor.

Independent Challenge 1

You have finished writing a paper about Prince Hal in Shakespeare's play *Henry IV*: Part 1. Now you use the References features to manage source information. You create a new AutoCorrect entry, insert and modify footnotes, and modify existing citations. You also work in the Source Manager dialog box to organize sources, and then you generate and modify a bibliography.

a. Start Word, open the file WD K-5.docx from the drive and folder where you store your Data Files, then save it as **WD K-English Term Paper**.

b. Create an AutoCorrect entry that replaces **ssh** with **Shakespeare**, then search for each instance of **xx** and replace it with the **ssh** AutoCorrect entry. (*Note*: The document contains three instances of "xx.")

c. Go to the top of the document, find the first instance of **chivalric code**, then add the footnote: **Chivalry is associated with the ideals of honor and courtly love held by medieval knights**.

d. Find footnote A, change the date 200 A.D. to **400 A.D.**, then change the number format for all the footnotes to 1, 2, 3.

e. Modify the footnote style so that the footnote text is single spaced and all the text is 9 pt.

f. Find the text **people and situations**, then insert a citation placeholder to the right of the ending quotation mark and before the ending period.

g. Find the text **by his involvements**, insert a citation after the ending quotation mark and before the period that refers to Quinones, then edit the citation to add the page number **74**.

h. Replace Placeholder 1 with a citation that refers to Quinones and page number **81**.

i. At the end of the document after the last paragraph, insert a new page, and then generate a new bibliography using the MLA style.

j. In the Source Manager dialog box, delete the placeholder, then edit the source for *Shakespeare's Tudor History* by Tom Allenham so that the last name is **McAlindon** instead of Allenham.

k. Update the bibliography.

l. Remove the **ssh** AutoCorrect entry from the AutoCorrect dialog box.

m. Type your name where indicated in the footer, use the (c) code to enter the copyright symbol (©) before your name, submit the file to your instructor, then save and close the document.

Independent Challenge 2

You decide to further explore using the Translate feature. You open a document containing a short message in English. You want to explore how accurate a translation is that goes through multiple translations. You translate the passage from English into French and then from French into Spanish, and finally from Spanish back to English. Then you compare the result of this last translation with the original English text to check the accuracy of the translation. You also work with captions and generate a table of figures.

a. Start Word, open the file WD K-6.docx from the drive and folder where you store your Data Files, then save it as **WD K-Translation Practice**.

b. Select the English message (begins "We are delighted..." and ends "beautiful countryside.") at the beginning of the document, then use the Translate Selected Text feature to translate the selected text to French.

Independent Challenge 2 (continued)

c. Click in the table cell under From English to French, then click Insert in the Research task pane to insert the French translation from the Research task pane into the From English to French cell in the table. (*Hint*: Scroll down the Research pane to see more of the translation and the Insert button.)

d. Close the Research task pane, select the French translation, then use the Translate feature to translate the selected French text into Spanish. (*Hint*: You will need to change the entry in the From text box to French (France) and the entry in the To text box to Spanish (Spain).

e. Click in the table cell under From French to Spanish, then click insert in the Research task pane to insert the Spanish translation from the Research task pane into the French to Spanish cell in the table.

f. Close the Research task pane, select the Spanish translation in the table cell, use the Translate feature to translate the selected text back into English, insert the English translation from the Research task pane into the table cell under From Spanish to English, then close the Research task pane. (*Hint*: Remember to change the entries in the From and To text boxes to reflect the correct languages - Spanish and English.)

g. Compare the paragraph at the beginning of the document with the translation you just inserted in the last cell of the table. Notice some of the ways in which the syntax of the original English message has changed after two translations.

h. Scroll to Figure b, which is the picture of snails in mushroom cream. Use the mini-translator to find the French translation for "snails", then type the French translation (escargots) to replace "snails."

i. Add a caption to the first picture (the sunflowers) that reads: **Figure A: Gorgeous sunflowers blanket the fields**. Make sure you select the A, B, C, Numbering style.

j. Change the style of the captions so they appear in bold with no italics and with After Spacing of 18 pt.

k. Below the last picture, type Table of Figures, format it with bold, centering and 14 pt, then generate a table of figures using the Formal format.

l. Delete the picture of the swimming pool and its caption, then update the figure references and update the table of figures. (*Hint*: Use [Ctrl][A] to select all the text then press F9 or update each of the figure references manually.)

m. Type your name in the footer, then save the document.

n. Export the document to a PDF file, scroll through the file after it opens in Adobe Reader, then close the PDF file.

o. Submit your files to your instructor.

Independent Challenge 3

You are helping a teacher to prepare a worksheet showing some of the equations related to circles and spheres for a high school geometry class. The teacher has already entered some of the formulas in Word. She asks you to use the Equation feature to add a new formula and then to create a table of figures to list the formulas used in the document.

a. Start Word, open the file WD K-7.docx from the drive and folder where you store your Data Files, then save it as **WD K-Geometry Equations**.

b. Increase the zoom to 150% so you can easily see the formula as you work, then click below the Volume of a Sphere heading and create the Volume of a Sphere equation as follows:

- Click Equation in the Symbols group on the INSERT tab, type **V**, then type an equal sign (=).
- Click the Fraction button in the Structures group, then select the first fraction style and highlight the top box.
- Type **4**, show the Basic Math symbols, then click the Pi (π) symbol (third row).
- Click the Script button in the Structures group, select the Superscript style (first selection), then type an **r** in the large box and a **3** in the small box.
- Highlight the bottom box in the fraction, type **3**, then compare the completed formula to **FIGURE K-27**.

FIGURE K-27

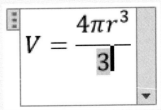

$$V = \frac{4\pi r^3}{3}$$

c. Format the equation for Perimeter of a Circle with the 16 pt font size and the Orange, Accent 1, Lighter 60% shading.

d. Use the Format Painter to apply the same formatting to the other two equations.

Independent Challenge 3 (continued)

e. Click the third equation, click the selection handle, then change the equation to a Linear equation. (*Hint*: Click Linear in the Tools group on the EQUATION TOOLS DESIGN tab.)

f. Add captions centered above each of the three equations so that each caption includes the caption number followed by a colon and the name of the equation. For example, caption 1 should be **EQUATION 1: PERIMETER OF A CIRCLE**.

- Make sure you select the entire equation by clicking the selection handle before you insert the caption.
- In the Caption dialog box, you need to select Equation as the label type, and then type a colon and the caption title in the Caption text box in the Caption dialog box. (*Hint*: If Equation is not available as a label type, create a new label. Click New Label in the Caption dialog box, type **Equation**, then click OK.)
- To center the caption, press [Ctrl][e] immediately after you insert the caption.)

g. Modify the Caption style so that the font is 10 point and the font color is Orange, Accent 1, Darker 25%.

h. Below the heading SAMPLE EQUATIONS... at the top of the document, insert a table of figures using the style of your choice, insert a page break, then update the table of figures.

i. Type your name in the document footer, save the file, submit a copy to your instructor, then close the file.

Independent Challenge 4: Explore

You have just started a job as a research assistant with Information Overload, a company in Tulsa, Oklahoma, that conducts research projects for local businesses. On your first day on the job, your supervisor asks you to demonstrate how you use the Research task pane to find answers to three questions he gives you. He then wants you to use the citation feature in Word to document each of the three Web sites you accessed to find the answers.

a. Start Word, open the file WD K-8.docx from the drive and folder where you store your Data Files, then save it as **WD K-Web Citations**.

b. Create an AutoCorrect entry called pb that will enter the text **Prepared by** followed by your name.

c. Use pb to enter its associated text under the heading "Web Research Practice" and in the footer, then remove the AutoCorrect entry.

d. Read the first question, then open the Research task pane. (*Hint*: Click anywhere in the document click the Translate button on the REVIEW tab), then click Translate Selected Text. The Research task pane opens).

e. Click in the Search for text box in the Research task pane, type **Mount Everest first climber**, click the Translation list arrow, then click All Research Sites.

f. Follow one of the links to find the answers to Question 1 in the document: Identify the names of the first team of climbers to scale Mount Everest, the date they did it, and their nationalities.

g. Write a short paragraph in the space provided below the question with the required information.

h. Set the citations and bibliography style to APA, then immediately following the text you typed, insert a citation based on a new source you create by entering information about the Web site you used as a source. (*Hint*: In the Create Source dialog box, set the Type of Source to Web site, click the Show All Bibliography Fields check box, then enter the information about the Web site you consulted in all fields starred with a red asterisk. To enter the Web site address in the URL field, switch to the Web site, select the Web site address, press [Ctrl][C], switch back to the Create Source dialog box, click in the URL text box, then press [Ctrl][V].)

i. Use the Research task pane to find an answer to the next question and then provide the appropriate citation based on a source you add. Make sure you consult a different Web site to find the answer.

j. For the final question, enter your description, then insert a Placeholder for the citation.

k. Following the placeholder, insert a footnote that contains the text: **This information is based on my own observations**.

l. Modify the footnote style so the text is bold, a color of your choice, and uses the footnote numbering A, B, C.

m. At the end of the document, generate a bibliography.

n. Submit the file to your instructor, then save and close the document.

Visual Workshop

Open the file WD K-9.docx from the drive and folder where you store your Data Files, then save it as **WD K-Contemporary Culture Bibliography**. Open the AutoCorrect dialog box, identify the keystrokes required to enter the ™ symbol, then type the sentence shown in **FIGURE K-28** and insert the symbol where indicated. Generate a bibliography. Open the Source Manager dialog box, edit the entry for Dawn Harrison so the information appears as shown in Figure K-28, update the bibliography, then select the bibliography style so the format of the entries matches Figure K-28. Type your name where shown, submit the file to your instructor, then save and close the document.

FIGURE K-28

CONTEMPORARY CULTURE SOURCES

Compiled by Your Name

The Center for Contemporary Culture Studies has developed the Research Buddy™ program to facilitate academic research. Here is a list of the sources consulted in the creation on the Research Buddy™.

BIBLIOGRAPHY

Harrison, Dawn. *Contemporary Media Issues*. Oxford: Three Rivers Publishing, 2015.

Heinrich, Joe. *Social Media and Contemporary Culture Studies*. Toronto: New Arcadia Publishing, 2014.

Ng, Sally. *Popular Culture on the Web*. Boston: Popular Press, 2013.

Singh, Jasjit. "Exploring Social Media Web Sites." *Popular Culture Studies* (2015): 82-84.

Integrating Word with Other Programs

CASE ▶ You have developed text for a report about how to market questspecialtytravel.com, QST's home on the World Wide Web. You need the report to include embedded objects from PowerPoint and Excel, information contained in another Word file, and data included in files created in Excel and Access. You also need to merge an Access data source with the cover letter that you will send with the report to all QST branch managers.

Unit Objectives

After completing this unit, you will be able to:

- Explore integration methods
- Embed an Excel file
- Link an Excel chart
- Embed a PowerPoint slide

- Insert a Word file and Hyperlinks
- Import a table from Access
- Manage document links
- Merge with an Access data source

Files You Will Need

WD L-1.docx	WD L-13.docx
WD L-2.xlsx	WD L-14.docx
WD L-3.docx	WD L-15.xlsx
WD L-4.accdb	WD L-16.docx
WD L-5.docx	WD L-17.accdb
WD L-6.docx	WD L-18.xlsx
WD L-7.xlsx	WD L-19.docx
WD L-8.docx	WD L-20.docx
WD L-9.accdb	WD L-21.accdb
WD L-10.docx	WD L-22.xlsx
WD L-11.docx	WD L-23.xlsx
WD L-12.xlsx	

Explore Integration Methods

You can integrate information created with other Office programs into a Word document in a variety of ways. **FIGURE L-1** shows a five-page Word document containing shared information from PowerPoint, Excel, Access, and another Word document. **TABLE L-1** describes four common Office programs and lists the associated file extensions and icons. **CASE** ▶ *You review the various ways you can share information between programs.*

DETAILS

You can share information in the following ways:

- **Copy and paste**

  You use the Copy and Paste commands to copy information from one program (the **source file**) and paste it into another program (the **destination file**). You usually use the Copy and Paste commands when you need to copy a small amount of text.

- **Append a Word file**

  You can use the Object/Text from File command on the INSERT tab to append the text from an entire file into a Word document. The file types you can insert into Word include Word documents (.docx) or templates (.dotx), documents from previous versions of Word (.doc or .dot), documents saved in Rich Text Format (.rtf), Portable Document Files (.pdf), and documents saved in a Web page format, such as .mht or .htm.

- **Object Linking and Embedding**

  The ability to share information with other programs is called **object linking and embedding (OLE)**. Two programs are involved in the OLE process. The **source program** is the program in which information is originally created, and the **destination program** is the program the information is copied to.

- **Objects**

  An **object** is self-contained information that can be in the form of text, spreadsheet data, graphics, charts, tables, or even sound and video clips. Objects are used to share information between programs. To insert an object, you use the Object command on the INSERT tab. This command opens the Object dialog box where you can create an object from a new file or from an existing file. You can insert an object either as an embedded object or as a linked object.

- **Embedded objects**

  An **embedded object** is created either within a source program and then inserted into the destination program, or it is created within a destination program and then modified in the destination program using the tools of the source program. For example, you can create a PowerPoint slide in a Word document as an embedded object. To make changes to the embedded PowerPoint slide in Word, you double-click the embedded object in Word, and the PowerPoint Ribbon opens in Word. You use the PowerPoint Ribbon in Word to make changes. Changes you make to an embedded object are not made to the object in the source file, and changes you make to an object in the source file are not reflected in the embedded object. Once the object is embedded, there is no connection between the object in the source file and the object in the destination file.

- **Linked objects**

  A **linked object** is created in a source file and inserted into a destination file. The link between the source file and the destination file is kept. When you link an object, changes you make to the data contained in the object in the source file are reflected in the destination file.

- **Exporting tables and reports from Access**

  You can export a table or a report from Access into Word using the Export command. This command produces a Rich Text Format (.rtf) file that you can open in Word and then modify using Word formatting tools. An Access table exported to an .rtf file and then opened in Word is the same as a Word table and can be formatted using Word table styles and other table features.

FIGURE L-1: Word document with shared information

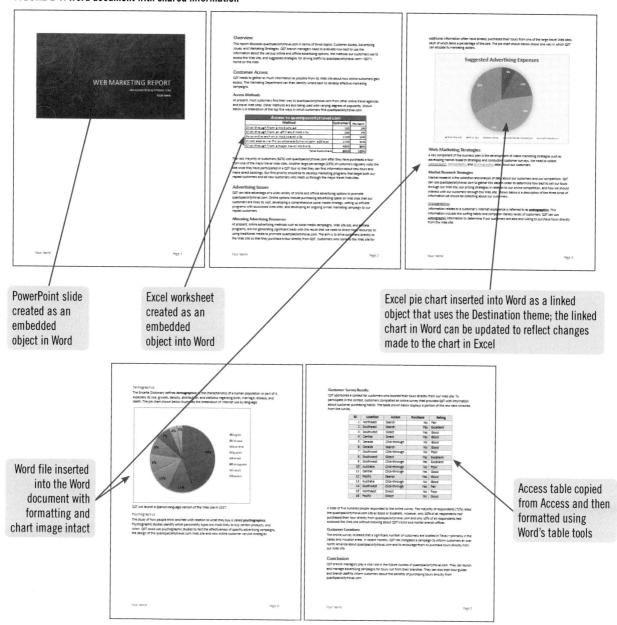

PowerPoint slide created as an embedded object in Word

Excel worksheet created as an embedded object into Word

Excel pie chart inserted into Word as a linked object that uses the Destination theme; the linked chart in Word can be updated to reflect changes made to the chart in Excel

Word file inserted into the Word document with formatting and chart image intact

Access table copied from Access and then formatted using Word's table tools

TABLE L-1: Common Office programs

icon	program	extension	purpose
Word	Word	.docx	To create documents and share information in print, e-mail, and on the Web
Excel	Excel	.xlsx	To create, analyze, and share spreadsheets and to analyze data with charts, PivotTable dynamic views, and graphs
PowerPoint	PowerPoint	.pptx	To organize, illustrate, and provide materials in an easy-to-understand graphics format for delivery in a presentation or over the Internet
Access	Access	.accdb	To store, organize, and share database information

Embed an Excel File

Learning Outcomes
• Embed an Excel file
• Edit an embedded Excel file

An embedded object uses the features of another program such as Excel, but it is stored as part of the Word document. You embed an object, such as an Excel worksheet or a PowerPoint slide, in Word when you want to be able to edit the embedded object in Word. You edit an embedded object directly in Word using commands on the Ribbon associated with the source program. The edits you make to an embedded object are not made to the object in the source file, and edits you make to the object in the source file are not made to the embedded object. **CASE** ▶ *The Web Marketing Report contains placeholder text and bookmarks to designate where you need to insert information created in other programs. Your first task is to embed an Excel worksheet.*

STEPS

1. **Start Word, open the file** WD L-1.docx **from the location where you store your Data Files, then save it as** WD L-Web Marketing Report

2. **Press [Ctrl][G] to open the Find and Replace dialog box with the Go To tab active, click** Bookmark **in the Go to what list, verify that "Customers" appears in the Enter bookmark name text box, click** Go To, **click** Close, **then delete the placeholder text** EXCEL WORKSHEET HERE **and position the insertion point on a blank line**

3. **Click the** INSERT tab, **then click the** Object button **in the Text group**
   The Object dialog box opens. You use the Object dialog box to create a new object using the commands of a program other than Word or to insert an object already created in another program.

4. **Click the** Create from File tab, **click the** Browse button, **navigate to the drive and folder where you store your Data Files, click** WD L-2.xlsx, **then click** Insert
   The path to the file WD L-2.xlsx is shown in the File name text box. Because you want to create an embedded object, you leave the Link to file check box blank as shown in **FIGURE L-2**.

5. **Click** OK, **then double-click the** embedded worksheet object
   The embedded object opens in an Excel object window, and the Excel Ribbon opens in place of the Word Ribbon. The title bar at the top of the window contains the Word filename, indicating that you are still working within a Word file.

6. **Click cell** B3, **type** 150, **press [Enter], click cell** B8, **then click the** Bold button **B in the Font group**
   The total number of customers shown in cell B8 increases by 55, from 7955 to 8010. Because you did not select the link option when you embedded the Excel file into the Word document, the changes you make to the embedded file are not made in the original Excel source file.

7. **Click the** PAGE LAYOUT tab, **click the** View check box **under Gridlines in the Sheet Options group to deselect the check box, click** Themes **in the Themes group, then select** Celestial
   You turned off the display of gridlines so that only borders show in the worksheet. Then, you formatted the embedded Excel file with the same theme (Celestial) that has been applied to the Word document. The completed worksheet object appears in Word as shown in **FIGURE L-3**.

8. **Click to the right of the worksheet object to return to Word**
   The Excel Ribbon closes and the Word Ribbon opens.

9. **Click the** worksheet object **to select it, click the** HOME tab, **click the** Center button ≡ **in the Paragraph group, click below the worksheet object, then save the document**

FIGURE L-2: Create from File tab in the Object dialog box

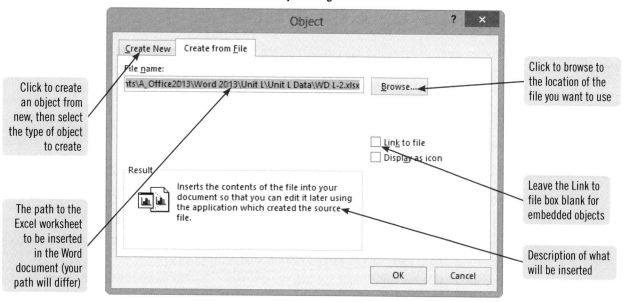

Click to create an object from new, then select the type of object to create

The path to the Excel worksheet to be inserted in the Word document (your path will differ)

Click to browse to the location of the file you want to use

Leave the Link to file box blank for embedded objects

Description of what will be inserted

FIGURE L-3: Excel Worksheet embedded in Word document

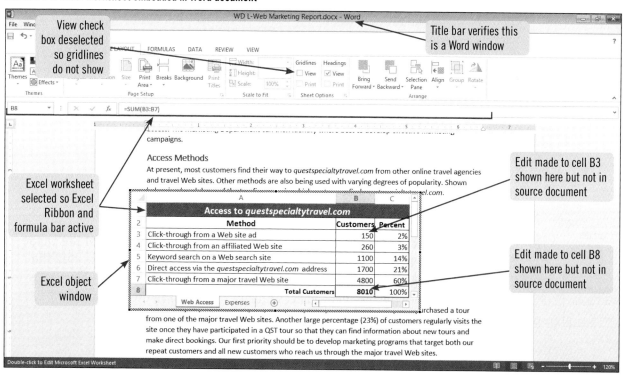

View check box deselected so gridlines do not show

Title bar verifies this is a Word window

Excel worksheet selected so Excel Ribbon and formula bar active

Excel object window

Edit made to cell B3 shown here but not in source document

Edit made to cell B8 shown here but not in source document

Integrating Word with Other Programs

Link an Excel Chart

Learning Outcomes
- Copy an Excel chart to Word
- Update a linked chart in Word

The Paste command on the HOME tab provides several options for integrating data from a source file into a destination file. When you select one of the paste link options, you create a linked object. The data copied from the source file in one program is pasted as a link into the destination file in another program. If you make a change to the data in the source file, the data in the linked object that you copied to the destination file is updated. **CASE** ▶ *You copy a pie chart from Excel and paste it into the Word report as a linked object.*

STEPS

1. **Press [Ctrl][G], click the** Enter bookmark name list arrow, **click** Resources, **click** Go To, **click** Close, **then delete the text** EXCEL PIE CHART HERE **but leave the blank line**

2. **Open** Windows Explorer **and navigate to the location where you store your files, double-click** WD L-2.xlsx, **then save it as** WD L-Web Marketing Data

   Notice that the values in cells B3 and B8, which you changed in the embedded Excel worksheet object in the previous lesson, have not changed. The value in cell B8 is still 7955.

3. **Click the** Expenses worksheet tab **at the bottom of the Excel worksheet, click any blank area of the chart to select the pie chart and all its components, then click the** Copy **button in the Clipboard group**

4. **Click the** Microsoft Word program button **on the taskbar to return to Word, click the** Paste button list arrow **in the Clipboard group on the HOME tab, then move your mouse over each of the Paste Options to read each ScreenTip and preview how the chart will be pasted into the document based on the selected option**

   Some of the options retain the formatting of the source program, and some options adopt the formatting of the destination program. The source program is Excel, which is currently formatted with the Office theme. The destination program is Word, which is currently formatted with the Celestial theme.

5. **Click the** Use Destination Theme & Link Data button **as shown in** FIGURE L-4, **then note that Web Site Ads (the purple slice) accounts for 5% of the advertising expenses**

   The chart is inserted using the destination theme, which is Celestial.

6. **Click the** Excel program button **on the taskbar to return to Excel, click cell** B2, **type** 9000, **then press [Enter]**

   The Web Site Ads slice increases to 8%.

7. **Return to Word, then verify that the Web Site Ads slice has increased to 8%**

8. **Click the** chart, **click the** CHART TOOLS FORMAT tab, **select the contents of the** Shape Width text box **in the Size group, type** 6, **press [Enter], click the** HOME tab, **click the** Center button ☰ **in the Paragraph group, click away from the pie chart object to deselect it, compare the pie chart object to** FIGURE L-5, **then save the document**

9. **Switch to Excel, save and close the workbook, then exit Excel**

   The WD L-Web Marketing Report in Word is again the active document.

FIGURE L-4: Selecting a link paste option

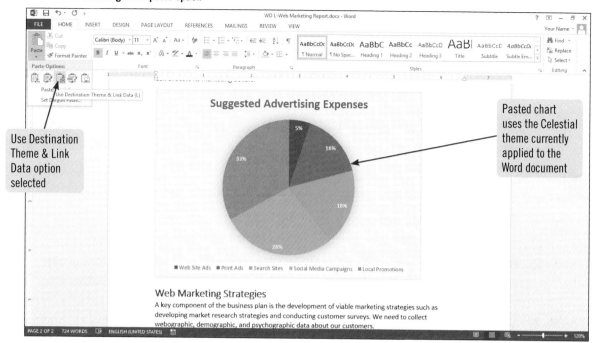

Use Destination Theme & Link Data option selected

Pasted chart uses the Celestial theme currently applied to the Word document

FIGURE L-5: Linked pie chart updated in Word

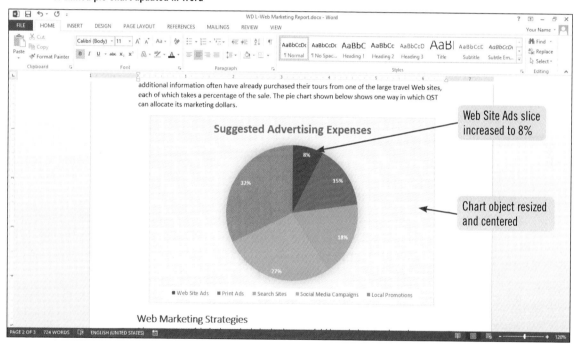

Web Site Ads slice increased to 8%

Chart object resized and centered

Using the Object dialog box to create a linked file

In addition to using the Paste options, you can create a linked object using the Object dialog box. You open the Object dialog box by clicking Object in the Text group on the INSERT tab, and then clicking the Create from File tab. You click the Browse button to navigate to and then select the file you want to link, click the Link to file check box to be sure that box is active (has a check mark), and then click OK. The file you select is inserted in the destination file as a linked object.

You create a linked object using one of the options available on the Paste menu when you want to copy only a portion of a file, such as selected cells or a chart in an Excel worksheet. You create a linked object using the Link to file check box in the Object dialog box when you want to insert the entire file, such as the entire worksheet in an Excel file.

Embed a PowerPoint Slide

Learning Outcomes
• Embed a PowerPoint slide in Word
• Customize colors

You can share information between Word and PowerPoint in a variety of ways. You can use the Paste Special command to insert a slide as a linked or an embedded object into a Word document. You can also use the Create New tab in the Object dialog box to create a PowerPoint slide as an embedded object in Word, and then use the tools on the PowerPoint Ribbon to modify the slide in Word. **CASE** > *You plan to distribute the Web Marketing Report at a conference where you will also deliver a PowerPoint presentation. You create a new PowerPoint slide and embed it in the title page, then you use the tools on the PowerPoint Ribbon to format the embedded object.*

STEPS

1. **Press [Ctrl][Home], then press [Ctrl][Enter]**
   A new blank page appears. You want to embed a PowerPoint slide on the new blank page.

2. **Press [Ctrl][Home] again, click the INSERT tab, then click Object in the Text group**
   The Object dialog box opens. The types of objects that you can create new in Word are listed in the Object type: list box.

3. **Scroll down, select Microsoft PowerPoint Slide in the Object type: list box as shown in FIGURE L-6, then click OK**
   A blank PowerPoint slide appears along with the PowerPoint Ribbon.

4. **Click the Click to add title text box, type Web Marketing Report, click the Click to add subtitle text box, type www.questspecialtytravel.com, press [Enter], then type your name**

5. **Click the DESIGN tab, click the More button [☰] in the Themes group to open the Themes gallery, then click the Celestial theme as shown in FIGURE L-7**

6. **Click outside the slide**
   The slide is inserted into Word as an object. To make changes to the slide, you double-click it to return to PowerPoint.

7. **Double-click the slide, click the DESIGN tab, then click the far right color variant (red-purple) in the Variants group**

8. **Click the More button in the Variants group, click Colors, click Customize Colors, click the list arrow for Hyperlink, click the White, Text 1 color box, click the Followed Hyperlink list arrow, click the White, Text 1, Darker 15% color box, then click Save**
   You change the hyperlink colors so the hyperlink is easy to read against the dark background.

9. **Click away from the slide object to deselect it, then save the document**
   The embedded PowerPoint slide appears in a Word document, as shown in FIGURE L-8.

Integrating Word with Other Programs

FIGURE L-6: Create New tab in Object dialog box

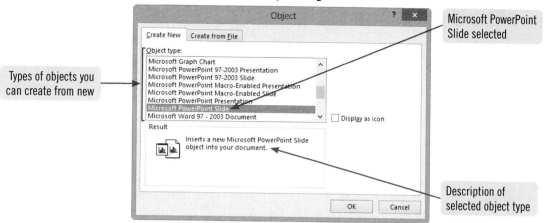

Types of objects you can create from new

Microsoft PowerPoint Slide selected

Description of selected object type

FIGURE L-7: Celestial theme selected

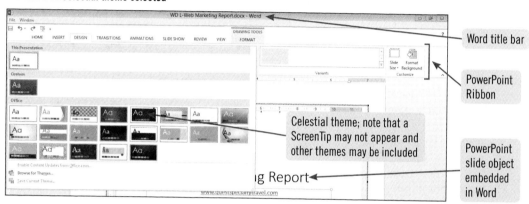

Word title bar

PowerPoint Ribbon

Celestial theme; note that a ScreenTip may not appear and other themes may be included

PowerPoint slide object embedded in Word

FIGURE L-8: Completed embedded PowerPoint slide object in Word

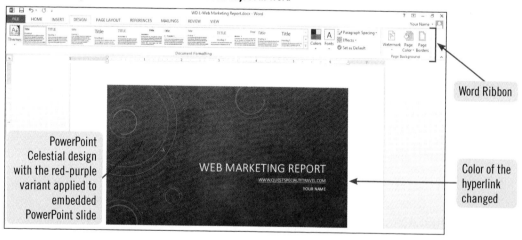

PowerPoint Celestial design with the red-purple variant applied to embedded PowerPoint slide

Word Ribbon

Color of the hyperlink changed

Creating a PowerPoint presentation from a Word outline

When you create a PowerPoint presentation from a Word outline, the Word document is the source file and the PowerPoint document is the destination file. Text formatted with heading styles in the Word source file are converted to PowerPoint headings in the PowerPoint destination file. For example, each line of text formatted with the Heading 1 style becomes its own slide. To create a PowerPoint presentation from a Word outline, create and then save the outline in Word, close the document, then launch PowerPoint. In PowerPoint, click the New Slide list arrow, click Slides from Outline, navigate to the location where you stored the Word document, then double-click the filename. The Word outline is converted to a PowerPoint presentation, which you can modify in the same way you modify any PowerPoint presentation. Any changes you make to the presentation in PowerPoint are *not* reflected in the original Word document.

Insert a Word File and Hyperlinks

Learning Outcomes
- Insert a Word file
- Insert hyperlinks

When you want to include the content of an entire Word document in another Word document, you use the Text from File Insert command to insert the entire Word file. When you insert an entire file into a document, the formatting applied to the destination file is also applied to the content you insert. The inserted file becomes part of the Word document, similar to an embedded object, and you cannot return to the original document from the inserted file. You can help readers navigate the content of a document quickly by creating hyperlinks from text in one part of the document to text in another location in the document. **CASE** ➤ *You insert a Word file, then you create hyperlinks and add ScreenTips to the hyperlinks.*

STEPS

1. **Press [Ctrl][G], select the Research bookmark, click Go To, click Close, delete the text WORD FILE HERE, then be sure the insertion point is on a blank line**

2. **Click the INSERT tab, click the Object list arrow in the Text group, then click Text from File**

3. **Navigate to the location where you store your Data Files, click WD L-3.docx, then click Insert**

   The content of the file WD L-3.docx file appears in your current document and is formatted with the Celestial theme. The pie chart was created in Word from the INSERT tab. If you make changes to the text you inserted in this destination file, the changes will *not* be reflected in the file WD L-3.docx source file.

4. **Scroll up, click to the right of Market Research Methods to select the entire line, press [Delete], select the Webographics heading, click the HOME tab, click the More button ▼ in the Styles group to show the Style gallery, click the Heading 3 style, then apply the Heading 3 style to the Demographics and Psychographics headings**

5. **Scroll up to the Web Marketing Strategies heading on page 3, select webographic in the third line of the paragraph, click the INSERT tab, then click the Hyperlink button in the Links section**

   The Insert Hyperlink dialog box opens, which you use to create a link to another file, to a Web page, or to a place in the current document. You can also create a link that creates a new document and a link that opens an e-mail client.

6. **Click Place in This Document**

   A list of headings and subheadings within the document that are formatted with styles, as well as bookmarks already included in the document, appear in the Insert Hyperlink dialog box. You can create a hyperlink to any place in the list.

7. **Click Webographics as shown in FIGURE L-9, click ScreenTip, type Click here to move to information about webographics. as shown in FIGURE L-10, click OK, then click OK**

   The text webographic appears light purple and underlined to indicate it is a hyperlink.

8. **Repeat Steps 5 through 7 to select and then create hyperlinks for the text demographic and psychographic, changing the ScreenTip as required so it matches its corresponding heading**

9. **Move the pointer over psychographic to show the ScreenTip as shown in FIGURE L-11, press [Ctrl]+Click as directed to move to the section on Psychographics, delete the extra blank link above the Customer Survey Results heading, then save the document**

FIGURE L-9: Insert Hyperlink dialog box

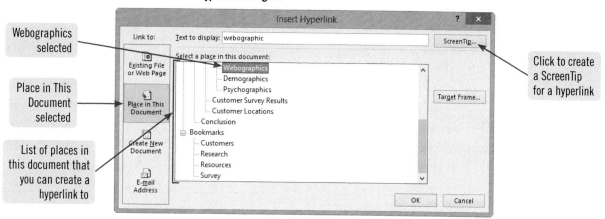

Webographics selected

Place in This Document selected

List of places in this document that you can create a hyperlink to

Click to create a ScreenTip for a hyperlink

FIGURE L-10: Entering text for a ScreenTip

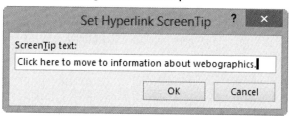

FIGURE L-11: Viewing a ScreenTip

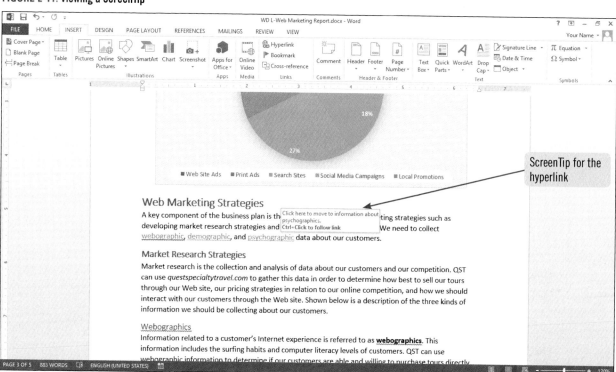

ScreenTip for the hyperlink

Import a Table from Access

Learning Outcomes
- Export an Access table to Word
- Format the exported table in Word

You can share information between Access and Word in a variety of ways. The most common method is to export an Access table or report to a Rich Text Format (.rtf) file. You can then open the .rtf file in Word and use Word's table features to format it just as you would format any table. **CASE** ▶ *You have already created an Access database that contains information related to online survey results. You open the Access database and export the table containing the survey results to an .rtf file that you then open in Word. Next you copy the Word table into the Marketing Online Report and then format the table with a built-in table style.*

STEPS

1. **Press [Ctrl][G], select the Survey bookmark, click Go To, delete ACCESS TABLE HERE, then be sure the insertion point is on a blank line**

2. **Use Windows Explorer to navigate to the location where you store your Data Files, double-click WD L-4.accdb, save the database as WD L-Web Marketing Database, enable content if prompted, then maximize the window if necessary**

3. **Click Online Survey: Table, click the EXTERNAL DATA tab, click the More button in the Export group as shown in FIGURE L-12, then click Word**
   The Export – RTF File dialog box opens, as shown in **FIGURE L-13**. You use this dialog box to designate where you will save the exported file. When you are exporting to Word, only the second option is available.

4. **Click Browse, navigate to the location where you save your files, change the filename to WD L-Web Survey, click Save, click the Open the destination file after the export operation is complete check box to select it, then click OK**
   The .rtf file opens in a Word window.

5. **Click the table move handle ⊞ in the upper-left corner of the table to select the entire table, click the Copy button in the Clipboard group on the HOME tab, show the Web Marketing Report document, then click the Paste button in the Clipboard group on the HOME tab**
   The Word table is copied into your Word document. The Word table is just that—a Word table; it is *not* an embedded object or a linked object.

6. **Scroll up and select the entire table again, click the TABLE TOOLS DESIGN tab, click the Banded Columns check box in the Table Style Options group to deselect it, click the More button ▼ in the Table Styles group to view the table styles available, then select the Grid Table 2 – Accent 1 (light purple) table style**

7. **Click the HOME tab, click the Center button ≡ in the Paragraph group, click away from the table to deselect it, add a page break to the left of Customer Survey Results, save your document, submit the file to your instructor, then close it**
   The formatted table appears as shown in **FIGURE L-14**.

8. **Show the WD L-Web Survey.rtf document, close the document without saving it, switch to Access, click Close to close the Export – RTF File dialog box, then exit Access**

FIGURE L-12: Options on the More menu in the Export group

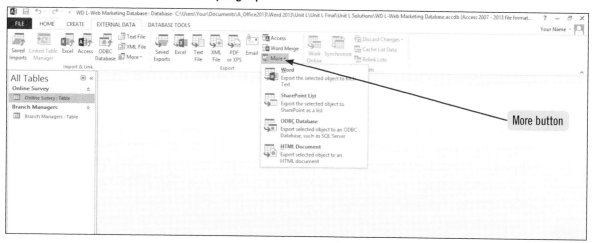

FIGURE L-13: Export – RTF file dialog box

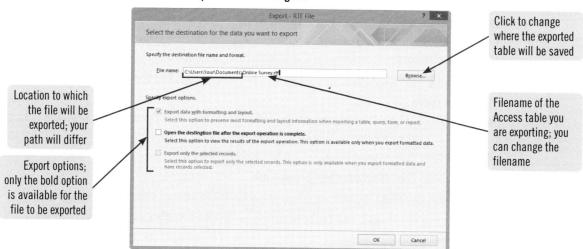

FIGURE L-14: Table created in Access, exported to Word, then formatted

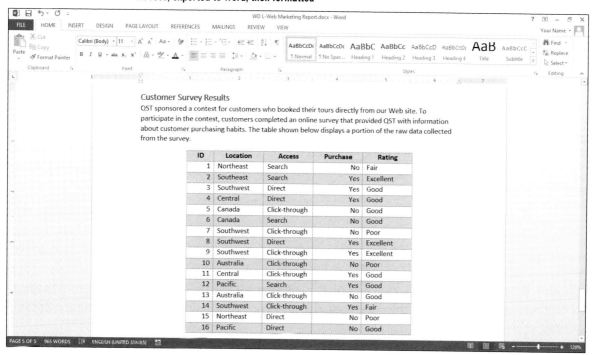

Manage Document Links

When you create a document that contains linked objects, you must include all source files when you copy the document to a new location or when you e-mail the document to a colleague. If you do not include source files, you (or your colleague) will receive error messages when trying to open the destination file. If you do not want to include source files when you move or e-mail a document containing links, then you should break the links before moving or e-mailing the document. After you break the links, the Update Links command cannot be used to update information in your destination file. Any changes you make to the source files after you break the links will not be reflected in the destination file. The objects in the destination file will appear as they do at the time the links are broken. **CASE** *You need to distribute the Word report to all QST branch managers. You keep a copy of the original report with the links intact, and then you save the report with a new name and break the links. You also view the entire report in Reading Layout view.*

STEPS

1. **Open the document** WD L-Web Marketing Report, **then save it as** WD L-Web Marketing Report_Managers

   You do not want to send along the source file for the Excel pie chart, so you break the link that was created when you copied the pie chart from Excel and pasted it into the Word report.

   TROUBLE
   You may need to scroll down to see the Edit Links to Files link in the lower-right corner of the screen.

2. **Click the** FILE **tab, then click** Edit Links to Files **in the Related Documents section of the Properties pane**

   The Links dialog box opens, as shown in **FIGURE L-15**. You can use the Links dialog box to update links, open source files, change source files, and break existing links. Notice that only one source file is listed in the Links dialog box—the Excel file called WD L-Online Marketing Data.xlsx.

3. **With the Excel file selected, click** Break Link

   A message appears asking if you are sure you want to break the selected link.

4. **Click** Yes, **click** OK **to exit the Links dialog box, then click** ⬅ **to exit Backstage view**

   The link between the Excel source file and the pie chart in the Word destination file is broken. Now if you make a change to the pie chart in the Excel source file, the pie chart in Word will not change.

5. **Scroll to the Suggested Advertising Expenses pie chart on page 3, then click the** pie chart

   The Word Ribbon is still active, and the CHART TOOLS contextual tabs are available. When you broke the link to the source file, Word converted the pie chart from a linked object to a chart object. You can use commands on the CHART TOOLS DESIGN and FORMAT tabs to modify the chart object, but you cannot change the content of the pie chart.

6. **Click the** CHART TOOLS DESIGN **tab, click the More button** ⬇ **in the Chart Styles group, then click** Style 12 **(last selection)**

   TROUBLE
   What you see on your screen may differ. Remember, Read Mode view shows the document so it is easy to read on the screen. Do not be concerned about page breaks or large areas of white space in this view.

7. **Click away from the chart, press [Ctrl][Home], click the** VIEW **tab, click the** Read Mode **button in the Views group to open the document in Read Mode, click the** VIEW **tab in the upper-left corner of the screen, then note the options available for working in Read Mode as shown in** FIGURE L-16

8. **Click the** Next Screen button ⊙ **on the right side of the screen to scroll through the report**

   In Read Mode, you can comfortably read the document text and scroll from screen to screen using the Next Screen ⊙ and Previous Screen ⊙ buttons. As you scroll through the report in Read Mode, you notice that page breaks appear differently than they do in Print Layout mode.

9. **Click the** VIEW **tab, click** Edit Document **on the VIEW menu that opens to return to Print Layout view, save the document, submit a copy to your instructor, then close the document**

FIGURE L-15: Links dialog box

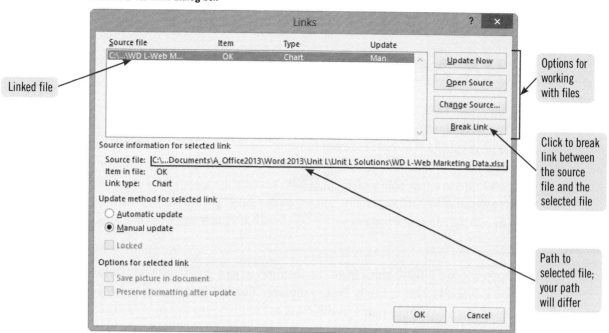

Linked file

Options for working with files

Click to break link between the source file and the selected file

Path to selected file; your path will differ

FIGURE L-16: VIEW menu in Read Mode

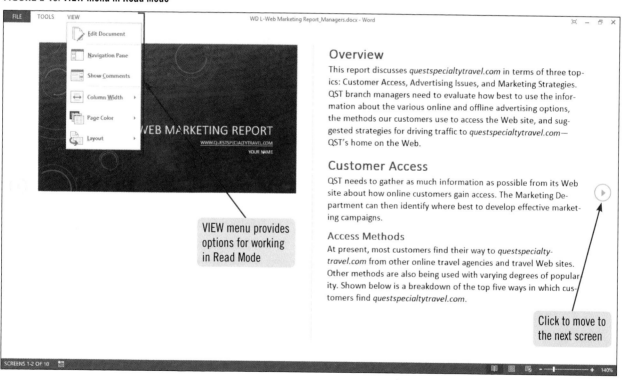

VIEW menu provides options for working in Read Mode

Click to move to the next screen

Merge with an Access Data Source

Learning
Outcomes
• Select Merge
  Recipients from
  Access
• Run a Merge

Many businesses store the names and addresses of contacts, employees, and customers in an Access database. You can merge information contained in an Access database with a letter, a sheet of labels, or any merge document that you've created in Word. The data you merge with the destination file is the **data source**. When you use an existing database as your data source, you save time because you do not need to create a new data source. **CASE ▶** *You need to mail a printed copy of the Online Marketing Report to all QST branch managers. First, you edit a cover letter to accompany the report, and then you merge the letter with the names and addresses of the QST branch managers that are stored in an Access database.*

STEPS

1. Open the file WD L-5.docx from the location where you store your Data Files, save it as WD L-Web Marketing Cover Letter, replace "Current Date" with today's date, scroll down, then type your name in the closing

2. Click the MAILINGS tab, click Select Recipients in the Start Mail Merge group, click Use an Existing List, navigate to the location where you store your files, click WD L-Web Marketing Database.accdb, then click Open

3. Verify that Branch Managers is selected, then click OK

   Most of the buttons on the MAILINGS tab are now active.

4. Delete the word Address near the top of the letter, be sure the insertion point is on a blank line, click the Address Block button in the Write & Insert Fields group, click the Always include the country/region in the address option button as shown in FIGURE L-17, then click OK

   The <<AddressBlock>> field is inserted in the letter.

5. Delete the word Greeting, be sure the insertion point is on a blank line, click the Greeting Line button in the Write & Insert Fields group, click the list arrow next to Mr. Randall, scroll down and click Joshua, then click OK

6. Scroll to the last paragraph, click to the left of Please, click the Insert Merge Field button in the Write & Insert Fields group, click FirstName, click Insert, click Close, type a comma (,), press [Spacebar], then change Please to please

7. Click the Preview Results button in the Preview Results group, select the text in the address block from "Ms. Marilyn Clancy" to "United States," click the HOME tab, click the Line and Paragraph Spacing button ⌃≡ ⌄ in the Paragraph group, click Remove Space After Paragraph, press the right arrow, then press [Enter] to move the greeting line down

   Sometimes you need to adjust spacing when you view the results of a merge.

8. Click the MAILINGS tab, then click the Next Record button ▶ in the Preview Results group until you have previewed all seven records

   You've successfully merged the cover letter with the names and addresses of the branch managers. Now you can save just a selection of the letters.

9. Click the Finish & Merge button in the Finish group, click Edit Individual Documents, click the From option button, enter 5 in the From box and 6 in the To box, click OK, click the VIEW tab, click Multiple Pages in the Zoom group, save the document as WD L-Web Marketing Cover Letter_Merged, compare the letters to FIGURE L-18, then close the document

10. Save the main document, submit all files to your instructor, close the file, then exit Word

Integrating Word with Other Programs

FIGURE L-17: Insert Address Block dialog box

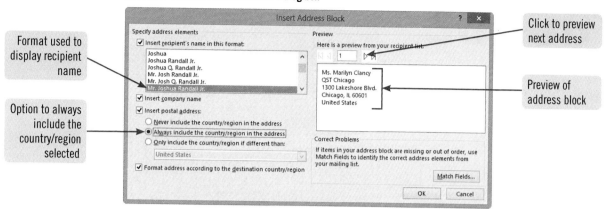

Format used to display recipient name

Option to always include the country/region selected

Click to preview next address

Preview of address block

FIGURE L-18: Merged cover letters

Opening a merge document

The file WD L-Online Marketing Cover Letter contains merge fields so when you open the document, Word will try to complete the merge. When you open the WD L-Online Marketing Cover Letter document, you will see a warning telling you that opening the document will run the SQL command: SELECT*FROM 'Branch Managers'. This warning means that Word will look for the list of recipients in the Branch Managers table in a database file. Click Yes. If the database is stored on your computer, the correct recipient list will be matched to the document. If the database is not stored in the location expected by Word, then you will need to navigate to the location where the database is stored and select it. If the database is not available, you will receive an error message and will not be able to complete the merge.

Practice

Concepts Review

Refer to FIGURE L-19 **to answer the questions that follow.**

FIGURE L-19

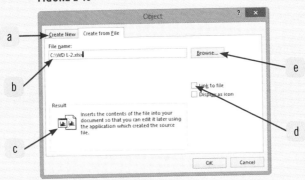

1. Which element do you click to create an Excel worksheet or PowerPoint slide directly in Word?
2. Which element describes the action being taken?
3. Which element do you click to link the inserted file to its source program?
4. Which element points to the name of the file that will be inserted?
5. Which element do you click to find the file you want to insert?

Match each term with the statement that best describes it.

6. Chart
7. Object
8. Update
9. Embedded object
10. Hyperlink
11. Data Source
12. Read Mode

a. Doesn't change if the source document is edited
b. Excel object pasted as a link by default
c. Self-contained information that can be in the form of text, graphics, and so on
d. Text that, when clicked, goes to another location in a document
e. The process of changing data in a linked file to match the source program
f. View in which Word text cannot be edited
g. Contains records used in a merge

Select the best answer from the list of choices.

13. What file format is an Access table saved to when it is exported to Word?
   a. .docx
   b. .tmp
   c. .rtf
   d. .txt
14. How do you open the Links dialog box?
   a. Click the VIEW tab, then click the Links check box in the Show group
   b. Click the FILE tab, then click Edit Links to Files.
   c. Click the PAGE LAYOUT tab, then click the Links button in the Arrange group
   d. Click the REVIEW tab, then click the Links button in the Proofing group
15. Which Paste command can be used to insert a linked object?
   a. Keep Source Formatting and Embed Workbook
   b. Keep Text Only
   c. Use Destination Theme & Link Data
   d. Picture

Skills Review

1. Embed an Excel worksheet.

a. Start Word, open the file WD L-6.docx from the drive and folder where you store your Data Files, then save it as **WD L-Cloud Nine Tours Report**.

b. Use the Go To command to find the Categories bookmark, then delete the placeholder text "Excel Worksheet Here" and be sure the insertion point is on a blank line. (*Note*: As you delete placeholder text throughout this Skills Review, always be sure the insertion point is on a blank line.)

c. Click Object in the Text group on the INSERT tab, click the Create from File tab, then use the Browse feature to insert the file WD L-7.xlsx file from the location where you store your Data Files into the Word document.

d. Edit the worksheet object by changing the value in cell B3 from 1800 to **2200**, then enhance the value in cell B8 with bold.

e. Apply the Frame theme to the Excel workbook. (*Note*: The themes are not listed in alphabetical order.)

f. In Word, center the worksheet object, then save the document.

2. Link an Excel chart.

a. Use the Go To command to find the Popularity bookmark, then delete the placeholder text "Excel Chart Here."

b. Use Windows Explorer to open the file WD L-7.xlsx from the location where you store your Data Files, then save it as **WD L-Cloud Nine Tours Data**.

c. Show the Popularity worksheet, change the number of Backpacking Tours sold to **1500**, copy the column chart, switch to Word, preview the paste options on the HOME tab, then paste the column chart using the Use Destination Theme & Link Data paste option.

d. Switch to Excel, change the value in cell C5 to **3000**, then save the workbook in Excel.

e. In Word, verify that the Wilderness Canoeing column for Available Tours is now 3000, refreshing the data if the data does not update automatically.

f. Switch to Excel, then exit the program.

3. Embed a PowerPoint slide.

a. Insert a blank page at the top of the Word document, then insert a PowerPoint slide as an embedded object on the new blank page.

b. Enter the text **Cloud Nine Tours - Vancouver** as the slide title, then enter **www.cloudninetours-vancouver.com** as the subtitle followed by your name, which should appear on the next line. Note that "vancouver" should not be capitalized.

c. Apply the Frame design to the embedded slide object (see **FIGURE L-20**).

d. Click below the embedded slide object.

e. Double-click the slide object so you can edit the slide using the tools on the PowerPoint Ribbon, select the gray-green variant (3rd from left), then customize the color applied to the hyperlink by changing it to Aqua, Accent 2, Lighter 80%.

FIGURE L-20

Frame design

f. Customize the color applied to the followed hyperlink by changing it to Aqua, Accent 2, Lighter 40%. Exit the embedded slide object, then save the document.

4. Insert a Word file and hyperlinks.

a. Use the Go To command to find the Tours bookmark in WD L-Cloud Nine Tours Report.

b. Remove the placeholder text "Word File Here," then insert the file WD L-8.docx as a Text from File from the location where you store your Data Files.

c. Scroll up to and delete the entire line containing the heading "Cloud Nine Tours" so no extra space appears, select the Sea Kayaking heading (currently formatted with the Heading 1 style), then apply the Heading 3 style to the heading. (*Hint*: Remember to turn the display of formatting marks on and off as needed to help you make selections.)

d. Apply the Heading 3 style to the remaining headings: Backpacking, Wildlife Photography, Wilderness Canoeing, and Mountain Biking.

e. Scroll up to the Category Descriptions heading, select Sea Kayaking in the first line in the paragraph, create a hyperlink to the Sea Kayaking heading, then create this ScreenTip: **Click here to move to the description of Sea Kayaking tours.**

f. Create hyperlinks and ScreenTips for each of the remaining four tour categories: Backpacking, Wildlife Photography, Wilderness Canoeing, and Mountain Biking. (*Hint*: Copy the text for the Sea Kayaking ScreenTip, paste it into the ScreenTip text box for each entry, then change the name of the tour.)

g. Test the hyperlinks, scroll to "Customer Profiles," remove any extra blank lines below the paragraph on mountain biking, then save the document.

5. **Import a table from Access.**

a. Use the Go To command to find the Profile bookmark, then remove the placeholder text "Access Table Here."

b. Use Windows Explorer to open the file WD L-9.accdb from the location where you store your Data Files, then save the database as **WD L-Cloud Nine Data.accdb**, enabling content when prompted.

c. Export the Customer Profile table as an .rtf file called **WD L-Cloud Nine Customer Profile.rtf** to the location where you store your files for this book, making sure to select the Open the destination file after the export operation is complete check box.

d. Copy the table from the .rtf file that opened in Word, and paste it into the Cloud Nine Tours Report document. (*Note*: The table breaks across two pages. You will adjust pagination in a later step.)

e. Apply the Grid Table 2 - Accent 3 table style (light green) to the table, deselect the Banded Rows check box, then reduce the column widths to fit the content.

f. Press [Ctrl][Home], scroll through the document and add a page break at the Tour Popularity heading and a page break at the Customer Survey Results heading.

g. Save the WD L-Cloud Nine Tours Report document, switch to and close the WD L-Cloud Nine Customer Profile.rtf file without saving it, switch to Access, click Close, then exit Access.

6. **Manage document links.**

a. Using the Word FILE tab, open the Links dialog box, then break the link to the WD L-Cloud Nine Tours Data.xlsx file.

b. Scroll to view the Tours Popularity column chart, then click the column chart.

c. Apply Chart Style 14.

d. Click away from the chart, switch to Read Mode, use the Next Screen and Previous Screen buttons to view the document in Read Mode, then return to Print Layout view.

e. Enter your name where indicated in the document footer, save the document, submit a copy to your instructor, then close the document.

f. The completed report appears as shown in **FIGURE L-21**.

FIGURE L-21

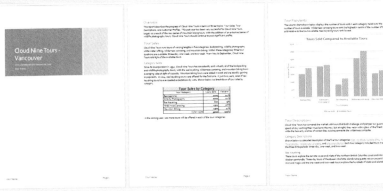

Skills Review (continued)

7. Merge with an Access data source.

    a. Open the file WD L-10.docx from the location where you store your Data Files, save it as **WD L-Cloud Nine Tours Cover Letter**, then replace the placeholder text Current Date and Your Name with the appropriate information.

    b. Click the MAILINGS tab, select the file WD L-Cloud Nine Data.accdb as the recipients list, then select the Tour Guides table.

    c. Insert the Address Block field to replace the word Address and accept the default settings.

    d. Insert the Greeting Line field to replace the word Greeting, then use Joshua as the greeting line format.

    e. Click to the left of Please in the last paragraph, insert the FirstName field, type a comma (,), insert a space, then change Please to **please**.

    f. Preview the merge results, select the text of the first address in the address block, then remove the After paragraph spacing so that no extra space appears between the lines in the inside address.

    g. Press [Enter] following the address so a blank line appears between the address and the greeting line.

    h. Preview all the records, then finish the merge so that you edit letters **5** and **6** (to Sandro Corelli and Grace Kwan).

    i. Save the two merged letters as **WD L-Cloud Nine Tours Cover Letter_Merged.docx**, then close the document.

    j. Save and close the main document, submit all files to your instructor, then exit Word.

Independent Challenge 1

As a member of the Recreation Commission in Helena, Montana, you are responsible for compiling the minutes of the monthly meetings. You have already written most of the text required for the minutes. Now you need to insert information from two sources. First, you insert a worksheet from an Excel file that shows the monies raised from various fundraising activities, and then you insert a Word file that the director of the commission has sent you for inclusion in the minutes.

    a. Start Word, open the file WD L-11.docx from the location where you store your Data Files, then save it as **WD L-Recreation Commission Minutes**.

    b. Select and delete the phrase EXCEL WORKSHEET, then insert the file WD L-12.xlsx from the location where you store your Data Files as an embedded object to replace EXCEL WORKSHEET. (*Hint*: Click the Create from File tab in the Object dialog box.)

    c. Edit the worksheet object changing the value in cell D3 from 300 to **500**, enhance the contents of cells A3:A5 with bold, then apply the Organic theme to the Excel workbook.

    d. Center the worksheet in Word.

    e. At the end of the document, insert a page break, then insert the file WD L-13.docx as a Text from File from the location where you store your Data Files.

    f. Apply the Heading 1 style to the text **Director's Report**.

    g. Find the heading "Recreation Council Report" then after the text "...was a success." (end of sentence under the heading), type the text **See the Director's Report for more details**.

    h. Create a hyperlink from the phrase "Director's Report" in the text you just typed to the heading Director's Report.

    i. From the DESIGN tab, click the Colors button in the Document Formatting group, then customize the color of the hyperlink by changing it to Green, Accent 1, Darker 50%.

    j. Type **Prepared by** followed by your name in the document footer.

    k. Save the document, submit all files to your instructor, close the document, then exit Word.

Independent Challenge 2

You run a summer camp in Yellowstone National Park for teenagers interested in taking on leadership roles at their schools and in their communities. You have started an outline for a report about this program in Word. You will continue to enhance the Word document so you can eventually use it to create a PowerPoint presentation.

Independent Challenge 2 (continued)

a. Start Word, open the file WD L-14.docx from the location where you store your Data Files, then save it as **WD L-Yellowstone Camp Report**.

b. Insert a new page above the first page in the document, then insert an embedded PowerPoint slide.

c. Add **Yellowstone Camp Report** as the title and your name as the subtitle, then format the slide with the slide design of your choice.

d. Deselect the slide, then edit the slide and apply the variant of your choice.

e. Use Windows Explorer to open the file WD L-15.xlsx from the location where you store your Data Files, then save it as **WD L-Yellowstone Camp Data**.

f. Copy the chart from Excel, then paste it into Word below the Student Enrollment heading and its associated text using the Use Destination Theme & Link Data paste option.

g. In Excel, change the value in cell B3 to **1800**, save and close the workbook, then exit Excel.

h. In Word, refresh the data if it did not update automatically, center the chart, add your name to the footer, then save the document.

i. Open the Links dialog box, and break the link to the chart.

j. Apply the same design you applied to the PowerPoint slide to the Word document. (*Hint*: In PowerPoint, you can determine the name of the theme by moving your mouse over the active variant on the DESIGN tab.)

k. View the document in Read Mode and scroll through to view how the chart and other elements appear.

l. Return to Print Layout view, save the document, submit both files to your instructor, close the document, then exit Word.

Independent Challenge 3

You own a small Web-based business that sells craft materials online. The business is growing—thanks in large part to the help you're receiving from several art stores in your area. You've decided to send a memo to the store managers every few months to describe the growth of the Web site. The memo will include a linked Excel worksheet and a table created in Access. Once you have completed the memo, you will merge it with a database containing the names of all the store managers who are helping to promote the Web site.

a. Start Word, open the file WD L-16.docx from the location where you store your Data Files and save it as **WD L-Crafts Online Memo**.

b. Use Windows Explorer to open the file WD L-17.accdb from the location where you store your Data Files, save the file as **WD L-Crafts Online Database.accdb**, then enable content when prompted.

c. Export the Access table called June 1 Sales to an .rtf file called **WD L-Crafts Online Sales** so the .rft file opens in Word.

d. In Word, copy the table in the .rtf file, then switch to the WD L-Crafts Online Memo document, and paste the table below the paragraph that starts The table illustrated below....

e. Apply a table design of your choice with Banded Columns deselected, automatically adjust the column widths, so that both Buyer Location and Sale Amount labels wrap to two lines, center the data in the Buyer Location column, then center the table.

f. Use Windows Explorer to open the file WD L-18.xlsx from the location where you store your Data Files, then save the Excel file as **WD L-Crafts Online Data**.

g. Click the pie chart to select it, copy the pie chart, switch to the Crafts Online Memo document, then paste the chart below the paragraph that starts The pie chart shown below... using the Use Destination Theme & Link Data paste option.

h. In Excel, click cell F3, change the sale generated by the Georgia customer to **350.00**, press [Enter], then save the worksheet.

i. In the WD L-Arts Crafts Memo document, refresh the chart data if it did not update automatically, change the height of the chart to **2.5"**, then center it. (*Hint*: You know the data refreshed if the GA slice is 24%.)

j. Break the link to the Excel chart.

k. Scroll to the top of the document, then replace the placeholder text with your name and today's date in the Memo heading.

l. Click after the To: in the Memo heading, open the MAILINGS tab, click the Select Recipients button, click Use an Existing List, browse to the location where you store your Data Files, double-click WD L-17.accdb, then select the Retail Outlets table.

Independent Challenge 3 (continued)

m. Insert an Address Block following To: that contains only the recipient's name. (*Hint*: Deselect the Insert company name check box and the Insert postal address check box in the Insert Address Block dialog box.)

n. Preview the recipients, then complete the merge so that only records **3** and **4** are merged.

o. Save the merged memos as **WD L-Crafts Online Memo_Merged**, then close the file.

p. Save and close the main document in Word, close the .rtf file without saving it, submit your files to your instructor, then exit all open applications.

Independent Challenge 4: Explore

You can use the various applications in the Office suite in combination with Word to help you plan a special event such as a party or a wedding. For example, you can enter the names and addresses of the people you plan to invite in an Access database and create a budget for the event in Excel. To keep track of all the information related to an event, you modify a party planning document in Word. You open a Word document that contains tables and placeholders that you complete with information and objects related to an end-of-term class celebration. You also explore how to create a chart in Word from data in an embedded Excel file.

a. Open the file WD L-19.docx from the location where you store your Data Files, save it as **WD L-Class Celebration Planning**, then apply the theme of your choice.

b. In the space under Event Information, insert the file WD L-20.docx, then format the table with the table design of your choice. Explore the various options available for further modifying the table design in the Table Style Options group. For example, you can choose to format the Header Row differently from the other rows, use banded rows or banded columns (or both), etc.

c. Enter the text **Budget Information** next to Expenses in the Event Information table, then create a hyperlink from the text to the Cost Breakdown heading.

d. Test the hyperlink, then from the DESIGN tab, change the color applied to the Followed Hyperlink.

e. Open WD L-21.accdb in Access, then export the Guests table to an .rtf document called **WD L-Class Celebration Guests**.

f. Copy the table in WD L-Class Celebration Guests.rtf to the appropriate location in the Word Event Planning document, then format it attractively to compliment the formatting you applied to the event information table. Delete the ID column and adjust the spacing of the column headings so none of the lines wrap and the information is easy to read.

g. Add a page break to the left of the Event Budget heading, embed WD L-22.xlsx to replace the text "Budget Items," then apply the theme you applied to the rest of the document.

h. Edit the data in the embedded file by changing the Catering cost to 4,000.

i. Follow the steps below to create a chart in Word using the data in the embedded worksheet.

- Double-click the embedded file, select the range A1:B7, click the Copy button, then click outside the embedded object.
- Delete the text "Breakdown of Expenses Pie Chart."
- Click the INSERT tab, click the Chart button in the Illustrations group, click Pie, then click OK.
- Click cell A1 in the datasheet that appears above the chart, then press [Ctrl][V] to paste the data from the embedded worksheet.
- Widen columns so all the data is visible, then close the datasheet.
- Delete the title of the chart, click the CHART TOOLS DESIGN tab, click the Quick Layout button, then select Layout 4.
- Click the Change Colors button, then select a new color scheme.

j. Add your name to the footer in the Word document, save all open files, submit your files to your instructor, close all documents, then exit all open applications.

Visual Workshop

Start a new document in Word, select the Integral theme, then embed the PowerPoint slide using the slide design (Integral) and the variant shown in **FIGURE L-22**. Add the title **Idaho Arts Foundation** to the slide along with the subtitle **Cell Phone Charges** and Your Name on two separate lines as shown. In Word add the text **The pie chart shown below breaks down cell phone usage from May 1 to June 15 by employees of the Idaho Arts Foundation.** below the PowerPoint slide as shown in **FIGURE L-22**. Start Excel, open the file WD L-23.xlsx from the location where you store your Data Files, then save it as **WD L-Idaho Arts Cell Phone Data**. Copy the pie chart, paste it into the Word document using the Use Destination Theme & Link Data paste option, apply the Color 4 color scheme (Hint: Click the Change Colors button in the Chart Styles group), then change the height of the chart to 3.7". Save the document as **WD L-Idaho Arts Cell Phone Report**. In Excel, change the value in cell B2 to **80**, then save the workbook. In Word, verify that the pie chart appears as shown in **FIGURE L-22**, then break the link to the Excel file. View the document in Read Mode, compare it to **FIGURE L-22**, return to Print Layout mode, save the document, submit your files to your instructor, close the document, close the workbook in Excel, then exit all programs.

FIGURE L-22

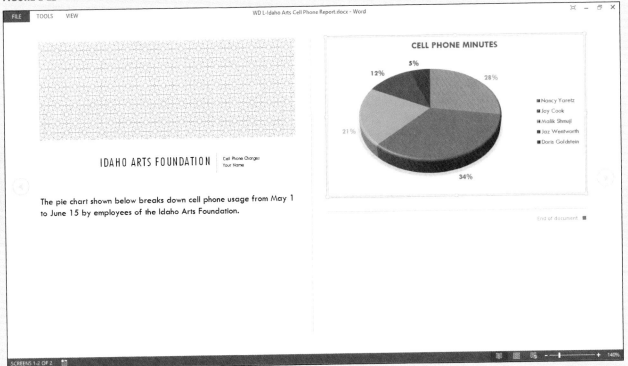

Exploring Advanced Graphics

CASE ▶ Sheila Barton, the manager of QST Sydney, has prepared a document reviewing activities during the past year at QST Sydney. She asks you to enhance the document with a variety of graphics including a screen shot of the Quest Specialty Travel Web site, modified pictures, SmartArt graphics, drawing objects, a watermark, and a page border.

Unit Objectives

After completing this unit, you will be able to:

- Create and modify screenshots
- Edit pictures
- Position pictures
- Remove the background from a picture

- Use artistic effects and layering options
- Arrange graphics
- Create SmartArt graphics
- Add a watermark and page border

Files You Will Need

WD M-1.docx	WD M-8.docx
WD M-2.jpg	WD M-9.docx
WD M-3.jpg	WD M-10.docx
WD M-4.docx	WD M-11.docx
WD M-5.docx	WD M-12.docx
WD M-6.jpg	WD M-13.docx
WD M-7.jpg	WD M-14.docx

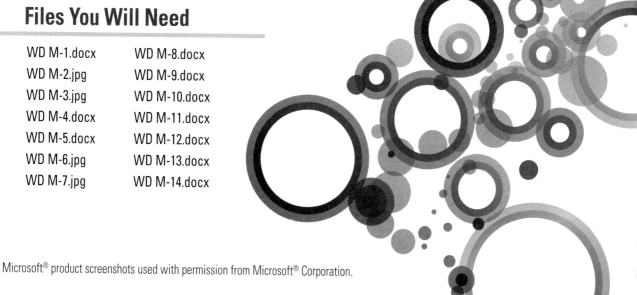

©Tumanyan/Shutterstock

Create and Modify Screenshots

Learning
Outcomes
• Insert a screenshot
• Create a screen
  clipping

The Illustrations group on the INSERT tab contains the buttons you use to create illustrations in six categories: pictures, online pictures, shapes, SmartArt, charts, and screenshots. The **Screenshot** command displays a gallery of thumbnails of all open program windows, such as a Web site window, an Excel worksheet window, or another Word window. You select the screenshot from the gallery and insert it into your document as a graphic object. In addition to inserting a screenshot, you can also use the Screen Clipping feature to insert just a portion of a window as a graphic object into your Word document. **CASE** *You want to include a screenshot of the Quest Specialty Travel Web site and a screen clipping of the company slogan in the QST Sydney Year in Review document.*

STEPS

1. **Start Word, open the file** WD M-1.docx **from the location where you store your Data Files, then save it as** WD M-QST Sydney Year in Review

2. **Start Internet Explorer or the Web browser you prefer, click in the** Address text box, **type** www.questspecialtytravel.com, **then press** [Enter]
   The Quest Specialty Travel Web site opens in the browser window.

QUICK TIP
A screenshot is a
static image,
which means the
screenshot does not
change even if the
contents of the Web
page change.

3. **Return to the document in Word, scroll to, then click to the left of the [Company Website] placeholder (below the WEB SITE heading), click the** INSERT tab, **then click the** Screenshot button **in the Illustrations group**
   A thumbnail of the QST Web page window appears in the Available Windows gallery, as shown in **FIGURE M-1**. If you have additional windows active, then thumbnails of those windows will also appear in the Available Windows gallery.

4. **Click the** thumbnail **of the QST Web site window in the Available Windows gallery, then click** No
   The screenshot of the QST Web site window is inserted in the Word document as a graphic object. If you answered Yes, the screenshot would include a hyperlink to the Web site so that when you click the image in the Word document, a browser window containing the Web site opens. You can resize, position, and format the object just like you would any graphic object, such as a picture or a chart.

5. **Select the contents of the** Width text box **in the Size group, type** 5, **press** [Enter], **then delete the [Company Website] placeholder**

6. **Click the** screenshot, **click the** Center button ≡ **in the Paragraph group on the HOME tab, then click away from the screenshot to deselect it**

7. **Scroll to the top of the document, click to the left of the [Company Logo] placeholder, click the** INSERT tab, **click** Screenshot, **then click** Screen Clipping
   In a few seconds, the window containing the Web site fills the screen and is dimmed.

8. **Drag the pointer to select just the company slogan as shown in** FIGURE M-2, **then release the mouse button**
   When you release the mouse button, the screen clipping appears in the Word document at the selected location. If you do not like the appearance of the clipped screen, click the Undo button, then repeat Steps 7 and 8.

9. **Delete the [Company Logo] placeholder, click the** screen clipping, **change its width to** 4", **save the document, click the** Web browser button **on the taskbar, then close the Web browser**

Exploring Advanced Graphics

FIGURE M-1: Thumbnail of window available for a screenshot

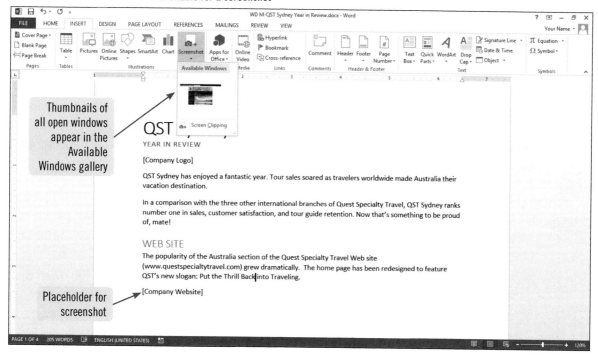

FIGURE M-2: Selecting content for a screen clipping

Inserting Videos

You can insert an online video clip directly into a Word document and then play it if you are connected to the Internet. To insert a video, click the Online Video button in the Media group on the INSERT tab. The Insert Video dialog box opens with three options available. You can find a video by entering keywords into the Bing Video Search box or by clicking the logo for YouTube. If you have already conducted a search on YouTube, the search box for YouTube will appear in the Insert Video dialog box below the search box for Bing Video Search. In the Insert Video dialog box, you can also paste the HTML code for a video currently stored on a Web site. Once you have selected and inserted a video into Word, you click it to play the video directly from the Word document.

Exploring Advanced Graphics

Edit Pictures

Learning Outcomes
• Crop a picture
• Add effects to a picture
• Add Alt text to a picture

You use the tools on the PICTURE TOOLS FORMAT tab and in the Format Picture pane to modify a picture in different ways. You can crop a picture, change the picture shape, modify the picture border, and apply picture effects such as the Glow and Bevel effects. You can even add **alternative text** (also known as alt text) to a picture to provide a description of the picture for people who are visually impaired and using a screen reader to read the document. **CASE** ▶ *The document describing QST Sydney's year in review contains a picture of a parrot. You use the picture tools to transform the picture into an interesting graphic object, then add Alt Text.*

STEPS

QUICK TIP
Click a picture to make the PICTURE TOOLS FORMAT tab available. Double-click a picture to make the PICTURE TOOLS FORMAT tab active.

1. **Scroll to the Top Tours heading on page 2, then double-click the** parrot picture

   When you double-click a picture, the PICTURE TOOLS FORMAT tab appears on the Ribbon and the Layout Options button appears outside the top right corner of the picture.

2. **Click the** Crop button **in the Size group on the PICTURE TOOLS FORMAT tab, then drag the middle-left and middle-right crop marks so the image appears as shown in** FIGURE M-3

   When you **crop** a picture, you drag the crop handle associated with the part of the picture you want to crop. A cropped picture is smaller than the original picture because you take away content from the top, bottom, and/or sides of the picture. When you resize a picture, the content of the picture stays the same even though the picture is made smaller or larger.

QUICK TIP
If you don't like the crop, you can click the Undo button ↶ to undo your last crop action.

3. **Click away from the picture to set the crop, click the** picture **again, click the** Crop button list arrow **in the Size group, point to** Crop to Shape, **then click the** Oval shape **in the top row of the Basic Shapes section (far-left selection)**

   The picture is cropped further in the shape of an oval.

4. **Click the** launcher ⌟ **in the Picture Styles group**

   The Format Picture pane opens with the Effects category active and the Effects subcategories listed.

5. **Click** 3-D FORMAT, **click the** Top bevel list arrow, **then click the** Circle bevel style (top left selection)

   The Circle bevel style is applied to the picture.

QUICK TIP
Use the Expand arrow ▷ next to categories in the Format Picture pane to show additional options and the Collapse arrow ◢ to hide them again.

6. **Change the Width of the top bevel to** 15 pt, **click the** Material list arrow **and select** Dark Edge **in the Special Effect area, scroll down, click the** Lighting list arrow **and select** Two Point **in the Special area, compare the 3-D FORMAT options to** FIGURE M-4, **then scroll up and click the** Collapse arrow ◢ **to the left of 3-D FORMAT**

7. **Click the** Layout & Properties button **to the right of the Effects button at the top of the Format Picture pane, then click** ALT TEXT

8. **Click the** Title text box, **type** Blue Parrot, **press [Tab], type the description:** Beautiful parrot in the tropical rainforest in northern Queensland., **then click** ◢ **next to ALT TEXT to collapse the Alt Text options**

   The Alt Text will be visible to users who view the document with a screen reader.

9. **Click the** Close button ✖ **to hide the Format Picture pane, click** Picture Effects **in the Picture Styles group on the Ribbon, point to** Shadow, **click the** Offset Diagonal Top Left **reflection option in the Outer area (third row, third column), then save the document**

FIGURE M-3: Cropping a picture

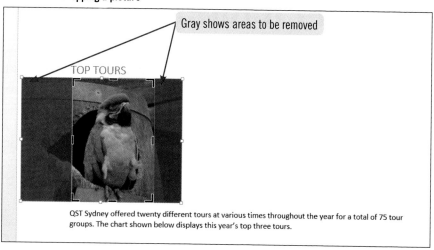

FIGURE M-4: 3-D effects applied to a picture

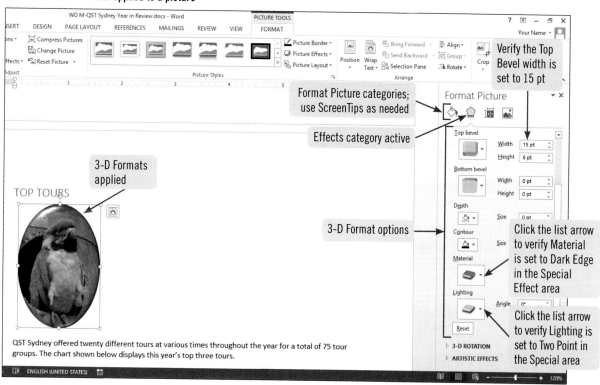

Inserting Online Pictures

You can insert a picture directly from the Internet into a Word document if you are connected to the Internet. To insert an online picture, click the Online Pictures button in the Illustrations group on the INSERT tab. The Insert Pictures dialog box opens with three options available. You can find a picture by entering keywords into the Office.com Clip Art search box or the Bing Image Search box. You can also insert a picture directly from your SkyDrive. Just click the Browse button to be taken directly to your SkyDrive, then navigate to the folder containing the picture you want to insert.

Position Pictures

Learning
Outcomes
• Change text
  wrapping
• Use advanced
  positioning
  options

When you insert a picture into a document, the default position is In Line with Text, which means that the picture is part of the line of text in which the picture was inserted. You can position the picture using the Left, Center, and Right buttons in the Paragraph group but you can't freely move the picture around the document. When you don't want the picture to be part of a line of text, you can modify how text wraps around it. When you change the wrapping option, the picture will no longer be part of a line of text and you can no longer use buttons in the Paragraph group to position the picture. Instead, you can move the picture using your mouse to drag the picture and the alignment guides to help you position the picture. You can also use the Position command in the Arrange group on the PICTURE TOOLS FORMAT tab to change the location of a picture that does not have In Line with Text wrapping applied. Finally, you can set a precise location for the picture by entering coordinates in the Position tab of the Layout dialog box. **CASE** *You change the wrapping of the parrot picture and position it using alignment guides, then you enter coordinates in the Layout dialog box to position it precisely on the page.*

STEPS

QUICK TIP

The Layout Options button ⌐ appears near the top right corner of the selected picture.

1. **Double-click the blue parrot picture to select it**

2. **Click the Layout Options button ⌐, click the Square wrap option (top left selection in the With Text Wrapping section)**

   Text wraps to the right of the picture. Notice that the two options below the With Text Wrapping area are now available. These options are only available when one of the With Text Wrapping options is active.

QUICK TIP

The green alignment guides appear as you drag an object and the object is aligned with a margin or other element on the page such as the top of a line of text or the side of another picture.

3. **Click the Align button in the Arrange group, be sure there is a check mark next to Use Alignment Guides or click Alignment Guides to show the check mark, click the parrot in the document, then use your mouse to drag the parrot up and to the right margin**

   Green alignment guides appear as you move your mouse toward the right margin and up toward the top margin.

4. **Continue to use your mouse and the green alignment guides to position the picture as shown in FIGURE M-5**

5. **Click the Layout Options button ⌐, click the Fix position on page option button, then click See more**

   The Layout dialog box opens with the Position tab active.

6. **Refer to FIGURE M-6 type 4.6 in the Absolute position text box in the Horizontal group, be sure "to the right of" is set to Margin, type 1.5 in Absolute position text box in the Vertical group, then be sure "below" is set to Page**

   You can position a graphic object horizontally and vertically on the page relative to a margin, column, line, or edge of the page. You've set the Absolute position of the picture as 4.6" to the right of the left margin and 1.5" below the top of the page.

7. **Click OK to close the Layout dialog box, click away from the image to deselect it, then compare the document to FIGURE M-7**

8. **Save the document**

FIGURE M-5: Using alignment guides to position a graphic object

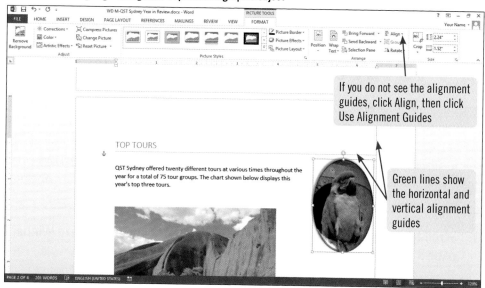

If you do not see the alignment guides, click Align, then click Use Alignment Guides

Green lines show the horizontal and vertical alignment guides

FIGURE M-6: Setting advanced positioning options for a graphic object

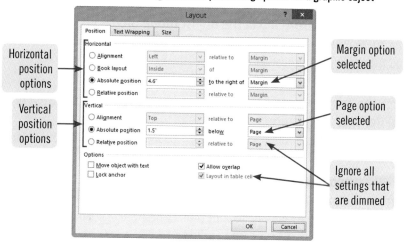

Horizontal position options

Vertical position options

Margin option selected

Page option selected

Ignore all settings that are dimmed

FIGURE M-7: Graphic object positioned precisely

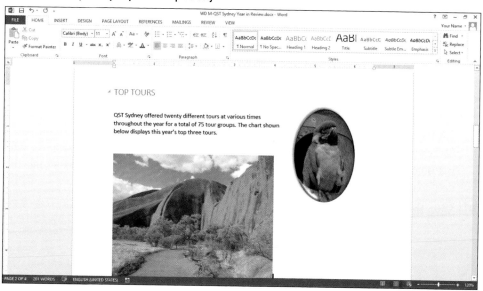

Word 2013

Remove the Background from a Picture

You use the Remove Background feature to remove background objects from a photograph. For example, you can remove the background from a photograph of a person standing in front of a landscape so that only the person is visible. **CASE** *The Year in Review document includes a photograph of a pink flower. You use the Remove Background feature to isolate just the flower from the surrounding lily pads and water, and then in the next lesson you use artistic effects to superimpose the isolated flower over a new picture.*

STEPS

1. **Scroll to and double-click the first picture of a flower under the Prize Winner heading on page 3**
   This document contains two pictures of the pink flower. You will use the second picture in the next lesson.

2. **Increase the zoom to 150%, then scroll so that all of the picture is visible in the document window**
   You increase the zoom percentage when working with graphics so you can see your changes more clearly.

3. **Click Remove Background in the Adjust group on the PICTURE TOOLS FORMAT tab**
   The BACKGROUND REMOVAL tab on the Ribbon becomes active and most of the picture turns purple. You use the buttons in the Refine group on the BACKGROUND REMOVAL tab to mark the areas of the photograph to keep and the areas to discard.

4. **Click the Mark Areas to Remove button in the Refine group, then move the mouse pointer over the picture**
   The mouse pointer changes to a pencil shape. You use this pointer to indicate the areas of the photograph to remove.

5. **Draw a diagonal line across the lily pad as shown by the dotted line in FIGURE M-8, then release the mouse button**
   The lily pad is removed and a dotted line shows where you dragged the pointer. The dotted line includes a Remove marker, which is a circle with a minus symbol.

TROUBLE
If some of the lily pad reappears, click Undo ↶ and try again, or use the Mark Areas to Remove command to remove the areas you don't want.

6. **Draw a second diagonal line across the lily pad to the right of the flower stem**
   If all of the lily pad is not removed, drag the pencil across the other shapes to remove them.

7. **Click the Mark Areas to Keep button in the Refine group, draw a vertical line up the stem and then release so the stem appears as shown in FIGURE M-9**
   The dotted line includes an Include marker that indicates that the line identifies the area of the picture to keep. An Include marker appears as a circle with a plus symbol.

QUICK TIP
If you want to start over, click the Reset Picture button in the Adjust group to return the picture to its original settings.

8. **When you are satisfied that the picture appears similar to FIGURE M-9, click the Keep Changes button in the Close group**
   The picture appears similar to **FIGURE M-10**. If you do not like the picture you have created, click the Remove Background button again and then use the Mark Areas to Keep, Mark Areas to Remove, and Undo buttons to further refine the picture. Note that the process of removing a background takes some time. You do not need to match **FIGURE M-10** exactly.

9. **Save the document**

Exploring Advanced Graphics

FIGURE M-8: Selecting an area of a photograph to remove

The pointer appears as an arrow when dragged

Drag the pointer across the lily pad; a dotted line shows the path drawn by the mouse pointer

Marquee handle; drag to include more of the picture immediately adjacent to the handle

Marquee shown as a framed area with marquee handles

FIGURE M-9: Selecting an area of a photograph to keep

Dotted line shows path to draw to keep stem

Remove marker is a minus sign that indicates areas marked for removal

Include marker is a plus sign that indicates areas marked for inclusion

The location of the Include and Remove markers will be different on your screen, depending on how you marked areas to keep and remove

FIGURE M-10: Portion of a picture isolated from the background

Even though the background has been removed, the canvas is still the size it would be if the background was still there

Compressing pictures

When you add a picture to a document, you increase the file size of your document—sometimes quite dramatically. You can use the Compress Pictures command to reduce the file size of the picture. When you apply this command, you can choose to reduce the image resolution and you can specify to delete all cropped areas of a picture. To compress a picture, select it, click the PICTURE TOOLS FORMAT tab, click the Compress Pictures button in the Adjust group, then specify the resolution you want to use. For example, you may choose 220 dpi (dots per inch) for pictures that you want to print and 96 dpi for a picture that you want to send in an e-mail. If you have more than one picture in a document, you can specify that you wish to apply the same compression options to every picture in the document.

Use Artistic Effects and Layering Options

Learning Outcomes
- Apply artistic effects
- Layer objects
- Work in the Selection pane

In the Adjust group on the PICTURE TOOLS FORMAT tab, you can choose to apply one of 23 artistic effects to a picture, correct the brightness and contrast, modify the color saturation, and sharpen or soften the appearance of a photograph. When you include two or more photographs or graphic objects in your document, you can use options in the Arrange group on the PICTURE TOOLS FORMAT tab to specify how the objects should appear in relation to each other. For example, you can choose to layer objects in order to show one object partially on top of another object. You can also use the **Selection pane** to layer objects. **CASE** *You apply an artistic effect to the untouched picture of the flower, and then use layering options to superimpose the picture of the flower with the background removed over the picture of the flower with the artistic effect applied.*

STEPS

1. Scroll to and click the untouched photograph of the flower, then click Artistic Effects in the Adjust group on the PICTURE TOOLS FORMAT tab

2. Click the Mosaic Bubbles effect as shown in FIGURE M-11

QUICK TIP
You can move the mouse pointer over each of the artistic effects to view how the photograph changes.

3. Click Corrections in the Adjust group, then click the Brightness: +20% Contrast: −20% option in the Brightness/Contrast area (second row, fourth column)

4. Reduce the zoom to 80%, click the Wrap Text button in the Arrange group, click Through, scroll up and click the picture of the flower with the background removed, click the Wrap Text button, then click Through

   You changed the wrapping of both pictures so you can superimpose one picture on top of the other picture.

5. Press the down arrow [↓] to move the selected picture down so that it exactly covers the flower with the Mosaic Bubbles artistic effect as shown in FIGURE M-12

   The picture of the flower with the background removed is superimposed over the picture formatted with the Mosaic Bubbles artistic effect.

QUICK TIP
You can rename objects in the Selection pane so they have meaningful names, such as "flower background removed".

6. Increase the zoom to 150%, click Selection Pane in the Arrange group, then click the eye icon 👁 to the right of Picture 2

   The photograph of the flower with the background is hidden from view. The Selection pane shows the objects on the current page and their stacking order. The picture listed at the top of the pane is the picture on top, which, in this example, is the photograph of the flower with the background removed.

7. Click Show All in the Selection pane, click Picture 1 in the Selection pane, click the PICTURE TOOLS FORMAT tab if necessary, click the Send Backward list arrow in the Arrange group, then click Send to Back

   Picture 1 moves below Picture 2 in the Selection pane and the flower picture with the background removed seems to disappear.

QUICK TIP
You can also use the re-order buttons at the top of the Selection pane or you can drag picture labels above and below other labels in the Selection pane to change the layering of pictures.

8. Click the Bring Forward list arrow, click Bring to Front, click Picture 2 in the Selection pane, click Color in the Adjust group, then click Saturation 200% in the Color Saturation area (top row)

   The colors in the flower picture with the background are now strongly saturated, which makes the flower picture with the background removed stand out even more.

9. Press and hold the [Ctrl] key, click Picture 1 in the Selection pane so both pictures are selected, click Group in the Arrange group, click Group, compare the picture to FIGURE M-13, close the Selection pane, then save the document

Exploring Advanced Graphics

FIGURE M-11: Applying the Mosaic Bubbles artistic effect

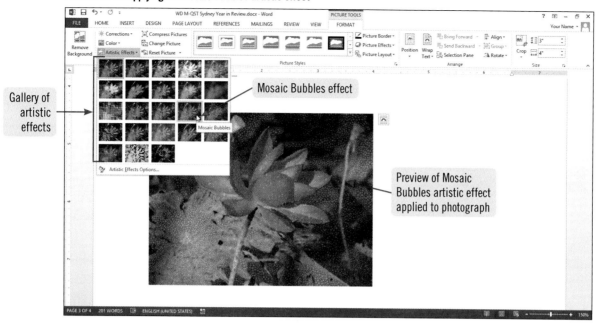

Gallery of artistic effects

Mosaic Bubbles effect

Preview of Mosaic Bubbles artistic effect applied to photograph

FIGURE M-12: Moving one picture on top of another picture

After applying text wrapping to both pictures, use the down arrow key to move the top picture down so it covers the bottom picture; the canvas of both pictures is the same size

The image of the flower without the background is superimposed on the picture with the background; the Through text wrapping allows both images to be seen

FIGURE M-13: Completed pictures grouped as one picture

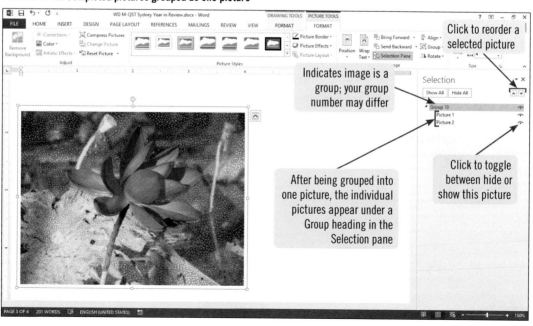

Click to reorder a selected picture

Indicates image is a group; your group number may differ

After being grouped into one picture, the individual pictures appear under a Group heading in the Selection pane

Click to toggle between hide or show this picture

Word 2013

Arrange Graphics

The Arrange group on the PICTURE TOOLS FORMAT tab includes commands you can use to align, group, and rotate objects. The Align Left command aligns several objects along their left sides. The Distribute Vertically or the Distribute Horizontally command displays three or more objects so the same amount of space appears between each object. The Group button combines two or more objects into one object. The Rotate button rotates or flips an object. **CASE** ▶ *You decide to include a series of small stars that are aligned and distributed horizontally below the flower picture. You also want to rotate the stars and group them into one object that you can position easily.*

STEPS

1. **Click the** INSERT **tab, click** Shapes **in the Illustrations group, then select the** 5-Point Star **shape in the Stars and Banners section (first row, fourth column)**

2. **Scroll up, if necessary, then draw a star similar to the star shown in** FIGURE M-14 **in a blank area to the right of the picture**

3. **Click the** More button ▼ **in the Shape Styles group, then click the** Moderate Effect – Gold, Accent 4 style **(second to last row, fifth column)**

   The star is filled with a gradient fill.

4. **Click the** launcher ⌐ **in the Size group, click the** Lock aspect ratio check box **to select it, set the Absolute Height at .4", press [Tab] to set the Width automatically, then click** OK

   By selecting the Lock aspect ratio check box, you make sure that the Width is calculated in proportion to the Height you enter (or vice versa).

5. **Press [Ctrl][C] to copy the star, press [Ctrl][V] to paste a copy of the star, repeat two times so you have four stars, then position the bottom star about halfway down the picture as shown in** FIGURE M-15

6. **Press and hold [Ctrl], click each** star **until all four stars are selected, click the** Align **button in the Arrange group, then click** Align Left

   The left edge of each star is on the same plane as the other stars.

7. **Verify all four stars are still selected, click the** Align button, **click** Distribute Vertically, **click the** Group button **in the Arrange group, then click** Group

   The Distribute Vertically command places the stars so that the distance between each star is equal. The Group command groups the stars into one shape.

8. **Click the** Rotate button **in the Arrange group, then click** Rotate Right 90°

   Before you can move the grouped object, you need to adjust the text wrapping.

9. **Click the** Layout Options button ⌷, **select the** Square Wrap **option, use your mouse to position the rotated stars below the flower picture as shown in** FIGURE M-16, **then save the document**

FIGURE M-14: Star shape drawn

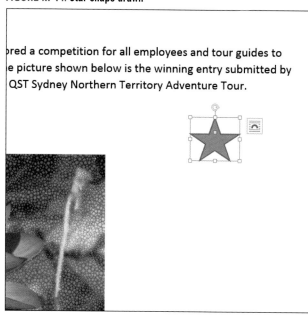

ored a competition for all employees and tour guides to
e picture shown below is the winning entry submitted by
QST Sydney Northern Territory Adventure Tour.

FIGURE M-15: Positioning a graphic object

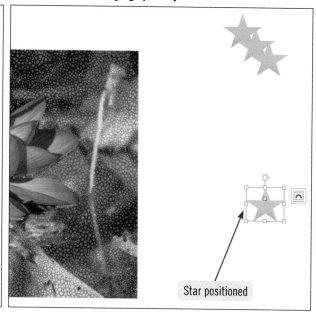

Star positioned

FIGURE M-16: Stars grouped, rotated, and positioned

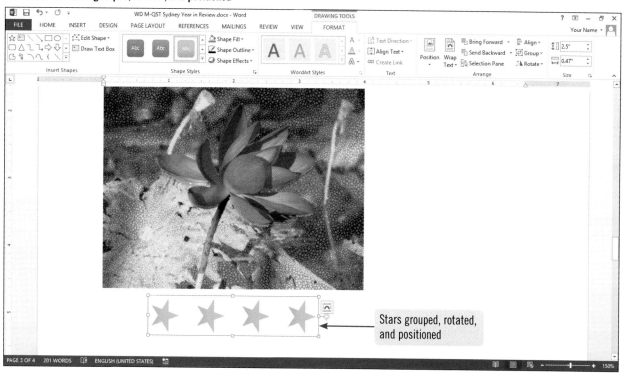

Stars grouped, rotated,
and positioned

Editing Clip Art

A clip art picture is made up of many drawn objects that are grouped together into one picture. When you edit a clip art picture, you are really editing the objects that make up the picture. You obtain a clip art picture by clicking the Online Pictures button in the Illustrations group on the INSERT tab, then searching for clipart on Office.com. If you want to be able to edit the picture, then you need to find and insert drawing pictures, not photographs. You know you can edit the clip art picture when you right-click it in Word and the Edit Picture option is available. When the Edit Picture option is greyed out, you cannot edit the individual objects in the clipart picture. After you click Edit Picture, you can click on and edit the individual drawing objects that make up the picture. For example, you can change the fill color of an object, delete it from the picture, rotate or resize it, move it, and enhance it the way you enhance any drawn object that you work with in Word.

Create SmartArt Graphics

Learning Outcomes
• Create a Picture SmartArt graphic
• Create a Hierarchy SmartArt graphic

You create a **SmartArt graphic** when you want to provide a visual representation of information. A SmartArt graphic combines shapes with text. SmartArt categories include List, Process, Cycle, Hierarchy, Relationship, Matrix, Pyramid, and Picture. You can also obtain special SmartArt graphics from Office.com. Once you have selected a SmartArt category, you select a layout and then type text in the SmartArt shapes or text pane. You can further modify a SmartArt graphic by changing fill colors, shape styles, and layouts. **CASE** *You create two SmartArt graphics: a picture graphic and an organizational chart.*

STEPS

1. **Scroll up to page 2, double-click the picture of the red rocks, then reduce the zoom to 120%**

   You can create a SmartArt picture graphic from any picture inserted in a document, and then you can add additional pictures to the graphic.

2. **Click Picture Layout in the Picture Styles group on the PICTURE TOOLS FORMAT tab, move your mouse pointer over each picture layout, then click the Bending Picture Caption List layout (second row, fifth column)**

   Two SMARTART TOOLS tabs appear on the Ribbon with the DESIGN tab active.

3. **Click Add Shape in the Create Graphic group, click Add Shape again, click the picture content control 🖼 for the blank shape in the top row, click Browse next to the top selection, navigate to the location where you store your Data Files, double-click WD M-2.jpg, click 🖼 in the last shape, click Browse, then double-click WD M-3.jpg**

QUICK TIP
You can also click Text Pane in the Create Graphic group on the SMARTART TOOLS DESIGN tab to open and close the text pane.

4. **Click the Expand button ⟨ at the left side of the pictures to show the text pane if the text pane is not open, click [Text] next to the top bullet in the text pane, type Red Centre Tour, press the [↓], enter Fraser Island Tour and Top End Tour in the text pane for the other two pictures as shown in FIGURE M-17, then close the text pane**

Trouble
If you do not see the Size button, then the Shape Height and Shape Width text boxes are already visible.

5. **Click the SmartArt object border to select the whole SmartArt object, click the SMARTART TOOLS FORMAT tab, click the Wrap Text button in the Arrange group, click Square, click the Size button, change the Height of the graphic to 4" and the Width to 6", click the SMARTART TOOLS DESIGN tab, click the More button ⏷ in the Layouts group, click the Titled Picture Blocks layout, then move the graphic below the parrot picture**

6. **Click away from the graphic to deselect it, press [Ctrl][End], select the [Organization Chart] placeholder, click the INSERT tab, click the SmartArt button in the Illustrations group, click Hierarchy in the left pane, select the Name and Title Organization Chart style, click OK, click in the top box, type Sheila Barton, click in the white box, then type Manager**

7. **Click the box below and to the left, press [Delete], click the far left box in the bottom row, click the Add Shape list arrow in the Create Graphic group, click Add Shape Below, then click the Add Shape button again to add another shape to the right of the shape you just inserted**

   The Add Shape menu provides options (such as below, after, and above) for adding more shapes to your SmartArt graphic. The new shapes are added based on the currently selected box and the menu selection.

8. **Click the Change Colors button in the SmartArt Styles group, select Colorful – Accent Colors (first selection in the Colorful section), click the More button ⏷ in the SmartArt Styles group, then click Inset (second selection in the 3-D section)**

9. **Enter text so the organization chart appears as shown in FIGURE M-18, then save the document**

FIGURE M-17: Text entered in the text pane for the Picture SmartArt graphic

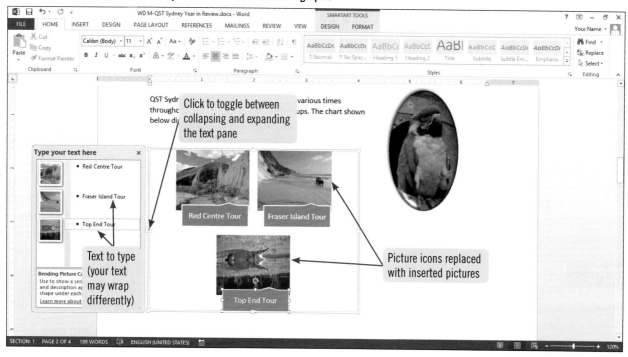

FIGURE M-18: Names and positions for the organization chart

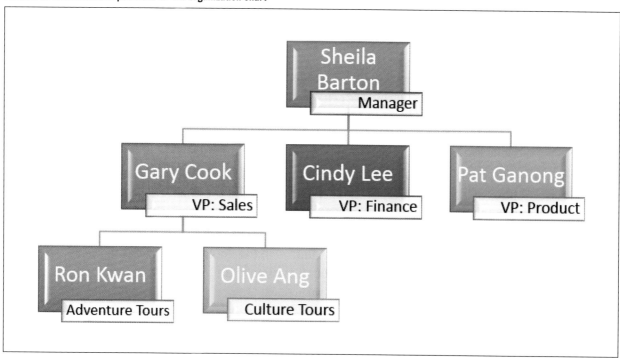

Add a Watermark and Page Border

Learning Outcomes
- Add and edit a watermark
- Add a page border

You can customize the appearance of a document by including a watermark and a page border. A **watermark** is a picture or other type of graphic object that appears lightly shaded behind text in a document. For example, you could include a company logo as a watermark on every page of a company report, or you could create "Confidential" as a WordArt object that appears in a very light gray behind the text of an important letter or memo. A **page border** encloses one or more pages of a document. You can create a box border using a variety of line styles and colors, or you can insert one of Word's preset page borders. **CASE** ▶ *You add a watermark consisting of the text "DRAFT" that will appear lightly shaded behind the document text, you change the size and position of the watermark, and then you add a page border.*

STEPS

1. **Press [Ctrl][Home] to go to the top of the document, then click the DESIGN tab**

2. **Click the Watermark button in the Page Background group, then scroll to and click DRAFT 2 as shown in FIGURE M-19**
   The word "DRAFT" appears lightly shaded behind the text of each page in the document.

3. **Switch to 70% view, then double-click above the document title to open the header area**
   The watermark is actually inserted into a header. If you want to make additional changes to the watermark, you can access it by opening the document header.

4. **Click any part of DRAFT, click the WORDART TOOLS FORMAT tab, select the contents of the Height text box in the Size group, type 1.7, then press [Enter]**
   The watermark is resized.

5. **Use the mouse to move the watermark toward the bottom of the page as shown in FIGURE M-20**

6. **Scroll up and double-click in the Header area, click the HEADER & FOOTER TOOLS DESIGN tab, click the Different First Page check box, then click the Close Header and Footer button in the Close group**
   The watermark does not appear on the first page of the document. It appears only on the second and subsequent pages of the document.

7. **Click the DESIGN tab, click the Page Borders button in the Page Background group, click the Box icon in the Setting area, scroll to and click the Thick-Thin border in the Style list box (ninth selection from the top), click the Color list arrow, click the Blue, Accent 5 color box, then click OK**

8. **Click the VIEW tab, click the Zoom button in the Zoom group, click the Many Pages option button, click the Many Pages list arrow, drag to show 1 x 4 pages, then click OK**
   The completed document appears as shown in FIGURE M-21

9. **Return to 100% view, enter your name where indicated in the footer starting on page 2, save the document, submit the file to your instructor, then close the document**

FIGURE M-19: Watermark gallery

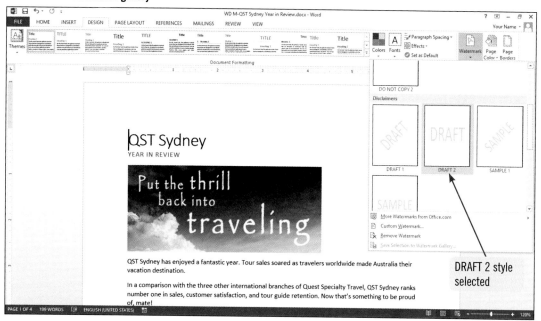

DRAFT 2 style selected

FIGURE M-20: Sized and positioned watermark

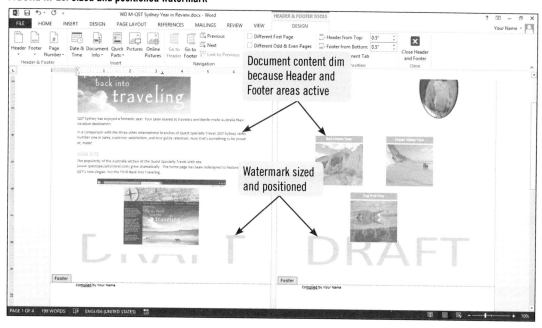

Document content dim because Header and Footer areas active

Watermark sized and positioned

FIGURE M-21: Completed document

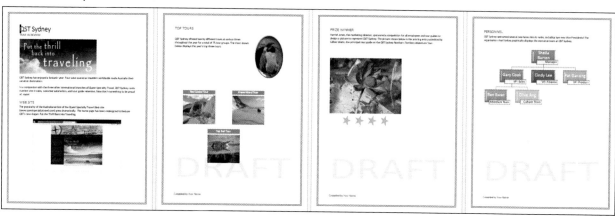

Practice

Concepts Review

Label the numbered items shown in FIGURE M-22.

FIGURE M-22

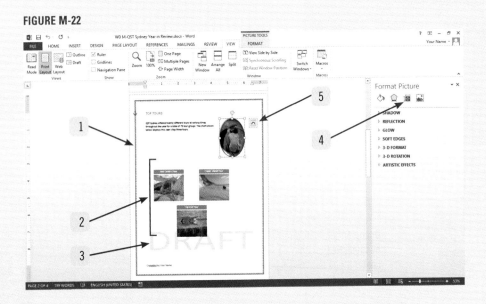

Match each term with the statement that best describes it.

6. **Screen clipping**
7. **Cropping**
8. **Wrapping**
9. **Distribute Vertically**
10. **Grouping**
11. **Hierarchy**
12. **Artistic Effects**

a. Procedure used to remove portions of a picture
b. Type of SmartArt graphic
c. Evenly spaces three or more objects
d. Describes how a picture is positioned with relation to text in a document
e. Combines two or more objects into one object
f. Portion of a window selected and inserted into a document
g. Preset options used to modify a picture

Select the best answer from the list of choices.

13. **Group in which the Remove Background option is included on the PICTURE TOOLS FORMAT tab.**
    a. Arrange
    b. Adjust
    c. Format
    d. Effects

14. **You can work in the _____ pane to layer objects.**
    a. 3-D Format
    b. Styles
    c. Format Picture
    d. Selection

15. **How do you edit a watermark?**
    a. Double-click the watermark in the document
    b. Double-click in the footer area, then click the watermark.
    c. Double-click in the header area, then click the watermark
    d. Click the DESIGN tab, then click Watermark in the Page Background group.

Exploring Advanced Graphics

Skills Review

1. Create and modify screenshots.

a. Start Word, open the file WD M-4.docx from the drive and folder where you store your Data Files, then save it as **WD M-Pacific Trading Report**.

b. Open WD M-5.docx from the drive and folder where you store your Data Files, then scroll down slightly so the graphic fills the window. (*Hint*: If necessary, change the zoom to 140% so the graphic fills the window.)

c. Return to the Pacific Trading Report in Word, then scroll down and click to the left of the [Home Page Design] placeholder below the Web Design heading on page 1.

d. Insert a screenshot of the Word document you just opened.

e. Change the width of the screenshot to **4.5**", then delete the [Home Page Design] placeholder.

f. Switch to the WD M-5 document, scroll to view the graphic containing the company slogan ("Your Home on the Web for the Very Best of the Islands"), return to the WD M-Pacific Trading Report, then replace the [Company Slogan] placeholder with a screen clipping of the company slogan.

g. Change the width of the screen clipping to **4.5**", save the document, then close WD M-5.docx without saving it.

2. Edit Pictures

a. Click the picture of the flower at the top of page 1, then crop it so that it appears as shown in **FIGURE M-23**.

b. Crop the picture to the Diamond shape.

FIGURE M-23

c. From the Format Picture pane, modify the 3-D format to use the Angle Top bevel with a top width of **10 pt** and Metal Material.

d. Open the ALT TEXT pane, then enter **Flower** in the Title text box and **A pink hibiscus from Fiji.** as the description.

e. Add an Offset Diagonal Bottom Left shadow to the picture, then save the document.

3. Position Pictures

a. Change the text wrapping of the flower picture to Square, then use your mouse to position the picture top aligned with the current paragraph and on the right side of the paragraph, using the alignment guides as needed. (*Hint*: If you do not see the alignment guides, click Align in the Arrange group on the PICTURE TOOLS FORMAT tab to open the Alignment menu, then click Use Alignment Guides. A check mark must be next to Use Alignment Guides for this feature to be active.)

b. Open the LAYOUT OPTIONS gallery, fix the position on the page, then open the Layout dialog box with the Position tab active.

c. Specify the Absolute horizontal position as 5.5" to the right of Margin and the Absolute vertical position at 2.5" below Page.

d. Save the document.

FIGURE M-24

4. Remove the background from a picture.

a. Scroll to the first picture of the sailboat on page 2 (below the New Graphic for Brochure paragraph).

b. Remove the background and make adjustments until only the sailboat appears as shown in **FIGURE M-24**.

c. Keep the changes, then save the document.

5. Use artistic effects and layering options.

a. Scroll down until both of the sailboat pictures are in the document window, adjust the zoom as needed to see both pictures, then apply the Watercolor Sponge artistic effect to the picture that includes two sailboats.

b. Apply the Brightness: 0% (Normal) Contrast: +20% correction.

c. Change the wrapping option to Through for both pictures, then move the picture of the single sailboat over the picture of the two sailboats.

    d. Use the Selection pane to select the photograph of the two sailboats, then use the Bring Forward command to view the picture of the two sailboats.

    e. Apply the 400% Saturation color effect to the picture of the two sailboats, then place the single sailboat in front.

    f. Group the two pictures into one picture, then close the Selection pane.

    g. Use the mouse and [Enter] to adjust spacing so that the sailboat picture appears below the New Graphic for Brochure heading and the New Supplier Countries heading appears below the sailboat picture, then save the document.

6. Arrange graphics.

    a. Draw a sun shape in a blank area to the right of the sailboat picture, then apply the Subtle Effect – Purple, Accent 1 shape style.

    b. Open the Size tab in the Layout dialog box, click the Lock aspect ratio check box to select it, then set the absolute height of the shape at **.5"**.

    c. Copy the sun shape twice so that there is a total of three sun shapes.

    d. Use the Align and Distribute functions to show all three suns evenly spaced above the sailboat picture. (*Note*: If necessary, add some space above the picture. Move one sun above and aligned to the right side of the picture, one sun to above and aligned to the left side, and the remaining sun between the other two suns, select all three suns, apply the align top option, then apply the distribute horizontally option.)

    e. Group the three suns into one object.

    f. Click the sailboat picture, view the rotate options, then click Flip Horizontal.

    g. Save the document.

7. Create SmartArt graphics.

    a. Click the photograph below the New Supplier Countries paragraph, then apply the Alternating Picture Circles picture layout.

    b. Add two new shapes using Add Shape After, then insert WD M-6.jpg in the second shape and WD M-7.jpg in the third shape from the location where you store your Data Files.

    c. In the text pane, enter three captions as follows: **Japan**, **Thailand**, **Australia**, then close the text pane.

    d. Change the height of the graphic to 3" and the width to 5".

    e. From the SMARTART TOOLS DESIGN tab, apply the Bending Picture Caption layout style.

    f. Turn on paragraph marks so you can see the Page Break, then move it up so it appears directly below the SmartArt graphic.

    g. Find the [Organization Chart] placeholder on the last page of the document, insert an organization chart using the Hierarchy layout in the Hierarchy category, type **Sue Lee** in the top box, press [Shift][Enter], then type **President**.

    h. Click the box below and to the left, add a shape after, then add a shape below the new box.

    i. Apply the Polished SmartArt style in the 3-D section, then change the colors of the organization chart to Colorful Range – Accent Colors 5 to 6.

    j. Enter text so the organization chart appears as shown in **FIGURE M-25**, making sure to press [Shift][Enter] after typing each name, then save the document.

FIGURE M-25

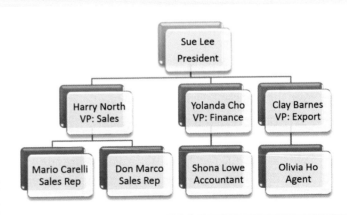

8. Add a watermark and page border.

    a. Go to the top of the document, then insert a watermark using the Confidential 1 watermark style.

    b. Access the header area, then edit the watermark by changing its height to **1.2**.

    c. Specify that the watermark appears only on the second and subsequent pages of the document.

Skills Review (continued)

d. Add a page border to the document using the Thin-Thick border style and the Purple, Accent 1 color.

e. View the document using the 1 X 3 Many Pages zoom setting, then compare the completed document to **FIGURE M-26**.

f. Enter your name where indicated at the top of the document, submit the file to your instructor, then close the document.

FIGURE M-26

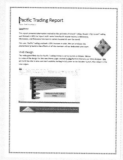  

Independent Challenge 1

You have just been hired to design a menu for Dolphin Bay Bistro, a new restaurant on a small island north of Seattle. You edit and position a picture that includes the name of the bistro, use the Remove Background and Artistic Effects features to modify a photograph, and add a watermark and page border.

a. Start Word, open the file WD M-8.docx from the drive and folder where you store your Data Files, then save it as **WD M-Dolphin Bay Bistro Lunch Menu**.

b. Refer to **FIGURE M-27** to transform the picture at the top of the document. You need to crop the picture, then crop the smaller image to a shape using the Flowchart: Document option.

FIGURE M-27

Dolphin Bay Lunch Menu

Your Name, Designer

c. With the image still selected, change the Text wrapping to Behind Text (the title will appear inside the picture), set the Absolute vertical position .2" below the paragraph, then enhance the picture by adding the Full Reflection, touching reflection option.

d. Add the following ALT TEXT: **Header Graphic** for the title and **Cropped photograph of Dolphin Bay.** for the description.

e. Scroll to the bottom of the document, select the picture of the kayak on page 1, then remove the background so only the orange kayak remains.

f. Scroll to the second page, apply the Cutout artistic effect to the second photograph of the kayak, then change the color to Turquoise, Accent color 1 Light in the Recolor area of the Color feature in the Adjust group, and use the Corrections feature to select the Brightness: +40% Contrast: -20% Correction.

g. Use the Picture Effects feature to apply the Bevel, Cool Slant effect. **FIGURE M-28**.

h. Change the wrapping to Through, then scroll up and change the wrapping of the kayak picture with the background removed to Through.

i. Use the mouse pointer and the arrow keys to position the orange kayak over the aqua picture.

j. Use the Selection pane and the Bring Forward and Send Backward features to help you position the two pictures in relation to each other so the completed picture appears as shown in **FIGURE M-28**.

k. Group the two pictures into one picture, then if necessary, reposition the picture as shown in **FIGURE M-28**.

l. Add a page border that is 3 pt wide and Turquoise, Accent 1.

m. Type your name where indicated at the top of the document, save and close the document, submit the file to your instructor, then close the document.

Exploring Advanced Graphics

Independent Challenge 2

You have just started working for Greenways Tours, a company based in Rhode Island that takes visitors on guided tours of local gardens and provides gardening advice. One of your jobs is to prepare the company's annual report. Before you format the entire report, you gather some of the information required. First, you insert and modify a screenshot of the graphic created by a coworker that will be featured on the report's title page, and then you create an organization chart to show the company personnel. The report also includes some drawn objects and a watermark.

a. Start Word, open the file WD M-9.docx from the drive and folder where you store your Data Files, then save it as **WD M-Greenways Tours Report** to the drive and folder where you store your Data Files.

b. Open WD M-10.docx, scroll so the picture fills the window, then view the WD M-Greenways Tours Report document again.

c. Click to the left of the [Screenshot] placeholder, use the Screenshot command to take a picture of WD M-10.docx, then delete the [Screenshot] placeholder.

d. In the WD M-Greenways Tours Report document, add a 3 pt Pink, Accent 5 border to the screenshot, change the picture's width to **6"**, then center it.

e. Click to the left of the heading "Graphic for Report Title Page", then take a screen clipping of the orange rose in the Home Page Graphic image in WD M-10.docx. (*Hint*: Close other open windows if WD M-10.docx is not the active window when you select Screen Clipping.)

f. Change the text wrapping to Square, change the height to 1.2", then use the alignment guides to position the rose so it is even with the top and right margins. (*Hint*: If you do not see the alignment guides, click Align in the Arrange group on the PICTURE TOOLS FORMAT tab to open the Alignment menu, then click Use Alignment Guides. A check mark must be next to Use Alignment Guides for this feature to be active.)

g. Insert a page break to move the Organization Chart heading to the next page, then use the information contained in the table to create a SmartArt graphic organization chart that uses the Horizontal Hierarchy style in the Hierarchy category. Remember to press [Shift][Enter] after you type a name so that you can enter the position.

h. Apply the Cartoon SmartArt style from the SMARTART TOOLS DESIGN tab and the color scheme of your choice.

i. When you have entered the names and positions for the organization chart, delete the table and the [Organization Chart] placeholder.

j. Below the organization chart, change the text wrapping of all four flowers to Square.

k. Use [Shift] to select all four of the flower pictures, align the flowers along their bottom edges, then distribute them horizontally across the page so the white flower is at the left margin and the orange rose is at the right margin.

l. Group the flowers into one object.

m. Insert a watermark using the SAMPLE 1 style, access the header, select the watermark, then change the fill color to Lavender, Accent 6, Lighter 40%.

n. Change the height of the watermark to 2", then move it down so the sizing handle of the bounding box just touches the dotted line that separates the footer area from the document.

o. Type your name in the document footer, save the document, close the WD M-10.docx document without saving it, submit the WD M-Greenways Tour Report to your instructor, then close the document.

Independent Challenge 3

You can use the many options available in the PICTURE TOOLS FORMAT tab to modify the appearance of your photographs. You can then use the modified photographs to enhance invitations, posters, and photo albums. You decide to explore the options on the PICTURE TOOLS FORMAT tab and then to use at least four different options to modify two photographs. As you format the photographs, you keep track of the options you have selected.

a. Open the file WD M-11.docx from the drive and folder where you store your Data Files, then save it as **WD M-Picture Effects**. This document contains two photographs and space for you to specify the options you use to modify the photographs.

b. Add Alt Text to each of the pictures. You choose appropriate text.

Independent Challenge 3 (continued)

c. Use the Rotate function to show the second of the two pictures vertically.

d. Modify each of the two pictures with picture effects and other picture-related settings. For example, you can choose to crop the picture; crop the picture to a shape; apply a picture style; modify picture effects such as glows, bevels, and reflections; apply a picture correction; change the picture color; or apply an artistic effect. As you work, note the modifications you make in the table provided under each photograph. For example, if you add a Cool Slant Bevel picture effect, enter **Picture Effects: Bevel** in the Feature column, then enter **Cool Slant** in the Setting column.

e. Add an art page border of your choice. (*Hint*: On the Page Border tab of the Borders and Shading dialog box, click the Art list arrow, then select one of the preset art border styles.) If you wish, apply a new color for the art border. (*Note*: You can't change the color of all the art border styles.)

f. Type your name where indicated in the footer, save the document, submit the file to your instructor, then close the document.

Independent Challenge 4: Explore

You work as a teacher's aide at an elementary school. Your supervisor has asked you to create a worksheet that children can color, according to the labels. You've downloaded a clip art picture to use in the worksheet. This clip art picture is composed of several drawn shapes that you can edit individually using the Edit Picture command. You explore how to edit the various components that make up a clip art picture by modifying some of the shapes in the picture, drawing and rotating an AutoShape, and then adding some text objects.

a. Start Word, open the file WD M-12.docx from the drive and folder where you store your Data Files, then save it as **WD M-Learning Colors Picture**.

b. Increase the size of the picture to 4" wide.

c. Right-click the picture of the balloons, then select Edit Picture. The picture of the balloons jumps to the top left corner of the screen.

d. Click anywhere in the picture to show the drawing canvas (a solid line appears around the picture), click the Layout Options button, then change the Wrapping to Square.

e. Fix the position on the page so that the absolute horizontal position is 1" to the right of the page and the absolute vertical position is 2" below the top of the page.

f. Click on and delete the colored shape from each balloon. (*Hint*: If you remove a shape that you want to keep, just click the Undo button on the Quick Access toolbar).

g. Refer to **FIGURE M-29** to complete the picture, according to the following instructions.

- Double-click a blank area of the page to the right of the balloons, then draw and format the three sun shapes: First draw one sun shape, and set the height at 1.3" with the lock aspect ratio option selected. (*Hint*: Select the Lock aspect ratio button in the Size dialog box before you enter 1.3 in the Height text box.)

- Remove the fill color and change the line color to black, copy and paste the two other sun AutoShapes, use the align left and vertical distribute option to align the suns along their left edges and set an equal space between each of the suns.

- As shown in **FIGURE M-29**, add text boxes (click Text Box on the INSERT tab). Type text in the text boxes and format it in Calibri, Bold, and 18 pt., copying and pasting where needed to reduce drawing time. (*Note*: Remove the border around each text box and move text boxes as needed to ensure they do not block other parts of the picture.)

- Draw black, 3 pt lines to connect each text box with its object or objects.

FIGURE M-29

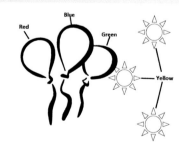

h. Type **Prepared by** followed by your name in the document footer.

i. Save the document, submit the file to your instructor, then close the document.

Visual Workshop

You are working with the Web Development Group at Snugglepets.com to plan and launch a new Web site that sells exotic stuffed animals. Open WD M-13.docx, then save it as **WD M-Web Launch Graphic**. Open WD M-14.docx, note the picture of the elephant and lion, then return to the WD M-Web Launch Graphic document. Modify the document so that it matches **FIGURE M-30**. Some useful hints follow: The graphic of the elephant and lion is a screen clipping from WD M-14.docx resized to 2" wide with the wrapping set to Square, the koala picture is created by removing the background from one picture and overlaying it on the other picture that is enhanced with the Pencil Sketch Artistic Effect. Remember to change the Wrapping to Through to position the two pictures, use the Selection pane to group the two pictures into one picture, change the Wrapping to Square, then position it as shown. Finally, create the SmartArt by selecting the Basic Target SmartArt graphic from the Relationship category. Be sure to use the text pane to enter the text and add shapes before you apply a color or style to the graphic. Select the Colorful Range Accent Colors 5 and 6 color scheme and the Intense Effect SmartArt. Enclose the SmartArt graphic in a 6 pt Dark Green, Accent 3, Darker 25% border. Change the wrapping to Square. Add your name in the footer, save the document, submit the file to your instructor, then close the document.

FIGURE M-30

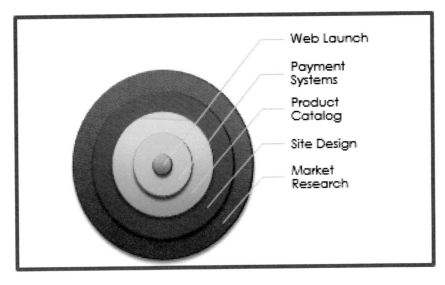

Building Forms

CASE ▶ Ron Dawson in the Marketing Department asks you to create a form to survey the managers of the various Quest Specialty Travel (QST) branches worldwide. You start by creating the form template, then you add content controls, format and protect the form, and fill it in as a user.

Unit Objectives

After completing this unit, you will be able to:

- Construct a form template
- Add Text content controls
- Add Date Picker and Picture content controls
- Add Repeating Section and Check Box content controls

- Add Drop-Down content controls
- Insert Legacy Tools controls
- Format and protect a form
- Fill in a form as a user

Files You Will Need

WD N-1.jpg   WD N-5.jpg
WD N-2.jpg   WD N-6.docx
WD N-3.jpg   WD N-7.jpg
WD N-4.docx

Construct a Form Template

Learning
Outcomes
• Create a table
  form
• Save a form as a
  template

A **form** is a structured document with spaces reserved for entering information. You create a form as a template that includes labeled spaces, called **form controls**, which are **fields** into which users type information. A Word form is created as a **form template**, which contains all the components of the form. The structure of a form template usually consists of a table that contains labels and form controls. A **label** is a word or phrase such as "Date" or "Location" that tells people who fill in the form the kind of information required for a given field. A **form control** is the placeholder that you, as the form developer, insert into the form. You insert a form control, often referred to simply as a control, to contain the data associated with the label. FIGURE N-1 shows a completed form template containing several different types of controls. Once you have created a form, you can protect it so that users can enter information into the form but they cannot change the structure of the form itself. **CASE** *You need to create the basic structure of the form in Word, and then you save the document as a template.*

STEPS

1. **Start Word, create a new blank document, click the** DESIGN **tab, click** Themes, **then click** Slice

   The Slice theme is applied to the document.

2. **Type** Marketing Survey, **press** [Enter] **two times, select the text, click the** HOME **tab, then apply the Title style**

3. **Change the zoom to** 150%, **click below the title, click the** INSERT **tab, click** Table, **click** Insert Table, **enter** 4 **for the number of columns and** 9 **for the number of rows, then click** OK

4. **Type** Name, **press** [Tab] **twice, then type** Position

5. **Select the first three rows of the table, then reduce the width of columns 1 and 3 as shown in** FIGURE N-2

6. **Enter the remaining labels and merge cells to create the form shown in** FIGURE N-3

   Once you have created the structure for your form, you can save it as a template.

7. **Click the** FILE **tab, click** Save As, **click** Computer, **click** Browse, **then type** WD N-Marketing Survey **in the File name box**

   You need to specify that the file is saved as a template so you can use it as the basis for a form that users will fill out.

8. **Click the** Save as type list arrow, **then select** Word Template (*.dotx) **from the list of file types**

   By default, the location to save the template switches to the Custom Office Templates folder in the My Documents folder on your computer's hard drive.

9. **Click** Save

   Word saves the template to the Custom Office Templates folder.

Building Forms

FIGURE N-1: Form construction

Rich Text content control

Legacy Tools Text Form Field into which users can enter only a three-digit number

Combo Box content control; a list arrow appears when users move to the field

Check Box content controls; a check mark appears when a user clicks the box

Plain Text content control formatted with the Strong style

Date Picker content control; a list arrow appears when users move to the field

Drop-Down List content control; a list arrow appears when users move to the field

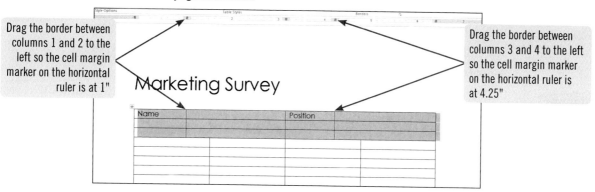

Legacy Tools Text Form Field formatted for upper case and includes a Help message that appears on the status bar when a user moves to the field

Picture content controls; a user can insert a picture file; the Picture content control is also in a Repeating Section content control so users can choose to insert more than one picture

FIGURE N-2: Modifying column widths

Drag the border between columns 1 and 2 to the left so the cell margin marker on the horizontal ruler is at 1"

Drag the border between columns 3 and 4 to the left so the cell margin marker on the horizontal ruler is at 4.25"

FIGURE N-3: Table form with labels and merged cells

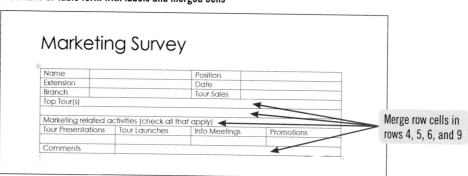

Merge row cells in rows 4, 5, 6, and 9

Word 2013

Add Text Content Controls

Learning Outcomes
- Add a Rich Text content control
- Add a Plain Text content control

Once you have created a structure for your form, you need to designate the locations where you want users to enter information. You insert text content controls in the table cells where users enter text information, such as their names or positions. Two types of text content controls are available. You use the **Rich Text content control** when you want formatting, such as bold or a different font size, automatically applied to text as users enter it in the content control. You can also apply a style, such as the Title style, to a Rich Text content control. You generally use the **Plain Text content control** when you do not need formatting applied to the text that users enter. However, if you want text entered in a Plain Text content control to be formatted, you can specify that a style be automatically applied to text as users enter it. You use the DEVELOPER tab to access all the commands you use to create and work with forms in Word. **CASE** ▶ *You display the DEVELOPER tab on the Ribbon, then you insert text content controls in the table cells where you need users to enter text.*

STEPS

1. **Click the FILE tab, click Options, click Customize Ribbon, click the Developer check box in the list of main tabs on the right side of the Word Options dialog box to select it, click OK, then click the DEVELOPER tab**

   The DEVELOPER tab becomes available on the Ribbon. The Controls group on the DEVELOPER tab contains the buttons you use to create and modify the various elements of a form. **TABLE N-1** describes each content control button in the Controls group.

2. **Click in the blank table cell to the right of Name, then click the Rich Text Content Control button ⎡Aa⎤ in the Controls group**

   A Rich Text content control is inserted. When completing the form, the user will be able to enter text into this content control.

3. **Click Properties in the Controls group**

   The Content Control Properties dialog box opens.

4. **Type Full Name as the title of the content control, click OK, then click the Design Mode button in the Controls group**

   Word automatically assigns "Full Name" to the title of the content control and to the content control tags.

5. **Select the text Click here to enter text. between the two tags, then type Enter your full name here.**

6. **Click the Full Name selection handle to select the entire content control, click the HOME tab, change the font size to 14 point, click the Bold button ⎡B⎤, click the Font Color list arrow ⎡A ▾⎤, select Red, Accent 6, Darker 25%, click the DEVELOPER tab, click anywhere in the content control, then compare the content control to FIGURE N-4**

7. **Press [Tab] two times to move to the blank cell to the right of Position, then click the Plain Text Content Control button ⎡Aa⎤ in the Controls group**

8. **Click Properties in the Controls group, type Job, click the Use a style to format text typed into the empty control check box, click the Style list arrow, select Strong as shown in FIGURE N-5, then click OK**

   If you want text entered in a Plain Text content control to appear formatted when the user fills in the form, you must apply a paragraph style. If you apply formats, such as bold and font size, to the Plain Text content control, the formatting will be lost when the form is opened and filled in by a user. You can format both Rich Text and Plain Text content controls with a paragraph style. The Strong paragraph style that you applied to the Plain Text content control will show when you fill in the form as a user.

9. **Select Click here to enter text. between the two Job tags, type Enter your job title here., then click the Save button ⎙ on the Quick Access toolbar to save the template**

Building Forms

FIGURE N-4: Rich Text content control

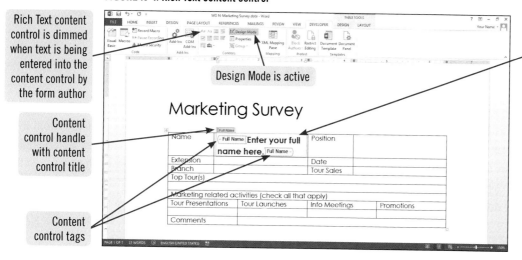

Rich Text content control is dimmed when text is being entered into the content control by the form author

Content control handle with content control title

Content control tags

Design Mode is active

Text provides direction to form user regarding what to type in this cell of the form

FIGURE N-5: Content Control Properties dialog box

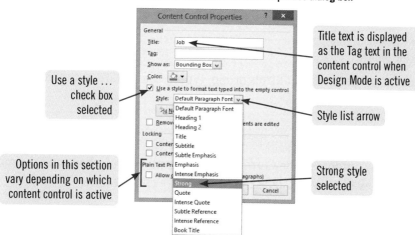

Use a style ... check box selected

Options in this section vary depending on which content control is active

Title text is displayed as the Tag text in the content control when Design Mode is active

Style list arrow

Strong style selected

TABLE N-1: Buttons in the Controls group

button	use to
Aa	Insert a Rich Text content control when you want to apply formatting, such as bold, to text users type
Aa	Insert a Plain Text content control to apply a style to text users type or to display text as plain, unformatted text
(picture)	Insert a Picture content control when you want users to be able to insert a picture file
(building block)	Insert a Building Block Gallery content control when you want to insert a custom building block, such as a cover page or a SmartArt graphic
✓	Insert a Check Box content control when you want to insert a check box that users can click to indicate a selection
(combo box)	Insert a Combo Box content control when you want users to select from a list or be able to add a new item
(drop-down)	Insert a Drop-Down List content control to provide users with a list of restricted choices
(date picker)	Insert a Date Picker content control when you want to include a calendar control that users can use to select a specific date
(repeating)	Insert a Repeating Section content control to enter any content that you want to repeat, including other content controls
(legacy tools)	Insert controls from the Legacy Tools options when you want additional control over the content that can be entered into a control; if you have programming experience, you can insert ActiveX Controls into forms using the Legacy Tools button

Building Forms

Add Date Picker and Picture Content Controls

Learning
Outcomes
• Add a Date Picker
  content control
• Add a Picture
  content control

The **Date Picker content control** provides users with a calendar from which they can select a date. The **Picture content control** inserts a placeholder that users can click to insert a picture from a file stored on their computer or SkyDrive or a file they search for on Office.com or another search engine. You can modify the appearance of the Picture content control by applying one of the preset Picture styles. **CASE** *You want the form to include a Date Picker content control that users click to enter the current date. You also want to include a Picture content control in the Top Tour table cell. When users fill in the form, they click the Picture content control and select a picture file stored on their computer or SkyDrive.*

STEPS

1. **Click the blank table cell to the right of Date, then click the** Date Picker Content Control **button** 🗓 **in the Controls group**

   You can modify the properties of the Date Picker content control so the date users enter appears in a specific format.

2. **Click** Properties **in the Controls group, type** Current Date **as the title, then click the date format shown in** FIGURE N-6

3. **Click** OK

   You will see the calendar in a later lesson when you complete the form as a user.

4. **Select the contents of the Current Date content control, then type the message** Click the down arrow to show a calendar and select the current date.

   Users see this message when they fill in the form.

5. **Click the cell below the Top Tour(s) label**

6. **Click the** Picture Content Control button 🖼 **in the Controls group**

   A Picture content control is inserted in the table cell. When users fill in the form, they click the picture icon to insert a picture file from their computer's hard drive, their SkyDrive, or from a Web site.

7. **Click** Properties, **type** Enter up to three pictures **as the title, then click** OK

   In the next lesson, you add a Repeating Section content control that will permit users to add additional pictures to the form. The title text advises users that they will be able to insert more than one picture.

8. **Click the** Design Mode button **in the Control group to toggle out of Design mode, compare the table form to** FIGURE N-7, **then save the template**

   You need to toggle out of Design mode so that you can work with the Repeating Section content control in the next lesson.

FIGURE N-6: Selecting a date format

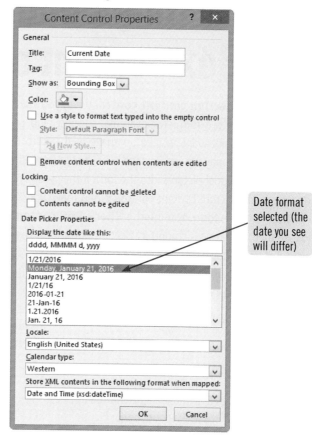

Date format selected (the date you see will differ)

FIGURE N-7: Picture content control

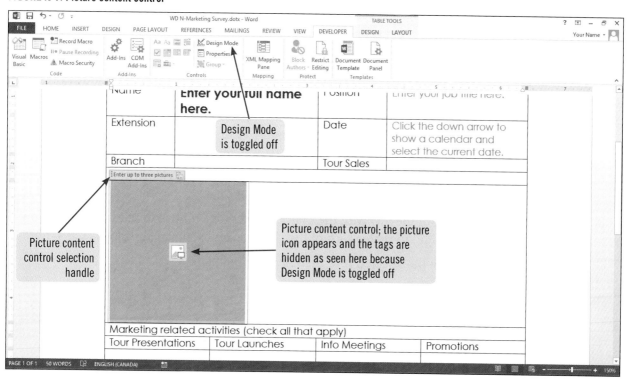

Picture content control selection handle

Picture content control; the picture icon appears and the tags are hidden as seen here because Design Mode is toggled off

Learning
Outcomes
• Use the Repeating
  Section content
  control
• Add Check Box
  content controls

Add Repeating Section and Check Box content controls

You insert a **Repeating Section content control** when you want to give users the option to add to the information they enter into a form. For example, suppose you create a form that includes one Picture content control. You do not want to take up space in the form template with multiple Picture content controls that users may or may not use. Instead, you use the Repeating Section content control to give users the option to insert additional pictures into the form if they wish. When users fill out the form, they see an Add button next to the Picture content control. When they click the Add button, another Picture content control is inserted into the form. You insert a **Check Box content control** when you want users to be able to indicate their preferences among a selection of options. Users click a check box to insert an "X" or another symbol of your choice such as a check mark. **CASE** *You want the form to provide users with the option to insert more than one picture into the form so you include the Repeating Section content control. You also want users to click check boxes to indicate their preferences so you include Check Box content controls.*

STEPS

TROUBLE
If the Repeating
Section Content
Control button is
dimmed, click the
Design Mode button
to toggle it off.

1. **Click the** Picture content control selection handle, **then click the** Repeating Section Content Control button

   An Add button appears in the lower right corner of the Picture content control, as shown in **FIGURE N-8**. A user who wishes to include more pictures in the form can click the Add button to insert another Picture content control and then add a picture to that Picture content control.

2. **Click in the blank table cell below Tour Presentations, then click the** Check Box Content Control button ✓ **in the Controls group**

3. **Click** Properties, **then type** Activity

4. **Click the** Use a style ... check box, **click the** Style list arrow, **then select** Title

   If you want the check box to appear larger than the default size in the form, you need to modify it with a style that includes a large font size. You can also choose which symbol is inserted in the check box when a user clicks it.

5. **Click** Change **next to the Checked symbol label, click the** Font list arrow **in the Symbol dialog box, click** Wingdings **if it is not the active font, select the contents of the** Character code text box, **type** 252, **then click** OK

6. **Compare the Content Control Properties dialog box to** FIGURE N-9, **then click** OK

   A check mark symbol will appear in the check box when a user filling in the form clicks it.

7. **Click the** Activity content control selection handle **to select it, press** [Ctrl][C], **click the cell below Tour Launches, press** [Ctrl][V], **then paste the Check Box content control into the cells below Info Meetings and Promotions**

8. **Click to the left of the row with the Check Box content control to select the entire row, then press** [Ctrl][E] **to center each of the check boxes as shown in** FIGURE N-10

9. **Click away from the selected row, then save the template**

FIGURE N-8: Add button for the Picture content control

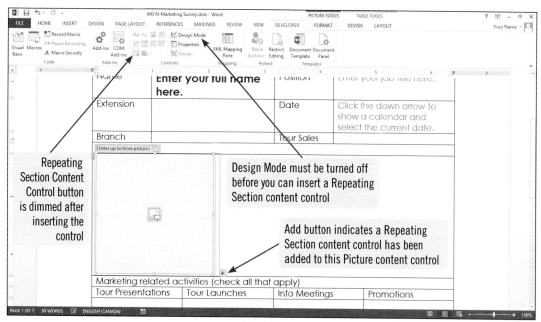

Repeating Section Content Control button is dimmed after inserting the control

Design Mode must be turned off before you can insert a Repeating Section content control

Add button indicates a Repeating Section content control has been added to this Picture content control

FIGURE N-9: Check Box content control properties

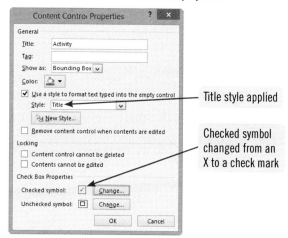

Title style applied

Checked symbol changed from an X to a check mark

FIGURE N-10: Table form with the Check Box content controls added

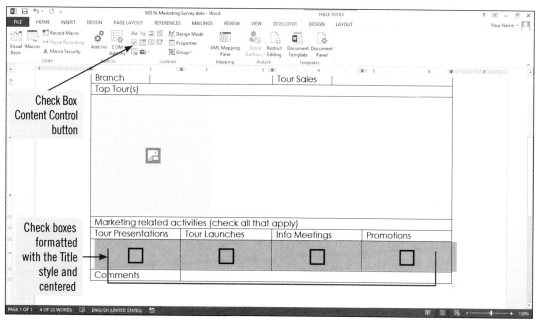

Check Box Content Control button

Check boxes formatted with the Title style and centered

Add Drop-Down Content Controls

Learning
Outcomes
• Add a Combo Box
content control
• Add a Drop-Down
List content
control

You can choose from two drop-down content controls: the **Combo Box content control** and the **Drop-Down List content control**. Both drop-down content controls provide users with a list of choices. In the Combo Box content control, users can select an item from the list of choices or they can type a new item. Users can only select from the list of choices in the Drop-Down List content control. **CASE** ▶ *As QST continues to grow, new branch locations are opening on a regular basis. You insert a Combo Box content control next to the Branch table cell so users can select the location of their QST branch if it is listed or type in the location of their branch if it is not listed. You then insert a Drop-Down List content control so users can select an adjective to describe overall tour sales.*

STEPS

QUICK TIP
With Design Mode
on, you can see
the tags associated
with each content
control.

1. **Scroll up and click in the blank table cell to the right of Branch, click the** Design Mode **button in the Controls group to turn Design Mode on, then click the** Combo Box **Content Control button** 🔲 **in the Controls group**

    You open the Content Control Properties dialog box to enter the items that users can select.

2. **Click** Properties **in the Controls group, type** Branch Location, **click** Add, **type** London, England, **then click** OK

    London, England, will be the first choice users see when they click the Combo Box content control.

3. **Click** Add, **type** San Diego, California, **then click** OK

4. **Add three more branch locations to the Content Control Properties dialog box:** Sydney, Australia; Vancouver, Canada; **and** New York, USA

5. **Click** San Diego, California, **click** Modify, **change California to** USA, **click** OK, **click** New York, USA, **then click** Move Up **until the entry appears immediately below London, England as shown in** FIGURE N-11.

    The list is now in alphabetical order.

6. **Click** OK

7. **Click in the blank table cell to the right of Tour Sales, click the** Drop-Down List Content Control button 🔲 **in the Controls group, then click** Properties

8. **Complete the Content Control Properties dialog box as shown in** FIGURE N-12, **then click** OK

9. **Save the template**

FIGURE N-11: Entries for the Combo Box content control

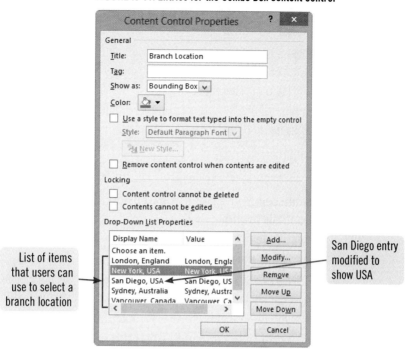

List of items that users can use to select a branch location

San Diego entry modified to show USA

FIGURE N-12: Entries for the Drop-Down List content control

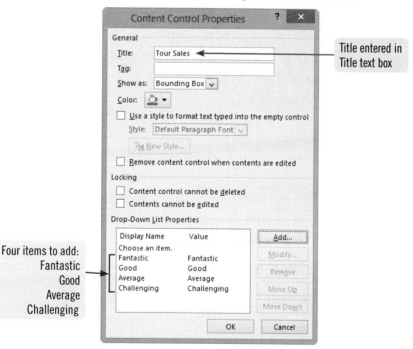

Title entered in Title text box

Four items to add:
Fantastic
Good
Average
Challenging

Building Block Gallery Content Controls

You can also insert a Building Block Gallery content control in a form. A Building Block Gallery content control can contain both text and objects, such as pictures and SmartArt graphics. You must follow several steps to use a Building Block Gallery content control. First, you create the content you want to be the building block in a new document. Next, you save the content as a Quick Part to the General gallery (or any gallery of your choice). Then, you use the Building Block Gallery content control in the Controls group to insert a Building Block Gallery content control into the form. Finally, you use the Quick Parts list arrow on the Building Block Gallery content control you inserted into the form to insert the Quick Part you created into the Building Block Gallery content control. You must work with Design Mode turned off when you are working with Building Block Gallery content controls.

Insert Legacy Tools Controls

The Legacy Tools button in the Controls group on the DEVELOPER tab provides access to a selection of **Legacy Tools controls**. Some of the Legacy Tools controls, such as the **Text control** and the **Drop-Down Form Field control**, are similar to the content controls you have already worked with. You use Legacy Tools when you need more control over how the content control is configured. **CASE** *First, you insert a Text Form Field control that you limit to three numerical characters, and then you insert another Text Form Field control to contain comments and a Help message.*

STEPS

1. **Click in the blank table cell to the right of Extension, then click the** Legacy Tools **button in the Controls group**

   The gallery of Legacy Forms controls and ActiveX controls opens, as shown in **FIGURE N-13**.

2. **Click the** Text Form Field button abl **to insert a form field**

   You use the Text Form Field control when you need to control exactly what data a user can enter into the placeholder. Like all Legacy Tools controls, the Text Form Field control is inserted into the table cell as a shaded rectangle and does not include a title bar or tags.

3. **Double-click the** Text Form Field control **to open the Text Form Field Options dialog box**

   In the Text Form Field Options dialog box, you define the type and characteristics of the data that users can enter into the Text Form Field control.

4. **Click the** Type list arrow, **click** Number, **then click the** Maximum length up arrow **three times to set the maximum length of the entry at** 3

5. **Click the** Default number text box, **type** 100, **compare your Text Form Field Options dialog box to FIGURE N-14, then click** OK

   Users will only be able to enter a 3-digit number in the Text Form Field control. If users do not enter a number, the default setting of 100 will appear.

6. **Scroll to the last row of the table (contains "Comments"), click in the blank table cell to the right of Comments, click the** Legacy Tools button, **click the** Text Form Field **button abl, double-click the** Text Form Field control, **click the** Text format list arrow, **then click** Uppercase

7. **Click the** Add Help Text button **to open the Form Field Help Text dialog box**

   In this dialog box, you can enter directions that will appear on the status bar when users click in the Text Form Field control.

8. **Click the** Type your own: option button, **then type** Provide suggestions to help us improve our marketing efforts. **as shown in FIGURE N-15**

9. **Click** OK, **click** OK, **then save the template**

   You will see the Help message when you fill in the form as a user in a later lesson.

ActiveX controls

The Legacy Tools button also provides you with access to ActiveX controls that you can use to offer options to users or to run macros or scripts that automate specific tasks. You need to have some experience with programming to use most of the ActiveX controls.

FIGURE N-13: Inserting a Text Form Field control

FIGURE N-14: Text Form Field Options dialog box

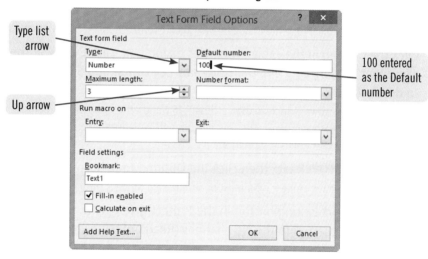

FIGURE N-15: Adding Help text

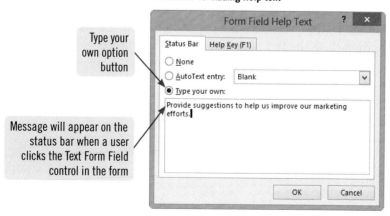

Format and Protect a Form

Learning Outcomes
- Format a form
- Protect a form

Forms should be easy to read on-screen so that users can fill them in quickly and accurately. You can enhance a table containing form fields, and you can modify the magnification of a document containing a form so that users can easily see the form fields. You can then protect a form so that users can enter only the data required and cannot change the structure of the form. When a form is protected, information can be entered only in form fields. **CASE** *You enhance the field labels, modify the table form, then protect and save the template.*

STEPS

1. Scroll up and select Name in the first cell of the table, click the HOME tab, click the Bold button **B** in the Font group, double-click the Format Painter button ⚡ in the Clipboard, then use the Format Painter to enhance all the labels with bold

2. Click the Format Painter button ⚡ to turn off the Format Painter, reduce the zoom to 80% so the entire form fits in the document window, select the first three rows in the table, press and hold [Ctrl], then select the last four rows in the table

3. Click the TABLE TOOLS LAYOUT tab, click Properties in the Table group, click the Row tab, click the Specify height check box, select the contents of the Specify height text box, then type .45

   You work in the Table Properties dialog box to quickly format nonadjacent rows in a table.

4. Click the Cell tab in the Table Properties dialog box, click Center in the Vertical alignment section, click OK, then click any cell containing a label (for example, Name) to deselect the rows

   The height of the rows is increased to at least .45", and all the labels and content controls are centered vertically within each table cell. The row heights will look even when the content control directions are removed after the user enters information.

5. Click the DEVELOPER tab, then click the Design Mode button to turn off Design Mode

   Before you protect a document, you must be sure Design Mode is turned off.

6. Click the Restrict Editing button in the Protect group, click the check box in the Editing restrictions section, click the No changes (Read only) list arrow, then click Filling in forms as shown in FIGURE N-16

7. Click Yes, Start Enforcing Protection in the Restrict Editing pane

8. Type cengage, press [Tab], then type cengage

   You enter a password so that a user cannot unprotect the form and change its structure. You can only edit the form if you enter the "cengage" password when prompted.

9. Click OK, close the Restrict Editing pane, click the form title (the Full Name content control appears to be selected), compare the completed form template to FIGURE N-17, save the template, then close the template but do not close Word

FIGURE N-16: Protecting a form

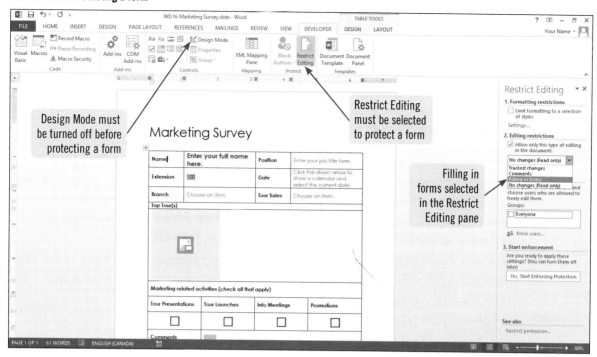

FIGURE N-16: Protecting a form

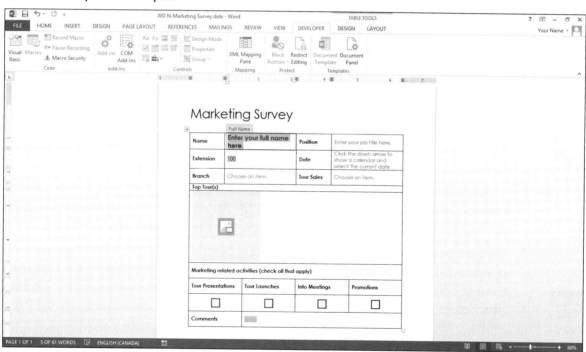

FIGURE N-17: Completed form template

Protecting documents with formatting and editing restrictions

You protect a form so that users can enter data only in designated areas. You can also protect a document. To protect a document, click the DEVELOPER tab, click the Restrict Editing button in the Protect group, then choose the restriction settings you wish to apply. To restrict formatting, you click the Limit formatting to a selection of styles check box, then click Settings. You then choose the styles that you do not want users to use when formatting a document. For example, you can choose to prevent users from using the Heading 1 style or some of the table styles. For editing restrictions, you can specify that users may only make tracked changes or insert comments, or you can select No changes (read only) when you want to prevent users from making any changes to a document.

Fill in a Form as a User

Learning Outcomes
• Edit a form
• Fill in a form

Before you distribute a form template to users, you need to test it to ensure that all the elements work correctly. For example, you want to make sure you can insert a picture in the Picture content control and that the Help text you entered appears in the status bar when you move to the Comments cell. **CASE** ➤ *You open and edit the form template by adding a shaded background to the table form, then you open a new document based on the template and fill in the form as if you were the Sydney branch manager.*

STEPS

QUICK TIP
Before you can edit any part of the template, you need to stop protection.

1. **Click the FILE tab, click Open, navigate to and open the Custom Office Templates folder in the Documents folder, click WD N-Marketing Survey.dotx, click Open, click the DEVELOPER TAB, click the Restrict Editing button in the Protect group, click Stop Protection in the Restrict Editing pane, type cengage, then click OK**

2. **Click anywhere in the table form, click the table select handle ⊞, click the TABLE TOOLS DESIGN tab, click the Shading list arrow in the Table Styles group, then click the Light Turquoise, Background 2, Lighter 80% color box**

   Now you can protect the form again and resave it.

3. **Click Yes, Start Enforcing Protection in the Restrict Editing pane, type cengage as the password, press [Tab], type cengage, click OK, then save and close the template but do not exit Word**

   You need to open the template as a new Word document so that you can fill it in as a user.

4. **Click the FILE tab, click New, click PERSONAL, then click the WD N-Marketing Survey icon**

   The document opens as a Word document (not a template) with only the content controls active. You will see Document 1 - Word in the title bar. The insertion point highlights the content control following Name. The form is protected, so you can enter information only in spaces that contain content controls or check boxes.

5. **Type your name, click the content control to the right of Position, type Marketing Manager, double-click 100 next to Extension, then type 240**

   Notice how Marketing Manager appears bold because you applied the Strong style when you inserted the Plain Text content control.

QUICK TIP
To enter a choice that is not listed in the Combo Box content control, select the text in the content control and type.

6. **Click the content control to the right of Date, click the down arrow, click Today, click the content control to the right of Branch, click the list arrow, click Sydney, Australia, click the content control to the right of Tour Sales, click the list arrow, then click Fantastic**

7. **Click the picture icon ⊡ in the Picture content control, click Browse next to From a file, navigate to the location where you store your Data Files, double-click WD N-1.jpg, click the Add button ⊕ next to the Picture content control, click the picture icon ⊡ in the new Picture content control, click Browse next to From a file, then insert WD N-2.jpg**

QUICK TIP
If you wish to submit the template file to your instructor, remember that it is stored in the Custom Office Templates folder in the Documents folder on your computer. You can copy it to the location where you store your files.

8. **Click the check box below Tour Launches, click the check box below Promotions, verify that the insertion point appears in the content control next to Comments, note the message that appears on the status bar, then type the comment text shown in FIGURE N-18, noting that it will appear in lower case as you type**

9. **Press [Tab] and scroll down to view the text in uppercase, compare the completed form to FIGURE N-19, save the document with the name WD N-Sydney Survey to the location where you save your files for this book, submit the file to your instructor, then close the document**

FIGURE N-18: Comment entry

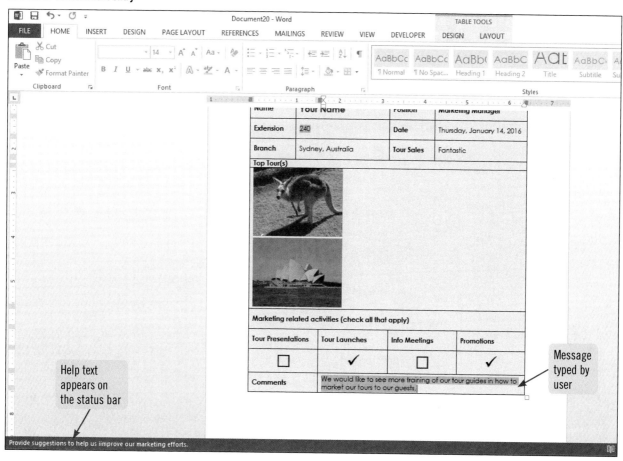

Help text
appears on
the status bar

Message
typed by
user

Provide suggestions to help us iimprove our marketing efforts.

FIGURE N-19: Completed form

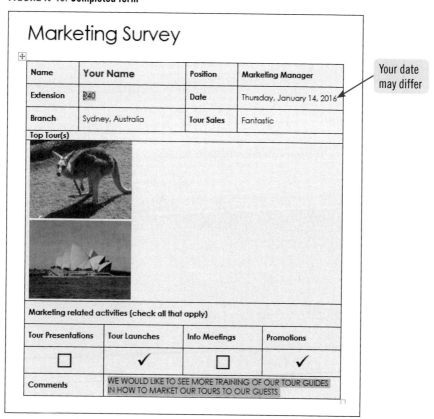

Your date
may differ

Practice

Put your skills into Practice with **SAM!** If you have a SAM account, go to www.cengage.com/sam2013 to access SAM assignments for this unit.

Concepts Review

Identify each of the numbered buttons in the Controls group shown in FIGURE N-20.

FIGURE N-20

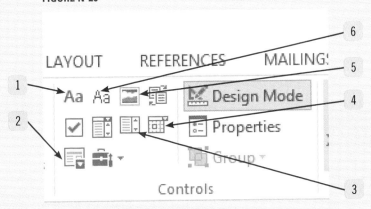

Match each term with the statement that best describes it.

7. **Text Form Field control**
8. **Check Box content control**
9. **Table**
10. **Template**
11. **Restrict Editing**

a. Use to provide users with an option to pick
b. One of the Legacy Tools options
c. Object used to contain the content controls and labels for a form
d. Uses the .dotx file extension
e. Click to protect a form

Select the best answer from the list of choices.

12. **Which of the following controls allows you to enter Help text that appears on the status bar?**
    a. Date Picker content control
    b. Text Form Field control
    c. Repeating Section content control
    d. Check Box content control

13. **Which of the following content controls allows you to select from a list or to type a new option?**
    a. Combo Box content control
    b. Drop-Down List content control
    c. Picture content control
    d. Text Form Field control

Skills Review

1. **Construct a form template.**
   a. Start a new blank document in Word, then apply the Parallax theme.
   b. Type **Change of Grade Notification**, press [Enter] two times, then enhance the text with the Title style.
   c. Create a table that has 4 columns and 12 rows.
   d. Type the text and merge cells where needed as shown in FIGURE N-21.

FIGURE N-21

Change of Grade Notification

Student Name		Student Picture	
Date		Student Number	
Course Name		Course Number	
Original Letter Grade		Revised Letter Grade	
A		A	
B		B	
C		C	
D		D	
F		F	
Grade Change Reason			
Comments			

Skills Review (continued)

    e. Save the file as a template called **WD N-Change of Grade Notification.dotx** to the Custom Office Templates folder on your computer's hard drive.

2. Add Text content controls.

    a. Show the DEVELOPER tab on the Ribbon if it is not already displayed, then turn on Design Mode.

    b. Insert a Rich Text content control in the table cell below Student Name.

    c. In the Properties dialog box for the content control, type **Full Name** as the title, exit the Properties dialog box, then click the HOME tab.

    d. Select the entire control, change the font size to 14 point, then change the font color to Lavender, Accent 6, Darker 25%.

    e. Between the two Full Name tags, enter **Type the student's full name.**

    f. Click the DEVELOPER tab, click in the blank cell to the right of Grade Change Reason in the second to last row of the table, then insert a Plain Text content control.

    g. In the Properties dialog box, enter **Description of Change** as the title, then specify that the text be formatted with the Intense Emphasis style.

    h. Between the two Description of Change tags, type **Enter the reasons for the grade change.**, then save the template.

3. Add Date Picker and Picture content controls.

    a. Insert a Date Picker content control in the blank cell to the right of Date.

    b. In the Properties dialog box, enter **Current Date** as the title, then change the date format to the format that corresponds to March 18, 2016.

    c. Between the two Current Date tags, type the message **Click the down arrow to show a calendar, then select the date of the last day of term.**

    d. In the blank cell below Student Picture, insert a Picture content control, then save the template.

4. Add Repeating Section and Check Box content controls.

    a. Select the row containing the Course Name and Course Number labels, then insert a Repeating Section content control. (*Note*: Turn off Design Mode to view the Add button.)

    b. Select the six rows from Original Letter Grade to the row containing "F", then insert a Repeating Section content control.

    c. Turn on Design Mode, insert a Check Box content control in the cell to the right of A under Original Letter Grade.

    d. In the Content Control Properties dialog box, apply the Heading 1 style to the Check Box content control, then change the Checked symbol to Character code **251** from the Wingdings font, which is a stylized *x*.

    e. Select the Check Box content control, copy it, then paste it in all the table cells to the right of each letter grade. (*Notes*: You will need to paste the Check Box content control nine times. The extra tags are the closing tags for the Repeat Section content control you added in step 4b.)

5. Add Drop-Down content controls.

    a. Insert a Combo Box content control in the blank cell to the right of Course Name.

    b. In the Content Control Properties dialog box, enter **Course Title** as the title.

    c. Add the following entries: **Accounting**, **Finance**, **Marketing**, and **Business**.

    d. Change Business to **Computers**, then move Computers up so it appears immediately after Accounting.

    e. Insert a Drop-Down List content control in the cell to the right of Course Number, before the closing tags for the Repeating Section content control you added in step 4a.

    f. In the Content Control Properties dialog box, enter **Course Number** as the title, then add the following entries: **100, 150, 200, 220, 300**.

    g. Save the template.

6. Insert Legacy Tools controls.

    a. Insert a Text Form Field control from the Legacy Tools gallery in the blank cell to the right of Student Number.

    b. Double-click the control to open the Text Form Field Options dialog box, change the Type to Number, change the Maximum length to **7**, then enter **1234567** as the default.

Skills Review (continued)

c. Insert a Text Form Field control from the Legacy Tools gallery in the blank cell to the right of Comments.

d. Specify that the text format should be uppercase, add the help text: **Provide additional details if necessary**, then save the template.

7. Format and protect a form.

a. Apply bold to all the labels in the form template except the letter grades.

b. Change the view to 90%, select the table, then change the row height to at least .3".

c. Vertically center align the text in all the cells. (*Hint*: Use the Cell tab in the Table Properties dialog box.)

d. Right-align all of the letter grades but not the check boxes. (*Hint*: Use the HOME tab.)

e. Protect the document for users filling in forms using the password **skills**, then save and close the template but do not exit Word. (*Note*: If you turned Design Mode on, it must be turned off to protect the document.)

8. Fill in a form as a user.

a. Open the WD N-Change of Grade Notification.dotx template from the Custom Office Templates folder, then stop protection using the **skills** password.

b. Fill the table form with the Lavender, Accent 6, Lighter 80% color.

c. Center the "Original Letter Grade" and "Revised Letter Grade" labels.

d. Protect the form again using the **skills** password.

e. Save and close the template but do not exit Word.

f. From the FILE tab, start a new document based on the Grade Notification template (verify that Document 1 (or another number) appears in the title bar), then refer to **FIGURE N-22** to complete the form using WD N-3.jpg (or your own picture if you wish) in the Picture content control.

g. Save the document as **WD N-Grade Change Completed** to the location where you store your files for this book, submit the file to your instructor, then close the document.

FIGURE N-22

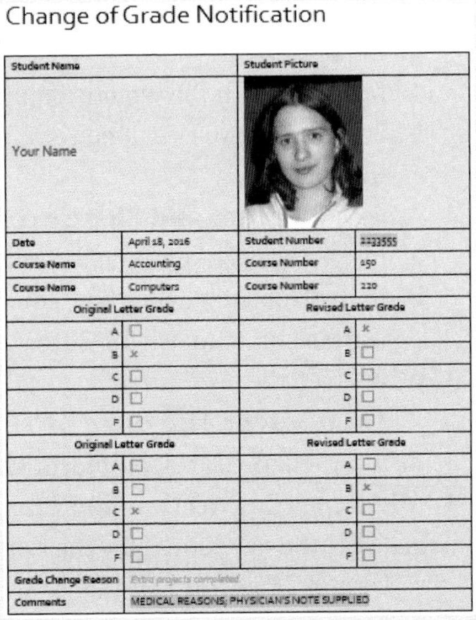

Change of Grade Notification

Independent Challenge 1

You work for the owner of Letson Consultants, a communications consulting company that assists businesses in the creation and development of business reports and proposals. The owner and some of the managers of the company often travel to meet with clients. Your boss asks you to create an itinerary form that managers can complete in Word to help them keep track of their travel details.

a. Start Word and open the file WD N-4.docx from the drive and folder where you store your Data Files. Save it as a template called **WD N-Itinerary Form** to the Custom Office Templates folder.

b. Make Design Mode active, then insert a Rich Text content control in the blank table cell to the right of the Name label. Enter **Full Name** as the title, then format the control with 14 pt, bold, italic.

c. Insert a Date Picker control in the blank table cell to the right of Report Date. Enter **Date** as the title, then select the date format that corresponds with June 30, 2016.

d. Insert a Drop-Down List content control in the blank table cell to the right of Department. Enter **Department** as the title, then add: **Sales**, **Accounting**, and **Human Resources**, and put in alphabetical order.

e. Insert a Text Form Field control from the Legacy Tools gallery in the blank table cell to the right of Extension. Specify the Type as Number, a Maximum length of **3**, and **200** as the Default number.

f. Insert a Plain Text content control in the blank table cell to the right of Purpose of Travel. Enter **Travel Purpose** for the title, then apply the Intense Emphasis style.

g. Select the Date Picker content control you inserted next to Report Date, copy it, then paste it below Date.

h. Insert a Combo Box content control in the first cell below Category. Enter **Category** as the title, then add three selections: **Transportation**, **Hotel**, **Meeting**. Enter the text **Choose an item or type your own** between the two tags.

Independent Challenge 1 (continued)

i. Insert a Rich Text content control in the first cell below Details. Enter the text **Click add button for more rows** as the title, then select the Gold color for the control in the Content Control Properties dialog box.

j. Select the last row in the form (contains three content controls), then click the Repeating Section Content Control button. When users fill in the form, they can click the plus sign to add more rows to supply more itinerary details.

k. Insert a Picture content control in the blank cell to the right of Picture of Location. Apply the Bevel Rectangle picture style. (*Hint*: Click the center of the Picture content control and not the content control selection handle, click the PICTURE TOOLS FORMAT tab, then select the picture style from the Styles gallery.)

l. Apply bold to all the form labels, then center the three labels: Date, Category, and Details.

m. Protect the form using the Filling in forms selection, enter **ic1** as the password, then save and close the template but do not exit Word.

n. Start a new document from the FILE tab based on the WD N-Itinerary Form template (verify that Document 1 or another number appears in the title bar), enter your name and the current date in row 1, then complete the form with the information shown in **TABLE N-2**.

o. Insert WD N-5.jpg in the Picture content control.

p. Enter itinerary information as shown in **TABLE N-3**, clicking the Add button after you've entered data for each row for a total of four rows.

q. Save the form as **WD N-Paris Itinerary**, submit a copy to your instructor, then close the document.

TABLE N-2

Department	Extension	Purpose of Travel
Human Resources	244	To attend an HR conference in Paris

TABLE N-3

Date	Category	Details
April 2, 2016	Transportation	AA Flight 300 from Seattle to Paris
April 3, 2016	Hotel	Hotel Miramar, Paris: 3 nights
April 5, 2016	Meeting	Attendance at the conference
April 6, 2016	Meeting	Presentation at the conference

Independent Challenge 2

You work for a company called Chatwick Communications that conducts business writing and communications courses. Clients complete a feedback form after they participate in a course. You create a Word form to e-mail clients.

a. Start Word and open the file WD N-6.docx from the location where your Data Files are located. Save it as a template called **WD N-Course Evaluation Form** to the Custom Office Templates folder.

b. Switch to Design Mode, then insert and format controls as described in **TABLE N-4**:

TABLE N-4

Location	Content Control	Title	Properties
Name	Rich Text content control	Full Name	Format with Heading 1 and bold
Course Date	Date Picker content control	Date	Format with the date format of your choice
Instructor	Drop-Down List content control	Instructor	Format with the names of four instructors (for example, Mary Prentiss, Doreen Jefferson); put the names in alphabetical order by last name
Subject	Combo Box content control	Subject	Format with entries for three subjects in alphabetical order: **Viral Marketing, Business Writing**, and **Leadership Skills**; type the text **Select an item or enter a new subject.** between the form tags as a direction to users
Course Element	Plain Text content control in the blank cell below Course Element	Course Element	Format with 16 pt font size; type the text: **Click the Add button to insert up to four more course elements.**
Rankings	Check Box content control in each of the 4 blank cells for the ranking of course elements.	Rank	Format with the Heading 1 style and the Wingdings 252 check mark character. (*Hint*: Insert and modify the first check box content control, then copy and paste it to the remaining table cells.)
Additional Comments	Text Form Field control from the Legacy Tools		Format to include the Help text: **Please add comments about the course and the instructor.**

Independent Challenge 2 (continued)

c. Select the row containing the Plain Text and Check Box content controls and make the row a Repeating Section. Turn off Design Mode and verify that the Add button appears to the right of the last cell in the row.

d. Protect the form for filling in forms, click OK to bypass password protection when prompted, then save and close the template but do not exit Word.

e. Open the form template and unprotect it, then delete one of the instructors from the Drop-Down List content control so the list includes three instructors.

f. Apply the table style of your choice to the entire table; experiment with the table style options until you are satisfied.

g. Protect the form again, then save and close the template but do not exit Word.

h. Start a new document from the FILE tab based on the WD N-Course Evaluation Form template, enter your name in the Name cell and the current date in the Seminar Date cell, select one of the three instructors, then enter **Listening Skills** in the Combo Box content control to the right of Subject.

i. In the content control below Course Element, type **Course Materials**.

j. Use the Add button to add another row, enter **Instructor** as the course element, then add another row and enter **Course Location** as the course element.

k. Assign a ranking to each of the three course elements by clicking the appropriate check box.

l. In the Additional Comments form field, type **Fantastic course. Thanks!**

m. Save the document as **WD N-Completed Course Evaluation Form** to the location where you store the files for this book, submit it to your instructor, then close the document.

Independent Challenge 3

You can learn a great deal about form design by studying how the form templates are constructed. To complete this independent challenge, download one of the form templates included with Microsoft Office Word, and then customize the form. (*Note: To complete these steps your computer must be connected to the Internet.*)

a. Start Word, open a blank document, click the FILE tab, click New, click in the Search for online templates text box, type **Forms** and press [Enter], then explore the various categories and forms available.

b. Enter **Employee performance** in the Search text box, then select the Employee performance evaluation form and click Create to download it to your computer.

c. Click the Design Mode button on the DEVELOPER tab to view the content control titles.

d. Click the Start date control, open the Content Control Properties dialog box, then select a different date format. Repeat for the End date control.

e. Add a Drop-Down list content control in the blank cell to the right of Department, add **Department** as the title, then enter four departments: **Sales**, **Administration**, **Finance**, and **Product Development**. Put the items in alphabetical order.

f. Delete the third entry in each of the six categories so that just two entries appear in each category.

g. Turn off Design Mode and verify that the form fits on one page.

h. Insert a footer with the text **Modified by** followed by your name.

i. Protect the form using the filling in forms setting, password protect the form or click OK to bypass password protection, save the document as a template called **WD N-Assessment Form** to the Custom Office Templates folder on your computer, then submit it to your instructor.

Independent Challenge 4: Explore

As the Office Manager at Maxwell Securities, you create a Word form that staff members complete to purchase a parking permit. You create the form as a Word template that includes three option buttons that are ActiveX controls found in the Legacy Tools. Staff can open a new Word document based on the template and complete the form in Word, or they can print the form and fill it in by hand.

a. Start Word, then create the table form shown in **FIGURE N-23**. (*Hint*: To create the Status label, select the four rows in column 3, merge them, then click the Text Direction button in the Alignment group on the TABLE TOOLS LAYOUT tab.)

FIGURE N-23

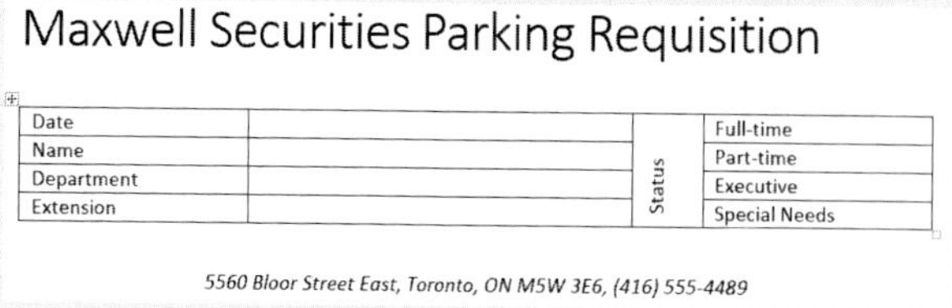

Maxwell Securities Parking Requisition

Date		Full-time
Name		Part-time
Department		Executive
Extension		Special Needs

5560 Bloor Street East, Toronto, ON M5W 3E6, (416) 555-4489

b. Save it as a template called **WD N-Parking Permit Requisition** to the Custom Office Templates folder on your computer.

c. Be sure Design Mode is active, then insert content controls with appropriate titles (you choose) and properties as described in **TABLE N-5**:

TABLE N-5

Location	Content Control
Date	Date Picker content control using the 5-Mar-16 format
Name	Plain Text content control formatted with the Heading 2 style
Department	Combo Box content control with four entries (for example, Accounting, Sales) in alphabetical order
Extension	Text Form field from the Legacy Tools with Number as the type, a limit of four characters and 1234 as the default characters
Full-time, Part-time, etc.	Check Box content control in each of the four Status cells formatted with the Heading 1 style and using the check mark symbol of your choice

d. Exit Design Mode, right-align the contents of all four of the Status cells, then apply bold to all the labels.

e. Add a new row at the bottom of the form.

f. Enter **Payment** in the first cell, then apply bold if necessary.

g. Select the next three blank cells, click the Clear All Formatting button on the HOME tab, merge the three cells into one cell, then split the newly merged cell into three columns with one row.

h. Click in the second cell in the last row, click the Design Mode button on the DEVELOPER tab to turn it on, show the selection of Legacy Tools, then click the Option (ActiveX Control) button in the ActiveX Controls section. (*Note*: In a form containing a selection of option buttons, users can select just one button.)

i. Click the Properties button, widen the Properties panel as needed to see all the text in column 2, select the OptionButton1 text next to Caption (*not* next to (Name)) in the list of properties, type **Payroll**, then close the Properties dialog box. (*Hint*: To enlarge the panel, move the pointer over the right side of the panel until the pointer changes, then drag the side of the panel to the right.)

j. Repeat to insert two more option button ActiveX controls in cells 3 and 4 with the captions **Debit** and **Cash**.

k. Click the cell containing Status, then reduce its width to .4".

l. Click the Design Mode button to exit design mode, protect the form for filling in forms, click OK to bypass password protection when prompted, then save and close the template.

m. Open the template from Windows Explorer, enter the current date and your name, select one of the departments (you choose), enter 2233 as the Extension, click the Full-time check box, then click the Debit option button.

n. Save the document as **WD N-Completed Parking Requisition** to the location where you store your files for this book, submit a copy to your instructor, close the document, then exit Word.

Word 2013

Visual Workshop

You work for Arts Alive Tours, Inc., a tour company that specializes in taking small groups of travelers on study tours that focus on the arts and culture of a region. You need to create a form that clients can complete after they have returned from a tour. Work in Design Mode to create and enhance a form template similar to the one shown in **FIGURE N-24**. (*Notes*: The Retrospect theme is applied to the document. Use appropriate controls where needed; it is OK to omit the titles and tags from the controls for this exercise.) Use these names for the tour names: **New York Culture, Renaissance Art, Asian History**, and **Chicago Architecture**. Use the Wingdings 171 symbol for the check box and format the Check Box content control with Heading 2. Include this Help text: **Describe some of the highlights of your trip.** for the Additional Comments. Apply shading where indicated. Save the template as **WD N-Tour Feedback Form** to the Custom Office Templates folder on your computer. Protect the form, do not password protect it, close the template, then open a new document based on the template. Complete the form as a user who took the Renaissance Art tour with the tour guide of your choice on the current date. Click one check box for each category, enter **Fabulous time!** as the comment, and insert WD N-7.jpg as the picture. Save the completed form as **WD N-Completed Tour Feedback Form** to the drive and folder where you store your files for this book, submit a copy to your instructor, then close the document.

FIGURE N-24

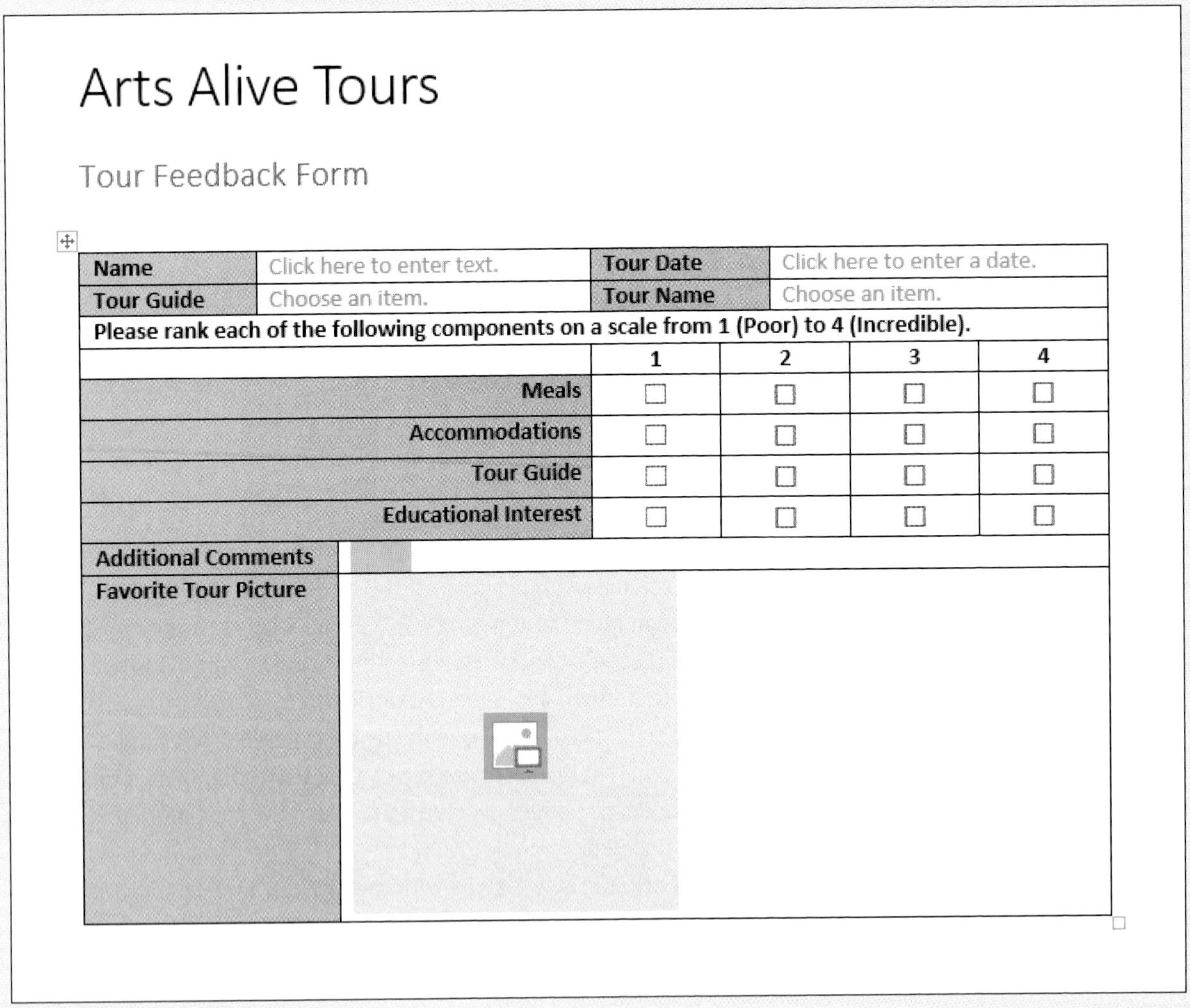

Arts Alive Tours

Tour Feedback Form

Name	Click here to enter text.	Tour Date	Click here to enter a date.		
Tour Guide	Choose an item.	Tour Name	Choose an item.		
Please rank each of the following components on a scale from 1 (Poor) to 4 (Incredible).					
			1	2	3	4
Meals			☐	☐	☐	☐
Accommodations			☐	☐	☐	☐
Tour Guide			☐	☐	☐	☐
Educational Interest			☐	☐	☐	☐
Additional Comments					
Favorite Tour Picture					

Collaborating with Coworkers

CASE ▶ Gloria Janzen in the Marketing Department at Quest Specialty Travel in New York has written several questions for an online survey that visitors to the Quest Specialty Travel Web site can complete. You collaborate with Gloria to refine the survey so you can submit it to other colleagues for additional input.

Unit Objectives

After completing this unit, you will be able to:

- Explore collaboration options
- Include comments in a document
- Track changes
- Work with tracked changes
- Manage reviewers
- Compare documents
- Use advanced find and replace options
- Sign a document digitally

Files You Will Need

Explore Collaboration Options

You can collaborate with colleagues in different ways. For example, you can distribute printed documents that show all the changes made by one or more colleagues, along with the comments they have made, or you can share the electronic file of the document, which also shows the changes and comments. In addition, you can collaborate with coworkers over the Internet by working with the Word Office Web Apps. **CASE** ➤ *Before you start working with Gloria to develop questions for an online survey, you investigate collaborative features available in Word.*

DETAILS

The collaborative features in Word include the following:

- **REVIEW tab**

  Commands on the REVIEW tab allow you to share a document with two or more people. The collaboration commands are included in four groups on the REVIEW tab: Comments, Tracking, Changes, and Compare.

- **Insert comments**

  You insert comments into a document when you want to ask questions or provide additional information. When several people work on the same document, their comments appear in balloons in the right margin of the document. Each reviewer is assigned a unique color automatically, which is applied to the bar, the picture icon, and the comment balloon outline when the comment is active. The comment balloons appear along the right side of the document in Print Layout view when All Markup is selected. **FIGURE O-1** shows a document containing comments made by two people. A Reply button appears in an active comment balloon.

- **Track changes**

  When you share documents with colleagues, you need to be able to show them where you have inserted and deleted text. In Word, inserted text appears in the document as underlined text in the color assigned to the person who made the insertion. This same color identifies that person's deletions and comment balloons. For example, if Cindy's comment balloons are blue, then the text she inserts in a document will also be blue, and the text she deletes will be marked with a blue strikethrough. **FIGURE O-1** includes both inserted text and deleted text. You use the commands in the Changes group to move through comments and tracked changes, and to accept or reject tracked changes.

- **Compare and combine documents**

  You use the Compare command to compare documents based on the same original document to show the differences between them. The Compare command is often used to show the differences between an original document and an edited copy of the original. The differences between the two documents are shown as tracked changes. The Combine command is also used to combine the changes and comments of multiple reviewers into a single document when each reviewer edits the document using a separate copy of the original.

- **Collaborate online**

  You can work collaboratively on a document with one or more people at the same time. You can edit files in real time, discuss revisions among team members, and review the work done by each person on the team. You can do these activities directly from Word using options available on the Person Card or you can work in the cloud via SkyDrive. The Person Card information is based on information contained in a Microsoft account or an Active Work Directory. **FIGURE O-2** shows a document open in the Word Web App in a Web browser. In the Word Web App, you can perform simple functions such as typing and formatting text, and inserting pictures, tables, clip art, and hyperlinks.

FIGURE O-1: Document showing tracked changes and comments

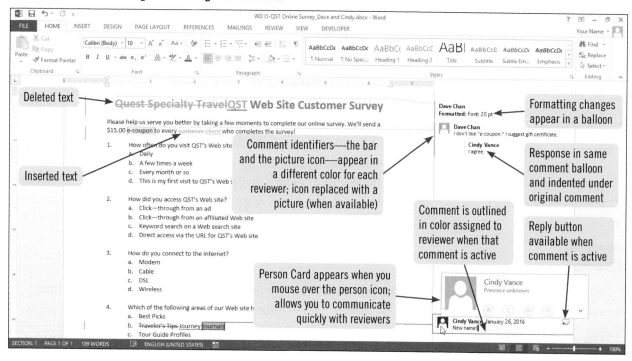

FIGURE O-2: Document in Word Web App

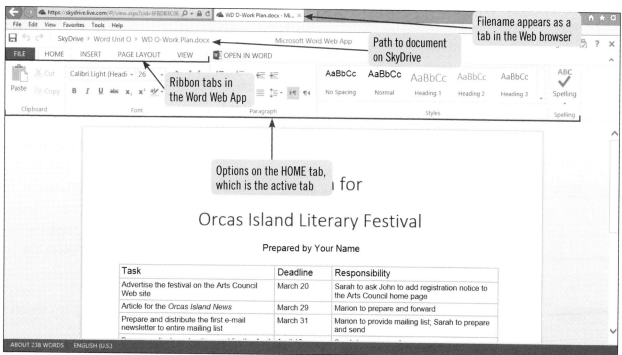

Word 2013

Learning Outcomes
- Add, edit, and delete comments

Include Comments in a Document

Sometimes when you review a document that someone else has written, you want to insert a comment about the document text, the document formatting, or any number of other related issues. A **comment** is contained in a comment balloon that appears along the right side of your document by default. Shading appears in the document at the point where you inserted the comment. A line connects the end comment mark and the comment balloon. The **Revisions pane** is used to view comments. **CASE** ▶ *Your colleague, Gloria Janzen, has prepared a document containing a list of survey questions, and she has inserted some comments for your review. You open the document, add a new comment, edit one of the comments that Gloria inserted, then delete a comment.*

STEPS

TROUBLE
A different markup option may be selected if another user was working on the computer before you.

1. **Start Word, open the file** WD O-1.docx **from the location where you store your Data Files, save it as** WD O-QST Online Survey_Gloria, **then click the** REVIEW **tab**

   Simple Markup is the default option in the Tracking group on the REVIEW tab. With this option, a comment balloon appears along the right side of the page. To see a comment in Simple Markup view, click the comment balloon. To see all comments in Simple Markup view, click Show Comments in the Comments group.

2. **Click the** Simple Markup button, **then click** All Markup

   The comments that Gloria inserted appear in the right margin of the document. The shading of $10.00 indicates the text referred to by the comment.

3. **Select the word** e-coupon **in the first paragraph, then click the** New Comment button **in the Comments group**

   The word "e-coupon" is shaded, and a comment balloon appears in the right margin. Your name or the name assigned to your computer appears in the box.

QUICK TIP
You can also click the New Comment button on the Ribbon or right-click the comment and click Reply To Comment to insert an indented reply to a comment.

4. **Type** Should we tell users where to spend their e-coupons?

   Your comment appears as shown in FIGURE O-3.

5. **Click in the first comment balloon (starts with "Too much?"), click the** Reply button 🗨 **in the comment, type** I suggest changing the amount to $15.00, pending management approval., **then click anywhere in the document text**

   Your response appears indented under the original comment.

QUICK TIP
When you click in a comment balloon, its colored outline appears.

6. **Click in Gloria's second comment balloon ("Should we say..."), click** 🗨 **in the comment, then type** I don't think so.

7. **Click in the comment you inserted in Steps 3 and 4 that contains the text "Should we tell users..." next to paragraph 1, select** users, **then type** clients

8. **Scroll down as needed, click the comment balloon containing the text "I'm using the new name..." attached to Best Picks in question 4, then click the** Delete button **in the Comments group**

   The comment is removed from the document.

QUICK TIP
The Revisions pane can also be displayed below the document window.

9. **Click** Reviewing Pane **in the Tracking group, reduce the zoom to 90% so you can see all the comments, then compare your screen to** FIGURE O-4

10. **Close the Revisions pane, return the zoom to 120%, then save the document**

FIGURE O-3: Comment balloons

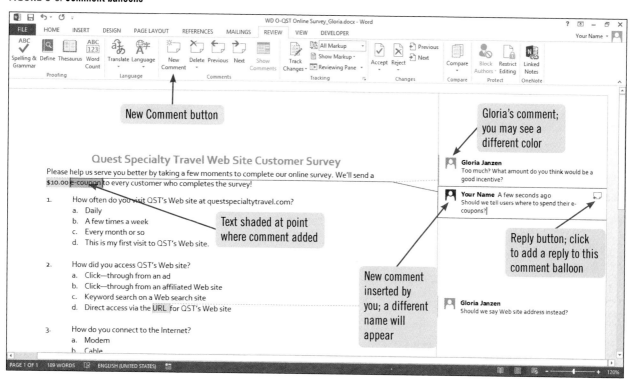

FIGURE O-4: Comments in the Revisions pane

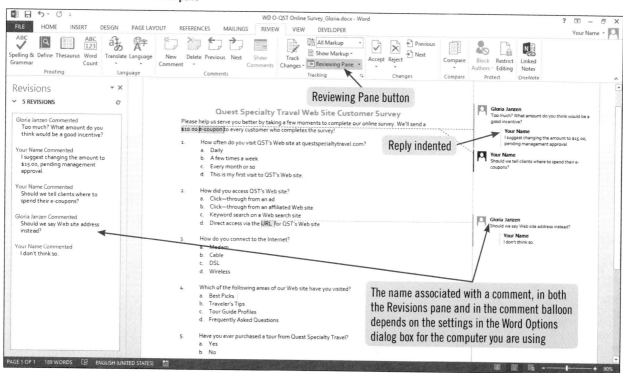

Distributing documents for revision

When you work with several people on a document, you can e-mail each person a copy of the document and ask for his or her input. To send the active document, click the FILE tab, click Share, click Email, then click the Send as Attachment button. If you are using Outlook as your e-mail client, the Outlook client window opens. The current document filename appears in the subject line, and the current document is attached to the e-mail message. If you are already connected to the Internet, you just enter the e-mail address(es) of the recipient(s) in the To: and Cc: text boxes, type a message in the message window, and then click Send.

Track Changes

Learning Outcomes
- Track insertions and deletions
- Track formatting changes

When you work on a document with two or more people, you want to be able to see all the changes they have made. You use the Track Changes command to show deleted text and inserted text. By default, deleted text appears as ~~strikethrough~~ and inserted text appears <u>underlined</u> in the document. Both insertions and deletions appear in the color assigned to the reviewer. **CASE** *You go through the survey that Gloria prepared and make some editing changes to the text and to some of the formatting. You also move selected text to a new location. All of these changes are tracked so that each person who opens the document next can see exactly what changes you made.*

STEPS

1. **Press [Ctrl][Home] to move to the top of the document, then click the Track Changes button in the Tracking group**

   When the Track Changes button is active, every change you make to the document will appear in colored text.

2. **Select $10.00 in the first paragraph, then press [Delete]**

   The deleted text appears as strikethrough.

3. **Type $15.00, then press [Spacebar]**

   As shown in **FIGURE O-5**, the inserted text appears underlined and in the same color as the color of the comment balloon you inserted in the previous lesson.

4. **Select often in question 1, then type frequently**

   The deleted text appears as strikethrough, and the text "frequently" appears in colored and underlined text.

5. **Scroll to question 5, select from "Have you" to the blank line after "No" as shown in FIGURE O-6, click the HOME tab, then click the Cut button in the Clipboard group**

   The text you selected appears as deleted text, and the questions have been renumbered.

   QUICK TIP
   You press [Backspace] to remove a lettered line in a list and to leave a blank line.

6. **Click the line below the new question 5, click the Paste button in the Clipboard group, click after "Improvement" (see 5d.), press [Enter], then press [Backspace]**

   As shown in **FIGURE O-7**, both the cut text and the pasted text appear in a new color and are double-underlined. The new color and the double underlining indicate that the text has been moved.

7. **Scroll to the top of the page, select the document title, click the Increase Font Size button $A^{\cdot}$ in the Font group once to increase the font to 18 pt, click the Font Color list arrow $\underline{A}^{\cdot}$, select Green, Accent 3, Darker 25%, then click in paragraph 1 to deselect the text**

   The formatting changes appear in a new balloon next to the selected text.

   QUICK TIP
   A comment balloon is not displayed in Simple Markup view for comments associated with deleted text.

8. **Click the REVIEW tab, click All Markup in the Tracking group, then click Simple Markup**

   The tracked changes and comments are no longer visible in the document. Instead, you see a bar in the left margin next to every line of text that includes a change, and a comment balloon in the right margin next to any line that includes a comment.

9. **Click the Show Comments button in the Comments group to show all comments in their balloons, click the Show Comments button to turn off this feature, click Simple Markup in the Tracking group, click All Markup, then save the document**

   The document appears as shown in **FIGURE O-8**.

Collaborating with Coworkers

FIGURE O-5: Text inserted with Track Changes feature active

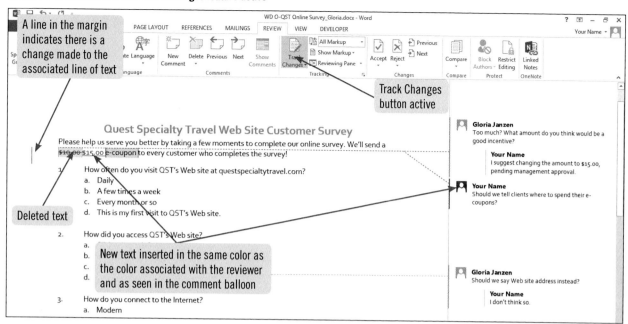

FIGURE O-6: Selected text

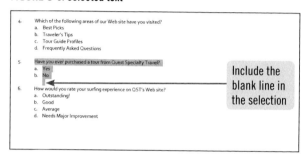

FIGURE O-7: Tracked changes shows formatting for moved text

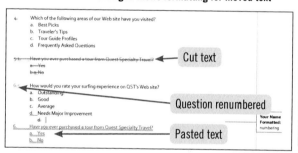

FIGURE O-8: Document with formatting and text tracked changes

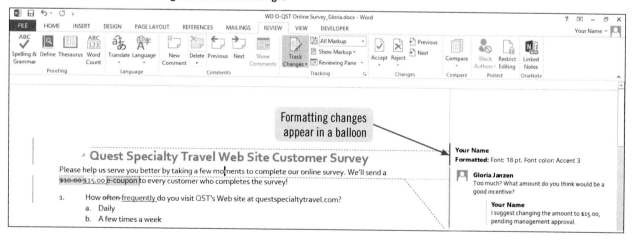

Track Changes and the Clipboard

If Track Changes is on when you are pasting items from the Clipboard, each item you paste is inserted in the document as a tracked change. If you cut an individual item and then paste it from the Clipboard into a new location, the item is inserted in a new color and with double underlining, which indicates that the item has been moved. If, however, you use the Paste All button on the Clipboard pane to paste all the items on the Clipboard at once, the items are pasted in the document as inserted text at the location of the insertion point. When you use the Paste All button, the items are pasted in the order in which you collected them, from the first item you collected (the item at the bottom of the Clipboard) to the most recent item you collected (the item at the top of the Clipboard).

Word 2013

Work with Tracked Changes

Learning Outcomes
- Change track change options
- Accept and reject changes

You can modify the appearance of tracked changes using the Track Changes Options dialog box. For example, you can change the formatting of insertions and select a specific color for them, and you can modify the appearance of the comment balloons. When you receive a document containing tracked changes, you can accept or reject the changes. When you accept a change, inserted text becomes part of the document and deleted text is permanently removed. You use the buttons in the Changes group on the REVIEW tab to accept and reject changes in a document, and you use the buttons in the Comments group to find and remove comments. **CASE** ➤ *You decide to modify the appearance of the tracked changes in the document. You then accept or reject the tracked changes and remove all the comments.*

STEPS

1. **Click the** launcher ⬛ **in the Tracking group to open the Track Changes Options dialog box**

   You can choose which tracking methods to show (comments, insertions, deletions, etc.), and you can explore advanced options to choose how to show tracking methods.

2. **Click the** Pictures By Comments check box, **click** Advanced Options, **click the** Insertions list arrow, **click** Double underline, **then at the bottom of the Track Changes Options dialog box, change the** Preferred width **of the balloon to** 2" **as shown in** FIGURE O-9, **click** OK, **then click** OK

3. **Press** [Ctrl][Home], **then click the** Next button **in the Changes group to move to the first tracked change in the document**

   The insertion point highlights the title because you modified the formatting.

4. **Click the** Accept list arrow **in the Changes group, then click** Accept and Move to Next

   The formatting changes to the title are accepted, and the insertion point moves to the next tracked change, which is deleted text ($10.00) in the first paragraph.

5. **Click the** Accept button **to accept the deletion and automatically move to the next change, click the** Accept button **again to accept $15.00, then click the** Delete button **in the Comments group**

   The comment is deleted, and $15.00 is formatted as black text to show it has been accepted.

6. **Click the** Next button **in the Changes group to highlight the next tracked change (deletion of "often"), click the** Reject button **in the Changes group, then click the** Reject button **again**

   Question 1 is restored to its original wording. You can continue to review and accept or reject changes individually, or you can choose to accept all of the remaining changes in the document.

7. **Click the** Accept list arrow, **click** Accept All Changes, **then scroll to the end of the document**

   All the tracked changes in the document are accepted, including the question that was moved and renumbered.

8. **Click the** Delete list arrow **in the Comments group, then click** Delete All Comments in Document

   Scroll through the document. Notice that all tracked changes and comments are removed from the document.

9. **Click the** Track Changes button **in the Tracking group to turn off Track Changes, scroll to the bottom of the document, type your name where indicated in the footer, then save and close the document, but do not exit Word**

   The completed document appears as shown in FIGURE O-10.

FIGURE O-9: Advanced Track Changes Options dialog box

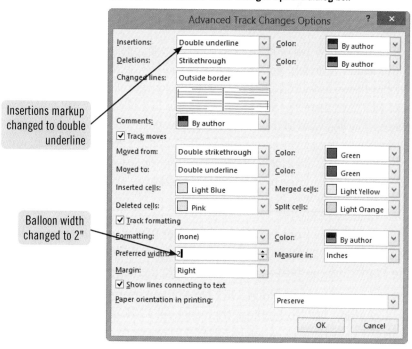

Insertions markup changed to double underline

Balloon width changed to 2"

FIGURE O-10: Completed document with tracked changes accepted and comments deleted

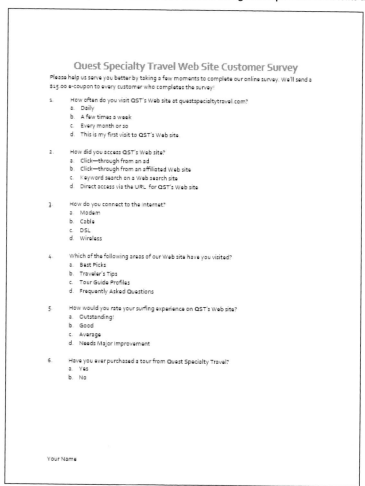

Manage Reviewers

You use commands on the REVIEW tab to help you collaborate with one or more people and to manage how you work with multiple reviewers. For example, you can choose to display tracked changes and comments associated with one reviewer, with several reviewers, or with all reviewers. You can also choose how you would like your own username and initials to appear in a document that you have reviewed. Finally, you can choose how you want to review the changes made to a document. **CASE** *You sent a copy of the QST Online Survey document you completed in the previous lesson to Dave Chan, who edited the document and then sent it to Cindy Vance for her input. Cindy then sent the edited document back to you. You view the changes they made and add a few more changes of your own.*

STEPS

1. **Open the file WD O-2.docx from the drive and folder where you store your Data Files, save the document as WD O-QST Online Survey_Dave and Cindy, click the REVIEW tab, then click the Track Changes button to turn on tracked changes**

2. **Click All Markup in the Tracking group, click No Markup, note that all the changes appear to be accepted, click No Markup, then click All Markup**

   All the comments and tracked changes are again visible.

3. **Click the Show Markup button in the Tracking group, point to Balloons, click Show All Revisions Inline, then move your pointer over cv2 in paragraph 1 to view the comment made by Cindy as shown in FIGURE O-11**

   Instead of being contained in balloons, the comments are contained within the document.

4. **Click the Show Markup button, point to Balloons, click Show Revisions in Balloons, note that both the comments and the deletions appear in balloons, click the Show Markup button, point to Balloons, then click Show Only Comments and Formatting in Balloons to return to the default view**

5. **Click the Show Markup button, then point to Specific People**

   A list of the people who worked on the document appears, as shown in FIGURE O-12.

6. **Click the check box next to Cindy Vance to deselect it, then scroll through the document**

   Only the tracked changes and comment made by Dave Chan are visible. You can choose to view comments made by each person who reviewed the document, a selection of people, or an individual.

QUICK TIP
You can also change the username and initials by clicking the FILE tab, and then clicking Options to open the Word Options dialog box.

7. **Click the launcher ⊡ in the Tracking group, click Change User Name to open the Word Options dialog box, select the contents of the User name text box, type your name, press [Tab], type your initials, click OK, then click OK**

8. **Press [Ctrl][Home], click the Accept button once to accept the deletion in the title, click the Accept button again to accept the insertion of QST, select e-coupon, then type gift certificate**

   The text "e-coupon" is marked as deleted, and the text "gift certificate" is marked as inserted.

TROUBLE
If you see a name other than the one you entered in step 7, then repeat step 7 and add a check mark to the Always use these values regardless of sign in to Office check box.

9. **Click the Show Markup button, point to Specific People, note that your name appears as one of the reviewers, click the check box next to Cindy Vance to select it, click the Accept list arrow, click Accept All Changes and Stop Tracking, then delete all comments in the document**

   The Tracked Changes button in the Tracking group is off. Tracked Changes is no longer active.

10. **Type your name where indicated at the bottom of the document, save the document, then close the document but do not exit Word**

FIGURE O-11: Showing a comment

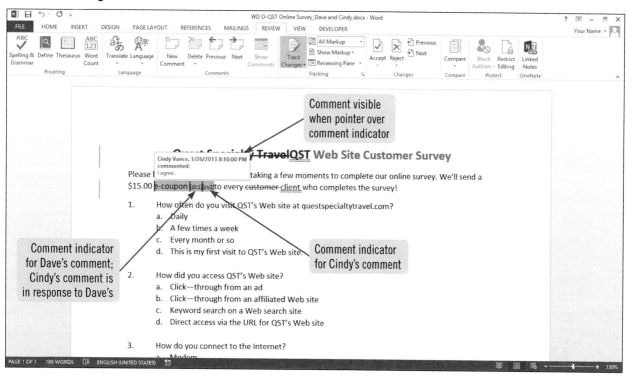

FIGURE O-12: Showing reviewers

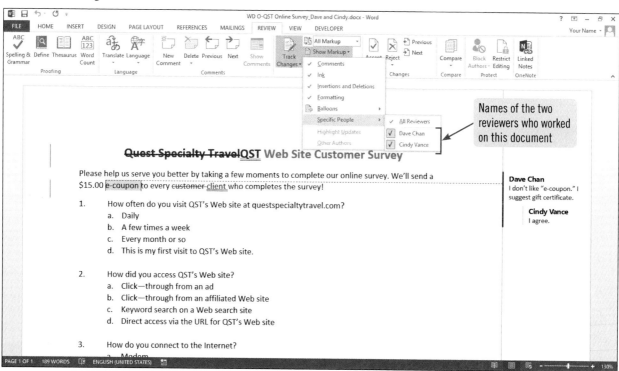

Compare Documents

Learning Outcomes
- Identify changes in compared documents

The Compare feature in Word allows you to compare two documents at one time so you can determine where changes have been made. Word shows the differences between the two documents as tracked changes. After identifying the documents you want to compare, you can choose to show the changes in the original document, in the revised document, or combined into one new document. **CASE** *Ron Dawson, your boss at QST, has reviewed the latest version of the QST Online Survey. You use the Compare feature to check the changes that Ron made against the WD O-QST Online Survey_Dave and Cindy document.*

STEPS

1. **Open the file** WD O-3.docx **from the drive and folder where you store your Data Files, type your name in the footer, then save it as** WD O-QST Online Survey_Ron

   Ron changed the value of the gift certificate from $15.00 to $25.00 before he turned on track changes. As a result, the change does not appear as a tracked change. After he turned on track changes, he added "within 30 days of receipt" to paragraph one and changed "Good" to "Very Good" in question 5b.

2. **Click the** FILE **tab, click** Close, **click the** REVIEW **tab, click the** Compare button **in the Compare group, then click** Compare

   The Compare Documents dialog box opens. In this dialog box, you specify which two documents you want to compare.

QUICK TIP
The Browse button looks like a file folder and is to the right of the filename text box.

3. **Click the** Browse button **in the Original document section, navigate to the location where you save the files for this unit, then double click** WD O-QST Online Survey_Dave and Cindy

4. **Click the** Browse button **in the Revised document section, then double-click** WD O-QST Online Survey_Ron

5. **Select the name in the Label changes with text box in the Revised document section, type** Ron Dawson, **then click** More, **if necessary, to show the options available for comparing documents**

   The edited Compare Documents dialog box is shown in **FIGURE O-13**. Check marks identify all the document settings that will be compared. If you do not want one of the settings to be included in the comparison, you can uncheck the check box next to that setting. By default, the changes are shown in a new document.

6. **Click** OK, **then click** Yes **to accept the warning**

   The new document that opens shows the differences between the two documents being compared as tracked changes, including the change Ron made to the price of the gift certificate price before he turned on tracked changes.

7. **Click the** Compare button **in the Compare group, point to** Show Source Documents **to see the options available for viewing compared documents, then click** Show Both **if it is not already selected**

   The Revisions pane opens and the two documents appear in a split screen, as shown in **FIGURE O-14**. The original document appears in the top pane to the right of the compared document and the revised document that incorporates Ron's changes appears in the lower pane.

8. **Click the** Close button ☒ **in the top right corner of the Original document to close it, close the Revised document, then close the Revisions pane**

   The revised document with tracked changes now fills the screen.

9. **Click the** Accept list arrow **in the Changes group, click** Accept All Changes, **then save the document as** WD O-QST Online Survey_Final

FIGURE O-13: Compare Documents dialog box

WD O-QST Online Survey_Dave and Cindy.docx

WD O-QST Online Survey_Ron.docx

Click to toggle between showing less options and more options

Insertions and deletions are compared by default and cannot be deselected

Changes in the document reviewed by Ron will be labeled with Ron Dawson's name

Document settings that can be compared or deselected and not compared

Where changes will appear

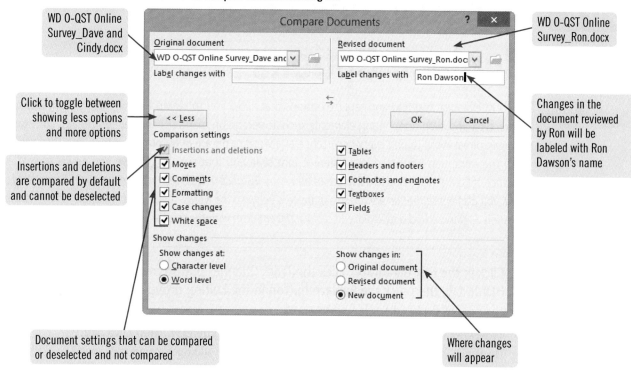

FIGURE O-14: Comparing documents

Original document

Revised document

All the changes Ron made, both tracked and untracked, are shown as tracked changes in the Compared Document

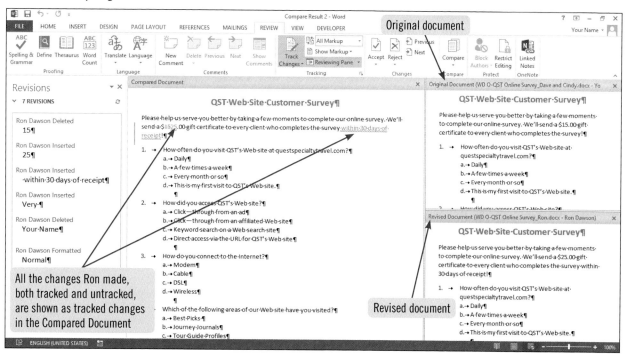

Use Advanced Find and Replace Options

Learning
Outcomes
• Find and replace
  formatting
• Find and replace
  special characters

Word offers advanced find and replace options that allow you to search for and replace formats, special characters, and even nonprinting elements such as paragraph marks (¶) and section breaks. For example, you can direct Word to find every occurrence of a word or phrase of unformatted text, and then replace it with the same text formatted in a different font style and font size. **CASE** *You decide to bold every instance of QST. You use Find and Replace to find every instance of QST, then replace it with QST formatted with bold. You also notice that an em dash (—) appears between the words "Click" and "through" in two entries in question 2. You use Find and Replace to replace the em dash with the smaller en dash (–).*

STEPS

1. **Click in the first paragraph, click the Track Changes button to deselect it, click the HOME tab, then click the Replace button in the Editing group**
   The Find and Replace dialog box opens.

2. **Type QST in the Find what text box, press [Tab], type QST, then click More**
   The Find and Replace dialog box expands, and a selection of additional commands appears.

3. **Click the Format button at the bottom of the Find and Replace dialog box, click Font to open the Replace Font dialog box, click Bold in the Font style list, then click OK**
   The format settings for the replacement text QST appear in the Find and Replace dialog box, as shown in FIGURE O-15.

4. **Click Find Next, move the dialog box as needed to see the selected text, click Replace All, click OK, click Close, then scroll up and click in the first paragraph to deselect the text**
   Every instance of QST is replaced with **QST**.

5. **Click the Replace button in the Editing group, press [Delete], click the Special button at the bottom of the dialog box, then click Em Dash**

6. **Press [Tab] to move to the Replace with text box, click Special, then click En Dash**
   Codes representing the em dash and en dash are entered in the Find what and Replace with text boxes on the Replace tab in the Find and Replace dialog box.

7. **Click the No Formatting button at the bottom of the Find and Replace dialog box**
   As shown in FIGURE O-16, the codes for special characters appear in the Find what and Replace with text boxes, and the formatting assigned to the text in the Replace with text box has been removed.

8. **Click Find Next, click Replace All, click Yes if prompted, click OK, then click Close**
   Two em dashes (—) are replaced with en dashes (–).

9. **Save the document**

FIGURE O-15: Find and Replace dialog box

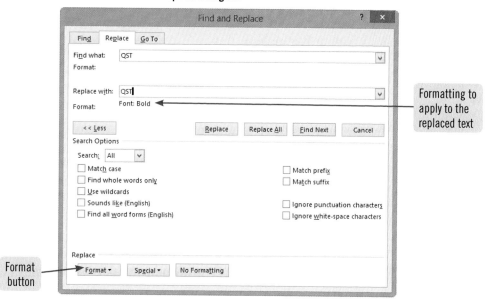

Formatting to apply to the replaced text

Format button

FIGURE O-16: Special characters entered

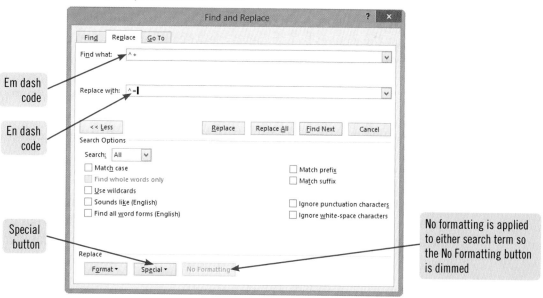

Em dash code

En dash code

Special button

No formatting is applied to either search term so the No Formatting button is dimmed

Word 2013

Sign a Document Digitally

Learning Outcomes
- Explore how to add a digital signature
- Restore track changes defaults

You can authenticate yourself as the author of a document by inserting a digital signature. A **digital signature** is an electronic stamp that you attach to a document to verify that the document is authentic and that the content of the document has not been changed or tampered with since it was digitally signed. When you insert a digital signature line into a Word document, you specify who can sign the document and include instructions for the signer. When the designated signer receives an electronic copy of the document, he or she sees the signature line and a notification that a signature is requested. The signer clicks the signature line to sign the document digitally, and then either types a signature, selects a digital image of his or her signature, or writes a signature on a touch screen such as those used with Tablet PCs. A document that has been digitally signed becomes read-only so that no one else can make changes to the content. **CASE** ▶ *You explore how to add a digital signature to the online survey.*

STEPS

1. Press [Ctrl][End] to move to the end of the document, select your name in the footer, then press [Delete]

2. Click the INSERT tab, then click Signature Line in the Text group

   The Signature Setup dialog box opens. You enter information about the person who can sign the document in this dialog box.

3. Type your name in the Suggested signer text box in the Signature Setup dialog box as shown in FIGURE O-17, then click OK

   A space for your signature appears in the footer at the position of the insertion point.

4. Double-click the signature line, read the message that appears, then click No

   If you click Yes, you are taken to a page on Microsoft's Web site that lists Microsoft partners that supply digital IDs. See the Clues for more information about acquiring a digital signature. Once you have obtained a Digital ID, you can enter it in the signature line. However, you will not be obtaining a Digital ID, so the signature line will remain blank.

5. Double-click in the document, click the REVIEW tab, click the launcher 🔲 in the Tracking group, click the Pictures by Comments check box to select it, then click Advanced Options

   As a courtesy to other users who might use the computer you are working on, you restore the default settings for track changes before saving and closing the document.

6. Return the options to the default settings: Underline for insertions and 3.7" for the balloon width, click OK, click Change User Name, then uncheck the Always use these values regardless of sign in to Office check box if you checked it in an earlier lesson

7. Click OK, then click OK

   The completed document appears as shown in FIGURE O-18.

8. Scroll to the bottom of the document and remove any extra blank lines so the document appears on one page, click the FILE tab, then click Close, submit a copy of the file and the other three files you created in this unit to your instructor, then exit Word

Acquiring a digital ID

You acquire a digital ID by purchasing one from a Microsoft partner. When you click Yes to acquire a digital ID, you are taken to a page of links of Microsoft partners. You can click on one of the links and purchase a digital ID. Other people can use this type of digital ID to verify that your digital signature is authentic. The Microsoft partner that issues the digital ID ensures the authenticity of the person or organization that acquires the digital ID.

FIGURE O-17: Signature Setup dialog box

FIGURE O-18: Final document with signature line

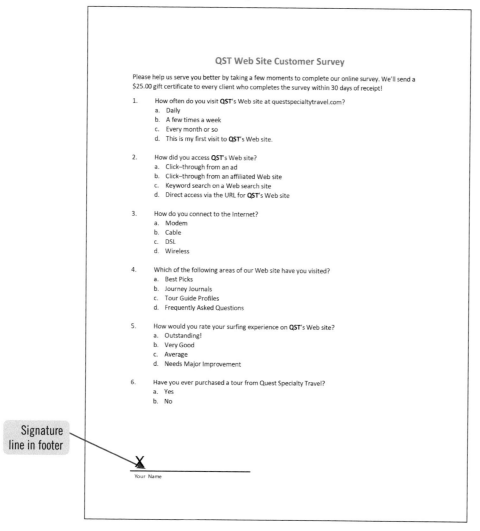

Practice

Put your skills into Practice with **SAM**! If you have a SAM account, go to www.cengage.com/sam2013 to access SAM assignments for this unit.

Concepts Review

Label each of the elements in FIGURE O-19.

FIGURE O-19

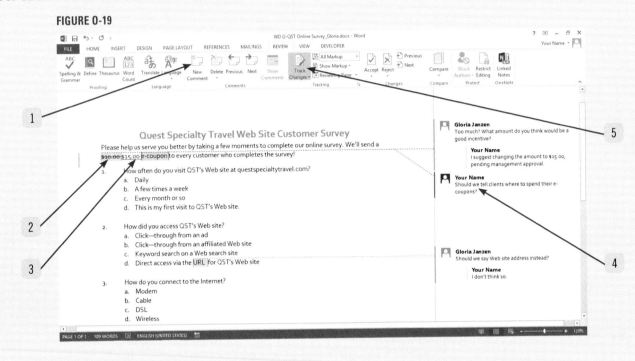

Match each term with the statement that best describes it.

6. **Balloon**
7. **Show All Revisions Inline**
8. **Next**
9. **Digital signature**
10. **More**
11. **Track Changes Options dialog box**

a. Use to move to another change
b. View that shows comments as shaded initials within a document
c. Contains a comment and appears in the right margin
d. Use to verify the identity of the person who created the document
e. Option to expand the Replace dialog box
f. Use to change the appearance of tracked changes

Select the best answer from the list of choices.

12. **How are comments that have been inserted by two or more individuals differentiated in a document?**
    a. The initials of the individual are inserted in the document next to the comment.
    b. The name and picture of the individual appears in the comment balloon.
    c. The comment balloon appears in a different location for each individual.
    d. The full name of the individual appears at the end of the comment text.

13. **What tab includes the options for collaborating on documents?**
    a. REFERENCES   c. DEVELOPER
    b. REVIEW   d. COLLABORATE

14. **By default, how is deleted text shown in All Markup view?**
    a. As strikethrough text that ~~looks like this~~
    b. As bold and colored text in the document
    c. As italic text in the document
    d. In a balloon along the right side of the document

15. **Which button do you click to create a new document out of two versions of an existing document?**
    a. Merge   c. Compare
    b. Show Source Documents   d. Browse

16. **By default, where do formatting changes appear in All Markup view?**
    a. Formatting changes are not shown in All Markup view   c. In a balloon along the right side of the document
    b. Within the text as shaded comments   d. In a balloon along the left side of the document

Skills Review

1. **Include comments in a Document.**
   a. Start Word, open the file WD O-4.docx from the drive and folder where you store your Data Files, then save it as **WD O-Designs Plus_Jorge**.
   b. Select the word **homeowners** in the first paragraph, then add a comment that contains the text **Let's include businesses as well.**
   c. Add a reply to Jorge's first comment (includes the text "I suggest we change…") that contains the text **How about we just say decorative items?**
   d. Add a reply to Jorge's second comment that begins "Should we mention…", that contains the text **I don't think so.**
   e. Click in the comment you inserted in Step b, and insert the word **local** before businesses.
   f. Delete Jorge's comment in the Expansion Plans section of the document, then save the document.

2. **Track changes.**
   a. Turn on Track Changes, delete the word "homeowners" in paragraph 1, then replace it with **homes and businesses**.
   b. Replace "objects d'art" in paragraph 1 with **decorative items**.
   c. Delete "-based" under "Company Background" so it reads: "home business" instead of "home-based business."
   d. Select the text from the Target Market heading to the end of the document, cut the text, then move it above the Expansion Plans section.
   e. Reduce the font size of the document title to 26 pt.
   f. Save the document.

3. **Work with tracked changes.**
   a. Open the Advanced Track Changes Options dialog box.
   b. Change the color of both the Moved from text and Moved to text from green to dark blue.
   c. Change the width of a balloon to 2.5", then close the Track Changes Options dialog box.

Skills Review (continued)

   d. Press [Ctrl][Home] to go to the top of the document, then use the buttons in the Changes group to accept or reject changes as follows:

- Reject the formatting change associated with the document title.
- Accept the deleted text ("homeowners") and the inserted text ("homes and businesses").
- Accept the deletion of "objects d'art" and the insertion of "decorative items."
- Reject the change to "home-based."
- Accept all the remaining changes in the document.

   e. Delete all the comments in the document.

   f. Turn off Track Changes, type your name in the document footer where indicated, then save and close the document.

4. Manage reviewers.

   a. Open the file WD O-5.docx from the drive and folder where you store your Data Files, then save the document as **WD O-Designs Plus_Will and Gail**.

   b. Show the document in No Markup view, scroll to view the document, return to All Markup view, change to Show All Revisions Inline, then mouse over an inline comment to view the comment in the document.

   c. Return to the Show Only Comments and Formatting in Balloons view.

   d. Show the list of specific people, then deselect Will Markham.

   e. Change the user name to your name and your initials if necessary. (*Hint*: Add a check mark to the Always use these values regardless of sign in to Office check box if you needed to do this step in the lessons.)

   f. Show the changes made by Will Markham.

   g. Move to the beginning of the document, use commands on the REVIEW tab to accept the addition of "and professional," delete the two comments in paragraph 1, then reject the change to "lifestyle."

   h. Accept all remaining changes in the document, then delete all comments in the document.

   i. Turn off track changes if it is active, save the document, then close the document.

5. Compare documents.

   a. Open the file WD O-6.docx from the drive and folder where you store your Data Files, then save it as **WD O-Designs Plus_Marta**. Note that Marta has made several changes, including changing the amount of the loan request in the Expansion Plans section from $50,000 to $80,000.

   b. Close the document but do not exit Word, open the Compare Documents dialog box, select WD O-Designs Plus_Will and Gail as the original document, then select WD O-Designs Plus_Marta as the revised document.

   c. Enter **Marta Owens** in the Label changes with text box in the Revised document area.

   d. Click OK to create the Compared Document, click Yes to accept tracked changes, then show both documents (Original and Revised) if they are not already open and close the Revisions pane if necessary.

   e. Scroll through, then close the original and revised documents.

   f. Accept all changes to the document, then save the document as **WD O-Designs Plus_Final**.

6. Use advanced find and replace options.

   a. Turn off Track Changes if it is still active, move to the top of the document, open the Find and Replace dialog box with the Replace tab active, then enter **Designs Plus** in the Find what text box.

   b. Type **Designs Plus** in the Replace with dialog box, then set the formatting as Bold Italic.

   c. Find and replace all instances of Designs Plus with ***Designs Plus***. (*Hint*: Expand the dialog box if necessary.)

   d. Move to the top of the document, replace the contents of the Find what text box with the symbol for an En dash. (*Hint*: Click Special, then click En dash.)

   e. Replace the contents in the Replace with text box with the symbol for the Em dash, then remove the formatting assigned to the text.

   f. Find and replace every En dash with an Em dash, close the Find and Replace dialog box, then save the document. (*Note*: You will make two replacements.)

Skills Review (continued)

7. Sign a document digitally.

a. Double-click in the document footer, then insert a signature line.

b. Type your name in the Signature Setup dialog box, then click OK.

c. Exit the footer area, then compare your document to the one shown in **FIGURE O-20**.

d Open the Advanced Track Changes Options dialog box, return the options to the default settings: Green for Moved text (two places), and 3.7" balloon width appearing in the right margin, and uncheck the Always use these values regardless of sign in to Office check box if you checked it in step 4e.

e. Close and save the document, submit the files you created in this Skills Review to your instructor, then exit Word.

Independent Challenge 1

You work for Digital Pal Solutions, a large application service provider based in Manchester, England. The company is sponsoring a conference called E-Business Solutions for local businesses interested in enhancing their online presence. Two of your coworkers have been working on a preliminary schedule for the conference. They ask for your input.

a. Start Word, open the file WD O-7.docx from the drive and folder where you store your Data Files, then save it as **WD O-Conference Schedule**.

b. Scroll through the document to read the comments and view the changes made by Patricia Jones and Jana McTavish.

c. Change the user name to your name and initials if necessary. (*Hint*: Add a check mark to the Always use these values regardless of sign in to Office check box if you checked this box when you completed the lessons.)

d. Change the color of inserted text to Violet.

e. In the 9:00 to 10:00 entry, select "E-Payment Systems: Future Trends," then insert a comment with the text **I suggest we change the name of this session to Micro Cash in the Second Decade.**

f. Be sure the Track Changes feature is active.

g. Starting with the first comment, make all the suggested changes, including the change you suggested in your comment. Be sure to capitalize "continental" in Continental Breakfast.

h. Accept all the changes, then delete all the comments in the document.

i. Turn off Track Changes, then find the two instances of Break and replace them with Break formatted with Bold. *Note*: Do not replace the "Break" in "Breakfast."

j. Restore the default setting for insertion to By author, and uncheck the Always use these values regardless of sign in to Office check box if you checked it in an earlier step.

k. Type your name where indicated in the document footer, save the document, submit a copy to your instructor, then close the document.

Independent Challenge 2

You work as an editor for Terry Marks, a freelance author currently writing a series of articles related to e-commerce. Terry sent you a draft of his Web Security Issues article that contains changes he has made and changes made by his colleague Parminder Singh. You need to review the changes made by Terry and Parminder and then prepare the final document. Terry has also asked you to use the Find and Replace feature to apply formatting to selected text included throughout the article.

a. Start Word, open the file WD O-8.docx from the drive and folder where you store your Data Files, then save it as **WD O-Web Security Issues Article**.

b. Turn on Track Changes, then scroll through the document to get a feeling for its contents. Notice there were two reviewers–Terry Marks and Parminder Singh.

c. Open the Reviewing pane. Notice there are 16 revisions, including one section break. Close the Revisions pane.

d. Change the user name to your name. (*Hint*: Add a check mark to the Always use these values regardless of sign in to Office check box if you needed to do this step in the lessons to display your name.)

e. Change the font color of the title to Dark Teal, Accent 1, Darker 50%.

f. Find and accept the first change that is not a comment or a section break–the addition of "Access Control."

g. Find, read, and then accept all the remaining changes.

h. Move back to the top of the document, move to the first comment, read it, then as requested in the comment, move the last sentence in paragraph 1 to the end of the article (following the Validity head and its paragraph), as its own paragraph.

i. Move to the comment about switching the Protection and Access Control sections, then perform the action requested.

j. Make the change requested in the Identification paragraph.

k. Delete all the comments from the document, accept all the changes, then turn off Track Changes.

l. Use the Find and Replace feature to find all instances of "Web" and replace it with "*Web*" formatted in Italic (eight replacements). (*Note*: Do not include the quotation marks.)

m. Use Find and Replace to find the section break (in the Special list) and replace it with nothing (one replacement).

n. In the footer, replace your name with a placeholder for a digital signature with your own name as the suggested signer.

o. Uncheck the Always use these values regardless of sign in to Office check box if you checked it in an earlier step, save the document, submit a copy to your instructor, then close it.

Independent Challenge 3

The Mountain Challenge School in Boulder, Colorado, offers courses in winter and summer mountain sports. Two colleagues, Jake Lee and Cecilia Ramirez, have each revised descriptions of the three summer courses. You use the Compare feature to review the changes and make some additional changes.

a. Start Word, open these files from the drive and folder where you store your Data Files, then save them as indicated: WD O-9.docx as **WD O-Summer Courses_Jake.docx**, and WD O-10.docx as **WD O-Summer Courses_Cecilia.docx**. Close both files.

b. Use the Compare feature to compare the WD O-Summer Courses_Jake (select as the Original document) and WD O-Summer Courses_Cecilia (select as the Revised document).

c. Show both documents used in the comparison to the right of the Compared Document and close the Revisions pane if it opened.

d. Show just the compared document.

e. Change the user name to your name. (*Hint*: Add a check mark to the Always use these values regardless of sign in to Office check box if you needed to do this step in the lessons.)

f. Turn on Track Changes, then make the following changes:

i. Replace "thrill" in the paragraph on Rock Climbing with an appropriate synonym. (*Hint*: Right-click "thrill," point to Synonyms, then select a synonym such as "excitement," or "delight.")

ii. Replace "expedition" in the Mountaineering paragraph with an appropriate synonym.

iii. Replace "proficient" in the Kayaking paragraph with an appropriate synonym.

Independent Challenge 3 (continued)

g. Accept all the changes and turn off Track Changes, then change the user name back to the default setting. (*Hint*: Uncheck the Always use these values regardless of sign in to Office check box if you checked it earlier in these steps.)

h. Save the document as **WD O-Summer Courses_Final.docx**, then submit a copy to your instructor and close the document.

Independent Challenge 4: Explore

From Word 2013 you can go directly to SkyDrive and work with a Word file using the Word Web App. The Word Web App does not include all of the features and functions included with the full Office version of its associated application. However, you can use the Word Web App from any computer that is connected to the Internet, even if Microsoft Word 2013 is not installed on that computer. You obtain a Microsoft account (if you do not already have one), upload a file from Word to SkyDrive, and then explore how you can work with the Word Web App to modify the file. (*Note: To complete these steps your computer must be connected to the Internet.*)

a. If you do not have a Microsoft account, Open your Web browser, and type **https://signup.live.com** in the Address bar, then press [Enter]. Follow the instructions to sign up for a Microsoft account using your e-mail address, then close your Web browser. If you do have a Microsoft account, use that account to complete the remaining steps.

b. Start Word, open the file WD O-11.docx from the drive and folder where you store your Data Files, then save it as **WD O-Work Plan**.

c. Click the FILE tab, click Save As, then click the link to your SkyDrive. (*Note*: This link is the first of the Save As options. When you are logged into your Microsoft account, the link will be called [Your Name's] SkyDrive (for example, Mary's SkyDrive).)

d. Click Browse to open the files and folders currently saved on your SkyDrive. If you have never used SkyDrive, you will not see any folders listed.

e. Click New folder on the Save As dialog box menu bar, type Word Unit O, press [Enter], click Open, then click Save. (*Note*: The WD O-Work Plan document is now saved into the Word Unit O folder on your own SkyDrive.)

f. Exit Word, open your Internet browser, type **www.skydrive.com** into the address box, then press [Enter]. The folders and files on your personal SkyDrive appear.

g. Double-click the Word Unit O folder, then double-click WD O-Work Plan to open the file in the Word Web App.

h. In the Word Web App, click EDIT DOCUMENT, then click Edit in Word Web App. (*Note*: Some of the formatting is removed when the document is opened in the Word Web App. You can perform limited editing functions in the Word Web App.)

i. Select "Marketing" in the heading and change it to **Work**, add your name in the subtitle, then change the deadline for the first task to **March 20**.

j. Click OPEN IN WORD to the right of the TABLE TOOLS LAYOUT tab, click Save, then click Yes in response to the message. (*Note*: The three changes you made in the Word Web App are retained. You are still working in SkyDrive.)

k. Use the FILE tab and the Save As command to download the file, click Allow if prompted, then click open in the message at the bottom of the window to open the file in Word when prompted. (The file opens in Protected View in Read Mode.)

m. Click Enable Editing, then save the document as **WD O-Work Plan Revised** to the location where you save files for this book.

n. Select the table in the WD O-Work Plan Revised file and apply a new table design of your choice, save the document, submit your file to your instructor, then close the document and exit the Web browser.

Visual Workshop

You work for a company called Natural Art that sells gardening supplies and plants. Your coworker has prepared a mission statement for the company, and she asks you to edit it. Open the file WD O-12.docx from the drive and folder where you store your Data Files, then save it as **WD O-Natural Art Mission Statement**. Turn on the Track Changes feature, then change the Track Changes Options to show your name as the user and insertions in red and double-underline. Make changes so that the edited mission statement appears as shown in FIGURE O-21. Turn off Track Changes, add a digital signature line containing your name, close the document, then submit a copy to your instructor. (Be sure to change the Track Changes Options back to the default: Underline insertions with the color set to By author and to uncheck the Always use these values regardless of sign in to Office check box if you checked it so your name would show in the comment balloons.)

FIGURE O-21

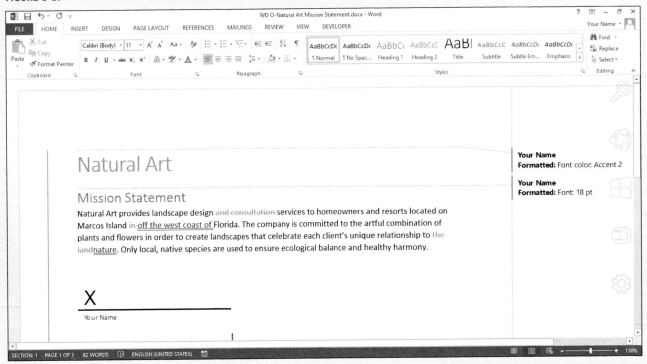

Customizing Word

CASE As a marketing assistant at QST San Diego, you need to create a booklet of excerpts from travel journals created by QST clients. All of the travel journals you have received are formatted differently. You create a macro to automate formatting tasks, add the macro and other buttons to a new tab for the Ribbon, modify default settings, and create keyboard shortcuts, then explore how to save a document in alternate file formats.

Unit Objectives

After completing this unit, you will be able to:

- Plan a macro
- Record macro steps
- Run a macro
- Edit a macro in Visual Basic

- Create a new tab
- Customize the Ribbon
- Modify Word options
- Save in alternate file formats

Files You Will Need

WD P-1.docx	WD P-7.docx
WD P-2.docx	WD P-8.docx
WD P-3.docx	WD P-9.docx
WD P-4.docx	WD P-10.docx
WD P-5.docx	WD P-11.docx
WD P-6.docx	

Plan a Macro

If you perform a task repeatedly in Microsoft Office Word, you can automate the task by using a macro. A **macro** is a series of Word commands and instructions that you group together as a single command to accomplish a task automatically. You create a macro when you want to perform multiple tasks quickly, usually in just one step, such as with the click of a button or the use of a shortcut key. **CASE** *You want to create a macro to consistently format each document that contains a travel journal, enter a title at the top of each document, and then save and close each document. You plan the steps you will perform to create the macro.*

DETAILS

- **Macro tasks**

  When planning a macro, the first step is to determine the tasks you want the macro to accomplish. For example, the macro could apply consistent formatting, insert a fill-in text field so users can enter text specific to each document, and then perform commands such as saving, printing, and closing the document. **TABLE P-1** lists all the tasks that you want your macro to perform.

QUICK TIP
You plan and practice the macro steps before you create a macro so that you can perform the steps without error when you create the macro.

- **Macro steps**

  TABLE P-1 also lists all the steps required to accomplish each task. If you make an error while recording the steps in the macro, you usually need to stop recording and start over because the recorded macro will include not only the correct steps but also the errors. By rehearsing the steps required before recording the macro, you ensure accuracy. While recording a macro, you can use the mouse to select options from drop-down lists and dialog boxes available via the Ribbon or you can use keystroke commands. For example, you could press [Ctrl][2] to turn on double spacing. When you are creating a macro it is also critical to know that you cannot use your mouse to select text. To select all the text in a document, you use the [Ctrl][A] or the Select button and the Select All command on the Select menu in the Editing group on the HOME tab. To select just a portion of text, first you use arrow keys to move the insertion point to the text, then you press the [F8] key to turn on select mode, and finally you use arrow keys to select the required text.

TROUBLE
If a debug warning appears, you need to click End and then record the macro steps again.

- **Macro Errors**

  As you work with macros, you discover which options you need to select from a dialog box and which options you can select from the Ribbon. When you select an option incorrectly, a "debug" warning appears when you run the macro (see **FIGURE P-1**). For example, the debug warning appears when you set line spacing by selecting 1.5 using the Line and Paragraph Spacing button in the Paragraph group on the HOME tab. To set the line spacing in a macro, you need to select 1.5 spacing either from the Paragraph dialog box, which you open using the launcher in the Paragraph group on the HOME tab or by pressing the keyboard shortcut for 1.5 spacing which is [Ctrl][5].

- **Macro information**

  Once you have practiced the steps required for the macro, you are ready to determine the information associated with the macro. You open the Record Macro dialog box and then you name the macro and enter a short description of the macro. This description is usually a summary of the tasks the macro will perform. You also use this dialog box to assign the location where the macro should be stored. The default location is in the Normal template so that the macro is accessible in all documents that use the Normal template.

- **Record macro procedure**

  When you click OK after completing the Record Macro dialog box, the Stop Recording button and the Pause Recording button appear in the Code group on the DEVELOPER tab as shown in **FIGURE P-2**. These buttons are toggle buttons. You click the Pause Recording button if, for example, you want to pause recording to perform steps not included in the macro. For example, you may need to pause to check information in another document or even attend to an e-mail. You click the Stop Recording button when you have completed all the steps required for the macro, or when you have made a mistake and want to start over.

FIGURE P-1: "Debug" warning that appears when the macro does not recognize a step

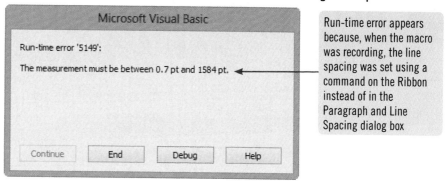

Run-time error appears because, when the macro was recording, the line spacing was set using a command on the Ribbon instead of in the Paragraph and Line Spacing dialog box

FIGURE P-2: Options available in the Code group when recording a macro

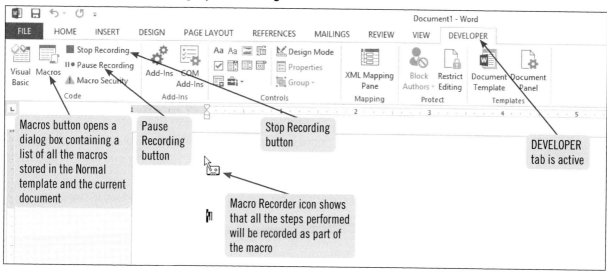

Macros button opens a dialog box containing a list of all the macros stored in the Normal template and the current document

Pause Recording button

Stop Recording button

DEVELOPER tab is active

Macro Recorder icon shows that all the steps performed will be recorded as part of the macro

TABLE P-1: Macro tasks and steps to complete the tasks

tasks	steps
Select all the text	Press [Ctrl][A]
Change the line spacing to 1.5	Press [Ctrl][5]
Select the Arial font	Click the Font list arrow in the Font group, then click Arial
Select 14 pt	Click the Font Size list arrow, then click 14
Insert a fill-in field text box	Press [↑] once to deselect the text and move to the top of the document, click the INSERT tab, click the Quick Parts button, click Field, scroll down the list of Field names, click Fill-in, click OK, then click OK
Add a blank line	Press [Enter]
Save the document	Click the Save button on the Quick Access toolbar
Close the document	Click the FILE tab, then click Close

© 2014 Cengage Learning

Record Macro Steps

Learning Outcomes
- Name a macro
- Record macro steps

Once you have created a macro and given it a name and a description, you need to record the macro steps. The macro recorder actually records each step you perform as a sequence of Visual Basic codes. When you record a macro, you can use the mouse to click commands and options, but you cannot use the mouse to select text. You can only use the keyboard to select text. For example, to select all the text in a document, you use the keystrokes [Ctrl][A]. **CASE** ▶ *Now that you have created the macro, you record the steps. You record the steps for the macro in a new blank document so that if you make errors, you do not affect the formatting of a completed document.*

STEPS

1. **Start a new blank document in Word, click the** FILE **tab, then click** Options, **click** Customize Ribbon, **click the** Developer check box **in the list of tabs on the right side of the Word Options dialog box if the box is not checked, then click** OK

2. **Click the** Show/Hide ¶ button ¶ **to turn on paragraph marks, then click the** DEVELOPER **tab**

   The Code group on the DEVELOPER tab contains the buttons you use to create and modify a macro.

3. **Save the blank document as** WD P-Journals_Macro Setup **to the location where you store your Data Files, press** [Enter] **three times, then click the** Record Macro button **in the Code group**

   The Record Macro dialog box opens. In this dialog box, you enter information about the macro, including the macro name, the location where you want to store the macro, and a description.

QUICK TIP

A macro name cannot contain spaces, so FormatJournals is acceptable, but Format Journals is not acceptable.

4. **Type** FormatJournals, **then press** [Tab] **three times to move to the Store macro in list box**

   You can store the macro in the Normal.dotm template so that it is available to all new documents or you can store the macro in the current document. Since you want the new macro to format several different documents, you accept the default storage location, which is the Normal.dotm template.

5. **Press** [Tab] **to move to the Description box, type the description shown in** FIGURE P-3, **then click** OK

   The Stop Recording and Pause Recording buttons become available in the Code group and the pointer changes to ⌨. This icon indicates that you are in record macro mode.

6. **Press** [Ctrl][A] **to select all the paragraph marks, press** [Ctrl][5] **to turn on 1.5 spacing, click the** HOME **tab, click the** Font list arrow, **scroll to and click** Arial, **click the** Font Size list arrow **in the Font group, then select** 14 pt

QUICK TIP

When you are recording a macro, you must use keystrokes to move around a document. You cannot use the mouse to position the insertion point.

7. **Press** [↑] **once to move to the top of the document, click the** INSERT **tab, click the** Quick Parts button **in the Text group, click** Field, **scroll down and select** Fill-in **from the list of Field names as shown in** FIGURE P-4, **then click** OK

   A fill-in field text box is inserted as shown in **FIGURE P-5**. When you run the macro, you will enter text in the fill-in field text box.

8. **Click** OK, **press** [Enter] **once, click the** Save button 🖫 **on the Quick Access toolbar, click the** FILE **tab, then click** Close

9. **Click the** DEVELOPER **tab, then click the** Stop Recording button **in the Code group**

   The WD P-Journals_Macro Setup file is saved and closed. The macro steps are completed, the Stop Recording button no longer appears in the Code group, and the Pause Recording button is dimmed. When you run the macro on a document that you open, the Save command saves the document with the filename already assigned to it. When you run the macro on a document that has not been saved, the Save command opens the Save As dialog box so that you can enter a filename in the File name text box and click Save.

FIGURE P-3: Record Macro dialog box

Macro name

You can assign a macro to a button or a keyboard shortcut before you record the macro or from the Word Options dialog box after you record the macro

By default, you store macros in the Normal template (Normal.dotm)

Macro description

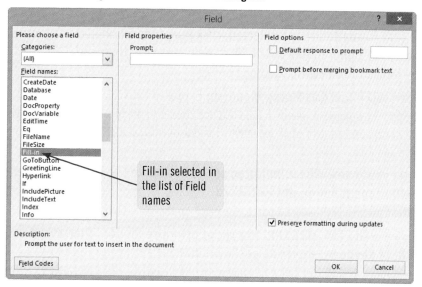

FIGURE P-4: Selecting the Fill-in field in the Field dialog box

Fill-in selected in the list of Field names

FIGURE P-5: Fill-in text box inserted

Fill-in text box

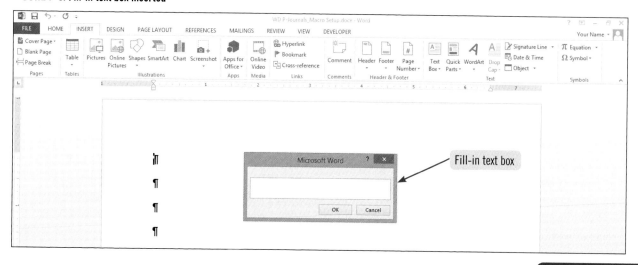

Word 2013

Run a Macro

Learning
Outcomes
• Run a macro
• Assign a keyboard
  shortcut to a
  macro

When you run a macro, the steps you recorded to create the macro are performed. You can choose to run a macro in three different ways. You can select the macro name in the Macros dialog box and click the Run button, you can click a button on the Quick Access toolbar if you have assigned a button to the macro, or you can press a keystroke combination if you have assigned shortcut keys to the macro. **CASE** *You open one of the journal documents you want to format and run the FormatJournals macro by selecting the macro name in the Macro dialog box and clicking Run. You then assign a keyboard shortcut to the macro.*

STEPS

1. **Open the file** WD P-1.docx **from the location where you store your Data Files, then save it as** WD P-Journals_Rocky Mountain Explorer Tour

   The file contains a journal entry made by a traveler who took QST's Rocky Mountain Explorer tour.

QUICK TIP
If others have created macros in the Normal template, you will see those marcos listed, too.

2. **Click the** DEVELOPER tab, **then click the** Macros button **in the Code group**

   The Macros dialog box opens. In this dialog box, you select a macro and then the action you want to perform, such as running, editing, or deleting the macro. The FormatJournals macro is listed. The name of the selected macro appears in the Macro name text box.

3. **Be sure** FormatJournals **is selected, click** Run, **type** Donna Long's Journal for Rocky Mountain Explorer Tour **in the fill-in field text box, then click** OK

   The document is formatted, saved, and closed.

4. **Open** WD P-Journals_Rocky Mountain Explorer Tour

   The text you entered in the fill-in field text box appears at the top of the page highlighted in gray. The gray will not appear in the printed document. The document text uses 1.5 spacing and the text is formatted in 14 pt and Arial.

QUICK TIP
Each time you are told to close a document in this unit, click the FILE tab, then click Close. Do not use the close button on the title bar.

5. **Enter your name where indicated at the bottom of the document, then save and close the document but do not exit Word**

   You can assign a keyboard shortcut to the macro in the Word Options dialog box.

6. **Click the** FILE tab, **click** Options, **click** Customize Ribbon, **then click** Customize **to the right of Keyboard shortcuts as shown in** FIGURE P-6

   The Customize Keyboard dialog box opens. In this dialog box, you can assign a keystroke combination to a macro or you can create a button for the macro and identify on which toolbar to place the button.

7. **Scroll to and click** Macros **in the list of Categories, then verify that** FormatJournals **is selected as shown in** FIGURE P-7

8. **Click in the** Press new shortcut key text box, **press** [Ctrl][J], **click** Assign, **click** Close, **then click** OK

9. **Open the file** WD P-2.docx **from the location where you store your Data Files, save it as** WD P-Journals_Japan Culture Tour, **press** [Ctrl][J], **type** Jim Grant's Journal for Japan Culture Tour **in the fill-in field text box, then click** OK

   The macro formats, saves, and closes the document.

Finding keyboard shortcuts

Word includes hundreds of keyboard shortcuts that you can use to streamline document formatting tasks and to help you work efficiently in Word. You access the list of Word's keyboard shortcuts from the Help menu. Click the Help button ? in the upper-right corner of the document window, type keyboard shortcuts, then press [Enter]. Click the link to Keyboard shortcuts for Microsoft Word. In the article that opens, all the keyboard shortcuts you can access in Word are described. You can also create your own keyboard shortcuts for procedures you use frequently. **TABLE P-2** shows some common keyboard shortcuts.

Customizing Word

FIGURE P-6: Word Options dialog box

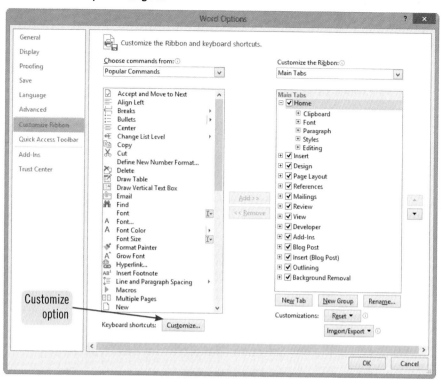

FIGURE P-7: Customize Keyboard dialog box

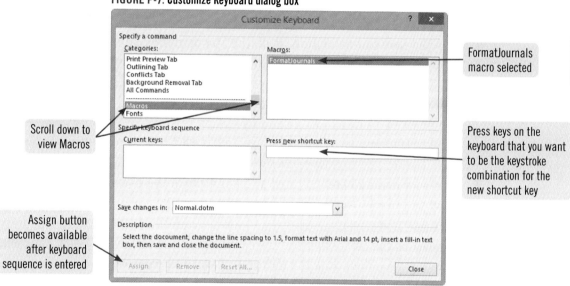

TABLE P-2: Some common keyboard shortcuts

function	keyboard shortcut	function	keyboard shortcut
Bold text	[Ctrl][B]	Print a document	[Ctrl][P]
Center text	[Ctrl][E]	Redo or repeat an action	[Ctrl][Y]
Copy text	[Ctrl][C]	Save a document	[Ctrl][S]
Cut text	[Ctrl][X]	Select all text	[Ctrl][A]
Open a document	[Ctrl][O]	Turn on double spacing	[Ctrl][2]
Paste text	[Ctrl][V]	Undo an action	[Ctrl][Z]

Customizing Word

Edit a Macro in Visual Basic

You can make changes to a macro in two ways. First, you can delete the macro and record the steps again, or second, you can edit the macro in the Microsoft Visual Basic window. You use the second method when the change you want to make to the macro is relatively minor—such as changing the font style or font size, or removing one of the commands. **CASE** ▸ *You decide to decrease the font size that the macro applies to text from 14 pt to 12 pt and then to remove the close document command.*

STEPS

1. **Click the DEVELOPER tab, then click the Macros button in the Code group**

   The Macros dialog box opens and the FormatJournals macro appears in the list of available macros.

2. **Verify that FormatJournals is selected, click Edit, then maximize the Microsoft Visual Basic window**

   The Microsoft Visual Basic window appears as shown in **FIGURE P-8**. The macro name and the description you entered when you created the macro appear in green text. A list of codes appears below the description. These codes were created as you recorded the steps for the FormatJournals macro. The text that appears to the left of the equal sign represents the code for a specific attribute, such as Selection.Font.Name or Selection. Font.Size. The text to the right of the equal sign represents the attribute setting, such as Arial or 14.

3. **Select 14 in the line Selection.Font.Size = 14, then type 12**

4. **Select ActiveDocument.Close, press [Delete], then press [Backspace] two times so the code appears as shown in FIGURE P-9**

   The font has been changed to 12 pt and the macro no longer includes the command to close the document.

5. **Click the Save Normal button 🖫 on the Standard toolbar in the Microsoft Visual Basic window, then click the Close button ☒ to close Microsoft Visual Basic**

6. **Open the file WD P-Journals_Japan Culture Tour.docx from the location where you store your Data Files, press [Ctrl][J] to run the macro, then click Cancel to close the fill-in field text box**

   The second time you run the macro you don't need to enter a title in the fill-in field text box. The font size of the document is now reduced to 12 pt and the document is saved.

7. **Type your name where indicated at the bottom of the document, then save and close it but do not exit Word**

8. **Click the DEVELOPER tab, click the Visual Basic button in the Code group, press [Ctrl][A] to select all the components of the FormatJounals macro in the Visual Basic window, press [Ctrl][C], then close the Microsoft Visual Basic window**

QUICK TIP
You save a copy of your macro code so you have a reference to verify the macro steps you performed.

9. **Press [Ctrl][N] to open a new blank Word document, press [Ctrl][V], press [Enter], type Created by followed by your name, save the document as WD P-Journals_Macro Codes, then close the document but do not exit Word**

Customizing Word

FIGURE P-8: Microsoft Visual Basic window

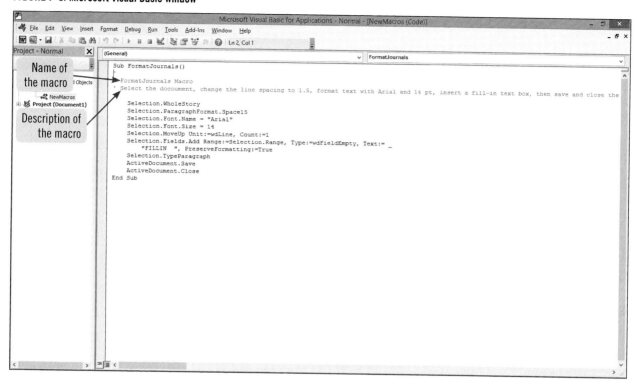

FIGURE P-9: Edited code in Visual Basic

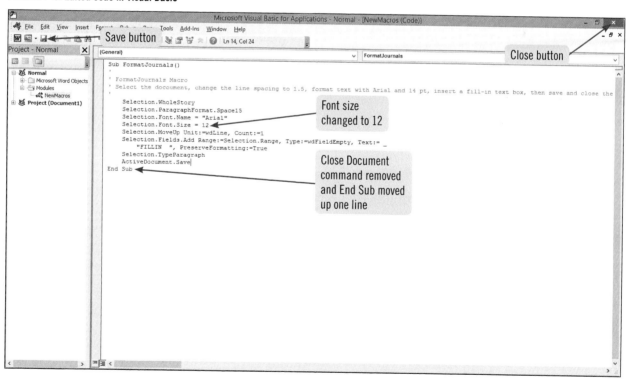

Word 2013

Create a New Tab

Learning Outcomes
- Create a custom tab
- Add groups and commands to a custom tab

You can create a new Ribbon tab that consists of groups containing only the commands you specify. You can also customize the Quick Access toolbar to include additional buttons that you use frequently. **CASE** ▸ *Over time, you will be formatting dozens of journals submitted by QST clients. The macro you created formats the text of the journal but now you also want to be able to perform other actions such as applying a consistent format to the document title, formatting a picture, and checking spelling and grammar. To save time, you create a new Ribbon tab that includes only the commands you need to format a journal entry.*

STEPS

1. **Click the FILE tab, click Options, then click Customize Ribbon**

   The Word Options dialog box opens with the Customize the Ribbon and keyboard shortcuts screen active. You use this screen to create a new tab and then to choose commands to place into groups on the new tab.

2. **Click the New Tab button under the Main Tabs list box, click New Tab (Custom) in the Main Tabs list, click the Rename button, type JOURNALS, then click OK**

   The new tab is called JOURNALS (Custom). You need to add groups to the tab to contain commands.

3. **Click New Group (Custom) under JOURNALS (Custom), click the Rename button, type Document in the Display name text box in the Rename dialog box, then click OK**

   Now that you have created a group for the JOURNALS tab, you can add commands to it. By default, the list of popular commands appears in the Choose commands from list box. You move commands from the list box on the left to the list box on the right of the Word Options dialog box.

4. **Click the Choose commands from list arrow, click Macros, click Normal.NewMacros. FormatJournals, then click Add**

   Normal.NewMacros.FormatJournals is the command to run the macro you created to format journal entries.

5. **Click Rename, type Format, click the icon shown in FIGURE P-10, then click OK**

   As shown in **FIGURE P-11**, you named the command to run the macro Format and you assigned an icon to the command, which will appear on the command button on the Ribbon.

6. **Click the Choose commands from list arrow, then click All Commands**

   The hundreds of commands you can use to develop and format documents in Word are listed in alphabetical order.

7. **Click JOURNALS (Custom) in the Main Tabs list box, click the New Group button, click the Rename button, type Text, click OK, then add the following commands to the Text group: Grow Font, Spelling & Grammar, and Text Effects**

8. **Click JOURNALS (Custom), create a new group called Graphics, add the Wrap Text button, then click OK**

   QUICK TIP
   This document contains several spelling and grammar errors. These errors are intentional and you'll fix them in a later lesson.

9. **Open the file WD P-3.docx from the location where you store your Data Files, save it as WD P-Journals_Pacific Odyssey Tour.docx, click the JOURNALS tab on the Ribbon, compare the JOURNALS tab to FIGURE P-12, then save the document**

Happy Face icon selected

FIGURE P-11: Group and command added to the JOURNALS custom tab

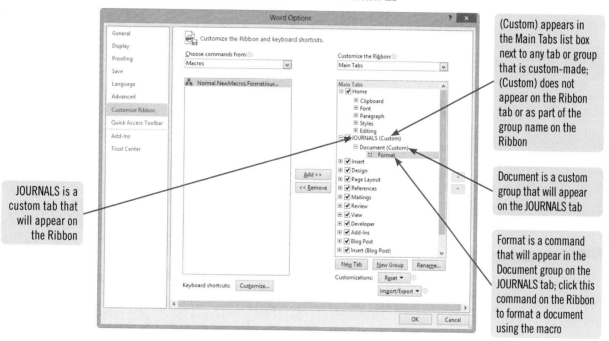

JOURNALS is a custom tab that will appear on the Ribbon

(Custom) appears in the Main Tabs list box next to any tab or group that is custom-made; (Custom) does not appear on the Ribbon tab or as part of the group name on the Ribbon

Document is a custom group that will appear on the JOURNALS tab

Format is a command that will appear in the Document group on the JOURNALS tab; click this command on the Ribbon to format a document using the macro

FIGURE P-12: Completed JOURNALS tab

Three groups and five commands on the new JOURNALS tab

Wrap Text command is dimmed when a picture is not selected

Customizing the Quick Access toolbar

To customize the Quick Access toolbar, click the FILE tab, click Options, then click Quick Access Toolbar. The three buttons included by default on the Quick Access toolbar appear in the list box on the right. These buttons are Save, Undo, and Redo. To add a new command to the Quick Access toolbar, select the command from the list box on the left, then click Add. To remove a button from the Quick Access toolbar, select the command in the list box, then click Remove.

Customize the Ribbon

Learning
Outcomes
• Browse commands
  associated
  with tabs
• Use buttons from
  a custom tab

While you cannot change the names of buttons or the icons associated with the buttons on the default Ribbon, you can change the name and icon associated with any button that you add to a custom group. You can also change the order in which buttons appear in a custom group, but you cannot change the order of buttons on the default Ribbon. **CASE** ▶ *Now that you have created the new JOURNALS tab and added commands to three new groups on this custom tab, you customize the commands on the JOURNALS tab and then use the buttons to format the document.*

STEPS

1. **Click the** FILE tab, **click** Options, **then click** Customize Ribbon

2. **Click the** Choose commands from list arrow, **then click** Tool Tabs
   The list of all the Tool tabs, such as the Drawing Tools tab and the SmartArt Tools tab, along with all the commands associated with each tab appears in the list box on the left. When you are not sure exactly what command you want to include on a custom Ribbon tab, you can browse the commands on the specific set of tabs that interests you.

3. **Click the** Format expand icon ⊞ **under Picture Tools, click the** Picture Styles expand icon ⊞, **then click the** Picture Effects expand icon ⊞
   All the commands associated with the Picture Effects command in the Picture Styles group on the Picture Tools tab are listed, as shown in **FIGURE P-13**.

4. **Click** Bevel **in the left list box, click** Graphics (Custom) **in the Main Tabs list box on the right, then click** Add
   The Graphics (Custom) group expands and you can see that the Bevel command has been added to the group.

5. **Click** Bevel **in the right list box, drag** Bevel **to move it above Wrap Text, click** OK **to exit the Word Options dialog box and return to the document, then click the picture**
   The revised JOURNALS tab appears as shown in **FIGURE P-14**.

6. **Click the** Format button **in the Document group, type** Dave Watson's Journal for Pacific Odyssey Tour, **then click** OK

7. **Scroll down, click the** picture, **click the** Bevel button, **select** Cool Slant **as shown in** FIGURE P-15, **click the** Wrap Text button, **click** Square, **then move the picture up so it top aligns with the paragraph and right aligns with the right margin**

8. **Select the document title, click the** Grow Font button **in the Text group two times, click the** Text Effects button **in the Text group, point to** Shadow, **then click** Offset Diagonal Bottom Left

9. **Deselect the document title, type your name where indicated at the end of the document, then save the document**

Customizing Word

FIGURE P-13: Commands associated with the Picture Effects command

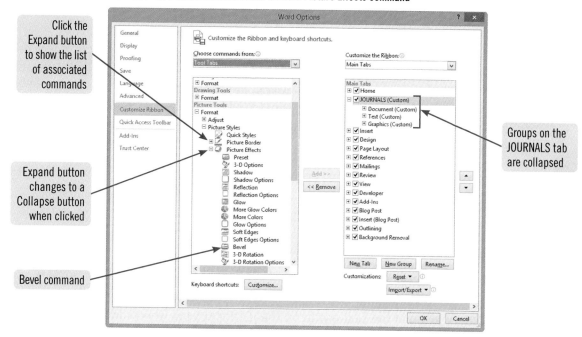

FIGURE P-14: Updated JOURNALS tab

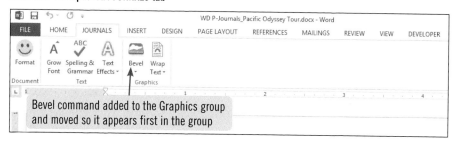

FIGURE P-15: Selecting the Cool Slant Bevel style

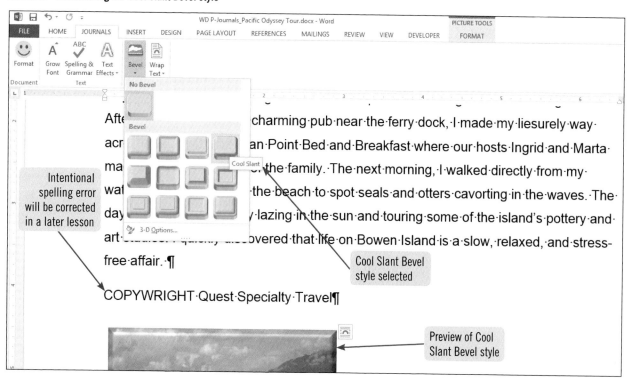

Modify Word Options

Learning Outcomes
• Modify Proofing options

Word includes many default settings designed to meet the needs of most users. You can modify default settings by selecting or deselecting options in the Word Options dialog box. **CASE** ▶ *After working with Word for several months, you have identified some default options that do not suit your working style. You work in the Word Options dialog box to modify a Spelling option, specify that the Show readability statistics dialog box appears each time you check the spelling, then set Word to check a document for both grammar and style errors.*

STEPS

1. **Click the** FILE **tab, then click** Options

   In addition to customizing the Ribbon and the Quick Access toolbar via the Word Options dialog box, you can access eight other categories that you can modify to meet your needs. **TABLE P-3** lists some of the other categories available via Options on the FILE tab.

2. **Click** Proofing**, then click the** Ignore words in UPPERCASE **check box to deselect it**

3. **Click the** Show readability statistics **check box to select it, click** OK**, click the** Spelling & Grammar **button in the Text group on the JOURNALS tab, then correct the four spelling errors**

   Notice that "COPYWRIGHT" is identified as a spelling error because you changed the option so that Word checks the spelling of words entered in uppercase. When the spell check is complete, the Readability Statistics dialog box opens.

QUICK TIP

If the number of characters in your dialog box differs from the number shown in the dialog box, it is because your name has a different number of characters than the text (Your Name) that it replaced.

4. **Compare your screen to the Readability Statistics dialog box shown in** FIGURE P-16

   In the Readability Statistics dialog box, Word displays the number of words in the document, the average number of words in each sentence, and the Flesch-Kincaid grade level.

5. **Click** OK**, click the** FILE **tab, click** Options**, click** Proofing**, click the** Writing Style list arrow **in the When correcting spelling and grammar in Word section of the dialog box, then click** Grammar & Style **if it is not already set to Grammar & Style**

6. **Click** Settings**, scroll down and view the default options that Word checks when Grammar & Style are selected, click the** Use of first person **check box to select it, click** OK**, click the** Recheck Document **button in the Word Options dialog box and click** Yes**, click** OK**, press** [Ctrl][Home] **to move to the top of the document, then click the** Spelling & Grammar **button**

   The first error identified is the use of the first person "I" in the first sentence. Since these are journal entries, you decide that you'd like to keep the first person after all.

7. **Click the** FILE **tab, click** Options**, click** Proofing**, click** Settings**, scroll to and click the** Use of first person **check box to deselect it, click** OK**, click** OK**, then click** Resume **in the Grammar pane**

   The next error is the use of "they're" instead of "their." The suggested correction does not work.

8. **Select** they're **in the document, type** their**, then click** Resume

   The next error is the use of passive voice.

9. **Select** The day was spent **in the document, type** I spent the day**, click** Resume**, click** OK **to close the Readability Statistics dialog box, then save the document**

FIGURE P-16: Readability Statistics dialog box

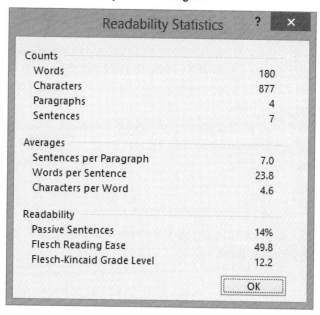

TABLE P-3: Some of the categories you can modify in the Word Options dialog box

category	options to change	category	options to change
General	• User Interface • Personalize • Start up	Language	• Editing languages • Display and Help languages • ScreenTip language
Display	• Page display • Formatting marks • Printing options	Advanced	• Editing options • Cut, copy, and paste • Image size and quality • Chart • Document content • Display • Print • Save • Fidelity • General • Layout • Compatibility
Proofing	• AutoCorrect • Spelling • Spelling and Grammar • Exceptions	Add-ins	• List of programs included with or added to Word
Save	• Save documents • Offline editing options • Fidelity for sharing	Trust Center	• Privacy • Security • Microsoft Word Trust Center

Creating and using custom dictionaries

You can use a custom dictionary to prevent Microsoft Word from flagging words that are spelled correctly but that do not appear in Word's main dictionary. For example, you can create a custom dictionary to contain terms you use frequently, such as medical terms, technical terms, or surnames. To create a new custom dictionary, click the FILE tab, click Options, click Proofing, click the Custom Dictionaries button, click New, type a name for the custom dictionary, save it, then click Edit Word List to add words to the new custom dictionary. If you do not want a custom dictionary to be activated for a particular document, you can remove the check mark that appears next to it in the Custom Dictionaries dialog box.

Save in Alternate File Formats

By default, Word saves all documents with the .docx extension. You also save a Word document in other formats such as PDF (covered in Unit K), Rich Text Format (RTF), and Plain Text (TXT). You use the **Rich Text Format (.rtf)** file type when you want to limit the file size of a document and you want to share it with people who may not have access to Word. An RTF file can be opened, viewed, and edited in virtually any word processing program. You save a document in the Plain Text (.txt) file type when you want to strip it of all formatting so only the text remains. **CASE** *You save the current document as a Rich Text Format file and then save another copy in the Plain Text format. Finally, you take a screenshot of the JOURNALS tab you created in this unit.*

STEPS

1. **Click the FILE tab, click** Save As, **click** Browse, **then browse to the location where you save your files for this book**

   The Save As dialog box opens.

2. **Click the** Save as type list arrow, **click** Rich Text Format (*.rtf), **click** Save, **then click** Continue

   The text effect you applied to the document title is removed in the .rtf file. However, the larger font size is retained. You can also use the Export command to change the file type of a document.

3. **Click the FILE tab, click** Export, **then click** Change File Type

   Options for changing file types appear as shown in **FIGURE P-17**.

4. **Click** Plain Text (*.txt), **click** Save As, **type** WD P-Journals_Plain Text Version, **click** Save, **click** OK, **click** FILE, **click** Close, **open** WD P-Journals_Plain Text Version.txt, **then click** OK

   All the formatting is stripped from the document and the picture is removed.

5. **Close the document, press** [Ctrl][N] **to start a new blank document, then click the JOURNALS tab**

6. **Press the Print Screen button on your computer keyboard, press** [Ctrl][V], **click the picture, click the** PICTURE TOOLS FORMAT tab, **click** Crop, **crop the screenshot and deselect the picture so that it appears similar to** FIGURE P-18, **click the** Picture Border list arrow **in the Picture Styles group, then click the black color box**

7. **Click the FILE tab, click** Options, **click** Customize Ribbon, **click** Reset, **click** Reset all customizations, **then click** Yes

8. **Click** Proofing, **then restore the default settings: select the** Ignore words in UPPERCASE check box, **deselect the** Show readability statistics check box, **select** Grammar Only **from the Writing Style list box, then click** OK

9. **Save the document as** WD P-Journals_Tab, **then close all documents and submit them to your instructor**

   You are returned to Word and both the DEVELOPER and the JOURNALS tabs are removed from the Ribbon.

FIGURE P-17: File type options in the Export dialog box

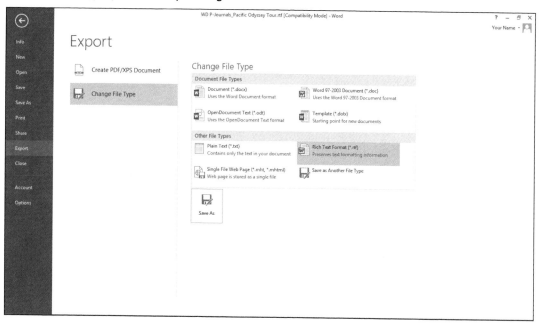

FIGURE P-18: Creating a print screen of the JOURNALS tab

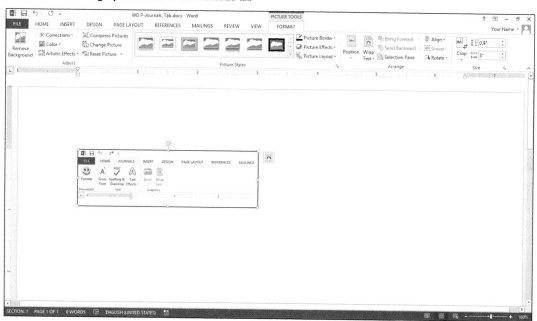

Maintain backward compatibility

When you open a Word document that was created in an earlier version of Microsoft Word, the document will always open in compatibility mode. You will see the words "Compatibility Mode" in brackets following the filename on the title bar as shown in **FIGURE P-19**. You can convert the document to Word 2013 by clicking the FILE tab, then clicking the Convert button on the Info screen. You can also choose not to convert the document to Word 2013 if you will be working on the file with users who have earlier versions of Word. With simple documents in particular, the changes between earlier versions and Word 2013 will not be noticeable.

FIGURE P-19: Title bar showing a file opened in Compatibility Mode

Practice

Concepts Review

Refer to FIGURE P-20 **to answer the following questions.**

FIGURE P-20

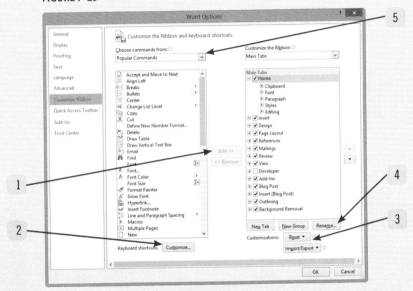

Which element do you click

a. to include a command on a Ribbon tab?

b. to show the list of command groups?

c. to rename a custom group?

d. to remove all customized tabs from your system?

e. when you want to create a shortcut such as [ALT][F]?

Match each term with the statement that best describes it.

6. Code group
7. Macros dialog box
8. Visual Basic
9. Customize
10. Word Options dialog box
11. RTF

a. Program where codes associated with macro steps are stored
b. Used to run macros
c. Contains the buttons used to stop and pause a macro
d. Button used to access the Customize Keyboard dialog box
e. File format that can be opened and edited in any word processing program
f. Contains categories such as General, Advanced, and Proofing

Select the best answer from the list of choices.

12. **What is a macro?**
    a. A small program, such as a dictionary, that you can download from the Internet
    b. Tasks that you cannot perform manually
    c. A series of Word commands and text selections made with a mouse that create buttons for a new group on the Ribbon
    d. A series of tasks that Word performs when you select Run from the Macros dialog box

13. **Which tab contains the Code group?**
    a. REFERENCES
    b. DEVELOPER
    c. VIEW
    d. REVIEW

Skills Review

1. Record macro steps.

a. Start Word, open the file WD P-4.docx from the location where you store your Data Files, then save it as **WD P-Press Release_Lake Towers Hotel**.

b. Show the DEVELOPER tab if it is not already displayed on the Ribbon and make it the active tab, open the Record Macro dialog box, then type **FormatPressRelease** as the macro name.

c. Enter the following description in the Description text box: **Select all the text, change the line spacing to single, enhance the title with Arial Black, 24 pt, then save the document**.

d. Exit the Record Macro dialog box.

e. Perform the macro steps as follows:

a. Press [Ctrl][A] to select all the text.

b. Press [Ctrl][1] to turn on single spacing.

c. Press [Ctrl][Home] to move to the top of the document.

d. Press [F8] to turn on text select mode.

e. Press [End] to select the title (Lake Towers Hotel).

f. Click the HOME tab, then select the Arial Black font.

g. Select the 24 pt font size.

h. Click the Save button.

f. From the DEVELOPER tab, stop the macro recording.

g. Type your name where indicated below the table, then save and close the document but do not exit Word.

2. Run a macro.

a. Open the file WD P-5.docx from the location where your Data Files are located, then save it as **WD P-Press Release_Saskatoon Classic Hotel**.

b. From the Macros dialog box, run the FormatPressRelease macro.

c. Open the Customize the Ribbon and keyboard shortcuts screen in the Word Options dialog box, click Customize, select Macros from the list of categories, then select the FormatPressRelease macro.

d. In the Press new shortcut key text box, assign the keystroke command **[Alt][H]** to the macro, click Assign, then close all open dialog boxes.

3. Edit a macro in Visual Basic.

a. Open the Macros dialog box, select the FormatPressRelease macro, then click Edit. Notice that two macros are listed—the FormatJournals macro you created in the lessons and the FormatPressRelease macro you just created. In the steps that follow, you make corrections to the FormatPressRelease macro.

b. Find Selection.Font.Name = "Arial Black", change the font to **Calibri** and keep the quotation marks around Calibri, then change Selection.Font.Size = 24 to **36**.

c. Save the macro, select all the components of the FormatPressRelease macro in the Visual Basic window, copy them, close the Visual Basic window, press [Ctrl][N] to open a new blank Word document, paste the code into the blank document, type **Created by** followed by your name below the last line, save the document as **WD P-Press Release_Codes** to the location where you store your files for this book, then close it.

d. Verify that WD P-Press Release_Saskatoon Classic Hotel is the active document, then use the [Alt][H] keystrokes to run the revised macro.

e. Verify that the font style of the document text is now Calibri and the font size of the title is 36 pt, type your name where indicated at the end of the document, then save and close the document but do not exit Word.

4. Create a new tab

a. Open the file WD P-6.docx from the location where your Data Files are located, then save it as **WD P-Press Release_John Cabot Hotel**.

b. Open the Customize the Ribbon and keyboard shortcuts screen in the Word Options dialog box.

c. Create a new tab called **HOTELS**.

d. Rename the new group on the HOTELS tab **Document**, then add the FormatPressRelease macro.

e. Change the name of the macro to **Format**, then select the checkmark symbol in the second to last row of the icons.

f. Add the Spelling & Grammar commands to the Document custom group.

g. Create a new group on the HOTELS tab called **Visuals**, then add the Shape Outline button.

h. Exit the Word Options dialog box, then save the document.

5. Customize the Ribbon

   a. Open the Customize the Ribbon and keyboard shortcuts screen in the Word Options dialog box.

   b. Show the list of Tool Tabs, expand the Drawing Tools Format, expand Shape Styles, expand Shape Outline (expand the first one if more than one is listed), add Weight to the Visuals group on the HOTELS tab, expand Shape Fill in the list of Tool Tabs, add Texture to the Visuals group, then move Texture so it appears above Weight.

   c. Change the name of the Visuals group to **Text Box** on the HOTELS tab.

   d. Click OK to accept the changes and close the Word Options dialog box, then display the HOTELS tab.

   e. Click the text box in the document (contains the text "We're thrilled..."), then compare your updated HOTELS tab to the one shown in **FIGURE P-21**.

FIGURE P-21

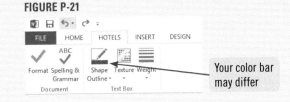

   f. Run the macro from the HOTELS toolbar, click the text box, use the buttons in the Text Box group to format the text box with a Gold, Accent 4, Darker 25% border line, the Parchment texture, and a 3 pt line weight.

   g. Save the document.

6. Modify Word options.

   a. From the Word Options dialog box, change the Proofing options as follows:

     • Check the spelling of words in UPPERCASE

     • Show the readability statistics

     • Select Grammar & Style in the Writing Style section, then in the Settings dialog box verify that the Passive sentences check box in the Style list is selected.

   b. Return to the document, use the Spelling & Grammar command on the HOTELS tab to correct all spelling errors and the passive sentences as follows: ignore the first two passive sentences ("No detail has been overlooked...is being described as..."), then correct the third passive sentence by changing "The hotel is owned by a consortium..." to "A consortium of businesspeople owns the hotel."

   c. Close the Grammar pane, then save the document.

7. Save in alternate file formats.

   a. Save the document in Rich Text Format.

   b. Use the Export option on the FILE tab to change the file type for the current document to Plain Text, then save and close the document but do not exit Word.

   c. Open the Plain Text version of the document, note that both the text box and all the formatting is removed, then save and close the document but do not exit Word.

   d. Start a new blank document, then use the Print Screen key on your keyboard to take a screenshot of your screen with the HOTELS tab active. Crop the screenshot so only the HOTELS tab is visible. Add a black Picture border around the image, then increase the size of the cropped screen so it is easy to read.

   e. Double-click below the screenshot and type **Created by** followed by your name.

   f. Save the document as **WD P-Press Release_Hotels Tab**.

   g. Reset all customizations, restore the default settings for Proofing: the Ignore words in UPPERCASE check box is selected, the Show readability statistics check box is deselected, and Grammar Only is listed as the Writing Style, save and close the document, submit your files to your instructor, then exit Word.

Independent Challenge 1

As the office manager of the Black Belt Academy, you prepare a gift certificate that you can e-mail to new members. You create a new Ribbon tab called ACADEMY that contains the commands you'll use most often to personalize each certificate and then you format a gift certificate and save it as an RTF document.

Independent Challenge 1 (continued)

a. Start Word, open a blank document, use the FILE tab to open the Word Options dialog box, view the Customize the Ribbon and keyboard shortcuts screen, create a new tab called **ACADEMY**, then change the name of the custom group to **Text**.

b. Add the following buttons to the Text group: Bold, Font Size, and Font Color. Move Font Color so the three buttons are in alphabetical order.

c. Create a new group on the ACADEMY tab called **Shapes**, then using the Choose commands from list arrow, show All Tabs.

d. From the Drawing Tools Format tab, expand all the categories and subcategories, then select and add the following buttons: Shapes, Change Shape, Shape Fill, and Weight. (*Hint*: Change Shape is a subcategory under Edit Shape.)

e. Put the four buttons into alphabetical order.

f. Close the Word Options dialog box, open the file WD P-7.docx, then save it as **WD P-Gift Certificate_ Gary Lee**.

g. Show the ACADEMY tab, click the hexagon shape, click the Change Shape button on the ACADEMY tab, then select the Explosion 2 shape in the Stars and Banners category.

h. Type **Gary** in the shape, press [Shift][Enter], type **Lee**, then select the text and use the buttons in the Text group on the ACADEMY tab to enhance the text with Bold, 14 pt, and the font color of your choice.

i. Use the Shape Fill button to select a light fill color of your choice.

j. Use the Shapes button to draw a straight line that starts to the right of "To:" and extends just to the left of the explosion shape.

k. Draw another line next to "Date:," then use the Weight button to change the width of the two lines to 1½.

l. Click next to "To:," type **Gary Lee, 300 East Street, Boulder, CO**, increase the font size to 14 pt, click next to "Date:," type the current date, then use your arrow keys as needed to move the lines under the text.

m. Type your name where indicated at the end of the document, then save the document.

n. Save the document again in Rich Text Format, then close it but do not exit Word.

o. Use [Ctrl][N] to start a new blank document, use the Print Screen command to insert a screenshot showing only the ACADEMY tab as the active tab, crop and format the screenshot with a black picture border, resize the image so the group names can be read, type **Created by** and your name below the cropped picture of the ACADEMY tab, save the document as **WD P-Gift Certificate_Academy Tab**, then close it.

p. Remove the ACADEMY tab from your system, then submit all documents to your instructor.

Independent Challenge 2

You work for Blossom Florists in Nashville. Recently, the company has moved to a new location. You create a macro that replaces the address and phone number of the old location with the correct contact information.

a. Start Word, open the file WD P-8.docx from the location where you store your Data Files, save it as **WD P-Catalog Request_McDonald**, then verify that the insertion point appears at the top of the document.

b. Show the DEVELOPER tab if it is not part of the Ribbon and make it the active tab, open the Record Macro dialog box, name the new macro **BlossomLetterhead**, then enter the following text in the Description text box: **Select the address, type a new address, change the zip code, then apply italic**.

c. Close the Record Macro dialog box.

d. Start recording the macro using the keystrokes listed below. If you make a mistake, you can either pause recording to correct the mistake, or you can stop recording and create the macro again.

- Press [↓] once to position the insertion point at the beginning of the address line.
- Press [F8] to turn on select mode, then press [→] repeatedly to select just 1801 Bower Avenue.

Independent Challenge 2 (continued)

- Press [Delete], then type **150 Cedar Street**.
- Press [→] to move just before the 0 in the ZIP Code, type **22**, then press [Delete] two times to delete 01.
- Press [Home] to move to the beginning of the line, press [F8], press [End], then press [↓] two times.
- Press [Ctrl][I] to turn on italic, press [→] once, then click the Stop Recording button in the Code group.

e. Enter your name in the closing where indicated, then save and close the document but do not exit Word.

f. Open the Macros dialog box, click BlossomLetterhead in the list of macros, click Edit to enter the Visual Basic window, then change the name of the macro from BlossomLetterhead to Letterhead (in two places).

g. Find the code Selection.Font.Italic = wdToggle, delete the line of code (*Note*: If you make a mistake, click Edit Undo), then delete the blank line and any extra spaces before the last line if necessary. (*Note*: The indented lines of code should left align.)

h. Save the revised macro, select all the components of the Letterhead macro in the Visual Basic window (from Sub Letterhead to End Sub), copy them, close the Visual Basic window, open a new blank Word document, paste the code, type **Created by** followed by your name at the bottom of the document, save the document as **WD P-Catalog Request_Codes**, then close the document but do not exit Word.

i. Open the file WD P-9.docx from the location where you store your Data Files, save it as **WD P-Catalog Request_Watson**, run the Letterhead macro, then press [→] to remove highlighting if necessary. Your letterhead should look similar to **FIGURE P-22**.

j. Type your name in the complimentary closing. (*Hint*: If the macro does not work (for example, if you receive a run-time error), click End, open the Macros dialog box, delete the Letterhead macro, then create it again.)

FIGURE P-22

k. Save and close the document, then submit all documents to your instructor.

Independent Challenge 3

You've just started working for Organics Forever, a company that delivers fresh organic fruits and vegetables to its customers in Seattle. The price lists distributed to customers are all contained within tables; however, the tables are not formatted very attractively. You decide to create a custom tab called ORGANICS that will contain all the commands you need to format the price list tables. The tab will also include commands for adding a theme.

a. Open the file WD P-10.docx from the location where you store your Data Files, then save it as **WD P-Price Lists_Produce**.

b. Create a new custom tab called **ORGANICS** that contains two groups: **Table** and **Document**.

c. In the list box on the left, show the commands associated with the Table Tools Design tab and expand all groups, then add the Borders command and the Shading command to the Table group.

d. Show the commands associated with the Table Tools Layout tab, expand all groups, then add the following commands to the Table group: Height, Align Center Left, and Sort.

e. Change the name of the Sort command to **Codes**, assign it an icon, then alphabetize the commands.

f. Change to show All Commands in the left list box, add the Themes command to the Document group, then return to the document.

g. Use the Themes command in the Document group on the ORGANICS tab to change the document theme to Quotable.

h. Select the table under the Fruit heading, then use the commands in the Table group on the ORGANICS tab as follows: sort all the entries in numerical order by code, set the row height to .4", apply the Red, Accent 6, Lighter 80% fill color to row 1.

i. Format the Vegetables table to match the Fruit table.

Independent Challenge 3 (continued)

j. Change the Proofing options so that Ignore words that contain numbers option is not selected, return to the document, then note in the document how all the codes have red wavy lines.

k. Restore the default setting for wording containing numbers (checked).

l. Create a new document containing a cropped and formatted screenshot of the ORGANICS tab, add the text **Created by** followed by your name under the graphic, then save the document as **WD P-Price Lists_ Organics Tab**.

m. Remove the ORGANICS tab, save and close all documents, then submit your documents to your instructor.

Independent Challenge 4: Explore

You can customize the Quick Access toolbar so that it includes buttons for additional commands. You create a macro, view it in Visual Basic, and then include a button to run the macro on the Quick Access toolbar.

a. Start Word, open a new blank document, then create a table consisting of 4 rows and 4 columns.

b. With the insertion point in the table, create a new macro called **FormatTable**.

c. For the description type **Select the table, change the row height to .3", change the cell alignment of each cell to center vertically, then change the fill to Green, Accent 6, Lighter 80%.** Do not close the Record Macro dialog box.

d. While still in the Record Macro dialog box, assign the macro to a button that will appear on the Quick Access toolbar as follows: click Button in the Record Macro dialog box to open the Word Options dialog box, click the name of the macro in the left pane, click Add, click Modify, give the button a default name of **Table** and assign the symbol of your choice, then click OK. (*Note*: If you closed the Record Macro dialog box in the previous step close the document without saving it and start again.)

e. Click OK to exit the Word Options dialog box and start the macro recording.

f. Perform the following steps to record the FormatTable macro:
- Click the TABLE TOOLS LAYOUT tab, click Select in the Table group, then click Select Table.
- Click Properties in the Table group, click the Row tab, click the Specify Height check box, select the contents of the Specify Height text box, then type **.3**.
- Click the Cell tab, click Center, then click OK.
- Click the TABLE TOOLS DESIGN tab, click the Shading list arrow, then click the Green, Accent 6, Lighter 80% color box.

g. Click the DEVELOPER tab and stop recording.

h. Create a new blank table under the existing table, then click the button you assigned to the Quick Access toolbar to run the macro to verify that it works. If the macro does not work (for example, if you receive a run-time error), click End, open the Macros dialog box, delete the FormatTable macro, then create it again.

i. View the macro in the Visual Basic window, select all the components of the FormatTable macro in the Visual Basic window, copy them, close the Visual Basic window, open a new blank Word document, paste the code, type Created by followed by your name at the bottom of the document, save the document as **WD P-FormatTable Codes** to the location where you store your files for this unit, then close the document.

j. Remove the button you assigned to the macro from the Quick Access toolbar.

k. Close the document without saving it, then submit a copy of the codes document to your instructor.

Visual Workshop

Open WD P-11.docx from the location where you store your Data Files, then save it as **WD P-Birthday Card**. Create a new tab called **CARD** that includes the buttons and groups shown in **FIGURE P-23**. (*Note*: Use the Center button in the Popular commands list.) Use the CARD tab to format the birthday card so that it appears as shown in **FIGURE P-24**. (*Notes*: Apply the Title style to "Happy Birthday," apply the Heading 1 style to "Continental Tours," center all the text and the graphic, then make other adjustments as needed so that your document matches **FIGURE P-24**.) Create a screenshot of the CARD tab, paste it in a new document, crop the image to show only the CARD tab and enlarge the cropped image so the text on the CARD tab can be read, then save the document as **WD P-Birthday Card Tab** to the location where you store your files for this book. Add your name to both documents, save the documents, submit them to your instructor, then close the documents. Remove the CARD tab from your system, then exit Word.

FIGURE P-23

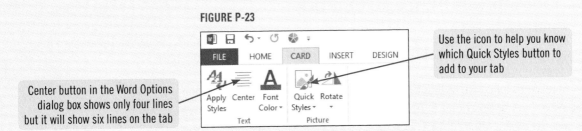

Center button in the Word Options dialog box shows only four lines but it will show six lines on the tab

Use the icon to help you know which Quick Styles button to add to your tab

FIGURE P-24

HAPPY BIRTHDAY

From all your friends at

Continental Tours
550 Skyline Avenue, Malibu, CA 90234
Phone: (310) 555-1000

Your Name

Automating Worksheet Tasks

CASE ▶ Kate Morgan, the North America regional vice president of sales at Quest, wants you to automate a task in the sales workbooks by creating a macro for the sales division. Kate sees this as a timesaver for the sales group. The macro will automatically insert text that identifies the worksheet as a sales division document.

Unit Objectives

After completing this unit, you will be able to:

- Plan a macro
- Enable a macro
- Record a macro
- Run a macro

- Edit a macro
- Assign keyboard shortcuts to macros
- Use the Personal Macro Workbook
- Assign a macro to a button

Files You Will Need

EX I-1.xlsx
EX I-2.xlsm
EX I-3.xlsx

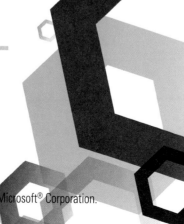

Plan a Macro

Learning
Outcomes
• Plan a macro
• Determine the
  storage location
  for a macro

A **macro** is a named set of instructions you can create that performs tasks automatically, in an order you specify. You create macros to automate Excel tasks that you perform frequently. For example, you can create a macro to enter and format text or to save and print a worksheet. To create a macro, you record the series of actions using the macro recorder built into Excel, or you write the instructions in a special programming language. Because the sequence of actions in a macro is important, you need to plan the macro carefully before you record it. **CASE** ▶ *Kate wants you to create a macro for the sales division that inserts the text "Quest Sales" in the upper-left corner of any worksheet. You work with her to plan the macro.*

DETAILS

To plan a macro, use the following guidelines:

• **Assign the macro a descriptive name**

  The first character of a macro name must be a letter; the remaining characters can be letters, numbers, or underscores. Letters can be uppercase or lowercase. Spaces are not allowed in macro names; use underscores in place of spaces. Press [Shift][-] to enter an underscore character. Kate wants you to name the macro "DivStamp". See **TABLE I-1** for a list of macros that could be created to automate other tasks at Quest.

• **Write out the steps the macro will perform**

  This planning helps eliminate careless errors. Kate writes a description of the macro she wants, as shown in **FIGURE I-1**.

• **Decide how you will perform the actions you want to record**

  You can use the mouse, the keyboard, or a combination of the two. Kate wants you to use both the mouse and the keyboard.

• **Practice the steps you want Excel to record, and write them down**

  Kate has written down the sequence of actions she wants you to include in the macro.

• **Decide where to store the description of the macro and the macro itself**

  Macros can be stored in an active workbook, in a new workbook, or in the **Personal Macro Workbook**, a special workbook used only for macro storage. Kate asks you to store the macro in a new workbook.

FIGURE I-1: Handwritten description of planned macro

Macro to create stamp with the division name

Name: DivStamp

Description: Adds a stamp to the top left of the worksheet, identifying it as a
               Quest sales worksheet

Steps: 1. Position the cell pointer in cell A1.
               2. Type Quest Sales, then click the Enter button.
               3. Click the Format button, then click Cells.
               4. Click the Font tab, under Font style, click Bold; under Underline, click
                  Single; under Color, click Blue; then click OK.

TABLE I-1: Possible macros and their descriptive names

description of macro	descriptive name for macro
Enter a frequently used proper name, such as "Kate Morgan"	KateMorgan
Enter a frequently used company name, such as Quest	Company_Name
Print the active worksheet on a single page, in landscape orientation	FitToLand
Add a footer to a worksheet	FooterStamp
Add totals to a worksheet	AddTotals

Enable a Macro

Learning Outcomes
- Create a macro-enabled workbook
- Enable macros by changing a workbook's security level

Because a macro may contain a **virus**—destructive software that can damage your computer files—the default security setting in Excel disables macros from running. Although a workbook containing a macro will open, if macros are disabled, they will not function. You can manually change the Excel security setting to allow macros to run if you know a macro came from a trusted source. When saving a workbook with a macro, you need to save it as a macro-enabled workbook with the extension .xlsm. **CASE** *Kate asks you to change the security level to enable all macros. You will change the security level back to the default setting after you create and run your macros.*

STEPS

QUICK TIP
If the DEVELOPER tab is displayed on your Ribbon, skip steps 2 and 3.

1. **Start Excel, open a blank workbook, click the** Save button 🖫 **on the Quick Access toolbar, navigate to the location where you store your Data Files, in the Save As dialog box click the** Save as type list arrow, **click** Excel Macro-Enabled Workbook (*.xlsm), **in the File name text box type** EX I-Macro Workbook, **then click** Save

   The security settings that enable macros are available on the DEVELOPER tab. The DEVELOPER tab does not appear by default, but you can display it by customizing the Ribbon.

2. **Click the** FILE tab, **click** Options, **then click** Customize Ribbon **in the category list**

   The Customize the Ribbon options open in the Excel Options dialog box, as shown in **FIGURE I-2**.

3. **Click the** Developer check box, **if necessary, in the Main Tabs area on the right side of the screen to select it, then click** OK

   The DEVELOPER tab appears on the Ribbon. You are ready to change the security settings.

4. **Click the** DEVELOPER tab, **then click the** Macro Security button **in the Code group**

   The Trust Center dialog box opens.

5. **Click** Macro Settings **if necessary, click the** Enable all macros (not recommended; potentially dangerous code can run) option button **to select it as shown in FIGURE I-3, then click** OK

   The dialog box closes. Macros remain enabled until you disable them by deselecting the Enable all macros option. As you work with Excel, you should disable macros when you are not working with them.

FIGURE I-2: Excel Options dialog box

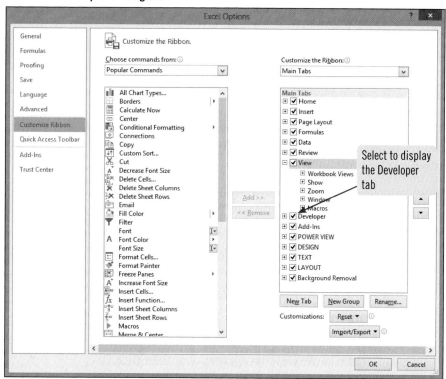

FIGURE I-3: Trust Center dialog box

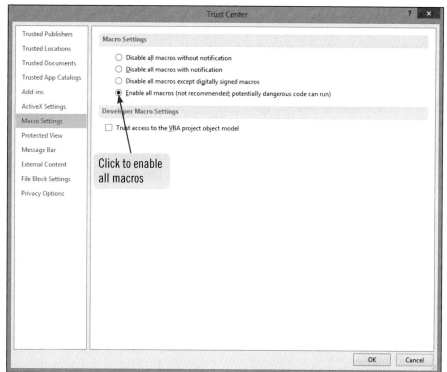

Disabling macros

To prevent viruses from running on your computer, you should disable all macros when you are not working with them. To disable macros, click the DEVELOPER tab, then click the Macro Security button in the Code group. Clicking any of the first three options disables macros. The first option disables all macros without notifying you. The second option notifies you when macros are disabled, and the third option allows only digitally signed macros to run.

Record a Macro

Learning Outcomes
• Choose a macro storage location
• Create a macro by recording steps

The easiest way to create a macro is to record it using the Excel Macro Recorder. You turn the Macro Recorder on, name the macro, enter the keystrokes and select the commands you want the macro to perform, then stop the recorder. As you record the macro, Excel automatically translates each action into program code that you can later view and modify. You can take as long as you want to record the macro; a recorded macro contains only your actions, not the amount of time you took to record it. **CASE** *Kate wants you to create a macro that enters a division "stamp" in cell A1 of the active worksheet. You create this macro by recording your actions.*

STEPS

1. **Click the Record Macro button 🖳 on the left side of the status bar**

   The Record Macro dialog box opens, as shown in **FIGURE I-4**. The default name Macro1 is selected. You can either assign this name or enter a new name. This dialog box also lets you assign a shortcut key for running the macro and assign a storage location for the macro.

2. **Type DivStamp in the Macro name text box**

3. **If the Store macro in list box does not display "This Workbook", click the list arrow and select This Workbook**

4. **Type your name in the Description text box, then click OK**

   The dialog box closes, and the Record Macro button on the status bar is replaced with a Stop Recording button 🔲. Take your time performing the steps below. Excel records every keystroke, menu selection, and mouse action that you make.

5. **Press [Ctrl][Home]**

   When you begin an Excel session, macros record absolute cell references. By beginning the recording with a command to move to cell A1, you ensure that the macro includes the instruction to select cell A1 as the first step, in cases where A1 is not already selected.

6. **Type Quest Sales in cell A1, then click the Enter button ✓ on the formula bar**

7. **Click the HOME tab, click the Format button in the Cells group, then click Format Cells**

8. **Click the Font tab, in the Font style list box click Bold, click the Underline list arrow and click Single, click the Color list arrow and click the Blue color in the Standard Colors row, then compare your dialog box to FIGURE I-5**

9. **Click OK, click the Stop Recording button 🔲 on the left side of the status bar, click cell D1 to deselect cell A1, then save the workbook**

   FIGURE I-6 shows the result of recording the macro.

FIGURE I-4: Record Macro dialog box

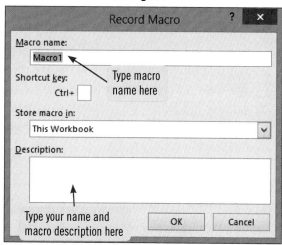

FIGURE I-5: Font tab of the Format Cells dialog box

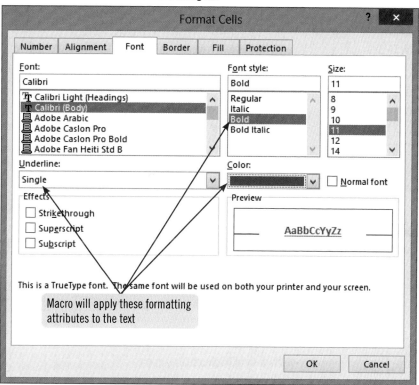

FIGURE I-6: Sales Division stamp

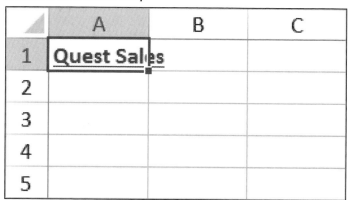

Run a Macro

Learning Outcomes
• Display selected macros
• Run a macro using the Macro dialog box

Once you record a macro, you should test it to make sure that the actions it performs are correct. To test a macro, you **run** (play) it. You can run a macro using the Macros button in the Code group of the DEVELOPER tab. **CASE** *Kate asks you to clear the contents of cell A1, and then test the DivStamp macro. After you run the macro in the Macro workbook, she asks you to test the macro once more from a newly opened workbook.*

STEPS

1. **Click cell A1, click the HOME tab if necessary, click the Clear button** ✐ **in the Editing group, click Clear All, then click any other cell to deselect cell A1**

   When you delete only the contents of a cell, any formatting still remains in the cell. By using the Clear All option you can be sure that the cell is free of contents and formatting.

2. **Click the DEVELOPER tab, click the Macros button in the Code group, click the Macros in list arrow, then click This Workbook**

   The Macro dialog box, shown in **FIGURE I-7**, lists all the macros contained in the workbook.

3. **Click DivStamp in the Macro name list if necessary, as you watch cell A1 click Run, then deselect cell A1**

   The macro quickly plays back the steps you recorded in the previous lesson. When the macro is finished, your screen should look like **FIGURE I-8**. As long as the workbook containing the macro remains open, you can run the macro in any open workbook.

4. **Click the FILE tab, click New, then click Blank workbook**

   Because the EX I-Macro Workbook.xlsm is still open, you can use its macros.

QUICK TIP

To create a custom button on the Quick Access toolbar that will run a macro, right-click the Ribbon, click Customize Quick Access Toolbar, click the Choose commands from list arrow, select Macros, select the macro to assign to a custom button in the macro list on the left, click Add to move the macro to the list of buttons on the Quick Access Toolbar, then click OK.

5. **Deselect cell A1, click the DEVELOPER tab, click the Macros button in the Code group, click the Macros in list arrow, then click All Open Workbooks, click 'EX I-Macro Workbook. xlsm'!DivStamp, click Run, then deselect cell A1**

   When multiple workbooks are open, the macro name in the Macro dialog box includes the workbook name between single quotation marks, followed by an exclamation point which is an **external reference indicator**, indicating that the macro is outside the active workbook. Because you only used this workbook to test the macro, you don't need to save it.

6. **Close Book2 without saving changes**

   The EX I-Macro Workbook.xlsm workbook remains open.

Automating Worksheet Tasks

FIGURE I-7: Macro dialog box

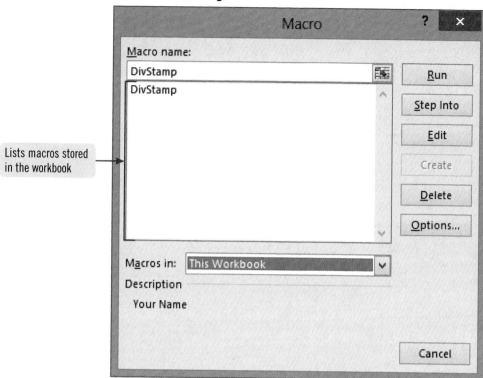

Lists macros stored in the workbook

FIGURE I-8: Result of running DivStamp macro

	A	B	C
1	Quest Sales	Formatted text inserted into cell A1	
2			
3			

Running a macro automatically

You can create a macro that automatically performs certain tasks when the workbook in which it is saved is opened. This is useful for actions you want to do every time you open a workbook. For example, you may import data from an external data source into the workbook or format the worksheet data in a certain way. To create a macro that will automatically run when the workbook is opened, you need to name the macro Auto_Open and save it in that workbook.

Edit a Macro

When you use the Macro Recorder to create a macro, the program instructions, called **program code**, are recorded automatically in the **Visual Basic for Applications (VBA)** programming language. Each macro is stored as a **module**, or program code container, attached to the workbook. After you record a macro, you might need to change it. If you have a lot of changes to make, it might be best to record the macro again. But if you need to make only minor adjustments, you can edit the macro code directly using the **Visual Basic Editor**, a program that lets you display and edit your macro code. **CASE** Kate wants you to modify the DivStamp macro to change the point size of the department stamp to 12.

STEPS

1. **Make sure the EX I-Macro Workbook.xlsm workbook is open, click the Macros button in the Code group, make sure DivStamp is selected, click Edit, then maximize the Code window, if necessary**

   The Visual Basic Editor starts, showing three windows: the Project Explorer window, the Properties window, and the Code window, as shown in FIGURE I-9.

2. **Click Module 1 in the Project Explorer window if it's not already selected, then examine the steps in the macro, comparing your screen to FIGURE I-9**

   The name of the macro and your name appear at the top of the Code window. Below this area, Excel has translated your keystrokes and commands into macro code. When you open and make selections in a dialog box during macro recording, Excel automatically stores all the dialog box settings in the macro code. For example, the line .FontStyle = "Bold" was generated when you clicked Bold in the Format Cells dialog box. You also see lines of code that you didn't generate directly while recording the DivStamp macro, for example, .Name = "Calibri".

3. **In the line .Size = 11, double-click 11 to select it, then type 12**

   Because Module1 is attached to the workbook and not stored as a separate file, any changes to the module are saved automatically when you save the workbook.

4. **Review the code in the Code window**

5. **Click File on the menu bar, then click Close and Return to Microsoft Excel**

   You want to rerun the DivStamp macro to make sure the macro reflects the change you made using the Visual Basic Editor. You begin by clearing the division name from cell A1.

6. **Click cell A1, click the HOME tab, click the Clear button 🖋 in the Editing group, then click Clear All**

7. **Click any other cell to deselect cell A1, click the DEVELOPER tab, click the Macros button in the Code group, make sure DivStamp is selected, click Run, then deselect cell A1**

   The department stamp is now in 12-point type, as shown in FIGURE I-10.

8. **Save the workbook**

FIGURE I-9: Visual Basic Editor showing Module1

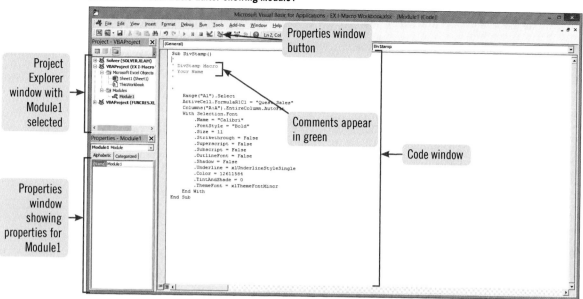

FIGURE I-10: Result of running edited DivStamp macro

	A	B	C
1	**Quest Sales**		
2			
3			
4			

Font size is enlarged to 12-point

Adding comments to Visual Basic code

With practice, you will be able to interpret the lines of macro code. Others who use your macro, however, might want to review the code to, for example, learn the function of a particular line. You can explain the code by adding comments to the macro. **Comments** are explanatory text added to the lines of code. When you enter a comment, you must type an apostrophe (') before the comment text. Otherwise, the program tries to interpret it as a command. On the screen, comments appear in green after you press [Enter], as shown in **FIGURE I-9**. You can also insert blank lines as comments in the macro code to make the code more readable. To do this, type an apostrophe, then press [Enter].

Assign Keyboard Shortcuts to Macros

For macros that you run frequently, you can run them by using shortcut key combinations instead of the Macro dialog box. You can assign a shortcut key combination to any macro. Using shortcut keys saves you time by reducing the number of actions you need to take to run a macro. You assign shortcut key combinations in the Record Macro dialog box. **CASE** ▶ *Kate also wants you to create a macro called Region to enter the company region into a worksheet. You assign a shortcut key combination to run the macro.*

STEPS

1. **Click cell B2**

   You want to record the macro in cell B2, but you want the macro to enter the region of North America anywhere in a worksheet. Therefore, you do not begin the macro with an instruction to position the cell pointer, as you did in the DivStamp macro.

2. **Click the Record Macro button 🖦 on the status bar**

   The Record Macro dialog box opens. Notice the option Shortcut key: Ctrl+ followed by a blank box. You can type a letter (A–Z) in the Shortcut key text box to assign the key combination of [Ctrl] plus that letter to run the macro. Because some common Excel shortcuts use the [Ctrl][*letter*] combination, such as [Ctrl][C] for Copy, you decide to use the key combination [Ctrl][Shift] plus a letter to avoid overriding any of these shortcut key combinations.

3. **With the default macro name selected, type Region in the Macro name text box, click the Shortcut key text box, press and hold [Shift], type C, then in the Description box type your name**

   You have assigned the shortcut key combination [Ctrl][Shift][C] to the Region macro. After you create the macro, you will use this shortcut key combination to run it. Compare your screen with **FIGURE I-11**. You are ready to record the Region macro.

4. **Click OK to close the dialog box**

5. **Type North America in cell B2, click the Enter button ✓ on the formula bar, press [Ctrl][I] to italicize the text, click the Stop Recording button ☐ on the status bar, then deselect cell B2**

   North America appears in italics in cell B2. You are ready to run the macro in cell A5 using the shortcut key combination.

6. **Click cell A5, press and hold [Ctrl][Shift], type C, then deselect the cell**

   The region appears in cell A5, as shown in **FIGURE I-12**. The macro played back in the selected cell (A5) instead of the cell where it was recorded (B2) because you did not begin recording the macro by clicking cell B2.

FIGURE I-11: Record Macro dialog box with shortcut key assigned

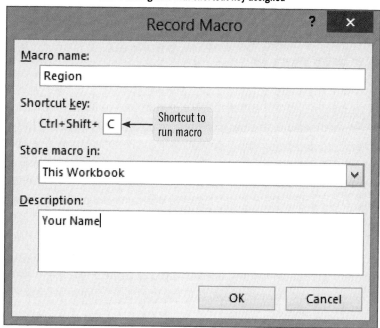

FIGURE I-12: Result of running the Region macro

◢	A	B	C	D	E	F	G
1	**Quest Sales**						
2		*North America* ←		Result of recording macro in cell B2			
3							
4							
5	*North America* ←		Result of running macro in cell A5				
6							
7							

Using relative referencing when creating a macro

By default, Excel records absolute cell references in macros. You can record a macro's actions based on the relative position of the active cell by clicking the Use Relative References button in the Code group prior to recording the action. For example, when you create a macro using the default setting of absolute referencing, bolding the range A1:D1 will always bold that range when the macro is run. However, if you click the Use Relative References button when recording the macro before bolding the range, then running the macro will not necessarily result in bolding the range A1:D1. The range that will be bolded will depend on the location of the active cell when the macro is run. If the active cell is A4, then the range A4:D4 will be bolded. Selecting the Use Relative

References button highlights the button name, indicating it is active, as shown in **FIGURE I-13**. The button remains active until you click it again to deselect it. This is called a toggle, meaning that it acts like an off/on switch: it retains the relative reference setting until you click it again to turn it off or you exit Excel.

FIGURE I-13: Use Relative References button selected

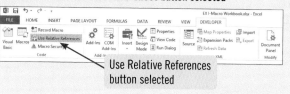

Use Relative References button selected

Use the Personal Macro Workbook

Learning Outcomes
• Determine when when to use the Personal Macro Workbook
• Save a macro in the Personal Macro Workbook

When you create a macro, it is automatically stored in the workbook in which you created it. But if you wanted to use that macro in another workbook, you would have to copy the macro to that workbook. Instead, it's easier to store commonly used macros in the Personal Macro Workbook. The **Personal Macro Workbook** is an Excel file that is always available, unless you specify otherwise, and gives you access to all the macros it contains, regardless of which workbooks are open. The Personal Macro Workbook file is automatically created the first time you choose to store a macro in it, and is named PERSONAL.XLSB. You can add additional macros to the Personal Macro Workbook by saving them in the workbook. By default, the PERSONAL.XLSB workbook opens each time you start Excel, but you don't see it because Excel designates it as a hidden file. **CASE** *Kate often likes to print her worksheets in landscape orientation with 1" left, right, top, and bottom margins. She wants you to create a macro that automatically formats a work-sheet for printing this way. Because she wants to use this macro in future workbooks, she asks you to store the macro in the Personal Macro Workbook.*

STEPS

1. **Click the Record Macro button ▦ on the status bar**
   The Record Macro dialog box opens.

2. **Type FormatPrint in the Macro name text box, click the Shortcut key text box, press and hold [Shift], type F, then click the Store macro in list arrow**
   You have named the macro FormatPrint and assigned it the shortcut combination [Ctrl][Shift][F]. The "This Workbook" storage option is selected by default, indicating that Excel automatically stores macros in the active workbook, as shown in **FIGURE I-14**. You can also choose to store the macro in a new workbook or in the Personal Macro Workbook.

3. ▶ **Click Personal Macro Workbook, in the Description text box enter your name, then click OK**
   The recorder is on, and you are ready to record the macro keystrokes.

4. **Click the PAGE LAYOUT tab, click the Orientation button in the Page Setup group, click Landscape, click the Margins button in the Page Setup group, click Custom Margins, then enter 1 in the Top, Left, Bottom, and Right text boxes**
   Compare your margin settings to **FIGURE I-15**.

5. **Click OK, then click the Stop Recording button ☐ on the status bar**
   You want to test the macro.

6. **Add a new worksheet, in cell A1 type Macro Test, press [Enter], press and hold [Ctrl][Shift], then type F**
   The FormatPrint macro plays back the sequence of commands.

7. **Preview Sheet2 and verify in the Settings that the orientation is landscape and the Last Custom Margins are 1" on the left, right, top, and bottom**

8. **Click the Back button ⬅ then save the workbook**

FIGURE I-14: Record Macro dialog box showing macro storage options

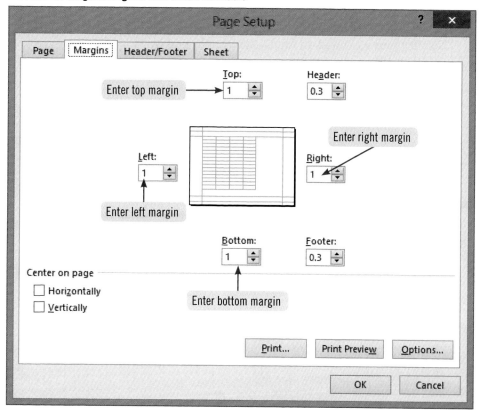

FIGURE I-15: Margin settings for the FormatPrint macro

Working with the Personal Macro Workbook

Once you use the Personal Macro Workbook, it opens automatically each time you start Excel so you can add macros to it. By default, the Personal Macro Workbook is hidden in Excel as a precautionary measure so you don't accidentally delete anything from it. If you need to delete a macro from the Personal Macro Workbook, click the VIEW tab, click Unhide in the Window group, click PERSONAL.XLSB, then click OK. To hide the Personal Macro Workbook, make it the active workbook, click the VIEW tab, then click Hide in the Window group. If you should see a message that Excel is unable to record to your Personal Macro Workbook, check to make sure it is enabled: Click the FILE tab, click Options, click Add-ins, click the Manage list arrow, click Disabled Items, then click Go. If your Personal Macro Workbook is listed in the Disabled items dialog box, click its name, then click Enable.

Assign a Macro to a Button

Learning
Outcomes
• Create a button
  shape in a
  worksheet
• Assign a macro to
  a button

When you create macros for others who will use your workbook, you might want to make the macros more visible so they're easier to use. In addition to using shortcut keys, you can run a macro by assigning it to a button on your worksheet. Then when you click the button the macro will run. **CASE** *To make it easier for people in the sales division to run the DivStamp macro, Kate asks you to assign it to a button on the workbook. You begin by creating the button.*

STEPS

1. **Add a new worksheet, click the INSERT tab, click the Shapes button in the Illustrations group, then click the first rectangle in the Rectangles group**
   The mouse pointer changes to a + symbol.

QUICK TIP
To format a macro
button using 3-D
effects, clip art,
photographs, fills,
and shadows,
right-click it, select
Format Shape from
the shortcut menu,
then select features
such as Fill, Line
Color, Line Style,
Shadow, Reflection,
Glow and Soft
Edges, 3-D Format,
3-D Rotation, Picture
Color, and Text
Box in the Format
Shape pane.

2. **Click at the top-left corner of cell A8, and drag the pointer to the lower-right corner of cell B9**
   Compare your screen to **FIGURE I-16**.

3. **Type Division Macro to label the button**
   Now that you have created the button, you are ready to assign the macro to it.

4. **Right-click the new button, then on the shortcut menu click Assign Macro**
   The Assign Macro dialog box opens.

5. **Click DivStamp under "Macro name", then click OK**
   You have assigned the DivStamp macro to the button.

6. **Click any cell to deselect the button, then click the button**
   The DivStamp macro plays, and the text Quest Sales appears in cell A1, as shown in **FIGURE I-17**.

7. **Save the workbook, preview Sheet3, close the workbook, then exit Excel, clicking Don't Save when asked to save changes to the Personal Macro Workbook**

8. **Submit the workbook to your instructor**

FIGURE I-16: Button shape

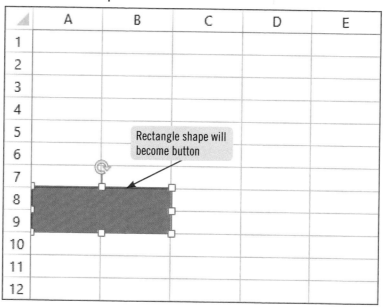

Rectangle shape will become button

FIGURE I-17: Sheet3 with the Sales Division text

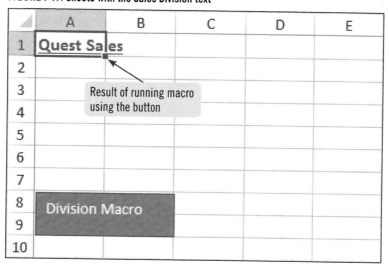

Result of running macro using the button

Creating and formatting a form control

You can add an object called a **form control** to an Excel worksheet to make it easier for users to enter or select data. Click the DEVELOPER tab on the Ribbon, click the Insert button in the Controls group, click the desired control in the Form Controls area of the Insert gallery, then draw the shape on the worksheet. After adding a control to a worksheet, you need to link it to a cell or cells in the worksheet. To do this, right-click it, select Format Control, then click the Control tab. For example, if you add a list box form control, the input range is the location of the list box selections and the cell link is the cell with the numeric value for the current position of the list control. To edit the form control's positioning properties (such as moving, sizing, and printing) right-click the form control, select Format Control and click the Properties tab. See **FIGURE I-18**.

FIGURE I-18: Properties tab of the Format Control dialog box

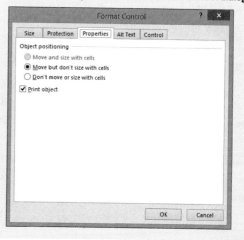

Practice

Concepts Review

FIGURE I-19

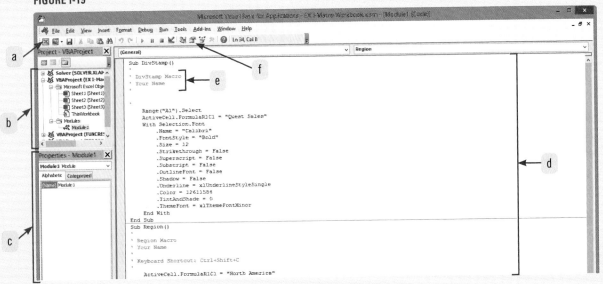

1. Which element points to comments?
2. Which element do you click to return to Excel without closing the module?
3. Which element points to the Code window?
4. Which element points to the Properties Window button?
5. Which element points to the Project Explorer window?
6. Which element points to the Properties window?

Match each term or button with the statement that best describes it.

7. Macro
8. Virus
9. Comments
10. Personal Macro Workbook
11. Visual Basic Editor

a. Set of instructions that performs a task in a specified order
b. Statements that appear in green explaining the macro
c. Destructive software that can damage computer files
d. Used to make changes to macro code
e. Used to store frequently used macros

Select the best answer from the list of choices.

12. Which of the following is the best candidate for a macro?
    a. Often-used sequences of commands or actions
    b. Nonsequential tasks
    c. Seldom-used commands or tasks
    d. One-button or one-keystroke commands

13. You can open the Visual Basic Editor by clicking the _____ button in the Macro dialog box.
    a. Edit
    b. Programs
    c. Modules
    d. Visual Basic Editor

14. A Macro named _____ will automatically run when the workbook it is saved in opens.
    a. Default
    b. Auto_Open
    c. Macro1
    d. Open_Macro

15. Which of the following is *not* true about editing a macro?

   a. You edit macros using the Visual Basic Editor.

   b. A macro cannot be edited and must be recorded again.

   c. You can type changes directly in the existing program code.

   d. You can make more than one editing change in a macro.

16. Why is it important to plan a macro?

   a. Macros can't be deleted.

   b. Planning helps prevent careless errors from being introduced into the macro.

   c. It is impossible to edit a macro.

   d. Macros won't be stored if they contain errors.

17. Macros are recorded with relative references:

   a. Only if the Use Relative References button is selected.

   b. In all cases.

   c. By default.

   d. Only if the Use Absolute References button is not selected.

18. You can run macros:

   a. From the Macro dialog box.

   b. From shortcut key combinations.

   c. From a button on the worksheet.

   d. Using all of the above.

19. Macro security settings can be changed using the _____ tab.

   a. Home

   b. Developer

   c. Security

   d. Review

Skills Review

1. Plan and enable a macro.

   a. You need to plan a macro that enters and formats your name and e-mail address in a worksheet.

   b. Write out the steps the macro will perform.

   c. Write out how the macro could be used in a workbook.

   d. Start Excel, open a new workbook, then save it as a Macro-Enabled workbook named **EX I-Macros** in the location where you store your Data Files. (*Hint*: The file will have the file extension .xlsm.)

   e. Use the Excel Options feature to display the DEVELOPER tab if it is not showing in the Ribbon.

   f. Using the Trust Center dialog box, enable all macros.

2. Record a macro.

   a. You want to record a macro that enters and formats your name and e-mail address in the range A1:A2 in a worksheet using the steps below.

   b. Name the macro **MyEmail**, store it in the current workbook, and make sure your name appears in the Description text box as the person who recorded the macro.

   c. Record the macro, entering your name in cell A1 and your e-mail address in cell A2. (*Hint*: You need to press [Ctrl][Home] first to ensure cell A1 will be selected when the macro runs.)

   d. Resize column A to fit the information entirely in that column.

   e. Add an outside border around the range A1:A2 and format the font using Green from the Standard Colors.

   f. Add bold formatting to the text in the range A1:A2.

   g. Stop the recorder and save the workbook.

3. Run a macro.

   a. Clear cell entries and formats in the range affected by the macro, resize the width of column A to 8.43, then select cell B3.

   b. Run the MyEmail macro to place your name and e-mail information in the range A1:A2.

   c. On the worksheet, clear all the cell entries and formats generated by running the MyEmail macro. Resize the width of column A to 8.43.

   d. Save the workbook.

Skills Review (continued)

4. Edit a macro.

a. Open the MyEmail macro in the Visual Basic Editor.

b. Change the line of code above the last line from Selection.Font.Bold = True to Selection.Font.Bold = False.

c. Use the Close and Return to Microsoft Excel command on the File menu to return to Excel.

d. Test the macro on Sheet1, and compare your worksheet to **FIGURE I-20** verifying that the text is not bold.

e. Save the workbook.

FIGURE I-20

	A
1	Your Name
2	yourname@yourschool.edu
3	
4	
5	

5. Assign keyboard shortcuts to macros.

a. Create a macro named **EmailStamp** in the current workbook, assign your macro the shortcut key combination [Ctrl][Shift][Q], enter your name in the description. (*Hint*: If you get an error when trying to use [Ctrl][Shift][Q], select another key combination.)

b. Begin recording, enter your e-mail address, format it in italics with a font color of red, without underlining, in the selected cell of the current worksheet. Stop recording.

c. After you record the macro, clear the contents and formats from the cell containing your e-mail address that you used to record the macro.

d. Use the shortcut key combination to run the EmailStamp macro in a cell other than the one in which it was recorded. Compare your macro result to **FIGURE I-21**. Your e-mail address may appear in a different cell.

e. Save the workbook.

FIGURE I-21

C	D	E
yourname@yourschool.edu		

6. Use the Personal Macro Workbook.

a. Using Sheet1, record a new macro called **FitToLand** and store it in the Personal Macro Workbook with your name in the Description text box. If you already have a macro named FitToLand replace that macro. The macro should set the print orientation to landscape.

b. After you record the macro, Add a new worksheet, and enter **Test data for FitToLand macro** in cell A1.

c. Preview Sheet2 to verify that the orientation is set to portrait.

d. Run the FitToLand macro. (You may have to wait a few moments.)

e. Add your name to the Sheet2 footer, then preview Sheet2 and verify that it is now in Landscape orientation.

f. Save the workbook.

7. Assign a macro to a button.

a. Add a new worksheet and enter **Button Test** in cell A1.

b. Using the rectangle shape, draw a rectangle in the range A7:B8.

c. Label the button with the text **Landscape**. Compare your worksheet to **FIGURE I-22**.

d. Assign the macro PERSONAL.XLSB!FitToLand to the button.

e. Verify that the orientation of Sheet3 is set to portrait.

f. Run the FitToLand macro using the button.

g. Preview the worksheet, and verify that it is in landscape view.

h. Add your name to the Sheet3 footer, then save the workbook.

i. Close the workbook, exit Excel without saving the FitToLand macro in the Personal Macro Workbook, then submit your workbook to your instructor.

FIGURE I-22

	A	B	C
1	Button Test		
2			
3			
4			
5			
6			
7		Landscape	
8			
9			
10			

Independent Challenge 1

As the office manager of Ocean Point Consulting Group, you need to develop ways to help your fellow employees work more efficiently. Employees have asked for Excel macros that can do the following:

- Adjust the column widths to display all column data in a worksheet.
- Place the company name of Ocean Point Consulting Group in the header of a worksheet.

a. Plan and write the steps necessary for each macro.

b. Start Excel, open the Data File EX I-1.xlsx from the location where you store your Data Files, then save it as a macro-enabled workbook called **EX I-Consulting**.

c. Check your macro security on the DEVELOPER tab to be sure that macros are enabled.

d. Create a macro named **ColumnFit**, save it in the EX I-Consulting.xlsm workbook, assign the ColumnFit macro a shortcut key combination of [Ctrl][Shift][X], and add your name in the description area for the macro. Record the macro using the following instructions:

- Record the ColumnFit macro to adjust a worksheet's column widths to display all data. (*Hint*: Select the entire sheet, click the HOME tab, click the Format button in the Cells group, select AutoFit Column Width, then click cell A1 to deselect the worksheet.)
- End the macro recording.

e. Format the widths of columns A through G to 8.43, then test the ColumnFit macro with the shortcut key combination [Ctrl][Shift][X].

f. Create a macro named **CompanyName**, and save it in the EX I-Consulting.xlsm workbook. Assign the macro a shortcut key combination of [Ctrl][Shift][Y], and add your name in the description area for the macro.

g. Record the CompanyName macro. The macro should place the company name of Ocean Point Consulting Group in the center section of the worksheet header.

h. Enter **CompanyName test data** in cell A1 of Sheet2, and test the CompanyName macro using the shortcut key combination [Ctrl][Shift][Y]. Preview Sheet2 to view the header.

i. Edit the CompanyName macro in the Visual Basic Editor to change the company name from Ocean Point Consulting Group to **Shore Consulting Group**. Close the Visual Basic Editor and return to Excel.

FIGURE I-23

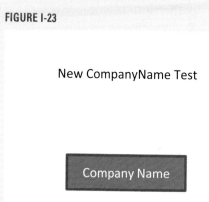

j. Add a rectangle button to Sheet3 in the range A6:B7. Label the button with the text **Company Name**.

k. Assign the CompanyName macro to the button.

l. Enter **New CompanyName Test** in cell A1. Compare your screen to **FIGURE I-23**. Use the button to run the CompanyName macro. Preview the worksheet, checking the header to be sure it is displaying the new company name.

m. Enter your name in the footers of all three worksheets. Save the workbook, close the workbook, then submit the workbook to your instructor and exit Excel.

Independent Challenge 2

You are an assistant to the VP of Sales at Twin Cities Beverage Company, a distributor of juices, water, and soda to 'super-markets. As part of your work, you create spreadsheets with sales projections for different regions of the company. You frequently have to change the print settings so that workbooks print in landscape orientation with custom margins of 1" on the top and bottom. You also add a header with the company name on every worksheet. You have decided that it's time to create a macro to streamline this process.

a. Plan and write the steps necessary to create the macro.

b. Check your macro security settings to confirm that macros are enabled.

Independent Challenge 2 (continued)

c. Start Excel, create a new workbook, then save it as a macro-enabled file named **EX I-Sales Macro** in the location where you store your Data Files.

d. Create a macro that changes the page orientation to landscape, adds custom margins of 1" on the top and bottom of the page, adds a header of **Twin Cities Beverage Company** in the center section formatted as Bold with a font size of 14 points. Name the macro **Format**, add your name in the description, assign it the shortcut key combination [Ctrl][Shift][W], and store it in the current workbook.

e. Add a new worksheet and enter the text **Format Test** in cell A1. Test the macro using the shortcut key combination of [Ctrl][Shift][W]. Preview Sheet2 to check the page orientation, margins, and the header.

f. Add a new worksheet, enter the text **Format Test** in cell A1 add a rectangular button with the text **Format Worksheet** to run the Format macro, then test the macro using the button.

g. Preview the Visual Basic code for the macro.

h. Save the workbook, close the workbook, exit Excel, then submit the workbook to your instructor.

Independent Challenge 3

You are the Northeast regional sales manager of New England Technology, a technology consulting firm. You manage the New England operations and frequently create workbooks with data from the office locations. It's tedious to change the tab names and colors every time you open a new workbook, so you decide to create a macro that will add the office locations and colors to the three office location worksheet tabs, as shown in **FIGURE I-24**.

FIGURE I-24

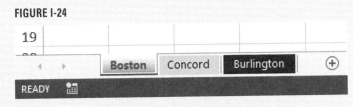

a. Plan and write the steps to create the macro described above.

b. Start Excel and open a new workbook.

c. Create the macro using the plan you created in Step a, name it **SheetFormat**, assign it the shortcut key combination [Ctrl][Shift][Q], store it in the Personal Macro Workbook, and add your name in the description area.

d. After recording the macro, close the workbook without saving it. Save the changes to the Personal Macro workbook.

e. Open a new workbook, then save it as a macro-enabled workbook named **EX I-Office Test** in the location where you store your Data Files. Use the shortcut key combination of [Ctrl][Shift][Q] to test the macro in the new workbook.

f. Unhide the PERSONAL.XLSB workbook. (*Hint:* Click the VIEW tab, click the Unhide button in the Window group, click PERSONAL.XLSB, then click OK.)

g. Edit the SheetFormat macro using **FIGURE I-25** as a guide, changing the Burlington sheet name to Portland. (*Hint:* There are three instances of Burlington that need to be changed.)

h. Open a new workbook, then save it as a macro-enabled workbook named **EX I-Office Test New** in the location where you store your Data Files. Test the edited macro using the shortcut key combination of [Ctrl][Shift][Q].

i. Add a new sheet in the workbook, and name it **Code**. Copy the SheetFormat macro code from the Personal Macro Workbook, and paste it in the Code sheet beginning in cell A1. Save the workbook, close the workbook, then submit the EX I-Office Test New workbook to your instructor.

FIGURE I-25

```
Sub SheetFormat()
'
' SheetFormat Macro
' Your Name
'
' Keyboard Shortcut: Ctrl+Shift+Q
'
    Sheets("Sheet1").Select
    Sheets("Sheet1").Name = "Boston"
    Sheets("Boston").Select
    With ActiveWorkbook.Sheets("Boston").Tab
        .Color = 12611584
        .TintAndShade = 0
    End With
    Sheets("Sheet2").Select
    Sheets("Sheet2").Name = "Concord"
    Sheets("Concord").Select
    With ActiveWorkbook.Sheets("Concord").Tab
        .Color = 65535
        .TintAndShade = 0
    End With
    Sheets("Sheet3").Select
    Sheets("Sheet3").Name = "Portland"
    Sheets("Portland").Select
    With ActiveWorkbook.Sheets("Portland").Tab
        .Color = 10498160
        .TintAndShade = 0
    End With
End Sub
```

Independent Challenge 3 (continued)

j. Hide the PERSONAL.XLSB workbook. (*Hint*: With the PERSONAL.XLSB workbook active, click the VIEW tab, then click the Hide button in the Window group.)

k. Close the workbook without saving changes to the PERSONAL.XLSB workbook, then exit Excel.

Independent Challenge 4: Explore

As the owner of a yoga studio you manage your courses using an Excel workbook. You have created a macro that will display available classes when a type of class is entered. You have been manually entering the class name and then running the macro. You have hired an assistant and would like to simplify the process of displaying class information by adding a form control to help select the data in the worksheet and then run the macro. Specifically, you will ask your assistant to use a list box which will return a numeric value for the current position of the control. That numeric value can be used with an Index function to insert the selected data in the necessary location for the macro which will use it as criteria to filter your data to return the requested course information.

a. Start Excel, open the Data File EX I-2.xlsm from the location where you store your Data Files, then save it as **EX I-Classes**.

b. Test the macro FindClass by entering **Power** in cell A20 and running the macro. Scroll down to cell A23 to see the results.

c. Insert a button form control in cells B19:C20 and assign the FindClass macro to the form control button. Label the button with the text **Find Classes**.

d. Enter **Basics** in cell A20 and test the button.

e. On the Controls sheet create a list for a List Box form control by entering **Basics** in cell A1, **Power** in cell A2, **Hatha** in cell A3, and **Kripalu** in cell A4.

f. On the Yoga Classes sheet enter **Select Class** in cell A1. Insert a list box form control in cells B1:B4. Format the control to set the Input range to A1:A4 of the Controls sheet and the Cell link to cell B1 in the Controls sheet. Compare your controls to **FIGURE I-26**.

FIGURE I-26

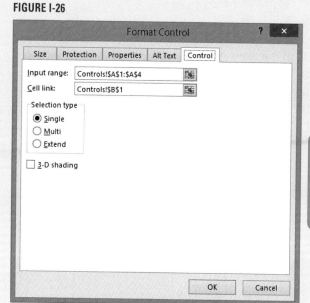

g. Test the list box by clicking different classes and viewing the position in the list displayed in cell B1 of the Controls sheet, the cell link used in the previous step.

h. Replace the class in cell A20 with the index formula **=INDEX(Controls!A1:A4,Controls!B1,0)**. This will use the list position displayed in cell B1 of the Controls sheet to find the class in the range A1:A4 of the Controls sheet and display the class name in cell A20. Test the index formula by selecting different classes in the list box and verifying cell A20 matches the selection.

i. Delete the form control button in cells B19:C20.

j. Assign the FindClass macro to the list box form control.

k. Select a class from the list box and verify the macro is working properly.

l. Enter your name in the footers of both worksheets. Save the workbook, close the workbook, then submit the workbook to your instructor and exit Excel.

Visual Workshop

Start Excel, open the Data File EX I-3.xlsx from the location where you store your Data Files, then save it as a macro-enabled workbook called **EX I-Payroll**. Create a macro with the name **TotalHours**, save the macro in the EX I-Payroll workbook that does the following:

- Totals the weekly hours for each employee by totaling the hours for the first employee and copying that formula for the other employees
- Adds a row at the top of the worksheet and inserts a label of **Hours** in a font size of 14 point, centered across all columns
- Adds your name in the worksheet footer

Test the TotalHours macro by opening the Data File EX I-3.xlsx from the location where you store your Data Files and running the macro. Compare your macro results to **FIGURE I-27**. Close the Data File EX I-3 without saving it, then save the EX I-Payroll workbook. Submit the EX I-Payroll workbook to your instructor.

FIGURE I-27

	A	B	C	D	E	F	G	H	I
1	Hours								
2		Monday	Tuesday	Wednesday	Thursday	Friday	Saturday	Sunday	Total
3	Mary Jacobs	7	8	6	8	5	0	1	35
4	John Malone	5	7	8	7	7	6	2	42
5	Ken Duffy	6	5	7	6	3	5	0	32
6	Sally Landry	8	7	6	5	5	1	0	32
7	Kathy Bane	8	7	5	8	7	7	0	42
8	Jacki Rand	8	7	5	5	7	8	0	40
9	Cindy Healy	7	5	2	6	8	5	3	36
10	Randy Thomas	2	7	8	6	7	2	0	32
11	Ken Yang	0	4	4	4	4	4	1	21
12	Linda Regan	7	8	2	8	8	1	0	34
13									

Enhancing Charts

CASE ▶ Quest's vice president of sales, Kate Morgan, has requested charts comparing sales and trends in the Quest regions over the first two quarters. You will produce these charts and enhance them to improve their appearance, clarify the display, and make the worksheet data more accessible.

Unit Objectives

After completing this unit, you will be able to:

- Customize a data series
- Change a data source and add a chart style
- Add chart elements
- Format chart axes
- Create a combination chart
- Enhance a chart
- Summarize data with sparklines
- Identify data trends

Files You Will Need

EX J-1.xlsx   EX J-5.xlsx
EX J-2.xlsx   EX J-6.xlsx
EX J-3.xlsx   EX J-7.xlsx
EX J-4.xlsx

Customize a Data Series

Learning Outcomes
- Switch row and column data
- Format a data series

A **data series** is the sequence of values that Excel uses to **plot**, or create, a chart. As with other Excel elements, you can change the data series presentation to get another view of your data. For example, you can reverse the data charted on the x and y axes. You can also format a chart's data series to make the chart more attractive and easier to read. **CASE** ▶ *Kate wants you to create a chart showing the sales for each region in January and February. You begin by creating a column chart, which you will customize to make it easier to compare the sales for each region.*

STEPS

1. **Start Excel, open the file EX J-1.xlsx from the location where you store your Data Files, then save it as EX J-Region Sales**

   To begin, Kate wants to see how each region performed over January and February. The first step is to select the data you want to appear in the chart.

2. **Select the range A2:C6**

3. **Click the Quick Analysis tool 📧 at the lower right corner of the selected range, click the CHARTS tab at the top of the Quick Analysis gallery, move the mouse pointer over the recommended charts to view your data in different visual presentations, then point to the Clustered Column option**

   A clustered column chart preview comparing the January and February sales for each branch appears, as shown in **FIGURE J-1**. You decide to use this option to compare the monthly sales for each branch.

4. **Click Clustered Column, then on the CHART TOOLS DESIGN tab in the Ribbon, click the Switch Row/Column button in the Data group**

   The legend now contains the region data, and the horizontal axis groups the bars by month. Kate can now easily compare the branch sales for each month. You want to see how the graph looks with the U.S. data series plotted in a green color.

5. **Double-click the Jan U.S. data series bar (the far-left bar on the graph), click the Fill & Line button 🖎 in the Format Data Series pane, click Fill, click the Solid fill option button, click the Fill Color list arrow 🖎 ▾, select Dark Green, Accent 5 in the Theme Colors group, then close the Format Data Series pane**

6. **Point to the edge of the chart, then drag the chart to place its upper-left corner in cell A8**

7. **Drag the chart's lower-right sizing handle to fit the chart in the range A8:H20, then compare your chart to FIGURE J-2**

   You can resize a chart by dragging its corner sizing handles.

8. **Save the workbook**

Adding width and depth to data series

You can change the gap depth and the gap width in column charts by double-clicking one of the chart's data series and dragging the Gap Width or depth sliders in the Format Data Series pane. Increasing the gap width adds space between each set of data on the chart by decreasing the width of the chart's data series. If you are working with 3-D charts, you will have the option to increase the gap depth to add depth to all categories of data.

FIGURE J-1: Clustered column chart comparing January and February sales for each region

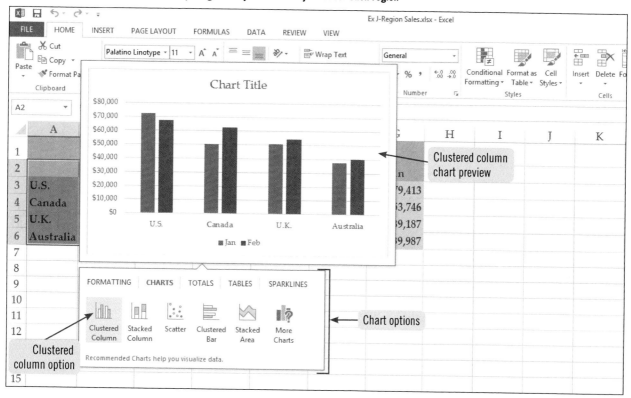

FIGURE J-2: Chart comparing region sales in January and February

	A	B	C	D	E	F	G	H
3	U.S.	$72,487	$67,506	$51,622	$67,706	$75,097	$79,413	
4	Canada	$50,226	$62,774	$65,012	$58,870	$56,311	$53,746	
5	U.K.	$50,632	$54,357	$52,992	$62,024	$51,278	$39,187	
6	Australia	$37,449	$39,998	$55,770	$49,576	$38,799	$39,987	

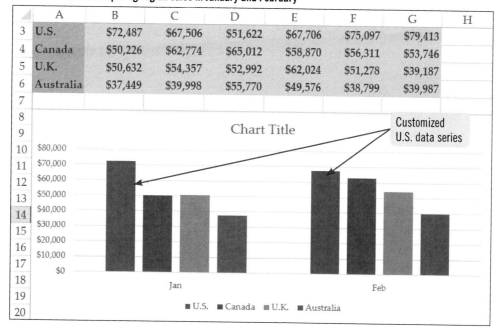

Enhancing Charts

Change a Data Source and Add a Chart Style

As you update your workbooks with new data, you may also need to add data series to (or delete them from) a chart. Excel makes it easy to revise a chart's data source and to rearrange chart data. Also, you can use preformatted styles to make a chart more attractive. **CASE** ▶ *Kate wants the chart to show branch sales for the first quarter, so you need to add the March data to your chart. She then asks you to add a chart style and modify the chart colors to make the chart more attractive. You begin by changing the data view to compare branch sales for each month.*

STEPS

1. **Click the CHART TOOLS DESIGN tab if necessary, then click the Switch Row/Column button in the Data group**

   The region data again appears on the horizontal axis. You want to add the March data to the chart.

2. **Drag the lower-right corner of the data border in worksheet cell C6 to the right to include the data in column D**

   The March data series appears on the chart, as shown in **FIGURE J-3**. You want to make the columns more attractive using one of the chart styles.

3. **With the chart selected, click Chart Styles button ⟋ outside the chart on the right side, then scroll down to and click Style 14 (the last style)**

   The data bars have an appearance of depth and the January data bars are now a blue color again. The menu remains open. You want to change the colors of the data bars.

4. **Click COLOR at the top of the Chart Styles gallery**

   There are colorful and monochromatic galleries available.

5. **Point to the color galleries and preview the data bar colors, click Color 2 (the second row from the top), then click the Chart Styles button again to close the gallery**

   The data bars appear in the new color scheme. Compare your chart to **FIGURE J-4**.

6. **Save the workbook**

FIGURE J-3: Chart with March data series added

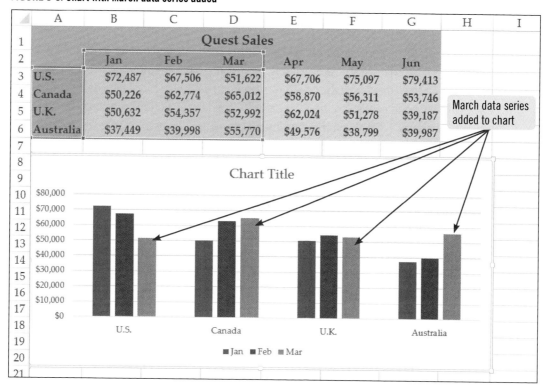

FIGURE J-4: Chart with new color scheme

Add Chart Elements

Learning
Outcomes
• Move a chart to a
  different work-
  sheet
• Add a data table
  to a chart
• Add data labels to
  a chart

When you create a chart, **chart elements** such as the chart title and legend often appear by default. You can add or remove chart elements by clicking the Chart Elements button on the right side of a selected chart to display an element list. Other chart elements you can choose include a data table and data labels. A **data table** is a grid containing the chart data, attached to the bottom of a chart. Data tables are useful because they display—directly on the chart itself—the values you used to generate a chart. **Data labels** also display series values, but value labels appear near or on the data markers. **CASE** *Kate wants you to move the chart to its own worksheet, add a data table to emphasize the chart's first-quarter data, and add data labels.*

STEPS

1. **Click the chart object to select it if necessary, click the** CHART TOOLS DESIGN tab **on the Ribbon, then click the** Move Chart button **in the Location group**

   The Move Chart dialog box opens. You want to place the chart on a new sheet named First Quarter.

2. **Click the** New sheet option button, **type** First Quarter **in the New sheet text box, then click** OK

   The chart moves to a separate sheet.

3. **Click the** Chart Elements button ⊞, **click the** Data Table check box **to select it, move the mouse pointer over the** Data Table list arrow, **click once, then verify that** With Legend Keys **is selected**

   A data table with the first-quarter data and a key to the legend appears at the bottom of the chart, as shown in **FIGURE J-5**. You will add data labels to clarify the exact amount of sales represented by each data bar.

4. **Click the** Data Labels check box **in the CHART ELEMENTS gallery**

   Data labels appear above the data bars. You don't need the legend keys in the data table so you decide to remove them.

5. **Point to** Data Table **on the CHART ELEMENTS gallery, click the** Data Table list arrow, **click** No Legend Keys, **click under the CHART ELEMENTS gallery to close it, then compare your chart to** FIGURE J-6

   The data table no longer shows the legend keys.

6. **Save the workbook**

FIGURE J-5: Chart with data table

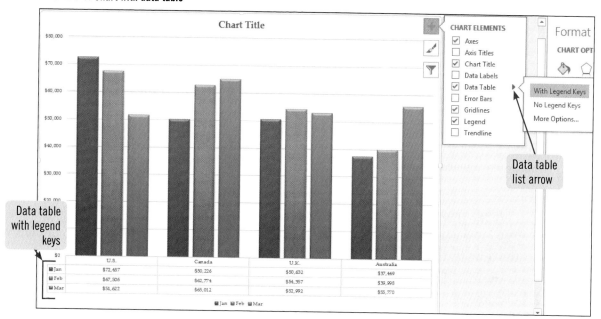

Data table with legend keys

Data table list arrow

FIGURE J-6: Chart with data table legend keys removed

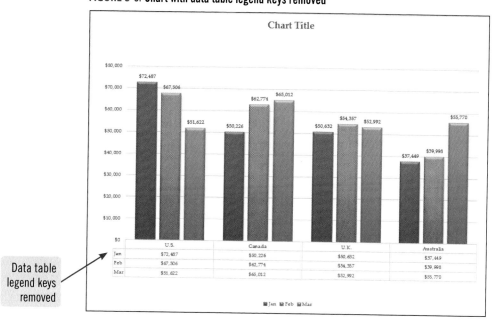

Data table legend keys removed

Formatting legends

To format a legend's fill, border, color, or shadows, click the Chart Elements button point to Legend, click the Legend list arrow, then click More Options. Using the options in the Format Legend pane, you can use the LEGEND OPTIONS tab and TEXT OPTIONS tab to customize the legend. For example, you can add a picture to the legend by clicking the Fill & Line button 🖫, clicking the Picture or texture fill option button, clicking the File button under Insert picture from, then browsing to your image. The legend in **FIGURE J-7** has a textured fill background. You can also drag a legend to any location. To change a legend's font size, color, or style right-click the legend text, click Font on the shortcut menu, then adjust the settings in the Font dialog box.

FIGURE J-7: Formatted legend

Learning
Outcomes
• Add axis titles
• Change the
  vertical axis
  maximum value

Format Chart Axes

Excel plots and formats chart data and places the chart axes within the chart's plot area. Data values in two-dimensional charts are plotted on the vertical y-axis (often called the value axis because it usually shows value levels). Categories are plotted on the horizontal x-axis (often called the category axis because it usually shows data categories). Excel creates a scale for the value (y) axis based on the highest and lowest values in the series and places intervals along the scale. **CASE** ▶ *Kate asks you to add axes titles to explain the plotted data. She would also like you to increase the maximum number on the value axis and change the axis number format.*

STEPS

1. **Click the chart to select it if necessary, click the Chart Elements button ⊞, click the Axis Titles check box to select it, then resize the chart and plot areas if necessary to display the titles text boxes**

   You decide to label the axes.

2. **Click the Horizontal axis title text box, type Regions, then press [Enter]**

   The word "Regions" appears as the Horizontal axis title after you press [Enter].

3. **Click the Vertical axis title text box, type Sales, then press [Enter]**

   The word "Sales" appears in the Vertical axis title as shown in **FIGURE J-8**. You decide to change the maximum number on the value axis. The maximum number on the value axis is currently $80,000.

4. **Click ⊞, point to Axes, click the Axes list arrow, then click More Options**

   The Format Axis pane opens.

5. **Click the AXIS OPTIONS list arrow near the top of the pane, click the Vertical (Value) Axis, in the Maximum text box type 90000, then press [Enter]**

   Now 90000.0 appears as the maximum value on the value axis, and the chart bar heights adjust to reflect the new value. Next, you want the vertical axis values to appear without additional zeroes to make the chart data easier to read.

6. **Click the Display units list arrow, click Thousands, then make sure the Show display units label on chart check box is selected**

   The values are reduced to two digits and the word "Thousands" appears in a text box to the left of the values. You will increase the font size of the axes titles and unit label to make them easier to see.

7. **Right-click the Sales title, in the shortcut menu click Font, enter 16 in the Size text box in the Font dialog box, click OK, right-click the Regions title, in the shortcut menu click Font, enter 16 in the Size text box in the Font dialog box, click OK, right-click the Thousands title, in the shortcut menu click Font, enter 12 in the Size text box in the Font dialog box, then click OK**

8. **Adjust the positioning of the Sales and Thousands titles to match FIGURE J-9, then save the workbook**

FIGURE J-8: Chart with axes titles

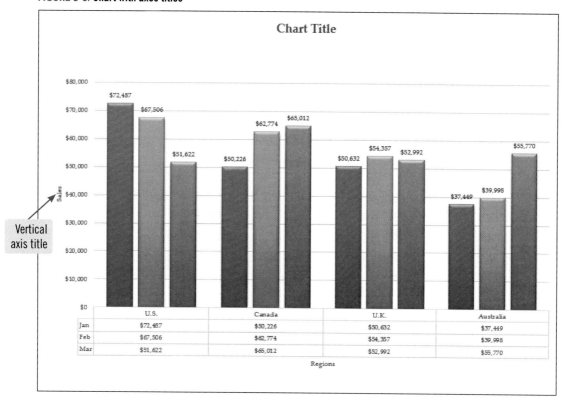

FIGURE J-9: Chart with formatted axes

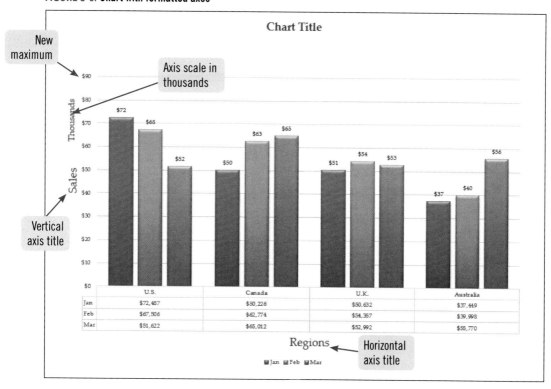

Create a Combination Chart

Learning
Outcomes
• Add chart data
• Create a chart
  with two types
  of graphs

A combination chart is a chart that combines two or more chart types in a single chart. This is helpful if you have different types of data in a chart and you want to emphasize the different data types. An example of a combination chart is a line and bar combination chart showing profits and sales. **CASE** *Kate wants you to create a combination chart by adding a line chart showing the averages of sales for the first quarter months.*

STEPS

1. **Click the** Sales sheet tab **to select it, select the range** A2:D6, **click the** Quick Analysis tool, **click the** TOTALS tab, **then click the** Average button

   Averages for the months appear in row 7.

2. **Click the** First Quarter sheet tab, **click the chart if necessary to select it, click the** CHART TOOLS DESIGN tab, **click the** Select Data button **in the Data group, edit the Chart data range to** =Sales!$A$2:$D$7, **then click** OK

   The average data bars are included in the chart as shown in **FIGURE J-10**. To create more room on the chart you will move the legend into the data table.

3. **Click the** Chart Elements button ⊞, **click the** Data Table list arrow, **click** With Legend Keys, **click the** Legend check box **to remove the legend, then click the** Chart Elements button **to close the gallery**

   You want to switch the axes data to show average amounts for each month.

4. **Click the** Switch Row/Column button **in the Data group**

   The average amounts for each month will be easier to distinguish if they are on a different type of graph.

QUICK TIP
You can plot two
data sets on different
axes by creating a
combination chart,
selecting the
Secondary Axis
checkbox next to one
of the data series,
then clicking OK.

5. **Click** Change Chart Type **in the Type group, click** Combo **in the Change Type dialog box, in the Chart Type column near the bottom of the dialog box, select** Clustered Column **for the US, Canada, UK, and Australia data series, select** Line **for the Average data series, then click** OK

6. **Click the** Chart Elements button ⊞, **click the** Data Labels check box **to remove the data labels on the chart, then close the Chart Elements gallery**

7. **Compare your chart to** FIGURE J-11, **then save the workbook**

Charting data accurately

The purpose of a chart is to help viewers interpret the worksheet data. When creating charts, make sure that your chart accurately portrays your data. Charts can sometimes misrepresent data and thus mislead people. For example, it is possible to change the y-axis units or its starting value to make charted sales values appear larger than they are. Even though you may have correctly labeled the sales values on the chart, the height of the data points will lead people viewing the chart to think the sales are higher than the labeled values. So use caution when you modify charts to make sure you accurately represent your data.

FIGURE J-10: Chart with average data series

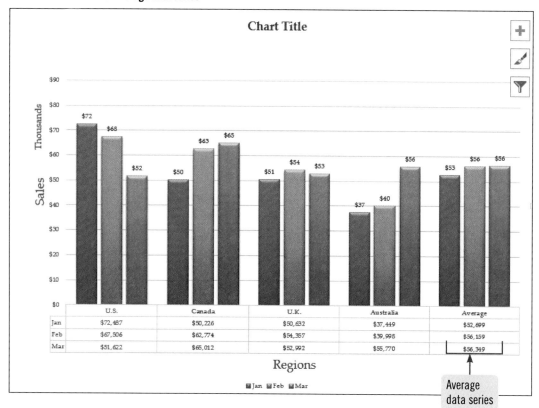

FIGURE J-11: Combination chart with two types of graphs

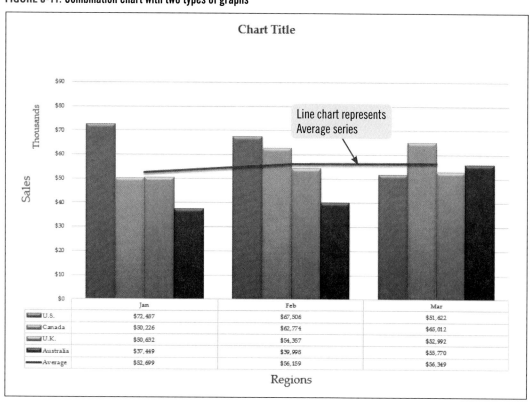

Excel 2013

Enhance a Chart

You can enhance your chart or worksheet titles using **WordArt**, which is preformatted text. Once you've added WordArt text, you can edit or format it by adding 3-D effects and shadows. WordArt text is a shape rather than text. This means that you cannot treat WordArt objects as if they were labels entered in a cell; that is, you cannot sort, use the spell checker, or use their cell references in formulas. You can further enhance your chart by adding a Shape Style to one of the chart elements. **CASE** *Kate wants you to add a WordArt title to the first-quarter chart. She also wants you to add a Shape Style to the plot area of the chart.*

STEPS

1. **Click the** Chart Title text box, **type** First Quarter Sales, **then press** [Enter]

2. **Click the** CHART TOOLS FORMAT tab, **then click the** More button ⥥ **in the WordArt Styles group**

   The Word Art styles gallery opens, as shown in **FIGURE J-12**. This is where you select the WordArt for your text.

3. **Click the** Fill - White, Outline - Accent 1, Shadow style

   The title text becomes formatted with green outlined letters. You decide the chart would look better if the gridlines were not visible.

4. **Click the** Chart Elements button, **click the** Gridlines checkbox **to deselect it, then click the Chart Elements button to close the gallery**

   Kate wants you to add a shape style to the plot area of the chart. Some chart elements cannot be selected using the CHART ELEMENTS gallery on the chart; instead you need to use the Chart Elements list arrow on the Ribbon.

5. **Click the chart to select it if necessary, click the** CHART TOOLS FORMAT tab, **click the** Chart Elements list arrow **in the Current Selection group, then click** Plot Area

   The plot area of the chart is selected, as shown by the four small circles on its corners.

6. **Click the** More button ⥥ **in the Shape Styles group, click the** Subtle Effect - Indigo, Accent 1 button **(in the fourth row), click the** Shape Effects button **in the Shape Styles group, point to** Preset, **then click** Preset 5

   The plot area of the chart is formatted in a light blue color with a slight 3-D effect.

7. **Click the** INSERT tab, **click the** Header & Footer button **in the Text group, click the** Custom Footer button, **enter your name in the Center section, click** OK, **then click** OK again

   Compare your chart to **FIGURE J-13**.

FIGURE J-12: WordArt Styles gallery

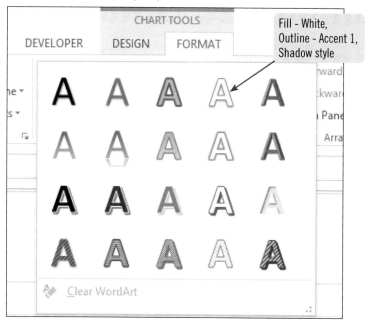

FIGURE J-13: Chart with formatted title and plot area

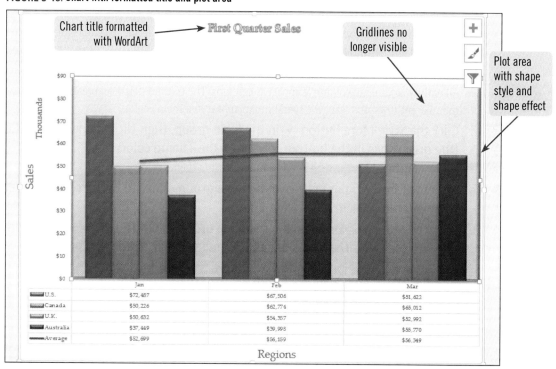

Working with Shapes

Shapes are wonderful additions to any worksheet, and can make your data more visually interesting. To create a shape, click the INSERT tab, click the Shapes button in the Illustrations group, click any shape, then drag across the worksheet to create a shape object. Once you create a shape, you can rotate it by selecting the shape if necessary, clicking the Rotate button in the Arrange group on the DRAWING TOOLS FORMAT tab, then clicking one of the rotation options. You can change a shape type by selecting it, clicking the Edit Shape button in the Insert Shapes group on the Drawing Tools Format tab, pointing to Change Shape, then clicking the new shape. To modify the shape of the existing shape, click the Edit Shape button in the Insert Shapes group, click Edit Points, then drag any of the existing points that appear as small black squares on the shape's perimeter to a new location. You can also add a new point by clicking the perimeter, then dragging the new point to a new location.

Learning Outcomes
• Add sparklines to a worksheet
• Format sparklines
• Add markers to sparklines

Summarize Data with Sparklines

You can create a quick overview of your data by adding sparklines to the worksheet cells. **Sparklines** are miniature charts that show data trends in a worksheet range, such as sales increases or decreases. Sparklines are also useful for highlighting maximum and minimum values in a range of data. Sparklines usually appear close to the data they represent. Any changes that you make to a worksheet are reflected in the sparklines that represent the data. After you add sparklines to a worksheet, you can change the sparkline and color. You can also format high and low data points in special colors. **CASE** ▶ *Kate wants you to add sparklines to the Sales worksheet to illustrate the sales trends for the first half of the year.*

STEPS

1. **Click the Sales sheet, click cell H3 to select it, click the INSERT tab if necessary, click the Line button in the Sparklines group, verify that the insertion point is in the Data Range text box, select the range B3:G3 on the worksheet, then click OK**

   A sparkline showing the sales trend for the U.S. appears in cell H3. You can copy the sparkline to cells representing other regions.

2. **With cell H3 selected, drag the fill handle to fill the range H4:H6**

   The sparklines for all four regions are shown in **FIGURE J-14**. You decide to change the sparklines to columns.

3. **Click cell H3, then click the Column button in the Type group of the SPARKLINE TOOLS DESIGN tab**

   All of the sparklines in column H appear as columns. The column heights represent the values of the data in the adjacent rows. You want the sparklines to appear in a theme color.

4. **Click the Style More button ⊽ in the Style group, then click Sparkline Style Colorful #4 (the green style in the bottom row) from the Theme colors**

   You want to highlight the high and low months using theme colors.

5. **Click the Marker Color button in the Style group, point to High Point, then select Dark Green, Accent 5 from the Theme Colors**

6. **Click the Marker Color button in the Style group, point to Low Point, select Indigo Accent 1 from the Theme Colors, then compare your screen to FIGURE J-15**

FIGURE J-14: Sales trend sparklines

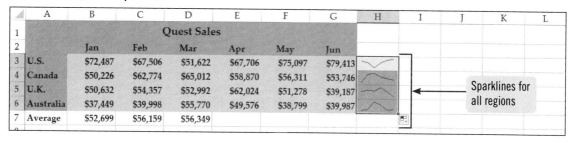

FIGURE J-15: Formatted sparklines

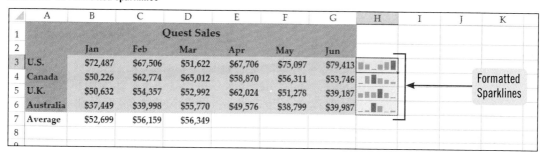

Identify Data Trends

Learning Outcomes
• Compare chart data using trendlines
• Format a trendline
• Forecast future trends using trendlines

You often use charts to visually represent data over a period of time. To emphasize patterns in data, you can add trendlines to your charts. A **trendline** is a series of data points on a line that shows data values representing the general direction in a data series. In some business situations, you can use trendlines to project future data based on past trends. **CASE** ▸ *Kate wants you to compare the U.S. and U.K. sales performance over the first two quarters and to project sales for each region in the following 3 months, assuming past trends. You begin by charting the 6-months sales data in a 2-D Column chart.*

STEPS

1. **On the Sales sheet, select the range A2:G6, click the** Quick Analysis tool, **click the** CHARTS tab, **then click the** Clustered Column button

2. **Drag the chart left until its upper-left corner is at the upper-left corner of cell A8, then drag the** middle-right sizing handle **right to the border between column G and column H**

   You are ready to add a trendline for the U.S. data series.

3. **Click the** Chart Elements button **click** Trendline, **verify that** U.S. **is selected in the Add Trendline dialog box, then click** OK

   A linear trendline identifying U.S. sales trends in the first 6 months is added to the chart, along with an entry in the legend identifying the line. You need to compare the U.S. sales trend with the U.K. sales trend.

4. **Make sure the U.S. trendline is not selected, click the** Chart Elements button **if necessary, point to** Trendline, **click the** Trendline list arrow, **click** Linear, **click** U.K. **in the Add Trendline dialog box, then click** OK

   The chart now has two trendlines, making it easy to compare the sales trends of the U.S. and the U.K. branches as show in **FIGURE J-16**. Now you want to project the next 3-months sales for the U.S. and U.K. sales branches based on the past 6-month trends.

5. **Double-click the** U.S. data series trendline, **enter** 3 **in the Forward textbox in the Format Trendline pane, press [Enter], click the** Fill & Line button ⬧, **click the** Color list arrow ⬧ ▾, **click** Indigo Accent 1, Darker 50%, **then close the Format Trendline pane**

   The formatted U.S. trendline projects an additional 3 months of future sales trends for the region, assuming that past trends continue.

6. **Double-click the** U.K. data series trendline, **enter** 3 **in the Forward textbox in the Format Trendline pane, press [Enter], click** ⬧, **click the** Color list arrow ⬧ ▾, **click** Orange, Accent 3, Darker 25%, **then click** Chart Title **in the CHART ELEMENTS gallery to deselect it**

   The formatted U.K. trendline also projects an additional 3 months of future sales trends for the region, assuming that past trends continue, and the chart title is removed. You will change the UK June data. When chart data is changed you will view the **chart animation** showing the resulting changes to the chart.

7. **Type** 80,000 **in cell G5, view the chart as you press [Enter], enter your name in the center section of the Sales sheet footer, save the workbook, preview the Sales sheet, close the workbook, submit the workbook to your instructor, then exit Excel**

   The completed worksheet is shown in **FIGURE J-17**.

FIGURE J-16: Chart with two trendlines

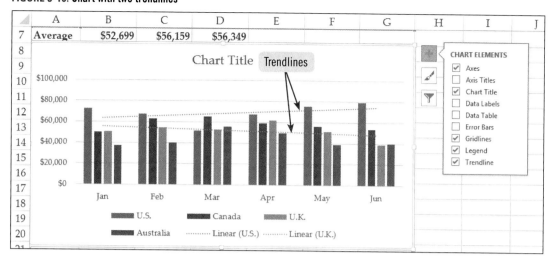

FIGURE J-17: Sales chart with trendlines for U.S. and U.K. data

Quest Sales	Jan	Feb	Mar	Apr	May	Jun	
U.S.	$72,487	$67,506	$51,622	$67,706	$75,097	$79,413	
Canada	$50,226	$62,774	$65,012	$58,870	$56,311	$53,746	
U.K.	$50,632	$54,357	$52,992	$62,024	$51,278	$80,000	
Australia	$37,449	$39,998	$55,770	$49,576	$38,799	$39,987	
Average	$52,699	$56,159	$56,349				

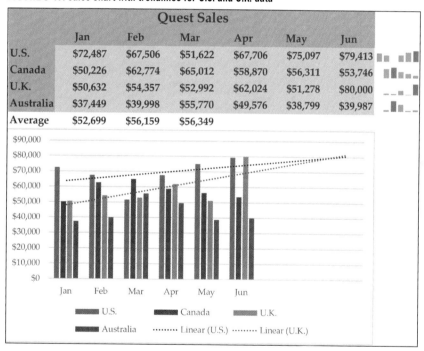

Choosing the right trendline for your chart

Trendlines can help you forecast where your data is headed and understand its past values. You can choose from six types of trendlines: Linear, Exponential, logarithmic, power, polynomial, and Two-Period Moving Average. A linear trendline is used for data series with data points that have the pattern of a line. An exponential or power trendline is a curved line that is used when data values increase or decrease in an arc shape. A polynomial trendline is also curved but changes direction more than one time. A two-period moving average smooths out fluctuations in data by averaging the data points. Logarithmic trendlines are useful for data that increases or decreases before leveling out.

Practice

 Put your skills into practice with SAM! If you have a SAM account, go to www.cengage.com/sam2013 to access SAM assignments for this unit.

Concepts Review

1. Which element points to the vertical axis?
2. Which element points to the vertical axis title?
3. Which element points to the chart legend?
4. Which element points to the chart title?
5. Which element points to the horizontal axis?
6. Which element points to a data label?

FIGURE J-18

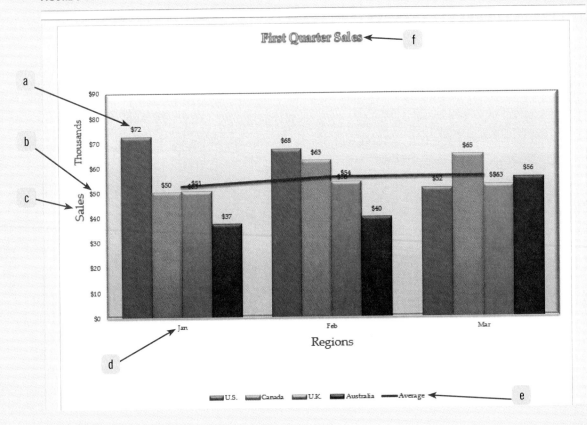

Match each term with the statement that best describes it.

7. Data series
8. Plot area
9. Sparklines
10. X-axis
11. Trendlines

a. Category axis
b. Miniature charts that show data trends
c. Line charts that can be used to project future data
d. Sequence of values plotted on a chart
e. Location holding data charted on the axes

Select the best answer from the list of choices.

12. **Which of the following is true regarding WordArt?**
    a. Cell references to WordArt can be used in formulas.
    b. WordArt is a shape.
    c. Spelling errors in WordArt can be detected by the spell checker.
    d. Cells containing WordArt can be sorted.

13. **Descriptive text that appears above a data marker is called a:**
    a. Data series.
    b. Data label.
    c. High point.
    d. Period.

14. **A chart's scale:**
    a. Can be adjusted.
    b. Always has a maximum of 80000.
    c. Always has a minimum of 0.
    d. Always appears in units of 10.

15. **Which Chart feature shows how a change in data values affects a chart?**
    a. Visualization
    b. Animation
    c. Update
    d. Format

16. **What is a data table?**
    a. A customized data series
    b. The data used to create a chart, displayed in a grid
    c. A grid with chart data displayed above a chart
    d. A three-dimensional arrangement of data on the y-axis

17. **A chart that combines two or more chart types is a:**
    a. Combination chart
    b. Grouped chart
    c. Clustered chart
    d. Complex chart

18. **Which of the following is false regarding trendlines?**
    a. Trendlines visually represent patterns in past data.
    b. Trendlines are used to project future data.
    c. Six types of trendlines can be added to a chart.
    d. Trendlines can be formatted to stand out on a chart.

Skills Review

1. **Customize a data series.**
   a. Start Excel, open the file EX J-2.xlsx from the location where you save your Data Files, then save it as **EX J-Pastry Sales**.
   b. On the Sales sheet select the range A2:D6.
   c. Create a clustered column chart using the selected data.
   d. Move and resize the chart to fit in the range A8:G20.
   e. Change the color of the January data series to Tan, Accent 1, Darker 50% in the Theme Colors.
   f. Change the chart view by exchanging the row and column data.
   g. Save the workbook.

2. **Change a data source and add a chart style.**
   a. Add the April, May, and June data to the chart.
   b. Resize the chart to fill the range A8:J20 to display the new data.
   c. Change the chart view back to show the months in the legend by exchanging the row and column data.
   d. Apply Chart Style 14.
   e. Save the workbook.

3. **Add chart elements.**
   a. Move the chart to its own sheet named **Sales Chart**.
   b. Add a data table with legend keys.
   c. Add data labels to your chart.

Skills Review (continued)

d. Remove the data table legend keys.

e. Save the workbook, then compare your screen to **FIGURE J-19**.

4. **Format chart axes.**

a. Remove the data table.

b. Set the value axis maximum to 5000.

c. Add a horizontal axis title and label it **Products**.

d. Add a vertical axis title and label it **Sales**.

e. Format both axes titles in 12-point bold.

f. Save the workbook.

5. **Create a combination chart.**

a. On the Sales sheet enter **Average** in cell A7.

b. Select the range B3:G6 and use the Quick Analysis tool to place averages in row 7.

c. On the Sales chart, change the chart data to **A2:G7** on the Sales sheet.

d. Switch the row and column chart view.

e. Create a combination chart with the muffins, cookies, brownies, and biscotti data as clustered column charts and the average data as a line chart.

f. Remove the data labels.

g. Save the workbook.

6. **Enhance a chart.**

a. Add a chart title of **Pastry Sales** to the top of the chart.

b. Format the chart title with the WordArt style Fill – Tan, Accent 1, Shadow.

c. Add a shape style of Subtle Effect - Lavender, Accent 6 to the plot area.

d. Remove the gridlines.

e. Compare your chart to **FIGURE J-20**.

f. Add your name to the chart footer, then save the workbook.

7. **Summarize data with Sparklines.**

a. On the Sales worksheet, add a Line sparkline to cell H3 that represents the data in the range B3:G3.

b. Copy the sparkline in cell H3 into the range H4:H6.

c. Change the sparklines to columns.

d. Apply the sparkline style Colorful #4.

e. Add high point markers with the color of Lavender, Accent 6 from the theme colors.

f. Save the workbook.

8. **Identify data trends.**

a. Create a line chart using the data in the range A2:G6, then move and resize the chart to fit in the range A8:G20.

b. Add linear trendlines to the Muffins and Cookies data series.

c. Change the Cookies trendline color to red and the Muffins trendline color to purple.

d. Set the forward option to six periods for both trendlines to view the future trend, increase the width of the chart to the border between columns J and K, remove the chart title, then compare your screen to **FIGURE J-21**.

FIGURE J-19

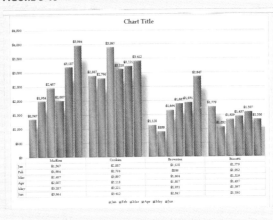

FIGURE J-20

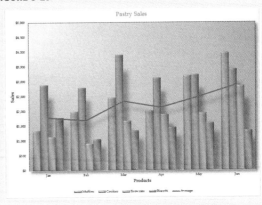

FIGURE J-21

	A	B	C	D	E	F	G	H	I	J
1				Main Street Pastry						
2		Jan	Feb	Mar	Apr	May	Jun			
3	Muffins	$1,347	$1,984	$2,457	$2,007	$3,187	$3,964			
4	Cookies	$2,887	$2,796	$3,897	$3,118	$3,221	$3,412			
5	Brownies	$1,128	$899	$1,664	$1,887	$1,931	$2,847			
6	Biscotti	$1,779	$1,052	$1,329	$1,437	$1,597	$1,330			
7	Average	$1,785	$1,683	$2,337	$2,112	$2,484	$2,888			

Skills Review (continued)

e. Add your name to the center footer section, save the workbook, preview the worksheet, close the workbook, then submit the workbook to your instructor.

f. Exit Excel.

Independent Challenge 1

You are the assistant to the vice president of marketing at a local radio station. The vice president has asked you to chart some information from a recent survey of the station's customers. Your administrative assistant has entered the survey data in an Excel worksheet, which you will use to create two charts.

a. Start Excel, open the file titled EX J-3.xlsx from the location where you store your Data Files, then save it as **EX J-Customer Demographics**.

b. Using the data in A2:B7 of the Education Data worksheet, create a pie chart on the worksheet.

c. Move the chart to a separate sheet named **Education Chart**. Format the chart using chart Style 9.

d. Add a title of **Education Data** above the chart. Format the title using WordArt Fill – White, Outline - Accent 1, Glow - Accent 1. Change the chart title font to a size of 28. (*Hint*: Right click the title and select Font from the shortcut menu.)

e. Add values to the data labels. (*Hint*: Double-click a data label and select the Value checkbox in the Format Data Labels pane.)

f. Select the Bachelor's degree pie slice by clicking the chart, then clicking the Bachelor's degree slice. Change the slice color to the light green Standard color.

g. Add a shape style of Subtle Effect - Blue Accent 5 to the chart area. Compare your chart to **FIGURE J-22**.

FIGURE J-22

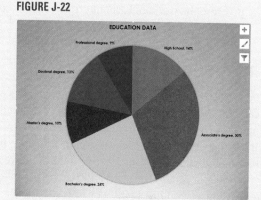

h. On the Income Data worksheet, use the data in A2:B6 to create a clustered column chart.

i. Place the chart on a new sheet named **Income Chart**. Format the chart using chart Style 16.

j. Add a chart title of **Income Data** above the chart, and format the title using WordArt Style Gradient Fill - Dark Purple, Accent 4, Outline - Accent 4.

k. Format the title in 28 point font.

l. Add horizontal and vertical axes titles. Change the title of the horizontal axis to **Income**. Change the title of the vertical axis to **Percent of Customers**. Format both axes' titles in 18-point bold. (*Hint*: Right-click the title and select Font from the shortcut menu.)

m. Enter your name in the center sections of the footers of the Income Chart and Education Chart sheets.

n. Save the workbook, preview the Income Chart and the Education Chart sheets.

o. Close the workbook, submit the workbook to your instructor, and exit Excel.

Independent Challenge 2

You manage the Atlanta Sports Club, which offers memberships for swimming, tennis, and fitness. You also offer a full membership that includes all of the activities at the club. The club owner has asked you to assemble a brief presentation on the membership data over the past 4 years while it has been under your management. You decide to include a chart showing the memberships in each category as well as an analysis of trends in memberships.

a. Start Excel, open the file titled EX J-4.xlsx from the location where you store your Data Files, then save it as **EX J-Memberships**.

b. Create a clustered bar chart on the worksheet, comparing the membership enrollments in the four types of memberships over the years 2013 - 2016. Format the chart using chart Style 12.

c. Change the row and column data so the years are shown in the legend.

d. Add a chart title of **Membership Data** above the chart, and format it using WordArt Style Gradient Fill - Dark Green, Accent 4, Outline - Accent 4.

Independent Challenge 2 (continued)

e. Move the chart to the region A9:H24.

f. Add Line sparklines to cells F4:F7 showing the membership trend from 2013 to 2016.

g. Format the sparklines using Sparkline Style Accent 5, (no dark or light).

h. Add high point markers to the sparklines with the color Red, Accent 2 from the theme colors.

i. Add a new membership type of **Family** in row 8 of the worksheet with the data in this table:

j. Add the data to the chart. Copy the sparklines to cell F8.

k. Move the chart to a sheet named **Membership Chart**.

l. Add a horizontal axis title of **Number of Memberships**, and format it in 18-point bold font. Delete the vertical axis title placeholder.

m. Add a data table with legend keys to the chart. Delete the chart legend.

n. Compare your chart to **FIGURE J-23**.

o. Add your name to the footers of the Membership and Membership Chart sheets, save the workbook, preview the Membership Chart and Membership sheets.

p. Close the workbook, submit the workbook to your instructor, and exit Excel.

Year	Membership
2013	1449
2014	1881
2015	1937
2016	2546

FIGURE J-23

Independent Challenge 3

You manage the East Side Golf Club. You meet twice a year with the store owner to discuss store sales trends. You decide to use a chart to represent the sales trends for the department's product categories. You begin by charting the sales for the first five months of the year. Then you add data to the chart and analyze the sales trend using a trendline. Lastly, you enhance the chart by adding a data table, titles, and a picture.

a. Start Excel, open the file EX J-5.xlsx from the location where you store your Data Files, then save the workbook as **EX J-Golf Sales**.

b. Create a clustered column chart on the worksheet showing the May through July sales information, using the first suggestion in the chart recommendations. Move the upper-left corner of the chart to cell A8 on the worksheet.

c. Format the May data series using the Lime, Accent 1, Lighter 40% color from the theme colors.

d. Add the Aug, Sep, and Oct data to the chart.

e. Move the chart to its own sheet named **May - Oct**.

f. Add the following profit data to the Sales sheet:

Cell	Data
A7	Profit
B7	$2,010
C7	$1,742
D7	$2,450
E7	$1,975
F7	$1,020
G7	$1,814

Independent Challenge 3 (continued)

g. Add the new profit data to the chart, then change the row and column view so the sales items are in the legend.

h. Create a combination chart placing clubs, apparel, footwear, and cart rentals in clustered column charts and profit in a line chart.

i. Add a chart title of **May - October Sales** in size 28-point font above the chart. Format the chart title using the WordArt Style Fill - Lime, Accent1, Shadow.

j. Add a title of **Sales** in 20-point to the vertical axis. Format it in the same WordArt style as the chart title. Delete the horizontal axis title placeholder.

k. Change the value axis scale to a maximum of **6000**, then save your workbook.

l. Add data labels to the profit data series. (*Hint*: Select the profit line chart before adding data labels.)

m. Compare your chart to **FIGURE J-24**.

n. Enter your name in the center footer section of the chart sheet, save the workbook, then preview the chart.

o. Close the workbook, submit the workbook to your instructor, then exit Excel.

FIGURE J-24

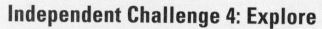

Independent Challenge 4: Explore

As the sales manager of Smith Motor Group you are interested in how sales at your company correlate with vehicles' fuel economy. Your administrative assistant has entered the January sales and mpg data in a worksheet and you decide to chart the data to visualize this relationship. You will use a combination chart because of the different types of data.

a. Start Excel, open the file EX J-6.xlsx from the location where you store your Data Files then save the workbook as **EX J-Car Sales**.

b. Create a clustered column chart using the data in cells A3:B10. Move and resize your chart to fill the range D1:L20.

c. Link the chart title to cell A1. (*Hint*: With the chart title selected, enter = in the formula bar, click cell A1, then press [Enter].)

d. Format the chart title text in WordArt style Fill - Blue, Accent 1, Shadow.

e. Add a vertical axis title and link it to cell A3. Format the axis title using a shape style of Subtle Effect - Blue, Accent 1. Add a shape effect of circle bevel.

f. Delete the horizontal axis title.

g. To improve the visibility of the combined MPG series, place it on a line chart and assign it to a secondary axis. (*Hint*: Change the chart type to Combo and select Secondary Axis for the Combined MPG line chart.)

h. Change the text in cell B3 from Combined MPG to MPG and verify that the legend changed.

i. Change the chart title link to cell A2 and verify the change in the chart title.

j. Change cell A5 to 52,500 and view the chart animation of the second bar to reflect this data change.

k. Add data labels to the MPG data series. (*Hint*: Select the MPG line chart before adding data labels.)

l. Assign the same shape style to the chart title that you assigned to the vertical axis.

m. Compare your chart to **FIGURE J-25**.

n. Enter your name in the center footer section of the worksheet, save the workbook, then preview the worksheet.

o. Close the workbook, submit the workbook to your instructor, then exit Excel.

FIGURE J-25

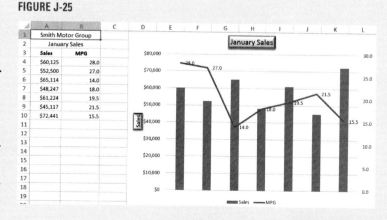

Visual Workshop

Open the file EX J-7.xlsx from the location where you store your Data Files, and create the custom chart shown in FIGURE J-26. (*Hint*: The trendlines forecast three periods forward and use the standard line colors red and purple.) Save the workbook as **EX J-Organic Sales**. Study the chart and worksheet carefully to make sure you select the displayed chart type with all the enhancements shown. Enter your name in the center section of the worksheet footer, then preview the worksheet in landscape orientation on one page. Submit the workbook to your instructor.

FIGURE J-26

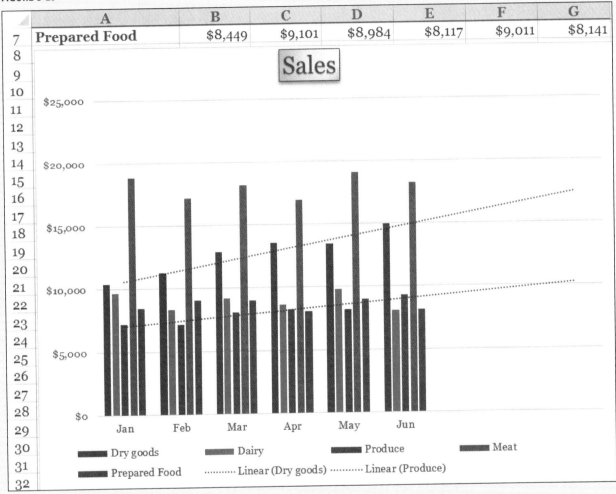

Using What-if Analysis

CASE ▶ Kate Morgan, the vice president of sales at Quest, is meeting with the U.S. region manager to discuss sales projections for the first half of the year. In preparation for her meeting, Kate asks you to help analyze the U.S. sales data using what-if scenarios, data tables, goal seek, Solver and the Analysis ToolPak.

Unit Objectives

After completing this unit, you will be able to:

- Define a what-if analysis
- Track a what-if analysis with Scenario Manager
- Generate a scenario summary
- Project figures using a data table
- Use Goal Seek
- Set up a complex what-if analysis with Solver
- Run Solver and summarize results
- Analyze data using the Analysis ToolPak

Files You Will Need

EX K-1.xlsx
EX K-2.xlsx
EX K-3.xlsx
EX K-4.xlsx

EX K-5.xlsx
EX K-6.xlsx
EX K-7.xlsx

Define a What-if Analysis

Learning
Outcomes
• Develop guidelines
for performing
what-if analysis
• Define what-if anal-
ysis terminology

By performing a what-if analysis in a worksheet, you can get immediate answers to questions such as "What happens to profits if we sell 25 percent more of a certain product?" or "What happens to monthly payments if interest rates rise or fall?". A worksheet you use to produce a what-if analysis is often called a **model** because it acts as the basis for multiple outcomes or sets of results. To perform a what-if analysis in a worksheet, you change the value in one or more **input cells** (cells that contain data rather than for-mulas), then observe the effects on dependent cells. A **dependent cell** usually contains a formula whose resulting value changes depending on the values in the input cells. A dependent cell can be located either in the same worksheet as the changing input value or in another worksheet. **CASE** *Kate Morgan has received projected sales data from regional managers. She has created a worksheet model to perform an initial what-if analysis, as shown in FIGURE K-1. She thinks the U.S. sales projections for the month of January should be higher. You first review the guidelines for performing a what-if analysis.*

DETAILS

When performing a what-if analysis, use the following guidelines:

- **Understand and state the purpose of the worksheet model**

  Identify what you want to accomplish with the model. What problem are you trying to solve? What questions do you want the model to answer for you? Kate's Quest worksheet model is designed to total Quest sales projections for the first half of the year and to calculate the percentage of total sales for each Quest region. It also calculates the totals and percentages of total sales for each month.

- **Determine the data input value(s) that, if changed, affect the dependent cell results**

  In a what-if analysis, changes in the content of the data input cells produces varying results in the output cells. You will use the model to work with one data input value: the January value for the U.S. region, in cell B3.

- **Identify the dependent cell(s) that will contain results**

  The dependent cells usually contain formulas, and the formula results adjust as you enter different values in the input cells. The results of two dependent cell formulas (labeled Total and Percent of Total Sales) appear in cells H3 and I3, respectively. The total for the month of January in cell B7 is also a dependent cell, as is the percentage in cell B8.

- **Formulate questions you want the what-if analysis to answer**

  It is important that you know the questions you want your model to answer. In the Quest model, you want to answer the following question: What happens to the U.S. regional percentage if the sales amount for the month of January is increased to $109,667?

- **Perform the what-if analysis**

  When you perform the what-if analysis, you explore the relationships between the input values and the dependent cell formulas. In the Quest worksheet model, you want to see what effect an increase in sales for January has on the dependent cell formulas containing totals and percentages. Because the sales amounts for this month is located in cell B3, any formula that references that cell is directly affected by a change in this sales amount—in this case, the total formula in cell H3. Because the formula in cell I3 references cell H3, a change in the sales amount affects this cell as well. The percentage formulas will also change because they reference the total formulas. **FIGURE K-2** shows the result of the what-if analysis described in this example.

FIGURE K-1: Worksheet model for a what-if analysis

	A	B	C	D	E	F	G	H	I	J	K
1				2017 Projected Sales							
2	Data input value	Jan	Feb	Mar	Apr	May	Jun	Total	Percent of Total Sales		
3	U.S.	$91,475	$67,189	$69,423	$61,664	$103,926	$100,244	$493,921	31.08%		
4	Canada	$64,868	$75,326	$77,244	$71,688	$67,015	$67,388	$423,529	26.65%		
5	U.K.	$61,573	$62,756	$64,681	$72,988	$61,191	$40,334	$363,523	22.88%		
6	Australia	$37,043	$57,657	$61,539	$60,708	$45,868	$45,224	$308,039	19.39%		
7	Total	$254,959	$262,928	$272,887	$267,048	$278,000	$253,190	$1,589,012			
8	Percent of Total Sales	16.05%	16.55%	17.17%	16.81%	17.50%	15.93%				
9											
10											
11											
12									Dependent cell formulas		
13											

FIGURE K-2: Changed input values and dependent formula results

	A	B	C	D	E	F	G	H	I	J
1				2017 Projected Sales						
2	Changed input value	Jan	Feb	Mar	Apr	May	Jun	Total	Percent of Total Sales	
3	U.S.	$109,667	$67,189	$69,423	$61,664	$103,926	$100,244	$512,113	31.86%	
4	Canada	$64,868	$75,326	$77,244	$71,688	$67,015	$67,388	$423,529	26.35%	
5	U.K.	$61,573	$62,756	$64,681	$72,988	$61,191	$40,334	$363,523	22.62%	
6	Australia	$37,043	$57,657	$61,539	$60,708	$45,868	$45,224	$308,039	19.17%	
7	Total	$273,151	$262,928	$272,887	$267,048	$278,000	$253,190	$1,607,204		
8	Percent of Total Sales	17.00%	16.36%	16.98%	16.62%	17.30%	15.75%			
9										
10										
11										
12										
13									Changed formula results	
14										
15										

Track a What-if Analysis with Scenario Manager

Learning
Outcomes
• Create scenarios to
  analyze Excel data
• Analyze scenarios
  using Scenario
  Manager

A **scenario** is a set of values you use to observe different worksheet results. For example, you might plan to sell 100 of a particular item, at a price of $5 per item, producing sales results of $500. But what if you reduced the price to $4 or increased it to $6? Each of these price scenarios would produce different sales results. A changing value, such as the price in this example, is called a **variable**. The Excel Scenario Manager simplifies the process of what-if analysis by allowing you to name and save multiple scenarios with variable values in a worksheet. **CASE** ▶ *Kate asks you to use Scenario Manager to create scenarios showing how a U.S. sales increase can affect total Quest sales over the 3-month period of February through April.*

STEPS

1. **Start Excel, open the file** EX K-1.xlsx **from the location where you store your Data Files, then save it as** EX K-Sales

   The first step in defining a scenario is choosing the changing cells. **Changing cells** are those that will vary in the different scenarios.

2. **With the Projected Sales sheet active, select range** C3:E3, **click the** DATA tab, **click the** What-If Analysis button **in the Data Tools group, then click** Scenario Manager

   You want to be able to easily return to your original worksheet values, so your first scenario contains those figures.

3. **Click** Add, **drag the Add Scenario dialog box to the right if necessary until columns A and B are visible, then type** Original Sales Figures **in the Scenario name text box**

   The range in the Changing cells box shows the range you selected, as shown in **FIGURE K-3**.

4. **Click** OK **to confirm the scenario range**

   The Scenario Values dialog box opens, as shown in **FIGURE K-4**. The existing values appear in the changing cell boxes. Because you want this scenario to reflect the current worksheet values, you leave these unchanged.

   QUICK TIP
   You can delete a scenario by selecting it in the Scenario Manager dialog box and clicking Delete.

5. **Click** OK

   You want to create a second scenario that will show the effects of increasing sales by $5,000.

6. **Click** Add; **in the Scenario name text box type** Increase Feb, Mar, Apr by 5000; **verify that the Changing cells text box reads** C3:E3, **then click** OK; **in the Scenario Values dialog box, change the value in the** $C$3 **text box to** 72189, **change the value in the** $D$3 **text box to** 74423, **change the value in the** $E$3 **text box to** 66664, **then click** Add

   You are ready to create a third scenario. It will show the effects of increasing sales by $10,000.

7. **In the Scenario name text box, type** Increase Feb, Mar, Apr by 10000 **and click** OK; **in the Scenario Values dialog box, change the value in the** $C$3 **text box to** 77189, **change the value in the** $D$3 **text box to** 79423, **change the value in the** $E$3 **text box to** 71664, **then click** OK

   The Scenario Manager dialog box reappears, as shown in **FIGURE K-5**. You are ready to display the results of your scenarios in the worksheet.

   QUICK TIP
   To edit a scenario, select it in the Scenario Manager dialog box, click the Edit button, then edit the Scenario.

8. **Make sure the Increase Feb, Mar, Apr by 10000 scenario is still selected, click** Show, **notice that the percent of U.S. sales in cell I3 changes from 31.08% to 32.36%; click** Increase Feb, Mar, Apr by 5000, **click** Show, **notice that the U.S. sales percent is now 31.73%; click** Original Sales Figures, **click** Show **to return to the original values, then click** Close

9. **Save the workbook**

FIGURE K-3: Add Scenario dialog box

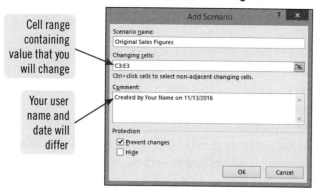

Cell range containing value that you will change

Your user name and date will differ

FIGURE K-4: Scenario Values dialog box

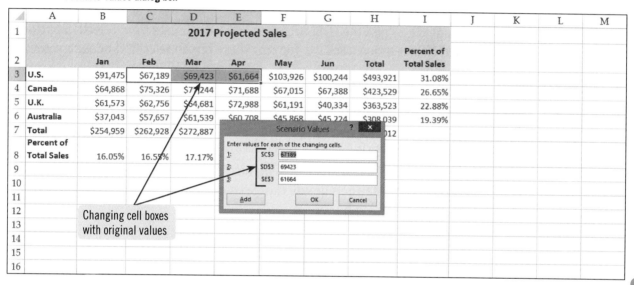

	A	B	C	D	E	F	G	H	I	J	K	L	M
1				**2017 Projected Sales**									
2		Jan	Feb	Mar	Apr	May	Jun	Total	Percent of Total Sales				
3	U.S.	$91,475	$67,189	$69,423	$61,664	$103,926	$100,244	$493,921	31.08%				
4	Canada	$64,868	$75,326	$71,244	$71,688	$67,015	$67,388	$423,529	26.65%				
5	U.K.	$61,573	$62,756	$64,681	$72,988	$61,191	$40,334	$363,523	22.88%				
6	Australia	$37,043	$57,657	$61,539	$60,708	$45,868	$45,224	$308,039	19.39%				
7	Total	$254,959	$262,928	$272,887									
8	Percent of Total Sales	16.05%	16.53%	17.17%									
9													
10													
11													
12													
13													
14													
15													
16													

Changing cell boxes with original values

FIGURE K-5: Scenario Manager dialog box with three scenarios listed

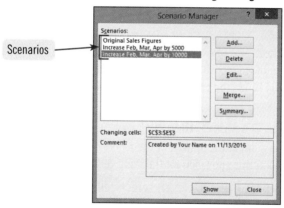

Scenarios

Merging scenarios

Excel stores scenarios in the workbook and on the worksheet in which you created them. To apply scenarios from another worksheet or workbook into the current worksheet, click the Merge button in the Scenario Manager dialog box. The Merge Scenarios dialog box opens, letting you select scenarios from other locations. When you click a sheet name in the sheet list, the text under the sheet list tells you how many scenarios exist on that sheet. To merge scenarios from another workbook, such as those sent to you in a workbook by a coworker, open the other workbook file, click the Book list arrow in the Merge Scenarios dialog box, then click the workbook name. When you merge workbook scenarios, it's best if the workbooks have the same structure, so that there is no confusion of cell values.

Generate a Scenario Summary

Learning
Outcomes
• Display scenarios in a scenario summary report
• Format a scenario summary report

Although it may be useful to display the different scenario outcomes when analyzing data, it can be difficult to keep track of them. In most cases, you will want to refer to a single report that summarizes the results of all the scenarios in a worksheet. A **scenario summary** is an Excel table that compiles data from the changing cells and corresponding result cells for each scenario. For example, you might use a scenario summary to illustrate the best, worst, and most likely scenarios for a particular set of circumstances. Using cell naming makes the summary easier to read because the names, not the cell references, appear in the report. **CASE** ▶ *Now that you have defined Kate's scenarios, she needs you to generate and print a scenario summary report. You begin by creating names for the cells in row 3 based on the labels in row 2, so that the report will be easier to read.*

STEPS

1. **Select the range B2:I3, click the FORMULAS tab, click the Create from Selection button in the Defined Names group, click the Top row check box to select it if necessary, then click OK**

   Excel creates the names for the data in row 3 based on the labels in row 2. You decide to review them.

2. **Click the Name Manager button in the Defined Names group**

   The eight labels appear, along with other workbook names, in the Name Manager dialog box, confirming that they were created, as shown in **FIGURE K-6**. Now you are ready to generate the scenario summary report.

3. **Click Close to close the Name Manager dialog box, click the DATA tab, click the What-If Analysis button in the Data Tools group, click Scenario Manager, then click Summary in the Scenario Manager dialog box**

   Excel needs to know the location of the cells that contain the formula results that you want to see in the report. You want to see the results for U.S. total and percentage of sales, and on overall Quest sales.

4. **With the Result cells text box selected, click cell H3 on the worksheet, type , (a comma), click cell I3, type , (a comma), then click cell H7**

   With the report type and result cells specified, as shown in **FIGURE K-7**, you are now ready to generate the report.

5. **Click OK**

   A summary of the worksheet's scenarios appears on a new sheet titled Scenario Summary. The report shows outline buttons to the left of and above the worksheet so that you can hide or show report details. Because the Current Values column shows the same values as the Original Sales Figures column, you decide to delete column D.

6. **Right-click the column D heading, then click Delete in the shortcut menu**

   Next, you notice that the notes at the bottom of the report refer to the column that no longer exists. You also want to make the report title and labels for the result cells more descriptive.

7. **Select the range B13:B15, press [Delete], select cell B2, edit its contents to read Scenario Summary for U.S. Sales, click cell C10, then edit its contents to read Total U.S. Sales**

8. **Click cell C11, edit its contents to read Percent U.S. Sales, click cell C12, edit its contents to read Total Quest Sales, then click cell A1**

   The completed scenario summary is shown in **FIGURE K-8**.

9. **Add your name to the center section of the Scenario Summary sheet footer, change the page orientation to landscape, then save the workbook and preview the worksheet**

FIGURE K-6: Name Manager dialog box displaying new names

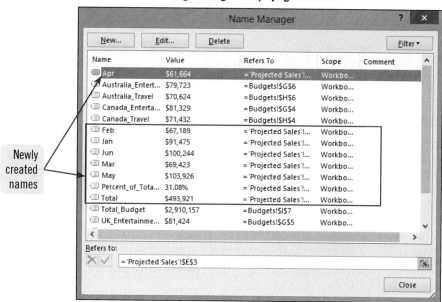

Newly created names

FIGURE K-7: Scenario Summary dialog box

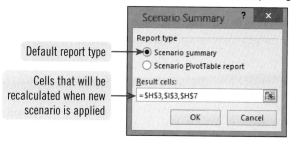

Default report type

Cells that will be recalculated when new scenario is applied

FIGURE K-8: Completed Scenario Summary report

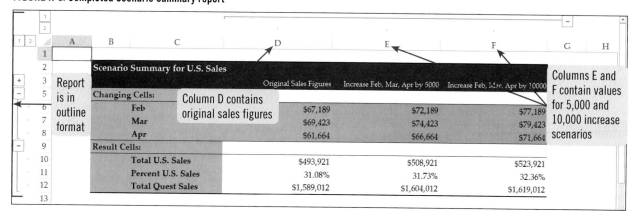

Report is in outline format

Column D contains original sales figures

Columns E and F contain values for 5,000 and 10,000 increase scenarios

Learning
Outcomes
• Develop a data
table structure
• Analyze options
using a data table

Project Figures Using a Data Table

Another way to answer what-if questions in a worksheet is by using a data table. A **data table** is a range of cells that simultaneously shows the varying resulting values when you change one or more input values in a formula. A **one-input data table** is a table that shows the result of varying one input value, such as the interest rate. **CASE** *Now that you have completed Kate's analysis, she wants you to find out how the U.S. sales percentage would change as U.S. total sales increased.*

STEPS

1. **Click the** Projected Sales sheet tab, **enter** Total U.S. Sales **in cell K1, widen column K to fit the label, in cell K2 enter** 481819, **in cell K3 enter** 531819, **select the range** K2:K3, **drag the fill handle to select the range** K4:K6, **then format the values using the Accounting number format with zero decimal places**

   You begin setting up your data table by entering total U.S. sales lower and higher than the total in cell H3 in increasing amounts of $50,000. These are the **input values** in the data table. With the varying input values listed in column K, you enter a formula reference to cell I3 that you want Excel to use in calculating the resulting percentages (the **output values**) in column L, based on the possible sales levels in column K.

2. **Click cell L1, type** =, **click cell** I3, **click the** Enter button ✔ **on the formula bar, then format the value in cell L1 using the Percentage format with two decimal places**

   The value in cell I3, 31.08%, appears in cell L1, and the cell name =Percent_of_Total_Sales appears in the formula bar, as shown in **FIGURE K-9**. Because it isn't necessary for users of the data table to see the value in cell L1, you want to hide the cell's contents from view.

3. **With cell L1 selected, click the** HOME tab, **click the** Format button **in the Cells group, click** Format Cells, **click the** Number tab **in the Format Cells dialog box if necessary, click** Custom **under Category, select any characters in the Type box, type** ;;; **(three semicolons), then click** OK

   Applying the custom cell format of three semicolons hides the values in a cell. With the table structure in place, you can now generate the data table showing percentages for the varying sales amounts.

4. **Select the range** K1:L6, **click the** DATA tab, **click the** What-If Analysis button **in the Data Tools group, then click** Data Table

   The Data Table dialog box opens, as shown in **FIGURE K-10**. Because the percentage formula in cell I3 (which you just referenced in cell L1) uses the total sales in cell H3 as input, you enter a reference to cell H3. You place this reference in the Column input cell text box, rather than in the Row input cell text box, because the varying input values are arranged in a column in your data table structure.

5. **Click the** Column input cell text box, **click cell** H3, **then click** OK

   Excel completes the data table by calculating percentages for each sales amount.

6. **Format the range** L2:L6 **with the Percentage format with two decimal places, then click cell** A1

   The formatted data table is shown in **FIGURE K-11**. It shows the sales percentages for each of the possible levels of U.S. sales. By looking at the data table, Kate determines that if she can increase total U.S. sales to over $700,000, the U.S. division will then comprise about 40% of total Quest sales for the first half of 2017.

7. **Add your name to the center section of the worksheet footer, change the worksheet orientation to landscape, then save the workbook and preview the worksheet**

FIGURE K-9: One-input data table structure

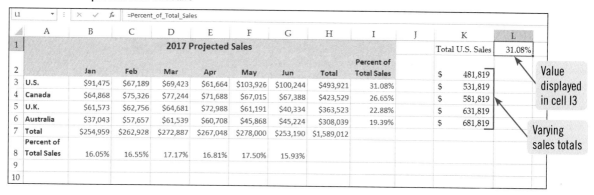

	A	B	C	D	E	F	G	H	I	J	K	L
L1	=Percent_of_Total_Sales											
1	2017 Projected Sales										Total U.S. Sales	31.08%
2		Jan	Feb	Mar	Apr	May	Jun	Total	Percent of Total Sales		$ 481,819	
3	U.S.	$91,475	$67,189	$69,423	$61,664	$103,926	$100,244	$493,921	31.08%		$ 531,819	
4	Canada	$64,868	$75,326	$77,244	$71,688	$67,015	$67,388	$423,529	26.65%		$ 581,819	
5	U.K.	$61,573	$62,756	$64,681	$72,988	$61,191	$40,334	$363,523	22.88%		$ 631,819	
6	Australia	$37,043	$57,657	$61,539	$60,708	$45,868	$45,224	$308,039	19.39%		$ 681,819	
7	Total	$254,959	$262,928	$272,887	$267,048	$278,000	$253,190	$1,589,012				
8	Percent of Total Sales	16.05%	16.55%	17.17%	16.81%	17.50%	15.93%					
9												
10												

Value displayed in cell I3

Varying sales totals

FIGURE K-10: Data Table dialog box

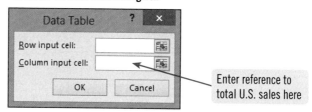

Data Table

Row input cell:

Column input cell:

OK   Cancel

Enter reference to total U.S. sales here

FIGURE K-11: Completed data table with resulting values

	A	B	C	D	E	F	G	H	I	J	K	L
1	2017 Projected Sales										Total U.S. Sales	
2		Jan	Feb	Mar	Apr	May	Jun	Total	Percent of Total Sales		$ 481,819	30.55%
3	U.S.	$91,475	$67,189	$69,423	$61,664	$103,926	$100,244	$493,921	31.08%		$ 531,819	32.69%
4	Canada	$64,868	$75,326	$77,244	$71,688	$67,015	$67,388	$423,529	26.65%		$ 581,819	34.70%
5	U.K.	$61,573	$62,756	$64,681	$72,988	$61,191	$40,334	$363,523	22.88%		$ 631,819	36.59%
6	Australia	$37,043	$57,657	$61,539	$60,708	$45,868	$45,224	$308,039	19.39%		$ 681,819	38.37%
7	Total	$254,959	$262,928	$272,887	$267,048	$278,000	$253,190	$1,589,012				
8	Percent of Total Sales	16.05%	16.55%	17.17%	16.81%	17.50%	15.93%					
9												
10												
11												
12												
13												

Input values in column K

Percentages (output values) in column L

Completed data table

Creating a two-input data table

A **two-input data table** shows the resulting values when two different input values are varied in a formula. You could, for example, use a two-input data table to calculate your monthly car payment based on varying interest rates and varying loan terms, as shown in **FIGURE K-12**. In a two-input data table, different values of one input cell appear across the top row of the table, while different values of the second input cell are listed down the left column. You create a two-input data table the same way that you created a one-input data table, except you enter both a row and a column input cell. In the example shown in **FIGURE K-12**, the two-input data table structure was created by first entering the number of payments in the range B6:D6 and rates in the range A7:A15. Then the data table values were created by first selecting the range A6:D15, clicking the DATA tab, clicking the What-If Analysis button in the Data Tools group, then clicking Data Table. In the Data Table dialog box, the row input value is the term in cell C2. The column input value is the interest rate in cell B2.

You can check the accuracy of these values by cross-referencing the values in the data table with those in row 2 where you can see that an interest rate of 4.5% for 36 months has a monthly payment of $594.94.

FIGURE K-12: Two-input data table

	A	B	C	D	E
1	Loan Amount	Interest Rate	# Payments	Monthly Payment	
2	$20,000.00	4.50%	36	$594.94	
3					
4		Car Payment for $20,000 Loan			
5			Term		
6		36	48	60	
7	4.00%	$590.48	$451.58	$368.33	
8	4.25%	$592.71	$453.82	$370.59	
9	4.50%	$594.94	$456.07	$372.86	
10	4.75%	$597.18	$458.32	$375.14	
11	5.00%	$599.42	$460.59	$377.42	
12	5.25%	$601.67	$462.85	$379.72	
13	5.50%	$603.92	$465.13	$382.02	
14	5.75%	$606.18	$467.41	$384.34	
15	6.00%	$608.44	$469.70	$386.66	
16					
17					

Use Goal Seek

Learning Outcomes
- Determine input values for a desired result using goal seek
- Answer questions about data using goal seek

You can think of goal seeking as a what-if analysis in reverse. In a what-if analysis, you might try many sets of values to achieve a certain solution. To **goal seek**, you specify a solution, then ask Excel to find the input value that produces the answer you want. "Backing into" a solution in this way, sometimes referred to as **backsolving**, can save a significant amount of time. For example, you can use Goal Seek to determine how many units must be sold to reach a particular sales goal or to determine what expense levels are necessary to meet a budget target. **CASE** ➤ *After reviewing her data table, Kate has a follow-up question: What January U.S. sales target is required to bring the January Quest sales percentage to 17%, assuming the sales for the other regions don't change? You use Goal Seek to answer her question.*

STEPS

1. **Click cell B8**

   The first step in using Goal Seek is to select a goal cell. A **goal cell** contains a formula in which you can substitute values to find a specific value, or goal. You use cell B8 as the goal cell because it contains the percent formula.

2. **Click the DATA tab, click the What-If Analysis button in the Data Tools group, then click Goal Seek**

   The Goal Seek dialog box opens. The Set cell text box contains a reference to cell B8, the percent formula cell you selected in Step 1. You need to indicate that the figure in cell B8 should equal 17%.

3. **Click the To value text box, then type 17%**

   The value 17% represents the desired solution you want to reach by substituting different values in the By changing cell.

4. **Click the By changing cell text box, then click cell B3**

   You have specified that you want cell B3, the U.S. January amount, to change to reach the 17% solution, as shown in **FIGURE K-13**.

5. **Click OK**

   The Goal Seek Status dialog box opens with the following message: "Goal Seeking with Cell B8 found a solution." By changing the sales amount in cell B3 to $109,667, Goal Seek achieves a January percentage of 17.

   QUICK TIP
   Before you select another command, you can return the worksheet to its status prior to the Goal Seek by pressing [Ctrl][Z].

6. **Click OK, then click cell A1**

   Changing the sales amount in cell B3 changes the other dependent values in the worksheet (B7, H3, I3, and H7) as shown in **FIGURE K-14**.

7. **Save the workbook, then preview the worksheet**

FIGURE K-13: Completed Goal Seek dialog box

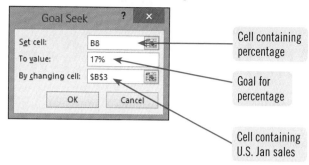

Cell containing percentage

Goal for percentage

Cell containing U.S. Jan sales

FIGURE K-14: Worksheet with new dependent values

	A	B	C	D	E	F	G	H	I	J
1					**2017 Projected Sales**					
2		Jan	Feb	Mar	Apr	May	Jun	Total	Percent of Total Sales	
3	U.S.	$109,667	$67,189	$69,423	$61,664	$103,926	$100,244	$512,113	31.86%	
4	Canada	$64,868	$75,326	$77,244	$71,688	$67,015	$67,388	$423,529	26.35%	
5	U.K.	$61,573	$62,756	$64,681	$72,988	$61,191	$40,334	$363,523	22.62%	
6	Australia	$37,043	$57,657	$61,539	$60,708	$45,868	$45,224	$308,039	19.17%	
7	Total	$273,151	$262,928	$272,887	$267,048	$278,000	$253,190	$1,607,204		
8	Percent of Total Sales	17.00%	16.36%	16.98%	16.62%	17.30%	15.75%			
9										
10										

New target values calculated by Goal Seek

New dependent values

13										
14										
15										

Excel 2013

Learning
Outcomes
• Develop an under-
standing of the
solver terminology
• Set up a worksheet
analysis using the
Solver Parameters
dialog box

Set up a Complex What-if Analysis with Solver

The Excel Solver is an **add-in** program that provides optional features. It must be installed before you can use it. Solver finds the best solution to a problem that has several inputs. The cell containing the formula is called the **target cell**, or **objective**. As you learned earlier, cells containing the values that vary are called "changing cells." Solver is helpful when you need to perform a complex what-if analysis involving multiple input values or when the input values must conform to specific limitations or restrictions called **constraints**. **CASE** *Kate decides to fund each region with the same amount, $775,000, to cover expenses. She adjusts the travel and entertainment allocations to keep expenditures to the allocated amount of $775,000. You use Solver to help Kate find the best possible allocation.*

STEPS

TROUBLE
If Solver is not on your DATA tab, click the FILE tab, click Options, click Add-Ins, click Go, in the Add-Ins dialog box click the Solver Add-in check box to select it, then click OK.

1. **Click the Budgets sheet tab**

   This worksheet is designed to calculate the travel, entertainment, and other budget categories for each region. It assumes fixed costs for communications, equipment, advertising, salaries, and rent. You use Solver to change the entertainment and travel amounts in cells G3:H6 (the changing cells) to achieve your target of a total budget of $3,100,000 in cell I7 (the target cell). You want your solution to include a constraint on cells G3:H6 specifying that each region is funded $775,000. Based on past budgets, you know there are two other constraints: the travel budgets must include at least $83,000, and the entertainment budgets must include at least $95,000. It is a good idea to enter constraints on the worksheet for documentation purposes, as shown in **FIGURE K-15**.

2. **Click the DATA tab, then click the Solver button in the Analysis group**

   If the Solver Parameters dialog box opens, you indicate the target cell with its objective, the changing cells, and the constraints under which you want Solver to work. You begin by entering your total budget objective.

QUICK TIP
If your Solver Parameters dialog box has entries in the By Changing Variable Cells box or in the Subject to the Constraints box, click Reset All, click OK, then continue with Step 3.

3. **With the insertion point in the Set Objective text box, click cell I7 in the worksheet, click the Value Of option button, double-click the Value Of text box, then type 3,100,000**

   You have specified an objective of $3,100,000 for the total budget. In typing the total budget figure, be sure to type the commas.

4. **Click the By Changing Variable Cells text box, then select the range G3:H6 on the worksheet**

   You have told Excel which cells to vary to reach the goal of $3,100,000 total budget. You need to specify the constraints on the worksheet values to restrict the Solver's answer to realistic values.

5. **Click Add, with the insertion point in the Cell Reference text box in the Add Constraint dialog box, select the range I3:I6 in the worksheet, click the list arrow in the dialog box, click =, then with the insertion point in the Constraint text box click cell C9**

   As shown in **FIGURE K-16**, the Add Constraint dialog box specifies that cells in the range I3:I6, the total region budget amounts, should be equal to the value in cell C9. Next, you need to add the constraint that the budgeted entertainment amounts should be at least $95,000.

QUICK TIP
If your solution needs to be an integer, you can select it in the Add Constraint dialog box.

6. **Click Add, with the insertion point in the Cell Reference text box select the range G3:G6 in the worksheet, click the list arrow, select >=, with the insertion point in the Constraint text box click cell C11**

   Next, you need to specify that the budgeted travel amounts should be greater than or equal to $83,000.

7. **Click Add, with the insertion point in the Cell Reference text box select the range H3:H6, select >=, with the insertion point in the Constraint text box click cell C10, then click OK**

   The Solver Parameters dialog box opens with the constraints listed, as shown in **FIGURE K-17**. In the next lesson, you run Solver and generate solutions to the budget constraints.

Using What-if Analysis

FIGURE K-15: Worksheet set up for a complex what-if analysis

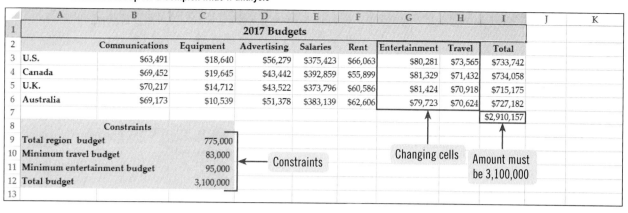

FIGURE K-16: Adding constraints

FIGURE K-17: Completed Solver Parameters dialog box

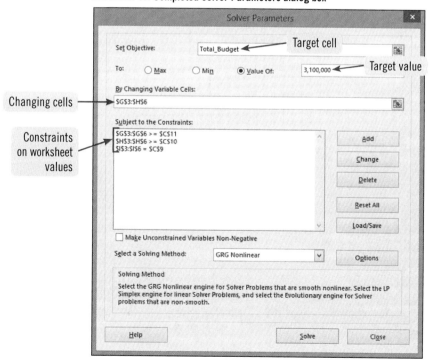

Run Solver and Summarize Results

Learning
Outcomes
• Run solver using
the parameters
in the Solver
Parameters
dialog box
• Create an answer
report using solver

After entering all the parameters in the Solver Parameters dialog box, you can run Solver to find a solution. In some cases, Solver may not be able to find a solution that meets all of your constraints. Then you would need to enter new constraints and try again. **CASE** *You have finished entering the parameters in the Solver Parameters dialog box. Kate wants you to run Solver and create a summary of the solution on a separate worksheet.*

STEPS

1. **Make sure your Solver Parameters dialog box matches FIGURE K-17 in the previous lesson**

2. **Click Solve**

   The Solver Results dialog box opens, indicating that Solver has found a solution, as shown in **FIGURE K-18**. The solution values appear in the worksheet, but you decide to save the solution values in a summary worksheet and display the original values in the worksheet.

3. **Click Save Scenario, enter Adjusted Budgets in the Scenario Name text box, click OK, in the Solver Results dialog box click the Restore Original Values option button, then click OK to close the Solver Results dialog box**

   The Solver Results dialog box closes, and the original values appear in the worksheet. You will display the Solver solution values on a separate sheet.

4. **Click the What-If Analysis button in the Data Tools group, click Scenario Manager, with the Adjusted Budgets scenario selected in the Scenario Manager dialog box click Summary, then click OK**

   The Solver results appear on the Scenario Summary 2 worksheet, as shown in **FIGURE K-19**. You want to format the solution values on the worksheet.

5. **Select Column A, click the HOME tab if necessary, click the Delete button in the Cells group, right-click the Scenario Summary 2 sheet tab, click Rename on the shortcut menu, type Adjusted Budgets, then press [Enter]**

6. **Select the range A16:A18, press [Delete], select the range A2:D3, click the Fill Color list arrow in the Font group, click Blue, Accent 2, select the range A5:D15, click the Fill Color list arrow, click Blue, Accent 2, Lighter 80%, right-click the row 1 header to select the row, click Delete, select cell A1, then enter Solver Solutions**

   The formatted Solver solution is shown in **FIGURE K-20**.

7. **Enter your name in the center section of the worksheet footer, save the workbook, then preview the worksheet**

Understanding Answer Reports

Instead of saving Solver results as a scenario, you can select from three types of answer reports in the Solver Results window. One of the most useful is the Answer Report, which compares the original values with the Solver's final values. The report has three sections. The top section has the target cell information; it compares the original value of the target cell with the final value. The middle section of the report contains information about the adjustable cells. It lists the original and final values for all cells that were changed to reach the target value. The last report section has information about the constraints. Each constraint you added into Solver is listed in the Formula column, along with the cell address and a description of the cell data. The Cell Value column contains the Solver solution values for the cells. The Status column contains information on whether the constraints were binding or not binding in reaching the solution.

FIGURE K-18: Solver Results dialog box

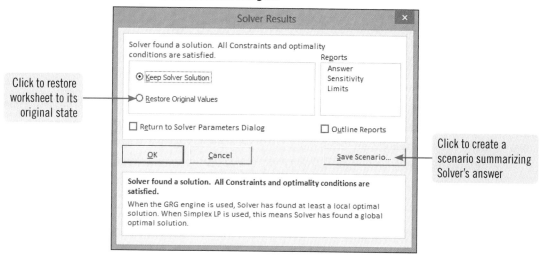

Click to restore worksheet to its original state

Click to create a scenario summarizing Solver's answer

FIGURE K-19: Solver Summary

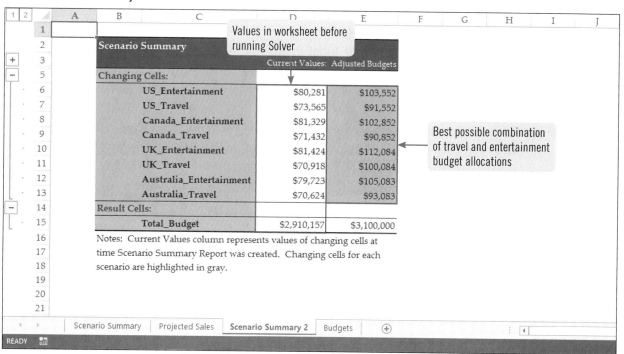

Values in worksheet before running Solver

Best possible combination of travel and entertainment budget allocations

FIGURE K-20: Formatted Solver Summary

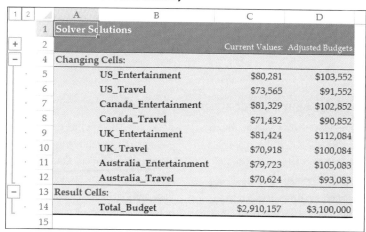

Using What-if Analysis

Analyze Data Using the Analysis ToolPak

Learning Outcomes
• Create a summary statistics worksheet
• Analyze worksheet data using descriptive statistics

The Analysis ToolPak is an Excel add-in that contains many statistical analysis tools. The Descriptive Statistics tool in the Data Analysis dialog box generates a statistical report including mean, median, mode, minimum, maximum, and sum for an input range you specify on your worksheet. **CASE** *After reviewing the projected sales figures for the Quest regions, Kate decides to statistically analyze the projected regional sales totals submitted by the managers. You use the Analysis ToolPak to help her generate the sales statistics.*

STEPS

TROUBLE
If Data Analysis is not on your DATA tab, click the FILE tab, click Options, click Add-Ins, click Go, in the Add-Ins dialog box click the Analysis ToolPak check box to select it, then click OK.

1. **Click the** Projected Sales sheet tab, **click the** DATA tab, **then click the** Data Analysis button **in the Analysis group**

   The Data Analysis dialog box opens, listing the available analysis tools.

2. **Click** Descriptive Statistics, **then click** OK

   The Descriptive Statistics dialog box opens, as shown in **FIGURE K-21**.

3. **With the insertion point in the Input Range text box, select the range** H3:H6 **on the worksheet**

   You have told Excel to use the total projected sales cells in the statistical analysis. You need to specify that the data is grouped in a column and the results should be placed on a new worksheet named Region Statistics.

QUICK TIP
Selecting the New Worksheet Ply option places the statistical output on a new worksheet in the workbook.

4. **Click the** Columns option button **in the Grouped By: area if necessary, click the** New Worksheet Ply option button **in the Output options section if necessary, then type** Region Statistics **in the text box**

   You want to add the summary statistics to the new worksheet.

5. **Click the** Summary statistics check box **to select it, then click** OK

   The statistics are generated and placed on the new worksheet named Region Statistics. **TABLE K-1** describes the statistical values provided in the worksheet. Column A is not wide enough to view the labels, and the worksheet needs a descriptive title.

QUICK TIP
If there are fewer than four data values, the Kurtosis will display the DIV/0! error value.

6. **Widen column A to display the row labels, then edit the contents of cell A1 to read** Total Projected Sales Jan – Jun

   The completed report is shown in **FIGURE K-22**.

7. **Enter your name in the center section of the Region Statistics footer, preview the report, save the workbook, close the workbook, then exit Excel**

8. **Submit the workbook to your instructor**

Choosing the right tool for your data analysis

The Analysis ToolPak offers 19 options for data analysis. Anova, or the analysis of variance, can be applied to one or more data samples. The Regression option creates a table of statistics from a least-squares regression. The Correlation choice measures how strong of a linear relationship exists between two random variables. A Moving Average is often calculated for stock prices or any other data that is time sensitive. Moving averages display long-term trends by smoothing out short-term changes. The Random Number Generation option creates a set of random numbers between values that you specify. The Rank and Percentile option creates a report of the ranking and percentile distribution.

FIGURE K-21: Descriptive Statistics dialog box

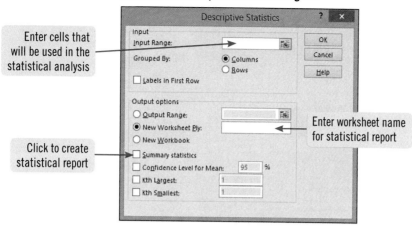

Enter cells that will be used in the statistical analysis

Enter worksheet name for statistical report

Click to create statistical report

FIGURE K-22: Completed report

Total Projected Sales Jan - Jun	
Mean	401801
Standard Error	43681.95
Median	393526
Mode	#N/A
Standard Deviation	87363.9
Sample Variance	7.63E+09
Kurtosis	-0.46892
Skewness	0.472144
Range	204074
Minimum	308039
Maximum	512113
Sum	1607204
Count	4

TABLE K-1: Descriptive statistics

statistic	definition
Mean	The average of a set of numbers
Standard Error	The deviation of the mean of your data from the overall population
Median	The middle value of a set of numbers
Mode	The most common value in a set of numbers
Standard Deviation	The measure of how widely spread the values in a set of numbers are; if the values are all close to the mean, the standard deviation is close to zero
Sample Variance	The measure of how scattered the values in a set of numbers are from an expected value
Kurtosis	The measure of the peakedness or flatness of a distribution of data
Skewness	The measure of the asymmetry of the values in a set of numbers
Range	The difference between the largest and smallest values in a set of numbers
Minimum	The smallest value in a set of numbers
Maximum	The largest value in a set of numbers
Sum	The total of the values in a set of numbers
Count	The number of values in a set of numbers

© 2014 Cengage Learning

Excel 2013

Using What-if Analysis

Practice

Concepts Review

FIGURE K-23

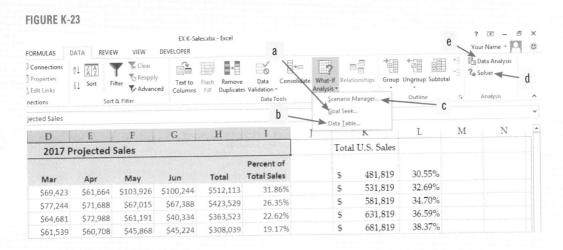

1. Which element do you click to create a range of cells showing the resulting values with varied formula input?
2. Which element do you click to perform a statistical analysis on worksheet data?
3. Which element do you click to name and save different sets of values to forecast worksheet results?
4. Which element do you click to perform a what-if analysis involving multiple input values with constraints?
5. Which element do you click to find the input values that produce a specified result?

Match each term with the statement that best describes it.

6. Solver
7. One-input data table
8. Scenario summary
9. Goal Seek
10. Two-input data table

   a. Add-in that helps you solve complex what-if scenarios with multiple input values
   b. Separate sheet with results from the worksheet's scenarios
   c. Generates values resulting from varying two sets of changing values in a formula
   d. Helps you backsolve what-if scenarios
   e. Generates values resulting from varying one set of changing values in a formula

Select the best answer from the list of choices.

11. To hide the contents of a cell from view, you can use the custom number format:
   a. —
   b. ;;;
   c. Blank
   d. " "
12. The _____ button in the Scenario Manager dialog box allows you to bring scenarios from another workbook into the current workbook.
   a. Combine
   b. Add
   c. Merge
   d. Import
13. When you use Goal Seek, you specify a _____, then find the values that produce it.
   a. Row input cell
   b. Column input cell
   c. Changing value
   d. Solution

14. In Solver, the cell containing the formula is called the:

   a. Target cell.

   b. Changing cell.

   c. Input cell.

   d. Output cell.

15. Which of the following Excel add-ins can be used to generate a statistical summary of worksheet data?

   a. Solver

   b. Lookup Wizard

   c. Conditional Sum

   d. Analysis ToolPak

Skills Review

1. Define a what-if analysis.

   a. Start Excel, open the file EX K-2.xlsx from the location where you store your Data Files, then save it as **EX K-Repair**.

   b. Examine the Auto Repair worksheet to determine the purpose of the worksheet model.

   c. Locate the data input cells.

   d. Locate any dependent cells.

   e. Examine the worksheet to determine problems the worksheet model can solve.

2. Track a what-if analysis with Scenario Manager.

   a. On the Auto Repair worksheet, select the range B3:B5, then use the Scenario Manager to set up a scenario called **Most Likely** with the current data input values.

   b. Add a scenario called **Best Case** using the same changing cells, but change the Labor cost per hour in the $B$3 text box to **70**, change the Parts cost per job in the $B$4 text box to **65**, then change the Hours per job value in cell $B$5 to **2.5**.

   c. Add a scenario called **Worst Case**. For this scenario, change the Labor cost per hour in the $B$3 text box to **95**, change the Parts cost per job in the $B$4 text box to **80**, then change the Hours per job in the $B$5 text box to **3.5**.

   d. If necessary, drag the Scenario Manager dialog box to the right until columns A and B are visible.

   e. Show the Worst Case scenario results, and view the total job cost.

   f. Show the Best Case scenario results, and observe the job cost. Finally, display the Most Likely scenario results.

   g. Close the Scenario Manager dialog box.

   h. Save the workbook.

3. Generate a scenario summary.

   a. Create names for the input value cells and the dependent cell using the range A3:B7.

   b. Verify that the names were created.

   c. Create a scenario summary report, using the Cost to complete job value in cell B7 as the result cell.

   d. Edit the title of the Summary report in cell B2 to read **Scenario Summary for Auto Repair**.

   e. Delete the Current Values column.

   f. Delete the notes beginning in cell B11. Compare your worksheet to FIGURE K-24.

   g. Return to cell A1, enter your name in the center section of the Scenario Summary sheet footer, save the workbook, then preview the Scenario Summary sheet.

4. Project figures using a data table.

   a. Click the Auto Repair sheet tab.

   b. Enter the label **Labor $** in cell D3.

FIGURE K-24

	Most Likely	Best Case	Worst Case
Scenario Summary for Auto Repair			
Changing Cells:			
Labor_cost_per_hour	$80.00	$70.00	$95.00
Parts_cost_per_job	$70.00	$65.00	$80.00
Hours_per_job	3.00	2.50	3.50
Result Cells:			
Cost_to_complete_job	$310.00	$240.00	$412.50

Skills Review (continued)

 c. Format the label so that it is boldfaced and right-aligned.

 d. In cell D4, enter **75**; then in cell D5, enter **80**.

 e. Select the range D4:D5, then use the fill handle to extend the series to cell D8.

 f. In cell E3, reference the job cost formula by entering **=B7**.

 g. Format the contents of cell E3 as hidden, using the ;;; Custom formatting type on the Number tab of the Format Cells dialog box.

 h. Generate the new job costs based on the varying labor costs. Select the range D3:E8 and create a data table. In the data table dialog box, make cell B3 (the labor cost) the column input cell.

 i. Format the range E4:E8 as currency with two decimal places. Compare your worksheet to **FIGURE K-25**.

 j. Enter your name in the center section of the worksheet footer, save the workbook, then preview the worksheet.

5. Use Goal Seek.

 a. Click cell B7, and open the Goal Seek dialog box.

 b. Assuming the labor rate and the hours remain the same, determine what the parts would have to cost so that the cost to complete the job is $290. (*Hint*: Enter a job cost of **290** as the To value, and enter **B4** (the Parts cost) as the By changing cell. Write down the parts cost that Goal Seek finds.

 c. Click OK, then use [Ctrl][Z] to reset the parts cost to its original value.

 d. Enter the cost of the parts that you found in step 5b into cell A14.

 e. Assuming the parts cost and hours remain the same, determine the fee for the labor so that the cost to complete the job is $250. Use [Ctrl][Z] to reset the labor cost to its original value. Enter the labor cost in cell A15.

 f. Save the workbook, then preview the worksheet.

6. Set up a complex what-if analysis with Solver.

 a. With the Brake Repair sheet active, open the Solver Parameters dialog box.

 b. Make B14 (the total repair costs) the objective cell, with a target value of 16,000.

 c. Use cells B6:D6 (the number of scheduled repairs) as the changing cells.

 d. Specify that cells B6:D6 must be integers. (*Hint*: Select int in the Add Constraint dialog box.)

 e. Specify a constraint that cells B6:D6 must be greater than or equal to 10.

7. Run Solver and summarize results.

 a. Use Solver to find a solution.

 b. Save the solution as a scenario named **Repair Solution**, and restore the original values to the worksheet.

 c. Create a scenario summary using the Repair Solution scenario, delete the notes at the bottom of the solution, and rename the worksheet **Repair Solution**. Compare your worksheet to **FIGURE K-26**.

 d. Enter your name in the center section of the worksheet footer, save the workbook, then preview the worksheet.

8. Analyze data using the Analysis ToolPak.

 a. With the Brake Repair sheet active, generate summary descriptive statistics for the repair cost per model, using cells B10:D10 as the input range. (*Hint*: The input is grouped in a row.) Place the new statistics on a worksheet named **Repair Cost Statistics**.

 b. Widen columns as necessary to view the statistics.

FIGURE K-25

	A	B	C	D	E
1	Auto Repair Model				
2					
3	Labor cost per hour	$80.00		Labor $	
4	Parts cost per job	$70.00		75	$295.00
5	Hours per job	3.00		80	$310.00
6				85	$325.00
7	Cost to complete job:	$310.00		90	$340.00
8				95	$355.00
9					
10					

FIGURE K-26

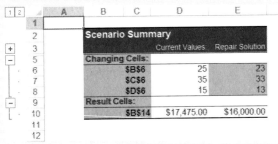

Skills Review (continued)

c. Change the contents of cell A1 to **Repair Cost Per Model**. Delete row 9 containing the kurtosis error information. (This was generated because you only have three data values.) Compare your worksheet to **FIGURE K-27**.

d. Add your name to the center section of the worksheet footer, then preview the worksheet.

e. Save and close the workbook, submit the workbook to your instructor, then exit Excel.

FIGURE K-27

	A	B
1	Repair Cost Per Model	
2		
3	Mean	5825
4	Standard Error	1517.467737
5	Median	6500
6	Mode	#N/A
7	Standard Deviation	2628.33122
8	Sample Variance	6908125
9	Skewness	-1.0794537
10	Range	5125
11	Minimum	2925
12	Maximum	8050
13	Sum	17475
14	Count	3
15		

Independent Challenge 1

You are the manager for Stern & Jones, an environmental consulting firm based in Boston. You are planning a computer hardware upgrade for the engineers in the company. The vice president of finance at the company has asked you to research the monthly cost for a $200,000 equipment loan to purchase the new hardware. You will create a worksheet model to determine the monthly payments based on several different interest rates and loan terms, using data from the company's bank. Using Scenario Manager, you will create the following three scenarios: a 4-year loan at 6.8 percent; a 3-year loan at 5.75 percent; and a 2-year loan at 5.5 percent. You will also prepare a scenario summary report outlining the payment details.

a. Start Excel, open the file EX K-3.xlsx from the location where you store your Data Files, then save it as **EX K-Hardware Loan**.

b. Create cell names for the cells B4:B11 based on the labels in cells A4:A11, using the Create Names from Selection dialog box.

c. Use Scenario Manager to create scenarios that calculate the monthly payment on a $200,000 loan under the three sets of loan possibilities listed below. (*Hint*: Create three scenarios using cells B5:B6 as the changing cells.)

Scenario Name	Interest Rate	Term
6.8% 4 Yr	.068	48
5.75% 3 Yr	.0575	36
5.5% 2 Yr	.055	24

d. Show each scenario to make sure it performs as intended, then display the 6.8% 4 Yr scenario.

e. Generate a scenario summary titled **Scenario Summary for Hardware Purchase**. Use cells B9:B11 as the Result cells.

f. Delete the Current Values column in the report, and delete the notes at the bottom of the report. Rename the sheet **Hardware Purchase**.

g. Enter your name in the center section of the Hardware Purchase sheet footer. Save the workbook, then preview the scenario summary.

h. Close the workbook, exit Excel, then submit the workbook to your instructor.

Independent Challenge 2

You are a CFO at Bay City Digital, an interactive media consulting company based in Michigan. The company president has asked you to prepare a loan summary report for a business expansion. You need to develop a model to show what the monthly payments would be for a $750,000 loan with a range of interest rates. You will create a one-input data table that shows the results of varying interest rates in 0.2% increments, then you will use Goal Seek to specify a total payment amount for this loan application.

a. Start Excel, open the file EX K-4.xlsx from the location where you store your Data Files, then save it as **EX K-Capital Loan Payment Model**.

Independent Challenge 2 (continued)

b. Use **FIGURE K-28** as a guide to enter the data table structure. Reference the monthly payment amount from cell B9 in cell E4, then format the contents of cell E4 as hidden.

FIGURE K-28

	A	B	C	D	E
1	Bay City Digital				
2					
3				Interest Rate	
4	Loan Amount	$750,000.00			
5	Annual Interest Rate	7.80%		7.00%	
6	Term in Months	60		7.20%	
7				7.40%	
8				7.60%	
9	Monthly Payment:	$15,135.61		7.80%	
10	Total Payments:	$908,136.58		8.00%	
11	Total Interest:	$158,136.58		8.20%	
12				8.40%	
13				8.60%	

c. Using cells D4:E13, create a one-input data table with varying interest rates for the loan.

d. Generate the data table that shows the effect of varying interest rates on the monthly payments. Use cell B5, the Annual Interest Rate, as the column input cell. Format the range E5:E13 as currency with two decimal places.

e. Select cell B10 and use Goal Seek to find the interest rate necessary for a total payment amount of $850,000. Use cell B5, the Annual Interest Rate, as the By changing cell. Note the interest rate, then cancel the solution found by Goal Seek. Enter the interest rate in cell B16.

f. Select cell B9 and use Goal Seek to find the interest rate necessary for a monthly payment amount of $13,000. Use cell B5, the Annual Interest Rate, as the By changing cell. Note the interest rate, then cancel the solution found by Goal Seek. Enter the interest rate in cell B17.

g. Enter your name in the center section of the worksheet footer, save the workbook, then preview the worksheet.

h. Close the workbook, exit Excel, then submit the workbook to your instructor.

Independent Challenge 3

You are the owner of Cape Medical, a home medical products company based in Boston. You are considering a purchase of vans, sedans, and compact cars to provide local delivery service. You want to use Goal Seek to look at how the interest rate affects the monthly payments for two of each type of vehicle. Next you want to look at options for expanding the delivery service by purchasing a combination of vans, sedans, and compact cars that can deliver a total of 1500 cubic feet of products. As you review your expansion options, you need to keep the total monthly payments for all of the vehicles at or below $6,500. You use Solver to help find the best possible combination of vehicles.

a. Start Excel, open the file EX K-5.xlsx from the location where you store your Data Files, then save it as **EX K-Vehicle Purchase**.

b. Use Goal Seek to find the interest rate that produces a monthly payment for the van purchase of $1,800, and write down the interest rate that Goal Seek finds. Reset the interest rate to its original value, record the interest rate in cell A19, then enter **Interest rate for $1800 van payment** in cell B19.

c. Use Goal Seek to find the interest rate that produces a monthly payment for the sedan purchase of $1000. Reset the interest rate to its original value, record the interest rate in cell A20, then enter **Interest rate for $1000 sedan payment** in cell B20.

Independent Challenge 3 (continued)

d. Use Goal Seek to find the interest rate that produces a monthly payment for the compact purchase of $650. Reset the interest rate to its original value, record the interest rate in cell A21, then enter **Interest rate for $650 compact payment** in cell B21.

e. Assign cell B8 the name **Quantity_Van**, name cell C8 **Quantity_Sedan**, name cell D8 **Quantity_Compact**, and name cell B15 **Total_Monthly_Payments**. Use Solver to set the total delivery capacity of all vehicles to 1500. Use the quantity to purchase, cells B8:D8, as the changing cells. Specify that cells B8:D8 must be integers. Make sure that the total monthly payments amount in cell B15 is less than or equal to $6,500.

f. Generate a scenario named **Delivery Solution** with the Solver values, and restore the original values in the worksheet. Create a scenario summary using the Delivery Solution scenario and the Total Monthly Payments as the result cells, delete the notes at the bottom of the solution, and edit cell B2 to contain **Total Capacity of 1500**.

g. Enter your name in the center footer section of both worksheets. Preview both worksheets, then save the workbook.

h. Close the workbook, then submit the workbook to your instructor.

Independent Challenge 4: Explore

You are researching various options for financing a new car loan. You haven't decided whether to finance the car for 3, 4, or 5 years. Each loan term carries a different interest rate. To help with the comparison, you will create a two-input data table using interest rates and terms available at your credit union.

a. Start Excel, open the file EX K-6.xlsx from the location where you store your Data Files, then save it as **EX K-Car Loan**.

b. Using FIGURE K-29 as a guide, enter the input values for a two-input data table with varying interest rates for 3-, 4-, and 5-year terms.

c. Reference the monthly payment amount from cell B9 in cell A13, and format the contents of cell A13 as hidden.

d. Generate the data table, using cells A13:D22, that shows the effect of varying interest rates and loan terms on the monthly payments. (*Hint*: Use cell B6, Term in Months, as the row input cell, and cell B5, the Annual Interest Rate, as the column input cell.)

e. Format the range B14:D22 as currency with two decimal places.

f. Enter your name in the center section of the Loan sheet footer, then preview the Loan sheet.

g. Save the workbook, close the workbook, then exit Excel and submit the workbook to your instructor.

FIGURE K-29

	A	B	C	D
1	**Car Financing Options**			
2				
3				
4	Loan Amount	$20,000.00		
5	Annual Interest Rate	3.50%		
6	Term in Months	60		
7				
8				
9	Monthly Payment:	$363.83		
10	Total Payments:	$21,830.09		
11	Total Interest:	$1,830.09		
12				
13			36	48	60
14		3.00%		
15		3.25%		
16		3.50%		
17		3.75%		
18		4.00%		
19		4.25%		
20		4.50%		
21		4.75%		
22		5.00%		
23				
24				

Excel 2013

Visual Workshop

Open the file EX K-7.xlsx from the location where you store your Data Files, then save it as **EX K-Columbus Manufacturing**. Create the worksheet shown in FIGURE K-30. (*Hint*: Use Goal Seek to find the Hourly labor cost to reach the total profit in cell H11 in the figure and accept the solution.) Then generate descriptive statistics for the products' total profits on a worksheet named **Manufacturing Profits**, as shown in FIGURE K-31. Add your name to the center footer section of each sheet, change the orientation of the Profit sheet to landscape, then preview and print both worksheets.

FIGURE K-30

	A	B	C	D	E	F	G	H
1				Columbus Manufacturing				
2				December Production				
3	Hourly Labor Cost	$51.76						
4								
5								
6	Product Number	Hours	Parts Cost	Cost to Produce	Retail Price	Unit Profit	Units Produced	Total Profit
7	NA425	9	$473	$ 938.85	$1,522.00	$ 583.15	425	$ 247,838.73
8	CX877	7	$230	$ 592.33	$ 974.00	$ 381.67	387	$ 147,707.14
9	QA287	2	$421	$ 524.52	$ 776.00	$ 251.48	127	$ 31,937.68
10	TQ894	11	$187	$ 756.37	$1,322.00	$ 565.63	305	$ 172,516.46
11	Total Profit							$ 600,000.00
12								
13								

FIGURE K-31

	A	B
1	Profit Statistics	
2		
3	Mean	150000
4	Standard Error	44743.1
5	Median	160112
6	Mode	#N/A
7	Standard Deviation	89486.3
8	Sample Variance	8E+09
9	Kurtosis	1.376
10	Skewness	-0.64908
11	Range	215901
12	Minimum	31937.7
13	Maximum	247839
14	Sum	600000
15	Count	4
16		

Analyzing Data with PivotTables

CASE ▶ Quest uses PivotTables to analyze sales data. Kate Morgan is preparing for the annual meeting for the United States region and asks you to analyze product sales in Quest's branches over the past year. You will create a PivotTable to summarize the 2016 sales data by quarter, product, and branch and illustrate the information using a PivotChart.

Unit Objectives

After completing this unit, you will be able to:

- Plan and design a PivotTable report
- Create a PivotTable report
- Change a PivotTable's summary function and design
- Filter and sort PivotTable data

- Update a PivotTable report
- Explore PivotTable Data Relationships
- Create a PivotChart report
- Use the GETPIVOTDATA function

Files You Will Need

EX L-1.xlsx   EX L-5.xlsx
EX L-2.xlsx   EX L-6.xlsx
EX L-3.xlsx   EX L-7.xlsx
EX L-4.xlsx

Learning
Outcomes
• Develop guidelines
for a PivotTable
• Develop an
understanding of
PivotTable
vocabulary

Plan and Design a PivotTable Report

The Excel **PivotTable Report** feature lets you summarize large amounts of columnar worksheet data in a compact table format. Then you can freely rearrange, or "pivot", PivotTable rows and columns to explore the relationships within your data by category. Creating a PivotTable report (often called a PivotTable) involves only a few steps. Before you begin, however, you need to review the data and consider how a PivotTable can best summarize it. **CASE** ▶ *Kate asks you to design a PivotTable to display Quest's sales information for its branches in the United States. You begin by reviewing guidelines for creating PivotTables.*

DETAILS

Before you create a PivotTable, think about the following guidelines:

- **Review the source data**

  Before you can effectively summarize data in a PivotTable, you need to understand the source data's scope and structure. The source data does not have to be defined as a table, but should be in a table-like format. That is, it should have column headings, should not have any blank rows or columns, and should have the same type of data in each column. To create a meaningful PivotTable, make sure that one or more of the fields has repeated information so that the PivotTable can effectively group it. Also be sure to include numeric data that the PivotTable can total for each group. The data columns represent categories of data, which are called **fields**, just as in a table. You are working with sales information that Kate received from Quest's U.S. branch managers, shown in **FIGURE L-1**. Information is repeated in the Product ID, Category, Branch, and Quarter columns, and numeric information is displayed in the Sales column, so you will be able to summarize this data effectively in a PivotTable.

- **Determine the purpose of the PivotTable and write the names of the fields you want to include**

  The purpose of your PivotTable is to summarize sales information by quarter across various branches. You want your PivotTable to summarize the data in the Product ID, Category, Branch, Quarter, and Sales columns, so you include those fields in your PivotTable.

- **Determine which field contains the data you want to summarize and which summary function you want to use**

  You want to summarize sales information by summing the Sales field for each product in a branch by quarter. You'll do this by using the Excel SUM function.

- **Decide how you want to arrange the data**

  The PivotTable layout you choose is crucial to delivering the message you intend. Product ID values will appear in the PivotTable columns, Branch and Quarter numbers will appear in rows, and the PivotTable will summarize Sales figures, as shown in **FIGURE L-2**.

- **Determine the location of the PivotTable**

  You can place a PivotTable in any worksheet of any workbook. Placing a PivotTable on a separate worksheet makes it easier to locate and prevents you from accidentally overwriting parts of an existing sheet. You decide to create the PivotTable as a new worksheet in the current workbook.

FIGURE L-1: Sales worksheet

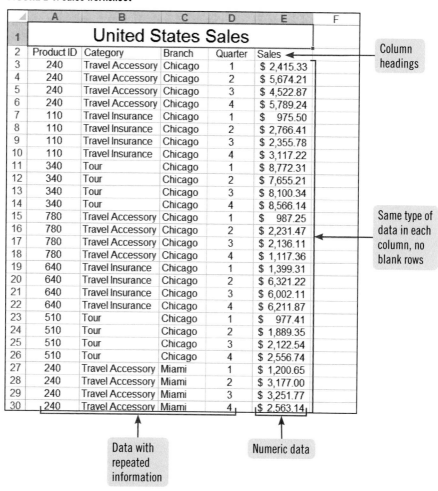

	A	B	C	D	E	F
1		United States Sales				
2	Product ID	Category	Branch	Quarter	Sales	
3	240	Travel Accessory	Chicago	1	$ 2,415.33	
4	240	Travel Accessory	Chicago	2	$ 5,674.21	
5	240	Travel Accessory	Chicago	3	$ 4,522.87	
6	240	Travel Accessory	Chicago	4	$ 5,789.24	
7	110	Travel Insurance	Chicago	1	$ 975.50	
8	110	Travel Insurance	Chicago	2	$ 2,766.41	
9	110	Travel Insurance	Chicago	3	$ 2,355.78	
10	110	Travel Insurance	Chicago	4	$ 3,117.22	
11	340	Tour	Chicago	1	$ 8,772.31	
12	340	Tour	Chicago	2	$ 7,655.21	
13	340	Tour	Chicago	3	$ 8,100.34	
14	340	Tour	Chicago	4	$ 8,566.14	
15	780	Travel Accessory	Chicago	1	$ 987.25	
16	780	Travel Accessory	Chicago	2	$ 2,231.47	
17	780	Travel Accessory	Chicago	3	$ 2,136.11	
18	780	Travel Accessory	Chicago	4	$ 1,117.36	
19	640	Travel Insurance	Chicago	1	$ 1,399.31	
20	640	Travel Insurance	Chicago	2	$ 6,321.22	
21	640	Travel Insurance	Chicago	3	$ 6,002.11	
22	640	Travel Insurance	Chicago	4	$ 6,211.87	
23	510	Tour	Chicago	1	$ 977.41	
24	510	Tour	Chicago	2	$ 1,889.35	
25	510	Tour	Chicago	3	$ 2,122.54	
26	510	Tour	Chicago	4	$ 2,556.74	
27	240	Travel Accessory	Miami	1	$ 1,200.65	
28	240	Travel Accessory	Miami	2	$ 3,177.00	
29	240	Travel Accessory	Miami	3	$ 3,251.77	
30	240	Travel Accessory	Miami	4	$ 2,563.14	

Column headings

Same type of data in each column, no blank rows

Data with repeated information

Numeric data

FIGURE L-2: PivotTable report based on Sales worksheet

Product ID values are column labels

	A	B	C	D	E	F	G	H	I	J
1										
2										
3										
4	Sum of Sales									
5		110	240	340	510	640	780	Grand Total		
6	Miami	$31,883.87	$10,192.56	$32,350.46	$9,567.18	$10,106.56	$10,001.51	$104,102.14		
7	1	$6,634.43	$1,200.65	$7,790.34	$2,310.34	$1,376.34	$1,766.34	$21,078.44		
8	2	$8,100.14	$3,177.00	$6,700.15	$2,524.87	$3,394.21	$3,524.21	$27,420.58		
9	3	$8,324.65	$3,251.77	$8,883.54	$2,183.54	$2,412.58	$2,307.53	$27,363.61		
10	4	$8,824.65	$2,563.14	$8,976.43	$2,548.43	$2,923.43	$2,403.43	$28,239.51		
11	New York	$15,057.69	$10,223.91	$29,818.65	$20,039.58	$8,856.97	$16,683.64	$100,680.44		
12	1	$4,921.45	$1,897.51	$6,258.21	$2,987.14	$1,305.47	$1,522.14	$18,891.92		
13	2	$3,319.92	$2,374.32	$7,628.78	$3,880.78	$2,183.98	$5,413.98	$24,801.76		
14	3	$4,176.89	$3,216.65	$8,198.90	$6,728.90	$2,577.98	$4,317.98	$29,217.30		
15	4	$2,639.43	$2,735.43	$7,732.76	$6,442.76	$2,789.54	$5,429.54	$27,769.46		
16	Chicago	$9,214.91	$18,401.65	$33,094.00	$7,546.04	$19,934.51	$6,472.19	$94,663.30		
17	1	$975.50	$2,415.33	$8,772.31	$977.41	$1,399.31	$987.25	$15,527.11		
18	2	$2,766.41	$5,674.21	$7,655.21	$1,889.35	$6,321.22	$2,231.47	$26,537.87		
19	3	$2,355.78	$4,522.87	$8,100.34	$2,122.54	$6,002.11	$2,136.11	$25,239.75		
20	4	$3,117.22	$5,789.24	$8,566.14	$2,556.74	$6,211.87	$1,117.36	$27,358.57		
21	Grand Total	$56,156.47	$38,818.12	$95,263.11	$37,152.80	$38,898.04	$33,157.34	$299,445.88		
22										
23										

PivotTable summarizes sales figures by product number, branch, and quarter

Branches and quarters are row labels

Create a PivotTable Report

Learning Outcomes
- Create a PivotTable
- Move PivotTable fields to rearrange data

Once you've planned and designed your PivotTable report, you can create it. After you create the PivotTable, you **populate** it by adding fields to areas in the PivotTable. A PivotTable has four areas: the Report Filter, which is the field by which you want to filter, or show selected data in, the PivotTable; the Row Labels, which contain the fields whose labels will describe the values in the rows; the Column Labels, which appear above the PivotTable values and describe the columns; and the Values, which summarize the numeric data. **CASE** ▶ *With the planning and design stage complete, you are ready to create a PivotTable that summarizes sales information.*

STEPS

1. **Start Excel if necessary, open the file EX L-1.xlsx from the location where you store your Data Files, then save it as EX L-US Sales**

   This worksheet contains the year's sales information for Quest's U.S. branches, including Product ID, Category, Branch, Quarter, and Sales. The records are sorted by branch. You decide to see what PivotTables Excel recommends for your data.

   QUICK TIP
   To create your own PivotTable without reviewing recommended ones, click the PivotTable button in the Tables group, verify your data range or enter an external data source such as a database, specify a PivotTable location, then click OK.

2. **Click the INSERT tab, click the Recommended PivotTables button in the Tables group, then click each of the recommended PivotTable layouts in the left side of the Recommended PivotTables dialog box, scrolling as necessary**

   The Recommended PivotTables dialog box opens, displaying recommended PivotTable layouts that summarize your data, as shown in **FIGURE L-3**. You decide to create your own PivotTable.

3. **Click Blank PivotTable at the bottom of the dialog box**

   A new, blank PivotTable appears on the left side of the worksheet and the PivotTable Fields List appears in a pane on the right, as shown in **FIGURE L-4**. You populate the PivotTable by clicking field check boxes in the PivotTable Fields List, often called the Field List. The diagram area at the bottom of the Field List represents the main PivotTable areas and helps you track field locations as you populate the PivotTable. You can also drag fields among the diagram areas to change the PivotTable layout.

4. **Click the Branch field check box in the Field List**

   Because the Branch field is a text, rather than a numeric field, Excel adds branch names to the rows area of the PivotTable, and adds the Branch field name to the ROWS area at the bottom of the Field List.

5. **Click the Product ID check box in the Field List**

   The Product ID information is automatically added to the PivotTable, and "Sum of Product ID" appears in the VALUES area in the diagram area. But because the data type of the Product ID field is numeric, the field is added to the VALUES area of the PivotTable and the Product ID values are summed, which is not meaningful. Instead, you want the Product IDs as column headers in the PivotTable.

6. **Click the Sum of Product ID list arrow in the VALUES area at the bottom of the PivotTable Fields List, then choose Move to Column Labels**

   The Product ID field becomes a column label, causing the Product ID values to appear in the PivotTable as column headers.

   QUICK TIP
   PivotTables containing a data field can be filtered by date: Click the PIVOTTABLE TOOLS ANALYZE tab, then click the Insert Timeline button in the Filter group.

7. **Drag the Quarter field from the top of the PivotTable Fields List and drop it below the Branch field in the ROWS area at the bottom, select the Sales field check box in the PivotTable Fields List, then save the workbook**

   You have created a PivotTable that totals U.S. sales, with the Product IDs as column headers and Branches and Quarters as row labels. SUM is the Excel default function for data fields containing numbers, so Excel automatically calculates the sum of the sales in the PivotTable. The PivotTable tells you that Miami sales of Product #110 were twice the New York sales level and more than three times the Chicago sales level. Product #340 was the best selling product overall, as shown in the Grand Total row. See **FIGURE L-5**.

FIGURE L-3: Recommended PivotTables dialog box

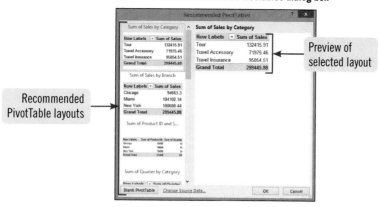

Recommended PivotTable layouts

Preview of selected layout

FIGURE L-4: Empty PivotTable ready to receive field data

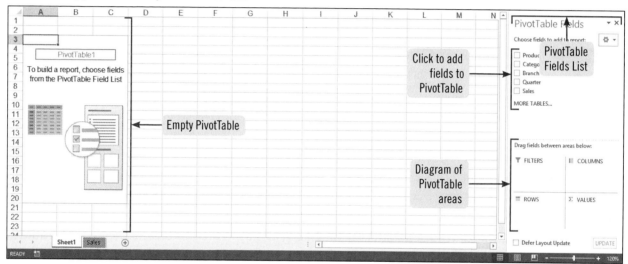

Empty PivotTable

Click to add fields to PivotTable

PivotTable Fields List

Diagram of PivotTable areas

FIGURE L-5: New PivotTable with fields in place

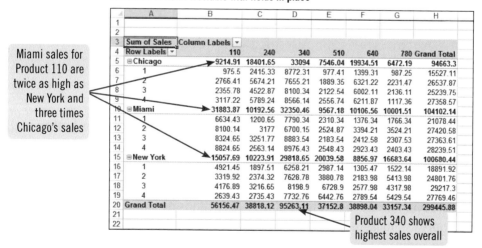

Miami sales for Product 110 are twice as high as New York and three times Chicago's sales

Product 340 shows highest sales overall

Changing the PivotTable layout

The default layout for PivotTables is the compact form; the row labels are displayed in a single column, and the second-level field items (such as the quarters in the U.S. Sales example) are indented for readability. You can change the layout of your PivotTable by clicking the PIVOTTABLE TOOLS DESIGN tab, clicking the Report Layout button in the Layout group, then clicking either Show in Outline Form or Show in Tabular Form. The tabular form and the outline form show each row label in its own column. The tabular and outline layouts take up more space on a worksheet than the compact layout.

Learning
Outcomes
• Change a
  PivotTable's
  summary function
• Format a PivotTable

Change a PivotTable's Summary Function and Design

A PivotTable's **summary function** controls what calculation Excel uses to summarize the table data. Unless you specify otherwise, Excel applies the SUM function to numeric data and the COUNT function to data fields containing text. However, you can easily change the default summary functions to different ones. **CASE** *Kate wants you to calculate the average sales for the U.S. branches using the AVERAGE function, and to improve the appearance of the PivotTable for her presentation.*

STEPS

QUICK TIP
You can also change the summary function by clicking the Field Settings button in the Active Field group on the PIVOTTABLE TOOLS ANALYZE tab.

1. **Right-click cell A3, then point to** Summarize Values By **in the shortcut menu**

   The shortcut menu shows that the Sum function is selected by default, as shown in **FIGURE L-6**.

2. **Click** Average

   The data area of the PivotTable shows the average sales for each product by branch and quarter, and cell A3 now contains "Average of Sales". You want to view the PivotTable data without the subtotals.

3. **Click the** PIVOTTABLE TOOLS DESIGN tab, **click the** Subtotals button **in the Layout group, then click** Do Not Show Subtotals

   After reviewing the data, you decide that it would be more useful to sum the sales information than to average it. You also want to redisplay the subtotals.

4. **Right-click cell A3, point to** Summarize Values By **in the shortcut menu, then click** Sum

   Excel recalculates the PivotTable—in this case, summing the sales data instead of averaging it.

QUICK TIP
You can control the display of grand totals by clicking the PIVOTTABLE TOOLS DESIGN tab, and clicking the Grand Totals button in the Layout group.

5. **Click the** Subtotals button **in the Layout group, then click** Show all Subtotals at Top of Group

   Just as Excel tables have styles that let you quickly format them, PivotTables have a gallery of styles to choose from. You decide to add a PivotTable style to the PivotTable to improve its appearance.

6. **Click the** More button ⮟ **in the PivotTable Styles gallery, then click** Pivot Style Light 20

   To further improve the appearance of the PivotTable, you will remove the unnecessary headers of "Column Labels" and "Row Labels".

7. **Click the** PIVOTTABLE TOOLS ANALYZE tab, **then click the** Field Headers button **in the Show group**

   The data would be more readable if it were in currency format.

TROUBLE
If you don't see the Active Field group, click the Active Field button to display the Field Settings button.

8. **Click any sales value in the PivotTable, click the** Field Settings button **in the Active Field group, click** Number Format **in the Value Field Settings dialog box, select** Currency **in the Category list, make sure Decimal places is 2 and Symbol is $, click OK, click OK again, then compare your PivotTable to** FIGURE L-7

   You decide to give the PivotTable sheet a more descriptive name. When you name a PivotTable sheet, it is best to avoid using spaces in the name. If a PivotTable name contains a space, you must put single quotes around the name if you refer to it in a function.

9. **Rename Sheet1** PivotTable, **add your name to the worksheet footer, save the workbook, then preview the worksheet**

FIGURE L-6: Shortcut menu showing Sum function selected

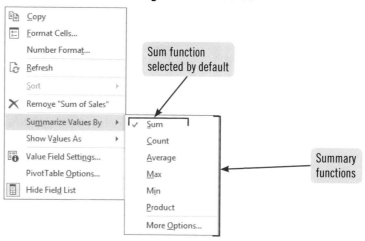

FIGURE L-7: Formatted PivotTable

	A	B	C	D	E	F	G	H
1								
2								
3	**Sum of Sales**							
4		110	240	340	510	640	780	Grand Total
5	⊟Chicago	$9,214.91	$18,401.65	$33,094.00	$7,546.04	$19,934.51	$6,472.19	$94,663.30
6	1	$975.50	$2,415.33	$8,772.31	$977.41	$1,399.31	$987.25	$15,527.11
7	2	$2,766.41	$5,674.21	$7,655.21	$1,889.35	$6,321.22	$2,231.47	$26,537.87
8	3	$2,355.78	$4,522.87	$8,100.34	$2,122.54	$6,002.11	$2,136.11	$25,239.75
9	4	$3,117.22	$5,789.24	$8,566.14	$2,556.74	$6,211.87	$1,117.36	$27,358.57
10	⊟Miami	$31,883.87	$10,192.56	$32,350.46	$9,567.18	$10,106.56	$10,001.51	$104,102.14
11	1	$6,634.43	$1,200.65	$7,790.34	$2,310.34	$1,376.34	$1,766.34	$21,078.44
12	2	$8,100.14	$3,177.00	$6,700.15	$2,524.87	$3,394.21	$3,524.21	$27,420.58
13	3	$8,324.65	$3,251.77	$8,883.54	$2,183.54	$2,412.58	$2,307.53	$27,363.61
14	4	$8,824.65	$2,563.14	$8,976.43	$2,548.43	$2,923.43	$2,403.43	$28,239.51
15	⊟New York	$15,057.69	$10,223.91	$29,818.65	$20,039.58	$8,856.97	$16,683.64	$100,680.44
16	1	$4,921.45	$1,897.51	$6,258.21	$2,987.14	$1,305.47	$1,522.14	$18,891.92
17	2	$3,319.92	$2,374.32	$7,628.78	$3,880.78	$2,183.98	$5,413.98	$24,801.76
18	3	$4,176.89	$3,216.65	$8,198.90	$6,728.90	$2,577.98	$4,317.98	$29,217.30
19	4	$2,639.43	$2,735.43	$7,732.76	$6,442.76	$2,789.54	$5,429.54	$27,769.46
20	**Grand Total**	$56,156.47	$38,818.12	$95,263.11	$37,152.80	$38,898.04	$33,157.34	$299,445.88
21								
22								

Using the Show buttons

To display and hide PivotTable elements, you can use the buttons in the Show group on the PIVOTTABLE TOOLS ANALYZE tab. For example, the Field List button will hide or display the PivotTable Fields List. The +/– Buttons button will hide or display the Expand and Collapse Outline buttons, and the Field Headers button will hide or display the Row and Column Label headers on the PivotTable.

Learning Outcomes
- Sort a PivotTable using the fields
- Filter a PivotTable using a slicer

Filter and Sort PivotTable Data

Just as you used filters to hide and display table data, you can restrict the display of PivotTable data. A **slicer** is a graphic object with a set of buttons that let you easily filter PivotTable data to show only the data you need. For example, you can use slicer buttons to show only data about a specific product. You can also filter a PivotTable using a **report filter**, which lets you filter PivotTable data using a list arrow to show data for one or more field values. For example, if you add a Month field to the FILTERS area, you can filter a PivotTable so that only January sales data appears in the PivotTable. You can also sort PivotTable data in ascending or descending order. **CASE** *Kate wants to see sales data about specific products for specific branches and quarters.*

1. **Right-click cell H5, point to Sort in the shortcut menu, then click More Sort Options**
   The Sort By Value dialog box opens. As you select options in the dialog box, the Summary information at the bottom of the dialog box changes to describe the sort results using your field names.

2. **Click the Largest to Smallest option button to select it in the Sort options section, make sure the Top to Bottom option button is selected in the Sort direction section, review the sort description in the Summary section of the dialog box, then click OK**
   The branches appear in the PivotTable in decreasing order of total sales from top to bottom. You want to easily display the sales for specific product IDs at certain branches.

> **QUICK TIP**
> To select an external data source for a slicer, click a cell outside the PivotTable, click the INSERT tab, click the Slicer button in the Filters group, click the Show list arrow in the Existing Connections dialog box, choose a connection, click the connection you want to use, then click Open.

3. **Click any cell in the PivotTable, click the PIVOTTABLE TOOLS ANALYZE tab if necessary, click the Insert Slicer button in the Filter group, click the Product ID check box and the Branch check box in the Insert Slicers dialog box to select both fields, click OK, then drag the slicers to the right of the PivotTable**
   Slicers appear, with buttons representing the Product ID numbers and Branch names, as shown in **FIGURE L-8**. You want to filter the data to show only Product IDs 110 and 510 in the New York and Chicago branches.

4. **Click the 110 button in the Product ID slicer, press [CTRL] then click the 510 button in the Product ID slicer, release [CTRL], click the New York button in the Branch slicer, press [CTRL], click the Chicago button in the Branch slicer, then release [CTRL]**
   The PivotTable displays only the data for Product IDs 110 and 510 in New York and Chicago, as shown in **FIGURE L-9**. In the slicers, the Filter symbol changes, indicating the PivotTable is filtered to display the selected fields. You decide to clear the filter and remove the slicers.

> **TROUBLE**
> If the PivotTable Fields List is not visible, click the PIVOTTABLE TOOLS ANALYZE tab, and click the Field List button in the Show group.

5. **Click the Clear Filter button [icon] in the Product ID slicer, click [icon] in the Branch slicer, click the top of the Branch slicer, press [CTRL], click the top of the Product ID slicer, release [CTRL], right-click the Product ID slicer, then click Remove Slicers on the shortcut menu**
   You want to display the PivotTable data by quarter using a Report Filter.

6. **In the PivotTable Fields List, click the Quarter field list arrow in the ROWS area, then select Move to Report Filter**
   The Quarter field moves to cell A1, and a list arrow and the word "(All)" appear in cell B1. The list arrow lets you filter the data in the PivotTable by Quarter. "(All)" indicates that the PivotTable currently shows data for all quarters. You decide to filter the data to show only data for the fourth quarter.

> **QUICK TIP**
> You can add a slicer style, edit a slicer caption, and change the button order using the SLICER TOOLS OPTIONS tab.

7. **In the PivotTable cell B1, click the Quarter list arrow, click 4, click OK, then save your work**
   The PivotTable filters the sales data to display the fourth quarter only, as shown in **FIGURE L-10**. The Quarter field list arrow changes to a filter symbol. A filter symbol also appears to the right of the Quarter field in the PivotTable Fields List, indicating that the PivotTable is filtered and summarizes only a portion of the PivotTable data.

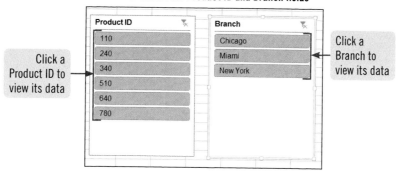

FIGURE L-8: Slicers for Product ID and Branch fields

Click a Product ID to view its data

Click a Branch to view its data

FIGURE L-9: PivotTable filtered by Product ID and Branch

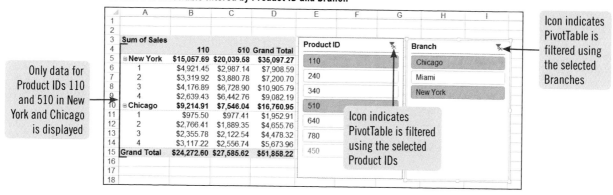

Only data for Product IDs 110 and 510 in New York and Chicago is displayed

Icon indicates PivotTable is filtered using the selected Branches

Icon indicates PivotTable is filtered using the selected Product IDs

FIGURE L-10: PivotTable filtered by fourth quarter

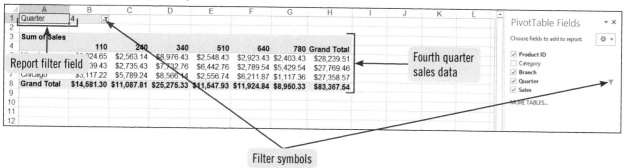

Report filter field

Fourth quarter sales data

Filter symbols

Filtering PivotTables using multiple values

You can select multiple values when filtering a PivotTable report using a report filter. After clicking a field's report filter list arrow in the top section of the PivotTable Fields List or in cell B1 on the PivotTable itself, click the Select Multiple Items check box at the bottom of the filter selections. This lets you select multiple values for the filter. For example, selecting 1 and 2 as the report filter in a PivotTable with quarters would display all of the data for the first two quarters. You can also select multiple values for the row and column labels by clicking the PIVOTTABLE TOOLS ANALYZE tab, clicking the Field Headers button in the Show group, clicking the Row Labels list arrow or the Column Labels list arrow in cells A4 and B3 on the PivotTable and selecting the data items that you want to display.

Update a PivotTable Report

The data in a PivotTable report looks like typical worksheet data. Because the PivotTable data is linked to a **data source** (the data you used to create the PivotTable), however, the values and results in the PivotTable are read-only values. That means you cannot move or modify a part of a PivotTable by inserting or deleting rows, editing results, or moving cells. To change PivotTable data, you must edit the items directly in the data source, then update, or **refresh**, the PivotTable to reflect the changes. **CASE** *Kate just learned that sales information for a custom group tour sold in New York during the fourth quarter was never entered into the Sales worksheet. Kate asks you to add information about this tour to the data source and PivotTable. You start by inserting a row for the new information in the Sales worksheet.*

STEPS

1. **Click the Sales sheet tab**

   By inserting the new row in the correct position by branch, you will not need to sort the data again.

2. **Scroll to and right-click the row 51 heading, then click Insert on the shortcut menu**

   A blank row appears as the new row 51, and the data in the old row 51, moves down to row 52. You now have room for the tour data.

3. **Enter the data for the new tour in row 51 using the following information**

Product ID	450
Category	Tour
Branch	New York
Quarter	4
Sales	3102.95

   The PivotTable does not yet reflect the additional data.

4. **Click the PivotTable sheet tab, then verify that the Quarter 4 data appears**

   The PivotTable does not currently include the new tour information, and the grand total is $83,367.54. Before you refresh the PivotTable data, you need to make sure that the cell pointer is located within the PivotTable range.

5. **Click anywhere within the PivotTable if necessary, click the PIVOTTABLE TOOLS ANALYZE tab, then click the Refresh button in the Data group**

   The PivotTable now contains a column for the new product ID, which includes the new tour information, in column H, and the grand total has increased by the amount of the tour's sales ($3,102.95) to $86,470.49, as shown in **FIGURE L-11**.

6. **Save the workbook**

Grouping PivotTable data

You can group PivotTable data to analyze specific values in a field as a unit. For example, you may want to group sales data for quarters one and two to analyze sales for the first half of the year. To group PivotTable data, first select the rows and columns that you want to group, click the PIVOTTABLE TOOLS ANALYZE tab, then click the Group Selection button in the Group group. To summarize grouped data, click the Field Settings button in the Active Field group, click the Custom option button in the Field Settings dialog box, select the function that you want to use to summarize the data, then click OK. To collapse the group and show the function results, click the Collapse Outline button ⊟ next to the group name. You can click the Expand Outline button ⊞ next to the group name to display the rows or columns in the group. To ungroup data, select the Group name in the PivotTable, then click the Ungroup button in the Group group.

Analyzing Data with PivotTables

FIGURE L-11: Updated PivotTable report

	A	B	C	D	E	F	G	H	I
1	Quarter	4	⊤					New data is added	
2									
3	**Sum of Sales**								
4		110	240	340	510	640	780	450	**Grand Total**
5	New York	$2,639.43	$2,735.43	$7,732.76	$6,442.76	$2,789.54	$5,429.54	$3,102.95	$30,872.41
6	Miami	$8,824.65	$2,563.14	$8,976.43	$2,548.43	$2,923.43	$2,403.43		$28,239.51
7	Chicago	$3,117.22	$5,789.24	$8,566.14	$2,556.74	$6,211.87	$1,117.36		$27,358.57
8	**Grand Total**	**$14,581.30**	**$11,087.81**	**$25,275.33**	**$11,547.93**	**$11,924.84**	**$8,950.33**	**$3,102.95**	**$86,470.49**
9									
10									

Totals are updated to include the new data

Adding a calculated field to a PivotTable

You can use formulas to analyze PivotTable data in a field by adding a calculated field. A calculated field appears in the Field List and can be manipulated like other PivotTable fields. To add a calculated field, click any cell in the PivotTable, click the PIVOTTABLE TOOLS ANALYZE tab, click the Fields, Items, & Sets button in the Calculations group, then click Calculated Field. The Insert Calculated Field dialog box opens. Enter the field name in the Name text box, click in the Formula text box, click a field name in the Fields list that you want to use in the formula, and click Insert Field. Use standard arithmetic operators to enter the formula you want to use. For example **FIGURE L-12** shows a formula to increase Sales data by 10 percent. After entering the formula in the Insert Calculated Field dialog box, click Add, then click OK. The new field with the formula results appears in the PivotTable, and the field is added to the PivotTable Fields List as shown in **FIGURE L-13**.

FIGURE L-12: Insert Calculated Field dialog box

New field name

Formula to increase sales by 10%

Fields that can be used in the formula

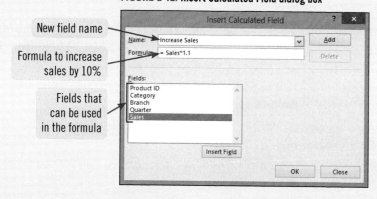

FIGURE L-13: PivotTable with calculated field

	A	B	C	D	E	F	G	H
1	Quarter	4	⊤			New calculated field		
2								
3		110		240		340		
4		Sum of Sales	Sum of Increase Sales	Sum of Sales	Sum of Increase Sales	Sum of Sales	Sum of Increase Sales	Sum of Sa
5	New York	$2,639.43	$ 2,903.37	$2,735.43	$ 3,008.97	$7,732.76	$ 8,506.04	$6,44
6	Miami	$8,824.65	$ 9,707.12	$2,563.14	$ 2,819.45	$8,976.43	$ 9,874.07	$2,54
7	Chicago	$3,117.22	$ 3,428.94	$5,789.24	$ 6,368.16	$8,566.14	$ 9,422.75	$2,55
8	Grand Total	$14,581.30	$ 16,039.43	$11,087.81	$ 12,196.59	$25,275.33	$ 27,802.86	$11,54
9								
10								
11								
12								

PivotTable Fields

Choose fields to add to report:

☑ Product ID
☐ Category
☑ Branch
☑ Quarter
☑ Sales
☑ Increase Sales

MORE TABLES...

Explore PivotTable Data Relationships

Learning
Outcomes
• Change a
PivotTable's
organization
• Add fields to a
PivotTable

What makes a PivotTable such a powerful analysis tool is the ability to change the way data is organized in the report. By moving fields to different positions in the report, you can explore relationships and trends that you might not see in the original report structure. **CASE** *Kate asks you to include category information in the sales report. She is also interested in viewing the PivotTable in different arrangements to find the best organization of data for her presentation.*

STEPS

1. **Make sure that the PivotTable sheet is active, that the active cell is located anywhere inside the PivotTable, and that the PivotTable Fields List is visible**

2. **Click the Category check box in the Field List**

   The category data is added to the ROWS area below the corresponding branch data. As you learned earlier, you can move fields within an area of a PivotTable by dragging and dropping them to the desired location.

3. **In the diagram section of the Field List, locate the ROWS area, then drag the Category field up and drop it above the Branch field**

   The category field is now the outer or upper field, and the branch field is the inner or lower field. The PivotTable is restructured to display the sales data by the category values and then the branch values within the category field. The subtotals now reflect the sum of the categories, as shown in **FIGURE L-14**. You can also move fields to new areas in the PivotTable.

4. **In the diagram area of the Field List, drag the Category field from the ROWS area to anywhere in the COLUMNS area, then drag the Product ID field from the COLUMNS area to the ROWS area below the Branch field**

   The PivotTable now displays the sales data with the category values in the columns and then the product IDs grouped by branches in the rows. The product ID values are indented below the branches because the Product ID field is the inner row label.

5. **In the diagram area of the Field List, drag the Category field from the COLUMNS area to the FILTERS area above the Quarter field, then drag the Product ID field from the ROWS area to the COLUMNS area**

   The PivotTable now has two report filters. The upper report filter, Category, summarizes data using all of the categories. Kate asks you to display the tour sales information for all quarters.

6. **Click the Category list arrow in cell B1 of the PivotTable, click Tour, click OK, click the Quarter filter list arrow in cell B2, click All, then click OK**

   The PivotTable displays sales totals for the Tour category for all quarters. Kate asks you to provide the sales information for all categories.

7. **Click the Category filter arrow, click All, then click OK**

   The completed PivotTable appears as shown in **FIGURE L-15**.

8. **Save the workbook, change the page orientation of the PivotTable sheet to Landscape, then preview the PivotTable**

Analyzing Data with PivotTables

FIGURE L-14: PivotTable structured by branches within categories

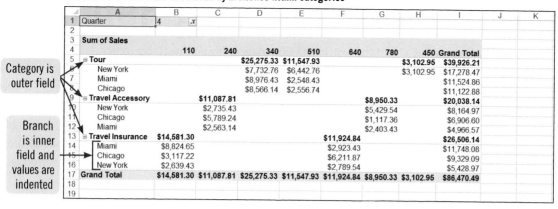

	A	B	C	D	E	F	G	H	I	J	K
1	Quarter	4	.T								
2											
3	**Sum of Sales**										
4		110	240	340	510	640	780		450	Grand Total	
5	⊟Tour			$25,275.33	$11,547.93				$3,102.95	$39,926.21	
6	New York			$7,732.76	$6,442.76				$3,102.95	$17,278.47	
7	Miami			$8,976.43	$2,548.43					$11,524.86	
8	Chicago			$8,566.14	$2,556.74					$11,122.88	
9	⊟Travel Accessory		$11,087.81				$8,950.33			$20,038.14	
10	New York		$2,735.43				$5,429.54			$8,164.97	
11	Chicago		$5,789.24				$1,117.36			$6,906.60	
12	Miami		$2,563.14				$2,403.43			$4,966.57	
13	⊟Travel Insurance	$14,581.30				$11,924.84				$26,506.14	
14	Miami	$8,824.65				$2,923.43				$11,748.08	
15	Chicago	$3,117.22				$6,211.87				$9,329.09	
16	New York	$2,639.43				$2,789.54				$5,428.97	
17	**Grand Total**	$14,581.30	$11,087.81	$25,275.33	$11,547.93	$11,924.84	$8,950.33	$3,102.95		$86,470.49	
18											
19											

Category is outer field

Branch is inner field and values are indented

FIGURE L-15: Completed PivotTable report

	A	B	C	D	E	F	G	H	I
1	Category	(All) ▼							
2	Quarter	(All) ▼							
3									
4	**Sum of Sales**								
5		110	240	340	510	640	780	450	Grand Total
6	Miami	$31,883.87	$10,192.56	$32,350.46	$9,567.18	$10,106.56	$10,001.51		$104,102.14
7	New York	$15,057.69	$10,223.91	$29,818.65	$20,039.58	$8,856.97	$16,683.64	$3,102.95	$103,783.39
8	Chicago	$9,214.91	$18,401.65	$33,094.00	$7,546.04	$19,934.51	$6,472.19		$94,663.30
9	**Grand Total**	$56,156.47	$38,818.12	$95,263.11	$37,152.80	$38,898.04	$33,157.34	$3,102.95	$302,548.83
10									
11									

Adding conditional formatting to a PivotTable

You can add conditional formatting to a PivotTable to make it easier to compare the data values. The conditional formatting is applied to cells in a PivotTable the same way as it is to non-PivotTable data. The conditional formatting rules follow the PivotTable cells when you move fields to different areas of the PivotTable. **FIGURE L-16** shows a PivotTable that uses data bars to visually display the sales data.

FIGURE L-16: PivotTable with conditional formatting

	A	B	C	D	E	F	G	H	I	J
1	Category	(All) ▼								
2	Quarter	(All) ▼								
3										
4	**Sum of Sales**									
5		110	240	340	510	640	780	450	Grand Total	
6	Miami	$31,883.87	$10,192.56	$32,350.46	$9,567.18	$10,106.56	$10,001.51		$104,102.14	
7	New York	$15,057.69	$10,223.91	$29,818.65	$20,039.58	$8,856.97	$16,683.64	$3,102.95	$103,783.39	
8	Chicago	$9,214.91	$18,401.65	$33,094.00	$7,546.04	$19,934.51	$6,472.19		$94,663.30	
9	**Grand Total**	$56,156.47	$38,818.12	$95,263.11	$37,152.80	$38,898.04	$33,157.34	$3,102.95	$302,548.83	
10										
11										
12										

Create a PivotChart Report

Learning Outcomes
- Create a PivotChart
- Format a PivotChart

A **PivotChart report** is a chart that you create from data or from a PivotTable report. **TABLE L-1** describes how the elements in a PivotTable report correspond to the elements in a PivotChart report. When you create a PivotChart directly from data, Excel automatically creates a corresponding PivotTable report. If you change a PivotChart report by filtering or sorting the charted elements, Excel updates the corresponding PivotTable report to show the new data values. You can move the fields of a PivotChart using the PivotTable Fields List window; the new layout will be reflected in the PivotTable. **CASE** ▶ *Kate wants you to chart the fourth quarter tour sales and the yearly tour sales average for her presentation. You create the PivotChart report from the PivotTable data.*

STEPS

1. **Click the** Category list arrow **in cell B1, click** Tour, **click** OK, **click the** Quarter list arrow, **click 4, then click** OK

   The fourth quarter tour sales information appears in the PivotTable. You want to create the PivotChart from the PivotTable information you have displayed.

2. **Click any cell in the PivotTable, click the** PIVOTTABLE TOOLS ANALYZE tab, **then click the** PivotChart button **in the Tools group**

   The Insert Chart dialog box opens and shows a gallery of chart types.

3. **Click the** Clustered Column chart **if necessary, then click** OK

   The PivotChart appears on the worksheet as shown in **FIGURE L-17**. The chart has Field buttons that let you filter and sort a PivotChart in the same way you do a PivotTable. It will be easier to view the PivotChart if it is on its own sheet.

4. **Click the** PIVOTCHART TOOLS DESIGN tab, **click the** Move Chart button **in the Location group, click the** New sheet option button, **type** PivotChart **in the text box, click** OK

   The chart represents the fourth quarter tour sales. Kate asks you to change the chart to show the average sales for all quarters.

5. **Click the** Quarter field button **at the top of the PivotChart, click** All, **then click** OK

   The chart now represents the sum of tour sales for the year as shown in **FIGURE L-18**. You can change a PivotChart's summary function to display averages instead of totals.

6. **Click the** Sum of Sales list arrow **in the VALUES area of the PivotTable Fields List, click** Value Field Settings, **click** Average **on the Summarize Values By tab, then click** OK

   The PivotChart report recalculates to display averages. The chart would be easier to understand if it had a title.

7. **Click the** PIVOTCHART TOOLS DESIGN tab, **click the** Add Chart Element button **in the Chart Layouts group, point to** Chart Title, **click** Above Chart, **type** Average Tour Sales, **press [Enter], then drag the chart title border to center the title over the columns**

   You are finished filtering the chart data and decide to remove the field buttons.

8. **Click the** PIVOTCHART TOOLS ANALYZE tab, **then click the** Field Buttons button **in the Show/Hide group**

9. **Enter your name in the PivotChart sheet footer, save the workbook, then preview the PivotChart report**

   The final PivotChart report displaying the average tour sales for the year is shown in **FIGURE L-19**.

FIGURE L-17: PivotChart with fourth quarter tour sales

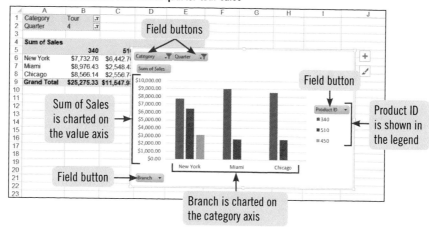

FIGURE L-18: PivotChart displaying tour sales for the year

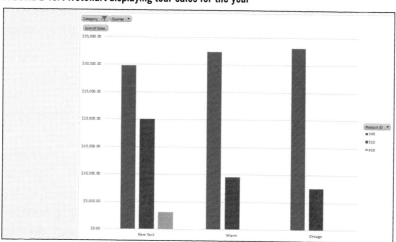

FIGURE L-19: Completed PivotChart report

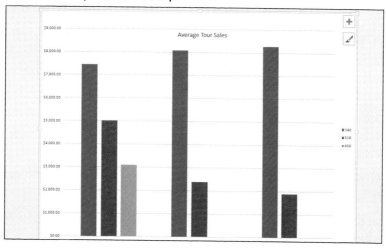

TABLE L-1: PivotTable and PivotChart elements

PivotTable items	PivotChart items
Row labels	Axis fields
Column labels	Legend fields
Report filters	Report filters

Analyzing Data with PivotTables

Use the GETPIVOTDATA Function

Learning
Outcomes
• Analyze the
GETPIVOTDATA
function
• Retrieve
information from
a PivotTable
using the
GETPIVOTDATA
function

Because you can rearrange a PivotTable so easily, you can't use an ordinary cell reference when you want to reference a PivotTable cell in another worksheet. The reason is that if you change the way data is displayed in a PivotTable, the data moves, making an ordinary cell reference incorrect. Instead, to retrieve summary data from a PivotTable, you need to use the Excel GETPIVOTDATA function. See **FIGURE L-20** for the GETPIVOTDATA function format. **CASE** *Kate wants to include the yearly sales total for the Chicago branch in the Sales sheet. She asks you to retrieve this information from the PivotTable and place it in the Sales sheet. You use the GETPIVOTDATA function to retrieve this information.*

STEPS

1. **Click the** PivotTable sheet tab

   The sales figures in the PivotTable are average values for tours. You decide to show sales information for all categories and change the summary information back to Sum.

2. **Click the** Category filter arrow **in cell B1, click** All, **then click** OK

   The PivotChart report displays sales information for all categories.

3. **Right-click cell** A4 **on the PivotTable, point to** Summarize Values By **on the shortcut menu, then click** Sum

   The PivotChart report recalculates to display sales totals. Next, you want to include the total for sales for the Chicago branch in the Sales sheet by retrieving it from the PivotTable.

4. **Click the** Sales sheet tab, **click cell** G1, **type** Total Chicago Sales:, **click the** Enter button ✓ **on the formula bar, click the** HOME tab, **click the** Align Right button ≡ **in the Alignment group, click the** Bold button **B** **in the Font group, then adjust the width of column G to display the label in cell G1**

   You want the GETPIVOTDATA function to retrieve the total Chicago sales from the PivotTable. Cell I8 on the PivotTable contains the data you want to display on the Sales sheet.

5. **Click cell** G2, **type** =, **click the** PivotTable sheet tab, **click cell** I8 **on the PivotTable, then click** ✓

   The GETPIVOTDATA function, along with its arguments, is inserted into cell G2 of the Sales sheet, as shown in **FIGURE L-21**. You want to format the sales total.

6. **Click the** Accounting Number Format button **$** **in the Number group**

   The current sales total for the Chicago branch is $94,663.30. This is the same value displayed in cell I8 of the PivotTable.

7. **Enter your name in the Sales sheet footer, save the workbook, then preview the Sales worksheet**

8. **Close the file, exit Excel, then submit the workbook to your instructor**

   The Sales worksheet is shown in **FIGURE L-22**.

FIGURE L-20: Format of GETPIVOTDATA function

GETPIVOTDATA("Sales",PivotTable!$A$4,"Branch","Chicago")

Field where data is extracted from

PivotTable name and cell in the report that contains the data you want to retrieve

Field and value pair that describe the data you want to retrieve

FIGURE L-21: GETPIVOTDATA function in the Sales sheet

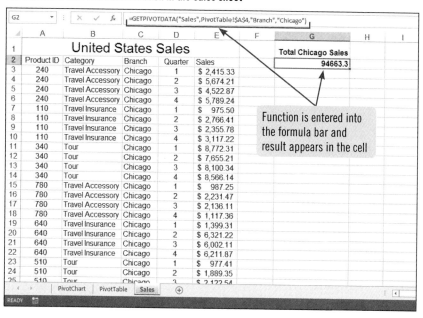

FIGURE L-22: Completed Sales worksheet showing total Chicago sales

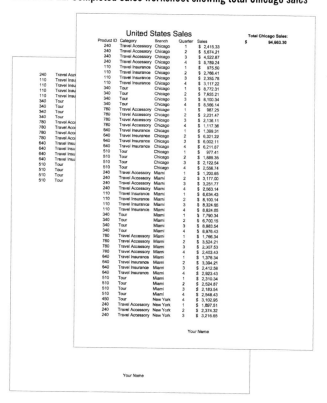

Practice

Concepts Review

FIGURE L-23

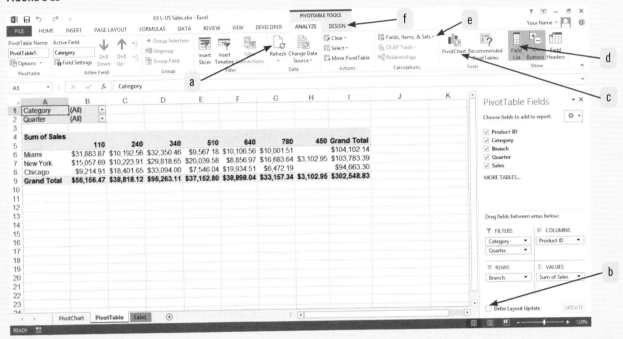

1. Which element do you click to create a calculated field in a PivotTable?
2. Which element do you click to create a chart based on the data in a PivotTable?
3. Which element do you click to display a gallery of PivotTable Styles?
4. Which element do you click to control when PivotTable changes will occur?
5. Which element do you click to display or hide the PivotTable Fields List pane?
6. Which element do you click to update a PivotTable?

Match each term with the statement that best describes it.

7. **PivotTable Row Label**
8. **Slicer**
9. **Compact form**
10. **Summary function**
11. **GETPIVOTDATA function**

a. Retrieves information from a PivotTable
b. Default layout for a PivotTable
c. PivotTable filtering tool
d. PivotChart axis field
e. Determines if data is summed or averaged

Select the best answer from the list of choices.

12. When a numeric field is added to a PivotTable, it is placed in the _____ area.

   a. VALUES

   b. ROWS

   c. COLUMNS

   d. FILTERS

13. Which PivotTable report area allows you to display only certain data using a list arrow?

   a. Values

   b. Column Labels

   c. Report Filter

   d. Row Labels

14. To make changes to PivotTable data, you must:

   a. Drag a column header to the column area.

   b. Create a page field.

   c. Edit cells in the PivotTable, then refresh the source list.

   d. Edit cells in the source list, then refresh the PivotTable.

15. When a nonnumeric field is added to a PivotTable, it is placed in the _____ area.

   a. VALUES

   b. Report Filter

   c. ROWS

   d. COLUMNS

Skills Review

1. Plan and design a PivotTable report.

   a. Start Excel, open the file titled EX L-2.xlsx from the location where you store your Data Files, then save it as **EX L-Product Sales**.

   b. Review the fields and data values in the worksheet.

   c. Verify that the worksheet data contains repeated values in one or more fields.

   d. Verify that there are not any blank rows or columns in the range A1:E25.

   e. Verify that the worksheet data contains a field that can be summed in a PivotTable.

2. Create a PivotTable report.

   a. Create a PivotTable report on a new worksheet using the Sales worksheet data in the range A1:E25.

   b. Add the Product ID field in the PivotTable Fields List pane to the COLUMNS area.

   c. Add the Sales field in the PivotTable Fields List pane to the VALUES Area.

   d. Add the Store field in the PivotTable Fields List pane to the ROWS area.

   e. Add the Sales Rep field in the PivotTable Fields List pane to the ROWS area below the Store field.

3. Change a PivotTable's summary function and design.

   a. Change the PivotTable summary function to Average.

   b. Rename the new sheet **Sales PivotTable**.

   c. Change the PivotTable Style to Pivot Style Light 20. Format the sales values in the PivotTable as Currency with a $ symbol and two decimal places.

   d. Enter your name in the center section of the PivotTable report footer, then save the workbook.

   e. Change the Summary function back to Sum. Remove the headers "Row Labels" and "Column Labels."

4. Filter and sort PivotTable data.

   a. Sort the stores in ascending order by total sales.

   b. Use slicers to filter the PivotTable to display sales for product IDs 100 and 200 in the DC and Seattle stores.

   c. Clear the filters and delete the slicers.

   d. Add the Region field to the FILTERS area in the PivotTable Fields List pane. Use the FILTERS list arrow to display sales for only the East region. Display sales for all regions.

   e. Save the workbook.

5. Update a PivotTable report.

   a. With the Sales PivotTable sheet active, note the NY total for Product ID 300.

   b. Activate the Sales sheet, and change K. Lyons's sales of Product ID 300 in cell D7 to **$9,000**.

   c. Refresh the PivotTable so it reflects the new sales figure.

   d. Verify the NY total for Product ID 300 decreased to $18,254. Save the workbook.

Excel 2013

Skills Review (continued)

6. **Explore PivotTable Data Relationships.**
   a. In the PivotTable Fields List, drag the Product ID field from the COLUMNS area to the ROWS area below the Sales Rep field. Drag the Sales Rep field from the ROWS area to the COLUMNS area.
   b. Drag the Store field from the ROWS area to the FILTERS area below the Region field. Drag the Product ID field back to the COLUMNS area.
   c. Drag the Store field back to the ROWS area.
   d. Remove the Sales Rep field from the PivotTable.
   e. Compare your completed PivotTable to **FIGURE L-24**, save the workbook.

7. **Create a PivotChart report.**
   a. Use the existing PivotTable data to create a Clustered Column PivotChart report.
   b. Move the PivotChart to a new worksheet, and name the sheet **PivotChart**.
   c. Add the title **Total Sales** above the chart.
   d. Filter the chart to display only sales data for the east region. Display the sales data for all regions. Hide all of the Field Buttons.
   e. Add your name to the center section of the PivotChart sheet footer. Compare your PivotChart to **FIGURE L-25**, save the workbook.

8. **Use the GETPIVOTDATA function.**
   a. In cell D27 of the Sales sheet type =, click the Sales PivotTable sheet, click the cell that contains the grand total for LA, then press [Enter].
   b. Review the GETPIVOTDATA function that was entered in cell D27.
   c. Enter your name in the Sales sheet footer, compare your Sales sheet to **FIGURE L-26**, save the workbook, then preview the sales worksheet.
   d. Close the workbook and exit Excel. Submit the workbook to your instructor.

FIGURE L-24

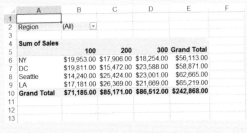

	100	200	300	Grand Total
NY	$19,953.00	$17,906.00	$18,254.00	$56,113.00
DC	$19,811.00	$15,472.00	$23,588.00	$58,871.00
Seattle	$14,240.00	$25,424.00	$23,001.00	$62,665.00
LA	$17,181.00	$26,369.00	$21,669.00	$65,219.00
Grand Total	$71,185.00	$85,171.00	$86,512.00	$242,868.00

FIGURE L-25

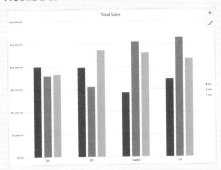

FIGURE L-26

	Product ID	Region	Store	Sales	Sales Rep
2	100	West	LA	$11,934	H. Jones
3	200	West	LA	$16,515	H. Jones
4	300	West	LA	$18,411	H. Jones
5	100	East	NY	$12,538	K. Lyons
6	200	East	NY	$6,052	K. Lyons
7	300	East	NY	$9,000	K. Lyons
8	100	West	Seattle	$12,098	M. Hale
9	200	West	Seattle	$15,550	M. Hale
10	300	West	Seattle	$17,690	M. Hale
11	100	East	DC	$11,850	J. Follen
12	200	East	DC	$14,225	J. Follen
13	300	East	DC	$18,254	J. Follen
14	100	West	LA	$5,247	D. Jacobs
15	200	West	LA	$9,854	D. Jacobs
16	300	West	LA	$3,258	D. Jacobs
17	100	East	NY	$7,415	L. Sorelle
18	200	East	NY	$11,854	L. Sorelle
19	300	East	NY	$9,254	L. Sorelle
20	100	West	Seattle	$2,142	T. Leonard
21	200	West	Seattle	$9,874	T. Leonard
22	300	West	Seattle	$5,311	T. Leonard
23	100	East	DC	$7,961	M. Grey
24	200	East	DC	$1,247	M. Grey
25	300	East	DC	$5,334	M. Grey
27			LA Sales for July:	$65,219	

Independent Challenge 1

You are the accountant for the Service Department of an HVAC company. The Service Department employs three technicians that service heating and air conditioning. Until recently, the owner had been tracking the technicians' hours manually in a log. You have created an Excel worksheet to track the following basic information: service date, technician name, job #, job category, hours, and warranty information. The owner has asked you to analyze the billing data to provide information about the number of hours being spent on the various job categories. He also wants to find out how much of the technicians' work is covered by warranties. You will create a PivotTable that sums the hours by category and technician. Once the table is completed, you will create a column chart representing the billing information.

a. Start Excel, open the file titled EX L-3.xlsx from the location where you store your Data Files, then save it as **EX L-Service**.
b. Create a PivotTable on a separate worksheet that sums hours by technician and category. Use **FIGURE L-27** as a guide.
c. Name the new sheet **PivotTable**, and apply the Pivot Style Medium 14.
d. Add slicers to filter the PivotTable using the category and technician data. Display only service data for Randal's category Level 1 jobs. Remove the filters, and remove the slicers.

FIGURE L-27

PivotTable Fields

Choose fields to add to report:

☐ Date
☑ Technician
☐ Job #
☑ Category
☑ Hours
☐ Warranty

MORE TABLES...

Drag fields between areas below:

▼ FILTERS   ▥ COLUMNS
                   Category ▼

☰ ROWS   Σ VALUES
Technician ▼   Sum of Hours ▼

☐ Defer Layout Update   UPDATE

Independent Challenge 1 (continued)

e. Add the Warranty field to the FILTERS area of the PivotTable. Display only the PivotTable data for jobs covered by warranties.

f. Remove the headers of "Column Labels" and "Row Labels" from the PivotTable.

g. Create a clustered column PivotChart that shows the warranty hours. Move the PivotChart to a new sheet named **PivotChart**.

h. Add the title **Warranty Hours** above the chart.

i. Change the PivotChart filter to display hours where the work was not covered by a warranty. Edit the chart title to read **Nonwarranty Hours**.

j. Hide the field buttons on the chart.

k. Add your name to the center section of the PivotTable and PivotChart footers, then save the workbook. Preview the PivotTable and the PivotChart. Close the workbook and exit Excel. Submit the workbook to your instructor.

Independent Challenge 2

You are the owner of an office supply store called Buffalo Office Supplies. You sell products at the store as well as online. You also take orders by phone from your catalog customers. You have been using Excel to maintain a sales summary for the second quarter sales of the different types of products sold by the company. You want to create a PivotTable to analyze and graph the sales in each product category by month and type of order.

a. Start Excel, open the file titled EX L-4.xlsx from the location where you store your Data Files, then save it as **EX L-Office Solutions**.

b. Create a PivotTable on a new worksheet named **PivotTable** that sums the sales amount for each category across the rows and each type of sale down the columns. Add the month field as an inner row label. Use **FIGURE L-28** as a guide.

c. Move the month field to the FILTERS area. Display the sum of sales data for the month of April.

FIGURE L-28

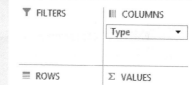

d. Turn off the grand totals for the columns. (*Hint*: Use the Grand Totals button in the Layout group on the PIVOTTABLE TOOLS DESIGN tab and choose On for Rows Only.)

e. Change the summary function in the PivotTable to Average.

f. Format the sales values using the Currency format with two decimal places and the $ symbol. Widen columns C and D to display the sales data.

g. On the Sales worksheet, change the April online paper sales in cell D3 to $20,221. Update the PivotTable to reflect this increase in sales.

h. Sort the average sales of categories from smallest to largest using the grand total of sales.

i. Create a stacked column PivotChart report for the average April sales data for all three types of sales.

j. Change the PivotChart to display the June sales data.

k. Move the PivotChart to a new sheet, and name the chart sheet **PivotChart**.

l. Add the title **Average June Sales** above your chart.

m. On the PivotTable, move the Month field from the FILTERS area to the ROWS area of the PivotTable below the Category field.

n. Add a slicer to filter the PivotTable by month. Use the slicer to display the average sales in April and May.

o. Check the PivotChart to be sure that the filtered data is displayed.

p. Change the chart title to **Average Sales April and May** to describe the charted sales.

q. Add your name to the center section of the PivotTable and PivotChart worksheet footers, save the workbook, then preview the PivotTable and the PivotChart. Close the workbook and exit Excel. Submit the workbook to your instructor.

Excel 2013

Independent Challenge 3

You are the North American sales manager for a drug store supply company with sales offices in the United States and Canada. You use Excel to keep track of the staff in the U.S. and Canadian offices. Management asks you to provide a summary table showing information on your sales staff, including their locations, status, and titles. You will create a PivotTable and PivotChart summarizing this information.

a. Start Excel, open the file titled EX L-5.xlsx from the location where you store your Data Files, then save it as **EX L-Sales Employees**.

b. Create a PivotTable on a new worksheet that shows the number of employees in each city, with the names of the cities listed across the columns, the titles listed down the rows, and the status indented below the titles. (*Hint*: Remember that the default summary function for cells containing text is Count.) Use **FIGURE L-29** as a guide. Rename the new sheet **PivotTable**.

FIGURE L-29

Count of Last Name	Column Labels									
Row Labels	Baltimore	Charlotte	Chicago	Los Angeles	Montreal	San Francisco	St. Louis	Toronto	Vancouver	Grand Total
Sales Manager	1	2	2	1	1	3	2	3	1	16
Full-time		2	2	1	1	2	1	2	1	12
Part-time						1	1	1		4
Sales Representative	4	7	2	5	4	7	2	3	3	37
Full-time	3	5	1	4	3	5	1	2	2	26
Part-time	1	2	1	1	1	2	1	1	1	11
Grand Total	5	9	4	6	5	10	4	6	4	53

c. Change the structure of the PivotTable to display the data as shown in **FIGURE L-30**.

d. Add a report filter using the Region field. Display only the U.S. employees.

e. Create a clustered column PivotChart from the PivotTable and move the chart to its own sheet named PivotChart. Rearrange the fields to create the PivotChart shown in **FIGURE L-31**.

f. Add the title **U.S. Sales Staff** above the chart.

g. Add the Pivot Style Light 18 style to the PivotTable.

h. Insert a new row in the Employees worksheet above row 7. In the new row, add information reflecting the recent hiring of Kate Conroy, a full-time sales manager at the Baltimore office. Update the PivotTable to display the new employee information.

i. Add the label **Total Chicago Staff** in cell G1 of the Employees sheet. Widen column G to fit the label.

j. Enter a function in cell H1 that retrieves the total number of employees located in Chicago from the PivotTable. Change the page orientation of the Employees sheet to landscape.

k. Use a slicer to filter the PivotTable to display only the data for the cities of Baltimore, Chicago, Los Angeles, and San Francisco.

l. Add another slicer for the Title field to display only the sales representatives.

m. Verify that the number of Chicago employees in cell H1 of the Employees sheet is now 2.

FIGURE L-30

Count of Last Name	Column Labels		
Row Labels	Full-time	Part-time	Grand Total
Sales Manager	12	4	16
Baltimore		1	1
Charlotte	2		2
Chicago	2		2
Los Angeles	1		1
Montreal	1		1
San Francisco	2	1	3
St. Louis	1	1	2
Toronto	2	1	3
Vancouver	1		1
Sales Representative	26	11	37
Baltimore	3	1	4
Charlotte	5	2	7
Chicago	1	1	2
Los Angeles	4	1	5
Montreal	3	1	4
San Francisco	5	2	7
St. Louis	1	1	2
Toronto	2	1	3
Vancouver	2	1	3
Grand Total	38	15	53

FIGURE L-31

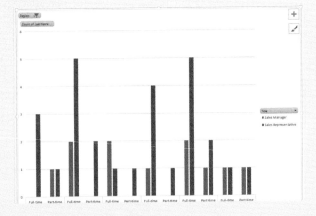

Independent Challenge 3 (continued)

n. Remove the slicers but do not remove the filters.

o. Add your name to the center section of all three worksheet footers, save the workbook, then preview the PivotTable, the first page of the Employees worksheet, and the PivotChart.

p. Close the workbook and exit Excel. Submit the workbook to your instructor.

Independent Challenge 4: Explore

You are the Regional sales manager for a Texas software support company with offices in Austin, Houston, and Dallas. You use Excel to keep track of the revenue generated by sales contracts in these offices. The CEO asks you to provide a summary table showing information on your offices' revenue over the past two years.

a. Start Excel, open the file EX L-6.xlsx, then save it as **EX L-Revenue** in the location where you save your Data Files.

FIGURE L-32

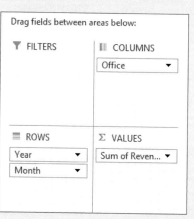

b. Create a PivotTable on a separate worksheet that sums revenue by office, year, and month. Use **FIGURE L-32** as a guide.

c. Name the new sheet **Summary**, and apply the Pivot Style Light 19.

d. Add slicers to filter the PivotTable using the Quarter and Office fields. Display only revenue data for Austin and Dallas for quarters 3 and 4. Remove the filters, but do not remove the slicers.

e. Format the Office slicer using the Slicer Style Light 4 in the Slicer Styles gallery on the SLICER TOOLS OPTIONS tab.

f. Change the Office slicer caption from Office to **Sales Office**. (*Hint*: Use the Slicer Caption text box in the Slicer group of the SLICER TOOLS OPTIONS tab.)

g. Change the Quarter slicer buttons to appear in two columns, with a button height of .3" and a button width of .56". (*Hint*: Use the options in the Buttons group of the SLICER TOOLS OPTIONS tab.)

h. Change the Quarter slicer shape to a height of 1.2" and width of 1.33". (*Hint*: Use the options in the Size group of the SLICER TOOLS OPTIONS tab.) Shorten the Sales Office slicer shape by dragging the lower slicer edge up to just below the bottom button.

i. Add a calculated field named **Average Sale** to the PivotTable to calculate the average sale using the formula =Revenue/Number of Contracts. Change the labels in cells C5, E5, and G5 to **Average** and format all of the Average labels as right justified.

j. Add the Quarter field to the PivotTable as a Report Filter.

k. Copy each quarter's data to a separate sheet. (*Hint*: Select the Quarter field in cell A1, click the Options list arrow in the PivotTable group of the PIVOTTABLE TOOLS ANALYZE tab, then select Show Report Filter Pages.) View the sheet for each quarter.

l. Group all of the worksheets, add your name to the center section of the footer for the worksheets, save the workbook, then preview the worksheets.

m. Close the workbook and exit Excel. Submit the workbook to your instructor.

Visual Workshop

Open the file EX L-7.xlsx from the location where you store your Data Files, then save it as **EX L-Real Estate**. Using the data in the workbook, create the PivotTable shown in FIGURE L-33 on a worksheet named PivotTable, then generate a PivotChart on a new sheet named PivotChart as shown in FIGURE L-34. (*Hint*: The PivotTable has been formatted using the Pivot Style Medium 2. Note that the PivotChart has been filtered.) Add your name to the PivotTable and the PivotChart footers, then preview the PivotTable and the PivotChart. Save the workbook, close the workbook, exit Excel, then submit the workbook to your instructor.

FIGURE L-33

	A	B	C	D	E	F
1						
2						
3	**Sum of Sales**					
4		Jan	Feb	Mar	Grand Total	
5	Commercial	$17,672,129.00	$18,851,236.00	$31,580,063.00	$68,103,428.00	
6	Boston	$10,018,009.00	$3,115,222.00	$12,025,664.00	$25,158,895.00	
7	DC	$4,711,899.00	$6,605,556.00	$9,504,845.00	$20,822,300.00	
8	Miami	$2,942,221.00	$9,130,458.00	$10,049,554.00	$22,122,233.00	
9	Land	$120,067,314.00	$165,020,142.00	$96,586,350.00	$381,673,806.00	
10	Boston	$75,518,444.00	$51,027,452.00	$41,025,444.00	$167,571,340.00	
11	DC	$18,505,645.00	$32,503,133.00	$37,515,452.00	$88,524,230.00	
12	Miami	$26,043,225.00	$81,489,557.00	$18,045,454.00	$125,578,236.00	
13	Residential	$76,578,375.00	$117,522,506.00	$182,574,063.00	$376,674,944.00	
14	Boston	$40,027,554.00	$29,011,550.00	$76,020,776.00	$145,059,880.00	
15	DC	$16,505,377.00	$68,508,511.00	$65,504,845.00	$150,518,733.00	
16	Miami	$20,045,444.00	$20,002,445.00	$41,048,442.00	$81,096,331.00	
17	**Grand Total**	**$214,317,818.00**	**$301,393,884.00**	**$310,740,476.00**	**$826,452,178.00**	
18						
19						
20						
21						
22						

FIGURE L-34

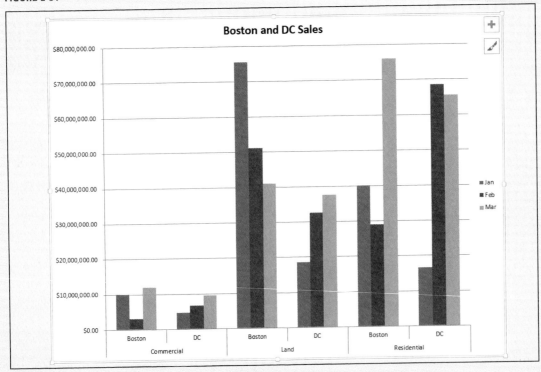

Exchanging Data with Other Programs

CASE ▶ Quest's upper management has asked Kate Morgan, the vice president of sales, to research the possible purchase of Service Adventures, a small company specializing in combining travel with volunteer work for corporate employees. Kate is reviewing the organization's files and developing a presentation on the feasibility of acquiring the company. She asks you to help set up the data exchange between Excel and other programs.

Unit Objectives

After completing this unit, you will be able to:

- Plan a data exchange
- Import a text file
- Import a database table
- Insert a graphic file in a worksheet

- Embed a workbook in a Word document
- Link a workbook to a Word document
- Link an Excel chart to a PowerPoint slide
- Import a table into Access

Files You Will Need

EX M-1.txt
EX M-2.accdb
EX M-3.jpg
EX M-4.docx
EX M-5.xlsx
EX M-6.pptx
EX M-7.xlsx
EX M-8.xlsx
EX M-9.txt
EX M-10.accdb
EX M-11.jpg
EX M-12.xlsx

EX M-13.pptx
EX M-14.xlsx
EX M-15.xlsx
EX M-16.pptx
EX M-17.txt
EX M-18.docx
EX M-19.xlsx
EX M-20.docx
EX M-21.xlsx
EX M-22.xlsx
EX M-23.accdb

©Katerina Havelkova/Shutterstock

Plan a Data Exchange

Learning
Outcomes
• Plan a data
exchange between
Office programs
• Develop an
understanding of
data exchange
vocabulary

Because the tools available in Microsoft Office programs are designed to be compatible, exchanging data between Excel and other programs is easy. The first step involves planning what you want to accomplish with each data exchange. **CASE** ▶ *Kate asks you to use the following guidelines to plan data exchanges between Excel and other programs in order to complete the business analysis project.*

DETAILS

To plan an exchange of data:

- **Identify the data you want to exchange, its file type, and, if possible, the program used to create it**

    Whether the data you want to exchange is a graphics file, a database file, a worksheet, or consists only of text, it is important to identify the data's **source program** (the program used to create it) and the file type. Once you identify the source program, you can determine options for exchanging the data with Excel. Kate needs to analyze a text file containing the Service Adventures tour sales. Although she does not know the source program, Kate knows that the file contains unformatted text. A file that consists of text but no formatting is sometimes called an **ASCII** or **text** file. Because ASCII is a universally accepted file format, Kate can easily import an ASCII file into Excel. See **TABLE M-1** for a partial list of other file formats that Excel can import.

- **Determine the program with which you want to exchange data**

    Besides knowing which program created the data you want to exchange, you must also identify which program will receive the data, called the **destination program**. This determines the procedure you use to perform the exchange. You might want to insert a graphic object into an Excel worksheet or add a spreadsheet to a Word document. Kate received a database table of Service Adventures' corporate customers created with the Access database program. After determining that Excel can import Access tables and reviewing the import procedure, she imports the database file into Excel so she can analyze it using Excel tools.

- **Determine the goal of your data exchange**

    Windows offers two ways to transfer data within and between programs that allow you to retain some connection with the source program. These data transfer methods use a Windows feature known as **object linking and embedding**, or **OLE**. The data to be exchanged, called an **object**, may consist of text, a worksheet, or any other type of data. You use **embedding** to insert a copy of the original object into the destination document and, if necessary, to then edit this data separately from the source document. This process is illustrated in **FIGURE M-1**. You use **linking** when you want the information you inserted to be updated automatically if the data in the source document changes. This process is illustrated in **FIGURE M-2**. You learn more about embedding and linking later in this unit. Kate has determined that she needs to use both object embedding and object linking for her analysis and presentation project.

- **Set up the data exchange**

    When you exchange data between two programs, it is often best to start both programs before starting the exchange. You might also want to tile the program windows on the screen either horizontally or vertically so that you can see both during the exchange. You will work with Excel, Word, Access, and PowerPoint when exchanging data for this project.

- **Execute the data exchange**

    The steps you use will vary, depending on the type of data you want to exchange. Kate is ready to have you start the data exchanges for the business analysis of Service Adventures.

FIGURE M-1: Embedded object

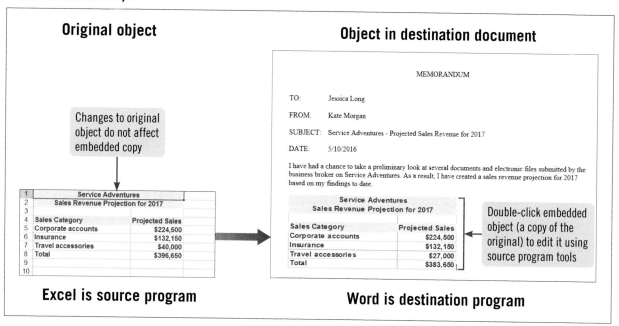

FIGURE M-2: Linked object

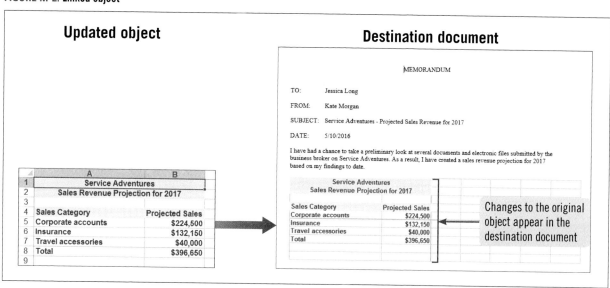

TABLE M-1: File formats Excel can import

file format	file extension(s)	file format	file extension(s)
Access	.mdb, .accdb	All Data Sources	.odc, .udl, .dsn
Text	.txt, .prn, .csv, .dif, .sylk	OpenDocument Spreadsheet	.ods
Query	.iqy, .dqy, .oqy, .rqy	XML	.xml
Web page	.htm, .html, .mht, .mhtml	dBASE	.dbf

Import a Text File

Learning Outcomes
- Import a text file into an Excel workbook
- Format text data

You can import text data into Excel and save the imported data in Excel format. Text files use a tab or space as the **delimiter**, or column separator, to separate columns of data. When you import a text file into Excel, the Text Import Wizard automatically opens and describes how text is separated in the imported file. **CASE** ▸ *Now that Kate has planned the data exchange, she wants you to import a tab-delimited text file containing branch and profit data from Service Adventures.*

STEPS

1. **Start Excel if necessary, create a blank workbook, click the DATA tab, click From Text in the Get External Data group, then navigate to the location where you store your Data Files**

   The Import Text File dialog box shows only text files.

2. **Click EX M-1.txt, then click Import**

   The first Text Import Wizard dialog box opens, as shown in **FIGURE M-3**. Under Original data type, the Delimited option button is selected. In the Preview of file box, line 1 indicates that the file contains two columns of data: Branch and Profit. No changes are necessary in this dialog box.

3. **Click Next**

   The second Text Import Wizard dialog box opens. Under Delimiters, Tab is selected as the delimiter, indicating that tabs separate the columns of incoming data. The Data preview box contains a line showing where the tab delimiters divide the data into columns.

4. **Click Next**

   The third Text Import Wizard dialog box opens with options for formatting the two columns of data. Under Column data format, the General option button is selected. The Data preview area shows that both columns will be formatted with the General format. This is the best formatting option for text mixed with numbers.

5. **Click Finish, then click OK**

   Excel imports the text file into the blank workbook starting in cell A1 of the worksheet as two columns of data: Branch and Profit.

6. **Click the FILE tab, click Save, navigate to the location where you store your Data Files, change the filename to EX M-Branch Profit, then click Save**

   The text file information is saved as an Excel workbook. The worksheet information would be easier to read if it were formatted and if it showed the total profit for all regions.

7. **Click cell A8, type Total Profit, click cell B8, click the HOME tab, click the AutoSum button in the Editing group, then click the Enter button ✓ on the formula bar**

8. **Rename the sheet tab Profit, center the column labels, apply bold formatting to them, format the data in column B using the Currency style with the $ symbol and no decimal places, then click cell A1**

   FIGURE M-4 shows the completed worksheet, which analyzes the text file data you imported into Excel.

9. **Add your name to the center section of the worksheet footer, save the workbook, preview the worksheet, close the workbook, then submit the workbook to your instructor**

FIGURE M-3: First Text Import Wizard dialog box

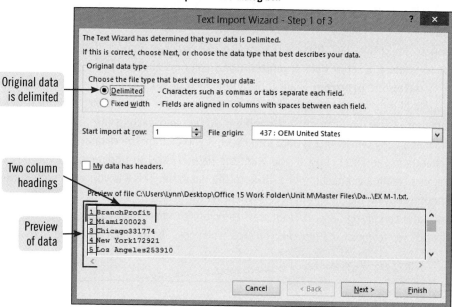

Original data is delimited

Two column headings

Preview of data

FIGURE M-4: Completed worksheet with imported text file

	A	B	
1	**Branch**	**Profit**	Columns from text file
2	Miami	$200,023	
3	Chicago	$331,774	
4	New York	$172,921	
5	Los Angeles	$253,910	
6	Boston	$264,512	
7	Portland	$199,531	
8	Total Profit	$1,422,671	
9			

Total profit added after importing data

Importing files using other methods

Another way to open the Text Import Wizard to import a text file into Excel is to click the FILE tab, click Open, then navigate to the location where you store your Data Files. In the Open dialog box you will see only files that match the file types listed in the Files of type box—usually Microsoft Excel files. To import a text file, you need to change the file type: click All Excel Files, click Text Files (*.prn; *.txt; *.csv), click the text file name, then click Open. You can also drag the icon representing a text file on the Windows desktop into a blank worksheet window. Excel will create a worksheet from the data without using the Wizard.

Import a Database Table

Learning Outcomes
- Import Access data into an Excel workbook
- Format imported data

In addition to importing text files, you can also use Excel to import data from database tables. A **database table** is a set of data organized using columns and rows that is created in a database program. A **database program** is an application, such as Microsoft Access, that lets you manage large amounts of data organized in tables. FIGURE M-5 shows an Access table. To import data from an Access table into Excel, you can copy the table in Access and paste it into an Excel worksheet. This method places a copy of the Access data into Excel; if you change the data in the Access file, the data will not change in the Excel copy. If you want the data in Excel to update when you edit the Access source file, you create a connection, or a **link**, to the database. This lets you work with current data in Excel without recopying the data from Access whenever the Access data changes. **CASE** *Kate received a database table containing Service Adventures' corporate customer information, which was created with Access. She asks you to import this table into an Excel workbook. She would also like you to format, sort, and total the data.*

STEPS

1. **Click the** File Tab, **click** New, **then click** Blank workbook

   A new workbook opens, displaying a blank worksheet for you to use to import the Access data.

2. **Click the** DATA tab, **click the** From Access button **in the Get External Data group, then navigate to the location where you store your Data Files**

3. **Click** EX M-2.accdb, **click** Open, **verify that the** Table option button **and the** Existing worksheet button **are selected in the Import Data dialog box, then click** OK

   Excel inserts the Access data into the worksheet as a table with the table style Medium 2 format applied, as shown in FIGURE M-6.

4. **Rename the sheet tab** Customer Information, **then format the data in columns F and G with the Currency format with the $ symbol and no decimal places**

   You are ready to sort the data using the values in column G.

5. **Click the cell** G1 list arrow, **then click** Sort Smallest to Largest

   The records are reorganized in ascending order according to the amount of the 2017 orders.

6. **Click the** TABLE TOOLS DESIGN tab **if necessary, click the** Total Row check box **in the Table Style Options group to select it, click cell** F19, **click the cell** F19 list arrow **next to cell F19, select** Sum **from the drop-down function list, then click cell** A1

   Your completed worksheet should match FIGURE M-7.

7. **Add your name to the center section of the worksheet footer, change the worksheet orientation to landscape, save the workbook as** EX M-Customer Information, **then preview the worksheet**

FIGURE M-5: Access Table

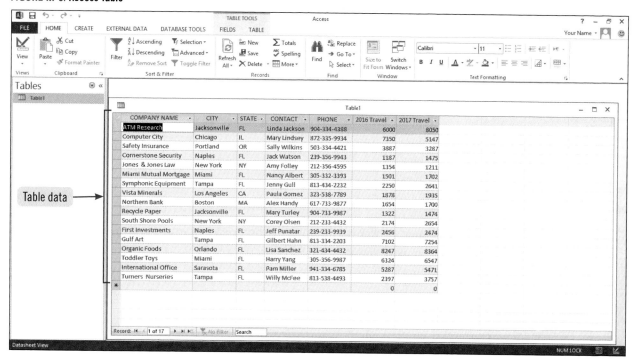

FIGURE M-6: Access table imported to Excel

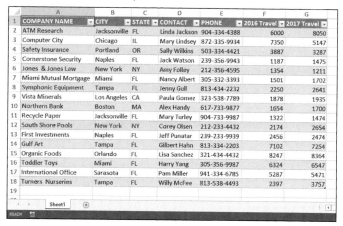

FIGURE M-7: Completed worksheet containing imported data

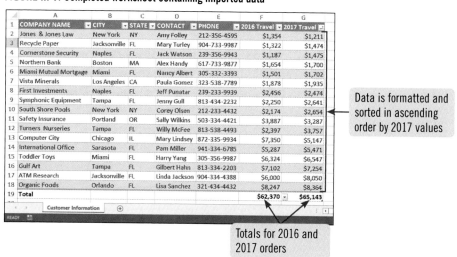

Data is formatted and sorted in ascending order by 2017 values

Totals for 2016 and 2017 orders

Insert a Graphic File in a Worksheet

Learning Outcomes
- Insert an image into an Excel worksheet
- Add a style to an image

A graphic object, such as a drawing, logo, or photograph, can greatly enhance your worksheet's visual impact. You can insert a graphic image into a worksheet and then format it using the options on the Format tab. **CASE** *Kate wants you to insert the Quest logo at the top of the customer worksheet. The company's graphic designer created the image and saved it in JPG format. You insert and format the image on the worksheet. You start by creating a space for the logo on the worksheet.*

STEPS

1. **Select rows 1 through 5, click the HOME tab, then click the Insert button in the Cells group**
   Five blank rows appear above the header row, leaving space to insert the picture.

2. **Click cell A1, click the INSERT tab, then click the Pictures button in the Illustrations group**
   The Insert Picture dialog box opens. You want to insert a picture that already exists in a file. The file has a .jpg file extension, so it is called a "jay-peg" file.

3. **Navigate to the location where you store your Data Files, click EX M-3.jpg, then click Insert**
   Excel inserts the image and displays the PICTURE TOOLS FORMAT tab. The small circles around the picture's border are sizing handles. Sizing handles appear when a picture is selected; you use them to change the size of a picture.

4. **Position the pointer over the sizing handle in the logo's lower-right corner until the pointer becomes ⤡, then drag the corner up and to the left so that the logo's outline fits within rows 1 through 5**
   Compare your screen to **FIGURE M-8**. You decide to remove the logo's white background.

QUICK TIP
You can correct an image by selecting it, clicking the Corrections button in the Adjust group on the PICTURE TOOLS FORMAT tab, then clicking an option in the Sharpen/Soften or Brightness/Contrast section.

5. **With the image selected, click the Color button in the Adjust group of the Picture Tools Format tab, click Set Transparent Color, then use ✐ to click the white background on the logo**
   The logo is now transparent, and shows the worksheet gridlines behind it. You decide that the logo will be more visually interesting with a frame and a border color.

6. **With the image selected, click the More button ⯆ in the Picture Styles group, point to several styles and observe the effect on the graphic, click the Reflected Bevel, White style (the third from the right in the last row), click the Picture Border list arrow in the Picture Styles group, then click Blue, Accent 1, Lighter 40% in the Theme Colors group**
   You decide to add a glow to the image.

7. **Click the Picture Effects button in the Picture Styles group, point to Glow, point to More Glow Colors, click Blue, Accent 1, Lighter 80% in the Theme Colors group, resize the logo as necessary to fit it in rows 1 through 5, then drag the logo above the column D data**
   You decide to add an artistic effect to the image.

8. **Click the Artistic Effects button in the Adjust group, click Light Screen (First effect in the third row), then click cell A1**
   Compare your worksheet to **FIGURE M-9**.

9. **Save the workbook, preview the worksheet, close the workbook, exit Excel, then submit the workbook to your instructor**

FIGURE M-8: Resized logo

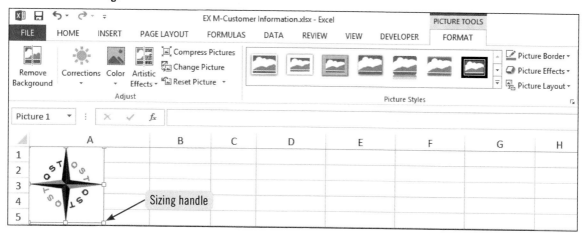

FIGURE M-9: Worksheet with formatted picture

	A	B	C	D	E	F	G	H	I
1									
2									
3					Formatted image				
4									
5									
6	COMPANY NAME	CITY	STATE	CONTACT	PHONE	2016 Travel	2017 Travel		
7	Jones & Jones Law	New York	NY	Amy Folley	212-356-4595	$1,354	$1,211		
8	Recycle Paper	Jacksonville	FL	Mary Turley	904-733-9987	$1,322	$1,474		
9	Cornerstone Security	Naples	FL	Jack Watson	239-356-9943	$1,187	$1,475		

Formatting SmartArt graphics

SmartArt graphics provide another way to visually communicate information on a worksheet. A **SmartArt graphic** is a professionally designed illustration with text and graphics. Each SmartArt type communicates a kind of information or relationship, such as a list, process, or hierarchy. Each type has various layouts you can choose. For example, you can choose from pyramid, process, picture, list, cycle, hierarchy, relationship and matrix layouts, allowing you to illustrate your information in many different ways. To insert a SmartArt graphic into a worksheet, click the INSERT tab, then click the SmartArt button in the Illustrations group. In the Choose a SmartArt Graphic dialog box, choose from eight SmartArt types: List, Process, Cycle, Hierarchy, Relationship, Matrix, Pyramid, and Picture. The dialog box also describes the type of information that is appropriate for each selected layout. After you choose a layout and click OK, a SmartArt object appears on your worksheet. As you enter text in the text entry areas, the font automatically resizes to fit the graphic. The SMARTART TOOLS DESIGN tab lets you choose

color schemes and styles for your SmartArt. You can add effects to SmartArt graphics using choices on the SMARTART TOOLS FORMAT tab. **FIGURE M-10** shows examples of SmartArt graphics. You can create a SmartArt graphic from an existing image by clicking the image, clicking the Picture Layout button in the Picture Styles group of the PICTURE TOOLS FORMAT tab, then selecting the SmartArt type.

FIGURE M-10: Examples of SmartArt graphics

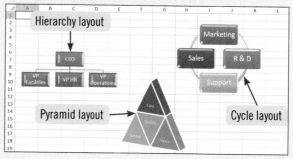

Learning Outcomes
- Embed Excel data in a Word document
- Edit an embedded file icon caption

Embed a Workbook in a Word Document

Microsoft Office programs work together to make it easy to copy an object (such as text, data, or a graphic) in a source program and then insert it into a document in a different program (the destination program). If you insert copied Excel data using a simple Paste command, however, you retain no connection to the source program. That's why it is often more useful to embed objects rather than simply paste them. Embedding allows you to edit an Excel workbook from within the source program using that program's commands and tools. If you send a Word document with an embedded workbook to another person, you do not need to send a separate Excel file with it. All the necessary information is embedded in the Word document. When you embed information, you can either display the data itself or an icon representing the data; users double-click the icon to view the embedded data. An icon is often used rather than the data when the worksheet data is too large to fit well on a Word document. **CASE** *Kate decides to update Jessica Long, the CEO of Quest, on the project status. She asks you to prepare a Word memo that includes the projected sales workbook embedded as an icon. You begin by starting Word and opening the memo.*

STEPS

1. **Open a File Explorer window, navigate to the location where you store your Data Files, then double-click the file EX M-4.docx to open the file in Word**
   The memo opens in Word.

2. **Click the FILE tab, click Save As, navigate to the location where you store your Data Files, change the file name to EX M-Service Adventures Memo, then click Save**
   You want to embed the workbook below the last line of the document.

3. **Press [Ctrl][End], click the INSERT tab, click the Object button in the Text group, then click the Create from File tab**
   FIGURE M-11 shows the Create from File tab in the Object dialog box. You need to indicate the file you want to embed.

4. **Click Browse, navigate to the location where you store your Data Files, click EX M-5.xlsx, click Insert, then select the Display as icon check box**
   You will change the icon label to a more descriptive name.

> **QUICK TIP**
> To display a different icon to represent the file, click the Change Icon button in the Object dialog box, scroll down the icon list in the Change Icon dialog box, and select any icon. You can also click Browse and choose an .ico file located on your computer.

5. **Click Change Icon, select the text in the Caption text box, type Projected Sales, click OK twice, then click anywhere in the Word document**
   The memo contains an embedded copy of the sales projection data, displayed as an icon, as shown in **FIGURE M-12**.

> **TROUBLE**
> If the Excel program window does not come to the front automatically, click the Excel icon in the taskbar.

6. **Double-click the Projected Sales icon on the Word memo, then maximize the Excel window and the worksheet window if necessary**
   The Excel program starts and displays the embedded worksheet, with its location displayed in the title bar, as shown in **FIGURE M-13**. Any changes you make to the embedded object using Excel tools are not reflected in the source document. Similarly, if you open the source document in the source program, changes you make are not reflected in the embedded copy.

7. **Click the FILE tab, click Close, exit Excel, click the Word FILE tab, then click Save to save the memo**

Exchanging Data with Other Programs

FIGURE M-11: Object dialog box

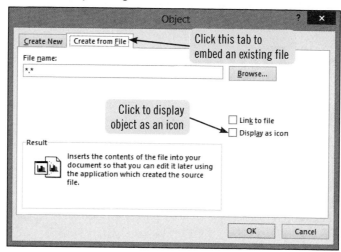

FIGURE M-12: Memo with embedded worksheet displayed as an icon

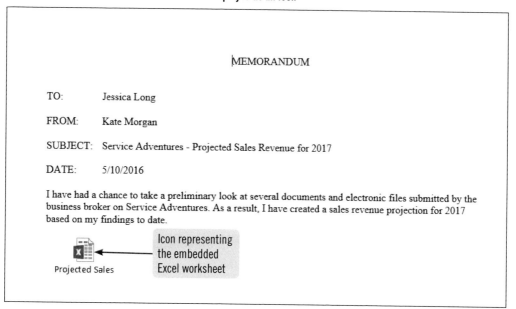

FIGURE M-13: Embedded worksheet open in Excel

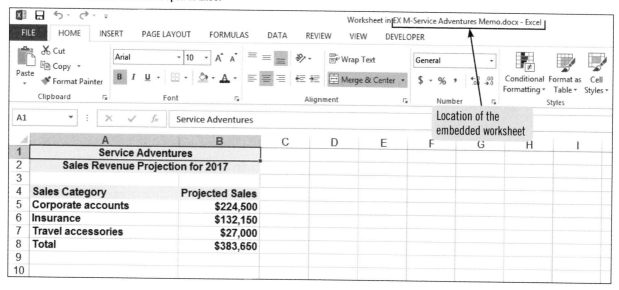

Link a Workbook to a Word Document

Learning
Outcomes
• Link data from an
Excel worksheet to
a Word document
• Update links in a
Word document

Linking a workbook to another file retains a connection with the original document as well as the original program. When you link a workbook to another program, the link contains a connection to the source document so that, when you double-click it, the source document opens for editing. In addition, any changes you make to the original workbook (the source document) are reflected in the linked object. **CASE** ▶ *Kate realizes she may need to edit the workbook she embedded in the memo to Jessica. To ensure that these changes will be reflected in the memo, she feels you should use linking instead of embedding. She asks you to delete the embedded worksheet icon and replace it with a linked version of the same workbook.*

STEPS

1. **With the Word memo still open, click the Projected Sales Worksheet icon to select it if necessary, then press [Delete]**

   The workbook is no longer embedded in the memo. The linking process is similar to embedding.

2. **Make sure the insertion point is below the last line of the memo, click the INSERT tab, click the Object button in the Text group, then click the Create from File tab in the Object dialog box**

3. **Click Browse, navigate to the location where you store your Data Files, click EX M-5.xlsx, click Insert, select the Link to file check box, then click OK**

   The memo now displays a linked copy of the sales projection data, as shown in **FIGURE M-14**. In the future, any changes made to the source file, EX M-5, will also be made to the linked copy in the Word memo. You verify this by making a change to the source file and viewing its effect on the memo.

4. **Click the File tab, click Save, close the Word memo, then exit Word**

5. **Start Excel, open the file EX M-5.xlsx from the location where you store your Data Files, click cell B7, type 40000, then press [Enter]**

   You want to verify that the same change was made automatically to the linked copy of the workbook.

6. **Start Word, open the EX M-Service Adventures Memo.docx file from the location where you store your Data Files, then click Yes if asked if you want to update the document's links**

   The memo displays the new value for Travel accessories, and the total has been updated as shown in **FIGURE M-15**.

7. **Click the INSERT tab, click the Header button in the Header & Footer group, click Edit Header, type your name in the Header area, then click the Close Header and Footer button in the Close group**

8. **Save the Word memo, preview it, close the file, exit Word, then submit the file to your instructor**

9. **Close the Excel worksheet without saving it, then exit Excel**

FIGURE M-14: Memo with linked worksheet

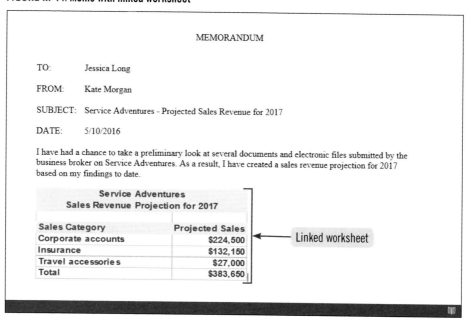

MEMORANDUM

TO: Jessica Long

FROM: Kate Morgan

SUBJECT: Service Adventures - Projected Sales Revenue for 2017

DATE: 5/10/2016

I have had a chance to take a preliminary look at several documents and electronic files submitted by the business broker on Service Adventures. As a result, I have created a sales revenue projection for 2017 based on my findings to date.

Service Adventures
Sales Revenue Projection for 2017

Sales Category	Projected Sales
Corporate accounts	$224,500
Insurance	$132,150
Travel accessories	$27,000
Total	$383,650

Linked worksheet

FIGURE M-15: Memo with updated values

MEMORANDUM

TO: Jessica Long

FROM: Kate Morgan

SUBJECT: Service Adventures - Projected Sales Revenue for 2017

DATE: 5/10/2016

I have had a chance to take a preliminary look at several documents and electronic files submitted by the business broker on Service Adventures. As a result, I have created a sales revenue projection for 2017 based on my findings to date.

Service Adventures
Sales Revenue Projection for 2017

Sales Category	Projected Sales
Corporate accounts	$224,500
Insurance	$132,150
Travel accessories	$40,000
Total	$396,650

Values update to match those in the source document

Managing links

When you open a document containing linked data, you are asked if you want to update the linked data. You can manage the updating of links by clicking the FILE tab, and clicking Edit Links to Files in the right pane. The Links dialog box opens, allowing you to change a link's update from the default setting of automatic to manual. The Links dialog box also allows you to change the link source, permanently break a link, open the source file, and manually update a link. If you send your linked files to another user, the links will be broken because the linked file path references the local machine where you inserted the links. Because the file path will not be valid on the recipient user's machine, the links will no longer be updated when the user opens the destination document. To correct this, recipients who have both the destination and source documents can use the Links dialog box to change the link's source in the destination document to their own machines. Then the links will be automatically updated when they open the destination document in the future.

Link an Excel Chart to a PowerPoint Slide

Microsoft PowerPoint is a **presentation graphics** program that you can use to create slide show presentations. PowerPoint slides can include a mix of text, data, and graphics. Adding an Excel chart to a slide can help to illustrate data and give your presentation more visual appeal. **CASE** ▶ *Kate asks you to add an Excel chart to one of the PowerPoint slides, illustrating the 2017 sales projection data. She wants you to link the chart in the PowerPoint file.*

STEPS

1. **Start PowerPoint, then open the file** EX M-6.pptx **from the location where you store your Data Files, then save it as** EX M-Management Presentation

    The presentation appears in Normal view and contains three panes, as shown in **FIGURE M-16**. You need to open the Excel file and copy the chart that you will paste in the PowerPoint presentation.

2. **Start Excel, open the file** EX M-7.xlsx **from the location where you store your Data Files, right-click the** Chart Area **on the Sales Categories sheet, click** Copy **on the shortcut menu, then click the** PowerPoint program button **on the taskbar to display the presentation**

    You need to add an Excel chart to Slide 2, "2017 Sales Projections". To add the chart, you first need to select the slide on which it will appear.

3. **Click** Slide 2 **in the Thumbnails pane, right-click** Slide 2 **in the Slide pane, then click the** Use Destination Theme & Link Data button **(third from the right) in the Paste Options group**

    A pie chart illustrating the 2017 sales projections appears in the slide. The chart matches the colors and fonts in the presentation, which is the destination document. You decide to edit the link so it will update automatically if the data source changes.

4. **Click the** FILE tab, **click** Edit Links to Files **at the bottom of the right pane, in the Links dialog box click the** Automatic Update check box **to select it, then click** Close

5. **Click the** Back to arrow button ⊙ **at the top of the pane to return to the presentation, click the** Save button 🖫 **on the Quick Access toolbar, then close the file**

    Kate has learned that the sales projections for the Travel accessories category has increased based on late sales for the current year.

6. **Switch to Excel, click the** Sales sheet tab, **change the Travel accessories value in cell B7 to** 45,000, **then press [Enter]**

    You decide to reopen the PowerPoint presentation to check the chart data.

7. **Switch to PowerPoint, open the file** EX M-Management Presentation.pptx, **click** Update Links, **click** Slide 2 **in the Thumbnails pane, then point to the** Travel accessories pie slice

    The ScreenTip shows that the chart has updated to display the revised Travel accessories value, $45,000, you entered in the Excel workbook. Slide Show view displays the slide on the full screen the way the audience will see it.

8. **Click the** Slide Show button 🖳 **on the status bar**

    The finished sales projection slide is complete, as shown in **FIGURE M-17**.

9. **Press [Esc] to return to Normal view; with Slide 2 selected click the** Insert tab, **click the** Header & Footer button **in the Text group, select the** Footer check box, **type your name in the Footer text box, click** Apply to All, **save and close the presentation, close the Excel file without saving it, exit PowerPoint and Excel, then submit the file to your instructor**

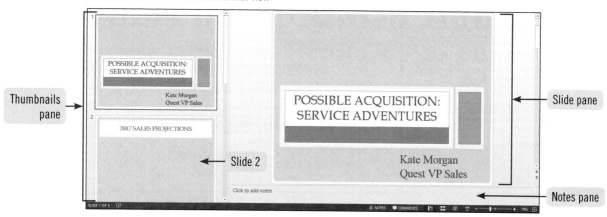

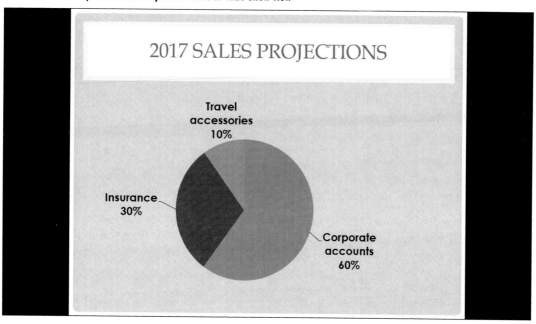

Excel 2013

Import a Table into Access

If you need to analyze Excel data using the more extensive tools of a database, you can import it into Microsoft Access. When you import Excel table data into Access, the data becomes an Access table using the same field names as the Excel table. In the process of importing an Excel table, Access specifies a primary key for the new table. A **primary key** is the field that contains unique information for each record (row) of information. **CASE** *Kate has just received a workbook containing salary information for the managers at Service Adventures, organized in a table. She asks you to convert the Excel table to a Microsoft Access table.*

STEPS

1. **Start Access, click the** Blank desktop database button, **change the filename in the File Name text box to** EX M-SA Management, **click the** Browse button 🖿 **next to the filename, navigate to the location where you store your Data Files, click OK, then click** Create

   The database window for the EX M-SA Management database opens. You are ready to import the Excel table data.

2. **Click the** EXTERNAL DATA tab, **then click the** Excel button **in the Import & Link group**

   The Get External Data - Excel Spreadsheet dialog box opens, as shown in **FIGURE M-18**. This dialog box allows you to specify how you want the data to be stored in Access.

3. **Click the** Browse button, **navigate to the location where you store your Data Files, click** EX M-8.xlsx, **click** Open, **if necessary click the** Import the source data into a new table in the current database option button, **click OK, then click** Open if necessary

   The first Import Spreadsheet Wizard dialog box opens, with a sample of the sheet data in the lower section. You want to use the column headings in the Excel table as the field names in the Access database.

4. **Make sure the** First Row Contains Column Headings check box **is selected, then click** Next

   The Wizard allows you to review and change the field properties by clicking each column in the lower section of the window. You will not make any changes to the field properties.

5. **Click** Next

   The Wizard allows you to choose a primary key for the table. The table's primary key field contains unique information for each record; the ID Number field is unique for each person in the table.

6. **Click the** Choose my own primary key option, **make sure "ID Number" appears in the text box next to the selected option button, click** Next, **note the name assigned to the new table, click** Finish, **then click** Close

   The name of the new Access table ("Compensation") appears in the left pane, called the Navigation pane.

7. **Double-click** Compensation: in the Navigation Pane

   The data from the Excel worksheet appears in a new Access table, as shown in **FIGURE M-19**.

8. **Double-click the** border **between the Monthly Salary and the Click to Add column headings to widen the Monthly Salary column, then use the last row of the table to enter your name in the First Name and Last Name columns and enter 0 for an ID Number**

9. **Click the** Save button 🖫 **on the Quick Access toolbar, close the file, then exit Access**

FIGURE M-18: Get External Data - Excel Spreadsheet dialog box

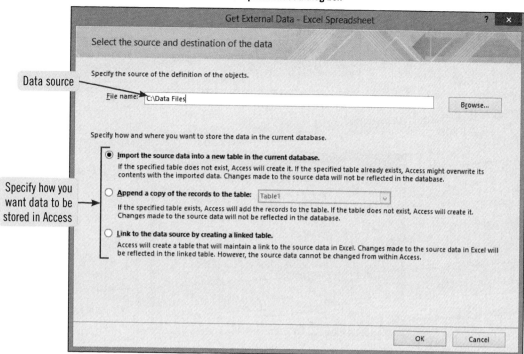

FIGURE M-19: Completed Access table with data imported from Excel

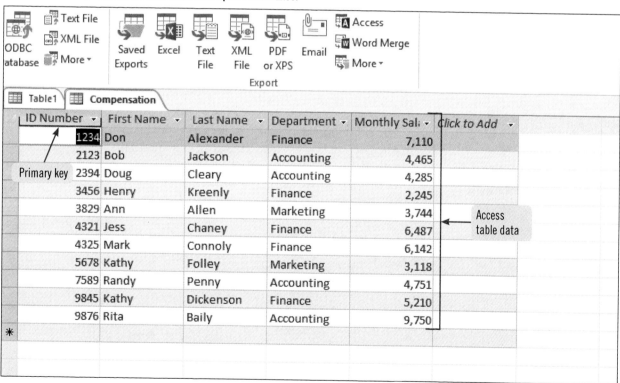

Practice

Put your skills into practice with SAM! If you have a SAM account, go to www.cengage.com/sam2013 to access SAM assignments for this unit.

Concepts Review

FIGURE M-20

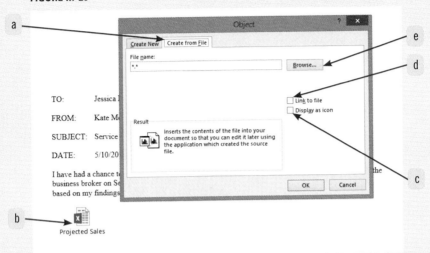

1. Which element do you click to embed information that can be viewed by double-clicking an icon?
2. Which element do you click to insert an existing object into a Word document rather than creating a new file?
3. Which element do you click to find a file to be embedded or linked?
4. Which element do you double-click to display an embedded Excel workbook?
5. Which element do you click to insert an object that maintains a connection to the source document?

Match each term with the statement that best describes it.

6. Source document
7. Embedding
8. Presentation graphics program
9. Destination document
10. OLE
11. Linking

a. File from which the object to be embedded or linked originates
b. Copies an object and retains a connection with the source program and source document
c. Document receiving the object to be embedded or linked
d. Data transfer method used in Windows programs
e. Copies an object and retains a connection with the source program only
f. Used to create slide shows

Select the best answer from the list of choices.

12. An ASCII file:
    a. Contains formatting but no text.
    b. Contains text but no formatting.
    c. Contains a PowerPoint presentation.
    d. Contains an unformatted worksheet.
13. An object consists of:
    a. Text, a worksheet, or any other type of data.
    b. A worksheet only.
    c. Text only.
    d. Database data only.
14. A column separator in a text file is called a(n):
    a. Object.
    b. Link.
    c. Primary key.
    d. Delimiter.

15. To view a workbook that has been embedded as an icon in a Word document, you need to:

a. Double-click the icon.

b. Drag the icon.

c. Click View, then click Worksheet.

d. Click File, then click Open.

16. A field that contains unique information for each record in a database table is called a(n):

a. Primary key.

b. ID Key.

c. First key.

d. Header key.

Skills Review

1. Import a text file.

a. Start Excel, open the tab-delimited text file titled EX M-9.txt from the location where you store your Data Files, then save it as a Microsoft Office Excel workbook with the name **EX M-East Campus Tea**.

b. Format the data in columns B and C using the Currency style with two decimal places.

c. Widen the columns if necessary so that all the data is visible.

d. Center the column labels and apply bold formatting, as shown in **FIGURE M-21**.

e. Add your name to the center section of the worksheet footer, save the workbook, preview the worksheet, close the workbook, then submit the workbook to your instructor.

FIGURE M-21

	A	B	C
1	**Item**	**Cost**	**Price**
2	Pot, small	$9.55	$18.50
3	Pot, large	$11.15	$25.00
4	Pot, decorated	$13.55	$23.70
5	Pot, china	$21.15	$30.90
6	Basket, small	$15.95	$26.80
7	Basket, large	$21.80	$32.90
8	Kettle, small	$16.75	$27.45
9	Kettle, large	$25.30	$33.75
10	Mug, large	$2.95	$4.70
11			

2. Import a database table.

a. Open a blank workbook in Excel, use the From Access button in the Get External Data group on the DATA tab to import the Access Data File EX M-10.accdb from the location where you store your Data Files, then save it as a Microsoft Excel workbook named **EX M-February Budget**.

b. Rename the sheet with the imported data **Budget**.

c. Delete the first data record in row 2.

d. Add a total row to the table to display the sum of the budgeted amounts in cell D25.

e. Apply the Medium 6 Table Style. Format range D2:D25 using the Currency style, the $ symbol, and two decimal places.

f. Save the workbook, and compare your screen to **FIGURE M-22**.

3. Insert a graphic file in a worksheet.

a. Add four rows above row 1 to create space for an image.

b. In rows 1 through 4, insert the picture file EX M-11.jpg from the location where you store your Data Files.

c. Resize and reposition the picture as necessary to make it fit in rows 1 through 4.

d. Apply the Beveled Matte, White Picture Style, and change the border color to Blue, Accent 5, Lighter 80%. Resize the picture to fit the image and the border in the first four rows. Move the picture to the center of the range A1:D4.

e. Compare your worksheet to **FIGURE M-23**, add your name to the center section of the worksheet footer, preview the workbook, save and close the workbook, then submit the workbook to your instructor.

FIGURE M-22

	A	B	C	D
1	**Category**	**Item**	**Month**	**Amount**
2	Compensation	Bonuses	Feb	$28,147.00
3	Compensation	Commissions	Feb	$22,574.00
4	Compensation	Conferences	Feb	$74,587.00
5	Compensation	Promotions	Feb	$62,354.00
6	Compensation	Payroll Taxes	Feb	$17,887.00
7	Compensation	Salaries	Feb	$42,057.00
8	Compensation	Training	Feb	$58,741.00
9	Facility	Lease	Feb	$47,324.00
10	Facility	Maintenance	Feb	$62,478.00
11	Facility	Other	Feb	$57,148.00
12	Facility	Rent	Feb	$77,634.00
13	Facility	Telephone	Feb	$62,748.00
14	Facility	Utilities	Feb	$57,964.00
15	Supplies	Food	Feb	$61,775.00
16	Supplies	Computer	Feb	$43,217.00
17	Supplies	General Office	Feb	$47,854.00
18	Supplies	Other	Feb	$56,741.00
19	Supplies	Outside Services	Feb	$41,874.00
20	Equipment	Computer	Feb	$49,874.00
21	Equipment	Other	Feb	$43,547.00
22	Equipment	Cash Registers	Feb	$55,987.00
23	Equipment	Software	Feb	$63,147.00
24	Equipment	Telecommunications	Feb	$58,779.00
25	**Total**			**$1,194,438.00**

Budget

FIGURE M-23

	A	B	C	D	E	F	G
1							
2							
3							
4							
5	**Category**	**Item**	**Month**	**Amount**			
6	Compensation	Bonuses	Feb	$28,147.00			
7	Compensation	Commissions	Feb	$22,574.00			
8	Compensation	Conferences	Feb	$74,587.00			
9	Compensation	Promotions	Feb	$62,354.00			
10	Compensation	Payroll Taxes	Feb	$17,887.00			
11	Compensation	Salaries	Feb	$42,057.00			
12	Compensation	Training	Feb	$58,741.00			
13	Facility	Lease	Feb	$47,324.00			
14	Facility	Maintenance	Feb	$62,478.00			
15	Facility	Other	Feb	$57,148.00			
16	Facility	Rent	Feb	$77,634.00			
17	Facility	Telephone	Feb	$62,748.00			
18	Facility	Utilities	Feb	$57,964.00			
19	Supplies	Food	Feb	$61,775.00			

Skills Review (continued)

4. Embed a workbook in a Word document.

a. Start Word, create a memo with a header addressed to your instructor, enter your name in the From line, enter **February Salaries** as the subject, and enter the current date in the Date line.

b. In the memo body, enter **The February salaries are provided in the worksheet below**:

c. In the memo body, use the Object dialog box to embed the workbook EX M-12.xlsx from the location where you store your Data Files, displaying it as an icon with the caption **Salary Details**.

d. Save the document as **EX M-February Salaries** in the location where you store your Data Files, then double-click the icon to verify that the workbook opens. (*Hint*: If the workbook does not appear after you double-click it, click the Excel icon on the taskbar.)

e. Close the workbook and return to Word.

f. Compare your memo to **FIGURE M-24**.

FIGURE M-24

To: Your Instructor

From: Your Name

Subject: February Sales

Date: 11/1/2016

The February salaries are provided in the worksheet below:

Salary Details

5. Link a workbook to a Word document.

a. Delete the icon in the memo body.

b. In the memo body, link the workbook EX M-12.xlsx, displaying the data, not an icon.

c. Save the document, then note that Mary Glenn's salary is $7,100. Close the document.

d. Open the EX M-12.xlsx workbook in Excel, and change Mary Glenn's salary to **$7500**.

e. Open the **EX M-February Salaries** document in Word, update the links, and verify that Mary Glenn's salary has changed to $7,500 and that the new total salaries amount is $48,057, as shown in **FIGURE M-25**. (*Hint*: If the dialog box does not open, giving you the opportunity to update the link, then right-click the worksheet object and click Update Link.)

f. Save the **EX M-February Salaries** document, preview the memo, close the document, exit Word, then submit the document to your instructor.

g. Close the EX M-12 workbook without saving changes, then exit Excel.

FIGURE M-25

To: Your Instructor

From: Your Name

Subject: February Sales

Date: 11/1/2016

The February salaries are provided in the worksheet below:

West Street Tea Salary Summary			
First Name	Last Name	Position	Salary
Mary	Glenn	Manager	$ 7,500
Jack	Cronin	Manager	$ 5,534
Mark	Donnolly	Manager	$ 6,754
Karen	Walker	Sales Associate	$ 7,132
Sandy	Jones	Custodian	$ 6,987
Keith	Allen	Sales Associate	$ 6,950
Gail	Henry	Sales Associate	$ 7,200
		Total	$ 48,057

6. Link an Excel chart to a PowerPoint slide.

a. Start PowerPoint.

b. Open the PowerPoint file EX M-13.pptx from the location where you store your Data Files, then save it as **EX M-Budget Meeting**.

c. Display Slide 2, February Expenditures.

d. Link the chart, using the theme of the destination file, from the Excel file EX M-14.xlsx from the location where you store your Data Files to Slide 2. Edit the link to be updated automatically. Save and close the Ex M-Budget Meeting file.

e. Change the Equipment amount on Sheet1 of the file EX M-14 to $207,000, open the EX M-Budget Meeting file, updating the links, and verify the Equipment percentage changed from 17% to 18% on Slide 2.

f. View the slide in Slide Show view.

g. Press [Esc] to return to Normal view. Resize and reposition the chart to fit on the slide if necessary. Compare your slide to **FIGURE M-26**.

FIGURE M-26

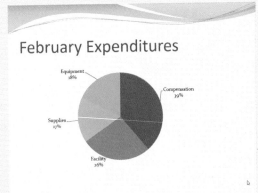

February Expenditures

Equipment 18%

Compensation 39%

Supplies 17%

Facility 26%

h. Add a footer to all of the slides with your name.

i. Save the presentation, exit PowerPoint, close EX M-14 without saving it, then submit the presentation to your instructor.

7. Import a table into Access.

a. Start Access.

b. Create a blank desktop database named **EX M-Budget** in the location where you store your Data Files.

c. Use the EXTERNAL DATA tab to import the Excel table in the file EX M-15.xlsx from the location where you store your Data Files. Store the data in a new table, use the first row as column headings, let Access add the primary key, and use the default table name February Budget.

d. Open the February Budget table in Access, and widen the columns as necessary to fully display the field names and field information.

e. Enter your name in the Budget Category column of row 25 in the table, save the database file, compare your screen to **FIGURE M-27**, exit Access, then submit the database file to your instructor.

FIGURE M-27

ID	Budget Category	Budget Item	Month	Budgeted Amount	Click to Add
1	Compensation	Benefits	Feb	$71,357	
2	Compensation	Bonuses	Feb	$65,874	
3	Compensation	Commissions	Feb	$59,847	
4	Compensation	Conferences	Feb	$57,894	
5	Compensation	Promotions	Feb	$51,034	
6	Compensation	Payroll Taxes	Feb	$32,674	
7	Compensation	Salaries	Feb	$34,228	
8	Compensation	Training	Feb	$54,879	
9	Facility	Lease	Feb	$35,789	
10	Facility	Maintenance	Feb	$37,845	
11	Facility	Other	Feb	$46,987	
12	Facility	Rent	Feb	$68,974	
13	Facility	Telephone	Feb	$54,698	
14	Facility	Utilities	Feb	$52,397	
15	Supplies	Food	Feb	$98,754	
16	Supplies	Computer	Feb	$86,478	
17	Supplies	General Office	Feb	$43,258	
18	Supplies	Other	Feb	$39,784	
19	Supplies	Outside Service	Feb	$30,254	
20	Equipment	Computer	Feb	$51,587	
21	Equipment	Other	Feb	$55,987	
22	Equipment	Cash Registers	Feb	$52,314	
23	Equipment	Software	Feb	$59,874	
24	Equipment	Telecommunic	Feb	$45,231	
25	Your Name				

Record: 25 of 25 | No Filter | Search

Independent Challenge 1

You are a real estate agent for the Naples office of West Coast Realty. You have been asked to give a presentation to the regional manager about your sales in the past month. To illustrate your sales data, you will add an Excel chart to one of your slides, showing the different types of property sales and the sales amounts for each type.

a. Start Excel, create a new workbook, then save it as **EX M-June Sales** in the location where you store your Data Files.

b. Enter the property types and the corresponding sales amounts shown below into the EX M-June Sales workbook. Name the sheet with the sales data **Sales**.

Property Type	Sales
Condominium	$2,300,500
Single-family	$8,100,200
Land	$1,210,000

c. Create a 3-D pie chart from the sales data. Format it using Chart Style 9.

d. Copy the chart to the Clipboard.

e. Start PowerPoint, open the Data File EX M-16.pptx from the location where you store your Data Files, then save it as **EX M-Sales Presentation**.

f. Link the Excel chart to Slide 2 using the destination theme. Use the sizing handles to change the size if necessary, and drag the edge of the chart to position it in the center of the slide if necessary.

g. View the slide in Slide Show view, then press [Esc] to end the show.

h. Add a footer to the slides with your name, then save the presentation. Slide 2 should look like **FIGURE M-28**.

i. Change the status of links in the PowerPoint file to update automatically.

j. Close the presentation, exit PowerPoint, then submit the PowerPoint file to your instructor.

k. Save the workbook, then close the workbook, and exit Excel.

FIGURE M-28

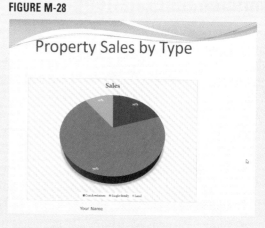

Property Sales by Type

Independent Challenge 2

You are opening a new fitness center, Total Sports, in Oakland, California. The owner of a fitness center in the area is retiring and has agreed to sell you a text file containing his list of supplier information. You need to import this text file into Excel so that you can manipulate the data. Later, you will convert the Excel file to an Access table so that you can give it to your business partner who is building a supplier database.

a. Start Excel, import the file EX M-17.txt from the location where you store your Data Files, then save it as an Excel file named **EX M-Fitness Suppliers**. (*Hint*: This is a tab-delimited text file.)

b. Adjust the column widths as necessary. Rename the worksheet **Suppliers**.

c. Sort the worksheet data in ascending order by Supplier.

d. Add your name to the center section of the worksheet footer, save and close the workbook, then exit Excel.

e. Start Access, create a new blank desktop database in the location where you store your Data Files. Name the new database **EX M-Suppliers**.

f. Use the EXTERNAL DATA tab to import the Excel file EX M-Fitness Suppliers from the location where you store your Data Files. Store the data in a new table, use the column labels as the field names, let Access add the primary key, and accept the default table name.

g. Open the Suppliers table and AutoFit the columns.

h. Enter your name in the Supplier column in row 13, then compare your database file to **FIGURE M-29**.

i. Save and then close the table, and exit Access.

j. Submit the database file to your instructor.

FIGURE M-29

Independent Challenge 3

You are the newly hired manager at NE Financial, a mutual funds firm specializing in consumer products. An employee, Kathy Hogan, has completed a two-year training period as an assistant and you would like to promote her to an associate position with a higher salary. You have examined the salaries of the other associates in the company and will present this information to the vice president of Human Resources, requesting permission to grant Kathy a promotion and an increase in salary.

a. Start Word, open the Word file EX M-18.docx from the location where you store your Data Files, then save it as **EX M-Promotion**.

b. Add your name to the From line of the memo, and change the date to the current date.

c. At the end of the memo, embed the workbook EX M-19.xlsx as an icon from the location where you store your Data Files. Change the caption for the icon to **Salaries**. Double-click the icon to verify that the workbook opens.

d. Close the workbook, return to Word, delete the Salaries icon, and link the workbook EX M-19 to the memo, displaying the data, not an icon.

e. Save the EX M-Promotion memo, and close the file.

f. Open the EX M-19.xlsx workbook in Excel, and change Kathy Hogan's salary to $51,000.

Independent Challenge 3 (continued)

g. Open the EX M-Promotion memo, update the links, and make sure Kathy Hogan's salary is updated.

h. Save and close the memo. Exit Word and submit the memo to your instructor.

i. Close EX M-19 without saving the changes to Karen Holden's information, then exit Excel.

Independent Challenge 4: Explore

You work as a technology manager at a local town office. Each Friday afternoon you are required to submit your hours to your supervisor in a Word document. You prefer to use Excel to track your daily hours so you will link your worksheet to a Word document for your supervisor.

a. Open the file EX M-20.docx from the location where you store your Data Files, then save it as **EX M-Hours**.

b. Change "Your Name" in the FROM line with your own name.

c. Open the file EX M-21.xlsx from the location where you store your Data Files. Copy the range A1:B8 to the Clipboard.

d. Return to the EX M-Hours document, and use the Paste Special in the Paste Options to paste the copied range as a linked worksheet object with the destination style. (*Hint*: Using **FIGURE M-30** as a guide, right-click below the line "My hours for this week are shown below.", then click the Link & Use Destination Styles option in the Paste Options group. It is the 4th option from the left.) Save and close the memo.

FIGURE M-30

e. In the EX M-21 workbook, change Sunday's hours to 5.

f. Return to Word, open the EX M-Hours memo, update links, then verify that the new hours information appears. Save and then close the memo and exit Word. Close the EX M-21 workbook without saving the file and exit Excel.

g. Using Access, create a new blank desktop database named **EX M-Week** in the location where you store your Data Files. Link the Excel data in the EX M-22.xlsx file to the EX M-Week database file using **FIGURE M-31** as a guide. View the data in the linked Hours table by double-clicking the object's name.

h. Close the database file, open the EX M-22.xlsx file, and change the hours for Sunday to 10. Save and close the Excel file.

i. Open the EX M-Week database, verify that the hours figure for Sunday was updated in the linked Hours table, then close the database and exit Access.

j. Submit the EX M-Hours Word document and the EX M-Week database file to your instructor.

FIGURE M-31

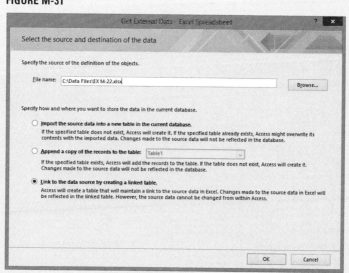

Visual Workshop

Create the worksheet shown in **FIGURE M-32** by opening a blank workbook, importing the Access data in file EX M-23.accdb, sorting the data in Excel, and formatting the price data. The image is from the Microsoft ClipArt. (*Hint*: Click the Online Pictures button in the Illustrations group of the INSERT tab and search for Dog. If you don't see the image shown, select another. Notice the image's transparent background.) Add your name to the center section of the Prices worksheet. Save the workbook as **EX M-Prices**, close the workbook, then exit Excel. Submit the file to your instructor.

FIGURE M-32

	A	B	C
1			
2			
3			
4			
5			
6	Item Code ▼	Product ▼	Price ↓↑
7	B755	Cat Post	$18.99
8	B132	Cat Collar	$22.36
9	A135	Dog Collar	$31.19
10	A884	Dog Toy Set	$37.54
11	A252	Dog Brush Set	$39.94
12	B211	Cat Play Set	$52.99
13	A410	Dog Crate Small	$112.57
14	A408	Dog Crate Medium	$115.22
15	B111	Cat Bed	$116.99
16	A327	Dog Bed Small	$130.57
17	A407	Dog Crate Large	$141.99
18	A321	Dog Bed Large	$155.99
19			

Sharing Excel Files and Incorporating Web Information

CASE ▶ Kate Morgan, the vice president of sales for Quest, wants to share information with corporate office employees and branch managers using the company's intranet and the Web. Kate wants the Quest sales department to use shared workbooks to collaborate on sales worksheet data.

Unit Objectives

After completing this unit, you will be able to:

- Share Excel files
- Set up a shared workbook for multiple users
- Track revisions in a shared workbook
- Apply and modify passwords

- Work with XML schemas
- Import and export XML data
- Share Web links
- Import and export HTML data

Files You Will Need

EX N-1.xlsx	EX N-9.xml
EX N-2.xlsx	EX N-10.htm
EX N-3.xsd	EX N-11.xlsx
EX N-4.xml	EX N-12.htm
EX N-5.xml	EX N-13.xsd
EX N-6.htm	EX N-14.xml
EX N-7.xlsx	EX N-15.htm
EX N-8.xsd	

Share Excel Files

**Learning
Outcomes**
• Determine the
best way to share
Excel workbooks
• Define XML and
HTML terms

Microsoft Excel provides many different ways to share spreadsheets with people in your office, in your organization, or anywhere on the Web. When you share workbooks, you have to consider how you will protect information that you don't want everyone to see and how you can control revisions others will make to your files. Also, some information you want to use might not be in Excel format. For example, there is a great deal of information published on the Web in HTML format, so Excel allows you to import HTML to your worksheets. You can also export your worksheet data in HTML format. However, many companies find the XML format to be more flexible than HTML for storing and exchanging data, so they are increasingly using XML to store and exchange data both internally and externally. Excel allows you to easily import and export XML data. You can also share data using links. **FIGURE N-1** shows methods of importing to and exporting from workbooks. **CASE** *Kate needs to decide the best way to share her Excel workbooks with corporate employees and branch managers.*

DETAILS

To share worksheet information, consider the following issues:

• **Allowing others to use a workbook**

While many of your workbooks are for your own use, you will want to share some of them with other users. When users **share** your workbooks, they can simultaneously open them from a network server, modify them electronically, and return their revisions to you for incorporation with others' changes. You can view each user's name and the date each change was made. To share a workbook, you need to turn on the sharing feature for that workbook. Kate wants to obtain feedback on Quest sales data from the branch managers, so she sets up her workbook so others can use it.

• **Controlling access to workbooks on a server**

When you place a workbook on a network server, you will probably want to control who can open and change it. You can do this using Excel passwords. Kate assigns a password to her workbook, then posts the workbook on the Quest server. She gives the corporate staff and branch managers the password, so only they can open the workbook and revise it.

• **HTML data**

You can paste data from a Web page into a worksheet and then manipulate and format it using Excel. You can also save Excel workbook information in HTML format so you can publish it on an intranet or on the Web. Kate decides to publish the worksheet with the North American sales information in HTML format on the company intranet, as shown in **FIGURE N-2**.

• **Working with XML data**

Importing and storing data in XML format allows you to use it in different situations. For example, a company might store all of its sales data in an XML file and make different parts of the file available to various departments such as marketing and accounting. These departments can extract information that is relevant to their purposes from the file. A subset of the same XML file might be sent to vendors or other business associates who only require certain types of sales data stored in the XML file. Kate decides to import XML files that contain sales information from the Miami and New York branches to get a sales summary for Quest's eastern region, as shown in **FIGURE N-3**.

• **Sharing workbooks in the Cloud**

After you save a workbook on your SkyDrive, you can use Excel sharing tools to email links to your workbook, invite people to access the workbook using the Excel Web App, and even post a workbook link on a social networking site. Kate decides to share the branch sales results with the managers by saving the workbook in the cloud and sending the managers a link to access the information.

FIGURE N-1: Importing and exporting data

© 2014 Cengage Learning

FIGURE N-2: North America sales information displayed in a Web browser

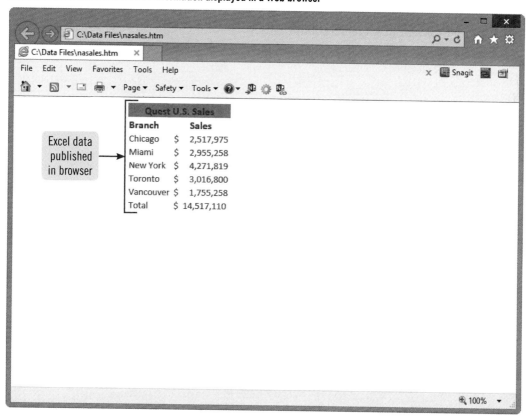

FIGURE N-3: Data imported from XML file

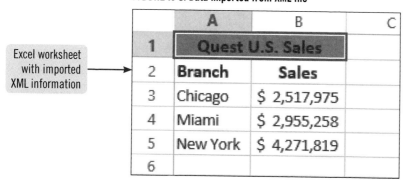

Sharing Excel Files and Incorporating Web Information

Set Up a Shared Workbook for Multiple Users

You can make an Excel file a **shared workbook** so that several users can open and modify it at the same time. This is useful for workbooks that you want others to review on a network server, where the workbook is equally accessible to all network users. When you share a workbook, you can have Excel keep a list of all changes to the workbook, which you can view and print at any time. Note that not all features are available in shared workbooks. **CASE** *Kate wants to get feedback from selected corporate staff and branch managers before presenting the information at the next corporate staff meeting. She asks you to help her put a shared workbook containing customer and sales data on the company's network. You begin by making her Excel file a shared workbook.*

STEPS

1. **Start Excel, open the file EX N-1.xlsx from the location where you store your Data Files, then save it as EX N-Sales Information**

   The workbook with the sales information opens, displaying two sheet tabs. The first contains tour sales data for the Quest U.S. branches; the second is a breakdown of the branch sales by sales associate.

2. **Click the REVIEW tab, then click the Share Workbook button in the Changes group**

   The Share Workbook dialog box opens, as shown in **FIGURE N-4**.

3. **Click the Editing tab, if necessary**

   The dialog box lists the names of people who are currently using the workbook. You are the only user, so your name, or the name of the person entered as the computer user, appears, along with the current date and time.

4. **Click to select the check box next to Allow changes by more than one user at the same time. This also allows workbook merging., then click OK**

   A dialog box appears, asking if you want to save the workbook. This will resave it as a shared workbook.

5. **Click OK**

   Excel saves the file as a shared workbook. The title bar now reads EX N-Sales Information.xlsx [Shared], as shown in **FIGURE N-5**. This version replaces the unshared version.

Adding Office Apps to a worksheet

To help manage information on your worksheets, you can add an Office App to Excel. The app will be available to use for all of your worksheets. For example, there are maps, dictionaries, and calendars that help personalize your worksheets. To insert an app into Excel, click the INSERT tab, click the Apps for Office list arrow in the Apps group, click See All, click FEATURED APPS, then select the app that you want to insert. Clicking More apps opens an Office store Web page with additional app information. If your app isn't open, click the INSERT tab, click the Apps for Office list arrow in the Apps group, click See All, click MY APPS, select the app that you want to insert, then click Insert. If you have used an app recently, open it by clicking the Apps for Office list arrow and clicking the app name in the Recently Used Apps list. Office Apps are not available in shared workbooks.

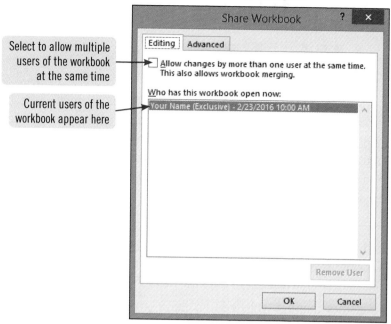

FIGURE N-5: Shared workbook

Merging workbooks

Instead of putting the shared workbook on a server to be shared simultaneously, you might want to distribute copies to your reviewers via e-mail. Once everyone has entered their changes and returned their workbook copies to you, you can merge the changed copies into one master workbook that contains everyone's changes. Each copy you distribute must be designated as shared, and the Change History feature on the Advanced tab of the Share Workbook dialog box must be activated. Occasionally a conflict occurs when two users are trying to edit the same cells in a shared workbook. In this case, the second person to save the file will see a Resolve Conflicts dialog box and need to choose Accept Mine or Accept Other. To merge workbooks, you need to add the Compare and Merge Workbooks command to the Quick Access toolbar by clicking the FILE tab, clicking Options, and clicking Quick Access toolbar. Click All Commands in the Choose commands from list, click Compare and Merge Workbooks, click Add, then click OK. Once you get the changed copies back, open the master copy of the workbook, then click the Compare and Merge Workbooks button on the Quick Access toolbar. The Select Files to Merge Into Current Workbook dialog box opens. Select the workbooks you want to merge (you can use the [Ctrl] key to select more than one workbook), then click OK.

Track Revisions in a Shared Workbook

Learning Outcomes
• Review changes to a shared workbook
• Create a change history worksheet

When you share workbooks, it is often helpful to **track** modifications, or identify who made which changes. You can accept the changes you agree with, and if you disagree with any changes you can reject them. In addition to highlighting changes, Excel keeps track of changes in a **change history**, a list of all changes that you can place on a separate worksheet. **CASE** ▶ *Kate asks you to set up the shared Sales Information workbook so that Excel tracks all future changes. You then open a workbook that is on the server and review its changes and the change history.*

STEPS

1. **Click the Track Changes button in the Changes group, then click Highlight Changes**

   The Highlight Changes dialog box opens, as shown in **FIGURE N-6**, allowing you to turn on change tracking. You can also specify which changes to highlight and where you want to display changes.

2. **Click to select the Track changes while editing check box if necessary, remove check marks from all other boxes except for Highlight changes on screen, click OK, then click OK in the dialog box that informs you that you have yet to make changes**

   Leaving the When, Who, and Where check boxes blank allows you to track all changes.

3. **Click the Sales by Rep sheet tab, change the sales figure for Sanchez in cell C3 to 250,000, press [Enter], then move the mouse pointer over the cell you just changed**

   A border with a small triangle in the upper-left corner appears around the cell you changed, and a ScreenTip appears with the date, the time, and details about the change, as shown in **FIGURE N-7**.

4. **Save and close the workbook**

   Jose Silva has made changes to a version of this workbook. You want to open this workbook and view the details of these changes and accept the ones that appear to be correct.

5. **Open the file EX N-2.xlsx from the location where you store your Data Files, save it as EX N-Sales Information Edits, click the REVIEW tab, click the Track Changes button in the Changes group, click Accept/Reject Changes, click the When check box in the Select Changes to Accept or Reject dialog box to deselect it, then click OK**

   You will accept the first four changes that Jose made to the workbook and reject his last change. You also want to see a list of all changes.

6. **Click Accept four times to approve the first four changes, click Reject to undo Jose's fifth change, click the Track Changes button in the Changes group, click Highlight Changes, click the When check box in the Highlight Changes dialog box to deselect it, click to select the List changes on a new sheet check box, then click OK**

   A new sheet named History opens, as shown in **FIGURE N-8**, with Jose's changes in a filtered list. Because saving the file closes the History sheet, you need to copy the information to a new worksheet.

7. **Copy the range A1:I6 on the History sheet, click the New sheet button ⊕ next to the History sheet tab, on the new sheet click the HOME tab, click the Paste button in the Clipboard group, widen columns E, F, H, and I to display the column information, then rename the new sheet tab Saved History**

8. **Add a footer with your name to the Saved History sheet, save and close the workbook, then submit the workbook to your instructor**

FIGURE N-6: Highlight Changes dialog box

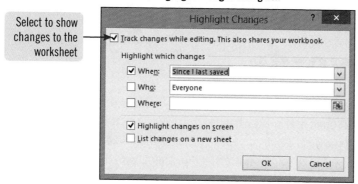

Select to show changes to the worksheet

FIGURE N-7: Tracked change

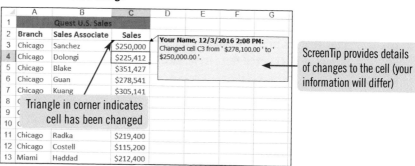

Triangle in corner indicates cell has been changed

ScreenTip provides details of changes to the cell (your information will differ)

FIGURE N-8: History sheet tab with change history

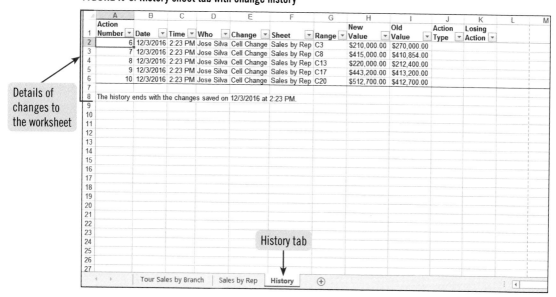

Details of changes to the worksheet

History tab

Apply and Modify Passwords

Learning Outcomes
• Create a password to open a workbook
• Create a password to modify a workbook

When you place a shared workbook on a server, you may want to use a password so that only authorized people will be able to open it or make changes to it. However, it's important to remember that *if you lose your password, you will not be able to open or change the workbook.* Passwords are case sensitive, so you must type them exactly as you want users to type them, with the same spacing and using the same case. For security, it is a good idea to include uppercase and lowercase letters and numbers in a password. **CASE** *Kate wants you to put the workbook with sales information on one of the company's servers. You decide to save a copy of the workbook with two passwords: one that users will need to open it, and another that they will use to make changes to it.*

STEPS

QUICK TIP
You can also use a password to encrypt the contents of a workbook: click the FILE tab, click Protect Workbook in the middle pane, click Encrypt with Password, then enter a password.

1. **Open the file EX N-1.xlsx from the location where you store your Data Files, click the FILE tab, click Save As, navigate to the location where you store your Data Files, click the Tools list arrow in the bottom of the Save As dialog box, then click General Options**

    The General Options dialog box opens, with two password boxes: one to open the workbook, and one to allow changes to the workbook, as shown in **FIGURE N-9**. You can also protect data using a password to encrypt it. **Encrypted data** is encoded in a form that only authorized people with a password can decode.

2. **In the Password to open text box, type QSTmanager01**

    Be sure to type the letters in the correct cases. This is the password that users must type to open the workbook. When you enter passwords, the characters you type are masked with bullets (• • •) for security purposes.

QUICK TIP
You can press [Enter] rather than clicking OK after entering a password. This allows you to keep your hands on the keyboard.

3. **Press [Tab], in the Password to modify text box, type QSTsales01, then click OK**

    This is the password that users must type to make changes to the workbook, also referred to as having **write access**. A dialog box asks you to verify the first password by reentering it.

4. **Enter QSTmanager01 in the first Confirm Password dialog box, click OK, enter QSTsales01 in the second Confirm Password dialog box, then click OK**

5. **Change the filename to EX N-Sales Information PW, if necessary navigate to the location where you store your Data Files, click Save, then close the workbook**

QUICK TIP
To delete a password, reopen the General Options dialog box, highlight the symbols for the existing password, press [Delete], click OK, change the filename, then click Save.

6. **Reopen the workbook EX N-Sales Information PW, enter the password QSTmanager01 when prompted for a password, click OK, then enter QSTsales01 to obtain write access**

    The Password dialog box is shown in **FIGURE N-10**.

7. **Click OK, change the sales figure for the Chicago branch in cell B3 to 3,500,000, then press [Enter]**

    You were able to make this change because you obtained write access privileges using the password "QSTsales01".

8. **Save and close the workbook**

FIGURE N-9: General Options dialog box

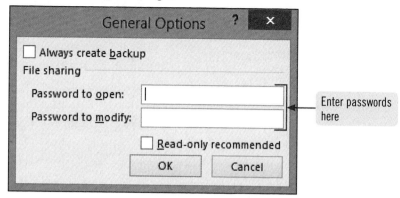

Enter passwords here

FIGURE N-10: Password entry prompt

Password is masked with bullets for security

Creating strong passwords for Excel workbooks

Strong passwords will help to protect your workbooks from security threats. **A strong password** has at least 14 characters that are not commonly used. Although your password needs to be easy to remember, it should be difficult for other people to guess. Avoid using your birthday, your pet's name, or other personal information in your password. Also avoid dictionary words and repeated characters. Instead, mix the types of characters using uppercase and lowercase letters, numbers, and special characters such as @ and %. Microsoft offers an online password checker to test your passwords for security. See **TABLE N-1** for rules and examples for creating strong passwords.

TABLE N-1: Rules for creating strong passwords

rule	example
Include numbers	5qRyz8O6w
Add symbols	IQx!u%z7q9
Increase complexity	4!%5Zq^c6#
Use long passwords	Z7#l%2!q9!6@i9&Wb

© 2014 Cengage Learning

Work with XML Schemas

Learning
Outcomes
- Apply an XML schema to a workbook
- Map XML properties to a workbook

Using Excel you can import and export XML data and analyze it using Excel tools. To import XML data, Excel requires a file called a schema that describes the structure of the XML file. A **schema** contains the rules for the XML file by listing all of the fields in the XML document and their characteristics, such as the type of data they contain. A schema is used to **validate** XML data, making sure the data follows the rules given in the file. Once a schema is attached to a workbook, a schema is called a **map**. When you map an element to a worksheet, you place the element name on the worksheet in a specific location. Mapping XML elements allows you to choose the XML data from a file with which you want to work in the worksheet. **CASE** ▶ *Kate has been given XML files containing sales information from the U.S. branches. She asks you to prepare a workbook to import the sales representatives' XML data. You begin by adding a schema to a worksheet that describes the XML data.*

STEPS

1. **Create a new workbook, save it as** EX N-Sales Reps **in the location where you store your Data Files, click the** DEVELOPER tab, **then click the** Source button **in the XML group**

   The XML Source pane opens. This is where you specify a schema, or map, to import. A schema has the extension .xsd. Kate has provided you with a schema she received from the IT Department describing the XML file structure.

2. **Click** XML Maps **at the bottom of the task pane**

   The XML Maps dialog box opens, listing the XML maps or schemas in the workbook. There are no schemas in the Sales Reps workbook at this time, as shown in **FIGURE N-11**.

3. **Click** Add **in the XML Maps dialog box, navigate to the location where you store your Data Files in the Select XML Source dialog box, click** EX N-3.xsd, **click** Open, **then click** OK

   The schema elements appear in the XML Source task pane. Elements in a schema describe data similarly to the way field names in an Excel table describe the data in their columns. You choose the schema elements from the XML Source pane with which you want to work on your worksheet and map them to the worksheet. Once on the worksheet, the elements are called fields.

4. **Click the** BRANCH element **in the XML Source task pane and drag it to cell** A1 **on the worksheet, then use** FIGURE N-12 **as a guide to drag the** FNAME, LNAME, SALES, **and** ENUMBER fields **to the worksheet**

   The mapped elements appear in bolded format in the XML Source pane. The fields on the worksheet have filter arrows because Excel automatically creates a table on the worksheet as you map the schema elements. You decide to remove the ENUMBER field from the table.

5. **Right-click the** ENUMBER element **in the XML Source task pane, then click** Remove element

   ENUMBER is no longer formatted in bold because it is no longer mapped to the worksheet. This means that when XML data is imported, the ENUMBER field will not be populated with data. However, the field name remains in the table on the worksheet.

6. **Drag the** table resizing arrow **to the left to remove cell** E1 **from the table**

   Because you plan to import XML data from different files, you want to be sure that data from one file will not overwrite data from another file when it is imported into the worksheet. You also want to be sure that Excel validates the imported data against the rules specified in the schema.

7. **Click any cell in the table, click the** DEVELOPER tab, **then click the** Map Properties button **in the XML group**

   The XML Map Properties dialog box opens, as shown in **FIGURE N-13**.

8. **Click the** Validate data against schema for import and export check box **to select it, click the** Append new data to existing XML tables option button **to select it, then click** OK

   You are ready to import XML data into your worksheet.

FIGURE N-11: XML Maps dialog box

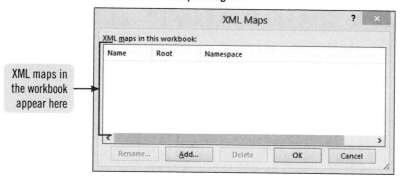

XML maps in the workbook appear here

FIGURE N-12: XML elements mapped to the worksheet

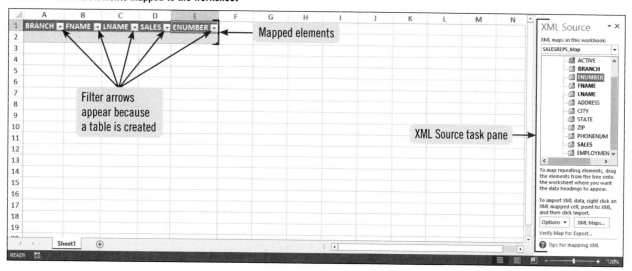

Mapped elements

Filter arrows appear because a table is created

XML Source task pane

FIGURE N-13: XML Map Properties dialog box

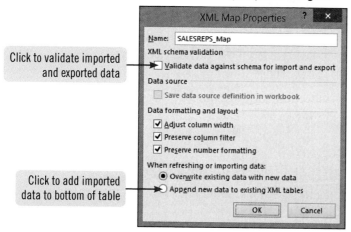

Click to validate imported and exported data

Click to add imported data to bottom of table

Learning more about XML

XML is a universal data format for business and industry information sharing. Using XML, you can store structured information related to services, products, or business transactions and easily share and exchange the information with others. XML provides a way to express structure in data. Structured data is tagged, or marked up, to indicate its content. For example, an XML data marker (tag) that contains an item's cost might be named COST. The ability of Excel to work with XML data lets you access the large amount of information stored in the XML format. For example, organizations have developed many XML applications with a specific focus, such as MathML (Mathematical Markup Language) and RETML (Real Estate Transaction Markup Language).

Import and Export XML Data

Learning Outcomes
• Import XML data into a workbook
• Export Excel data into an XML file

After the mapping is complete, you can import any XML file with a structure that conforms to the workbook schema. The mapped elements on the worksheet will fill with (or be **populated** with) data from the XML file. If an element is not mapped on the worksheet, then its data will not be imported. Once you import the XML data, you can analyze it using Excel tools. You can also export data from an Excel workbook to an XML file. **CASE** *Kate asks you to combine the sales data for the Miami and New York branches that are contained in XML files. She would like you to add a total for the combined branches and export the data from Excel to an XML file.*

STEPS

1. **Click cell A1, click the DEVELOPER tab if necessary, then click the Import button in the XML group**

   The Import XML dialog box opens.

2. **Navigate to the location where you store your Data Files if necessary, click EX N-4.xml, then click Import**

   The worksheet is populated with data from the XML file that contains the Miami sales rep information. Excel only imports data for the mapped elements. You decide to add the sales rep data for the New York branch to the worksheet.

3. **Click the Import button in the XML group, navigate to the location where you store your Data Files in the Import XML dialog box if necessary, click EX N-5.xml, then click Import**

   The New York branch sales rep data is added to the worksheet, below the Miami branch data. You decide to total the sales figures for all sales reps.

4. **Click the TABLE TOOLS DESIGN tab, then click the Total Row check box to select it**

   The total sales amount of 4974777 appears in cell D25. You decide to format the table.

5. **Select the range D2:D25, click the HOME tab, click the Accounting Number Format button $ in the Number group, click the Decrease Decimal button ⬚ in the Number group twice, click the TABLE TOOLS DESIGN tab, click the More button ⬚ in the Table Styles group, select Table Style Light 14, then click cell A1**

   Compare your completed table to **FIGURE N-14**.

6. **Enter your name in the center section of the worksheet footer, then preview the table**

   You will export the combined sales rep data as an XML file. Because not all of the elements in the schema were mapped to fields in your Excel table, you do not want the data exported from the table to be validated against the schema.

7. **Click any cell in the table, click the DEVELOPER tab, click the Map Properties button in the XML group, then click the Validate data against schema for import and export check box to deselect it**

   The Map Properties dialog box with the validation turned off is shown in **FIGURE N-15**. You are ready to export the XML data.

8. **Click OK, click the Export button in the XML group, navigate to the location where you store your Data Files in the Export XML dialog box, enter the name EX N-East Reps in the File name text box, click Export, then save and close the workbook**

   The sales data is saved in your Data File location in XML format, in the file called EX N-East Reps.xml.

FIGURE N-14: Completed table with combined sales rep data

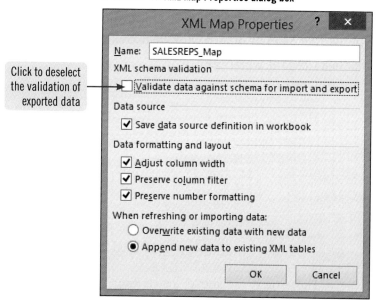

	A	B	C	D	E
1	BRANCH	FNAME	LNAME	SALES	
2	Miami	Cate	Monroe	$ 193,998	
3	Miami	Don	Greenway	$ 125,670	
4	Miami	Lee	Conolly	$ 313,200	
5	Miami	Bob	Neeley	$ 209,400	
6	Miami	Kathy	Deveney	$ 302,700	
7	Miami	Meg	Lyons	$ 302,345	
8	Miami	Elaine	Hansen	$ 181,345	
9	Miami	Deb	Mulligan	$ 159,300	
10	New York	Peg	Lions	$ 203,200	
11	New York	Brad	Benson	$ 100,400	
12	New York	Molly	Donnolly	$ 219,200	
13	New York	Paul	Neely	$ 702,200	
14	New York	Julio	Sallby	$ 125,300	
15	New York	Ann	Lincoln	$ 304,200	
16	New York	Jack	Bloomberg	$ 210,400	
17	New York	Peg	Harrington	$ 215,300	
18	New York	William	Galvin	$ 113,452	
19	New York	Kelvin	McCarthy	$ 209,300	
20	New York	Paul	Reilly	$ 102,300	
21	New York	Rod	Stedman	$ 123,567	
22	New York	Al	Tessier	$ 218,200	
23	New York	Kathy	Vodel	$ 210,400	
24	New York	Ken	Perkins	$ 129,400	
25	**Total**			**$ 4,974,777**	

Imported data is formatted

Total sales

Sheet1

FIGURE N-15: XML Map Properties dialog box

XML Map Properties ? ✕

Name: SALESREPS_Map

XML schema validation

☐ Validate data against schema for import and export

Click to deselect the validation of exported data

Data source

☑ Save data source definition in workbook

Data formatting and layout

☑ Adjust column width
☑ Preserve column filter
☑ Preserve number formatting

When refreshing or importing data:

◯ Overwrite existing data with new data
● Append new data to existing XML tables

OK   Cancel

Importing XML data without a schema

You can import XML data without a schema, and Excel will create one for you. In this situation all of the XML elements are mapped to the Excel worksheet, and the data in all of the fields is populated using the XML file. When a schema is not used, you are unable to validate the data that is imported. You also need to delete all of the fields in the table that you will not use in the worksheet, which can be time consuming.

Share Web Links

Learning Outcomes
• Save a workbook on a SkyDrive
• Copy a workbook web link

Often you'll want to share your Excel workbooks with co-workers. You can do this by sending them a link to your workbook. When you send a link to your workbook that is saved on your Sky Drive, your co-workers can use the Excel Web App to work with your file in the cloud. When you create the link, you can allow users to view the workbook, or to view and edit it. **CASE** ▶ *Kate is working on the sales results with the branch managers. She asks you to save the sales information in the cloud and give her a link that she can share with the managers.*

STEPS

1. **Open the file EX N-1.xlsx from the location where you store your Data Files, then save it as EX N-Tour Sales**

   You need to save the file to your Sky Drive account before you can send a link to it.

2. **Click the FILE tab, click Share, then click Invite People if necessary**

   The Share window opens, showing the steps to invite people to use your workbook as shown in **FIGURE N-16**.

3. **Click Save To Cloud, click Save As if necessary, navigate to your Sky Drive location, then click Save in the Save As dialog box**

4. **Click Get a Sharing Link**

   You will see more options in the Share window as shown in **FIGURE N-17**. You can choose to get a **View Link** which allows people to view your Excel file, or you can select an **Edit Link** which allows people to edit the file. You decide to create a View Link.

5. **Click the Create Link button next to the View Link, then copy the View Link URL**

   You decide to test the web link address by pasting it in your browser.

6. **Open your browser, paste the View Link URL in the address text box, then press [Enter]**

   The workbook opens in the Excel WebApp as shown in **FIGURE N-18**.

7. **Close your browser, return to the Excel EX N-Tour Sales.xlsx file, then paste the copied link in cell A7 of the Tour Sales by Branch worksheet**

8. **Save your work, then close the workbook**

Creating your own Web queries

The easiest way to retrieve data from a particular Web page on a regular basis is to create a customized Web query. Click the DATA tab, click the From Web button in the Get External Data group (or click the Get External Data button and click the From Web button). In the Address text box in the New Web Query dialog box, type the address of the Web page from which you want to retrieve data, then click Go. Click the yellow arrows next to the information you want to bring into a worksheet or click the upper-left arrow to import the entire page, verify that the information that you want to import has a green checkmark next to it, then click Import. The Import Data dialog box opens and allows you to specify where you want the imported data to appear in the worksheet or workbook. You can save a query for future use by clicking the Save Query button 🖫 in the New Web Query dialog box before you click Import. The query is saved as a file with an .iqy file extension.

FIGURE N-16: Share window with invite options

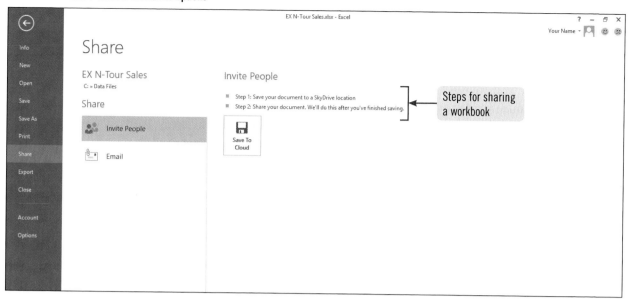

FIGURE N-17: Share window with link options

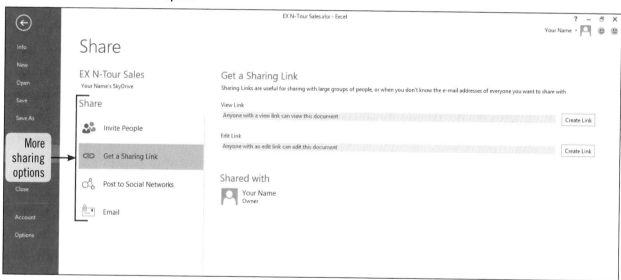

FIGURE N-18: Workbook in the Excel Web App

Learning Outcomes
• Import HTML data into a workbook
• Export Excel data into an HTML file

Import and Export HTML Data

Although you can open HTML files directly in Excel, most often the information that you want to include in a worksheet is published on the Web and you don't have the HTML file. In this situation you can import the HTML data by copying the data on the Web page and pasting it into an Excel worksheet. This allows you to bring in only the information that you need from the Web page to your worksheet. Once the HTML data is in your worksheet, you can analyze the imported information using Excel features. You can also export worksheet data as an HTML file that you can then share on a Web site. **CASE** *The Toronto and Vancouver branch managers have published the Canada branch sales information on the company intranet. Kate asks you to import the published sales data into an Excel worksheet so she can summarize it using Excel tools. She also wants you to export the summarized data to an HTML file she can post on the company intranet.*

STEPS

QUICK TIP
You need to use Internet Explorer as your browser for this lesson.

1. **In File Explorer, navigate to the location where you store your Data Files, double-click the file EX N-6.htm to open it in your browser, then copy the two table rows on the Web page containing the Toronto and Vancouver sales information**
   You are ready to paste the information from the Web page into an Excel worksheet.

2. **Open the file EX N-1.xlsx from the location where you store your Data Files, then save it as EX N-North America Sales**

TROUBLE
Pasting the data doesn't match all of the destination formats. You will fix the formatting of the pasted data in Step 5.

3. **Right-click cell A6 on the Tour Sales by Branch sheet, click the Match Destination Formatting button 📋 in the Paste Options list**
   The Canada sales information is added to the U.S. sales data.

4. **Click cell A8, type Total, press [Tab], click the AutoSum button in the Editing group, then press [Enter]**
   You want the font to be uniform throughout the worksheet.

5. **Select the range A5:B5, click the Format Painter button in the Clipboard group, select the range A6:B8, then click cell A1**
   Compare your worksheet to **FIGURE N-19**. Kate is finished with the analysis and formatting of the North America branches. She wants the combined worksheet information published in a Web page.

6. **Click the FILE tab, click Save As, then browse to the location where you store your Data Files**
   The Save As dialog box lets you specify what workbook parts you want to publish.

7. **Click the Save as type list arrow, click Web Page (*.htm;*.html), edit the filename to read nasales.htm, click the Selection: Sheet option button, click Publish, then click Publish again**
   The HTML file, containing only the tour Sales by Branch worksheet, is saved in your Data Files location. To avoid problems when publishing pages to a Web server, use lowercase characters, omit special characters and spaces, and limit your filename to eight characters plus a three-character extension.

8. **In File Explorer, navigate to the location where you store your Data Files, then double-click the file nasales.htm**
   The HTML version of your worksheet opens in your default browser, similar to **FIGURE N-20**.

9. **Close your browser window, click the Excel window to activate it if necessary, enter your name in the center footer section of the Tour Sales by Branch worksheet, save the workbook, preview the worksheet, close the workbook, exit Excel, then submit the workbook and the Web page file to your instructor**

FIGURE N-19: Worksheet with North America sales data

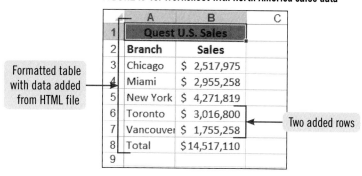

Formatted table with data added from HTML file

Two added rows

FIGURE N-20: North America Sales as Web page

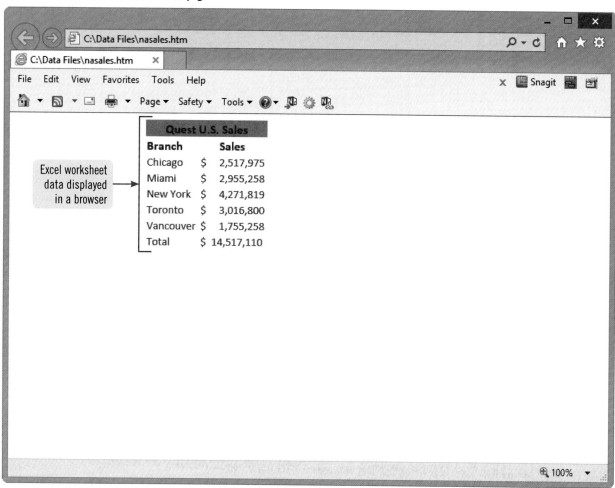

Excel worksheet data displayed in a browser

Adding Web hyperlinks to a worksheet

In Excel worksheets, you can create hyperlinks to information on the Web. Every Web page is identified by a unique Web address called a Uniform Resource Locator (URL). To create a hyperlink to a Web page, click the cell for which you want to create a hyperlink, click the INSERT tab, click the Hyperlink button in the Links group, under Link to: make sure Existing File or Web Page is selected, specify the target for the hyperlink (the URL) in the Address text box, then click OK. If there is text in the cell, the text format changes to become a blue underlined hyperlink or the color the current workbook theme uses for hyperlinks. If there is no text in the cell, the Web site's URL appears in the cell.

Practice

Concepts Review

FIGURE N-21

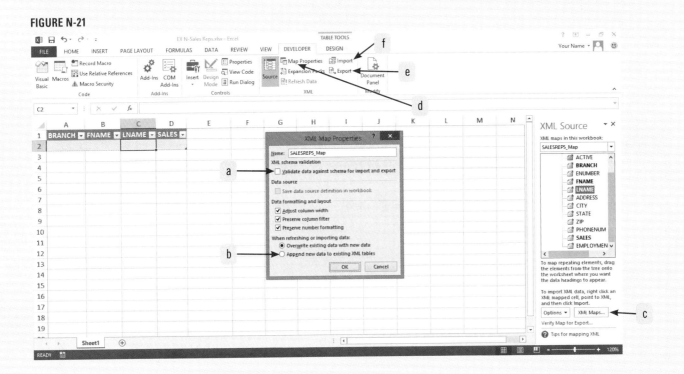

1. **Which element do you click to save workbook data to an XML file?**
2. **Which element do you click to add imported XML data below existing data in a table?**
3. **Which element do you click to check imported XML data using the schema rules?**
4. **Which element do you click to change the way XML data is imported and exported?**
5. **Which element do you click to add a schema to an Excel workbook?**
6. **Which element do you click to bring in XML data to a workbook table?**

Match each item with the statement that best describes it.

7. **Password**
8. **Change history**
9. **Shared workbook**
10. **xsd**
11. **iqy**

a. The file extension for an XML schema
b. A record of edits others have made to a worksheet
c. Used to protect a workbook from unauthorized use
d. The file extension for a Web query
e. A file used by many people on a network

Select the best answer from the list of choices.

12. Which of the following is the best example of a strong password for a workbook?

a. myfile

b. MollY

c. MYFILE

d. my%File95gz

13. Which of the following sharing links allows people to make changes to your Excel data?

a. Change Link

b. Edit Link

c. View Link

d. Import Link

14. The process of selecting XML elements to include on a worksheet is called:

a. Sharing.

b. Selecting.

c. Mapping.

d. Loading.

15. A file that describes the structure of XML data is called a:

a. Query.

b. Schema.

c. Layout.

d. Detail File.

Skills Review

1. Set up a shared workbook for multiple users.

a. Start Excel, open the file EX N-7.xlsx from the location where you store your Data Files, then save it as **EX N-Sales**.

b. Use the Share Workbook command on the REVIEW tab to set up the workbook so that more than one person can use it at one time.

c. Save the workbook when asked to save it.

d. Verify the workbook is marked as Shared in the title bar.

e. Review the regional sales data for the first two quarters of the year.

2. Track revisions in a shared workbook.

a. Change the Seattle sales to **$50,000** for the first quarter and **$45,000** for the second quarter.

b. Save the file.

c. Display the History sheet by opening the Highlight Changes dialog box, deselecting the When check box, then selecting the option for List changes on a new sheet.

d. Compare your History sheet to FIGURE N-22.

e. Copy the range A1:I3 in the History sheet, add a new worksheet and paste the range in the new worksheet. Widen the columns to

FIGURE N-22

	A	B	C	D	E	F	G	H	I	J	K	L
1	Action Number	Date	Time	Who	Change	Sheet	Range	New Value	Old Value	Action Type	Losing Action	
2	1	12/3/2016	2:38 PM	Your Name	Cell Change	Sales	C2	$50,000.00	$32,988.00			
3	2	12/3/2016	2:38 PM	Your Name	Cell Change	Sales	D2	$45,000.00	$28,364.00			
4												
5	The history ends with the changes saved on 12/3/2016 at 2:38 PM.											
6												

display all of the information, then rename the new worksheet to **History Sheet**.

f. Enter your name in the History Sheet footer, then preview the History Sheet.

g. Save the workbook, close it, then submit the workbook to your instructor.

3. Apply and modify passwords.

a. Open the file EX N-7.xlsx from the location where you store your Data Files, open the Save As dialog box, then open the General Options dialog box.

b. Set the password to open the workbook as **Sales11** and the password to modify it as **FirstHalf11**.

c. Save the password-protected file as **EX N-Sales PW** in the location where you store your Data Files.

d. Close the workbook.

e. Use the assigned passwords to reopen the workbook and verify that you can change it by adding your name in the center section of the Sales sheet footer, save the workbook, preview the Sales worksheet, close the workbook, then submit the workbook to your instructor.

Skills Review (continued)

4. Work with XML schemas.

   a. Open a new blank workbook, then save it as **EX N-Contact Information** in the location where you store your Data Files.

   b. Open the XML Source pane, and add the XML schema EX N-8.xsd to the workbook.

   c. Map the FNAME element to cell A1 on the worksheet, LNAME to cell B1, PHONENUM to cell C1, and EMPLOYMENT_DATE to cell D1.

   d. Remove the EMPLOYMENT_DATE element from the map, and delete the field from the table.

   e. Use the XML Map Properties dialog box to make sure imported XML data is validated using the schema.

5. Import and export XML data.

   a. Import the XML file EX N-9.xml into the workbook.

   b. Sort the worksheet list in ascending order by LNAME.

   c. Add the Table Style Light 13 to the table, and compare your screen to **FIGURE N-23**.

   d. Enter your name in the center section of the worksheet footer, save the workbook, then preview the worksheet.

   e. Use the XML Map Properties dialog box to turn off the validation for imported and exported worksheet data, export the worksheet data to an XML file named **EX N-Contact**, save and close the workbook.

FIGURE N-23

	A	B	C
1	FNAME	LNAME	PHONENUM
2	Kathy	Conolly	503-302-1163
3	Jack	Green	503-367-4156
4	Elaine	Jackson	503-392-8163
5	Linda	MacNeal	503-932-9966
6	Kelly	Maguire	503-272-9456
7	Kris	Malone	503-722-9163
8	Bruce	Nangle	503-322-3163
9	Meg	Shelly	503-322-3163
10			

6. Share Web Links.

   a. Open the file EX N-7.xlsx from the location where you store your Data Files, then save it as **EX N-Region Sales**.

   b. Save the EX-Region Sales file to your SkyDrive.

   c. Enter **View Link** in cell A24. Get a sharing link that allows the recipient to view the workbook. Paste the link in cell B24.

   d. Enter **Edit Link** in cell A25. Get a sharing link that allows the recipient to edit the workbook. Paste the link in cell B25.

   e. Compare your screen to **FIGURE N-24**. (Your links will be different.)

   f. Change the page orientation to landscape, enter your name in the center section of the worksheet header, preview the worksheet, then save the workbook in the location where you store your Data Files.

FIGURE N-24

	A	B	C	D	E	F	G	H
16	South	Tampa	$17,662	$21,854				
17	South	Dallas	$16,557	$19,633				
18	South	San Diego	$19,551	$16,855				
19	South	Santa Fe	$25,448	$42,887				
20	South	Charlotte	$21,662	$21,996				
21	South	Biloxi	$20,335	$16,833				
22	South	Houston	$25,700	$17,627				
23								
24	View Link	https://skydrive.live.com/redir?page=view&resid=123456789!123&authkey=!QWTYUo75P						
25	Edit Link	https://skydrive.live.com/redir?page=view&resid=123456789!123&authkey=!ABZS147B87						
26								

   g. Close the workbook, and submit the workbook to your instructor.

7. Import and export HTML data.

   a. Open the file EX N-7.xlsx from the location where you store your Data Files, then save it as **EX N-Sales2**.

   b. Open the file EX N-10.htm in your browser from the location where you store your Data Files. Copy the data in the four rows of the Web page (not the column headings), and paste it below the data in the Sales sheet of the EX N-Sales2 workbook.

   c. On the Sales sheet, enter **Total** in cell A27, and use **AutoSum** in cells C27 and D27 to total the values in columns C and D.

Skills Review (continued)

d. Adjust the formatting for the new rows to match the other rows on the Sales sheet, add your name to the center section of the worksheet footer, save the workbook, then preview the Sales sheet.

e. Save the data on the Sales sheet as an HTML file with the name **sales2.htm**.

f. Close the workbook, exit Excel, open the sales2.htm file in your browser, compare your screen to **FIGURE N-25**, close your browser, then submit the sales2.htm file to your instructor.

FIGURE N-25

Region	Store	Quarter 1	Quarter 2
North	Seattle	$32,988	$28,364
North	Portland	$29,302	$25,100
North	Minneapolis	$31,805	$21,601
North	Madison	$32,669	$22,471
North	Billings	$30,410	$25,445
North	Columbus	$32,577	$21,877
North	Boston	$42,358	$26,647
North	Hartford	$31,633	$22,541
North	Concord	$30,000	$32,145
North	New York	$18,521	$32,451
North	Newark	$16,201	$29,365
North	San Francisco	$19,105	$20,100
South	Miami	$17,511	$23,654
South	New Orleans	$14,652	$29,654
South	Tampa	$17,662	$21,854
South	Dallas	$16,557	$19,633
South	San Diego	$19,551	$16,855
South	Santa Fe	$25,448	$42,887
South	Charlotte	$21,662	$21,996
South	Biloxi	$20,335	$16,833
South	Houston	$25,700	$17,627
West	Los Angeles	$34,675	$46,789
West	Las Vegas	$37,175	$47,119
West	Denver	$34,175	$57,841
West	Salt Lake	$31,024	$45,127
Total		$663,696	$715,976

Independent Challenge 1

You are the registrar at West End College. One of your responsibilities is to work with the school's Academic Dean on the course schedule. You use shared Excel workbooks to help you with this scheduling by sharing the workbook with your first draft schedule with the Dean. You have received the shared workbook from the Dean with her changes that include location edits and you will review the workbooks and accept the changes which have your approval.

a. Start Excel, open the file EX N-11.xlsx from the location where you store your Data Files, then save it as **EX N-Fall Quarter**.

b. Use the Accept or Reject dialog box to accept the first three changes and reject the fourth change to the workbook.

c. Use the Highlight Changes dialog box to highlight the change on the screen. Review the ScreenTip details.

d. Use the Highlight Changes dialog box to create a History worksheet detailing the changes to the workbook.

e. Copy the information about the change in the range A1:I5, and paste it in a new worksheet.

f. Widen the columns as necessary, and rename the new sheet **History Sheet**. Compare your History Sheet to **FIGURE N-26**.

g. Add your name to the center section of the History sheet footer, then preview the History worksheet.

h. Remove the Shared status of the workbook. (*Hint*: In the Share Workbook dialog box, deselect the "Allow changes by more than one user at the same time." checkbox.)

FIGURE N-26

	A	B	C	D	E	F	G	H	I
1	Action Number	Date	Time	Who	Change	Sheet	Range	New Value	Old Value
2	1	12/3/2016	3:39 PM	Maria Gonzalez	Cell Change	Fall Semester	F2	N102	N122
3	2	12/3/2016	3:39 PM	Maria Gonzalez	Cell Change	Fall Semester	F5	S210	S214
4	3	12/3/2016	3:39 PM	Maria Gonzalez	Cell Change	Fall Semester	F8	N100	N101
5	4	12/3/2016	3:39 PM	Maria Gonzalez	Cell Change	Fall Semester	F13	S217	S215
6									

i. Add a password of **Fall%2016** to open the workbook and **Courses%2016** to modify it.

j. Save and close the workbook. Submit the EX N-Fall Quarter.xlsx workbook to your instructor.

Independent Challenge 2

The North Shore Health Club is a fitness center with five fitness facilities. As the general manager you are responsible for setting and publishing the membership rate information. You decide to run a special promotion offering a 10 percent discount off the current membership prices. You will also add two new membership categories to help attract younger members. The membership rate information is published on the company Web site. You will copy the rate information from the Web page and work with it in Excel to calculate the special discounted rates. You will save the new rate information as an HTML file so it can be published on the Web.

Independent Challenge 2 (continued)

a. Open the file EX N-12.htm from the location where you store your Data Files to display it in your browser.

b. Start Excel, create a new workbook, then save it as **EX N-Rates** in the location where you store your Data Files.

c. Return to the browser, copy the five rows of data, including the column headings from the table in the EX N-12 file, and paste them in the EX N-Rates workbook. Adjust the column widths as necessary. Close the EX N-12.htm file.

d. Add the new membership data from the table below in rows 6 and 7 of the worksheet.

Membership	Price
Teen	250
Youth	175

e. Remove the borders around the cells in columns A and B. (*Hint*: Select the range A1:B7, click the Border list arrow, then click No Border.)

f. Enter **Special** in cell C1, and calculate each special rate in column C by discounting the prices in column B by 10%. (*Hint*: Multiply each price by .90.)

g. Format the price information in columns B and C with the Accounting format using the $ symbol with two decimal places. Widen the columns as necessary.

h. Add the passwords **Members11** to open the EX N-Rates workbook and **Gym11** to modify it. Save the workbook, replacing the existing file, close the workbook, then reopen it by entering the passwords.

i. Verify that you can modify the workbook by formatting the worksheet using the Office Theme font color Green, Accent 6, Darker 50%.

j. Format the label in cell C1 as bold. Compare your worksheet data to **FIGURE N-27**.

k. Add your name to the center footer section of the worksheet, save the workbook, then preview the worksheet.

l. Save the worksheet data in HTML format using the name **prices.htm**. Close the workbook and exit Excel.

m. Open the prices.htm page in your browser and print the page.

n. Close your browser. Submit the prices.htm and the EX N-Rates file to your instructor.

FIGURE N-27

	A	B	C
1	Membership	Price	Special
2	Family	$875.00	$787.50
3	Adult	$675.00	$607.50
4	Senior	$275.00	$247.50
5	College	$280.00	$252.00
6	Teen	$250.00	$225.00
7	Youth	$175.00	$157.50
8			

Independent Challenge 3

You are the director of development at a local hospital. You are preparing the phone lists for your annual fundraising event. The donor information for the organization is in an XML file, which you will bring into Excel to organize. You will use an XML schema to map only the donors' names and phone numbers to the worksheet. This will allow you to import the donor data and limit the information that is distributed to the phone-a-thon volunteers. You will also import information about the donors from another XML file. You will export your worksheet data as XML for future use.

a. Start Excel, create a new workbook, then save it as **EX N-Donors** in the location where you store your Data Files.

b. Add the map EX N-13.xsd from the location where you store your Data Files to the workbook.

c. Map the FNAME element to cell A1, LNAME to cell B1, and PHONENUM to cell C1. Make sure that imported XML data will be validated using the schema rules.

d. Import the XML data in file EX N-14.xml from the location where you store your Data Files. Add the Table Style Light 20 to the table. Change the field name in cell A1 to **FIRST NAME**, change the field name in cell B1 to **LAST NAME**, and change the field name in cell C1 to **PHONE NUMBER**. Widen the columns as necessary to accommodate the full field names.

Independent Challenge 3 (continued)

e. Sort the table in ascending order by LAST NAME. Compare your sorted table to **FIGURE N-28**.

f. Open the XML Map Properties dialog box to verify the Overwrite existing data with new data option button is selected. Map the ACTIVE element to cell D1. Import the XML data in file EX N-14.xml again.

g. Map the CONTRIB_DATE element to cell E1. Import the XML data in file EX N-14.xml a third time. Change the field name in cell E1 to **LAST DONATION**, and widen the column to accommodate the full field name.

h. Filter the table to show only active donors. Compare your filtered table to **FIGURE N-29**.

i. Export the worksheet data to an XML file named **EX N-Phone List**.

j. Enter your name in the center section of the worksheet footer, preview the worksheet in landscape orientation, then save the workbook.

k. Close the workbook, exit Excel, then submit the workbook and the XML file to your instructor.

FIGURE N-28

	A	B	C
1	FIRST NAME	LAST NAME	PHONE NUMBER
2	Peg	Allen	312-765-8756
3	Ellen	Atkins	773-167-4156
4	Kathy	Breen	773-220-9456
5	Sally	Colby	312-322-3163
6	Betty	Daly	312-322-3163
7	Ken	Gonzales	773-379-0092
8	Julio	Herandez	312-765-8756
9	Ann	Land	312-299-4298
10	Lynn	Neal	312-932-9966
11	Mark	Zoll	312-765-8756
12			

FIGURE N-29

	A	B	C	D	E
1	FIRST NAME	LAST NAME	PHONE NUMBER	ACTIVE	LAST DONATION
2	Kathy	Breen	773-220-9456	TRUE	Jan-15
4	Lynn	Neal	312-932-9966	TRUE	Jan-14
7	Ken	Gonzales	773-379-0092	TRUE	Nov-14
9	Mark	Zoll	312-765-8756	TRUE	Dec-13
10	Peg	Allen	312-765-8756	TRUE	Nov-12
11	Julio	Herandez	312-765-8756	TRUE	Dec-13
12					

Independent Challenge 4: Explore

You will explore the Apps for Office available to use in worksheets and share your results in the Cloud by inviting people to view your workbook saved on your SkyDrive.

a. Start Excel, create a new blank workbook, then save it as **EX N-WebApp** in the location where you store your Data Files.

b. View the featured apps for Office. (*Hint*: Click the INSERT tab, click the Apps for Office button in the Apps group, then click FEATURED APPS at the top of the window if necessary.)

c. Insert a free app from the Featured Apps collection.

d. Explore the app to develop an understanding of its purpose.

e. If you have data in rows one, two, or three from your app, insert three rows above the data. In cell A1 of your worksheet, enter App Name. Enter the name of your app in cell B1.

f. In rows 2 and 3 of the worksheet enter information about the purpose of the app.

g. Enter your name in the center section of the worksheet footer.

h. Save your EX N-WebApp workbook on your SkyDrive.

i. Share your EX N-WebApp workbook by inviting a classmate to view it. If you don't have a classmate's email address you can use your own email address. (*Hint*: Click the FILE tab, click Share, click Invite People, enter the email address, click the Can edit list arrow, select Can view, then click Share.)

j. Get sharing links to view the workbook and to edit the workbook.

k. Create a new worksheet, name the worksheet Links, then copy the sharing links and paste them into the new worksheet with labels identifying each one.

l. Save the workbook to the location where you store your Data Files replacing the previously saved workbook.

m. Close the workbook, exit Excel, then submit the workbook to your instructor.

Excel 2013

Visual Workshop

Start Excel, create a new workbook, then save it as **EX N-Shore.xlsx** in the location where you store your Data Files. Open the file EX N-15.htm in your browser from the location where you store your Data Files. Create the worksheet shown in **FIGURE N-30** by pasting the information from the Web page into your EX N-Shore.xlsx file, formatting it, adding the fourth quarter information, adding the totals, and replacing Your Name with your name. (*Hint*: The colors are in the Office theme, the font size of the first three rows is 14 and the remaining font size is 12.) Add your name to the footer of Sheet1, preview the worksheet, then save the workbook. Submit the EX N-Shore.xlsx workbook to your instructor.

FIGURE N-30

	A	B	C	D	E	F
1	Shore Catering					
2	Sales Report					
3	Your Name					
4	Category	1st Quarter	2nd Quarter	3rd Quarter	4th Quarter	Totals
5	Corporate	$ 13,267	$ 11,345	$ 12,212	$ 11,542	$ 48,366
6	Weddings	$ 9,340	$ 11,876	$ 14,876	$ 15,247	$ 51,339
7	Home Celebrations	$ 7,023	$ 9,154	$ 9,423	$ 13,274	$ 38,874
8	Functions	$ 9,432	$ 9,331	$ 11,213	$ 10,284	$ 40,260
9	Delivery	$ 6,432	$ 5,331	$ 6,713	$ 21,874	$ 40,350
10	Totals	$ 45,494	$ 47,037	$ 54,437	$ 72,221	$ 219,189
11						

Customizing Excel and Advanced Worksheet Management

CASE ▶ Quest's vice president of sales, Kate Morgan, asks you to review sales worksheet formulas, customize Excel workbooks, and create a sales template. You will use Excel tools and options to help Kate and the sales staff work quickly and efficiently in a customized environment.

Unit Objectives

After completing this unit, you will be able to:

- Audit a worksheet
- Control worksheet calculations
- Group worksheet data
- Work with cell comments

- Create custom AutoFill lists
- Create and apply a template
- Customize Excel workbooks
- Customize the Excel screen

Files You Will Need

EX O-1.xlsx EX O-5.xlsx
EX O-2.xlsx EX O-6.xlsx
EX O-3.xlsx EX O-7.xlsx
EX O-4.xlsx

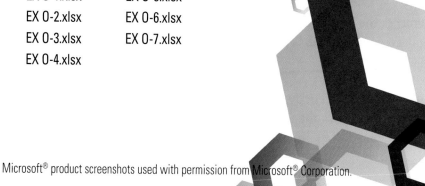

©Katerina Havelkova/Shutterstock

Audit a Worksheet

Learning Outcomes
- Locate formula errors
- Correct formula errors

Because errors can occur at any stage of worksheet development, it is important to include auditing as part of your workbook-building process. The Excel **auditing** feature helps you track errors and check worksheet logic to make sure your worksheet is error free and the data is arranged sensibly. The Formula Auditing group on the FORMULAS tab contains several error-checking tools to help you audit a worksheet. **CASE** *Kate asks you to help identify errors in the worksheet that tracks sales for the two Canadian branches to verify the accuracy of year-end totals and percentages.*

STEPS

TROUBLE
You will fix the formula errors that appear in cells O5 and O6.

1. **Start Excel, open the file EX O-1.xlsx from the location where you store your Data Files, then save it as EX O-Canada Sales**

2. **Click the FORMULAS tab, then click the Error Checking button in the Formula Auditing group**

   The Error Checking dialog box opens and alerts you to a Divide by Zero Error in cell O5, as shown in **FIGURE O-1**. The formula reads =N5/N8, indicating that the value in cell N5 will be divided by the value in cell N8. In Excel formulas, blank cells have a value of zero. This error means the value in cell N5 cannot be divided by the value in cell N8 (zero) because division by zero is not mathematically possible. To correct the error, you must edit the formula so that it references cell N7, the total of sales, not cell N8.

3. **Click Edit in Formula Bar in the Error Checking dialog box, edit the formula in the formula bar to read =N5/N7, click the Enter button ✓, then click Resume in the Error Checking dialog box**

   The edited formula produces the correct result, .5547, in cell O5. The Error Checking dialog box indicates another error in cell N6, the total Vancouver sales. The formula reads =SUM(B6:L6) and should be =SUM(B6:M6). The top button in the Error Checking dialog box changes to "Copy Formula from Above". Since this formula in the cell N5 is correct, you will copy it.

QUICK TIP
You can use the Trace Error tool to high-light the cells used to calculate a formula by clicking the FORMULAS tab on the Ribbon, clicking the Error Checking list arrow in the Formula Auditing group, then clicking Trace Error to view the cells used in the formula calculations.

4. **Click Copy Formula from Above**

   The Vancouver total changes to $318,130 in cell N6. The Error Checking dialog box finds another division-by-zero error in cell O6. You decide to use another tool in the Formula Auditing group to get more information about this error.

5. **Close the Error Checking dialog box, then click the Trace Precedents button in the Formula Auditing group**

   Blue arrows called **tracer arrows** point from the cells referenced by the formula to the active cell as shown in **FIGURE O-2**. The arrows help you determine if these cell references might have caused the error. The tracer arrows extend from the error to cells N6 and N8. To correct the error, you must edit the formula so that it references cell N7 in the denominator, the sales total, not cell N8.

QUICK TIP
To locate invalid data that may lead to errors in formula calculations, click the DATA tab, click the Data Validation list arrow, then click Circle Invalid Data. Red circles appear around cells that are not consistent with data validation criteria.

6. **Edit the formula in the formula bar to read =N6/N7, then click ✓ on the formula bar**

   The result of the formula, .4453, appears in cell O6. The November sales for the Vancouver branch in cell L6 is unusually high compared with sales posted for the other months. You can investigate the other cells in the sheet that are affected by the value of cell L6 by tracing the cell's **dependents**—the cells that contain formulas referring to cell L6.

7. **Click cell L6, then click the Trace Dependents button in the Formula Auditing group**

   The tracer arrows run from cell L6 to cells L7 and N6, indicating that the value in cell L6 affects the total November sales and the total Vancouver sales. You decide to remove the tracer arrows and format the percentages in cells O5 and O6.

8. **Click the Remove Arrows button in the Formula Auditing group, select the range O5:O6, click the HOME tab, click the Percent Style button % in the Number group, click the Increase Decimal button ⬚ twice, return to cell A1, then save the workbook**

Customizing Excel and Advanced Worksheet Management

FIGURE O-1: Error Checking dialog box

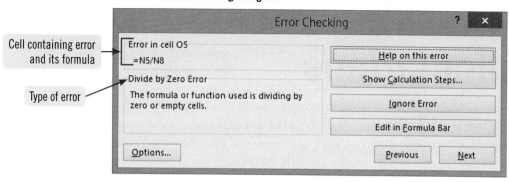

Cell containing error and its formula

Type of error

FIGURE O-2: Worksheet with traced error

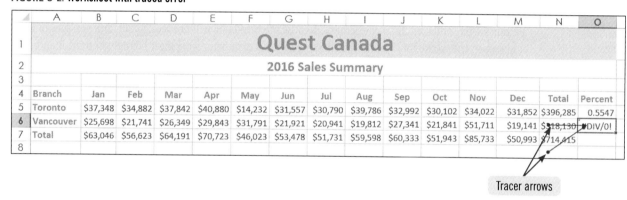

Tracer arrows

Watching and evaluating formulas

As you edit your worksheet, you can watch the effect that cell changes have on selected worksheet formulas. Select the cell or cells that you want to watch, click the FORMULAS tab, click the Watch Window button in the Formula Auditing group, click Add Watch in the Watch Window, then click Add. The Watch Window displays the workbook name, worksheet name, the cell address you want to watch, the current cell value, and its formula. As cell values that "feed into" the formula change, the resulting formula value in the Watch Window changes. To delete a watch, select the cell information in the Watch Window, then click Delete Watch. You can also step through a formula, and its results: Select a cell that contains a formula, then click the Evaluate Formula button in the Formula Auditing group. The formula appears in the Evaluation Window of the Evaluate Formula dialog box. As you click the Evaluate button, the cell references are replaced with their values and the formula result.

Customizing Excel and Advanced Worksheet Management

Control Worksheet Calculations

Learning Outcomes
- Control formula calculations
- Calculate worksheet formulas

Whenever you change a value in a cell, Excel automatically recalculates all the formulas in the worksheet based on that cell. This automatic calculation is efficient until you create a worksheet so large that the recalculation process slows down data entry and screen updating. Worksheets with many formulas, data tables, or functions may also recalculate slowly. In these cases, you might want to selectively determine if and when you want Excel to perform calculations. You do this by applying the **manual calculation** option. Once you change the calculation mode to manual, Excel applies manual calculation to all open worksheets. **CASE** ▸ *Because Kate knows that using specific Excel calculation options can help make worksheet building more efficient, she asks you to review the formula settings in the workbook and change the formula calculations from automatic to manual calculation.*

STEPS

1. **Click the FILE tab, click Options, then click Formulas in the list of options**

   The options related to formula calculation and error checking appear, as shown in **FIGURE O-3**.

2. **Under Calculation options, click to select the Manual option button**

   When you select the Manual option, the Recalculate workbook before saving check box automatically becomes active and contains a check mark. Because the workbook will not recalculate until you save or close and reopen the workbook, you must make sure to recalculate your worksheet before you print it and after you finish making changes.

3. **Click OK**

   Kate informs you that the December total for the Toronto branch is incorrect. You adjust the entry in cell M5 to reflect the actual sales figure.

4. **Click cell M5**

   Before changing cell M5, notice that in cell N5 the total for the Toronto branch is $396,285, and the Toronto percent in cell O5 is 55.47%.

5. **Type 40,000, then click the Enter button ☑ on the formula bar**

   The total and percent formulas are *not* updated. The total in cell N5 is still $396,285 and the percentage in cell O5 is still 55.47%. The word "Calculate" appears in the status bar to indicate that a specific value in the worksheet did indeed change and that the worksheet must be recalculated.

6. **Click the FORMULAS tab, click the Calculate Sheet button in the Calculation group, click cell A1, then save the workbook**

   The total in cell N5 is now $404,433 instead of $396,285 and the percentage in cell O5 is now 55.97% instead of 55.47%. The other formulas in the worksheet affected by the value in cell M5 changed as well, as shown in **FIGURE O-4**. Because this is a relatively small worksheet that recalculates quickly, you will return to automatic calculation.

7. **Click the Calculations Options button in the Calculation group, then click Automatic**

   Now any additional changes you make will automatically recalculate the worksheet formulas.

8. **Place your name in the center section of the worksheet footer, then save the workbook**

FIGURE O-3: Excel formula options

Click to select manual calculation of worksheet formulas

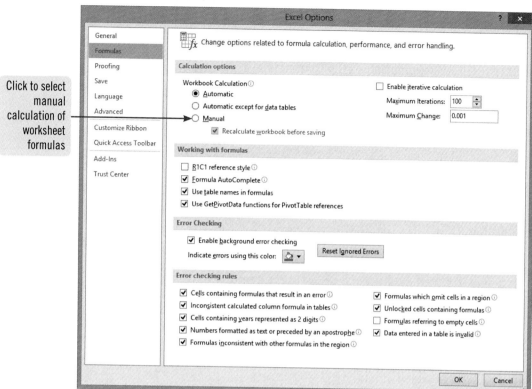

FIGURE O-4: Worksheet with updated values

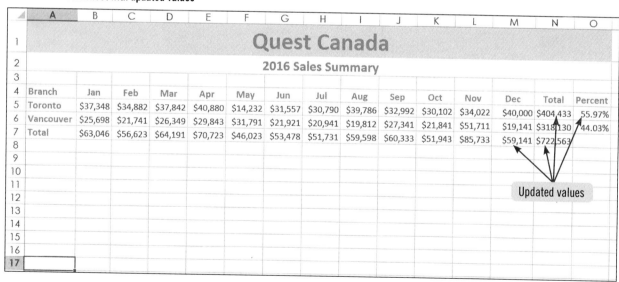

Updated values

Excel 2013

Group Worksheet Data

Learning Outcomes
- Group worksheet data
- Outline worksheet data

You can create groups of rows and columns on a worksheet to manage your data and make it easier to work with. The Excel grouping feature provides an outline with symbols that allow you to easily expand and collapse groups to show or hide selected worksheet data. You can turn off the outline symbols if you are using the condensed data in a report. **CASE** ▶ *Kate needs to give Jessica Long, the Quest CEO, the quarterly sales totals for the Canadian branches. She asks you to group the worksheet data by quarters.*

STEPS

> **QUICK TIP**
> You can also group worksheet data by rows to show and hide related information in rows.

1. **Click the** Quarterly Summary sheet, **select the range** B4:D7, **click the** DATA tab, **click the** Group button **in the Outline group, click the** Columns option button **in the Group dialog box, then click** OK

   The first quarter information is grouped, and **outline symbols** that are used to hide and display details appear over the columns, as shown in **FIGURE O-5**. You continue to group the remaining quarters.

2. **Select the range** F4:H7, **click the** Group button **in the Outline group, click the** Columns option button **in the Group dialog box, click** OK, **select the range** J4:L7, **click the** Group button **in the Outline group, click the** Columns option button **in the Group dialog box, click** OK, **select the range** N4:P7, **click the** Group button **in the Outline group, click the** Columns option button **in the Group dialog box, click** OK, **then click cell** A1

   All four quarters are grouped. You decide to use the outline symbols to expand and collapse the first quarter information.

> **QUICK TIP**
> If you want to summarize your data using subtotals, you need to sort your data on the field that you will subtotal, click the DATA tab, click the Subtotal button in the Outline group, then choose the subtotal field.

3. **Click the** Collapse Outline button ⊟ **above the column E label, then click the** Expand Outline button ⊞ **above the column E label**

   Clicking the (−) symbol temporarily hides the Q1 detail columns, and the (−) symbol changes to a (+) symbol. Clicking the (+) symbol expands the Q1 details and redisplays the hidden columns. The Column Level symbols in the upper-left corner of the worksheet are used to display and hide levels of detail across the entire worksheet.

4. **Click the** Column Level 1 button ①

   All of the group details collapse, and only the quarter totals are displayed.

5. **Click the** Column Level 2 button ②

   You see the quarter details again. Kate asks you to hide the quarter details and the outline symbols for her summary report.

> **QUICK TIP**
> You can ungroup a range of cells by clicking Ungroup in the Outline group.

6. **Click** ①, **click the** FILE tab, **click** Options, **click** Advanced **in the list of options, scroll to the Display options for this worksheet section, verify that** Quarterly Summary **is displayed as the worksheet name, click the** Show outline symbols if an outline is applied **check box to deselect it, then click** OK

   The quarter totals without outline symbols are shown in **FIGURE O-6**.

7. **Enter your name in the center footer section, save the workbook, then preview the worksheet**

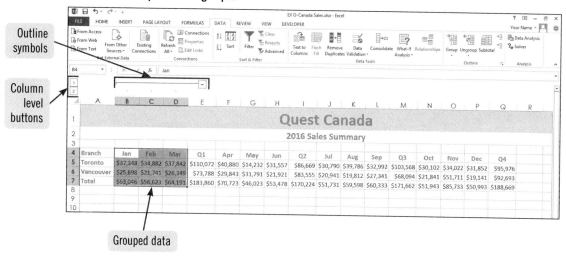

FIGURE O-5: First quarter data grouped

Outline symbols

Column level buttons

Grouped data

FIGURE O-6: Quarter summary

Breaks in column letter sequence indicate data is grouped

Branch	Q1	Q2	Q3	Q4
Toronto	$110,072	$86,669	$103,568	$95,976
Vancouver	$73,788	$83,555	$68,094	$92,693
Total	$183,860	$170,224	$171,662	$188,669

Applying and viewing advanced workbook properties

You can add summary information to your workbook, such as a subject, manager name, company name, or a category, using advanced properties. To view a workbook's advanced properties, click the FILE tab, click Info, click the Properties list arrow on the right side of Backstage view, then click Advanced Properties.

The General tab displays file information. Use the Summary tab to add additional properties to the workbook. The Statistics tab displays file information and the Contents tab lists the file's worksheets. You can create and enter additional information fields on the Custom tab.

Work with Cell Comments

Learning
Outcomes
• Insert a new
comment
• Show worksheet
comments
• Print worksheet
comments

If you plan to share a workbook with others, it's a good idea to **document**, or make notes about, basic assumptions, complex formulas, or questionable data. By reading your documentation, a coworker can quickly become familiar with your workbook. The easiest way to document a workbook is to use **cell comments**, which are notes attached to individual cells that appear when you place the pointer over a cell. When you sort or copy and paste cells, any comments attached to them will move to the new location. In PivotTable reports, however, the comments do not move with the worksheet data. **CASE** ▸ *Kate thinks one of the figures in the worksheet may be incorrect. She asks you to add a comment for Mark Ng, the Toronto branch manager, pointing out the possible error. You will start by checking the default settings for comments in a workbook.*

STEPS

1. **Click the FILE tab if necessary, click Options, click Advanced in the list of options, scroll to the Display section, click the Indicators only, and comments on hover option button to select it in the "For cells with comments, show:" section if necessary, then click OK**

   The other options in the "For cells with comments, show:" area allow you to display the comment and its indicator or no comments.

QUICK TIP
To copy only com-
ments into a cell,
copy the cell con-
tents, right-click the
destination cell, point
to Paste Special, click
Paste Special on the
shortcut menu, click
Comments in the
Paste Special dialog
box, then click OK.

2. **Click the Sales sheet tab, click cell F5, click the REVIEW tab, then click the New Comment button in the Comments group**

   The Comment box opens, as shown in **FIGURE O-7**. Excel automatically includes the computer's username at the beginning of the comment. The **username** is the name that appears in the User name text box of the Excel Options dialog box. The white sizing handles on the border of the Comment box let you resize it.

3. **Type Is this figure correct? It looks low to me., then click outside the Comment box**

   A red triangle appears in the upper-right corner of cell F5, indicating that a comment is attached to the cell. People who use your worksheet can easily display comments.

4. **Place the pointer over cell F5**

   The comment appears next to the cell. When you move the pointer outside of cell F5, the comment disappears. Kate asks you to add a comment to cell L6.

5. **Right-click cell L6, click Insert Comment on the shortcut menu, type Is this increase due to the new marketing campaign?, then click outside the Comment box**

   Kate asks you to delete a comment and edit a comment. You start by displaying all worksheet comments.

6. **Click cell A1, then click the Show All Comments button in the Comments group**

   The two worksheet comments are displayed on the screen, as shown in **FIGURE O-8**.

7. **Click the Next button in the Comments group, with the comment in cell F5 selected click the Delete button in the Comments group, click the Next button in the Comments group, click the Edit Comment button in the Comments group, type Mark - at the beginning of the comment in the Comment box, click cell A1, then click the Show All Comments button in the Comments group**

   The Show All Comments button is a toggle button: You click it once to display comments, then click it again to hide comments. You decide to fit the worksheet to print on one page and preview the worksheet and the cell comment along with its associated cell reference on separate pages.

8. **Click the FILE tab, click Print, click Page Setup at the bottom of the Print pane, click the Fit to option button on the Page tab, click the Sheet tab, under Print click the Comments list arrow, click At end of sheet, click OK, then click the Next Page arrow ▶ at the bottom of the preview pane to view the comments**

   Your comment appears on a separate page after the worksheet.

9. **Save the workbook**

Customizing Excel and Advanced Worksheet Management

FIGURE O-7: Comment box

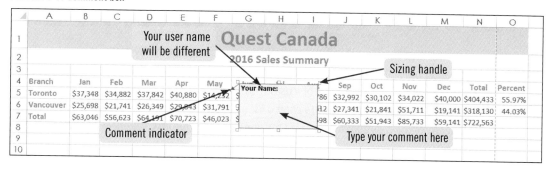

FIGURE O-8: Worksheet with comments displayed

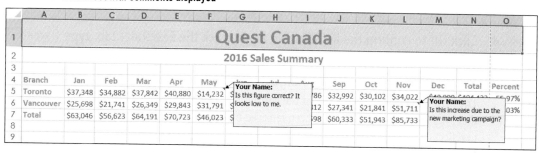

Working with Excel files

To increase your productivity, you can personalize the way recently used files and folders appear in Backstage view. For example, you can keep a workbook displayed in the Recent list of workbooks by clicking the FILE tab, clicking Open, right-clicking the file you want to keep, then clicking Pin to list. You can unpin the file by clicking the pin button to the right of the workbook name. If you want to clear the unpinned workbooks from the Recent list, click the FILE tab, click Open, click Recent Workbooks, right-click a file you want to remove from the list, click Clear unpinned Workbooks, then click Yes.

If you accidently close a file without saving it, if an unstable program causes Excel to close abnormally, or if the power fails,

you can recover your workbook, provided the AutoRecover feature is enabled. To enable AutoRecover, click the FILE tab, click Options, click Save in the Excel Options dialog box, verify that the Save AutoRecover information check box is selected; if necessary, modify the number of minutes AutoRecover saves your files by clicking the up or down arrow to adjust the number of minutes, then click OK. The AutoSave feature automatically saves your work at predetermined intervals, while the AutoRecover feature allows you to recover an AutoSaved file. If you need to restore an AutoRecovered file, click the FILE tab, click Info, click Manage Versions, then click Recover Unsaved Workbooks to see a list of any AutoRecovered files.

Create Custom AutoFill Lists

**Learning
Outcomes**
• Create a custom
  list
• Use a custom list

Whenever you need to type a list of words regularly, you can save time by creating a custom list. Then you can simply enter the first value in a blank cell and drag the fill handle. Excel enters the rest of the information for you. **FIGURE O-9** shows examples of custom lists that are built into Excel as well as a user-created custom list. **CASE** ▶ *Kate often has to enter a list of Quest's sales representatives' names in her worksheets. She asks you to create a custom list to save time in performing this task. You begin by selecting the names in the worksheet.*

STEPS

1. **Click the** Jan sheet tab, **then select the range** A5:A24

2. **Click the** FILE tab, **click** Options, **click** Advanced, **scroll down to the General section, then click** Edit Custom Lists

   The Custom Lists dialog box displays the custom lists that are already built into Excel, as shown in **FIGURE O-10**. You want to define a custom list containing the sales representatives' names you selected in column A. The Import list from cells text box contains the range you selected in Step 1.

3. **Click** Import

   The list of names is highlighted in the Custom lists box and appears in the List entries box. You decide to test the custom list by placing it in a blank worksheet.

4. **Click** OK **to confirm the list, click** OK **again, click the** Feb sheet tab, **type** Garceau **in cell A1, then click the** Enter button ✓ **on the formula bar**

5. **Drag the fill handle to fill the range** A2:A20

   The highlighted range now contains the custom list of sales representatives you created. Kate informs you that sales representative Brady has been replaced by a new representative, Perez. You update the custom list to reflect this change.

6. **Click the** FILE tab, **click** Options, **click** Advanced, **scroll down to the General section, click** Edit Custom Lists, **click the list of sales representatives names in the Custom lists box, change Brady to** Perez **in the List entries box, click** OK **to confirm the change, then click** OK **again**

   You decide to check the new list to be sure it is accurate.

7. **Click cell** C1, **type** Garceau, **click** ✓ **on the formula bar, drag the fill handle to fill the range** C2:C20

   The highlighted range contains the updated custom list of sales representatives, as shown in **FIGURE O-11**. You've finished creating and editing your custom list, and you need to delete it from the Custom Lists dia-log box in case others will be using your computer.

8. **Click the** FILE tab, **click** Options, **click** Advanced, **scroll down to the General section, click** Edit Custom Lists, **click the list of sales representatives' names in the Custom lists box, click** Delete, **click** OK **to confirm the deletion, then click** OK **two more times**

9. **Save the workbook**

FIGURE O-9: Sample custom lists

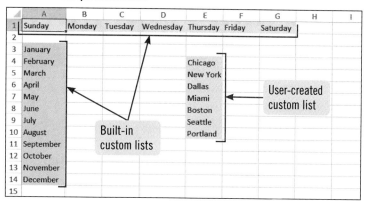

FIGURE O-10: Custom Lists dialog box

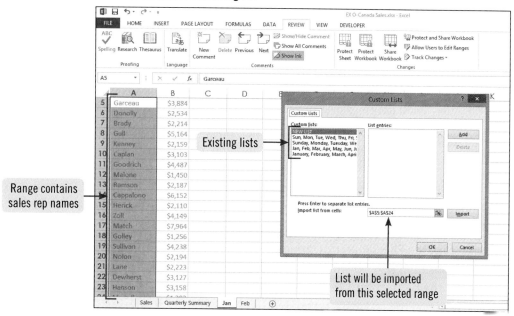

FIGURE O-11: Custom lists with sales rep names

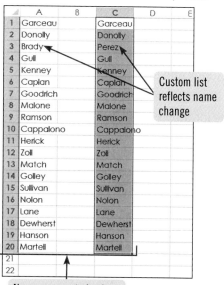

Create and Apply a Template

A template is a workbook with an .xltx file extension that contains text, formulas, macros, and formatting that you use repeatedly. Once you save a workbook as a template, it provides a model for creating a new workbook without your having to reenter standard data. To use a template, you **apply** it, which means you create workbooks *based on* the template. A workbook based on a template has the same content, formulas, and formatting you defined in the template, and is saved in the .xlsx format. The template file itself remains unchanged. **CASE** *Kate plans to use the same formulas, titles, and row and column labels from the Sales worksheet for subsequent yearly worksheets. She asks you to create a template that will allow her to quickly prepare these worksheets.*

STEPS

1. **Delete the Quarterly Summary, Jan, and Feb sheets**

   The workbook now contains only the Sales sheet. You decide to use the Sales sheet structure and formulas as the basis for your new template. You want to leave the formulas in row 7 and in columns N and O so future users will not have to re-create them. But you want to delete the comment, the sales data, and the year 2016.

2. **Right-click cell L6, click Delete Comment, select the range B5:M6, press [Delete], double-click cell A2, delete 2016, delete the space before "Sales", then click cell A1**

   You will create a folder named Templates to save the template.

3. **Open a File Explorer window, navigate to, then right-click, the location where you store your Data Files, point to New on the shortcut menu, click Folder, enter the name Templates as the new folder name, right click the new Templates folder, click Properties on the shortcut menu, click the General tab if necessary, select the path of the folder to the right of Location:, press and hold [CTRL], press [C], release both keys, then click OK**

   You need to enter the path to your Templates folder as the destination for your saved templates.

4. **In Excel, click the FILE tab, click Options, click Save, click in the Default personal templates location text box, press and hold [CTRL], press [V], release both keys, scroll to the end of the path, enter \Templates\, then click OK**

   Templates will now be saved to the path of your Templates folder. You will save the completed template shown in **FIGURE O-12** so Kate can use it for next year's sales summary.

5. **Click the FILE tab, click Save As, click Browse navigate to the location where you store your Data Files, double-click the Templates folder to open it, click the Save as type list arrow, click Excel Template (*.xltx), then click Save**

   Excel adds the .xltx extension to the filename.

6. **Close the workbook and exit Excel**

   Now you open a workbook based on the Canada Sales template.

7. **Navigate to the location where you store your Data Files, double-click the Templates folder to open it, then double-click the EX O-Canada Sales.xltx to open a workbook based on the template**

   The workbook name is EX O-Canada Sales1 as shown in **FIGURE O-13**. A workbook based on a template opens with the template name with a "1" at the end of the name. You want to make sure the formulas are working correctly.

8. **Click cell B5, enter 200, click cell B6, enter 300, select the range B5:B6, copy the data into the range C5:M6, compare your workbook to FIGURE O-14, save the workbook as EX O-Template Test, close the workbook, then submit the workbook to your instructor**

Customizing Excel and Advanced Worksheet Management

FIGURE O-12: Completed template

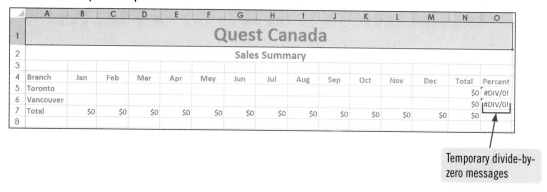

Temporary divide-by-zero messages

FIGURE O-13: Workbook based on template

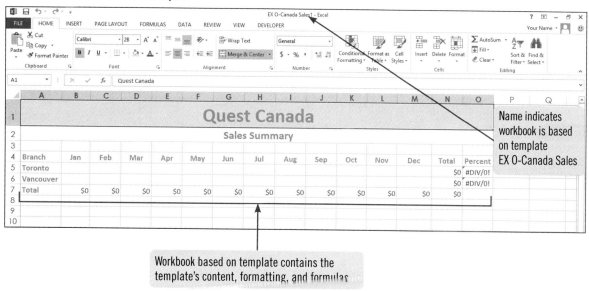

Name indicates workbook is based on template EX O-Canada Sales

Workbook based on template contains the template's content, formatting, and formulas

FIGURE O-14: Completed template test

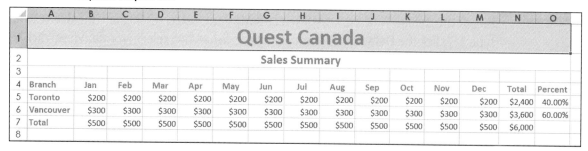

Customize Excel Workbooks

Learning Outcomes
- Change the number of default worksheets
- Change the default workbook font and view

The Excel default settings for editing and viewing a worksheet are designed to meet the needs of the majority of Excel users. You may find, however, that a particular setting doesn't always fit your particular needs, such as the default number of worksheets in a workbook, the default worksheet view, or the default font. You have already used the Advanced category in the Excel Options dialog box to create custom lists and the Formulas category to switch to manual calculation. The General category contains features that are commonly used by a large number of Excel users, and you can use it to further customize Excel to suit your work habits and needs. The most commonly used categories of the Excel Options are explained in more detail in **TABLE O-1.** **CASE** *Kate is interested in customizing workbooks to allow her to work more efficiently. She asks you to use a blank workbook to explore features that will help her better manage her data. In the last workbook you prepared for Kate you had to add a second worksheet. You would like to have two worksheets displayed rather than one when a new workbook is opened.*

STEPS

1. **Open a new blank workbook, click the FILE tab, then click Options**

   The Excel Options dialog box displays the default options that Excel uses in new workbooks, as shown in **FIGURE O-15**. You will change the number of worksheets in a new workbook.

2. **Select 1 in the Include this many sheets text box, in the "When creating new workbooks" area of the Excel Options dialog box, then type 2**

   You can change the default font Excel uses in new workbooks.

QUICK TIP

The default Excel text style is the body font, which is Calibri unless it is changed by the user. To change a workbook's default heading and body text font, click the PAGE LAYOUT tab, click the Fonts button in the Themes group, click Customize Fonts, select the fonts for the Heading and Body in the Create New Theme Fonts dialog box, enter a name, then click Save.

3. **Click the Use this as the default font list arrow, then select Arial**

   You can also change the standard workbook font size.

4. **Click the Font size list arrow, then select 12**

   Kate would rather have new workbooks open in Page Layout view.

5. **Click the Default view for new sheets list arrow, select Page Layout View, click OK to close the Excel Options dialog box, then click OK to the message about quitting and restarting Excel**

   These default settings take effect after you exit and restart Excel.

6. **Close the workbook, exit Excel, start Excel again, then open a new blank workbook**

   A new workbook opens with two sheet tabs in Page Layout view and a 12-point Arial font, as shown in **FIGURE O-16**. Now that you have finished exploring the Excel workbook Options, you need to restore the original Excel settings.

7. **Click the FILE tab, click Options, in the "When creating new workbooks" area of the General options, select 2 in the Include this many sheets text box, enter 1, click the Use this as the default font list arrow, select Body Font, select 12 in the Font size text box, type 11, click the Default view for new sheets list arrow, select Normal View, click OK, then close the workbook and exit Excel**

FIGURE O-15: General category of Excel options

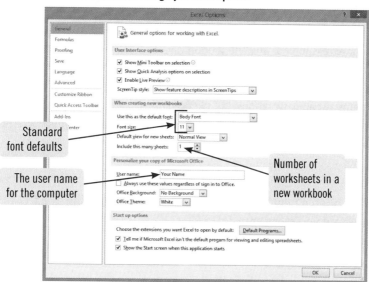

Standard font defaults

The user name for the computer

Number of worksheets in a new workbook

FIGURE O-16: Workbook with new default settings

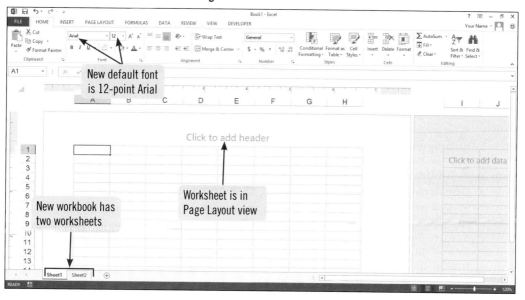

New default font is 12-point Arial

Worksheet is in Page Layout view

New workbook has two worksheets

TABLE O-1: Categories of Excel options

category	allows you to
General	Change the user name and the workbook screen display
Formulas	Control how the worksheet is calculated, how formulas appear, and error checking settings and rules
Proofing	Control AutoCorrect and spell-checking options
Save	Select a default format and location for saving files, and customize AutoRecover settings
Language	Control the languages displayed and allows you to add languages
Advanced	Create custom lists as well as customize editing and display options
Customize Ribbon	Add tabs and groups to the Ribbon
Quick Access Toolbar	Add commands to the Quick Access toolbar
Add-Ins	Install Excel Add-in programs such as Solver and Analysis ToolPak
Trust Center	Change Trust Center settings to protect your Excel files

Customize the Excel Screen

While the Quick Access toolbar and the Ribbon give you easy access to many useful Excel features, you might have other commands that you want to have readily available to speed your work. The Excel Options dialog box allows you to customize the Quick Access toolbar and Ribbon, either for all workbooks (the default) or for a specific workbook. **CASE** *Kate is interested in customizing the Quick Access toolbar to include spell checking. She would also like you to add a new tab to the Ribbon with accessibility tools.*

STEPS

1. **Start Excel, open a new, blank workbook, then save the file as** EX O-Customized **in the location where you store your Data Files**

2. **Click the** Customize Quick Access Toolbar button ⤓ **on the Quick Access toolbar, then click** More Commands

   The Excel Options dialog box opens with the Quick Access Toolbar option selected as shown in **FIGURE O-17**. You want to add the spell checking feature to the Quick Access toolbar for the EX O-Customized workbook.

3. **Make sure** Popular Commands **is displayed in the Choose commands from list, click the** Customize Quick Access Toolbar list arrow, **select** For EX O-Customized.xlsx, **click the** Spelling command **in the Popular Commands list, click** Add, **then click** OK

   The Spelling button now appears on the Quick Access toolbar to the right of the Save, Undo, and Redo buttons, which appear by default. Kate wants you to add a tab to the Ribbon with a group of accessibility tools.

4. **Click the** FILE tab, **click** Options, **click** Customize Ribbon, **on the lower-right side of the Excel Options dialog box click** New Tab

   A new tab named New Tab (Custom) appears in the listing of Main Tabs below the HOME tab. Under the new tab is a new group named New Group (Custom). You want to add accessibility tools to the new group.

5. **Click the** Choose commands from list arrow, **click** Commands Not in the Ribbon, **click the** Accessibility Checker command, **click** Add, **click** Alt Text, **click** Add, **scroll down, click** Zoom In, **click** Add, **click** Zoom Out, **then click** Add

   Four accessibility tools now appear in the custom group on the new custom tab. Clicking the Check Accessibility button inspects your worksheet for features that need additional description for people with disabilities. Warnings are issued for worksheets with the default names as well as objects such as images and hyperlinks without alternative text. You can also check a worksheet's accessibility features by clicking the FILE tab, clicking Info, clicking the Check for Issues list arrow, then clicking Check Accessibility. You decide to rename the tab and the group to identify the buttons.

6. **Click** New Tab (Custom) **in the Main Tabs area, click** Rename, **in the Rename dialog box type** ACCESSIBILITY, **click** OK, **click** New Group (Custom) **below the ACCESSIBILITY tab, click** Rename, **in the Rename dialog box type** Accessibility Tools **in the Display name text box, click** OK, **then click** OK **again**

   The new custom tab appears in the Ribbon, just to the right of the HOME tab. You can change the order of the tabs using the Move Up ▲ and Move Down ▼ buttons. You decide to check it to verify it contains the buttons you want.

7. **Click the** ACCESSIBILITY tab, **compare your tab to** FIGURE O-18, **click the** Zoom In button, **then click the** Zoom Out button

   You will reset the Ribbon to the default settings.

8. **Click the** FILE tab, **click** Options, **click** Customize Ribbon, **on the lower-right side of the Excel Options dialog box click** Reset, **click** Reset all customizations, **click** Yes, **click** OK, **save the workbook, then close it and exit Excel**

FIGURE O-17: Quick Access Toolbar category of Excel options

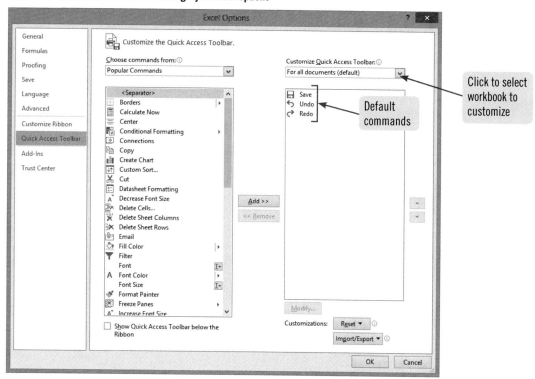

FIGURE O-18: Workbook with new toolbar button and Accessibility Tab

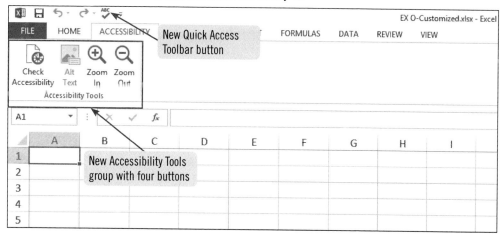

Customizing the Quick Access toolbar

You can quickly add a button from the Ribbon to the Quick Access toolbar by right-clicking it and selecting Add to Quick Access Toolbar. Right-clicking a Ribbon button also allows you to quickly customize the Ribbon and the Quick Access toolbar. You can also move the Quick Access toolbar from its default position and minimize the Ribbon.

Practice

Concepts Review

FIGURE O-19

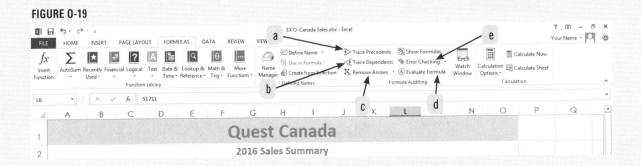

Which element do you click to:

1. Locate cells that reference the active cell?
2. Eliminate tracers from a worksheet?
3. Step through a formula in a selected cell?
4. Locate formula errors in a worksheet?
5. Find cells that may have caused a formula error?

Match each term with the statement that best describes it.

6. [Shift][F9]
7. Outline symbols
8. Custom list
9. Template
10. Comment

a. Note that appears when you place the pointer over a cell

b. Used to hide and display details in grouped data

c. Calculates the worksheet manually

d. A workbook with an .xltx file extension that contains text, formulas, and formatting

e. Entered in a worksheet using the fill handle

Select the best answer from the list of choices.

11. Which of the following categories of Excel options allows you to change the number of default worksheets in a workbook?
    - a. General
    - b. Proofing
    - c. Advanced
    - d. Formulas
12. Which of the following categories of Excel options allows you to create Custom Lists?
    - a. Add-Ins
    - b. Advanced
    - c. Customize
    - d. Formulas
13. The _____ displays the fewest details in grouped data.
    - a. Column Level 2 button
    - b. Column Level 1 button
    - c. Column Level 3 button
    - d. Column Level 4 button
14. To apply a custom list, you:
    - a. Click the Fill tab in the Edit dialog box.
    - b. Type the first cell entry and drag the fill handle.
    - c. Press [Shift][F9].
    - d. Select the list in the worksheet.

Skills Review

1. Audit a worksheet.

  a. Start Excel, open the file EX O-2.xlsx from the location where you store your Data Files, then save it as **EX O-Chatham**.

  b. Select cell B10, then use the Trace Dependents button to locate all the cells that depend on this cell.

  c. Clear the arrows from the worksheet.

  d. Select cell B19, use the Trace Precedents button to find the cells on which that figure is based, then correct the formula in cell B19. (*Hint*: It should be B7–B18.)

  e. Use the Error Checking button to check the worksheet for any other errors. Correct any worksheet errors using the formula bar. (*Hint*: If you get an inconsistent formula error for cell F18, make sure it is totaled vertically or horizontally, then ignore the error.)

2. Control worksheet calculations.

  a. Open the Formulas category of the Excel Options dialog box.

  b. Change the worksheet calculations to manual.

  c. Change the figure in cell B6 to **22,000**.

  d. Recalculate the worksheet manually, using an appropriate key combination or button.

  e. Change the worksheet calculations back to automatic using the Calculation Options button, and save the workbook.

3. Group worksheet data.

  a. Group the income information in rows 5 and 6.

  b. Group the expenses information in rows 10 through 17.

  c. Hide the income details in rows 5 and 6.

  d. Hide the expenses details in rows 10 through 17.

  e. Enter your name in the center section of the worksheet footer, then preview the worksheet with the income and expenses detail hidden.

  f. Redisplay the income and expenses details.

  g. Remove the row grouping for the income and expenses details. (*Hint*: With the grouped rows selected, click the DATA tab, then click the Ungroup button in the Outline group.)

  h. Save the workbook.

4. Work with cell comments.

  a. Insert a comment in cell E12 that reads **Does this include newspaper advertising?**.

  b. Click anywhere outside the Comment box to close it.

  c. Display the comment by moving the pointer over cell E12, then check it for accuracy.

  d. Edit the comment in cell E12 to read **Does this include newspaper and magazine advertising?**.

  e. Preview the worksheet and your comment, with the comment appearing at the end of the sheet.

  f. Save the workbook.

5. Create custom AutoFill lists.

  a. Select the range A4:A19.

  b. Open the Custom Lists dialog box, and import the selected text.

  c. Close the dialog box.

  d. Add a worksheet to the workbook. On Sheet2, enter **Income** in cell A1.

  e. Use the fill handle to enter the list through cell A15.

  f. Enter your name in the center section of the Sheet2 footer, then preview the worksheet.

  g. Open the Custom Lists dialog box again, delete the custom list you just created, then save the workbook.

6. Create and apply a template.

  a. Delete Sheet2 from the workbook.

  b. Delete the comment in cell E12.

  c. Delete the income and expense data for all four quarters. Leave the worksheet formulas intact.

d. Save the workbook as a template with the name **EX O-Chatham.xltx** in the template folder in the location where you store your Data Files. (*Hint*: If you don't have a template folder you will need to create one.)

e. Close the template, then open a workbook based on the template by opening File Explorer, then double-clicking the template in the template folder in the location where you store your Data Files.

f. Test the template by entering the data for all four quarters and in every budget category shown in **FIGURE O-20**.

g. Save the workbook as **EX O-Chatham1.xlsx** in the location where you store your Data Files.

h. Preview the worksheet, close the workbook, then submit the workbook to your instructor.

FIGURE O-20

	A	B	C	D	E	F	G
1	Chatham Chowder House						
2							
3		Q1	Q2	Q3	Q4	Total	% of Total
4	**Income**						
5	Beverages	$2,000	$2,000	$2,000	$2,000	$8,000	40%
6	Chowder	$3,000	$3,000	$3,000	$3,000	$12,000	60%
7	**Net Sales**	$5,000	$5,000	$5,000	$5,000	$20,000	
8							
9	**Expenses**						
10	Salaries	$100	$100	$100	$100	$400	3%
11	Rent	$200	$200	$200	$200	$800	6%
12	Advertising	$300	$300	$300	$300	$1,200	8%
13	Cleaning	$400	$400	$400	$400	$1,600	11%
14	Fish	$500	$500	$500	$500	$2,000	14%
15	Dairy	$600	$600	$600	$600	$2,400	17%
16	Beverages	$700	$700	$700	$700	$2,800	19%
17	Paper Products	$800	$800	$800	$800	$3,200	22%
18	**Total Expenses**	$3,600	$3,600	$3,600	$3,600	$14,400	100%
19	**Net Profit**	$1,400	$1,400	$1,400	$1,400	$5,600	

7. Customize Excel workbooks.

a. Open a new workbook, then open the General options of the Excel Options dialog box.

b. Change the number of sheets in a new workbook to **3**.

c. Change the default font of a new workbook to 14-point Times New Roman.

d. Close the workbook and exit Excel.

e. Start Excel and verify that the new workbook's font is 14-point Times New Roman and that it has three worksheets.

f. Reset the default number of worksheets to **1** and the default workbook font to 11-point Body Font.

8. Customize the Excel screen.

a. Use the Quick Access Toolbar category of the Excel Options dialog box to add the Print Preview and Print button to the Quick Access toolbar.

b. Use the Customize Ribbon category to add a tab named **MATH** to the Ribbon with a group named **Math Tools** containing the buttons Equation and Equation Symbols. (*Hint*: These buttons are in the All Commands list.)

FIGURE O-21

c. Compare your Quick Access Toolbar and Ribbon to **FIGURE O-21**.

d. Reset all customizations of the workbook, close the workbook then exit Excel.

Independent Challenge 1

You are the VP of Human Resources at Connect, a PR firm with offices in the east and the west regions of the United States. You are tracking the overtime hours for workers using total and percentage formulas. Before you begin your analysis, you want to check the worksheet for formula errors. Then, you group the first quarter data, add a comment to the worksheet, and create a custom list of the east and west locations and total labels.

a. Start Excel, open the file titled EX O-3.xlsx from the location where you store your Data Files, then save it as **EX O-Hours**.

b. Audit the worksheet, ignoring warnings that aren't errors and correcting the formula errors in the formula bar.

c. Select cell R5 and use the Trace Precedents button to show the cells used in its formula.

d. Select cell B10 and use the Trace Dependents button to show the cells affected by the value in the cell.

Independent Challenge 1 (continued)

e. Remove all arrows from the worksheet.

f. Group the months Jan, Feb, and March, then use the Outline symbols to hide the first quarter details.

g. Add the comment **This looks low.** to cell P11. Display the comment on the worksheet so it is visible even when you are not hovering over the cell.

h. Create a custom list by importing the range A5:A15. Add a new worksheet to the workbook, then test the list in cells A1:A11 of the new worksheet. Delete the custom list.

i. Change the comment display to show only the comment indicators and the comments when hovering over the cell with the comment.

j. Add your name to the center section of the worksheet footer, preview the worksheet with the comment on a separate page, then save the workbook.

k. Close the workbook, exit Excel, then submit the workbook to your instructor.

Independent Challenge 2

You are the property manager of The Eastern Group, a commercial retail property located in Baltimore. One of your responsibilities is to keep track of the property's regular monthly expenses. You have compiled a list of fixed expenses in an Excel workbook. Because the expense categories don't change from month to month, you want to create a custom list including each expense item to save time in preparing similar worksheets in the future. You will also temporarily switch to manual formula calculation, check the total formula, and document the data.

a. Start Excel, open the file titled EX O-4.xlsx from the location where you store your Data Files, then save it as **EX O-Expenses**.

b. Select the range of cells A4:A15 on the Fixed Expenses sheet, then import the list to create a Custom List.

c. Add a new worksheet to the workbook, then use the fill handle to insert your list in cells A1:A12 in the new sheet.

d. Add your name to the center section of the new worksheet footer, save the workbook, then preview the worksheet.

e. Delete your custom list, then return to the Fixed Expenses sheet.

f. Switch to manual calculation for formulas. Change the expense for Gas to $9,500.00. Calculate the worksheet formula manually. Turn on automatic calculation again.

g. Add the comment **This may increase.** to cell B4. Display the comment on the worksheet so it is visible even when the mouse pointer is not hovering over the cell.

h. Use the Error Checking dialog box for help in correcting the error in cell B16. Verify that the formula is correctly totaling the expenses in column B.

i. Trace the precedents of cell B16. Compare your worksheet to **FIGURE O-22**.

j. Remove the arrow and the comment display from the worksheet, leaving only the indicator displayed. Do not delete the comment from the worksheet cell.

k. Trace the dependents of cell B4. Remove the arrow from the worksheet.

l. Edit the comment in cell B4 to **This shouldn't change much with rate lock.**, and add the comment **This seems low.** to cell B10.

FIGURE O-22

	A	B	C	D	E
1	**The Eastern Group**				
2	**Fixed Monthly Expenses**				
3	Item	Amount			
4	Gas	$ 9,500.00	**Your Name:** This may increase.		
5	Electricity	$ 2,657.00			
6	Water & Sewer	$ 3,011.00			
7	Rubbish Removal	$ 2,159.00			
8	Parking & Garage	$ 923.00			
9	Alarm Service	$ 232.00			
10	Cleaning	$ 277.00			
11	Maintenance	$ 2,140.00			
12	Payroll	$ 5,311.00			
13	Supplies	$ 1,209.00			
14	Landscaping	$ 2,521.00			
15	Legal	$ 2,795.00			
16	Total	$ 32,735.00			
17					

Independent Challenge 2 (continued)

m. Use the Next and Previous buttons in the Comments group of the REVIEW tab to move between comments on the worksheet. Delete the comment in cell B10.

n. Add your name to the center section of the Fixed Expenses worksheet footer, save the workbook, then preview the Fixed Expenses worksheet with the comment appearing at the end of the sheet.

o. Close the workbook, exit Excel, then submit your workbook to your instructor.

Independent Challenge 3

As the business manager of a local historic museum you are responsible for the annual budget. You use Excel to track income and expenses using formulas to total each category and to calculate the net cash flow for the organization. You want to customize your workbooks and settings in Excel so you can work more efficiently. You are also interested in grouping your data and creating a template that you can use to build next year's budget.

a. Start Excel, open the file titled EX O-5.xlsx from the location where you store your Data Files, then save it as **EX O-Budget**.

b. Add an icon to the Quick Access toolbar for the EX O-Budget.xlsx workbook to print preview and print a worksheet.

c. Add a tab to the Ribbon named SHAPES with a group named Shape Tools. Add the buttons Down Arrow, Straight Arrow Connector, Straight Connector, and Zoom from the Commands Not in the Ribbon list to the new group. Compare your Ribbon and Quick Access toolbar to **FIGURE O-23**.

FIGURE O-23

d. Add a new worksheet to the workbook, name the new sheet Shapes. Test the new Shape Tools buttons on the Shapes worksheet by clicking each one and dragging an area to test the shapes. Add your name to the center footer section of the Shapes sheet.

e. Test the Print Preview button on the Quick Access toolbar by previewing the Shapes sheet.

f. On the Budget sheet, group rows 4–6 and 9–14, then use the appropriate row-level button to hide the expense and income details, as shown in **FIGURE O-24**.

FIGURE O-24

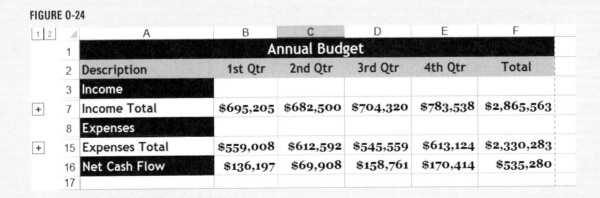

	A	B	C	D	E	F
1	Annual Budget					
2	Description	1st Qtr	2nd Qtr	3rd Qtr	4th Qtr	Total
3	Income					
7	Income Total	$695,205	$682,500	$704,320	$783,538	$2,865,563
8	Expenses					
15	Expenses Total	$559,008	$612,592	$545,559	$613,124	$2,330,283
16	Net Cash Flow	$136,197	$69,908	$158,761	$170,414	$535,280
17						

Independent Challenge 3 (continued)

g. Add your name to the center section of the worksheet footer, save the workbook, then use the Print Preview button on the Quick Access toolbar to preview the Budget worksheet. Redisplay all rows, using the Outline symbols, then save the workbook.

h. Delete the Shapes worksheet and all data in the Budget sheet, leaving the formulas and labels.

i. Save the workbook as a template named **EX O-Budget** in the Templates folder in the location where you store your Data Files. Close the template file, and open a workbook based on the template. Save the workbook as **EX O-New Budget**.

j. Test the template by entering data for the four quarters. Save the workbook, then preview the worksheet using the Print Preview button on the Quick Access toolbar.

k. Customize Excel so that your workbooks will open with two worksheets in Page Layout view and use 12-point Trebuchet MS font.

l. Reset the Ribbon, close your workbook, exit Excel, and then open a new workbook to confirm the new default workbook settings. Reset the default Excel workbook to open with one sheet in Normal view and the 11-point Body Font. Close the new workbook.

m. Exit Excel, then submit the EX O-Budget and EX O-New Budget workbooks and the template to your instructor.

Independent Challenge 4: Explore

As the east coast sales manager of a marine supply company, you monitor the sales of the sales representatives in your region. You use Excel to track sales using formulas to total each office. Your assistant has created an Excel workbook tracking the sales of the offices in your region with percentages of total sales. You will check the workbook for errors and add features before sending it back to your assistant for his review.

a. Start Excel, open the file titled EX O-6.xlsx from the location where you store your Data Files, then save it as **EX O-Sales**.

b. Audit the worksheet, ignoring warnings that aren't errors and correcting the formula errors in the formula bar.

c. Select cell S5 on the Sales sheet, then open the Evaluate Formula dialog box.

d. In the Evaluate Formula dialog box, click Evaluate three times to see the process of substituting values for cell addresses in the formula and the results of the formula calculations. Close the Evaluate Formula window.

e. Select cell S6, open the Watch Window. (*Hint:* Click the Watch Window button in the Formula Auditing group on the Formulas tab.)

f. Click Add Watch to add cell S6 to the Watch Window, and observe its value in the window as you change cell G6 to $1000. Close the Watch Window.

g. Add the comment **Please recheck this number.** to cell K7. Copy the comment in cell K7 and paste it in cell P5. (*Hint:* After copying cell K7, use the Paste Special option to copy the comment into cell P5.)

h. Using the Summary tab of advanced workbook properties, add your name as the author, and **Annual Sales** as the Category. Create a custom property of Forward to with a value of John Green. (*Hint:* Click the File tab, click Info, click the Properties list arrow, then click Advanced Properties.)

i. Pin the **EX O-Sales** workbook to the Recent list. Unpin the workbook. Clear all unpinned workbooks from the Recent list.

j. Save the workbook. View any unsaved workbooks.

k. Add your name to the center section of the worksheet footer, save the workbook, then preview the worksheet. Close the workbook, exit Excel, then submit the workbook to your instructor.

Visual Workshop

Open the Data File EX O-7.xlsx from the location where you store your Data Files, then save it as **EX O-Supply**. Group the data as shown after removing any errors in the worksheet. Your grouped results should match **FIGURE O-25**. (*Hint*: The Outline symbols have been hidden for the worksheet.) The new buttons on the Quick Access toolbar have only been added to the EX O-Supply workbook. Add your name to the center section of the worksheet footer, save the workbook, then preview the worksheet. Close the workbook, exit Excel, then submit the workbook to your instructor.

FIGURE O-25

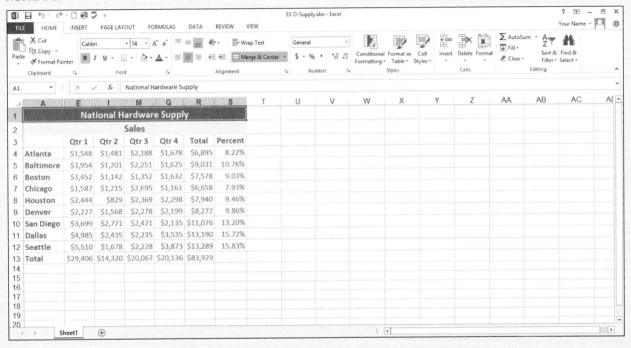

Programming with Excel

CASE ▶ Quest's vice president of sales, Kate Morgan, has used recorded macros to insert worksheet text. Now she would like to automate some more of the division's time-consuming tasks for the sales group. She plans to create macros that she enters manually. You help Kate by creating five new Excel macros using the Visual Basic for Applications (VBA) programming language.

Unit Objectives

After completing this unit, you will be able to:

- View VBA code
- Analyze VBA code
- Write VBA code
- Add a conditional statement

- Prompt the user for data
- Debug a macro
- Create a main procedure
- Run a main procedure

Files You Will Need

EX P-1.xlsm	EX P-5.xlsm
EX P-2.xlsx	EX P-6.xlsm
EX P-3.xlsm	EX P-7.xlsm
EX P-4.xlsm	EX P-8.xlsm

Microsoft® product screenshots used with permission from Microsoft® Corporation.

View VBA Code

**Learning
Outcomes**
• Identify the VBA
  windows
• Define VBA
  procedure terms

As you learned in Unit I, you can create macros using the Excel macro recorder, which automatically writes Visual Basic for Applications (VBA) instructions for you as you perform actions. For additional flexibility, you can also create entire Excel macros by typing VBA program code. To enter and edit VBA code, you work in the **Visual Basic Editor**, a tool you can start from within Excel. A common method of learning any programming language is to view existing code. In VBA macro code, a sequence of VBA statements is called a **procedure**. The first line of a procedure, called the **procedure header**, defines the procedure's type, name, and arguments. **Arguments** are variables used by other procedures that the main procedure might run. **CASE** *Each month, Kate receives text files containing tour sales information from the Quest branches. Kate has already imported the text file for the Miami January sales into a worksheet, but she still needs to format it. She asks you to work on a macro to automate the process of formatting the imported information.*

STEPS

1. **Start Excel if necessary, open a blank workbook, click the DEVELOPER tab, then click the Macro Security button in the Code group**

   The Trust Center dialog box opens, as shown in **FIGURE P-1**. You know the Quest branch files are from a trusted source, so you decide to allow macros to run in the workbook.

2. **Click the Enable all macros option button if necessary, then click OK**

   You are ready to open a file and view its VBA code. A macro-enabled workbook has the extension .xlsm. Although a workbook containing a macro will open if macros are disabled, they will not function.

3. **Open the file EX P-1.xlsm from the location where you store your Data Files, save it as EX P-Monthly Sales, click the DEVELOPER tab if necessary, then click the Macros button in the Code group**

   The Macro dialog box opens with the FormatFile macro procedure in the list box. If you have any macros saved in your Personal Macro workbook, they are also listed in the Macro dialog box.

4. **If it is not already selected click the FormatFile macro, then click Edit**

   The Microsoft Visual Basic for Applications window opens, containing three windows, shown in **FIGURE P-2**. See **TABLE P-1** to make sure your screen matches the ones shown in this unit. See also the yellow box on the next page for more information about the VBA window.

5. **Make sure both the Visual Basic window and the Code window are maximized to match FIGURE P-2**

   In the Code window, the different parts of the FormatFile procedure appear in various colors. **Comments** are notes explaining the code; they are displayed in green.

6. **Examine the top three lines of code, which contain comments, and the first line of code beginning with Sub FormatFile( )**

   The first two comment lines give the procedure name and tell what the procedure does. The third comment line explains that the keyboard shortcut for this macro procedure is [Ctrl][Shift][F]. Items that appear in blue are **keywords**, which are words Excel recognizes as part of the VBA programming language. The keyword Sub in the procedure header indicates that this is a **Sub procedure**, or a series of Visual Basic statements that perform an action but do not return (create and display) a value. An empty set of parentheses after the procedure name means the procedure doesn't have any arguments. In the next lesson, you will analyze the procedure code to see what each line does.

FIGURE P-1: Macro settings in the Trust Center dialog box

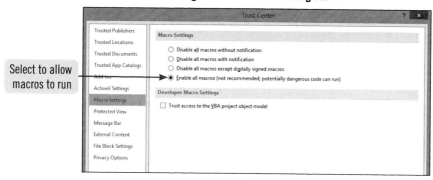

Select to allow macros to run

FIGURE P-2: Procedure displayed in the Visual Basic Editor

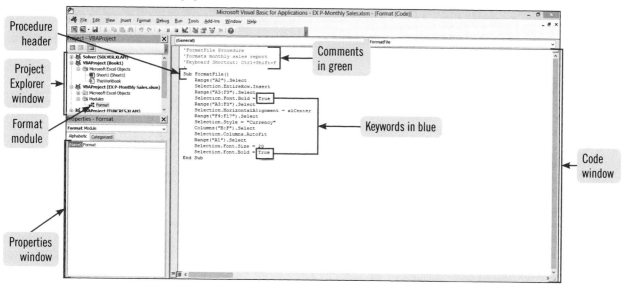

Procedure header

Project Explorer window

Format module

Properties window

Comments in green

Keywords in blue

Code window

TABLE P-1: Matching your screen to the unit figures

if...	do this...
The Properties window is not displayed	Click the Properties Window button on the toolbar
The Project Explorer window is not displayed	Click the Project Explorer button on the toolbar
You see only the Code window	Click Tools on the menu bar, click Options, click the Docking tab, then make sure the Project Explorer and Properties Window options are selected
You do not see folders in the Explorer window	Click the Toggle Folders button on the Project Explorer window Project toolbar

Understanding the Visual Basic Editor

A **module** is the Visual Basic equivalent of a worksheet. In it, you store macro procedures, just as you store data in worksheets. Modules, in turn, are stored in workbooks (or projects), along with worksheets. A **project** is the collection of all procedures in a workbook. You view and edit modules in the Visual Basic Editor, which is made up of the Project Explorer window (also called the Project window), the Code window, and the Properties window. **Project Explorer** displays a list of all open projects (or workbooks) and the worksheets and modules they contain. To view the procedures stored in a module, you must first select the module in Project Explorer (just as you would select a file in Windows Explorer). The **Code window** then displays the selected module's procedures. The **Properties window** displays a list of characteristics (or properties) associated with the module. A newly inserted module has only one property, its name.

Analyze VBA Code

Learning
Outcomes
• Examine the struc-
ture of VBA code
• Run a procedure

You can learn a lot about the VBA language simply by analyzing the code generated by the Excel macro recorder. The more VBA code you analyze, the easier it is for you to write your own programming code. **CASE** ▶ *Before writing any new procedures, you analyze a previously written procedure that applies formatting to a worksheet. Then you open a worksheet that you want to format and run the macro.*

STEPS

1. **With the FormatFile procedure still displayed in the Code window, examine the next four lines of code, beginning with Range("A2"). Select**

   Refer to **FIGURE P-3** as you analyze the code in this lesson. Every Excel element, including a range, is considered an **object**. A **range object** represents a cell or a range of cells. The statement Range("A2").Select selects the range object cell A2. Notice that several times in the procedure, a line of code (or **statement**) selects a range, and then subsequent lines act on that selection. The next statement, Selection.EntireRow. Insert, inserts a row above the selection, which is currently cell A2. The next two lines of code select range A3:F3 and apply bold formatting to that selection. In VBA terminology, bold formatting is a value of an object's Bold property. A **property** is an attribute of an object that defines one of the object's characteristics (such as size) or an aspect of its behavior (such as whether it is enabled). To change the characteristics of an object, you change the values of its properties. For example, to apply bold formatting to a selected range, you assign the value True to the range's Bold property. To remove bold formatting, assign the value False.

2. **Examine the remaining lines of code, beginning with the second occurrence of the line Range("A3:F3"). Select**

   The next two statements select the range object A3:F3 and center its contents, then the following two statements select the F4:F17 range object and format it as currency. Column objects B through F are then selected, and their widths set to AutoFit. Finally, the range object cell A1 is selected, its font size is changed to 20, and its Bold property is set to True. The last line, End Sub, indicates the end of the Sub procedure and is also referred to as the **procedure footer**.

3. **Click the View Microsoft Excel button ⊠ on the Visual Basic Editor toolbar to return to Excel**

   Because the macro is stored in the EX P-Monthly Sales workbook, Kate can open this workbook and repeatedly use the macro stored there each month after she receives that month's sales data. She wants you to open the workbook containing data for Chicago's January sales and run the macro to format the data. You must leave the EX P-Monthly Sales workbook open to use the macro stored there.

4. **Open the file EX P-2.xlsx from the location where you store your Data Files, then save it as EX P-January Sales**

   This is the workbook containing the data you want to format.

5. **Press [Ctrl][Shift][F] to run the procedure**

   The FormatFile procedure formats the text, as shown in **FIGURE P-4**.

6. **Save the workbook**

   Now that you've successfully viewed and analyzed VBA code and run the macro, you will learn how to write your own code.

FIGURE P-3: VBA code for the FormatFile procedure

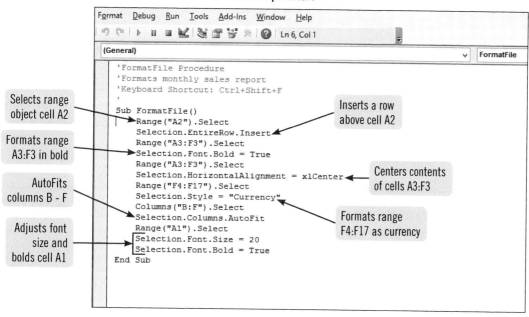

Format Debug Run Tools Add-Ins Window Help

Ln 6, Col 1

(General)   FormatFile

```
'FormatFile Procedure
'Formats monthly sales report
'Keyboard Shortcut: Ctrl+Shift+F
'
Sub FormatFile()
    Range("A2").Select
    Selection.EntireRow.Insert
    Range("A3:F3").Select
    Selection.Font.Bold = True
    Range("A3:F3").Select
    Selection.HorizontalAlignment = xlCenter
    Range("F4:F17").Select
    Selection.Style = "Currency"
    Columns("B:F").Select
    Selection.Columns.AutoFit
    Range("A1").Select
    Selection.Font.Size = 20
    Selection.Font.Bold = True
End Sub
```

- Selects range object cell A2
- Formats range A3:F3 in bold
- AutoFits columns B - F
- Adjusts font size and bolds cell A1
- Inserts a row above cell A2
- Centers contents of cells A3:F3
- Formats range F4:F17 as currency

FIGURE P-4: Worksheet formatted using the FormatFile procedure

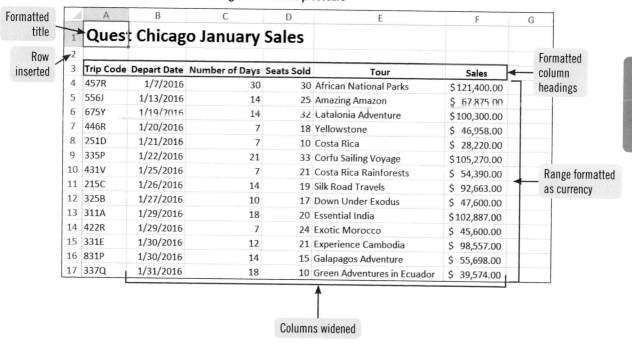

	A	B	C	D	E	F	G
1	**Quest Chicago January Sales**						
2							
3	**Trip Code**	**Depart Date**	**Number of Days**	**Seats Sold**	**Tour**	**Sales**	
4	457R	1/7/2016	30	30	African National Parks	$ 121,400.00	
5	556J	1/13/2016	14	25	Amazing Amazon	$ 67,875.00	
6	675Y	1/19/2016	14	32	Catalonia Adventure	$ 100,300.00	
7	446R	1/20/2016	7	18	Yellowstone	$ 46,958.00	
8	251D	1/21/2016	7	10	Costa Rica	$ 28,220.00	
9	335P	1/22/2016	21	33	Corfu Sailing Voyage	$ 105,270.00	
10	431V	1/25/2016	7	21	Costa Rica Rainforests	$ 54,390.00	
11	215C	1/26/2016	14	19	Silk Road Travels	$ 92,663.00	
12	325B	1/27/2016	10	17	Down Under Exodus	$ 47,600.00	
13	311A	1/29/2016	18	20	Essential India	$ 102,887.00	
14	422R	1/29/2016	7	24	Exotic Morocco	$ 45,600.00	
15	331E	1/30/2016	12	21	Experience Cambodia	$ 98,557.00	
16	831P	1/30/2016	14	15	Galapagos Adventure	$ 55,698.00	
17	337Q	1/31/2016	18	10	Green Adventures in Ecuador	$ 39,574.00	

- Formatted title
- Row inserted
- Formatted column headings
- Range formatted as currency
- Columns widened

Write VBA Code

Learning Outcomes
• Create a VBA module
• Enter VBA code

To write your own code, you first need to open the Visual Basic Editor and add a module to the workbook. You can then begin entering the procedure code. In the first few lines of a procedure, you typically include comments indicating the name of the procedure, a brief description of the procedure, and shortcut keys, if applicable. When writing Visual Basic code for Excel, you must follow the formatting rules, or **syntax**, of the VBA programming language. A misspelled keyword or variable name causes a procedure to fail. **CASE** ▶ *Kate would like to total the monthly sales. You help her by writing a procedure that automates this routine task.*

STEPS

TROUBLE
If the Code window is empty, verify that the workbook that contains your procedures (EX P-Monthly Sales) is open.

1. **With the January worksheet still displayed, click the** DEVELOPER **tab, then click the Visual Basic button in the Code group**

   Two projects are displayed in the Project Explorer window, EX P-Monthly Sales.xlsm (which contains the FormatFile macro) and EX P-January Sales.xlsx (which contains the monthly data). The FormatFile procedure is again displayed in the Visual Basic Editor. You may have other projects in the Project Explorer window.

2. **Click the** Modules folder **in the EX P-Monthly Sales.xlsm project**

   You need to store all of the procedures in the EX P-Monthly Sales.xlsm project, which is in the EX P-Monthly Sales.xlsm workbook. By clicking the Modules folder, you have activated the workbook, and the title bar changes from EX P-January Sales to EX P-Monthly Sales.

3. **Click** Insert **on the Visual Basic Editor menu bar, then click** Module

   A new, blank module with the default name Module1 appears in the EX P-Monthly Sales.xlsm project, under the Format module. You think the property name of the module could be more descriptive.

4. **Click (Name) in the Properties window, then type** Total

   The module name is Total. The module name should not be the same as the procedure name (which will be AddTotal). In the code shown in **FIGURE P-5**, comments begin with an apostrophe, and the lines of code under Sub AddTotal( ) have been indented using the Tab key. When you enter the code in the next step, after you type the procedure header Sub AddTotal( ) and press [Enter], the Visual Basic Editor automatically enters End Sub (the procedure footer) in the Code window.

TROUBLE
As you type, you may see words in drop-down lists. This optional feature is explained in the Clues to Use titled "Entering code using AutoComplete" on the next page. For now, just continue to type.

5. **Click in the** Code window, **then type the procedure code exactly as shown in** FIGURE P-5, **entering your name in the second line, pressing [Tab] to indent text and [Shift][Tab] to move the insertion point to the left**

   The lines that begin with ActiveCell.Formula insert the information enclosed in quotation marks into the active cell. For example, ActiveCell.Formula = "Monthly Total:" inserts the words "Monthly Total:" into cell E18, the active cell. As you type each line, Excel adjusts the spacing.

6. **Compare the procedure code you entered in the Code window with** FIGURE P-5, **make any corrections if necessary, then click the** Save EX P-Monthly Sales.xlsm button 🖫 **on the Visual Basic Editor toolbar**

7. **Click the** View Microsoft Excel button 🖾 **on the toolbar, click** EX P-January Sales.xlsx **on the taskbar to activate the workbook if necessary, with the January worksheet displayed click the** DEVELOPER **tab, then click the** Macros button **in the Code group**

   Macro names have two parts. The first part ('EX P-Monthly Sales.xlsm'!) indicates the workbook where the macro is stored. The second part (AddTotal or FormatFile) is the name of the procedure, taken from the procedure header.

TROUBLE
If an error message appears, click Debug. Click the Reset button ▣ on the toolbar, correct the error, then repeat Steps 6–8.

8. **Click** 'EX P-MonthlySales.xlsm'!AddTotal **to select it if necessary, then click** Run

   The AddTotal procedure inserts and formats the monthly total in cell F18, as shown in **FIGURE P-6**.

9. **Save the workbook**

FIGURE P-5: VBA code for the AddTotal procedure

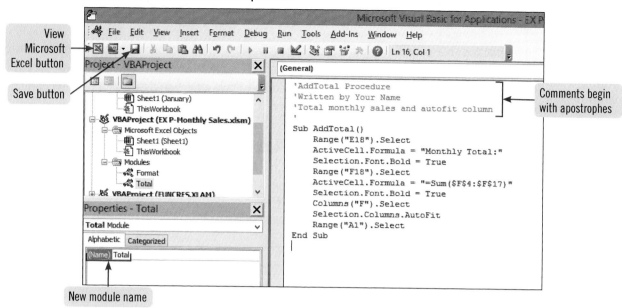

View Microsoft Excel button

Save button

New module name

Comments begin with apostrophes

```
'AddTotal Procedure
'Written by Your Name
'Total monthly sales and autofit column
'
Sub AddTotal()
    Range("E18").Select
    ActiveCell.Formula = "Monthly Total:"
    Selection.Font.Bold = True
    Range("F18").Select
    ActiveCell.Formula = "=Sum($F$4:$F$17)"
    Selection.Font.Bold = True
    Columns("F").Select
    Selection.Columns.AutoFit
    Range("A1").Select
End Sub
```

FIGURE P-6: Worksheet after running the AddTotal procedure

	A	B	C	D	E	F	G
1	Quest Chicago January Sales						
2							
3	Trip Code	Depart Date	Number of Days	Seats Sold	Tour	Sales	
4	457R	1/7/2016	30	30	African National Parks	$ 121,400.00	
5	556J	1/13/2016	14	25	Amazing Amazon	$ 67,875.00	
6	675Y	1/19/2016	14	32	Catalonia Adventure	$ 100,300.00	
7	446R	1/20/2016	7	18	Yellowstone	$ 46,958.00	
8	251D	1/21/2016	7	10	Costa Rica	$ 28,220.00	
9	335P	1/22/2016	21	33	Corfu Sailing Voyage	$ 105,270.00	
10	431V	1/25/2016	7	21	Costa Rica Rainforests	$ 54,390.00	
11	215C	1/26/2016	14	19	Silk Road Travels	$ 92,663.00	
12	325B	1/27/2016	10	17	Down Under Exodus	$ 47,600.00	
13	311A	1/29/2016	18	20	Essential India	$ 102,887.00	
14	422R	1/29/2016	7	24	Exotic Morocco	$ 45,600.00	
15	331E	1/30/2016	12	21	Experience Cambodia	$ 98,557.00	
16	831P	1/30/2016	14	15	Galapagos Adventure	$ 55,698.00	
17	337Q	1/31/2016	18	10	Green Adventures in Ecuador	$ 39,574.00	
18					Monthly Total:	$ 1,006,992.00	

Result of AddTotal procedure

Entering code using AutoComplete

To assist you in entering the VBA code, the Editor uses **AutoComplete**, a list of words that can be used in the macro statement and match what you type. The list usually appears after you press [.] (period). To include a word from the list in the macro statement, select the word in the list, then double-click it or press [Tab]. For example, to enter the Range("E12").Select instruction, type Range("E12"), then press [.] (period). Type s to bring up the words beginning with the letter "s", select the Select command in the list, then press [Tab] to enter the word "Select" in the macro statement.

Add a Conditional Statement

The formatting macros you entered in the previous lesson could have been created using the macro recorder. However, there are some situations where you cannot use the recorder and must type the VBA macro code, such as when you want a procedure to take an action based on a certain condition or set of conditions. One way of adding this type of conditional statement in Visual Basic is to use an **If...Then...Else statement**. For example, *if* a salesperson's performance rating is a 5 (top rating), *then* calculate a 10% bonus; otherwise (*else*), there is no bonus. The syntax for this statement is: "If *condition* Then *statements* Else [*else statements*]." The brackets indicate that the Else part of the statement is optional. **CASE** *Kate wants the worksheet to point out if the total sales figure meets or misses the $1,000,000 monthly quota. You use Excel to add a conditional statement that indicates this information. You start by returning to the Visual Basic Editor and inserting a new module in the Monthly Sales project.*

STEPS

1. With the January worksheet still displayed, click the DEVELOPER tab if necessary, then click the Visual Basic button in the Code group

2. Verify that the Total module in the Modules folder of the EX P-Monthly Sales VBAProject is selected in the Project Explorer window, click Insert on the Visual Basic Editor menu bar, then click Module

   A new, blank module named Module1 is inserted in the EX P-Monthly Sales workbook.

3. In the Properties window click (Name), then type Sales

4. Click in the Code window, then type the code exactly as shown in FIGURE P-7, entering your name in the second line

   Notice the green comment lines in the middle of the code. These lines help explain the procedure.

5. Compare the procedure you entered with FIGURE P-7, make any corrections if necessary, click the Save EX P-Monthly Sales.xlsm button 🖫 on the Visual Basic Editor toolbar, then click the View Microsoft Excel button 🗵 on the toolbar

6. If necessary, click EX P-January Sales.xlsx in the taskbar to display it, click the Macros button in the Code group, in the Macro dialog box click 'EX P-Monthly Sales.xlsm'!SalesStatus, then click Run

   The SalesStatus procedure indicates the status "Met Quota", as shown in FIGURE P-8.

7. Save the workbook

FIGURE P-7: VBA code for the SalesStatus procedure

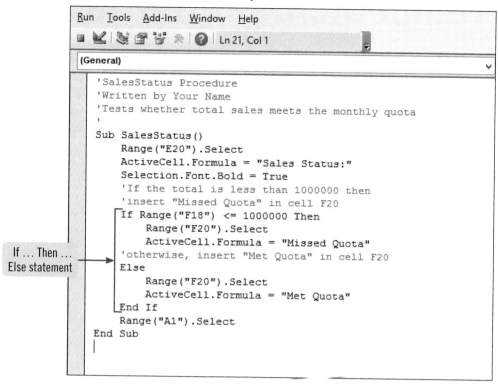

```
Run   Tools   Add-Ins   Window   Help

■ ☒ ☒ ☞ ☜ ☼ | ❓ | Ln 21, Col 1

(General)

'SalesStatus Procedure
'Written by Your Name
'Tests whether total sales meets the monthly quota
'
Sub SalesStatus()
    Range("E20").Select
    ActiveCell.Formula = "Sales Status:"
    Selection.Font.Bold = True
    'If the total is less than 1000000 then
    'insert "Missed Quota" in cell F20
    If Range("F18") <= 1000000 Then
        Range("F20").Select
        ActiveCell.Formula = "Missed Quota"
    'otherwise, insert "Met Quota" in cell F20
    Else
        Range("F20").Select
        ActiveCell.Formula = "Met Quota"
    End If
    Range("A1").Select
End Sub
```

If ... Then ... Else statement →

FIGURE P-8: Result of running the SalesStatus procedure

1 Quest Chicago January Sales

	Trip Code	Depart Date	Number of Days	Seats Sold	Tour	Sales
3	Trip Code	Depart Date	Number of Days	Seats Sold	Tour	Sales
4	457R	1/7/2016	30	30	African National Parks	$ 121,400.00
5	556J	1/13/2016	14	25	Amazing Amazon	$ 67,875.00
6	675Y	1/19/2016	14	32	Catalonia Adventure	$ 100,300.00
7	446R	1/20/2016	7	18	Yellowstone	$ 46,958.00
8	251D	1/21/2016	7	10	Costa Rica	$ 28,220.00
9	335P	1/22/2016	21	33	Corfu Sailing Voyage	$ 105,270.00
10	431V	1/25/2016	7	21	Costa Rica Rainforests	$ 54,390.00
11	215C	1/26/2016	14	19	Silk Road Travels	$ 92,663.00
12	325B	1/27/2016	10	17	Down Under Exodus	$ 47,600.00
13	311A	1/29/2016	18	20	Essential India	$ 102,887.00
14	422R	1/29/2016	7	24	Exotic Morocco	$ 45,600.00
15	331E	1/30/2016	12	21	Experience Cambodia	$ 98,557.00
16	831P	1/30/2016	14	15	Galapagos Adventure	$ 55,698.00
17	337Q	1/31/2016	18	10	Green Adventures in Ecuador	$ 39,574.00
18					Monthly Total:	$ 1,006,992.00
19						
20					Sales Status:	Met Quota
21						
22						

Indicates status of monthly total →

Prompt the User for Data

Another situation where you must type, not record, VBA code is when you need to pause a macro to allow user input. You use the VBA InputBox function to display a dialog box that prompts the user for information. A **function** is a predefined procedure that returns (creates and displays) a value; in this case the value returned is the information the user enters. The required elements of an InputBox function are as follows: *object*.InputBox(*"prompt"*), where *"prompt"* is the message that appears in the dialog box. For a detailed description of the InputBox function, use the Visual Basic Editor's Help menu. **CASE** *You decide to create a procedure that will insert the user's name in the left footer area of the worksheet. You use the InputBox function to display a dialog box in which the user can enter his or her name. You also type an intentional error into the procedure code, which you will correct in the next lesson.*

STEPS

1. **With the January worksheet displayed, click the DEVELOPER tab if necessary, click the Visual Basic button in the Code group, verify that the Sales module is selected in the EX P-Monthly Sales VBAProject Modules folder, click Insert on the Visual Basic Editor menu bar, then click Module**

   A new, blank module named Module1 is inserted in the EX P-Monthly Sales workbook.

2. **In the Properties window click (Name), then type Footer**

3. **Click in the Code window, then type the procedure code exactly as shown in FIGURE P-9 entering your name in the second line**

   Like the SalesStatus procedure, this procedure also contains comments that explain the code. The first part of the code, Dim LeftFooterText As String, **declares**, or defines, LeftFooterText as a text string variable. In Visual Basic, a **variable** is a location in memory in which you can temporarily store one item of information. Dim statements are used to declare variables and must be entered in the following format: Dim *variablename* As *datatype*. The datatype here is "string." In this case, you plan to store the information received from the input box in the temporary memory location called LeftFooterText. Then you can place this text in the left footer area. The remaining statements in the procedure are explained in the comment line directly above each statement. Notice the comment pointing out the error in the procedure code. You will correct this in the next lesson.

4. **Review your code, make any necessary changes, click the Save EX P-MonthlySales.xlsm button 🖫 on the Visual Basic Editor toolbar, then click the View Microsoft Excel button 🗷 on the toolbar**

5. **With the January worksheet displayed, click the Macros button in the Code group, in the Macro dialog box click 'EX P-Monthly Sales.xlsm'!FooterInput, then click Run**

   The procedure begins, and a dialog box generated by the InputBox function opens, prompting you to enter your name, as shown in FIGURE P-10.

6. **With the cursor in the text box, type your name, then click OK**

7. **Click the File tab, click Print, then view the worksheet preview**

   Although the customized footer with the date is inserted on the sheet, because of the error your name does *not* appear in the left section of the footer. In the next lesson, you will learn how to step through a procedure's code line by line. This will help you locate the error in the FooterInput procedure.

8. **Click the Back button ⊙, then save the workbook**

   You return to the January worksheet.

FIGURE P-9: VBA code for the FooterInput procedure

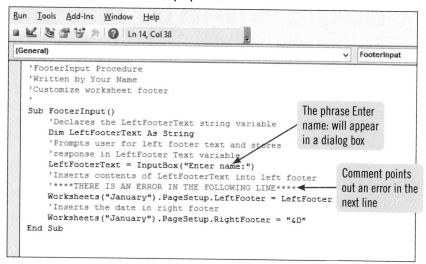

FIGURE P-10: InputBox function's dialog box

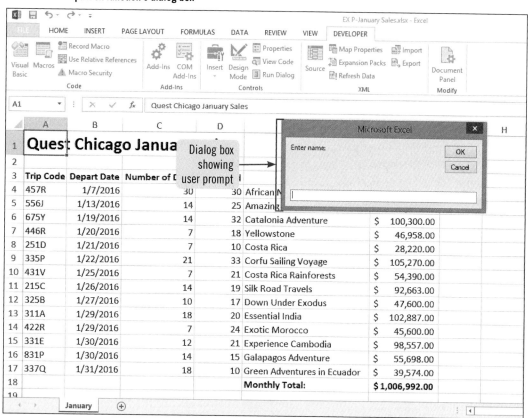

Naming variables

Variable names in VBA must begin with a letter. Letters can be uppercase or lowercase. Variable names cannot include periods or spaces, and they can be up to 255 characters long. Each variable name in a procedure must be unique. Examples of valid and invalid variable names are shown in **TABLE P-2**.

TABLE P-2: Variable names

valid	invalid
Sales_Department	Sales Department
SalesDepartment	Sales Department
Quarter1	1stQuarter

Debug a Macro

When a macro procedure does not run properly, it can be due to an error, referred to as a **bug**, in the code. To help you find the bug(s) in a procedure, the Visual Basic Editor lets you step through the procedure's code, one line at a time. When you locate the error, you can then correct, or **debug**, it. **CASE** *You decide to debug the macro procedure to find out why it failed to insert your name in the worksheet footer.*

STEPS

1. **With the January worksheet displayed, click the** DEVELOPER **tab if necessary, click the** Macros button **in the Code group, in the Macro dialog box click** 'EX P-Monthly Sales. xlsm'!FooterInput, **then click** Step Into

   The Visual Basic Editor opens with the yellow statement selector positioned on the first statement of the procedure, as shown in **FIGURE P-11**.

2. **Press [F8] to step to the next statement**

   The statement selector skips over the comments and the line of code beginning with Dim. The Dim statement indicates that the procedure will store your name in a variable named LeftFooterText. Because Dim is a declaration of a variable and not a procedure statement, the statement selector skips it and moves to the line containing the InputBox function.

3. **Press [F8] again, with the cursor in the text box in the Microsoft Excel dialog box type your name, then click** OK

   The Visual Basic Editor opens. The statement selector is now positioned on the statement that reads Worksheets("January").PageSetup.LeftFooter = LeftFooter. This statement should insert your name (which you just typed in the text box) in the left section of the footer. This is the instruction that does not appear to be working correctly.

4. **If necessary scroll right until the end of the LeftFooter instruction is visible, then place the mouse pointer on** LeftFooter

   The value of the LeftFooter variable is displayed as shown in **FIGURE P-12**. Rather than containing your name, the variable LeftFooter at the end of this line is empty. This is because the InputBox function assigned your name to the LeftFooterText variable, not to the LeftFooter variable. Before you can correct this bug, you need to turn off the Step Into feature.

5. **Click the** Reset button ▣ **on the Visual Basic Editor toolbar to turn off the Step Into feature, click at the end of the statement containing the error, then replace the variable** LeftFooter **with** LeftFooterText

   The revised statement now reads Worksheets("January").PageSetup.LeftFooter = LeftFooterText.

6. **Delete the comment line pointing out the error**

7. **Click the** Save EX P-Monthly Sales.xlsm button 🖫 **on the Visual Basic Editor toolbar, then click the** View Microsoft Excel button 🗷 **on the toolbar**

8. **With the January worksheet displayed click the** Macros button **in the Code group, in the Macro dialog box click** 'EX P-Monthly Sales.xlsm'!FooterInput, **click** Run **to rerun the procedure, when prompted type your name, then click** OK

9. **Click the** File tab, **click** Print, **then view the worksheet preview**

   Your name now appears in the left section of the footer.

10. **Click the** Back button ⊙, **then save the workbook**

FIGURE P-11: Statement selector positioned on first procedure statement

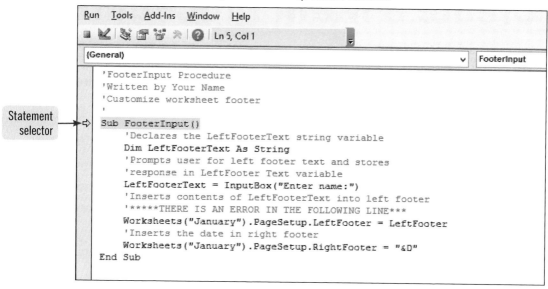

FIGURE P-12: Value contained in LeftFooter variable

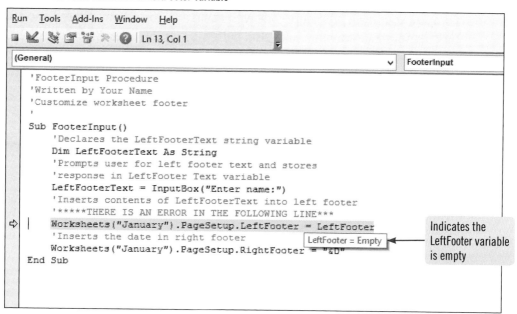

Adding security to your macro projects

To add security to your projects, you can add a digital signature to the project. A digital signature guarantees the project hasn't been altered since it was signed. Sign macros only after you have tested them and are ready to distribute them. If the code in a digitally signed macro project is changed in any way, its digital signature is removed. To add a digital signature to a Visual Basic project, select the project that you want to sign in the Visual Basic Project Explorer window, click the Tools menu in the Visual Basic Editor, click Digital Signature, click Choose, select the certificate, then click OK twice. When you add a digital signature to a project, the macro project is automatically re-signed whenever it is saved on your computer. You can get a digital certificate from your administrator. There are also third-party certification authorities that issue certificates that are trusted by Microsoft.

Excel 2013

Create a Main Procedure

When you routinely need to run several macros one after another, you can save time by combining them into one procedure. The resulting procedure, which processes (or runs) multiple procedures in sequence, is referred to as the **main procedure**. To create a main procedure, you type a **Call statement** for each procedure you want to run. The syntax of the Call statement is Call *procedurename*, where *procedurename* is the name of the procedure you want to run. **CASE** ▶ *To avoid having to run her macros one after another every month, Kate asks you to create a main procedure that will run (or call) each of the procedures in the EX P-Monthly Sales workbook in sequence.*

STEPS

1. **With the January worksheet displayed, click the DEVELOPER tab if necessary, then click the Visual Basic button in the Code group**

2. **Verify that EX P-Monthly Sales is the active project, click Insert on the menu bar, then click Module**

   A new, blank module named Module1 is inserted in the EX P-Monthly Sales workbook.

3. **In the Properties window click (Name), then type MainProc**

4. **In the Code window enter the procedure code exactly as shown in FIGURE P-13, entering your name in the second line**

5. **Compare your main procedure code with FIGURE P-13, correct any errors if necessary, then click the Save EX P-Monthly Sales.xlsm button 🖫 on the Visual Basic Editor toolbar**

   To test the new main procedure, you need an unformatted version of the EX P-January Sales worksheet.

6. **Click the View Microsoft Excel button 🖾 on the toolbar, then save and close the EX P-January Sales workbook**

   The EX P-Monthly Sales workbook remains open.

7. **Open the file EX P-2.xlsx from the location where you store your Data Files, then save it as EX P-January Sales 2**

   In the next lesson, you'll run the main procedure.

Copying a macro to another workbook

If you would like to use a macro in another workbook, you can copy the module to that workbook using the Visual Basic Editor. Open both the source and destination Excel workbooks, then open the Visual Basic Editor and verify that macros are enabled. In Project Explorer, drag the module that will be copied from the source workbook to the destination workbook.

FIGURE P-13: VBA code for the MainProcedure procedure

```
'MainProcedure Procedure
'Written by Your Name
'Calls sub procedures in sequence
'
Sub MainProcedure()
    Call FormatFile
    Call AddTotal
    Call SalesStatus
    Call FooterInput
End Sub
```

MainProcedure calls each procedure in the order shown

Writing and documenting VBA code

When you write VBA code in the Visual Basic Editor, you want to make it as readable as possible. This makes it easier for you or your coworkers to edit the code when changes need to be made. The procedure statements should be indented, leaving the procedure name and its End statement easy to spot in the code. This is helpful when a module contains many procedures. It is also good practice to add comments at the beginning of each procedure that describe its purpose and any assumptions made in the procedure, such as the quota amounts. You should also explain each code statement with a comment. You have seen comments inserted into VBA code by beginning the statement with an apostrophe. You can also add comments to the end of a line of VBA code by placing an apostrophe before the comment, as shown in FIGURE P-14.

FIGURE P-14: VBA code with comments at the end of statements

Run   Tools   Add-Ins   Window   Help

Ln 10, Col 8

(General)   MainProcedure

```
'MainProcedure Procedure
'Written by Your Name
'Calls sub procedures in sequence
'
Sub MainProcedure()
    Call FormatFile 'Run FormatFile procedure
    Call AddTotal   'Run AddTotal procedure
    Call SalesStatus  'Run SalesStatus procedure
    Call FooterInput  'Run FooterInput procedure
End Sub
```

Comments at the end of the statements in green

Run a Main Procedure

Running a main procedure allows you to run several macros in sequence. You can run a main procedure just as you would any other macro procedure. **CASE** ▸ *You have finished creating Kate's main procedure, and you are ready to run it. If the main procedure works correctly, it should format the worksheet, insert the sales total, insert a sales status message, and add your name and date to the worksheet footer.*

STEPS

TROUBLE
If an error message
appears, click
Debug, click the
Reset button ▪
on the toolbar, then
correct your error.

1. **With the January worksheet displayed, click the DEVELOPER tab, click the Macros button in the Code group, in the Macro dialog box click 'EX P-Monthly Sales.xlsm'!MainProcedure, click Run, when prompted type your name, then click OK**

   The MainProcedure runs the FormatFile, AddTotal, SalesStatus, and FooterInput procedures in sequence. You can see the results of the FormatFile, AddTotal, and SalesStatus procedures in the worksheet window, as shown in **FIGURE P-16**. To view the results of the FooterInput procedure, you need to switch to the Preview window.

2. **Click the File tab, click Print, view the worksheet preview and verify that your name appears in the left footer area and the date appears in the right footer area, click the Back button ⬅, then click the DEVELOPER tab**

3. **Click the Visual Basic button in the Code group**

   You need to add your name to the Format module.

4. **In the Project Explorer window, double-click the Format module, add a comment line after the procedure name that reads Written by [Your Name], then click the Save EX P-Monthly Sales.xlsm button 🖫**

   You want to see the options for printing VBA code.

QUICK TIP
When you complete
your work with
macros, you should
disable macros to
prevent macros
containing viruses
from running on
your computer. To
disable macros, click
the DEVELOPER tab,
click the Macro
Security button in
the Code group, click
one of the Disable all
macros options, then
click OK.

5. **Click File on the Visual Basic Editor menu bar, then click Print**

   The Print - VBAProject dialog box opens, as shown in **FIGURE P-17**. The Current Module is selected which will print each procedure separately. It is faster to print all the procedures in the workbook at one time by clicking the Current Project option button to select it. You can also create a file of the VBA code by selecting the Print to File check box. You do not want to print the modules at this time.

6. **Click Cancel in the Print - VBAProject dialog box**

7. **Click the View Microsoft Excel button 🗵 on the toolbar**

8. **Save the EX P-January Sales 2 workbook, then preview the worksheet**

   Compare your formatted worksheet to **FIGURE P-18**.

9. **Close the EX P-January Sales 2 workbook, close the EX P-Monthly Sales workbook, then exit Excel**

Running a macro using a button

You can run a macro by assigning it to a button on your worksheet. Create a button by clicking the Insert tab, clicking the Shapes button in the Illustrations group, choosing a shape, then drawing the shape on the worksheet. After you create the button, right-click it, click Assign Macro, then click the macro the button will run and click OK. It is a good idea to label the button with descriptive text; select it and begin typing. You can also format macro buttons using clip art, photographs, fills, and shadows. You format a button using the buttons on the DRAWING TOOLS FORMAT tab. To add a fill to the button, click the Shape Fill list arrow and select a fill color,

picture, texture, or gradient. To add a shape effect, click the Shape Effects button and select an effect. You can also use the WordArt styles in the WordArt Styles group. **FIGURE P-15** shows a button formatted with a gradient, bevel and WordArt.

FIGURE P-15: Formatted macro button

FIGURE P-16: Result of running MainProcedure procedure

Formatted title

Row inserted

1	**Quest Chicago January Sales**					
2						
3	Trip Code	Depart Date	Number of Days	Seats Sold	Tour	Sales
4	457R	1/7/2016	30	30	African National Parks	$ 121,400.00
5	556J	1/13/2016	14	25	Amazing Amazon	$ 67,875.00
6	675Y	1/19/2016	14	32	Catalonia Adventure	$ 100,300.00
7	446R	1/20/2016	7	18	Yellowstone	$ 46,958.00
8	251D	1/21/2016	7	10	Costa Rica	$ 28,220.00
9	335P	1/22/2016	21	33	Corfu Sailing Voyage	$ 105,270.00
10	431V	1/25/2016	7	21	Costa Rica Rainforests	$ 54,390.00
11	215C	1/26/2016	14	19	Silk Road Travels	$ 92,663.00
12	325B	1/27/2016	10	17	Down Under Exodus	$ 47,600.00
13	311A	1/29/2016	18	20	Essential India	$ 102,887.00
14	422R	1/29/2016	7	24	Exotic Morocco	$ 45,600.00
15	331E	1/30/2016	12	21	Experience Cambodia	$ 98,557.00
16	831P	1/30/2016	14	15	Galapagos Adventure	$ 55,698.00
17	337Q	1/31/2016	18	10	Green Adventures in Ecuador	$ 39,574.00
18					Monthly Total:	$ 1,006,992.00
19						
20					Sales Status:	Met Quota
21						

Total sales calculated

Sales status message inserted

FIGURE P-17: Printing options for macro procedures

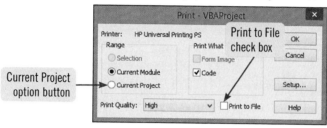

Current Project option button

Print to File check box

FIGURE P-18: Formatted January worksheet

Quest Chicago January Sales

Trip Code	Depart Date	Number of Days	Seats Sold	Tour	Sales
457R	1/7/2016	30	30	African National Parks	$ 121,400.00
556J	1/13/2016	14	25	Amazing Amazon	$ 67,875.00
675Y	1/19/2016	14	32	Catalonia Adventure	$ 100,300.00
446R	1/20/2016	7	18	Yellowstone	$ 46,958.00
251D	1/21/2016	7	10	Costa Rica	$ 28,220.00
335P	1/22/2016	21	33	Corfu Sailing Voyage	$ 105,270.00
431V	1/25/2016	7	21	Costa Rica Rainforests	$ 54,390.00
215C	1/26/2016	14	19	Silk Road Travels	$ 92,663.00
325B	1/27/2016	10	17	Down Under Exodus	$ 47,600.00
311A	1/29/2016	18	20	Essential India	$ 102,887.00
422R	1/29/2016	7	24	Exotic Morocco	$ 45,600.00
331E	1/30/2016	12	21	Experience Cambodia	$ 98,557.00
831P	1/30/2016	14	15	Galapagos Adventure	$ 55,698.00
337Q	1/31/2016	18	10	Green Adventures in Ecuador	$ 39,574.00
				Monthly Total:	$ 1,006,992.00
				Sales Status:	Met Quota

Your Name

11/30/2016

Practice

Concepts Review

1. Which element do you click to return to Excel from the Visual Basic Editor?
2. Which element points to the Project Explorer window?
3. Which element points to the Code window?
4. Which element do you click to turn off the Step Into feature?
5. Which element points to comments in the VBA code?

FIGURE P-19

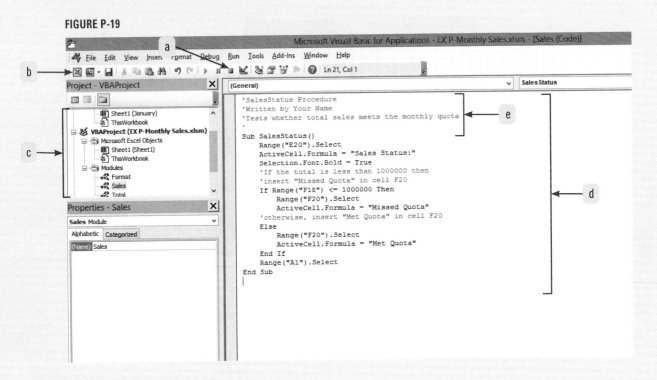

Match each term with the statement that best describes it.

6. **Sub procedure**

7. **Function**

8. **Keywords**

9. **Procedure**

10. **Comments**

a. Another term for a macro in Visual Basic for Applications (VBA)

b. A procedure that returns a value

c. Words that are recognized as part of the programming language

d. A series of statements that perform an action but don't return a value

e. Descriptive text used to explain parts of a procedure

Select the best answer from the list of choices.

11. **A location in memory where you can temporarily store information is a:**
   a. Variable.
   b. Procedure.
   c. Sub procedure.
   d. Function.

12. **You enter the statements of a macro in:**
   a. The Macro dialog box.
   b. Any blank worksheet.
   c. The Properties window of the Visual Basic Editor.
   d. The Code window of the Visual Basic Editor.

13. **If your macro doesn't run correctly, you should:**
   a. Select the macro in the Macro dialog box, click Step Into, then debug the macro.
   b. Create an If...Then...Else statement.
   c. Click the Project Explorer button.
   d. Click the Properties button.

14. **Comments are displayed in _____ in VBA code.**
   a. Black
   b. Blue
   c. Red
   d. Green

15. **Keywords are displayed in _____ in VBA code.**
   a. Black
   b. Blue
   c. Green
   d. Red

Skills Review

1. **View and analyze VBA code.**
   a. Start Excel, open the file EX P-3.xlsm from the location where you store your Data Files, enable macros, then save it as **EX P-Home Products**.
   b. Review the unformatted December worksheet.
   c. Open the Visual Basic Editor.
   d. Select the DataFormat module, and review the Format procedure.
   e. Insert comments in the procedure code describing what action you think each line of code will perform. (*Hint*: One of the statements will sort the list by Store #.) Add comment lines to the top of the procedure to describe the purpose of the macro and to enter your name.
   f. Save the macro, return to the worksheet, then run the Format macro.
   g. Compare the results with the code and your comments.
   h. Save the workbook.

2. **Write VBA code.**
   a. Open the Visual Basic Editor, and insert a new module named **Total** in the EX P-Home Products project.
   b. Enter the code for the SalesTotal procedure exactly as shown in **FIGURE P-20**. Enter your name in the second line.
   c. Save the macro.
   d. Return to the December worksheet, then run the SalesTotal macro.
   e. Save the workbook.

FIGURE P-20

```
'SalesTotal Procedure
'Written by Your Name
'Totals December sales
Sub SalesTotal()
    Range("E17").Select
    ActiveCell.Formula = "=SUM($E$3:$E$16)"
    Selection.Font.Bold = True
    With Selection.Borders(xlTop)
        .LineStyle = xlSingle
    End With
    Columns("E").Select
    Selection.Columns.AutoFit
    Range("A1").Select
End Sub
```

Skills Review (continued)

3. Add a conditional statement

a. Open the Visual Basic Editor, and insert a new module named **Goal** in the EX P-Home Products project.

b. Enter the SalesGoal procedure exactly as shown in **FIGURE P-21**. Enter your name on the second line.

c. Save the macro.

d. Return to the December worksheet, and run the SalesGoal macro. The procedure should enter the message **Missed goal** in cell E18. Save the workbook.

FIGURE P-21

```
'SalesGoal Procedure
'Written by Your Name
'Tests whether sales goal was met
Sub SalesGoal()
    'If the total is >=100000, then insert "Met Goal"
    'in cell E18
    If Range("E17") >= 100000 Then
        Range("E18").Select
        ActiveCell.Formula = "Met goal"
    'otherwise, insert "Missed goal" in cell E18
    Else
        Range("E18").Select
        ActiveCell.Formula = "Missed goal"
    End If
    Range("A1").Select
End Sub
```

4. Prompt the user for data.

a. Open the Visual Basic Editor, and insert a new module named **Header** in the EX P-Home Products project.

b. Enter the HeaderFooter procedure exactly as shown in **FIGURE P-22**. You are entering an error in the procedure that will be corrected in Step 5.

c. Save the macro, then return to the December worksheet, and run the HeaderFooter macro.

d. Preview the December worksheet. Your name should be missing from the left section of the footer.

e. Save the workbook.

FIGURE P-22

```
'HeaderFooter Procedure
'Written by Your Name
'Procedure to customize the header and footer
Sub HeaderFooter()
    'Inserts the filename in the header
    Worksheets("December").PageSetup.CenterHeader = "&F"
    'Declares the variable LeftFooterText as a string
    Dim LeftFooterText As String
    'Prompts user for left footer text
    LeftFooter = InputBox("Enter your full name:")
    'Inserts response into left footer
    Worksheets("December").PageSetup.LeftFooter = LeftFooterText
    'Inserts the date into right footer
    Worksheets("December").PageSetup.RightFooter = "&D"
End Sub
```

5. Debug a macro.

a. Return to the Visual Basic Editor and use the Step Into feature to locate where the error occurred in the HeaderFooter procedure. Use the Reset button to turn off the debugger.

b. Edit the procedure in the Visual Basic Editor to correct the error. (*Hint*: The error occurs on the line: LeftFooter = InputBox("Enter your full name:"). The variable that will input the response text into the worksheet footer is LeftFooterText. The line should be: LeftFooterText = InputBox("Enter your full name:").)

c. Save the macro, then return to the December worksheet, and run the HeaderFooter macro again.

d. Verify that your name now appears in the left section of the footer, then save the file.

6. Create and run a main procedure.

a. Return to the Visual Basic Editor, insert a new module, then name it **MainProc**.

b. Begin the main procedure by entering comments in the code window that provide the procedure's name (MainProcedure) and explain that its purpose is to run the Format, SalesTotal, SalesGoal, and HeaderFooter procedures. Enter your name in a comment.

c. Enter the procedure header **Sub MainProcedure()**.

d. Enter four Call statements that will run the Format, SalesTotal, SalesGoal, and HeaderFooter procedures in sequence.

e. Save the procedure and return to Excel.

f. Open the file EX P-3.xlsm, then save it as **EX P-Home Products 2**.

g. Run the MainProcedure macro, entering your name when prompted. (*Hint*: In the Macro dialog box, the macro procedures you created will now have EX P-Home Products.xlsm! as part of their names. This is because the macros are stored in the EX P-Home Products workbook, not in the EX P-Home Products 2 workbook.)

Skills Review (continued)

h. Verify that the macro ran successfully by comparing your worksheet to **FIGURE P-23**.

i. Save the EX P-Home Products 2 workbook, preview the December worksheet to check the header and footer, then close the EX P-Home Products 2 workbook.

j. Save the EX P-Home Products workbook, close the workbook, exit Excel, then submit the EX P-Home Products workbook to your instructor.

FIGURE P-23

	A	B	C	D	E
1	Home Products December Sales				
2	Store #	City	State	Manager	Sales
3	11405	Juno	FL	Clifford	$ 8,645.93
4	19404	Palm Beach	FL	Cloutier	$ 8,656.83
5	29393	Tampa	FL	Nelson	$ 7,654.32
6	29396	Cape Coral	FL	Enos	$ 9,583.66
7	29399	Daytona	FL	DiBenedetto	$ 9,228.33
8	29402	Vero Beach	FL	Guapo	$ 5,534.34
9	29406	Miami	FL	Monroe	$ 4,987.36
10	39394	Naples	FL	Hamm	$ 6,715.68
11	39395	Bonita Springs	FL	Handelmann	$ 4,225.22
12	39397	Clearwater	FL	Erickson	$ 7,594.22
13	39398	Delray Beach	FL	Dever	$ 8,442.90
14	39400	Stuart	FL	Hahn	$ 8,001.34
15	39401	Neptune	FL	Pratt	$ 5,251.22
16	39403	Sanibel	FL	Lo	$ 4,643.93
17					$99,165.28
18					Missed goal
19					

Independent Challenge 1

You are the development director at a private school. The information systems manager asks you to document and test an Excel procedure that the previous director wrote for the school's accountant. You will first run the macro procedure to see what it does, then add comments to the VBA code to document it. You will also enter data to verify that the formulas in the macro work correctly.

a. Start Excel, open the file EX P-4.xlsm from the location where you store your Data Files, then save it as **EX P-First Quarter**.

b. Run the First macro, noting anything that you think should be mentioned in your documentation.

c. Review the First procedure in the Visual Basic Editor. It is stored in the FirstQtr module.

d. Document the procedure by adding comments to the code, indicating the actions the procedure performs and the objects (ranges) that are affected.

e. Enter your name in a comment line, then save the procedure.

f. Return to the Jan-Mar worksheet, and use **FIGURE P-24** as a guide to enter data in cells B4:D6. The totals will appear as you enter the income data.

g. Format the range B4:D8 using the Accounting Number format with no decimals, as shown in **FIGURE P-24**.

h. Check the total income calculations in row 8 to verify that the macro is working correctly.

i. Enter your name in the center section of the Jan-Mar sheet footer, save the workbook, then preview the worksheet.

j. Close the workbook, exit Excel, then submit the workbook to your instructor.

FIGURE P-24

	A	B	C	D	E
1		January	February	March	
2	Income				
3					
4	Donations	$ 1,700	$ 1,700	$ 1,500	
5	Fundraisers	$ 3,000	$ 2,100	$ 2,700	
6	Grants	$ 21,000	$ 51,000	$ 92,000	
7					
8	Total Income	$ 25,700	$ 54,800	$ 96,200	
9					

Independent Challenge 2

You work in the Miami branch of Medical Resources, a medical employment recruitment agency. You have three locations where you have monthly quotas for placements. Each month you are required to produce a report stating whether placement quotas were met for the following three medical facilities: Central Hospital, Shore Clinic, and Assisted Home. The quotas for each month are as follows: Central Hospital 12, Shore Clinic 8, and Assisted Home 5. Your placement results this month were 8, 9, and 6, respectively. You decide to create a procedure to automate your monthly task of determining the placement quota status for the placement categories. You would like your assistant to take this task over when you go on vacation next month. Because he has no previous experience with Excel, you decide to create a second procedure that prompts a user with input boxes to enter the actual placement results for the month.

a. Start Excel, open the file EX P-5.xlsm from the location where you store your Data Files, then save it as **EX P-Placements**.

Independent Challenge 2 (continued)

b. Use the Visual Basic Editor to insert a new module named **Quotas** in the EX P-Placements workbook. Create a procedure in the new module named **PlacementQuota** that determines the quota status for each category and enters Yes or No in the Status column. The VBA code is shown in **FIGURE P-25**.

c. Add comments to the PlacementQuota procedure, including the procedure name, your name, and the purpose of the procedure, then save it.

d. Insert a new module named **MonthlyPlacement**. Create a second procedure named **Placement** that prompts a user for placement data for each placement category, enters the input data in the appropriate cells, then calls the PlacementQuota procedure. The VBA code is shown in **FIGURE P-26**. (*Hint*: The procedure's blank lines group the macro code in related units. These blank lines are optional and their purpose is to make the procedure easier to understand.)

e. Add a comment noting the procedure name on the first line. Add a comment with your name on the second line. Add a third comment line at the top of the procedure describing its purpose. Enter comments in the code to document the macro actions. Save the procedure.

f. Run the Placement macro, and enter **8** for hospital placement, **9** for clinic placements, and **6** for assisted placements. Correct any errors in the VBA code.

g. Add your name to the center section of the worksheet footer, save the workbook, then preview the worksheet. Close the workbook, exit Excel, then submit your workbook to your instructor.

FIGURE P-25

```
Sub PlacementQuota()

    If Range("C4") >= 12 Then
        Range("D4").Select
        ActiveCell.Formula = "Yes"
    Else
        Range("D4").Select
        ActiveCell.Formula = "No"
    End If

    If Range("C5") >= 8 Then
        Range("D5").Select
        ActiveCell.Formula = "Yes"
    Else
        Range("D5").Select
        ActiveCell.Formula = "No"
    End If

    If Range("C6") >= 5 Then
        Range("D6").Select
        ActiveCell.Formula = "Yes"
    Else
        Range("D6").Select
        ActiveCell.Formula = "No"
    End If

End Sub
```

FIGURE P-26

```
Sub Placement()

    Dim Hospital As String
    Hospital = InputBox("Enter Hospital Placements")
    Range("C4").Select
    Selection = Hospital

    Dim Clinic As String
    Clinic = InputBox("Enter Clinic Placements")
    Range("C5").Select
    Selection = Clinic

    Dim Assisted As String
    Assisted = InputBox("Enter Assisted Placements")
    Range("C6").Select
    Selection = Assisted

    Call PlacementQuota

End Sub
```

Independent Challenge 3

You are the marketing director at a car dealership business based in Cincinnati. You have started to advertise using an area magazine, billboards, TV, radio, and local newspapers. Every month you prepare a report with the advertising expenses detailed by source. You decide to create a macro that will format the monthly reports. You add the same footers on every report, so you will create another macro that will add a footer to a document. Finally, you will create a main procedure that calls the macros to format the report and adds a footer. You begin by opening a workbook with the January data. You will save the macros you create in this workbook.

a. Start Excel, open the file EX P-6.xlsm from the location where you store your Data Files, then save it as **EX P-Auto**.

b. Insert a module named **Format**, then create a procedure named **Formatting** that:

- Selects a cell in row 3, and inserts a row in the worksheet above it.
- Selects the cost data in column C, and formats it as currency. (*Hint*: After the row is inserted, this range is C5:C9.)
- Selects cell A1 before ending.

c. Save the Formatting procedure.

d. Insert a module named **Foot**, then create a procedure named **Footer** that:

- Declares a string variable for text that will be placed in the left footer.
- Uses an input box to prompt the user for his or her name, and places the name in the left footer.
- Places the date in the right footer.

Independent Challenge 3 (continued)

e. Save the Footer procedure.

f. Insert a module named **Main**, then create a procedure named **MainProc** that calls the Footer procedure and the Formatting procedure.

g. Save your work, then run the MainProc procedure. Debug each procedure as necessary. Your worksheet should look like **FIGURE P-27**.

h. Document each procedure by inserting a comment line with the procedure name, your name, and a description of the procedure.

i. Preview the January worksheet, save the workbook, close the workbook, exit Excel, then submit the workbook to your instructor.

FIGURE P-27

	A	B	C	D
1	Cincinnati Auto			
2	Ad Campaign			
3				
4	**Advertising Type**	**Source**	**Cost**	
5	Magazine	Ohio Magazine	$ 350.00	
6	Newspaper	Tribune	$ 150.00	
7	Billboard	Main Street	$ 450.00	
8	TV	Local Access Station	$ 170.00	
9	Radio	WAQV	$ 575.00	
10				

Independent Challenge 4: Explore

You decide to create a log of your monthly expenses in an effort to budget your income. You have received a workbook with a macro that tracks your major expenses for the first three months of the year. You want to expand this macro to track six months of expenses.

a. Start Excel, open the file EX P-7.xlsm from the location where you store your Data Files, then save it as **EX P-Expenses**.

b. Run the MonthExpenses macro and enter expense numbers to verify the macro is working properly, then clear all the expense entries in cells E2:E7.

c. Edit the MonthExpenses procedure to add the abbreviated month entries of Apr, May, and Jun. Remember to edit the selected cells, total cells and the formatting ranges in the procedure.

d. Run the macro and debug the procedure as necessary. Enter expense numbers to verify the macro is working properly. Widen columns where necessary.

e. Save your work.

f. Verify that the totals are correct for each month and each category.

g. Enter your name as a comment in the second line of the procedure, then save the procedure.

h. Change the page orientation to landscape, enter your name in the center section of the worksheet footer, then preview the worksheet.

i. Insert a module named **Preview** with a procedure named **PreviewSheetdata** that previews a worksheet. The VBA code is shown in **FIGURE P-28**.

j. Save the macro and return to the worksheet.

k. Assign the macro PreviewSheetdata to a button on the worksheet. (*Hint*: Use the Rectangle tool to create the button, label the button **Print Preview**, then right-click the button to assign the macro.)

l. Format the button and its label with a style of your choice.

m. Test the button, then close the Print Preview.

n. Save the workbook, close the workbook, exit Excel, then submit the workbook to your instructor.

FIGURE P-28

```
Sub PreviewSheetdata()

ActiveSheet.PrintPreview

End Sub
```

Visual Workshop

Open the file EX P-8.xlsm from the location where you store your Data Files, then save it as **EX P-Florist**. Create a macro procedure named **Formatting** in a module named **FormatFile** that will format the worksheet as shown in **FIGURE P-29**. (*Hints*: The font size of the first two rows is 12 pt and the other rows are 11 pt. Notice that there is an added row.) Run the macro and debug it as necessary to make the worksheet match **FIGURE P-29**. Insert your name in a comment line under the procedure name and in the worksheet footer, then preview the worksheet. Submit the workbook to your instructor.

FIGURE P-29

	A	B	C
1	Blossoms		
2	Monthly Sales		
3			
4	Flowers	$857.89	
5	Plants	$622.87	
6	Silks	$424.58	
7	Home Décor	$469.88	
8			
9			

Importing and Exporting Data

CASE At Quest Specialty Travel, Jacob Thomas, director of staff development, has asked you to develop an Access database that tracks professional staff continuing education. First, you will explore the Access templates for creating a new database. Then, you will work with Access tools that allow you to share Access data with other software programs so that each Quest department can have the necessary data in a format they can use.

Unit Objectives

After completing this unit, you will be able to:

- Use database templates
- Use Application Parts
- Import data from Excel
- Link data

- Export data to Excel
- Publish data to Word
- Merge data with Word
- Export data to PDF

Files You Will Need

Education-I.accdb	Vendors.xlsx
DepartmentData.xlsx	Basketball-I.accdb
CourseMaterials.xlsx	2015-2016Schedule.xlsx
Machinery-I.accdb	Languages-I.accdb
MachineryEmp.xlsx	

Use Database Templates

Learning
Outcomes
• Create a database
  from a template
• Set a startup form

A **database template** is a tool that you use to quickly create a new database based on a particular subject, such as assets, contacts, events, or projects. When you install Access 2013 on your computer, Microsoft provides many database templates for you to use. Additional templates are available from Microsoft Office Online, where they are organized by category, such as business, personal, and education. **CASE** ▸ *Jacob Thomas, director of staff development, asks you to develop a new Access database to track the continuing education of Quest employees. You explore Microsoft database templates to fill this request.*

STEPS

QUICK TIP
Database templates
are also called
database wizards.

1. **Start Access 2013**

   As shown in **FIGURE I-1**, Microsoft provides many Web and desktop database templates to help you create a new database. A custom **Web app** is an Access database that you publish to a Web server so that it is available to users who work with a browser over the Internet. Web apps will be covered in Unit P.

   A **desktop database** is a traditional Access database available to users who work with Access on their computers over a local area network and is identified by the word *desktop* in the template name. All templates are **online**, meaning they are available to download from the Microsoft Office Online Web site. Templates change over time as more are added and enhancements to existing templates are provided by Microsoft. The database you want to create should track employees and the continuing education courses they have completed, so you search for database templates using Education as the search phrase.

QUICK TIP
To review the video
later, open the
Getting Started form.

2. **Click the Search for online templates box, type education, click the Start searching button ⌕ , then double-click the Desktop student database**

   The Desktop student database template builds a new database that includes several sample tables, queries, forms, reports, macros, and a module object. You can use or modify these objects to meet your needs.

QUICK TIP
When using a
template, the
database is created
in the default file
location shown in
the title bar.

3. **Click the Enable Content button (if it is presented), then close the Getting Started window to explore the actual database, as shown in FIGURE I-2**

   The Student List form opens automatically, and the other objects in the database are presented in the Navigation Pane.

4. **Right-click the Student List form tab, click Close, then double-click the Student Details form in the Navigation Pane**

   Objects created by database templates are rich in functionality and can be modified for your specific needs or analyzed to learn more about Access.

5. **Close the Student Details form, then double-click the Guardian Details form to open it**

   If you wanted to use this database, your next step would be to enter data and continue exploring the other objects in the database.

6. **Close the Guardian Details form, then open, explore, and close the other objects of the Desktop student database**

   Because this database is designed for a traditional school rather than a corporate educational environment, you won't be using it at Quest. However, you can still learn a great deal by exploring the objects that the template created. You will also keep using this sample database to learn about Application Parts.

FIGURE I-1: **Creating a database from a template**

FIGURE I-1: **Creating a database from a template**

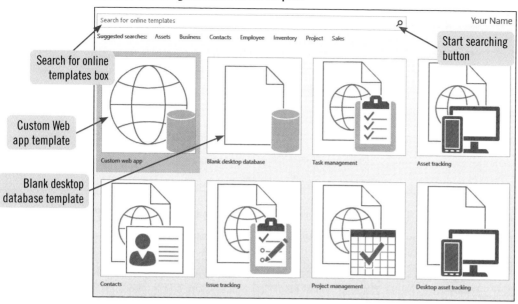

FIGURE I-2: **Desktop student database template**

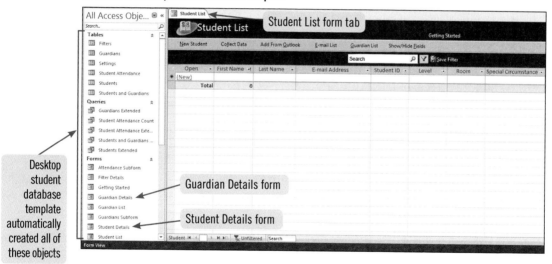

Setting a startup form

To specify that a particular form automatically opens when the database opens, click the FILE tab, click Options, then click the Current Database category in the Access Options dialog box. Use the Display Form drop-down list to specify which form should automatically open when the database is started. Another way to set startup options is to create an AutoExec macro. Macros will be covered in Unit M.

Use Application Parts

Application Parts are object templates that create objects such as tables and forms. Application Parts include several table, form, and report templates, tools you can use to quickly create these individual objects within an existing database. As with database templates, Microsoft is constantly updating and improving this part of Access. **CASE** ▶ *You continue your study of templates by exploring the Access 2013 Application Parts in the new database.*

STEPS

1. **Click the CREATE tab, then click the Application Parts button, as shown in FIGURE I-3, click Contacts, click the There is no relationship option button, click Create, then close the Getting Started window**

   The Contacts Application Part created a new table named Contacts; a new query named ContactsExtended; three new forms named ContactDetails, ContactDS, and ContactList; and four new reports named ContactAddressBook, ContactList, ContactPhoneBook, and Label that you can modify and relate to the other tables in the database as needed.

   Anytime you create a database or objects using Access templates, it's a good practice to check the Relationships window to make sure the objects are related correctly and that you understand the relationships.

2. **Close the Student List form, click the DATABASE TOOLS tab, then click the Relationships button**

   The Desktop student database template did not create relationships between the tables. You'll connect four of the main tables.

3. **Double-click Guardians, Students and Guardians, Students, and Student Attendance; click Close; then resize the Guardians and Students field lists to view as many fields as possible**

   With the four field lists for the main tables in the database positioned in the Relationships window so that you can see nearly all of the fields, you will build the one-to-many relationships between the tables.

4. **Drag the ID field from the Guardians table to the GuardianID field in the Students and Guardians table, click the Enforce Referential Integrity check box, then click Create**

5. **Create the other two relationships, as shown in FIGURE I-4**

   Note that in this database, the linking fields do not have the same name in both the "one" and "many" tables. Also recall that referential integrity helps prevent orphan records—records in the "many" table that don't have a matching record in the "one" table.

6. **Save and close the Relationships window, click the FILE tab, click Save As, click the Save As button, navigate to the location where you store your Data Files, enter Students as the filename, click Save, then close the Getting Started dialog box and exit Access 2013**

   Access database templates and Application Parts provide powerful tools to build databases and objects quickly. Templates are also an exciting way to learn more about Access features and possibilities.

FIGURE I-3: Application Parts list

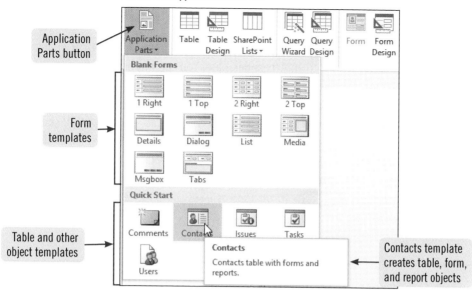

Application Parts button

Form templates

Table and other object templates

Contacts template creates table, form, and report objects

FIGURE I-4: Major relationships for the Students database

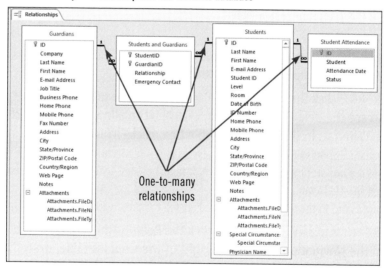

One-to-many relationships

Referential integrity cascade options

When connecting tables in one-to-many relationships, apply referential integrity whenever possible. This feature prevents orphan records from being created in the database and lets you select cascade options. **Cascade Update Related Fields** means that if a value in the primary key field (the field on the "one" side of a one-to-many relationship) is modified, all values in the foreign key field (the field on the "many" side of a one-to-many relationship) are automatically updated as well.

Cascade Delete Related Records means that if a record on the "one" side of a one-to-many relationship is deleted, all related records in the "many" table are also deleted. Because both of these options automatically change or delete data in the "many" table behind the scenes, they should be used carefully. Often these features are not employed as standard options, but are used temporarily to correct a problem in the database.

Import Data from Excel

Learning Outcomes
• Import data from Excel
• Describe other data import options

Access can share data with many other Microsoft Office programs. **Importing** enables you to quickly copy data from an external file into an Access database. You can import data from many sources, such as another Access database; Excel spreadsheet; SharePoint site; Outlook email; or text files in an HTML, XML, or delimited text file format. A **delimited text file** stores one record on each line. Field values are separated by a common character, the **delimiter**, such as a comma, tab, or dash. A **CSV (comma-separated value)** file is a common example of a delimited text file. An **XML file** is a text file containing **Extensible Markup Language (XML)** tags that identify field names and data. One of the most common file formats from which to import data into an Access database is **Microsoft Excel**, the spreadsheet program in the Microsoft Office suite. **CASE** ▶ *Jacob Thomas gives you an Excel spreadsheet that contains a list of supplemental materials used for various courses, and asks you to import the information in the new internal training database.*

STEPS

1. **Start Access, open the** Education-I.accdb **database from the location where you store your Data Files, enable content if prompted, click the** EXTERNAL DATA tab, **click the** Excel button **in the Import & Link group, click the** Browse button, **navigate to the location where you store your Data Files, then double-click** CourseMaterials.xlsx

   The **Get External Data - Excel Spreadsheet** dialog box opens. You can import the records, **append** the records (add the records to an existing table), or link to the data source. In this case, you want to import the records into a new table.

2. **Click** OK

   The **Import Spreadsheet Wizard** helps you import data from Excel into Access and presents a sample of the data to be imported, as shown in **FIGURE I-5**.

3. **Click** Next, **click the** First Row Contains Column Headings **check box, click** Next, **click** Next **to accept the default field options, click** Next **to allow Access to add a primary key field, type** Materials **in the Import to Table box, click** Finish, **then click** Close

   To save the import steps so that they can be easily repeated, click the Save import steps check box on the last step of the import process. You run a saved import process by clicking the **Saved Imports** button on the EXTERNAL DATA tab.

   One record in the Courses table can be related to many records in the Materials table.

4. **Click the** DATABASE TOOLS tab, **click the** Relationships button, **drag the** Materials table **from the Navigation Pane to the right of the Courses table, drag the** CourseID field **in the Courses table to the** CourseID field **in the Materials table, click the** Enforce Referential Integrity **check box, then click** Create

   The final Relationships window is shown in **FIGURE I-6**. One employee record is related to many enrollments. One course record is related to many enrollments and to many materials.

5. **Click the** Close button, **then click** Yes **to save the changes to the database relationships**

Importing from another database

If you import from an Access database using the Access button on the EXTERNAL DATA tab, you are presented with a dialog box that allows you to import selected objects from the database. This provides an excellent way to develop new queries, forms, and reports in an external "development" database, and then import them into the "production" database only after they have been fully developed and tested.

FIGURE I-5: Import Spreadsheet Wizard

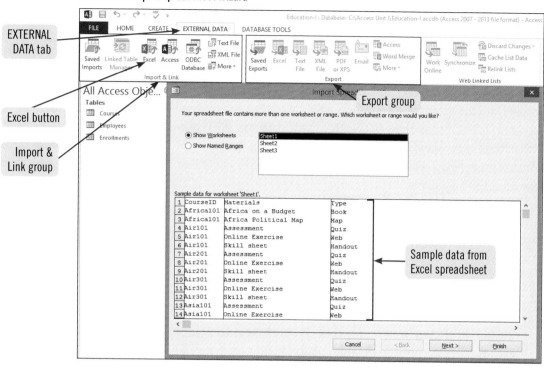

FIGURE I-6: Relationships window with imported Materials table

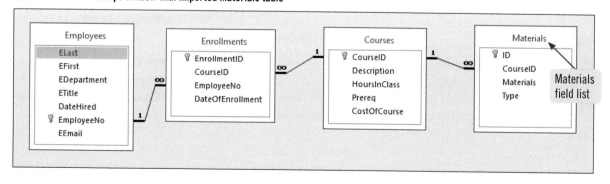

Access 2013

Link Data

Learning
Outcomes
• Link data from
  Excel
• Describe linking
  versus importing

Linking connects an Access database to data in an external file such as another Access database, Excel spreadsheet, text file, HTML file, XML file, or other data sources that support **ODBC (Open Database Connectivity)** standards. Linking is different from importing in that linked data is not copied into the database. If you link, data is only stored and updated in the original file. Importing, in contrast, makes a copy of the data in the Access database. **CASE** *Jacob Thomas has created a small spreadsheet with information about the departments at Quest. He wants to use the information in the Education-I database while maintaining it in Excel. He asks you to help create a link to this Excel file from the Education-I database.*

STEPS

1. **Click the EXTERNAL DATA tab, then click the Excel button in the Import & Link group**

   The Get External Data - Excel Spreadsheet dialog box opens. This dialog box allows you to choose whether you want to import, append, or link to the data source.

2. **Click Browse, navigate to the location where you store your Data Files, double-click DepartmentData.xlsx, click the Link to the data source by creating a linked table option button, as shown in FIGURE I-7, click OK, click Next to accept the default range selection, click Next to accept the default column headings, type Departments as the linked table name, click Finish, then click OK**

   The **Link Spreadsheet Wizard** guides you through the process of linking to a spreadsheet. The linked Departments table appears in the Navigation Pane with a linking Excel icon, as shown in **FIGURE I-8**. Like any other table, in order for the linked table to work with the rest of a database, a one-to-many relationship between it and another table should be created.

3. **Click the DATABASE TOOLS tab, click the Relationships button, drag the Departments table from the Navigation Pane to the left of the Employees table, then drag a border of the Departments table to display all fields**

   The Dept field in the Departments table is used to create a one-to-many relationship with the EDepartment field in the Employees table. One department may be related to many employees.

4. **Drag the Dept field in the Departments table to the EDepartment field in the Employees table, then click Create in the Edit Relationships dialog box**

   Your Relationships window should look like **FIGURE I-9**. A one-to-many relationship is established between the Departments and Employees tables, but because referential integrity is not enforced, the one and many symbols do not appear on the link line. You cannot establish referential integrity when one of the tables is a linked table. Now that the linked Departments table is related to the rest of the database, it can participate in queries, forms, and reports that select fields from multiple tables.

5. **Click the Close button, then click Yes when prompted to save changes**

   You work with a linked table just as you work with any other table. The data in a linked table can be edited through either the source program (in this case, Excel) or in the Access database, even though the data is only physically stored in the original source file.

FIGURE I-7: Get External Data - Excel Spreadsheet dialog box

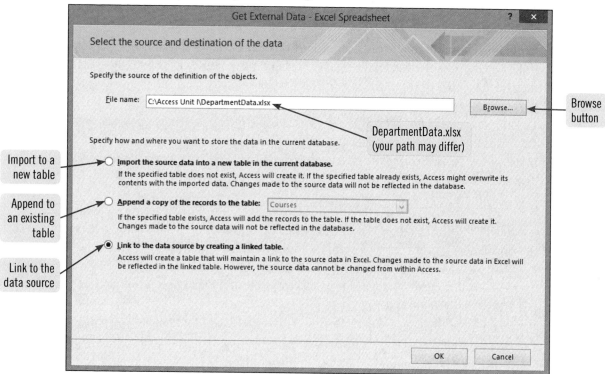

Import to a
new table

Append to
an existing
table

Link to the
data source

DepartmentData.xlsx
(your path may differ)

Browse
button

FIGURE I-8: Departments table is linked from Excel

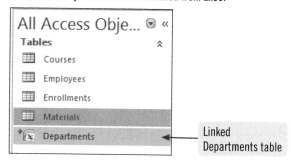

Linked
Departments table

FIGURE I-9: Relationships window with linked Departments table

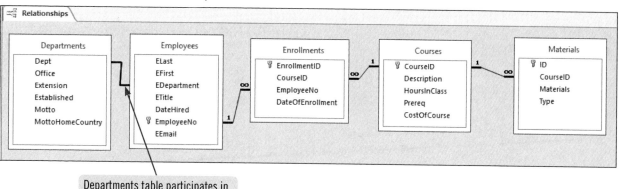

Departments table participates in
one-to-many relationship but
referential integrity is not enforced

Access 2013

Export Data to Excel

Learning Outcomes
• Export data to Excel
• Describe other data export options

Exporting is a way to copy Access information to another database, spreadsheet, or file format. Exporting is the opposite of importing. You can export data from an Access database to other file types, such as those used by Excel or Word, and in several general file formats, including text, HTML, and XML. Given the popularity of analyzing numeric data in Excel, it is common to export Access data to an Excel spreadsheet for further analysis. **CASE** *The Finance Department asks you to export some Access data to an Excel spreadsheet so the finance personnel can use Excel to analyze how increases in the cost of the courses would affect departments. You can gather the fields needed in an Access query, then export the query to an Excel spreadsheet.*

STEPS

1. **Click the CREATE tab, click the Query Design button, double-click Employees, double-click Enrollments, double-click Courses, then click Close**

   The fields you want to export to Excel—EDepartment and CostOfCourse—are in the Employees and Courses tables. You also need to include the Enrollments table in this query because it provides the connection between the Employees and Courses tables.

2. **Double-click EDepartment in the Employees field list, double-click CostOfCourse in the Courses field list, click the Sort cell for the EDepartment field, click the Sort cell list arrow, click Ascending, then click the View button to display the query datasheet**

   The resulting datasheet has 403 records. You want to summarize the costs by department before exporting this to Excel.

3. **Click the View button to return to Design View, click the Totals button in the Show/Hide group, click Group By for the CostOfCourse field, click the Group By list arrow, click Sum, click to display the query datasheet, then widen the SumOfCostOfCourse column, as shown in FIGURE I-10**

   Save the query with a meaningful name to prepare to export it to Excel.

4. **Click the Save button on the Quick Access toolbar, type DepartmentCosts, click OK, right-click the DepartmentCosts tab, then click Close**

   Before you start an export process, be sure to select the object you want to export in the Navigation Pane.

QUICK TIP

To quickly export an object, right-click it in the Navigation Pane, point to Export, then click the file type for the export.

5. **Click the DepartmentCosts query in the Navigation Pane, click the EXTERNAL DATA tab, click the Excel button in the Export group, click Browse, navigate to the location where you store your Data Files, click Save to accept the default filename, click OK, then click Close**

   The data in the DepartmentCosts query has now been exported to an Excel spreadsheet file named DepartmentCosts and saved in the location where you store your Data Files. As with imports, you can save and then repeat the export process by saving the export steps when prompted by the last dialog box in the Export Wizard. Run the saved export process using the **Saved Exports** button on the EXTERNAL DATA tab or by assigning the export process to an Outlook task.

   Access can work with data in a wide variety of file formats. Other file formats that Access can import from, link with, and export to are listed in **TABLE I-1**.

FIGURE I-10: New query selects and summarizes data to be exported to Excel

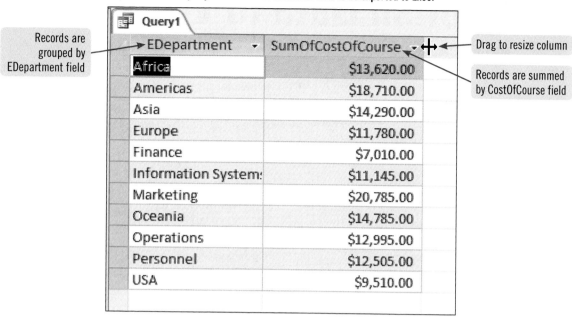

Records are grouped by EDepartment field

Drag to resize column

Records are summed by CostOfCourse field

EDepartment	SumOfCostOfCourse
Africa	$13,620.00
Americas	$18,710.00
Asia	$14,290.00
Europe	$11,780.00
Finance	$7,010.00
Information Systems	$11,145.00
Marketing	$20,785.00
Oceania	$14,785.00
Operations	$12,995.00
Personnel	$12,505.00
USA	$9,510.00

TABLE I-1: File formats that Access can link to, import, and export

file format	import	link	export
Access	•	•	•
Excel	•	•	•
Word			•
SharePoint site	•	•	•
Email file attachments			•
Outlook folder	•	•	
ODBC database (such as SQL Server)	•	•	•
dBASE	•	•	•
HTML document	•	•	•
PDF or XPS file			•
Text file (delimited or fixed width)	•	•	•
XML file	•		•

Publish Data to Word

Learning
Outcomes
• Export data to
  Word
• Describe techni-
  ques to share
  Access data

Microsoft Word, the word-processing program in the Microsoft Office suite, is a premier program for entering, editing, and formatting text. You can easily export data from an Access table, query, form, or report into a Word document. This is helpful when you want to use Word's superior text-editing features to combine the information in a Word document with Access data. **CASE** ▸ *You are asked to write a memo to the management committee describing departmental costs for continuing education. You export an Access query with this data to a Word document where you finish the memo.*

STEPS

1. **Click the DepartmentCosts query in the Navigation Pane, click the EXTERNAL DATA tab, click the More button in the Export group, click Word, click Browse, navigate to the location where you store your Data Files, click Save to accept the default filename DepartmentCosts.rtf, click OK, then click Close**

   The data in the DepartmentCosts query is exported as an **RTF (Rich Text Format)** file, which can be opened and edited in Word.

2. **Start Word, then open DepartmentCosts.rtf from the location where you store your Data Files**

   Currently, the document contains only a table of information, the data you exported from the DepartmentCosts query. Use Word to add the memo information.

3. **Press [Enter], then type the following text, pressing [Tab] after typing each colon**

To:	Management Committee
From:	*Your* Name
Re:	Analysis of Continuing Education Courses
Date:	*Today's date*

   The following information shows the overall cost for continuing education subtotaled by department. The information shows that the Americas and Marketing departments are the highest consumers of continuing education.

4. **Proofread your document, which should now look like FIGURE I-11, then preview and print it**

   The **word wrap** feature in Word determines when a line of text extends into the right margin of the page and automatically forces the text to the next line without you needing to press [Enter]. This allows you to enter and edit large paragraphs of text in Word very efficiently.

5. **Save and close the document, then exit Word**

   In addition to exporting data, **TABLE I-2** lists other techniques you can use to copy Access data to other applications.

FIGURE I-11: Word document with Access data

To: Management Committee

From: Student Name

Re: Analysis of Continuing Education Courses

Date: 12/2/2015

The following information shows the overall cost for continuing education subtotaled by department. The information shows that the Americas and Marketing departments are the highest consumers of continuing education.

EDepartment	SumOfCostOfCourse
Africa	$13,620.00
Americas	$18,710.00
Asia	$14,290.00
Europe	$11,780.00
Finance	$7,010.00
Information Systems	$11,145.00
Marketing	$20,785.00
Oceania	$14,785.00
Operations	$12,995.00
Personnel	$12,505.00
USA	$9,510.00

Enter this information into a Word document

DepartmentCosts query exported from Access

TABLE I-2: Techniques to copy Access data to other applications

technique	button or menu option	description
Drag and drop	Resize the Access window so that the target location (Word or Excel, for example) can also be seen on the screen	With both windows visible, drag the Access table, query, form, or report object icon from the Access window to the target (Excel or Word) window
Export	Use the buttons in the Export group on the EXTERNAL DATA tab	Copy information from an Access object into a different file format
Office Clipboard	Copy and Paste	Click the Copy button to copy selected data to the Office Clipboard (the Office Clipboard can hold multiple items); open a Word document or Excel spreadsheet, click where you want to paste the data, then click the Paste button

Merge Data with Word

Learning
Outcomes
• Merge data to a
  Word document
• Save a main docu-
  ment with merge
  fields

Another way to export Access data is to merge it to a Word document as the data source for a mail-merge process. In a **mail merge**, data from an Access table or query is combined into a Word form letter, label, or envelope to create mass mailing documents. **CASE** ➤ *Jacob Thomas wants to send Quest employees a letter announcing two new continuing education courses. You merge Access data to a Word document to customize a letter to each employee.*

STEPS

1. **Click the Employees table in the Navigation Pane, click the EXTERNAL DATA tab, then click the Word Merge button in the Export group**

   The **Microsoft Word Mail Merge Wizard** dialog box opens asking whether you want to link to an existing document or create a new one.

2. **Click the Create a new document and then link the data to it option button, click OK, then click the Word button on the taskbar**

   Word starts and opens the **Mail Merge task pane**, which steps you through the mail-merge process. Before you merge the Access data with the Word document, you must create the **main document**, the Word document that contains the standard text for each form letter.

   TROUBLE
   The "Next" links are
   at the bottom of the
   Mail Merge task
   pane.

3. **Type the standard text shown in FIGURE I-12, click the Next: Starting document link in the bottom of the Mail Merge task pane, click the Next: Select recipients link to use the current document, click the Next: Write your letter link to use the existing list of names, press [Tab] after To: in the letter, then click the Insert Merge Field arrow button in the Write & Insert Fields group on the MAILINGS tab**

   The Insert Merge Field drop-down list shows all of the fields in the original data source, the Employees table. You use this list to insert **merge fields**, codes that are replaced with the values in the field that the code represents when the mail merge is processed.

   TROUBLE
   You cannot type the
   merge codes directly
   into the document.
   You must use the
   Insert Merge Field
   button.

4. **Click EFirst, press [Spacebar], click the Insert Merge Field arrow button, click ELast, then click the Next: Preview your letters link**

   With the main document and merge fields inserted, you are ready to complete the mail merge.

5. **Click the Next: Complete the merge link as shown in FIGURE I-13, click the Edit individual letters link to view the letters on the screen, then click OK to complete the merge**

   The mail-merge process combines the EFirst and ELast field values from the Employees table with the main document, creating a 24-page document, as shown in the Word status bar. Each page is a customized letter for each record in the Employees table. The first page is a letter to Ron Dawson. "Ron" is the field value for the EFirst field in the first record in the Employees table, and "Dawson" is the field value for the ELast field.

   QUICK TIP
   The total number of
   pages in the docu-
   ment is displayed in
   the lower-left corner
   of the Word window.

6. **Press [Page Down] several times to view several pages of the final merged document, then close the merged document, Letters1, without saving it**

   You generally don't need to save the final, large merged document. Saving the one-page main document, however, is a good idea in case you need to repeat the merge process.

7. **Click the Save button 🔲 on the Quick Access toolbar, navigate to the location where you store your Data Files, enter Employees in the File name text box, click Save, then close Word**

FIGURE I-12: Creating the main document in Word

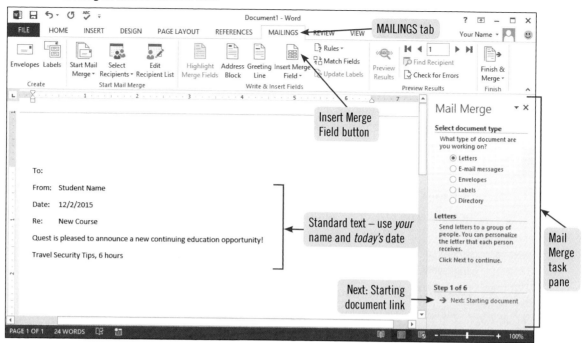

FIGURE I-13: Inserting merge fields

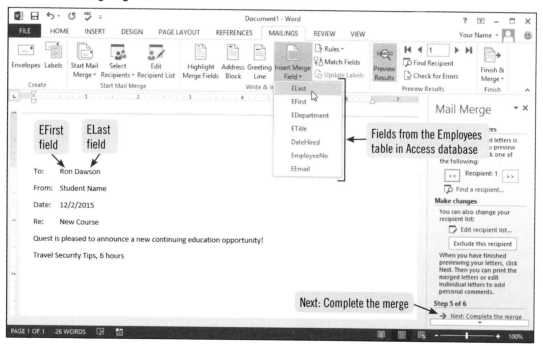

Access 2013

Export Data to PDF

Learning
Outcomes
• Publish data to PDF
• Export a report
  as an email
  attachment

Access data can be exported to a PDF document. **PDF** stands for **Portable Document Format**, a file format developed by Adobe that has become a standard format for exchanging documents. By sharing information in a PDF format, anyone can read the document using free **Adobe Reader software**, but they cannot edit or change the information. PDF files look on the screen just like they would look if printed. **CASE** ▸ *Jacob Thomas asks you to export the Courses table to a PDF document for later distribution to employees as an email attachment.*

STEPS

1. **Click the** CourseRosters report **in the Navigation Pane, click the** EXTERNAL DATA tab, **then click the** PDF or XPS button **in the Export group**

   The Publish as PDF or XPS dialog box opens asking you to choose a name and location for the file. **XPS** (structured XML) is a file format that is similar to a PDF file, but is based on the **XML** (Extensible Markup Language) instead of the PostScript language used by PDF files.

2. **Navigate to the location where you store your Data Files, as shown in** FIGURE I-14

   The Publish as PDF or XPS dialog box provides a check box to automatically open the file after publishing so you can double-check the results.

TROUBLE
If you do not have the free Adobe PDF Reader software installed on your computer, you may be prompted to download it.

3. **Click** Publish **to save the file with the default name** CourseRosters.pdf

   The CourseRosters.pdf file automatically opens, as shown in **FIGURE I-15**.

4. **Press [Alt][Tab] to return to the Access window, then click** Close **to close the Export - PDF dialog box**

   The CourseRosters.pdf file is now available for you to attach to an email. Because it is a PDF file, users can open, view, and print the report even if they don't have Access on their computers. PDF files are common because they provide an easy way to share information that cannot be modified.

   Another way to email an Access report (or any other Access object) as a PDF file is to click the report in the Navigation Pane, then click the Email button in the Export group of the EXTERNAL DATA tab on the Ribbon. You are presented with the Send Object As dialog box that allows you to choose the desired file format, such as .xlsx, .pdf, .htm, or .rtf, for the report. Once you select the desired file format and click OK, Outlook opens with the report attached to the email in the chosen file format. You must have Microsoft Outlook installed and configured to use this option.

5. **Close the Education-I.accdb database and Access 2013, then close the CourseRosters.pdf file**

FIGURE I-14: Publish as PDF or XPS dialog box

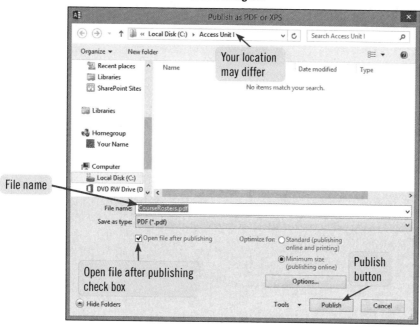

File name

Open file after publishing check box

FIGURE I-15: Previewing the CourseRosters.pdf file

Course Rosters by Deparment

Africa

PDF files can be viewed and printed but not modified

Employee	Description	Hours
Boyd Hosta	Air Reservations I	12
	Air Reservations II	12
	Air Reservations III	12
	Corporate Sales I	12
	Cruising I	24
	Ecological Tours I	12
	Ecological Tours II	12
	European Travel I	12
	European Travel II	12
	European Travel III	12
	Hotel Reservations I	12
	Time Management I	16
	Travel Sales and Trends	16
	USA Biking I	12
	USA Biking II	12
	USA Hiking I	12
	USA Hiking II	12
		224
Gail Owen	African Travel I	16
	African Travel II	16
	African Travel III	16
	Air Reservations I	12
	All Inclusives I	12
	Asian Travel I	12
	Asian Travel II	12
	Bus Travel I	12
	Cruising I	24
	Cruising II	12
	Customer Service Skills I	16
	Customer Service Skills II	16

Importing and Exporting Data

Practice

Concepts Review

Identify each element of the EXTERNAL DATA tab shown in FIGURE I-16.

FIGURE I-16

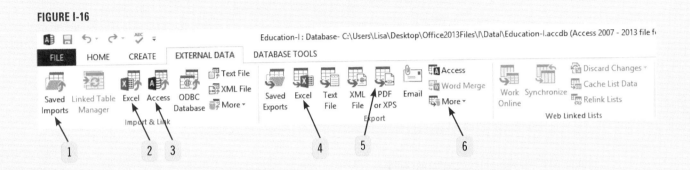

Match each term with the statement that best describes its function.

7. **Table template**
8. **Database template**
9. **Exporting**
10. **Main document**
11. **Linking**
12. **Delimited text file**
13. **Mail merge**
14. **Importing**

a. A tool used to quickly create a single table within an existing database

b. A file used to determine how a letter and Access data will be combined

c. A file that stores one record on each line, with the field values separated by a common character such as a comma, tab, or dash

d. A way to copy Access information to another database, spreadsheet, or file format

e. The process of converting data from an external source into an Access database

f. A way to connect to data in an external source without copying it

g. A tool used to quickly create a new database based on a particular subject, such as assets, contacts, events, or projects

h. To combine data from an Access table or query into a Word form letter, label, or envelope to create mass mailing documents

Select the best answer from the list of choices.

15. **Which of the following is *not* true about database templates?**
    a. They cover a wide range of subjects, including assets, contacts, events, or projects.
    b. Microsoft provides online templates in areas such as business and personal database applications.
    c. They create multiple database objects.
    d. They analyze the data on your computer and suggest database applications.

16. **Which of the following is *not* true about exporting?**
    a. Access data can be exported into Excel.
    b. Access data can be exported to Word.
    c. Exporting creates a copy of data.
    d. Exporting retains a link between the original and target data files.

17. **Which of the following is *not* a file format that Access can import?**
    a. Word
    b. Excel
    c. Access
    d. HTML

18. **Which of the following file formats allows you to send information that cannot be modified?**
    a. XLS
    b. HTM
    c. RTF
    d. PDF

19. **Which is *not* true about enforcing referential integrity?**
    a. It is required for all one-to-many relationships.
    b. It prevents records from being deleted on the "one" side of a one-to-many relationship that have matching records on the "many" side.
    c. It prevents records from being created on the "many" side of a one-to-many relationship that do not have a matching record on the "one" side.
    d. It prevents orphan records.

20. **Which of the following is *not* true about linking?**
    a. Linking copies data from one data file to another.
    b. Access can link to data in an HTML file.
    c. Access can link to data in an Excel spreadsheet.
    d. You can edit linked data in Access.

Skills Review

1. **Use database templates.**
   a. Start Access 2013 and use the Desktop asset tracking template to build a new Access database. (*Hint*: Be sure to use the *Desktop* asset tracking database, and not the Asset tracking database, which is a Web app.) Save the database with the name **Assets-I** in the location where you store your Data Files.
   b. Enable content if prompted, close the Getting Started with Assets dialog box, then explore the forms in the database by opening and closing the Asset Details form, the Contact Details form, the Contact List form, and the Getting Started form.
   c. Close all open forms, and then explore the relationships between tables by opening the Relationships window. Expand field lists as needed to view all fields.
   d. Note the arrow on the "one" side of the one-to-many relationship between Contacts and Assets. Double-click the link line to open the Edit Relationships dialog box, click Join Type, click option 1 Only include rows where the joined fields from both tables are equal, click OK, and then click OK in the Edit Relationships dialog box. Because there are no records in the Assets or Contacts tables yet, you do not need a modified relationship. Given referential integrity is applied to this relationship, no records can be entered in the Assets table without a matching record in the Contacts table. Save and close the Relationships window.
   e. Close all objects but leave the new Assets-I.accdb database open.

Skills Review (continued)

2. Use Application Parts.

   a. Use the Issues table template in Application Parts to create a new table in the Assets-I.accdb database named Issues. Choose the One 'Assets' to many 'Issues' relationship, choose the ID field from 'Assets', do not choose a sorting field, and name the lookup column as **AssetID**.

   b. Close all open forms, reopen the Relationships window then click the All Relationships button to show the new relationship you just created between the new Issues table and the Assets table.

   c. Double-click the link line between the Assets and Issues tables, click the Enforce Referential Integrity check box, then click OK.

   d. Click the Relationship Report button to create a relationships report for this database, then print it if requested by your instructor.

   e. Save and close the **Relationships for Assets-I** report with that name.

   f. Save and close the Relationships window, and then close the Assets-I.accdb database.

3. Import data from Excel.

   a. Open the Machinery-I.accdb database from the location where you store your Data Files. Enable content if prompted.

   b. Import the MachineryEmp.xlsx spreadsheet from the location where you store your Data Files to a new table in the current database using the Import Spreadsheet Wizard to import the data. Make sure that the first row is specified as the column headings.

   c. Choose the EmployeeNo field as the primary key, and import the data to a table named **Employees**. Do not save the import steps.

   d. In Table Design View for the Employees table, change the Data Type of the EmployeeNo field to Number. Save the table and click Yes when prompted. The EmployeeNo field values are from 1 to 6. No data will be lost. Close the Employees table.

4. Link data from Excel.

   a. Link to the Vendors.xlsx Excel file in the location where you store your Data Files.

   b. In the Link Spreadsheet Wizard, specify that the first row contains column headings.

   c. Name the linked table **Vendors**.

   d. Open the Relationships window and display all five field lists in the window. Link the tables together with one-to-many relationships, as shown in **FIGURE I-17**. Be sure to enforce referential integrity on all relationships except for the relationship between Products and the linked Vendors table.

   e. Save and close the Relationships window.

FIGURE I-17

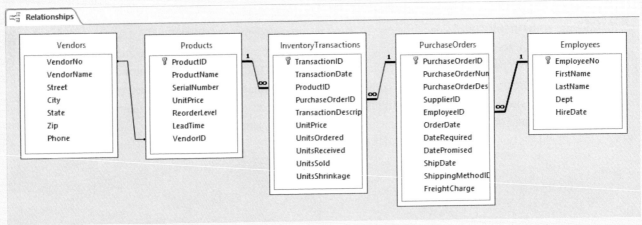

5. Export data to Excel.

   a. Open the Products table to view the datasheet, then close it.

   b. Export the Products table data to an Excel spreadsheet named **Products.xlsx**. Save the spreadsheet to the location where you store your Data Files. Do not save the export steps.

6. Publish data to Word.

   a. In the Machinery-I.accdb database, export the Products table to a Word document named **Products.rtf**. Save the Products.rtf file in the location where you store your Data Files. Do not save the export steps.

   b. Start Word, then open the Products.rtf document from the location where you store your Data Files. Press [Enter] twice, press [Ctrl][Home] to return to the top of the document, then type the following text:

   INTERNAL MEMO

From:	***Your* Name**
To:	**Sales Staff**
Date:	***Today's* date**

   Do not forget to check the lead times on the Back Hoe, Thatcher, and Biodegrader when you get an order for these items. We usually do not keep these items in stock.

   c. Proofread the document, then save and print it. Close the document, then exit Word.

7. Merge data with Word.

   a. In the Machinery-I.accdb database, merge the data from the Employees table to a new Word document.

   b. Use the "Create a new document and then link the data to it" option in the Microsoft Word Mail Merge Wizard dialog box. In the Word document, enter the following text as the main document for the mail merge:

Date:	***Today's* date**
To:	
From:	***Your* Name**
Re:	**CPR Training**

   The annual CPR Training session will be held on Friday, February 26, 2016. Please sign up for this important event in the lunchroom. Friends and family who are at least 18 years old are also welcome.

   c. To the right of To:, press [Tab] to position the insertion point at the location for the first merge field.

   d. Click the Insert Merge Field button arrow, click FirstName, press [Spacebar], click the Insert Merge Field button arrow, then click LastName.

   e. Click the links at the bottom of the Mail Merge task pane to move through the steps of the mail-merge process, Steps 1 through 6, click Edit individual letters, then click OK to make sure that your final document has six pages for the six records in your Access Employees table.

   f. Print the first page of the merged document if required by your instructor (the letter to Melissa Lenox), then close the six-page final merged document without saving changes.

   g. Save the main document with the name **CPR.docx**, then exit Word.

8. Export data to PDF.

   a. Use the Report Wizard to create a new report based on all of the fields in the Products table. Do not specify any grouping levels, choose an ascending sort order on ProductName, choose a Tabular layout and a Landscape orientation, and title the report **Product List**.

   b. Use Layout View to resize the columns so that all data is clearly visible, then save and close the report.

   c. Export the Product List report with the name **Product List.pdf** to the location where you store your Data Files.

   d. Close the Product List report, close the Machinery-I database, then exit Access 2013.

Independent Challenge 1

As the manager of a women's college basketball team, you have created a database called Basketball-I that tracks the players, games, and player statistics. You want to export a report to a Word document.

a. Open the database Basketball-I.accdb from the location where you store your Data Files. Enable content if prompted.

b. In the Relationships window, connect the Games and Stats tables with a one-to-many relationship based on the common GameNo field. Connect the Players and Stats tables with a one-to-many relationship based on the common PlayerNo field. Be sure to enforce referential integrity on both relationships. Save and close the Relationships window.

c. Export the Player Statistics report to a Word file with the name **Player Statistics.rtf**. Save the Player Statistics. rtf document in the location where you store your Data Files. Do not save the export steps.

d. Start Word, then open the Player Statistics.rtf document.

e. Press [Enter] three times to enter three blank lines at the top of the document, then press [Ctrl][Home] to position the insertion point at the top of the document.

f. Type *your* name on the first line of the document, enter *today's* date as the second line, then write a sentence or two that explains the Player Statistics data that follows. Save, print, and close the Player Statistics document.

g. Exit Word. Close the Basketball-I.accdb database, then exit Access.

Independent Challenge 2

As the manager of a women's college basketball team, you have created a database called Basketball-I that tracks the players, games, and player statistics. The 2015–2016 basketball schedule has been provided to you as an Excel spreadsheet file. You will import that data and append it to the current Games table.

a. Open the database Basketball-I.accdb from the location where you store your Data Files. Enable content if prompted.

b. If the relationships haven't already been established in this database, create relationships as described in Step b of Independent Challenge 1.

c. Open the Games table to observe the datasheet. It currently contains 22 records with scores for the 2014–2015 basketball season.

d. Start Excel and open the 2015-2016Schedule.xlsx file from the location where you store your Data Files. Note that it contains 22 rows of data indicating the opponent, mascot, home or away status, and date of the games for the 2015–2016 season. You have been told that the data will import more precisely if it is identified with the same field names as have already been established in the Games table in Access, so you'll insert those field names as a header row in the Excel spreadsheet.

e. Click anywhere in row 1 of the 2015-2016Schedule.xlsx spreadsheet, click the Insert button arrow in the Cells group, then click Insert Sheet Rows to insert a new blank row.

f. In the new blank row 1, enter the field names that correspond to the field names in the Games table for the same data above each column: **Opponent**, **Mascot**, **Home-Away**, and **GameDate**. Be careful to enter the names precisely as shown.

g. Save and close the 2015-2016Schedule.xlsx spreadsheet, exit Excel, and return to the Basketball-I.accdb database.

h. Close the Games table, click the EXTERNAL DATA tab, click the Excel button in the Import & Link group, browse for the 2015-2016Schedule.xlsx spreadsheet in your Data Files, then choose the Append a copy of the records to the table option button. Be sure that Games is selected as the table to use for the append process.

i. Follow the steps of the Import Spreadsheet Wizard process through completion (do not save the import steps), then open the Games table. It should contain the original 22 records for the 2014–2015 season plus 22 more from the 2015-2016Schedule.xlsx spreadsheet with default values of 0 for both the CycloneScore and OpponentScore fields.

j. Change the Opponent value in the first record to *your* last name's College, then print the first page of the Games table if requested by your instructor.

k. Save and close the Games table, close the Basketball-I.accdb database, then exit Access.

Independent Challenge 3

You have been asked by a small engineering firm to build a database that tracks projects. You decide to explore Microsoft database templates to see if there is a template that could help you get started.

a. Start Access and start a new database with the Desktop project management template. Save and name the database **Project Tracking.accdb**, store it in the location where you store your Data Files, then enable content if prompted.

b. Click the Navigation Pane title bar, then choose Object Type to organize the objects in this database by type.

c. Open and review the Relationships window. Rearrange the field lists as shown in FIGURE I-18, then print the Relationships report in landscape orientation. Save the report with the default name, **Relationships for Project Tracking**, then close it.

FIGURE I-18

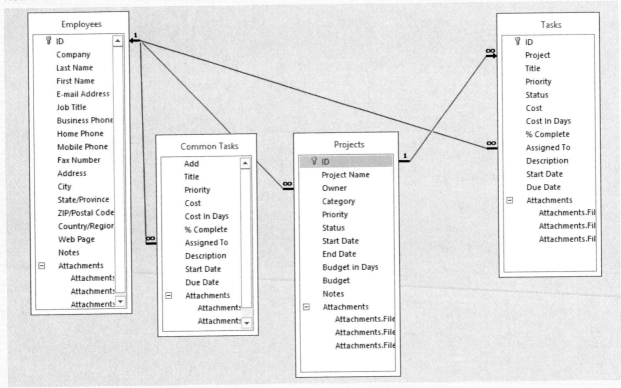

d. Save and close the Relationships window.

e. Open the Project List form (if it's not already open), and enter the following data: Project Name: **Web Site Update**, Owner: *Your* **Name**.

f. Click Yes to add your name to the list, then enter the Street, City, State/Province, Zip/Postal Code, and Country/Region information for your school in the Employee Details form.

g. Close the Employee Details form and the Project List form.

h. Open the Employee List form and add another record for your instructor. Enter your instructor's school email address, school phone, and school name for the E-mail Address, Business Phone, and Company fields. Enter **Professor** in the Job Title field for your instructor.

i. Close the Employee List form, then open the Employee Address Book report. If requested by your instructor, print the report and then close it.

j. Explore the other objects of the Project Tracking database, close the database, then exit Access.

Independent Challenge 4: Explore

Learning common phrases in a variety of foreign languages is extremely valuable if you travel or interact with people from other countries. As a volunteer with the foreign student exchange program at your college, you have created a database that documents the primary and secondary languages used by foreign countries. The database also includes a table of common words and phrases that you can use to practice basic conversation skills. (*Note: To complete this Independent Challenge, make sure you are connected to the Internet.*)

a. Open the Languages-I.accdb database from the location where you store your Data Files. Enable content if prompted.

b. Open the datasheets for each of the three tables to familiarize yourself with the fields and records. The Primary and Secondary fields in the Countries table represent the primary and secondary languages for that country. Close the datasheets for each of the three tables.

c. Open the Relationships window, then create a one-to-many relationship between the Languages and Countries table using the LanguageID field in the Languages table and the Primary field in the Countries table. Enforce referential integrity on the relationship.

d. Create a one-to-many relationship between the Languages and Countries tables using the LanguageID field in the Languages table and the Secondary field in the Countries table. Click No when prompted to edit the existing relationship, and enforce referential integrity on the new relationship. The field list for the Languages table will appear twice in the Relationships window with Languages_1 as the title for the second field list, as shown in FIGURE I-19. The Words table is used for reference and does not have a direct relationship to the other tables.

FIGURE I-19

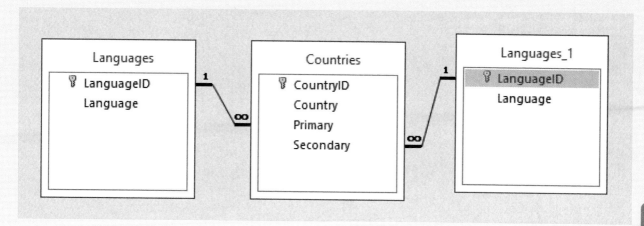

e. Create a Relationships report, then display it in Design View.

f. Add a label to the Report Header section with *your* name, change the font color of the new label to black, then save the report with the name **Relationships for Language-I**.

g. Print the report if requested by your instructor, then close it.

h. Save and close the Relationships window.

i. Connect to the Internet and go to www.ask.com, www.about.com, or any search engine. Your goal is to find a Web site that translates English to other languages, and to print the home page of that Web site.

j. Add a new field to the Words table with a new language that isn't already represented. Use the Web site to translate the existing six words into the new language.

k. Add three new words or phrases to the Words table, making sure that the translation is made in all of the represented languages: English, French, Spanish, German, Italian, Portuguese, Polish, and the new language you added.

l. If requested by your instructor, print the updated datasheet for the Words table, close the Words table, close the Languages-I.accdb database, then exit Access.

Visual Workshop

Start Access and open the Basketball-I.accdb database from the location where you store your Data Files. Enable content if prompted. Merge the information from the Players table to a new Word form letter. The first page of the merged document is shown in **FIGURE I-20**. Notice that the player's first and last names have been merged to the first line and that the player's first name is merged a second time in the first sentence of the letter. Be very careful to correctly add spaces as needed around the merge fields. Print the last page of the merged document if requested by your instructor, close the 13-page final merged document without saving it, save the main document as **Champs.docx**, then close it.

FIGURE I-20

To: Sydney Freesen

From: *Your* Name

Date: *Current Date*

Re: Conference Champions!

Congratulations, Sydney, for an outstanding year at State University! Your hard work and team contribution have helped secure the conference championship for State University for the second year in a row.

Thank you for your dedication!

Analyzing Database Design Using Northwind

CASE ▶ You work with Jacob Thomas, director of staff development at Quest Specialty Travel, to examine the Microsoft Northwind database and determine what features and techniques could be applied to improve the Education database.

Unit Objectives

After completing this unit, you will be able to:

- Normalize data
- Analyze relationships
- Evaluate tables
- Improve fields

- Use subqueries
- Modify joins
- Analyze forms
- Analyze reports

Files You Will Need

Education-J.accdb
Northwind.mdb
Northwind2.mdb
Basketball-J.accdb

RealEstate-J.accdb
JobSearch-J.accdb
Dives-J.accdb

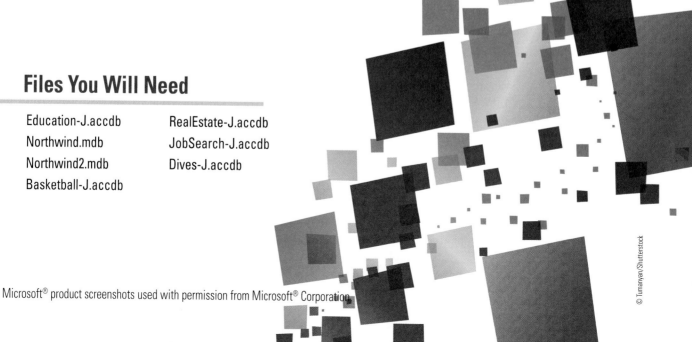

© Tumanyan/Shutterstock

Normalize Data

Learning
Outcomes
• Describe
normalization
• Create Lookup
fields

Normalizing data means to structure and link the tables in a well-designed relational database. A normalized database reduces inaccurate and redundant data, decreases storage requirements, improves database speed and performance, and simplifies overall database maintenance. **CASE** ▶ *Jacob Thomas asks you to study and improve the Education-J database.*

STEPS

1. **Open the Education-J.accdb database from the location where you store your Data Files, then enable content if prompted**

2. **Double-click the Employees table in the Navigation Pane**

   The EDepartment and ETitle fields both contain repeating data. You decide to further normalize the database by creating lookup tables for these fields. A **lookup table** is a small table that stores values used in a field of another table.

3. **Close the Employees datasheet, click the CREATE tab, click the Table Design button in the Tables group, type Department as the field name, press [Tab], click the Primary Key button in the Tools group, save the table with the name Departments, then open it in Datasheet View and enter the values shown in FIGURE J-1**

   QUICK TIP

   Use the ↔ pointer to resize columns.

4. **Close the Departments datasheet, click the CREATE tab, click the Table Design button in the Tables group, type Titles as the field name, press [Tab], click the Primary Key button in the Tools group, save the table with the name Titles, then open it in Datasheet View and enter the values shown in FIGURE J-2**

5. **Save and close the Titles datasheet, right-click the Employees table in the Navigation Pane, then click Design View**

   Next, you use the Lookup Wizard to establish a one-to-many relationship between the Department field in the Departments table and the EDepartment field in the Employees table. The Lookup Wizard also creates a drop-down list of values for the Lookup field.

   TROUBLE

   If you receive an error message, compare the values in your Departments table to **FIGURE J-1**, then redo Step 6.

6. **Click Short Text in the Data Type column for the EDepartment field, click the list arrow, click Lookup Wizard, click Next to look up values in a table, click Table: Departments, click Next, double-click Department as the selected field, click Next, click the first sort arrow, click Department, click Next, click Next, click the Enable Data Integrity check box, click Finish, then click Yes**

   The Departments and Employees tables are now linked in a one-to-many relationship with referential integrity enforced.

   TROUBLE

   If you receive an error message, compare the values in your Titles table to **FIGURE J-2**, then redo Step 7.

7. **Click Short Text in the Data Type column for the ETitle field, click the list arrow, click Lookup Wizard, click Next to look up values in a table, click Table: Titles, click Next, double-click Titles as the selected field, click Next, click the first sort arrow, click Titles, click Next, click Next, click the Enable Data Integrity check box, click Finish, click Yes, then click Yes again**

   The Titles and Employees tables are now linked in a one-to-many relationship with referential integrity enforced.

8. **Click the View button ⊞ to switch to Datasheet View, click any value in the EDepartment field, click the list arrow, as shown in FIGURE J-3, click any value in the ETitle field, then click its list arrow to test its Lookup properties as well**

   Lookup properties mean that data entry will be faster, more consistent, and more accurate.

FIGURE J-1: Departments datasheet

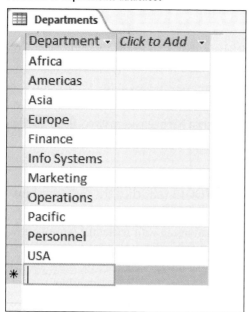

FIGURE J-2: Titles datasheet

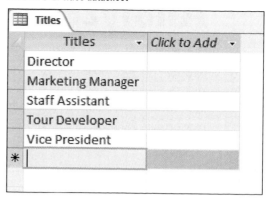

FIGURE J-3: EDepartment field of the Employees table has Lookup properties

List arrow for EDepartment

ETitle is now a Lookup field

EDepartment is now a Lookup field

ELast	EFirst	EDepartment	ETitle	DateHired	EmployeeNo
⊞ Dawson	Ron	Marketing	Vice President	2/15/2000	11-55-77
⊞ Lane	Keisha	Africa	Vice President	3/22/2000	13-47-88
⊞ Wong	Grace	Americas	Vice President	8/20/2002	17-34-22
⊞ Ramirez	Juan	Asia	Director	8/6/2003	22-33-44
	Gail	Europe	Tour Developer	1/3/2007	23-45-67
	Ellen	Finance	Tour Developer	7/1/2004	32-10-68
⊞ Hoppengarth	Wim	Info Systems	Tour Developer	1/1/2005	33-38-37
⊞ McDonald	Nancy	Marketing	Tour Developer	9/23/2010	33-44-09
⊞ Opazo	Derek	Operations	Tour Developer	4/8/2003	34-58-99
⊞ Long	Jessica	Pacific	Marketing Manager	3/1/2004	34-78-13
⊞ Rock	Mark	Personnel	Tour Developer	2/25/2007	42-42-42
⊞ Rice	Julia	USA / Personnel	Vice President	1/10/2001	45-99-11

Understanding third normal form

The process of normalization can be broken down into degrees, which include **first normal form (1NF)**, a single two-dimensional table with rows and columns; **second normal form (2NF)**, where redundant data in the original table is extracted, placed in a new table, and related to the original table; and **third normal form (3NF)**, where calculated fields (also called derived fields) such as totals or taxes are removed. In an Access database, calculated fields can be created "on the fly" using a query, which means that the information in the calculation is automatically produced and is always accurate based on the latest updates to the database. Strive to create databases that adhere to the rules of third normal form.

Analyze Relationships

Learning Outcomes
• Analyze table relationships
• Analyze junction tables

One of the best ways to teach yourself advanced database skills is to study a well-developed database. Microsoft provides a fully developed, well-designed database example called **Northwind** that tracks worldwide orders for a specialty food wholesale business. Northwind was created in the 1990s but is still used to learn about Access today. The relationships between tables determine the health and effectiveness of a database because the Relationships window shows how well the data has been normalized. **CASE** ▸ *You study the Relationships window of the Education-J and the Northwind databases.*

STEPS

1. **Close the Employees table, click the DATABASE TOOLS tab, click the Relationships button, then click the All Relationships button**

   You used the Lookup Wizard to create a one-to-many relationship with referential integrity between the Departments and Employees tables using the Department and EDepartment fields. You also used the Lookup Wizard to create a one-to-many relationship with referential integrity between the Titles and Employees tables using the Titles and ETitle fields. Move the field lists to better view the relationships.

   QUICK TIP
   Move field lists by dragging their title bars.

2. **Drag and resize the field lists in the Relationships window to look like FIGURE J-4**

   When the relationship lines are clear, the database design is easier to read. A **many-to-many relationship** exists when two tables are related to the same intermediate table, called the **junction table**, with one-to-many relationships. The Employees and Courses tables have a many-to-many relationship (one employee can take many courses and one course can be taken by many employees). This relationship is resolved with the junction table, Enrollments.

3. **Save and close the Relationships window, close the Education-J database, open the Northwind.mdb database from the location where you store your Data Files, click the Close button to close the welcome message, enable content if prompted, read the welcome message, then click OK**

   Northwind.mdb is a database in the Access 2000 file format. Access 2013 can open and work with an Access database in a 2000 or 2002-2003 file format, both of which have the **.mdb** file extension. Databases with a 2007 through 2013 file format have an **.accdb** file extension.

4. **Double-click the Categories table in the Navigation Pane; note the number of fields and records in the table; then open, observe, and close each of the eight tables**

   Now that you're familiar with the data in each table, view their relationships.

   QUICK TIP
   Double-click the link line between two tables to open the Edit Relationships dialog box, which shows all aspects of a relationship, including the referential integrity and cascade options.

5. **Click the DATABASE TOOLS tab, click the Relationships button, scroll to the top of the window as needed, then resize and move the field lists so that all fields are visible, as shown in FIGURE J-5**

   Note that the Employees and Shippers tables have a many-to-many relationship, as do the Employees and Customers and the Shippers and Customers tables in the Northwind database. In each case, the Orders table is the junction table.

   Also note that the Order Details table has a **multifield primary key** that consists of the OrderID and ProductID fields. In other words, the combination of a particular OrderID value plus a ProductID value should be unique for each record.

Multivalued fields

Access allows you to store multiple values in one field by setting the **Allow Multiple Values property** to Yes. This property is found on the Lookup tab in Table Design View. For example, you might be tempted to create an Ingredients field in a Products table to list all of the major ingredients for each product. A better way to handle this, however, is to create an Ingredients table and relate it to the Products table using a one-to-many relationship. The latter approach may take a little more time up front, but it respects fundamental database design rules and gives you the most flexibility in the long run.

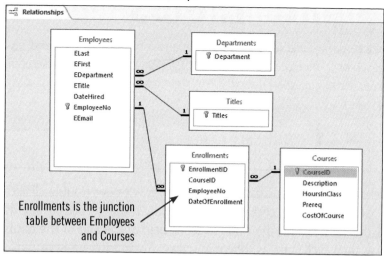

Enrollments is the junction table between Employees and Courses

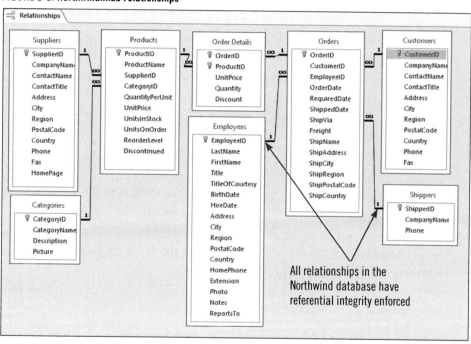

All relationships in the Northwind database have referential integrity enforced

More about Cascade options

When referential integrity is enforced on a relationship, two options become available in the Edit Relationships dialog box, as shown in **FIGURE J-6**: Cascade Update Related Fields and Cascade Delete Related Records. Checking the **Cascade Update Related Fields** check box means that if you change the primary key field value in the table on the "one" side of a one-to-many relationship, all foreign key field values in the "many" table automatically update as well. Checking the **Cascade Delete Related Records** check box means that if you delete a record in the table on the "one" side of a relationship, all related records in the "many" table are automatically deleted as well. Therefore, the cascade options both automatically change data in the "many" table based on changes in the "one" table.

FIGURE J-6: Edit Relationships dialog box

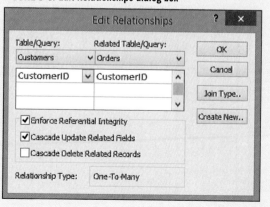

Access 2013

Evaluate Tables

Learning Outcomes
• Apply the Totals row in a datasheet
• Modify table properties

Access offers several table features that make analyzing existing data and producing results, such as datasheet subtotals, much easier and faster. **CASE** ▶ *You review the tables of the Northwind database to analyze data and to study table properties.*

STEPS

QUICK TIP
Scroll to the right to find the Units In Stock field. Scroll to the bottom of the datasheet to find the Totals row.

1. **Save and close the Northwind Relationships window, double-click the Products table in the Navigation Pane, click the Totals button in the Records group on the HOME tab, click the Total cell for the Units In Stock field at the end of the datasheet, click the list arrow, then click Sum, as shown in** FIGURE J-7

   A subtotal of the units in stock, 3119, appears in the Total cell for the Units In Stock field. As shown in the Totals list, a numeric field allows you to calculate the Average, Sum, Count, Maximum, Minimum, Standard Deviation, or Variance statistic for the field. If you were working in the Total cell of a Text field, you could choose only the Count statistic. Notice that the Current Record box displays the word "Totals" to indicate that you are working in the Total row. You can use the Current Record box to quickly move to a record.

2. **Double-click Totals in the Current Record box, type 6, then press [Enter]**

   Access moves the focus to the Units In Stock field of the sixth record.

3. **Click the record selector button of the sixth record to select the entire record, then press [Delete]**

   Working with a well-defined relational database with referential integrity enforced on all relationships, you are prevented from deleting a record in a "one" (parent) table if the record is related to many records in a "many" (child) table. In this case, the sixth record in the Products table is related to records in the Order Details table, and therefore it cannot be deleted. Next, you examine table properties.

4. **Click OK, save and close the Products table, right-click the Employees table, click Design View, then click the Property Sheet button in the Show/Hide group to open the Property Sheet if it is not already open**

   For the Products table, you can prevent data entry errors by specifying that the HireDate field value is always greater than the BirthDate field value.

5. **Click the Validation Rule box, type [HireDate]>[BirthDate], click the Validation Text box, type Hire date must be greater than birth date, as shown in** FIGURE J-8, **click the Save button** 🖫 **on the Quick Access toolbar, click Yes, then click the View button** 🏢 **to switch to Datasheet View**

   Test the new table validation rule.

6. **Tab to the Hire Date field, type 4/4/40, then press [↓]**

   A dialog box opens, displaying the text entered in the Validation Text property.

7. **Click OK, then press [Esc] to remove the incorrect hire date entry for the first record**

Analyzing Database Design Using Northwind

FIGURE J-7: Products datasheet with Total row

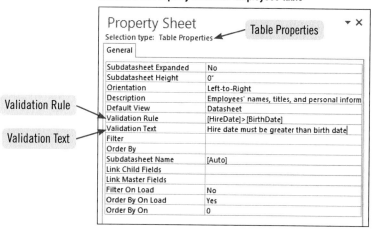

FIGURE J-8: Property Sheet for Employees table

Property Sheet ▾ ✕
Selection type: Table Properties   Table Properties

General

Subdatasheet Expanded	No
Subdatasheet Height	0"
Orientation	Left-to-Right
Description	Employees' names, titles, and personal inform
Default View	Datasheet
Validation Rule	[HireDate] > [BirthDate]
Validation Text	Hire date must be greater than birth date|
Filter	
Order By	
Subdatasheet Name	[Auto]
Link Child Fields	
Link Master Fields	
Filter On Load	No
Order By On Load	Yes
Order By On	0

Validation Rule

Validation Text

Modifying fields in Datasheet View

When working in Table Datasheet View, the FIELDS tab on the Ribbon contains buttons that allow you to add or delete a field, or change the name or data type of an existing field. You can also modify certain field properties such as Caption, Field Size, Format, Required, Validation Rule, and Validation Text. For full access to all of the properties for a field, however, work in Table Design View.

Improve Fields

To improve and enhance database functionality, the Northwind database also employs several useful field properties, such as Caption, Allow Zero Length, and Index. **CASE** *You review the Northwind database to study how lesser-used field properties have been implemented in the Employees table.*

STEPS

1. **Click the View button ⊻ to switch to Design View, close the Property Sheet, click the EmployeeID field, then press [↓] to move through the fields of the Employees table while observing the Caption property in the Field Properties pane**

   The **Caption** property text is displayed as the default field name in datasheets and labels.

2. **Select Reports To in the Caption property of the ReportsTo field, then type Manager**

   Use the Caption property when you want to clarify a field for the users, but prefer not to change the actual field name.

3. **Click the HireDate field, then change the Indexed property to Yes (Duplicates OK)**

   An **index** keeps track of the order of the values in the indexed field as data is being entered and edited. The **Indexed property** is used to improve database performance when a field is often used for sorting. Fields that are not often used for sorting should have their Indexed property set to No, but you can still sort on any field at any time, whether the Indexed property is set to Yes or No.

4. **Click the HomePhone field and examine the Allow Zero Length property**

   Currently, the **Allow Zero Length property** is set to No, meaning zero-length strings ("") are not allowed. A zero-length string is an *intentional* "nothing" entry (as opposed to a **null** entry, which also means that the field contains nothing, but doesn't indicate intent). For example, some employees might *intentionally* not want to provide a home phone number. In those instances, a zero-length string entry is appropriate. Note that you query for zero-length strings using "" criteria, whereas you query for null values using the operator **Is Null**.

5. **Double-click the Allow Zero Length property to switch the choice from No to Yes, as shown in FIGURE J-9**

   With the field changes in place, you test them in Datasheet View.

6. **Click the View button ▦ to switch to Datasheet View, click Yes to save the table, tab to the Home Phone field, enter "" (two quotation marks without a space), tab to the Extension field, enter "", then press [Tab]**

   An error message appears, as shown in **FIGURE J-10**, indicating that you cannot enter a zero-length string in the Extension field.

7. **Click OK to acknowledge the error message, press [Esc], press [Tab] three more times to observe the Manager caption for the ReportsTo field, then save and close the Employees table**

FIGURE J-9: Changing field properties in the Employees table

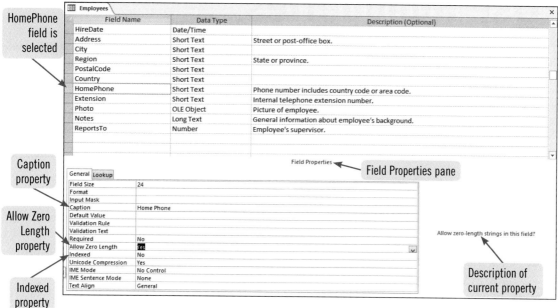

HomePhone field is selected

Field Properties pane

Caption property

Allow Zero Length property

Indexed property

Allow zero-length strings in this field?

Description of current property

FIGURE J-10: Testing field properties in the Employees table

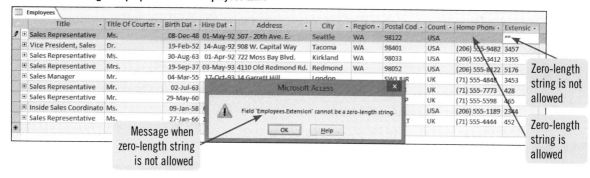

Zero-length string is not allowed

Message when zero-length string is not allowed

Zero-length string is allowed

Using Long Text fields

Use Long Text fields when you need to store more than 256 characters in a field, which is the maximum Field Size value for a Short Text field. Fields that store comments, reviews, notes, or other ongoing conversational information are good candidates for the Long Text data type. Set the **Append Only** property to Yes to allow users to add data to a Memo field, but not to change or remove existing data. The Append Only property is available for Memo or Long Text fields in Access 2007 databases created in Access 2007, 2010, or Access 2013.

Analyzing Database Design Using Northwind

Use Subqueries

Learning Outcomes
• Use subqueries
• Use advanced functions

The Northwind database contains several interesting queries that demonstrate advanced query techniques, such as grouping on more than one field, using functions in calculated fields, and developing subqueries, which you might not have studied yet. **CASE** ▶ *You work in the Northwind database to learn how to use advanced query techniques, including subqueries.*

STEPS

1. **Double-click the Product Sales for 1995 query to view the datasheet**

   This query summarizes product sales by product name for the year 1995. The datasheet includes 77 records, and each record represents one product name. The third column summarizes product sales for that product. To analyze the construction of the query, switch to Design View.

   QUICK TIP
   Right-click a field in the query grid, then click Build on the shortcut menu to open the Expression Builder dialog box.

2. **Click the View button ☒, then resize the columns in the query grid to better view the data, as shown in FIGURE J-12**

   Several interesting techniques have been used in the construction of this query. The records are grouped by both the CategoryName and the ProductName fields. A calculated field, ProductSales, is computed by first multiplying the UnitPrice field from the Order Details table by the Quantity field, then subtracting the Discount. The result of this calculation is subtotaled using the Sum function. In addition, the ShippedDate field contains criteria so that only those sales between the dates of 1/1/1995 and 12/31/1995 are selected.

3. **Save and close the Product Sales for 1995 query, then double-click the Category Sales for 1995 query in the Navigation Pane to open the query datasheet**

   This query contains only eight records because the sales are summarized (grouped) by the Category field and there are only eight unique categories. The Category Sales field summarizes total sales by category. To see how this query was constructed, switch to Design View.

4. **Click ☒ to switch to Design View, then resize the field list and the columns in the query grid to display all of the fields**

   Note that the field list for the query is based on the Product Sales for 1995 query, as shown in **FIGURE J-13**. When a query is based on another query's field list, the field list is called a **subquery**. In this case, the Category Sales for 1995 query used the Product Sales for 1995 as its subquery to avoid having to re-create the long ProductSales calculated field.

5. **Save and close the Category Sales for 1995 query**

Using Expression Builder

The **Expression Builder** is a dialog box that helps you evaluate and create expressions. The full expression is displayed at the top of the dialog box. The three panes at the bottom of the dialog box help you find and enter parts of the expression. The left pane shows all objects and built-in functions in the database. The middle and right panes further break down the options for the element selected in the left pane. **FIGURE J-11** shows how to find the built-in CCur function used in the ProductSales calculated field. The **CCur** function is used to convert an expression to Currency.

FIGURE J-11: Expression Builder dialog box

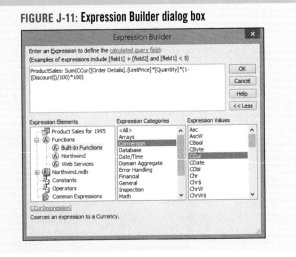

FIGURE J-12: Design View of the Product Sales for 1995 query

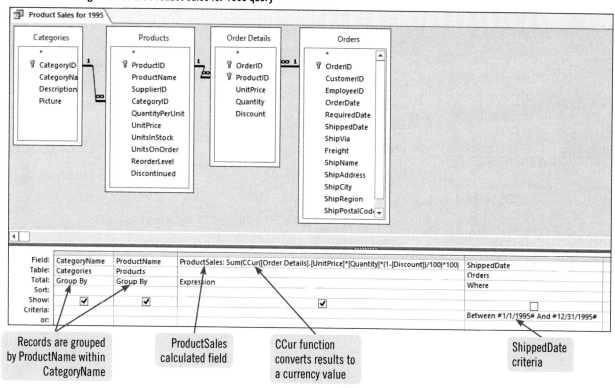

Records are grouped by ProductName within CategoryName

ProductSales calculated field

CCur function converts results to a currency value

ShippedDate criteria

FIGURE J-13: Using a subquery

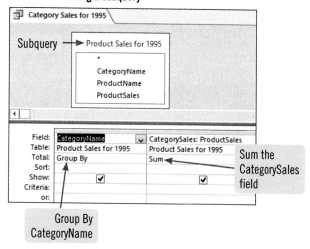

Subquery

Sum the CategorySales field

Group By CategoryName

Modify Joins

When you create a query based on multiple tables, only records that have matching data in each of the field lists present in the query are selected. This is due to the default **inner join** operation applied to the one-to-many relationship between two tables. Other join types are described in TABLE J-1. They help select records that do not have a match in a related table. **CASE** ▶ *You use the Northwind database and modify the join operation to find records in the Customers table that do not have a matching record in the Orders table.*

STEPS

1. Click the CREATE tab, click the Query Design button in the Queries group, double-click Customers, double-click Orders, then click Close

2. Resize the field list so that you can see all the fields in the Orders table, double-click CompanyName in the Customers table, double-click OrderDate in the Orders table, double-click Freight in the Orders table, then click the View button 🔲 to view the datasheet

   This query selects 830 records using the default inner join between the tables. An inner join means that records are selected only if a matching value is present in both tables. Therefore, any records in the Customers table that did not have a related record in the Orders table would not be selected. You modify the join operation to find those customers.

3. Click the View button 🔲 to switch to Design View, then double-click the middle of the one-to-many relationship line between the tables to open the Join Properties dialog box shown in FIGURE J-14

   The Join Properties dialog box provides information regarding how the two tables are joined and allows you to change from the default inner join (option 1) to a left outer join (2) or right outer join (3).

4. Click the 2 option button, then click OK as shown in FIGURE J-15

   The arrow pointing to the Orders table indicates that the join line has been modified to be a left outer join. With join operations, "left" always refers to the "one" table of a one-to-many relationship regardless of where the table is physically positioned in Query Design View. A **left outer join** means that all of the records in the "one" table will be selected for the query regardless of whether they have matching records in the "many" table.

5. Click 🔲 to view the datasheet

   The datasheet now shows 832 records, two more than when an inner join operation was used. To find the two new records quickly, use Is Null criteria.

6. Click 🔲 to return to Design View, click the Criteria cell for the OrderDate field, type Is Null, then click 🔲 to view the datasheet again

   The datasheet now contains only two records, as shown in FIGURE J-16, the two customers who do not have any matching order records. Left outer joins are very useful for finding records on the "one" side of a relationship (parent records) that do not have matching records on the "many" side (child records).

   When referential integrity is enforced on a relationship before data is entered, it is impossible to create new records on the "many" side of a relationship that do not have matching records on the "one" side (orphan records). Therefore, a **right outer join** is very useful to help find orphan records in a poorly designed database, but a right outer join operation would not be useful in the Northwind database because referential integrity was applied on all relationships before any records were entered.

7. Close the query and save with the name CustomersWithoutOrders

FIGURE J-14: Join Properties dialog box

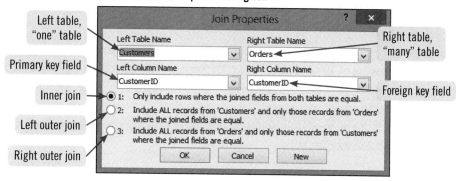

Left table, "one" table

Primary key field

Inner join

Left outer join

Right outer join

Right table, "many" table

Foreign key field

FIGURE J-15: Left outer join line

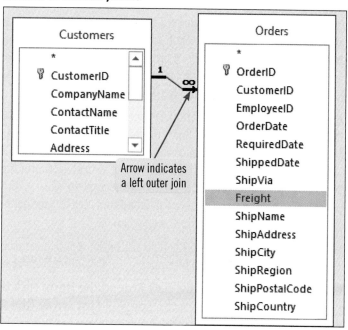

Arrow indicates a left outer join

FIGURE J-16: Customers without orders

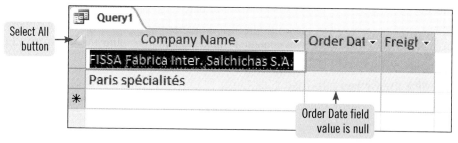

Select All button

Order Date field value is null

TABLE J-1: Join operations

join operation	description
inner	Default join; selects records from two related tables in a query that have matching values in a field common to both tables
left outer	Selects all the records from the left table (the "one" table in a one-to-many relationship) even if the "one" table doesn't have matching records in the related "many" table
right outer	Selects all the records from the right table (the "many" table in a one-to-many relationship) even if the "many" table doesn't have matching records in the related "one" table

Analyze Forms

Learning
Outcomes
• Work with form
  properties
• Work with a splash
  screen form
• Work with a
  switchboard form

Database developers create forms to provide a fast and easy-to-use interface for database users. In a fully developed database, users generally do not work with individual objects or the Navigation Pane. Rather, they use forms to guide all of their activities. The Northwind database provides several examples of sophisticated forms used to easily navigate and work with the data in the underlying database. **CASE** ▶ *You examine Northwind forms to gain an understanding of how well-designed forms could be applied to the databases at Quest Specialty Travel.*

STEPS

1. **Double-click the Startup form in the Navigation Pane**

   The Startup form opens, as shown in **FIGURE J-17**. The Startup form is a **splash screen**, a special form used to announce information. To create a splash screen, you create a new form in Form Design View with the labels, graphics, and command buttons desired, plus you set the **Border Style** property of the form to None. You also set the following form properties to No: **Record Selectors**, **Navigation Buttons**, **Scroll Bars** (Neither), **Control Box**, and **Min Max Buttons** (None).

2. **Click OK, then double-click the Main Switchboard form in the Navigation Pane**

   The Main Switchboard form opens, as shown in **FIGURE J-18**. A **switchboard** is a special form used to help users navigate throughout the rest of the database. A switchboard contains command buttons to give users fast and easy access to the database objects they use. A switchboard form is created in Form Design View using many of the same form properties used to create a splash screen. Also note that the Record Source property for the splash screen and switchboard forms is not used because neither form is used for data entry.

3. **Click the Orders command button**

   The Orders form opens for the first of 830 orders. This form shows the attractiveness and sophistication of a well-developed form. You modify the first order to learn about the form's capabilities.

4. **Click the Bill To: combo box arrow, click Around the Horn, click the Salesperson combo box arrow, click King, Robert, click the Spegesild list arrow (the first product in the order), click Steeleye Stout, press [Tab], type 20 for the Quantity value, press [Tab], enter 50 for the Discount value, then press [Tab]**

   The first order in the Orders form should look like **FIGURE J-19**. The Orders form is a traditional Access form in that it is used to enter and edit data. The form uses combo boxes and calculations to make data entry fast, easy, and accurate. Also notice the Print Invoice command button used to print the current record, the current invoice. Well-designed forms contain a command button to print the *current* record because the regular Print button will print *all* records (in this case, all 830 orders).

5. **Right-click the Orders tab, then click Close**

   Northwind contains many other forms you can explore later to learn more about form design and construction.

Analyzing Database Design Using Northwind

FIGURE J-17: Northwind splash screen form, Startup

Welcome to Northwind Traders, a sample database you can use to learn about Microsoft Access. You can experiment with the data stored in Northwind, and use the forms, reports, and other database objects as models for your own database.

All the objects in Northwind are available from the Database window, which will be displayed when you click OK. In the Database window, you can display descriptions of the objects by clicking Details on the View menu.

OK

The names of companies, products, people, characters, and/or data mentioned herein are fictitious and are in no way intended to represent any real individual, company, product, or event, unless otherwise noted.

FIGURE J-18: Northwind startup form, Main Switchboard

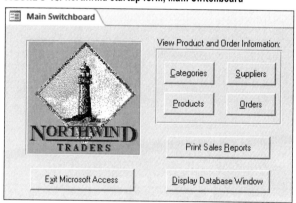

FIGURE J-19: Northwind Orders form

Salesperson combo box

Spegesild changed to Steeleye Stout

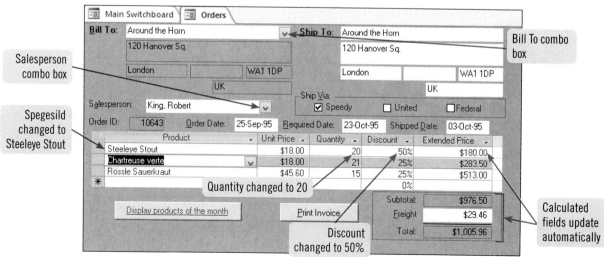

Quantity changed to 20

Discount changed to 50%

Bill To combo box

Calculated fields update automatically

Analyzing Database Design Using Northwind

Analyze Reports

Learning
Outcomes
• Run a report from
a dialog box
• Add a background
image to a report

In a fully developed database, the database designer creates reports for the printed information needs of the users. In a well-designed database, the user can select what data he or she wants the report to display by making choices in a dialog box or by using parameter criteria in a query on which the report is based. **CASE** *You study some reports in the Northwind database to gain new ideas and skills.*

STEPS

1. **Click the Print Sales Reports command button on the Main Switchboard form**

   A form, the Sales Reports dialog box shown in **FIGURE J-20**, opens. A **dialog box** is a type of form used to make choices to modify the contents of another query, form, or report. In this case, the selections you make in the Sales Reports dialog box will help you create a specific report.

2. **Click the Sales by Category option button to enable the Category list box**

   In a well-designed form, controls are often enabled and disabled based on choices the user makes. In this case, the Category list box is enabled only if the Sales by Category option button is selected. You will learn how to modify a form to respond to user interaction when you work with Visual Basic for Applications (VBA).

3. **Click the Employee Sales by Country option button, click Preview, type 1/1/1995 in the Beginning Date text box, click OK, type 12/31/1995 in the Ending Date text box, click OK, then click the report to display it at 100% zoom**

   The Employee Sales by Country report opens in Print Preview, as shown in **FIGURE J-21**. It is based on the Employee Sales by Country query, which contains parameter criteria that prompted you for the beginning and ending dates to select the desired data for this report.

   The Employee Sales by Country report presents several advanced report techniques, including a calculated date expression in the Report Header section, multiple grouping levels, and a background picture also called a watermark. The **watermark** is achieved by specifying the desired watermark image, in this case Confidential.bmp, in the report's **Picture** property.

QUICK TIP
The Record Source
property of a report
identifies the
recordset (table or
query) on which the
report is based.

4. **Right-click the Employee Sales by Country report tab, click Design View, click the Property Sheet button to open the property sheet for the report, click the Data tab to observe Employee Sales by Country in the Record Source property, then click the Format tab to observe Confidential.bmp in the Picture property**

   By studying the Design View of Northwind's advanced tables, queries, and reports, you can reverse engineer the enhancements and apply them to your own database.

5. **Right-click the Employee Sales by Country report tab, click Close All, then close the Northwind.mdb database and exit Access**

   Northwind.mdb is the most common database in the history of Access. Experienced database developers often use Northwind to discuss and share database ideas.

FIGURE J-20: Sales Reports dialog box

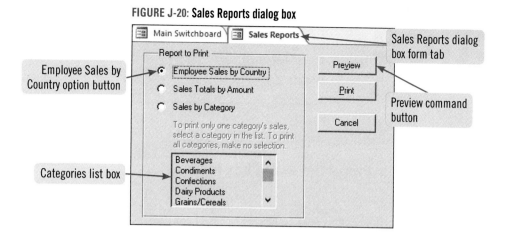

Employee Sales by Country option button

Categories list box

Sales Reports dialog box form tab

Preview command button

FIGURE J-21: Report with background picture and date criteria

Expression based on date criteria

Records are grouped by country and salesperson

Confidential background picture

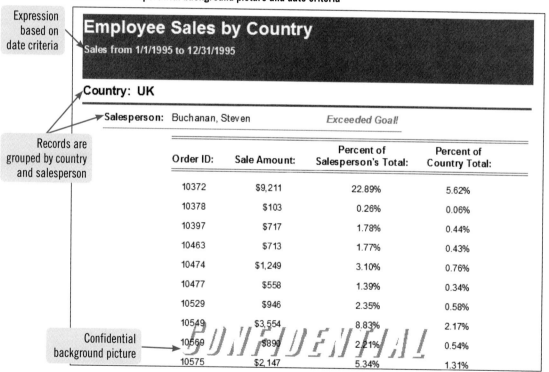

Practice

Concepts Review

Identify each element of the Join Properties dialog box in FIGURE J-22.

FIGURE J-22

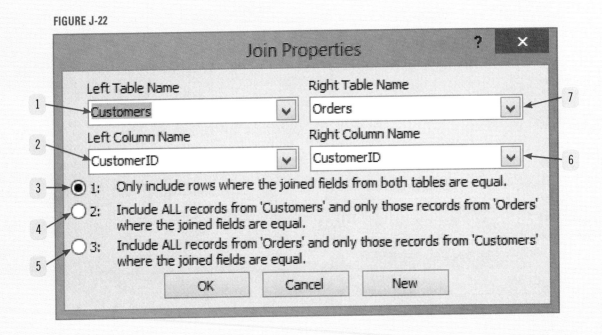

Match each term with the statement that best describes it.

8. Normalization
9. Caption
10. Index
11. Zero-length string

a. An *intentional* "nothing" entry
b. Displayed as the default field name at the top of the field column in datasheets as well as in labels that describe fields on forms and reports
c. Keeps track of the order of the values in the indexed field as data is entered and edited
d. The process of structuring data into a well-formed relational database

Select the best answer from the list of choices.

12. **Which of the following is *not* a benefit of a well-designed relational database?**
    - **a.** Reduces redundant data
    - **b.** Has lower overall storage requirements
    - **c.** Improves reporting flexibility
    - **d.** Is easier to create than a single-table database

13. **First normal form can be described as:**
    - **a.** A well-functioning, fully developed relational database.
    - **b.** Any collection of data in any form.
    - **c.** A single two-dimensional table with rows and columns.
    - **d.** A series of queries and subqueries.

14. **Which of the following activities occurs during the creation of second normal form?**
    - **a.** Redundant data is removed from one table, and relationships are created.
    - **b.** Calculated fields are removed from tables.
    - **c.** Additional calculated fields are added to tables.
    - **d.** All data is organized in one master table.

15. **Which of the following activities occurs during the creation of third normal form?**
    - **a.** All data is organized in one master table.
    - **b.** Calculated fields are removed from tables.
    - **c.** Additional calculated fields are added to tables.
    - **d.** Redundant data is removed from one table, and relationships are created.

16. **Which report property is used to add a watermark to a report?**
    - **a.** Record Source
    - **c.** Default View
    - **b.** Caption
    - **d.** Picture

17. **A multifield primary key consists of:**
    - **a.** Two or more fields.
    - **c.** An AutoNumber field.
    - **b.** One field.
    - **d.** A primary key field that also serves as a foreign key field.

18. **Which of the following is *not* true for the Caption property?**
    - **a.** It is the default field name at the top of the field column in datasheets.
    - **b.** The value of the Caption property is the default label that describes a field on a report.
    - **c.** The value of the Caption property is the default label that describes a field on a form.
    - **d.** It is used instead of the field name when you build expressions.

19. **Which of the following fields would most likely be used for an index?**
    - **a.** MiddleName
    - **c.** ApartmentNumber
    - **b.** FirstName
    - **d.** LastName

20. **Which of the following phrases best describes the need for both null values and zero-length strings?**
    - **a.** They represent two different conditions.
    - **b.** Having two different choices for "nothing" clarifies data entry.
    - **c.** Null values speed up calculations.
    - **d.** They look different on a query datasheet.

Skills Review

1. **Normalize data.**
   - **a.** Start Access, open the Northwind2.mdb database from the location where you store your Data Files, close the splash screen, enable content if prompted, then click OK to close the splash screen again.
   - **b.** Double-click the Employees table to view its datasheet. Notice the repeated data in the Title of Courtesy field. Close the Employees datasheet. You will build a lookup table to better manage the values in this field.

Skills Review (continued)

c. Click the CREATE tab, click Table Design, then create a table with one field, **TitleName**. Give it a Short Text data type, and set it as the primary key field.

d. Save the table with the name **TitlesOfCourtesy**, and enter the data in the datasheet, as shown in **FIGURE J-23**. Be very careful to type the data exactly as shown. Save and close the TitlesOfCourtesy table when you are finished.

e. Open the Employees table in Design View, click the TitlesOfCourtesy field, then choose Lookup Wizard using the Data Type list arrow.

f. Choose the "I want the lookup field to get the values..." option, choose Table: TitlesOfCourtesy, select the TitleName field for the list and specify an ascending sort order on the TitleName field, accept the column width, accept the TitlesOfCourtesy label, then click Yes to save the table.

g. Switch to Datasheet View, and then click the Title Of Courtesy field's list arrow to make sure all four values from the TitlesOfCourtesy table are listed as values.

h. Close the Employees table, open the Relationships window, click the All Relationships button, then double-click the link line between the TitlesOfCourtesy and Employees tables to open the Edit Relationships dialog box. Click the Enforce Referential Integrity check box, then click OK.

i. Move and resize the field lists to match **FIGURE J-24**.

FIGURE J-23

TitleName	Click to Add
Dr.	
Mr.	
Mrs.	
Ms.	

FIGURE J-24

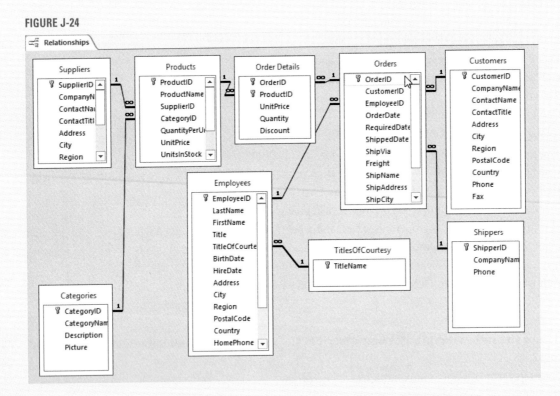

2. Analyze relationships.

a. It is easy to see that all of the relationships in the Northwind2.mdb database are one-to-many relationships with referential integrity enforced due to the presence of the "1" and "infinity" symbols. When two parent tables both have a one-to-many relationship with the same child table, they are said to have a many-to-many relationship with each other. This database has five many-to-many relationships. Use the following table to identify the tables involved. One many-to-many relationship is provided as an example.

Table 1	Junction Table	Table 2
Employees	Orders	Customers

Analyzing Database Design Using Northwind

Skills Review (continued)

b. Create a Relationship report. Use landscape orientation so that the report is only one page long, and insert your name as a label in the Report Header using black text and a 12-point font size. Save and close the report using the default name, **Relationships for Northwind2**.

c. Save and close the Relationships window.

3. Evaluate tables.

a. Open the datasheet for the Order Details table.

b. Tab to the Quantity field, then click the Totals button to open the Total row at the end of the datasheet.

c. Use the Total row to find the sum of the Quantity field, 51317, which represents the total quantity of products sold for this database.

d. Save and close the Order Details table.

4. Improve fields.

a. Open the Products table in Design View.

b. Change the Caption property for the UnitPrice field to **Retail Price**.

c. At the end of the field list, add a new field named **StandardQuantity** with a Number data type and a Caption property of **Standard Quantity**.

d. At the end of the field list, add a new field named **UnitOfMeasure** with a Short Text data type and a Caption property of **Unit of Measure**.

e. Save the table, then display it in Datasheet View.

f. Referring to the existing data in the Quantity Per Unit field, enter the correct information into the new Standard Quantity and Unit of Measure fields for the first 10 records. The first five records are completed for you in **FIGURE J-25**.

FIGURE J-25

Category	Quantity Per Unit	Retail Pr	Units In Stoc	Units On Orde	Reorder Leve	Discontinue	Standard Qu	Unit of Meas
⊞ Beverages	10 boxes x 20 bags	$18.00	39	0	10	☐	10	boxes x 20 bag:
⊞ Beverages	24 - 12 oz bottles	$19.00	17	40	25	☐	24	12 oz bottles
⊞ Condiments	12 - 550 ml bottles	$10.00	13	70	25	☐	12	550 ml bottles
⊞ Condiments	48 - 6 oz jars	$22.00	53	0	0	☐	48	6 oz jars
⊞ Condiments	36 boxes	$21.35	0	0	0	☑	36	boxes
⊞ Condiments	12 - 8 oz jars	$25.00	120	0	25	☐		
⊞ Produce	12 - 1 lb pkgs.	$30.00	15	0	10	☐		
⊞ Condiments	12 - 12 oz jars	$40.00	6	0	0	☐		
⊞ Meat/Poultry	18 - 500 g pkgs.	$97.00	29	0	0	☑		
⊞ Seafood	12 - 200 ml jars	$31.00	31	0	0	☐		
⊞ Dairy Products	1 kg pkg.	$21.00	22	30	30	☐		
⊞ Dairy Products	10 - 500 g pkgs.	$38.00	86	0	0	☐		
⊞ Seafood	2 kg box	$6.00	24	0	5	☐		

g. Explain the benefits of separating quantities from their units of measure. (*Hint*: Think about how you find, filter, sort, and calculate data.) If these benefits were significant to your company, you would want to convert the rest of the data from the Quantity Per Unit field to the new Standard Quantity and Unit of Measure fields, too. Once all of the new data was in place, you could delete the original Quantity Per Unit field.

h. Close the Products table datasheet.

5. Use subqueries.

a. Click the CREATE tab, then click the Query Design button.

b. Double-click Orders, Order Details, and Products, then click Close.

c. Double-click the OrderDate field in the Orders table, the Quantity and UnitPrice fields in the Order Details table, and the ProductName field in the Products table.

Skills Review (continued)

   d. In the fifth column, enter the following calculated field: **GrossRevenue:[Quantity]*[Products].
    [UnitPrice]**. Because the UnitPrice field is given the same name in two tables present in this query, you use the
    [TableName].[FieldName] syntax to specify which table supplies this field.

   e. Save the query with the name **GrossRevenueCalculation**, open it in Datasheet View to test and review the
    results, and then close it.

   f. Click the CREATE tab, then click the Query Design button.

   g. Click the Queries tab in the Show Table dialog box, double-click GrossRevenueCalculation, then click Close.

   h. Double-click the ProductName and GrossRevenue fields, then click the Totals button.

   i. Change Group By in the GrossRevenue field to Sum.

   j. Open the Property Sheet for the GrossRevenue field, change the Format property to Currency, change the Caption
    property to **Total Gross Revenue**, then view the resulting datasheet.

   k. Save the query with the name **GrossRevenueByProduct**, then close it.

6. Modify joins.

   a. Open the Suppliers table in Datasheet View, and enter a record using your own last name as the company name.
    Enter realistic but fictitious data for the rest of the record, then close the Suppliers table.

   b. Click the CREATE tab, click the Query Design button, double-click Suppliers, double-click Products, then click Close.

   c. Double-click CompanyName from the Suppliers table and ProductName from the Products table. Add an ascending
    sort order for both fields, then view the datasheet. Note that there are 77 records in the datasheet.

   d. Return to Query Design View, then change the join properties to option 2, which will select all Suppliers records
    even if they don't have matching data in the Products table.

   e. View the datasheet, and note it now contains 78 records.

   f. Return to Query Design View, and add **Is Null** criteria to the ProductName field.

   g. View the datasheet noting that the only supplier without matching product records is the one you entered in Step a.
    That tells you that every other supplier in the database is related to at least one record in the Products table.

   h. Save the query with the name **SuppliersWithoutProducts**, then close it.

7. Analyze forms.

   a. Open the Customer Orders form in Form View.

   b. Notice that this form contains customer information in the main form and in two subforms. The first subform is for
    order information, and the second subform shows order details. Navigate to the fourth company name in the main
    form, which shows the orders for the company named Around the Horn.

   c. Click the Order ID value 10692 in the upper subform, and notice that the order details automatically change in the
    lower subform as you move from order to order.

   d. Explore the form by moving through customer and order records, then answer this question: How would someone
    use this form? As navigation, information, data entry, or as a dialog box?

   e. Continue exploring the rest of the forms in the Northwind2 database and identify at least one form that is used as a
    navigation form, an information form, a data entry form, and a dialog box form.

   f. Close all open forms.

8. Analyze reports.

   a. Double-click the Sales by Year report.

   b. The Sales by Year dialog form appears. Enter **1/1/95** in the Enter beginning date text box, enter **6/30/95** in the
    Enter ending date text box, then click OK.

   c. The Sales by Year report for the first two quarters of 1995 appears, indicating that 186 orders were shipped during
    this period. A subreport is used in the ShippedDate Header section to provide summary information for the entire
    report before the Detail section prints.

   d. Continue to explore the other reports in the Northwind2 database and identify at least three new features or
    techniques that you would like to learn more about.

   e. Close all open reports, close the Northwind2 database, and exit Access.

Independent Challenge 1

As the manager of a basketball team, you have created an Access database called Basketball-J.accdb to track players, games, and statistics. You have recently learned how to create lookup tables to better control the values of a field that contain repeated data and to apply your new skills to your database.

a. Start Access, open the Basketball-J.accdb database from the location where you store your Data Files, and enable content if prompted.

b. Double-click the Players table to view its datasheet. Notice the repeated data in the YearInSchool and Position fields. You will build lookup tables to better describe and manage the values in those fields. Close the Players datasheet.

c. Click the CREATE tab, click Table Design, then create a two-field table with the field names **PositionDescription** and **PositionID**. Both fields should have a Short Text data type. Set PositionID as the primary key field. Save the table with the name **Positions**, and enter the data in the datasheet shown in **FIGURE J-26**. Save and close the Positions table.

FIGURE J-26

PositionDescription	PositionID
Center	C
Forward	F
Guard	G

d. Open the Players table in Design View, click the Position field, then choose Lookup Wizard using the Data Type list arrow.

e. Choose the "I want the lookup field to get the values..." option, choose Table: Positions, choose both fields, choose PositionDescription for an ascending sort order, do not hide the key column, choose PositionID as the field that uniquely identifies the row, accept the Position label, click the Enable Data Integrity check box, finish the Lookup Wizard, then click Yes to save the table. Close the Players table.

f. Repeat Step c creating a **ClassRanks** table instead of a Positions table using the field names and data shown in **FIGURE J-27**. The ClassRankDescription and ClassRankID fields are both Short Text fields. The SortOrder field is a Number field. Make the ClassRankID field the primary key field, then close the ClassRanks table.

FIGURE J-27

ClassRankDescription	ClassRankID	SortOrder
Freshman	Fr	1
Sophomore	So	2
Junior	Jr	3
Senior	Sr	4
		0

g. Repeat Step d by using the Lookup Wizard with the YearInSchool field in the Players table to look up data in the ClassRanks table. Choose all three fields, choose the SortOrder field for an ascending sort order, do not hide the key column, choose ClassRankID as the field that uniquely identifies the row, accept the YearInSchool label, click the Enable Data Integrity check box, finish the Lookup Wizard, then click Yes to save the table.

h. Click the Lookup tab and change the Column Widths property to 1;1;0 to hide the SortOrder field, then save the Players table.

i. Open the Players table datasheet to test the drop-down lists for the YearInSchool and Position fields.

j. Open the Relationships window, click the All Relationships button to make sure you're viewing all relationships, and resize field lists as needed to show all fields. The final Relationships window should look like **FIGURE J-28**.

FIGURE J-28

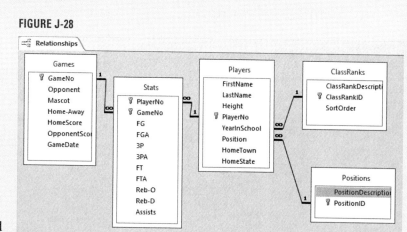

k. Create a Relationship report with the default name **Relationships for Basketball-J**.

l. Save and close the Relationships window, close the Basketball-J.accdb database, then exit Access.

Independent Challenge 2

You have been asked to create a query that displays employees as well as their manager in the same datasheet. Because each employee, regardless of title and rank, is entered as a record in the Employees table, you know that you will need to relate each record in the Employees table to another record in the same table to show the employee–manager relationship. You will work in the Northwind2 database to learn how to join a table to itself in order to answer this challenge.

a. Start Access, open the Northwind2.mdb database from the location where you store your Data Files, enable content if prompted, and click OK when prompted with the splash screen.

b. Click the CREATE tab, click the Query Design button, double-click Employees, double-click Employees a second time, click Close, right-click the Employees_1 field list, click Properties to open the Property Sheet for the Employee_1 field list, select Employees_1 in the Alias text box, type **Managers**, press [Enter], then close the Property Sheet.

c. Drag the EmployeeID field from the Managers field list and drop it on the ReportsTo field in the Employees table because each employee record reports to another employee whose EmployeeID value has been entered in the ReportsTo field. By creating this relationship using the primary key field of the Managers table, one record in the Managers table can be related to many records in the Employees table.

d. In the Managers field list, double-click the LastName field, then double-click the FirstName field.

e. In the Employees field list, double-click the LastName field, then double-click the FirstName field.

f. Add an ascending sort order on both LastName fields, as shown in **FIGURE J-29**.

g. Display the query datasheet, then widen each column to display all data. The datasheet shows that three employees report to Buchanan and five report to Fuller.

h. Save the query as **ManagerList**, close the query, then close the Northwind2 database and exit Access.

FIGURE J-29

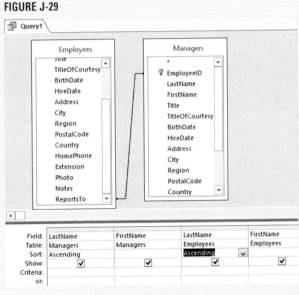

Independent Challenge 3

As the manager of a regional real estate information system, you've been asked to enhance the database to keep track of offers for each real estate listing. To do this, you will need to create a new table to track the offers, and relate it to the rest of the database in an appropriate one-to-many relationship.

a. Start Access, open the RealEstate-J.accdb database from the location where you store your Data Files, and enable content if prompted.

b. Create a table named **Offers** with the fields, data types, descriptions, and primary key shown in **FIGURE J-30**.

FIGURE J-30

Field Name	Data Type	Description
OfferID	AutoNumber	primary key field
ListingNo	Number	foreign key field to Listings table
OfferDate	Date/Time	date of offer
OfferAmount	Currency	dollar value of the offer
Buyer	Short Text	last name or company name of entity making the offer
Accepted	Yes/No	was offer accepted? Yes or No
AcceptanceDate	Date/Time	date the offer was accepted

Analyzing Database Design Using Northwind

Independent Challenge 3 (continued)

c. Use the Lookup Wizard on the ListingNo field in the Offers table to connect the Offers table to the Listings table. Select all the fields from the Listings table; sort in ascending order on the Type, Area, then SqFt fields; hide the key column; accept the ListingNo label for the lookup field; enable data integrity; and finish the wizard. Save the table when prompted.

d. In Table Design View, on the Lookup tab (Field Properties) for the ListingNo field, change the value for the Column Heads property from No to Yes.

e. In Table Design View, on the Lookup tab (Field Properties) for the ListingNo field, change the value for the List Rows property from 16 to **100**.

f. Save the table, click Yes when asked to check the data, then display it in Datasheet View.

g. Enter the record shown in the first row of **FIGURE J-31**, using the new combo box for the ListingNo field as shown.

h. Close the Offers table, close the RealEstate-J.accdb database, then exit Access.

FIGURE J-31

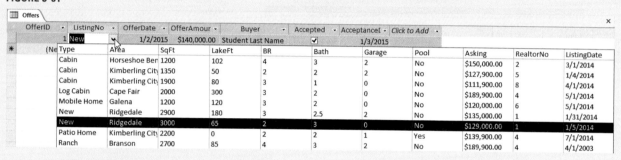

Independent Challenge 4: Explore

An Access database can help record and track your job search efforts. In this exercise, you work with a database that tracks employers and job positions to better normalize and present the data.

a. Start Access, open the JobSearch-J.accdb database from the location where you store your Data Files, and enable content if prompted.

b. Open both the Employers and Positions tables in Datasheet View to review the data. One employer may offer many positions, so the tables are related by the common EmployerID field. You decide to add Lookup properties to the EmployerID field in the Positions table to better identify each employer in this view.

c. Close both table datasheets, open the Relationships window, right-click the join line between the Employers and Positions tables, then click Delete. Click Yes to confirm you want to delete the relationship. Before you can start the Lookup Wizard on the EmployerID field in the Positions table, all existing relationships to that field must be deleted.

d. Save and close the Relationships window, then open the Positions table in Design View.

e. Start the Lookup Wizard for the EmployerID field to look up values in the Employers table. Select all fields, sort in ascending order on the CompanyName field, hide the key column, select EmployerID if asked to select the field containing the value you want to store, use the EmployerID label, enable data integrity, finish the wizard, then save the table.

f. Display the Positions table in Datasheet View, then test the new Lookup properties on the EmployerID field by changing the EmployerID for both of the "Professor" positions to **JCCC**.

g. Close the Positions table, then start a new query in Query Design View. Add both the Employers and Positions tables.

h. Add the CompanyName field from the Employers table, and the Title and CareerArea fields from the Positions table.

i. Modify the join line to include all records from Employers, then view the datasheet.

j. Save the query with the name **EmployerPositions**, then close it.

k. Close the JobSearch-J.accdb database, then exit Access.

Visual Workshop

Start Access, open the Dives-J.accdb database from the location where you store your Data Files, and enable content if prompted. Add Lookup properties to the DiveMasterID field of the DiveTrips table to achieve the result shown in **FIGURE J-32**, which looks up every field from the DiveMasters table for the lookup list and sorts the information on the LName field. Hide the key column, accept the DiveMasterID label, and enforce referential integrity. But in order to use the Lookup Wizard, first you'll have to delete the existing relationship between the DiveMasters and DiveTrips tables. Once you've finished reestablishing the relationship with the Lookup Wizard, you'll also want to modify the Lookup properties of the DiveMasterID field so that Column Heads is set to **Yes** and List Rows is set to **100**. The final DiveTrips datasheet with Lookup properties applied to the DiveMasterID field will look like **FIGURE J-32**.

FIGURE J-32

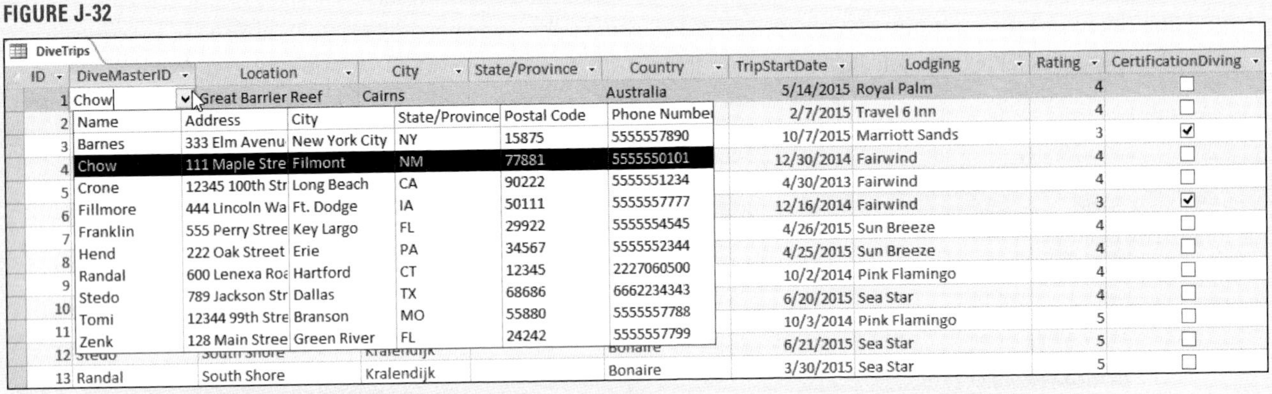

Creating Advanced Queries

CASE You use advanced query techniques to help Jacob Thomas handle the requests for information about data stored in the Education database.

Unit Objectives

After completing this unit, you will be able to:

- Query for top values
- Create a parameter query
- Modify query properties
- Create a Make Table query
- Create an Append query
- Create a Delete query
- Create an Update query
- Specify join properties
- Find unmatched records

Files You Will Need

Education-K.accdb   Basketball-K.accdb
Seminar-K.accdb   Chocolate-K.accdb

Query for Top Values

Learning Outcomes
• Apply Top Values criteria
• Apply the Totals row

After you enter a large number of records into a database, you may want to select only the most significant records by choosing a subset of the highest or lowest values from a sorted query. Use the **Top Values** feature in Query Design View to specify a number or percentage of sorted records that you want to display in the query's datasheet. **CASE** ▶ *Employee attendance at continuing education classes has grown at Quest Specialty Travel. To help plan future classes, Jacob Thomas wants a listing of the top five classes, sorted in descending order by the number of attendees for each class. You can create a summary query to find and sort the total number of attendees for each class, then use the Top Values feature to find the five most attended classes.*

STEPS

1. **Start Access, open the** Education-K.accdb database, **enable content if prompted, click the** CREATE tab, **then click the** Query Design button **in the Queries group**

   You need fields from both the Enrollments and Courses tables.

   TROUBLE
   If you add a table's field list to Query Design View twice by mistake, click the title bar of the extra field list, then press [Delete].

2. **Double-click** Enrollments, **double-click** Courses, **then click** Close **in the Show Table dialog box**

   Query Design View displays the field lists of the two related tables in the upper pane of the query window.

3. **Double-click** EnrollmentID **in the Enrollments field list, double-click** Description **in the Courses field list, then click the** View button ▦ **to switch to Datasheet View**

   The datasheet shows 404 total records. You want to know how many people took each course, so you need to group the records by the Description field and count the EnrollmentID field.

4. **Click the** View button ⊿ **to switch to Query Design View, click the** Totals button **in the Show/Hide group, click** Group By **for the EnrollmentID field, click the** Group By list arrow, **then click** Count

   Sorting is required in order to find the top values.

   QUICK TIP
   You must sort the records to get the highest (or lowest) values at the "top" before the Top Values feature makes sense.

5. **Click the** EnrollmentID **field Sort cell, click the** EnrollmentID **field Sort list arrow, then click** Descending

   Your screen should look like **FIGURE K-1**. Choosing a descending sort order lists the courses with the highest count value (the most attended courses) at the top of the datasheet.

6. **Click the** Top Values list arrow **in the Query Setup group, then click** 5

   The number or percentage specified in the Top Values list box determines which records the query returns, starting with the first record on the sorted datasheet. This is why you *must sort* your records before applying the Top Values feature. See **TABLE K-1** for more information on Top Values options.

7. **Click** ▦ **to display the resulting datasheet, then use the** ✛ **pointer to widen the first column to show the complete field name**

   Your screen should look like **FIGURE K-2**. The datasheet shows the seven most attended continuing education courses. The query selected the top seven, rather than the top five courses because there is a three-way tie for fifth place. Three courses that had 17 enrollments are all tied for fifth place, so each of those courses is listed in the datasheet.

8. **Click the** Save button 🖫 **on the Quick Access toolbar, type** TopCourses, **click** OK, **then close the datasheet**

   As with all queries, if you enter additional enrollment records into this database, the count statistics in the TopCourses query are automatically updated.

FIGURE K-1: Designing a summary query for top values

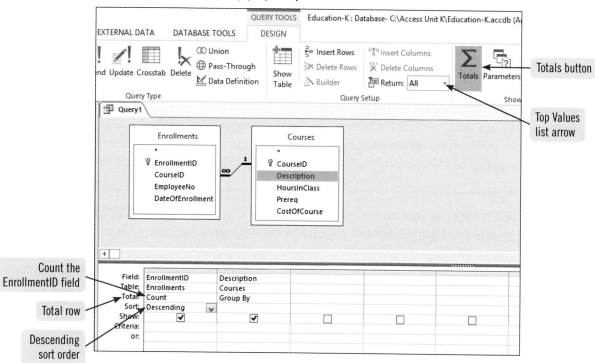

FIGURE K-2: Top Values datasheet

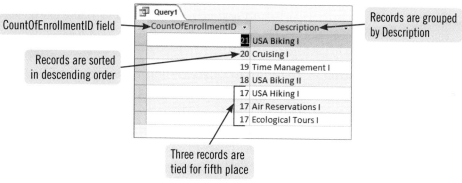

TABLE K-1: Top Values options

action	displays
Click 5, 25, or 100 in the Top Values list	Top 5, 25, or 100 records
Enter a number, such as 10, in the Top Values box	Top 10, or whatever value is entered, records
Click 5% or 25% in the Top Values list	Top 5 percent or 25 percent of records
Enter a percentage, such as 10%, in the Top Values text box	Top 10 percent, or whatever percentage is entered, of records
Click All	All records

Access 2013

Create a Parameter Query

Learning
Outcomes
• Enter parameter
  criteria
• Apply the Like
  operator

A **parameter query** displays a dialog box that prompts you for field criteria. Your entry in the dialog box determines which records appear on the final datasheet, just as if you had entered that criteria directly in the query design grid. You can also build a form or report based on a parameter query. When you open the form or report, the parameter dialog box opens. The entry in the dialog box determines which records the query selects in the recordset for the form or report. **CASE** *You want to create a query to display the courses for an individual department that you specify each time you run the query. To do so, you copy the TopCourses query then modify it to remove the Top Values option and include parameter prompts.*

STEPS

1. **Right-click the** TopCourses query **in the Navigation Pane, click** Copy, **right-click a blank spot in the Navigation Pane, click** Paste, **type** DepartmentParameter **as the Query Name, then click** OK

   You modify the DepartmentParameter query to remove the top values and to include the parameter prompt.

2. **Right-click** DepartmentParameter, **click** Design View **on the shortcut menu, click the** Show Table button **in the Query Setup group, double-click** Employees, **then click** Close

   The Employees table contains the Department field needed for this query.

3. **Drag the** title bar of the Courses field list **to the left, then drag the** title bar of the Enrollments field list **to the right so that the relationship lines do not cross behind a field list**

   You are not required to rearrange the field lists of a query, but doing so can help clarify the relationships between them.

4. **Double-click the** EDepartment **field in the Employees field list, click the** Top Values list arrow **in the Query Setup group, click** All, **delete the** Descending sort order **in the** EnrollmentID **field, then click the** View button 🖩 **to display the datasheet**

   The query now counts the EnrollmentID field for records grouped by course description as well as by employee department. Because you only want to query for one department at a time, however, you need to add parameter criteria to the Department field.

QUICK TIP
To enter a long crite-
rion, right-click the
Criteria cell, then
click Zoom.

5. **Click the** View button 🖩 **to return to Query Design View, click the** EDepartment field Criteria cell, **type** [Enter department:], **then click** 🖩 **to display the Enter Parameter Value dialog box, as shown in** FIGURE K-3

   In Query Design View, you must enter parameter criteria within [square brackets]. The parameter criterion you enter appears as a prompt in the Enter Parameter Value dialog box. The entry you make in the Enter Parameter Value dialog box is used as the final criterion for the field that contains the parameter criterion. You can combine logical operators such as greater than (>) or less than (<) as well as wildcard characters such as an asterisk (*) with parameter criteria to create flexible search options. See **TABLE K-2** for more examples of parameter criteria.

QUICK TIP
Query criteria are
not case sensitive, so
"marketing,"
"Marketing," and
"MARKETING" all
yield the same
results.

6. **Type** Marketing **in the Enter department: text box, then click** OK

   Only those records with "Marketing" in the Department field are displayed, a portion of which are shown in **FIGURE K-4**.

7. **Save and close the DepartmentParameter query**

FIGURE K-3: Using parameter criteria for the EDepartment field

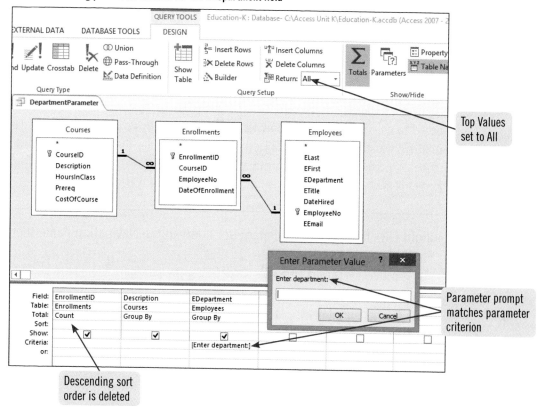

FIGURE K-4: Datasheet for parameter query when EDepartment field equals Marketing

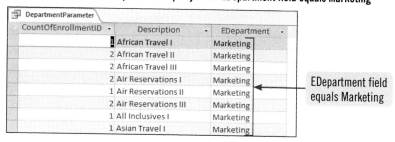

EDepartment field equals Marketing

TABLE K-2: Examples of parameter criteria

field data type	parameter criteria	description
Date/Time	>=[Enter start date:]	Searches for dates on or after the entered date
Date/Time	>=[Enter start date:] and <=[Enter end date:]	Prompts you for two date entries and searches for dates on or after the first date and on or before the second date
Short Text	Like [Enter the first character of the last name:] & "*"	Searches for any name that begins with the entered character
Short Text	Like "*" & [Enter any character(s) to search by:] & "*"	Searches for words that contain the entered characters anywhere in the field

© 2014 Cengage Learning

Modify Query Properties

Learning Outcomes
• Modify the Description property
• Define the Recordset Type property
• Create a backup

Properties are characteristics that define the appearance and behavior of items in the database, such as objects, fields, sections, and controls. You can view the properties for an item by opening its Property Sheet. **Field properties**, those that describe a field, can be changed in either Table Design View or Query Design View. If you change field properties in Query Design View, they are modified for that query only (as opposed to changing the field properties in Table Design View, which affects that field's characteristics throughout the database). Query objects also have properties that you might want to modify to better describe or protect the information they provide. **CASE** *You want to modify the query and field properties of the DepartmentParameter query to better describe and present the data.*

STEPS

1. **Right-click the DepartmentParameter query in the Navigation Pane, then click Object Properties**

   The DepartmentParameter Properties dialog box opens, providing information about the query and a text box where you can enter a description for the query.

2. **Type Counts enrollments per course description and prompts for department, then click OK**

   The **Description** property allows you to better document the purpose or author of a query. The Description property also appears on **Database Documenter** reports, a feature on the DATABASE TOOLS tab that helps you create reports with information about the database.

TROUBLE
The title bar of the Property Sheet always indicates which item's properties are shown. If it shows anything other than "Query Properties," click a blank spot beside the field lists to display query properties.

3. **Right-click the DepartmentParameter query in the Navigation Pane, click Design View on the shortcut menu, click the Property Sheet button in the Show/Hide group, then click a blank spot in the upper pane to show Query Properties in the Property Sheet**

   The Property Sheet for the query is shown in **FIGURE K-5**. It shows a complete list of the query's properties, including the Description property that you modified earlier. The **Recordset Type** property determines if and how records displayed by a query are locked and has two common choices: Snapshot and Dynaset. **Snapshot** locks the recordset (which prevents it from being updated). **Dynaset** is the default value and allows updates to data. Because a summary query's datasheet summarizes several records, you cannot update the data in a summary query regardless of the Recordset Type property value. For regular Select queries, you can specify Snapshot in the Recordset Type property to give users read (but not write) access to that datasheet.

   To change the field name, you modify the field's **Caption** property in the Property Sheet for field properties. When you click a property in a Property Sheet, a short description of the property appears in the status bar. Press [F1] to open Access Help for a longer description of the selected property.

4. **Click the EnrollmentID field, click the Caption property in the Property Sheet, type Total Enrollment, click the View button [img], type Personnel as the parameter value, then click OK**

   The Total Enrollment Caption clarifies the first column of data, as shown in **FIGURE K-6**, which displays a portion of the datasheet.

QUICK TIP
To add a description to a table, form, or other object, close it, right-click it in the Navigation Pane, then click View Properties on the shortcut menu.

5. **Save and close the DepartmentParameter query**

   The next few lessons work with action queries that modify data. In preparation for these lessons, you create a backup. A **backup** is a copy of the database that you could use if an error occurs in the current database that cannot be fixed. Businesses typically back up their database files each night.

6. **Click the FILE tab, click Save As, click Back Up Database, click the Save As button, navigate to the location where you store your Data Files, and click Save**

   A copy of the database has been placed in the selected folder with the name Education-K_*current date*.accdb.

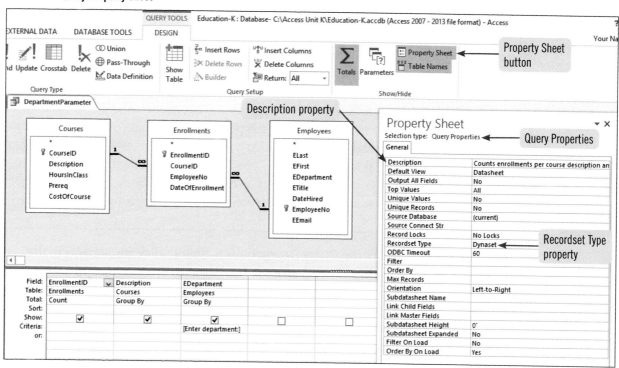

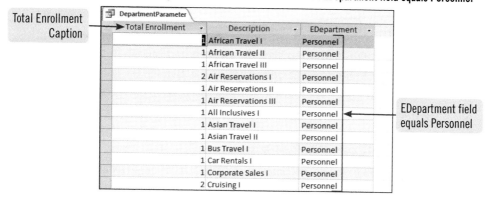

Creating an Alias

The **Alias** property renames a field list in Query Design View. An Alias doesn't change the actual name of the underlying object, but it can be helpful when you are working with a database which uses technical or outdated names for tables and queries. To create an alias, right-click the field list in Query Design View, click Properties on the shortcut menu, and then modify the Alias property.

Create a Make Table Query

Learning
Outcomes
• Define action
 queries
• Create a Make
 Table query

A **Select query** selects fields and records that match specific criteria and displays them in a datasheet. Select queries start with the SQL keyword **SELECT** and have many variations, such as summary, crosstab, top values, and parameter queries. Another very powerful type of query is the action query. Unlike Select queries that only *select* data, an **action query** *changes* all of the selected records when it is run. Access provides four types of action queries: Delete, Update, Append, and Make Table. See **TABLE K-3** for more information on action queries. A **Make Table query** is a type of action query that creates a new table of data for the selected datasheet. The location of the new table can be the current database or another Access database. Sometimes a Make Table query is used to back up data. **CASE** ▸ *You decide to use a Make Table query to archive the first quarter's records for the year 2015 that are currently stored in the Enrollments table.*

STEPS

1. **Click the CREATE tab, click the Query Design button, double-click Enrollments in the Show Table dialog box, click Close, then close the Property Sheet if it is open**

   Given you cannot undo the changes made by an action query, it's a good idea to create a backup copy of the database before running an action query. You created a backup copy of the database in the last step of the previous lesson.

2. **Double-click the * (asterisk) at the top of the Enrollments field list**

   Adding the asterisk to the query design grid includes in the grid all of the fields in that table. Later, if you add new fields to the Enrollments table, they are also added to this query.

3. **Double-click the DateOfEnrollment field to add it to the second column of the query grid, click the DateOfEnrollment field Criteria cell, type >=1/1/15 and <=3/31/15, click the DateOfEnrollment field Show check box to uncheck it, then use the resize pointer ↔ to widen the DateOfEnrollment column to view the entire Criteria entry, as shown in FIGURE K-7**

   Before changing this query into a Make Table query, it is always a good idea to run the query as a Select query to view the selected data.

4. **Click the View button ▦ to switch to Datasheet View, click any entry in the DateOfEnrollment field, then click the Descending button in the Sort & Filter group**

   Sorting the records in descending order based on the values in the DateOfEnrollment field allows you to confirm that only records in the first quarter of 2015 appear in the datasheet.

5. **Click the View button ☑ to return to Design View, click the Make Table button in the Query Type group, type ArchiveEnrollments in the Table Name text box, then click OK**

   The Make Table query is ready, but action queries do not change data until you click the Run button. All action query icons include an exclamation point in their buttons to remind you that they *change* data when you run them and you must *run* the queries for the action to occur. To prevent running an action query accidentally, use the Datasheet View button ▦ to *view* the selected records, and use the Run button only when you are ready to *run* the action.

6. **Click the View button ▦ to double-check the records you have selected, click the View button ☑ to return to Query Design View, click the Run button to execute the make table action, click Yes when prompted that you are about to paste 154 rows, then save the query with the name MakeArchiveEnrollments and close it**

   When you run an action query, Access prompts you with an "Are you sure?" message before actually updating the data. The Undo button cannot undo changes made by action queries.

7. **Double-click the ArchiveEnrollments table in the Navigation Pane to view the new table's datasheet as shown in FIGURE K-8, then close the ArchiveEnrollments table**

FIGURE K-7: Creating a Make Table query

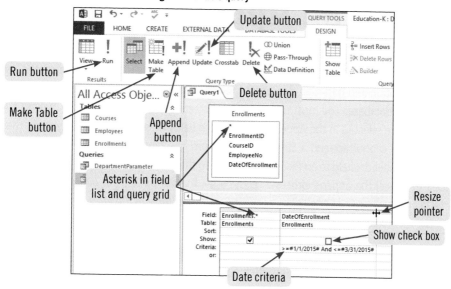

FIGURE K-8: ArchiveEnrollments table

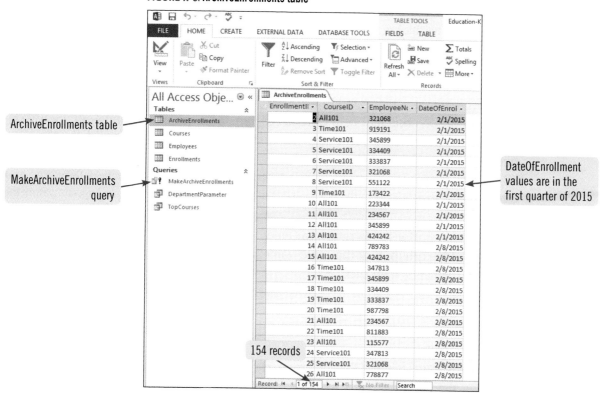

TABLE K-3: Action queries

action query	query icon	description	example
Delete		Deletes a group of records from one or more tables	Remove products that are discontinued or for which there are no orders
Update		Makes global changes to a group of records in one or more tables	Raise prices by 10 percent for all products
Append		Adds a group of records from one or more tables to the end of another table	Append the employee address table from one division of the company to the address table from another division of the company
Make Table		Creates a new table from data in one or more tables	Export records to another Access database or make a backup copy of a table

© 2014 Cengage Learning

Create an Append Query

An **Append query** is an action query that adds selected records to an existing table. The existing table is called the **target table**. The Append query works like an export feature because the records are copied from one location and pasted in the target table. The target table can be in the current database or in any other Access database. The most difficult part of creating an Append query is making sure that all of the fields you have selected in the Append query match fields with the same data types in the target table. For example, you cannot append a Short Text field from one table to a Number field in another table. If you attempt to append a field to an incompatible field in the target table, an error message appears and you are forced to cancel the append process. **CASE** ▶ *You use an Append query to append the records with a DateOfEnrollment value in April 2015 from the Enrollments table to the ArchiveEnrollments table.*

STEPS

1. **Click the CREATE tab, click the Query Design button, double-click Enrollments in the Show Table dialog box, then click Close**

2. **Double-click the title bar in the Enrollments table's field list, then drag the highlighted fields to the first column of the query design grid**

   Double-clicking the title bar of the field list selects all of the fields, allowing you to add them to the query grid very quickly. To successfully append records to a table, you need to identify how each field in the query is connected to an existing field in the target table. Therefore, the technique of adding all of the fields to the query grid by using the asterisk does not work when you append records, because using the asterisk doesn't list each field in a separate column in the query grid.

3. **Click the DateOfEnrollment field Criteria cell, type Between 4/1/15 and 4/30/15, use ✛ to widen the DateOfEnrollment field column to view the criteria, then click the View button ▦ to display the selected records**

   The datasheet should show 106 records with an April date in the DateOfEnrollment field. **Between...and** criteria select all records between the two dates, including the two dates. Between...and operators work the same way as the >= and <= operators.

4. **Click the View button ☒ to return to Query Design View, click the Append button in the Query Type group, click the Table Name list arrow in the Append dialog box, click ArchiveEnrollments, then click OK**

   The **Append To row** appears in the query design grid, as shown in **FIGURE K-9**, to show how the fields in the query match fields in the target table, ArchiveEnrollments. Now that you are sure you selected the right records and set up the Append query, you're ready to click the Run button to append the selected records to the table.

5. **Click the Run button in the Results group, click Yes to confirm that you want to append 106 rows, then save the query with the name AppendArchiveEnrollments and close it**

6. **Double-click the ArchiveEnrollments table in the Navigation Pane, click any entry in the DateOfEnrollment field, then click the Descending button in the Sort & Filter group**

   The 106 April records are appended to the ArchiveEnrollments table, which previously had 154 records for a new total of 260 records, as shown in **FIGURE K-10**.

7. **Save and close the ArchiveEnrollments table**

FIGURE K-9: Creating an Append query

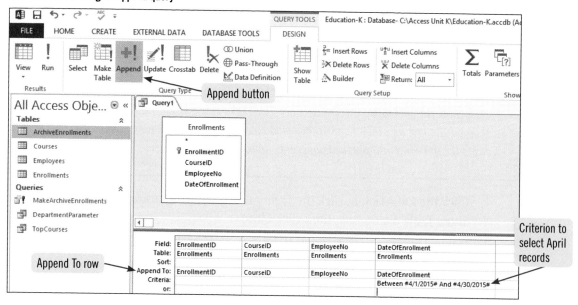

FIGURE K-10: ArchiveEnrollments table with appended records

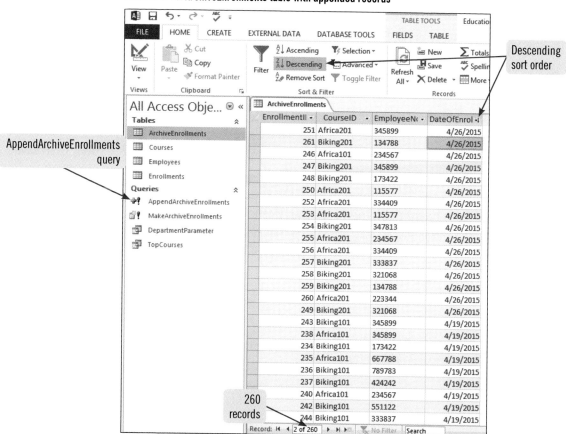

1900 versus 2000 dates

If you type only two digits of a date, Access assumes that the digits 00 through 29 are for the years 2000 through 2029. If you type 30 through 99, Access assumes the years refer to 1930 through 1999. If you want to specify years outside these ranges, you must type all four digits of the year.

Create a Delete Query

Learning
Outcomes
• Create a Delete
query

A **Delete query** deletes selected records from one or more tables. Delete queries delete entire records, not just selected fields within records. If you want to delete a field from a table, you open Table Design View, click the field name, then click the Delete Rows button. As in all action queries, you cannot reverse the action completed by the Delete query by clicking the Undo button. **CASE** ▶ *Now that you have archived the first four months of Enrollments records for 2015 in the ArchiveEnrollments table, you want to delete the same records from the Enrollments table. You can use a Delete query to accomplish this task.*

STEPS

1. **Click the CREATE tab, click the** Query Design button, **double-click** Enrollments **in the Show Table dialog box, then click** Close

2. **Double-click the * (asterisk) at the top of the Enrollments table's field list, then double-click the** DateOfEnrollment field

   Using the asterisk adds all fields from the Enrollments table to the first column of the query design grid. You add the DateOfEnrollment field to the second column of the query design grid so you can enter limiting criteria for this field.

3. **Click the** DateOfEnrollment field Criteria cell, **type** Between 1/1/15 and 4/30/15, **then use ↔ to widen the DateOfEnrollment field column to view the criteria**

   Before you run a Delete query, be sure to check the selected records to make sure you selected the same 260 records that you previously added to the ArchiveEnrollments table.

QUICK TIP
The View button
is always a safe
way to view selected
records for both
Select and action
queries.

4. **Click the** View button **to confirm that the datasheet has 260 records, click the** View button **to return to Design View, then click the** Delete button **in the Query Type group**

   Your screen should look like **FIGURE K-11**. The **Delete row** now appears in the query design grid. You can delete the selected records by clicking the Run button.

QUICK TIP
Remember that the
action taken by the
Run button for an
action query cannot
be undone.

5. **Click the** Run button, **click** Yes **to confirm that you want to delete 260 rows, then save the query with the name** DeleteEnrollments **and close it**

6. **Double-click the** Enrollments table **in the Navigation Pane, click any entry in the** DateOfEnrollment field, **then click the** Ascending button **in the Sort & Filter group**

   The records should start in May, as shown in **FIGURE K-12**. The Delete query deleted all records from the Enrollments table with dates between 1/1/2015 and 4/30/2015.

7. **Save and close the Enrollments table**

FIGURE K-11: Creating a Delete query

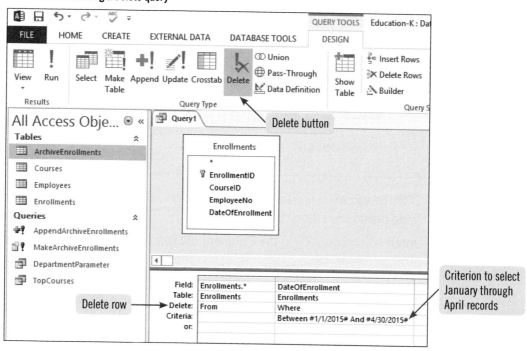

FIGURE K-12: Final Enrollments table after deleting 260 records

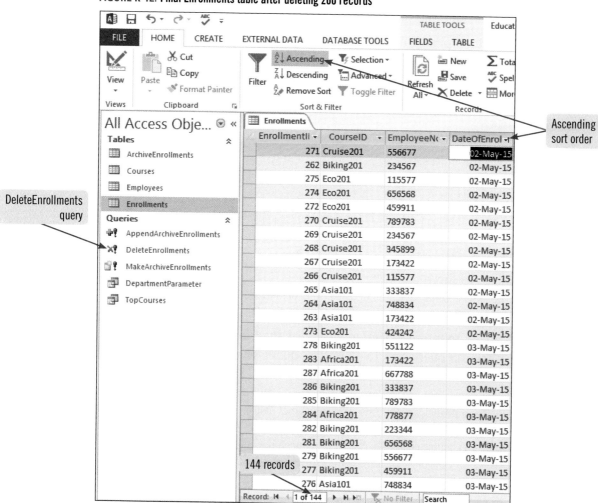

Access 2013

Create an Update Query

Learning Outcomes
- Create an Update query
- Hide and restore objects

An **Update query** is a type of action query that updates the values in a field. For example, you might want to increase the price of a product in a particular category by 10 percent. Or you might want to update information such as assigned sales representative, region, or territory for a subset of customers. **CASE** *Jacob Thomas has just informed you that the cost of continuing education is being increased by $20 for each class effective immediately. You can create an Update query to quickly calculate and update the new course costs.*

STEPS

1. **Click the CREATE tab, click the Query Design button, double-click Courses in the Show Table dialog box, then click Close**

2. **Double-click CourseID in the Courses field list, double-click Description, then double-click CostofCourse**

   Every action query starts as a Select query. Always review the datasheet of the Select query before initiating any action that changes data to double-check which records are affected.

3. **Click the View button ⊞ to display the query datasheet, note that the values in all three of the Africa courses are $450, then click the View button ☑ to return to Design View**

   After selecting the records you want to update and reviewing the values in the CostOfCourse field, you're ready to change this Select query into an Update query.

4. **Click the Update button in the Query Type group**

   The **Update To row** appears in the query design grid. To add $20 to the values in the CostOfCourse field, you need to enter the appropriate expression in the Update To cell for the CostOfCourse field.

5. **Click the Update To cell for the CostOfCourse field, then type 20+[CostOfCourse]**

   Your screen should look like **FIGURE K-13**. The expression adds 20 to the current value of the CostOfCourse field, but the CostOfCourse field is not updated until you run the query.

6. **Click the View button ⊞ to see the datasheet, click the View button ☑ to return to Design View, click the Run button, then click Yes to confirm that you want to update 32 rows**

   When you view the datasheet of an Update query, only the field being updated appears on the datasheet. To view all fields in the query, change this query back into a Select query, then view the datasheet.

7. **Click the Select button in the Query Type group, then click ⊞ to display the query datasheet, as shown in FIGURE K-14**

   The Africa records have been updated from $450 to $470. All other CostOfCourse values have increased by $20 as well.

TROUBLE
If you double-click an action query in the Navigation Pane, you initiate that action.

8. **Click ☑ to return to Design View, click the Update button in the Query Type group to switch this query back to an Update query, save the query with the name UpdateCost, then close it**

   Often, you do not need to save action queries because after the data has been updated, you generally won't use the same query again. Also, it is sometimes dangerous to leave action queries in the Navigation Pane because if you double-click an action query, you run that action (as opposed to opening its datasheet). When you double-click a Select query, you open the query's datasheet. You can keep an action query in the Navigation Pane but hide it using the **Hidden property**.

9. **Right-click the UpdateCost query in the Navigation pane, click Object Properties, click the Hidden check box, then click OK**

Creating Advanced Queries

FIGURE K-13: Setting up an Update query

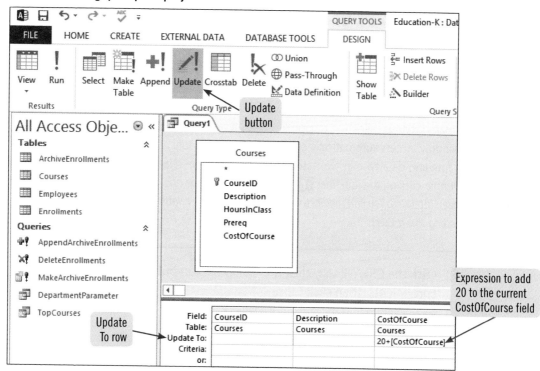

FIGURE K-14: Updated CostOfCourse values

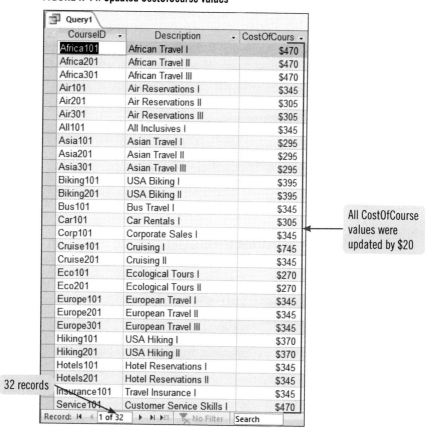

Restoring hidden objects

To view hidden objects, right-click a blank spot in the Navigation Pane, and then choose Navigation Options. In the Navigation Options dialog box, check the Show Hidden Objects check box, then click OK.

Creating Advanced Queries

Access 283

Access 2013

Specify Join Properties

Learning
Outcomes
•Create a left join
•Define left and
  right joins

When you use the Relationships window to define table relationships, the tables are joined in the same way in Query Design View. If referential integrity is enforced on a relationship, a "1" appears next to the field that serves as the "one" side of the one-to-many relationship, and an infinity symbol (∞) appears next to the field that serves as the "many" side. The "one" field is the primary key field for its table, and the "many" field is called the foreign key field. If no relationships have been established in the Relationships window, Access automatically creates **join lines** in Query Design View if the linking fields have the same name and data type in two tables. You can edit table relationships for a query in Query Design View by double-clicking the join line. **CASE** *Jacob Thomas asks what courses have been created that have never been attended. You can modify the join properties of the relationship between the Enrollments and Courses table to find this answer.*

STEPS

1. **Click the CREATE tab, click the Query Design button, double-click Courses, double-click Enrollments, then click Close**

   Because the Courses and Enrollments tables have already been related with a one-to-many relationship with referential integrity enforced in the Relationships window, the join line automatically appears in Query Design View.

TROUBLE
Double-click the
middle portion of
the join line, not the
"one" or "many"
symbol, to open the
Join Properties dialog
box.

2. **Double-click the one-to-many join line between the field lists**

   The Join Properties dialog box opens and displays the characteristics for the join, as shown in **FIGURE K-15**. The dialog box shows that option 1 is selected, the default join type, which means that the query displays only records where joined fields from *both* tables are equal. In **SQL (Structured Query Language)**, this is called an **inner join**. This means that if the Courses table has any records for which there are no matching Enrollments records, those courses do not appear in the resulting datasheet.

3. **Click the 2 option button**

   By choosing option 2, you are specifying that you want to see *all* of the records in the Courses table (the "one," or parent table), even if the Enrollments table (the "many," or child table) does not contain matching records. In SQL, this is called a **left join**. Option 3 selects all records in the Enrollments (the "many," or child table) even if there are no matches in the Courses table. In SQL, this is called a **right join**.

4. **Click OK**

   The join line's appearance changes, as shown in **FIGURE K-16**. With the join property set, you add fields to the query grid.

5. **Double-click CourseID in the Courses field list, double-click Description in the Courses field list, double-click EnrollmentID in the Enrollments field list, click the EnrollmentID Criteria cell, type Is Null, then click the View button [⊞] to display the datasheet**

   The query finds 14 courses that currently have no matching records in the Enrollments table, as shown in **FIGURE K-17**. These courses contain a null (nothing) value in the EnrollmentID field. To select these records, you had to change the join property between the tables to include *all* records from the Courses table because the default join type, the inner join, requires a matching record in *both* tables to display a record in the resulting datasheet.

6. **Save the query with the name CoursesWithoutEnrollments, then close it**

FIGURE K-15: Join Properties dialog box

Default join (inner join)

Selects parent records even if they have no matching child records (left join)

Selects child records even if they have no matching parent records (right join)

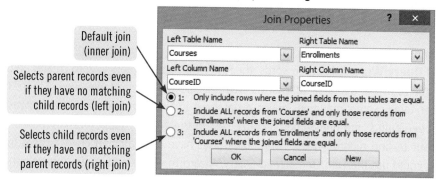

FIGURE K-16: Left join between tables

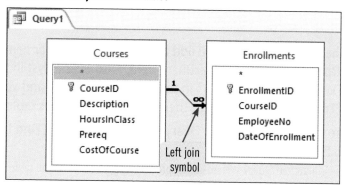

FIGURE K-17: Courses without matching enrollments

These courses have no matching records in the Enrollments table

EnrollmentID is null for each record

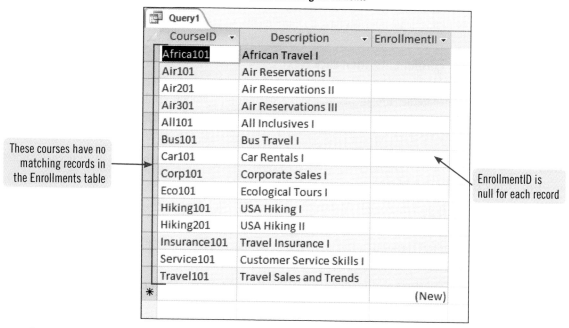

Null and zero-length string values

The term **null** describes a field value that does not exist because it has never been entered. In a datasheet, null values look the same as a zero-length string value but have a different purpose. A **zero-length string** value is a *deliberate* entry that contains no characters. You enter a zero-length string by typing two quotation marks ("") with no space between them. A null value, on the other hand, indicates *unknown* data.

By using null and zero-length string values appropriately, you can later query for the records that match one or the other condition. To query for zero-length string values, enter two quotation marks ("") as the criterion. To query for null values, use **Is Null** as the criterion. To query for any value other than a null value, use **Is Not Null** as the criterion.

Access 2013

Find Unmatched Records

Another way to find records in one table that have no matching records in another is to use the **Find Unmatched Query Wizard**. In other words, the Find Unmatched Query Wizard creates an outer join between the tables in the query so that *all* records are selected in one table even if there is no match in the other table. Sometimes you inherit a database in which referential integrity was not imposed from the beginning, and unmatched records exist in the "many" table (orphan records). Or sometimes you want to find records in the "one" table that have no matching child records in the "many" table. You could use the Find Unmatched Query Wizard to create a query to answer either of these questions. **CASE** *Jacob Thomas wonders if there are any employees who have never enrolled in a class. You can use the Find Unmatched Query Wizard to create a query to answer this question.*

STEPS

1. **Open the Employees table, and add a new record with *your* name in the ELast and EFirst fields, Operations in the EDepartment field, Business Analyst in the ETitle field, 1/1/15 in the DateHired field, 93-93-93 in the EmployeeNo field, and *your* school email address in the EEmail field, press [Enter], then close the Employees table**

2. **Click the CREATE tab, click the Query Wizard button, click Find Unmatched Query Wizard, then click OK**

   The Find Unmatched Query Wizard starts, prompting you to select the table or query that may contain no related records.

3. **Click Table: Employees, then click Next**

   You want to find which employees have no enrollments, so you select the Enrollments table as the related table.

4. **Click Table: Enrollments, then click Next**

   The next question asks you to identify which field is common to both tables. Because the Employees table is already related to the Enrollments table in the Relationships window via the common EmployeeNo field, those fields are already selected as the matching fields, as shown in **FIGURE K-18**.

5. **Click Next**

   You are prompted to select the fields from the Employees table that you want to display in the query datasheet.

6. **Click the Select All Fields button** `>>`

7. **Click Next, type EmployeesWithoutEnrollments, click Finish, then resize the columns of the datasheet to view all data**

   The final datasheet is shown in **FIGURE K-19**. One existing employee plus the record you entered in Step 1 have not yet enrolled in any class.

8. **Save and close the EmployeesWithoutEnrollments query, then close the Education-K. accdb database**

Reviewing referential integrity

Recall that you can establish, or enforce, **referential integrity** between two tables when joining tables in the Relationships window. Referential integrity applies a set of rules to the relationship that ensures that no orphaned records currently exist, are added to, or are created in the database. A table has an **orphan record** when information in the foreign key field of the "many" table doesn't have a matching entry in the primary key field of the "one" table. The term "orphan" comes from the analogy that the "one" table contains **parent records**, and the "many" table contains **child records**. Referential integrity means that a Delete query would not be able to delete records in the "one" (parent) table that has related records in the "many" (child) table.

Creating Advanced Queries

FIGURE K-18: Using the Find Unmatched Query Wizard

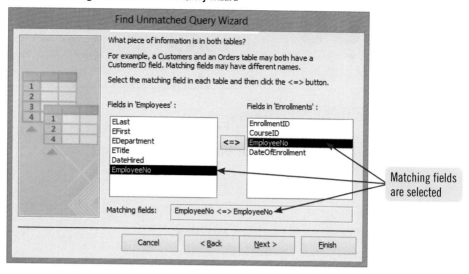

FIGURE K-19: Employees without matching Enrollments records

ELast	EFirst	EDepartment	ETitle	DateHired	EmployeeNo	EEmail
James	Kayla	Marketing	Staff Assistant	1/1/2015	90-90-90	kjames@quest.com
Student Last Name	Student First Name	Operations	Business Analyst	1/1/2015	93-93-93	student@college.edu

Find Duplicates Query Wizard

The Find Duplicates Query Wizard is another query wizard that is only available from the New Query dialog box. As you would suspect, the **Find Duplicates Query Wizard** helps you find duplicate values in a field, which can assist in finding and correcting potential data entry errors. For example, if you suspect that the same customer has been entered with two different names in your Customers table, you could use the Find Duplicates Query Wizard to find records with duplicate values in the Street or Phone field. After you isolated the records with the same values in a field, you could then edit incorrect data and delete redundant records.

Practice

Put your skills into practice with SAM! If you have a SAM account, go to www.cengage.com/sam2013 to access SAM assignments for this unit.

Concepts Review

Identify each element of the Query Design View shown in FIGURE K-20.

FIGURE K-20

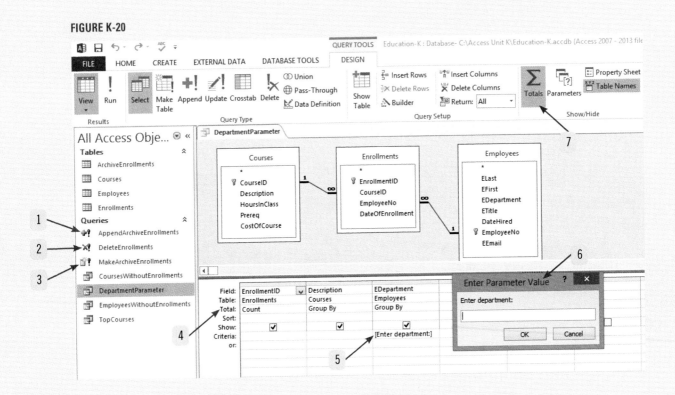

Match each term with the statement that best describes it.

8. **Null**

9. **Parameter**

10. **Top Values query**

11. **Inner join**

12. **Action query**

13. **Properties**

a. Characteristics that define the appearance and behavior of items within the database

b. Displays only a number or percentage of records from a sorted query

c. Displays a dialog box prompting you for criteria

d. Means that the query displays only records where joined fields from both tables are equal

e. Makes changes to data

f. A field value that does not exist

Select the best answer from the list of choices.

14. **Which join type selects all records from the "one" (parent) table?**
    a. Inner
    b. Left
    c. Central
    d. Right

15. **Which of the following is a valid parameter criterion entry in the query design grid?**
    a. >=[Type minimum value here:]
    b. >=Type minimum value here:
    c. >=(Type minimum value here:)
    d. >={Type minimum value here: }

16. **You *cannot* use the Top Values feature to:**
    a. Select the bottom 10 percent of records.
    b. Show the top 30 records.
    c. Display a subset of records.
    d. Update a field's value by 5 percent.

17. **Which of the following is *not* an action query?**
    a. Union query
    b. Delete query
    c. Make Table query
    d. Append query

18. **Which of the following precautions should you take before running a Delete query?**
    a. Check the resulting datasheet to make sure the query selects the right records.
    b. Understand the relationships between the records you are about to delete in the database.
    c. Have a current backup of the database.
    d. All of the above

19. **When querying tables in a one-to-many relationship with referential integrity enforced, which records appear (by default) on the resulting datasheet?**
    a. Only those with matching values in both tables.
    b. All records from both tables will appear at all times.
    c. All records from the "one" table, and only those with matching values from the "many" side.
    d. All records from the "many" table, and only those with nonmatching values from the "one" side.

20. **Which of the following is *not* a type of Select query?**
    a. Crosstab
    b. Update
    c. Summary
    d. Parameter

Skills Review

1. **Query for top values.**
    a. Start Access, then open the Seminar-K.accdb database from the location where you store your Data Files. Enable content if prompted.
    b. Create a new query in Query Design View with the EventName field from the Events table and the RegistrationFee field from the Registration table.
    c. Add the RegistrationFee field a second time, then click the Totals button. In the Total row of the query grid, Group By the EventName field, Sum the first RegistrationFee field, then Count the second RegistrationFee field.
    d. Sort in descending order by the summed RegistrationFee field.
    e. Enter **3** in the Top Values list box to display the top three seminars in the datasheet, then view the datasheet.
    f. Save the query as **Top3Revenue**, then close the datasheet.

2. **Create a parameter query.**
    a. Create a new query in Query Design View with the AttendeeLastName field from the Attendees table, the RegistrationDate field from the Registration table, and the EventName field from the Events table.
    b. Add the parameter criteria **Between [Enter Start Date:] and [Enter End Date:]** in the Criteria cell for the RegistrationDate field.
    c. Specify an ascending sort order on the RegistrationDate field.
    d. Click the Datasheet View button, then enter **5/1/15** as the start date and **5/31/15** as the end date to find everyone who has attended a seminar in May 2015. You should view five records.
    e. Save the query as **RegistrationDateParameter**, then close it.

Skills Review (continued)

3. Modify query properties.

    a. Right-click the RegistrationDateParameter query in the Navigation Pane, click Object Properties, then add the following description: **Prompts for a starting and ending registration date. Created by Your Name.**

    b. Close the RegistrationDateParameter Properties dialog box, then open the RegistrationDateParameter query in Query Design View.

    c. Right-click the RegistrationDate field in the query grid, then click Properties on the shortcut menu to open the Property Sheet for the Field Properties. Enter **Date of Registration** for the Caption property, change the Format property to Medium Date, then close the Property Sheet.

    d. View the datasheet for records between **1/1/15** and **1/31/15**, then widen the fields as needed to view the caption and the Medium Date format applied to the RegistrationDate field.

    e. Change Pham to *your* last name, then print the RegistrationDateParameter datasheet if requested by your instructor.

    f. Save and close the RegistrationDateParameter query.

4. Create a Make Table query.

    a. Create a new query in Query Design View, add the Registration table, then select all the fields from the Registration table by double-clicking the Registration field list's title bar and dragging the selected fields to the query design grid.

    b. Enter <=3/31/15 in the Criteria cell for the RegistrationDate field to find those records in which the RegistrationDate is on or before 3/31/2015.

    c. View the datasheet. It should display 23 records.

    d. In Query Design View, change the query into a Make Table query that creates a new table in the current database. Give the new table the name **BackupRegistration**.

    e. Run the query to paste 23 rows into the BackupRegistration table.

    f. Save the Make Table query with the name **MakeBackupRegistration**, then close it.

    g. Open the BackupRegistration table, view the 23 records to confirm that the Make Table query worked correctly, then close the table.

5. Create an Append query.

    a. Create a new query in Query Design View, add the Registration table, and select all the fields from the Registration table by double-clicking the Registration field list's title bar and dragging the selected fields to the query design grid.

    b. Enter >=4/1/15 and <=4/30/15 in the Criteria cell for the RegistrationDate field to find those records in which the RegistrationDate is in April 2015.

    c. View the datasheet, which should display one record.

    d. In Query Design View, change the query into an Append query that appends records to the BackupRegistration table.

    e. Run the query to append the one record into the BackupRegistration table.

    f. Save the Append query with the name **AppendBackupRegistration**, then close it.

    g. Open the BackupRegistration table to confirm that it now contains the additional April record for a total of 24 records, then close the table.

6. Create a Delete query.

    a. Create a new query in Query Design View, add the Registration table, and select all the fields from the Registration table by double-clicking the Registration field list's title bar and dragging the selected fields to the query design grid.

    b. Enter <5/1/15 in the Criteria cell for the RegistrationDate field to find those records in which the RegistrationDate is before May 1, 2015.

    c. View the datasheet, which should display 24 records, the same 24 records you added to the BackupRegistration table.

    d. In Query Design View, change the query into a Delete query.

    e. Run the query to delete 24 records from the Registration table.

    f. Save the query with the name **DeleteRegistration**, then close it.

    g. Open the Registration table in Datasheet View to confirm that it contains only five records, all with RegistrationDate values greater than or equal to 5/1/2015, then close the table.

Skills Review (continued)

7. Create an Update query.

a. Create a query in Query Design View, add the Registration table, then add the RegistrationFee field in the query grid.

b. Sort the records in descending order on the RegistrationFee field, then view the datasheet, which should display five records. Note the values in the RegistrationFee field.

c. In Query Design View, change the query to an Update query, then enter **[RegistrationFee]*2** in the RegistrationFee field Update To cell to double the RegistrationFee value in each record.

d. Run the query to update the five records.

e. Save the query with the name **UpdateRegistrationFee**, then close it.

f. Open the Registration table to confirm that the RegistrationFee for the five records has doubled, then close it.

8. Specify join properties.

a. Create a new query in Query Design View with the following fields: AttendeeFirstName and AttendeeLastName from the Attendees table, and EventID and RegistrationFee from the Registration table.

b. Double-click the join line between the Attendees and Registration tables to open the Join Properties dialog box. Click the 2 option button to include *all* records from Attendees and only those records from Registration where the joined fields are equal.

c. View the datasheet, add *your* first and last name as a new, last record, but do not enter anything in the EventID or RegistrationFee fields for your record.

d. In Query Design View, add **Is Null** criteria to either field from the Registration table to select only those names who have never registered for an event.

e. Save this query as **PeopleWithoutRegistrations**, then view and close the query.

9. Find unmatched queries.

a. Start the Find Unmatched Query Wizard.

b. Select the Events table, then the Registration table to indicate that you want to view the Events records that have no related records in the Registration table.

c. Specify that the two tables are related by the EventID field.

d. Select all of the fields from the Events table in the query results.

e. Name the query **EventsWithoutRegistrations**, then view the results. Change one of the entries in the Location field to **Your Name College**, as shown in FIGURE K-21.

f. If requested by your instructor, print the EventsWithoutRegistrations query, then close the query, close the Seminar-K.accdb database, and exit Access.

FIGURE K-21

Event I	Event Name	Location	Start Date	Available Sp
1	Estate Planning	Student Name College	5/1/2015	100
5	Wealth Management	Millen Civic Center	5/5/2015	25
6	Planning for College	Greenfield High School	5/6/2015	25
7	Live Debt Free	Wells Fargo Center	5/7/2015	75
*	(New)			

Access 2013

Independent Challenge 1

As the manager of a college women's basketball team, you want to create several queries using the Basketball-K database.

a. Start Access, then open the Basketball-K.accdb database from the location where you store your Data Files. Enable content if prompted.

b. Create a query in Query Design View with the FirstName and LastName fields from the Players table, the FG (field goal), 3P (three pointer), and FT (free throw) fields from the Stats table, and the Opponent and GameDate fields from the Games table.

c. Enter **Between [Enter start date:] and [Enter end date:]** in the Criteria cell for the GameDate field.

d. View the datasheet for all of the records between **12/1/14** and **12/31/14**. It should display 18 records.

e. Save the query with the name **StatsParameter**, change Lindsey Swift's name to *your* name, then print the datasheet if requested by your instructor.

f. In Query Design View of the StatsParameter query, insert a new calculated field named **TotalPoints** between the FT and Opponent fields with the expression **TotalPoints:[FG]*2+[3P]*3+[FT]**, then sort the records in descending order on the TotalPoints field.

g. Apply the 25% Top Values option, and view the datasheet for all of the records between **1/1/15** and **1/31/15**. It should display five records.

h. Use the Save Object As feature to save the revised query as **StatsParameterTopValues**. Print the datasheet if requested by your instructor, then close it.

i. Create a new query in Query Design View with the Opponent, Mascot, CycloneScore, and OpponentScore fields from the Games table, then add a new calculated field as the last field with the following field name and expression: **WinRatio:[CycloneScore]/[OpponentScore]**

j. View the datasheet to make sure that the WinRatio field calculates properly, and widen all columns as necessary to see all of the data. Because the CycloneScore is generally greater than the OpponentScore, most values are greater than 1.

k. In Query Design View, change the Format property of the WinRatio field to Percent and the Decimal Places property to **0**. View the datasheet, a portion of which is shown in **FIGURE K-22**.

l. Save the query as **WinPercentage**, change the first opponent's name (Northern Iowa) and mascot to *your* name and a mascot of your choice, print the WinPercentage datasheet if requested by your instructor, then close the WinPercentage query.

m. Close the Basketball-K.accdb database, then exit Access.

FIGURE K-22

Opponent	Mascot	CycloneScor	OpponentSc	WinRatio
Northern Iowa	Panthers	81	65	125%
Creighton	Bluejays	106	60	177%
Northern Illinois	Huskies	65	60	108%
Louisiana Tech	Red Raiders	69	89	78%
Drake	Bulldogs	80	60	133%
Northern Iowa	Panthers	38	73	52%
Buffalo	Bulls	50	55	91%
Oklahoma	Sooners	53	60	88%
Texas	Longhorns	57	60	95%
Kansas	Jayhawks	74	58	128%
Colorado	Buffaloes	90	84	107%

Independent Challenge 2

As the manager of a college women's basketball team, you want to enhance the Basketball-K database by creating several action queries.

a. Start Access, then open the Basketball-K.accdb database from the location where you store your Data Files. Enable content if prompted.

b. Create a new query in Query Design View, and select all the fields from the Stats table by double-clicking the field list's title bar and dragging the selected fields to the query design grid.

c. Add criteria to find all of the records with the GameNo field equal to **1**, **2**, or **3**, then view the datasheet. It should display 26 records.

d. In Query Design View, change the query to a Make Table query to paste the records into a table in the current database called **StatsForGames123**.

e. Run the query to paste the 26 rows, save the query with the name **MakeStatsBackup**, then close it.

f. Open the datasheet for the StatsForGames123 table to confirm that it contains 26 records, then close it.

g. In Query Design View, create another new query that includes all of the fields from the Stats table by double-clicking the field list's title bar and dragging the selected fields to the query design grid.

h. Add criteria to find all of the statistics for those records with the GameNo field equal to **4** or **5**, then view the datasheet. It should display 12 records.

i. In Query Design View, change the query to an Append query to append the records to the StatsForGames123 table.

j. Run the query to append the 12 rows, save it with the name **AppendStatsBackup**, then close it.

k. Open the StatsForGames123 table to confirm that it now contains 38 records (26 original records plus 12 appended records), print it if requested by your instructor, then close it.

l. Right-click the StatsForGames123 table in the Navigation Pane, click Rename, then edit the name to **StatsForGames12345**.

m. Close the Basketball-K.accdb database, then exit Access.

Independent Challenge 3

As the manager of a college women's basketball team, you want to query the Basketball-K database to find specific information about each player.

a. Start Access, then open the Basketball-K.accdb database from the location where you store your Data Files. Enable content if prompted.

b. Create a query in Query Design View using the Players and Stats tables. Resize the field lists to view all of the fields in each table.

c. Double-click the join line to open the Join Properties dialog box, then change the join properties to option 2 to include *all* records from Players and only those from Stats where the joined fields are equal.

d. Add the FirstName and LastName fields from the Players table and the Assists field from the Stats table.

e. Type **Is Null** in the Criteria cell for the Assists field, as shown in **FIGURE K-23**, then view the datasheet to find those players who have never recorded an Assist value in the Stats table. It should display one record.

f. Change the last name to *your* last name.

g. Print the datasheet if requested by your instructor, save the query as **NoAssists**, then close the query.

h. Close Basketball-K.accdb, then exit Access.

FIGURE K-23

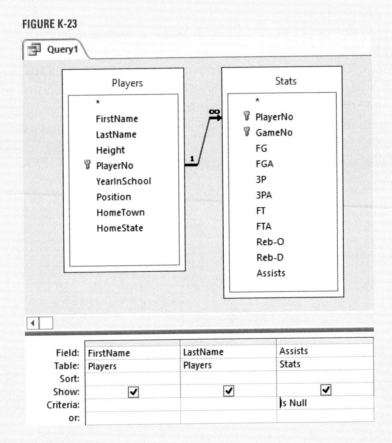

Independent Challenge 4: Explore

(*Note: To complete this Independent Challenge, make sure you are connected to the Internet.*)

One way to use Access to support your personal interests is to track the activities of a club or hobby. For example, suppose you belong to a culinary club that specializes in cooking with chocolate. The club collects information on international chocolate factories and museums and asks you to help build a database to organize the information.

a. Start Access, then open the Chocolate-K.accdb database from the location where you store your Data Files. Enable content if prompted.

b. Open the Countries table, then add two more country records, allowing the CountryID field to automatically increment because it is an AutoNumber data type. Close the Countries table.

c. Create a query in Query Design View with the Country field from the Countries table, and the PlaceName, City, and State fields from the ChocolatePlaces query.

d. Name the query **PlacesOfInterest**, double-click the join line between the Countries and ChocolatePlaces tables, then choose the 2 option that includes *all* records from the Countries table.

e. Save the PlacesOfInterest query and view the datasheet. Expand each column to show all of the data.

f. Print the PlacesOfInterest query if requested by your instructor, then close it.

g. Using the Internet, research a chocolate-related place of interest (a factory or museum) for one of the countries you entered in Step b.

h. Open the Countries table, and use the subdatasheet for the country you selected to enter the data for the chocolate-related place of interest. Enter **F** for factory or **M** for museum in the FactoryorMuseum field.

i. Close the Countries table, and open the PlacesOfInterest query in Design View. Modify the link line to option 1, so that records that have a match in both tables are selected.

j. Save and open the PlacesOfInterest query in Datasheet View, as shown in **FIGURE K-24**, and print the resulting datasheet if requested by your instructor. Note that the last record will show the unique data you entered.

k. Close Chocolate-K.accdb, then exit Access.

FIGURE K-24

Country	PlaceName	City	State
Germany	Lindt factory	Aachen	
Germany	Imhoff Stollwerk Chocolate Museum	Cologne	
Switzerland	Lindt factory	Kilchberg	
Switzerland	Museum del Cioccolato Alprose	Caslano	Canton Ticino
Switzerland	Nestle	Broc	Canton Fribourg
France	Lindt Factory	Oloron	
France	Atelier Musee du Chocolat, Biarritz	Biarritz	
Italy	Lindt Factory	Induno	
Italy	Lindt Factory	Luserna	
Italy	Museo Storico della Perugina	Perugia	
Italy	Museo del Cioccolato Antia Norba	Norma	Latina Province
Austria	Lindt Factory	Gloggnitz	
USA	Lindt Factory	San Leandro	CA
USA	Lindt Factory	Stratham	NH
Belgium	Musee du Cacao et du Chocolat	Brussels	
Great Britian	Cadbury World	Bourneville	
Japan	Shiroi Koibito Park	Sapporo	

Visual Workshop

As the manager of a college women's basketball team, you want to create a query from the Basketball-K.accdb database with the fields from the Players, Stats, and Games tables as shown. The query is a parameter query that prompts the user for a start and end date using the GameDate field from the Games table. **FIGURE K-25** shows the datasheet where the start date of **11/13/14** and end date of **11/16/14** are used. Also note that the records are sorted in ascending order first by GameDate, and then by LastName. The TotalRebounds field is calculated by adding the Reb-O (rebounds offense) and Reb-D (rebounds defense) values. Save and name the query **Rebounds**, then print the datasheet if requested by your instructor. Be sure to change one player's name to *your* name if you haven't previously done this to identify your printout.

FIGURE K-25

GameDate	FirstName	LastName	Reb-O	Reb-D	TotalRebounds
11/13/2014	Kristen	Czyenski	2	2	4
11/13/2014	Denise	Franco	2	3	5
11/13/2014	Theresa	Grant	1	3	4
11/13/2014	Megan	Hile	1	2	3
11/13/2014	Amy	Hodel	5	3	8
11/13/2014	Ellyse	Howard	1	2	3
11/13/2014	Jamie	Johnson	0	1	1
11/13/2014	Student First Name	Student Last Name	1	2	3
11/13/2014	Morgan	Tyler	4	6	10
11/16/2014	Kristen	Czyenski	3	2	5
11/16/2014	Denise	Franco	5	3	8
11/16/2014	Sydney	Freesen	2	3	5
11/16/2014	Theresa	Grant	3	3	6
11/16/2014	Megan	Hile	1	5	6
11/16/2014	Amy	Hodel	1	4	5
11/16/2014	Ellyse	Howard	3	3	6
11/16/2014	Sandy	Robins	0	1	1
11/16/2014	Student First Name	Student Last Name	2	2	4
11/16/2014	Morgan	Tyler	3	6	9
11/16/2014	Abbey	Walker	2	4	6

Creating Advanced Reports

CASE Jacob Thomas, coordinator of training at Quest Specialty Travel, wants to enhance existing reports to more professionally and clearly present the information in the Education-L database.

Unit Objectives

After completing this unit, you will be able to:

- Apply advanced formatting
- Control layout
- Set advanced print layout
- Create multicolumn reports
- Use domain functions
- Create charts
- Modify charts
- Apply chart types

Files You Will Need

Education-L.accdb   Basketball-L.accdb
RealEstate-L.accdb

Apply Advanced Formatting

Learning Outcomes
- Set margins
- Remove a layout
- Apply the Format property

You use Print Preview to see how a report will fit on paper and to make overall layout modifications such as changes to margins and page orientation. You use Layout and Design Views to modify the layout and characteristics of individual controls on a report. For example, the **Format property** provides several ways to format dates and numbers. Dates may be formatted as **Medium Date** (19-Jun-16), **Short Date** (6/19/2016), or **Long Date** (Friday, June 19, 2016). Numbers may be formatted as **Currency** ($7), **Percent** (700%), or **Standard** (7). **CASE** *You review the Departmental Summary Report to identify and correct formatting and page layout problems.*

STEPS

1. **Start Access, open the Education-L.accdb database from the location where you store your Data Files, enable content if prompted, then double-click DeptSummary in the Navigation Pane**

   Double-clicking a report in the Navigation Pane opens it in Report View, which doesn't show margins and page breaks. Switch to Print Preview to see how the report will look on paper.

2. **Right-click the Departmental Summary Report tab, then click Print Preview**

   Print Preview shows that data is cut off on the right side of the report. You fix this problem by modifying the margins and page orientation.

3. **Click the Margins button in the Page Size group, click the Narrow option, click the Page Setup button in the Page Layout group, select 0.25 in the Left margin box, then type 0.5, as shown in FIGURE L-1**

   The Narrow margin option set all four margins to 0.25". To customize individual margin settings, you use the Page Setup dialog box.

4. **Click OK, then click the Landscape button in the Page Layout group**

   Now that the report fits nicely on the printed page, you want to make some modifications to the controls themselves. You want to widen the text box that contains the name expression and format the Cost fields to show a currency symbol.

5. **Right-click the Departmental Summary Report tab, click Design View, click the =[ELast]&", "&[EFirst] text box, then use ◄─► to drag the right edge to the right to widen the text box**

   Many of the controls are grouped together in a report table layout, which means that resizing one control resizes the entire group. To modify an individual control in the group, you must first remove the layout.

6. **Click the Undo button 🔄 on the Quick Access toolbar, click the ARRANGE tab, click Remove Layout in the Table group, then use ◄─► to drag the right edge of the name expression text box to the right to widen it to about the 4" mark**

   Your last improvement will be to modify the Format property of the four text boxes that display Cost information in the last column of the report to include a currency symbol, $.

7. **Click the CostOfCourse text box in the Detail section, press and hold [Shift], click the three =Sum([CostOfCourse]) text boxes in the footer sections, release [Shift], click the DESIGN tab, click the Property Sheet button, click the Format property list arrow, click Currency, right-click the DeptSummary tab, click Print Preview, then scroll and zoom to the bottom of the last page of the report, as shown in FIGURE L-2**

   The report is more professional and informative with the Cost values formatted as Currency.

8. **Save and close the report**

FIGURE L-1: Page Setup dialog box

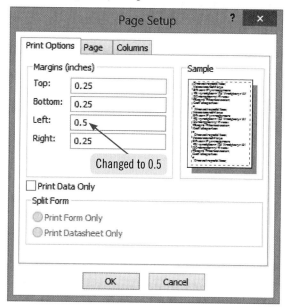

FIGURE L-2: Applying the Currency format

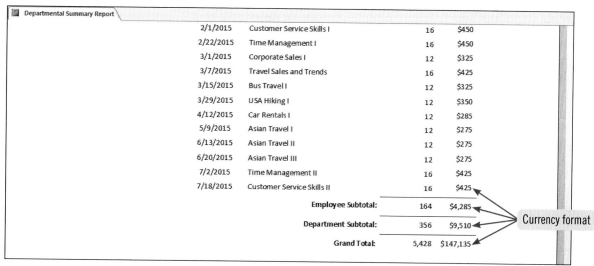

Access 2013

Control Layout

Learning Outcomes
- Change table layouts
- Open header and footer sections
- Insert page numbers

When you create a report using the Report button or Report Wizard, sometimes controls are automatically grouped together in a table layout. A **table layout** is a way of connecting controls together so that when you move or resize them in Layout or Design View, the action you take on one control applies to all controls in the layout. The different types of layouts are described in **TABLE L-1**. Another important report modification skill is your ability to open and close various header and footer sections. **CASE** ▶ *Jacob Thomas asks you to modify the CourseListing report to improve its format.*

STEPS

1. **Right-click the** CourseListing report **in the Navigation Pane, then click** Layout View

   Controls that are grouped together in the same layout can be resized easily in Layout View.

2. **Click** Africa101, **use** ←→ **to drag the** right edge **of the column to the left, click** African Travel I, **use** ←→ **to drag the** right edge **of the column to the left, and continue** resizing the columns **so that they all fit within the right border of the report, as shown in** FIGURE L-3

   Controls in the same layout move to provide space for the control you are moving. This report contains no title or page numbers. You add controls and open report sections in Design View.

3. **Right-click the** CourseListing tab, **then click** Design View

   You want to add a title to the Report Header section. Before you can add a label for the report title to the Report Header section, you must open it.

   QUICK TIP
   Recall that you open and close Group Header and Footer sections in the Group, Sort, and Total pane.

4. **Right-click the** Detail section bar, **click** Report Header/Footer, **click the** Label button Aa **on the DESIGN tab, click at the** 1″ mark **in the Report Header section, type** Course Listing Report, **press [Enter], click the HOME tab, click the** Font Color list arrow $\underline{A}$ ▾ **in the Text Formatting group, then click** Automatic (black) **to make the title more visible**

   You also want to add page numbers to the Page Footer section. You can open the Page Footer section and insert the page number at the same time.

5. **Click the** DESIGN tab, **click the** Page Numbers button **in the Header/Footer group, click the** Page N of M option button, **click the** Bottom of Page [Footer] option button, **click the** Alignment list arrow, **click** Right **in the Page Numbers dialog box, as shown in** FIGURE L-4, **then click** OK

   The Page N of M option creates the expression in the text box on the right side of the Page Footer, as shown in **FIGURE L-5**. This expression displays the current page number and total pages in the Page Footer. Because neither the Page Header nor Report Footer sections have any controls, you close them.

6. **Use** ‡ **to drag the** bottom edge of the report **up to close the Report Footer section, then use** ‡ **to drag the** top edge of the Detail section **up to close the Page Header section**

   QUICK TIP
   You cannot see the Page Header or Page Footer sections in Report View. You must use Print Preview.

7. **Right-click the** CourseListing report tab, **click** Print Preview, **then zoom and navigate back and forth to observe the Report Header on page one and the Page Footer on pages one and two**

   Always review your reports in Print Preview to see the contents of the Page Header and Page Footer sections as well as to see how the report fits on a printed piece of paper.

8. **Save and close the CourseListing report**

FIGURE L-3: Resizing columns in a layout

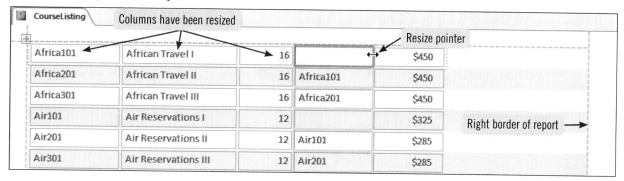

FIGURE L-4: Page Numbers dialog box

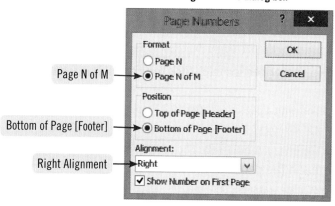

FIGURE L-5: Opening sections in Design View

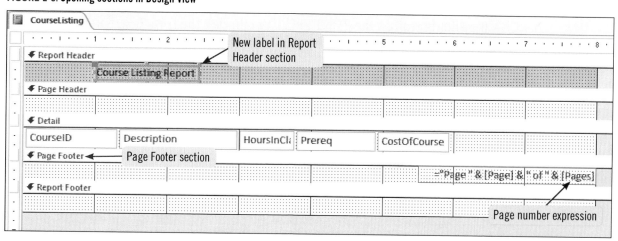

TABLE L-1: Layouts

layout	description
Stacked	Labels are positioned to the left of the text box; most often used in forms
Tabular	Labels are positioned across the top in the Page Header section forming columns of data with text boxes positioned in the Detail section; most often used in reports

Access 2013

Set Advanced Print Layout

Learning
Outcomes
• Modify Force New
  Page property
• Modify Repeat
  Section property

Setting advanced print layout in a report means controlling print options such as where page breaks occur and how report sections span multiple pages. **CASE** *In the Departmental Summary Report, Jacob asks you to print each person's information on a separate page, and to repeat the EDepartment Header information at the top of each page.*

STEPS

1. **Right-click the** DeptSummary report **in the Navigation Pane, click** Design View, **double-click the** EDepartment Header section bar **to open its Property Sheet, double-click the** Repeat Section property **to change the property from No to** Yes, **then double-click the** Force New Page property **to change the property from None to** Before Section, **as shown in** FIGURE L-6

   The controls in the EDepartment Header section will now repeat at the top of every page.

2. **Click the** EmployeeNo Footer section bar, **click the** Force New Page property list arrow, **then click** After Section

   Access will format the report with a page break after each EmployeeNo Footer. This means each employee's records will start printing at the top of a new page.

3. **Right-click the** DeptSummary report tab, **click** Print Preview, **then use the navigation buttons to move through the pages of the report**

   Previewing multiple pages helps you make sure that the department name repeats at the top of every page and that each employee starts on a new page.

4. **Navigate to page** 2, **then click the** top of the page **if you need to zoom in, as shown in** FIGURE L-7

   To print only page 2 of the report, you use the Print dialog box.

5. **Click the** Print button **on the** PRINT PREVIEW **tab, click the** From box, **enter** 2, **click the** To box, **enter** 2, **then if requested by your instructor to create a printout, click** OK, **but if not, click** Cancel

   Only page 2 of the 30+ page report is sent to the printer.

6. **Save and close the DeptSummary report**

FIGURE L-6: Working with section properties in Report Design View

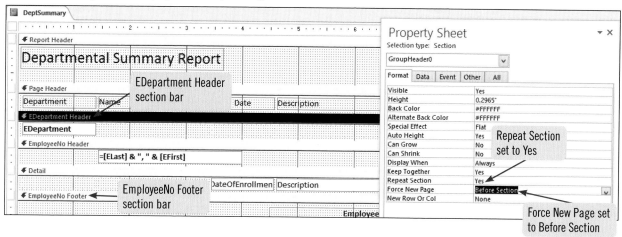

FIGURE L-7: Previewing the final Departmental Summary Report

Create Multicolumn Reports

Learning Outcomes
- Modify a report for multiple columns
- Set column layout

A **multicolumn report** repeats information in more than one column on the page. To create multiple columns, you use options in the Page Setup dialog box. **CASE** *Jacob asks you to create a report that shows employee names sorted in ascending order for each course. A report with only a few fields is a good candidate for a multicolumn report.*

STEPS

1. **Click the CREATE tab, click the Report Wizard button, click the Tables/Queries list arrow, click Table: Courses, double-click Description, click the Tables/Queries list arrow, click Table: Employees, double-click EFirst, double-click ELast, click Next, click Next to view the data by Courses, click Next to bypass adding any more grouping levels, click the first sort list arrow, click ELast, click Next, click the Stepped option button, click the Landscape option button, click Next, type Attendance List for the title, click Finish, then click the Last Page button ▶| on the navigation bar**

   The initial report is displayed in Print Preview as a 17- or 18-page report. This report would work well as a multicolumn report because only three fields are involved. You also decide to combine the first and last names into a single expression.

2. **Right-click the report, click Design View, close the Property Sheet or Field List if it is open, click the ELast label, press [Delete], click the EFirst label, press [Delete], click the ELast text box, press [Delete], click the EFirst text box, press [Delete], click the Page expression text box in the Page Footer section, press [Delete], click the =Now() text box in the Page Footer section, press [Delete], then drag the right edge of the report as far to the left as possible**

   When designing a multicolumn report, Report Design View should display the width of only the first column. Your next task is to add a new text box to the Detail section with an expression that contains both the first and last names.

3. **Click the Text Box button |abl| in the Controls group, click at about the 1" mark of the Detail section to insert a new text box control, then delete the accompanying Text9 label**

   TROUBLE
   Do not forget to enter a space after the comma so the expression creates Dawson, Ron versus Dawson,Ron.

4. **Click the Unbound text box to select it, click Unbound, type =[ELast]&", "&[EFirst], press [Enter], widen the new control to about 2" wide, right-click the Attendance List report tab, then click Print Preview**

   With the information clearly presented in a single, narrow column, you're ready to specify that the report print multiple columns.

5. **Click the Page Setup button, click the Columns tab, double-click 1 in the Number of Columns box, type 3, then click the Down, then Across option button, as shown in FIGURE L-8**

   The content of the report is now set to print in three newspaper-style columns. The Column Size Width value is based on 0.25" left and right margins, which leaves room for three, 3" columns. The Height value is based on the Height property of the Detail section.

   QUICK TIP
   You must use Print Preview to view report columns. Report View doesn't display multiple columns.

6. **Click OK**

   The final Attendance List report is shown in **FIGURE L-9**. By specifying that the report is three columns wide, the number of pages in the report is significantly reduced.

7. **Save and close the Attendance List report**

FIGURE L-8: Page Setup dialog box

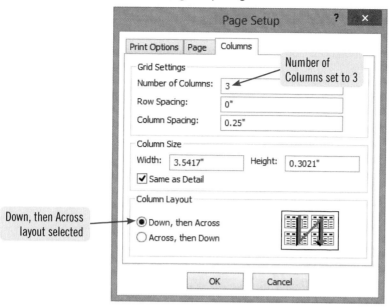

FIGURE L-9: Attendance List report in three columns

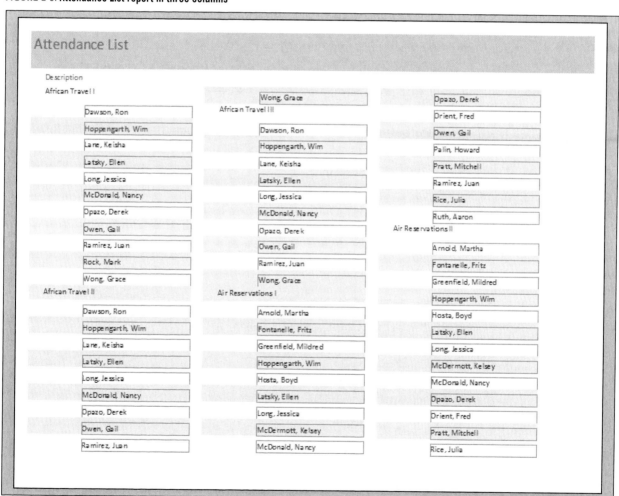

Use Domain Functions

Domain functions, also called domain aggregate functions, are used in an expression to calculate a value based on a field that is not included in the Record Source property for the form or report. All Domain functions start with a "D" for "domain" such as DSum, DAvg, or DCount. The DSum, DAvg, and DCount functions perform the same calculations as their Sum, Avg, and Count function counterparts. The **DLookup** function returns or "looks up" a value from a specified domain. All domain functions have two required arguments: the field that is used for the calculation or "look up" and the domain. The **domain** is the table or query that contains the field. A third optional argument allows you to select records from the domain based on criteria you specify. **CASE** ▶ *Jacob asks you to add a standard disclaimer to the bottom of every report. This is an excellent opportunity to use the DLookup function.*

STEPS

1. **Click the CREATE tab, click the Table Design button, then build a new table with the fields, data types, and primary key field, as shown in FIGURE L-10**

   With the design of the Disclaimers table established, you add two records of standard text used at Quest Specialty Travel.

2. **Save the table as Disclaimers, click the View button 📋, then enter the two records shown in FIGURE L-11**

   The first disclaimer is used with any report that contains employee information for Quest Specialty Travel, QST. The second is added to all internal reports that do not contain employee information. With the data in place, you're ready to use the DLookup function on a report to insert standard text.

3. **Save and close the Disclaimers table, right-click the Attendance List report in the Navigation Pane, then click Design View**

   You can now add a text box using the DLookup function in an expression to return the correct disclaimer.

4. **Click the Text Box button 🔲, click the Page Footer section, delete the Text11 label, click Unbound, type the expression =DLookup("[StandardText]","Disclaimers", "[StandardID]=1"), press [Enter], then widen the text box to about 3"**

   The expression is too wide to be completely displayed in Design View, but you must switch to Print Preview to see if it works anyway.

5. **Display the report in Print Preview and zoom and scroll to the Page Footer to view the result of the DLookup function, as shown in FIGURE L-12**

   By entering standard company disclaimers in one table, the same disclaimer text can be consistently added to each report.

6. **Save and close the Attendance List report, double-click the Disclaimers table to open its datasheet, change QST to Quest Specialty Travel in the first record for the StandardID of 1, close the Disclaimers table, right-click the Attendance List report, then click Print Preview**

   When the StandardText field is changed in the Disclaimers table, all reports that reference that value using the DLookup function in an expression are automatically updated as well.

7. **Close the Attendance List report**

FIGURE L-10: Disclaimers table

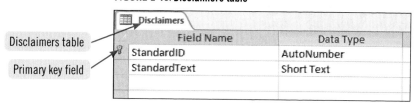

Disclaimers table ⟶

Primary key field ⟶

FIGURE L-11: Records in the Disclaimers table

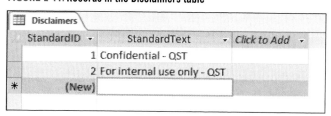

FIGURE L-12: Standard disclaimer in Report Footer section created with DLookup expression

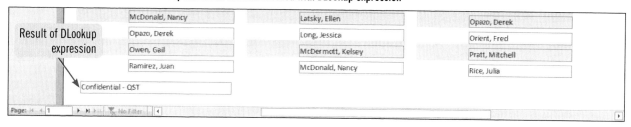

Result of DLookup expression ⟶

Adding page numbers or the date and time to a report

You can quickly add page numbers to a report by clicking the Page Numbers button on the DESIGN tab of the ribbon. The Page Numbers dialog box prompts you for a page number format and whether you want to insert the information into the Page Header or Page Footer section. To quickly add the current date and time to the report, click the Date and Time button on the DESIGN tab. Several date and time formats are available. Date and time information is always inserted on the right side of the Report Header section.

Create Charts

Learning Outcomes
• Define common chart types
• Add charts to a report

Charts, also called graphs, are visual representations of numeric data that help users see comparisons, patterns, and trends in data. Charts can be inserted on a form or report. Access provides a **Chart Wizard** that helps you create the chart. Common **chart types** that determine the presentation of data on the chart, such as column, pie, and line, are described in **TABLE L-2**. **CASE** ▶ *Jacob wants you to create a chart of the total number of course enrollments by department.*

STEPS

1. **Click the CREATE tab, click the Query Design button, double-click Employees, double-click Enrollments, then click Close**

   The first step in creating a chart is to select the data that the chart will graph and collect those fields and records in one query object.

2. **Double-click EDepartment in the Employees field list, double-click EnrollmentID in the Enrollments field list, save the query with the name DepartmentEnrollments, then close it**

   Charts can be added to forms or reports.

3. **Click the CREATE tab, click the Report Design button, click the More button ⊽ in the Controls group on the DESIGN tab, click the Chart button ▥, then click in the Detail section of the report**

   The Chart Wizard starts by asking which table or query holds the fields you want to add to the chart, then asks you to select a chart type.

4. **Click the Queries option button, click Next to choose the DepartmentEnrollments query, click the Select All Fields button ⟩⟩ , click Next, click Next to accept Column Chart, then drag the EnrollmentID field from the Series area to the Data area, as shown in FIGURE L-13**

   The **Data area** determines what data the chart graphs. If you drag a Number or Currency field to the Data area, the Chart Wizard automatically sums the values in the field. For Text or AutoNumber fields (such as EnrollmentID), the Chart Wizard automatically counts the values in that field.

5. **Click Next, type Department Enrollment Totals as the chart title, click Finish, use ⬉ to drag the lower-right corner of the chart to fill the Detail section, right-click the Report1 tab, then click Print Preview**

   When charts are displayed in Design View or Layout View, they appear as a generic Microsoft chart placeholder. The chart in Print Preview should look similar to **FIGURE L-14**. The chart is beginning to take shape, but some of the labels on the x-axis may not have room to display all of their text depending on the size of the chart. You enhance this chart in the next lesson.

Using the Blank Report button versus the Report Design button

Access provides several buttons on the CREATE tab to create a new report. The Blank Report button creates a new, blank report in Layout View. The Report Design button creates a new, blank report in Design View. The only difference between these two buttons is the initial view presented when you start building a new report. The same is true for Blank Form button, which creates a new, blank form in Layout View, and the Form Design button, which creates a new, blank form in Design View.

FIGURE L-13: Choosing the chart areas

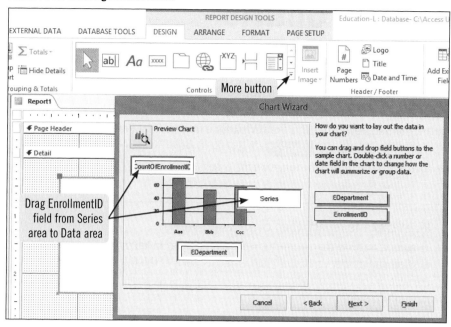

FIGURE L-14: Initial Department Enrollment Totals column chart

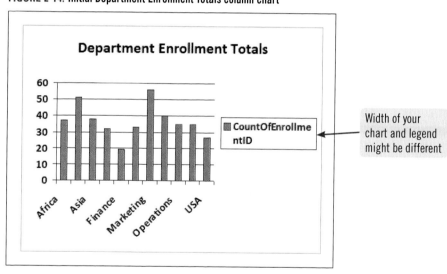

Width of your chart and legend might be different

TABLE L-2: Common chart types

chart type	chart icon	used to show most commonly	example
Column		Comparisons of values (vertical bars)	Each vertical bar represents the annual sales for a different product for the year 2016
Bar		Comparisons of values (horizontal bars)	Each horizontal bar represents the annual sales for a different product for the year 2016
Line		Trends over time	Each point on the line represents monthly sales for one product for the year 2016
Pie		Parts of a whole	Each slice represents total quarterly sales for a company for the year 2016
Area		Cumulative totals	Each section represents monthly sales by representative, stacked to show the cumulative total sales effort for the year 2016

Access 2013

Modify Charts

Learning Outcomes
- Define chart areas
- Modify a chart legend
- Modify chart bar colors

You modify charts in Design View of the form or report that contains the chart. Modifying a chart is challenging because Design View doesn't always show you the actual chart values, but instead, displays a chart placeholder that represents the embedded chart object. To modify the chart, you modify the chart elements and chart areas within the chart placeholder. To view the changes as they apply to the real data you are charting, return to either Form View for a form or Print Preview for a report. See **TABLE L-3** for more information on chart areas. **CASE** *You want to resize the chart, change the color of the bars, and remove the legend to better display the values on the x-axis.*

STEPS

1. **Right-click the report, then click Design View**

   To make changes to chart elements, you open the chart in Edit mode by double-clicking it. Use **Edit mode** to select and modify individual chart elements, such as the title, legend, bars, or axes. If you double-click the edge of the chart placeholder, you open the Property Sheet for the chart instead of opening the chart itself in Edit mode.

2. **Double-click the chart**

   The hashed border of the chart placeholder control indicates that the chart is in Edit mode, as shown in **FIGURE L-15**. The Chart Standard and Chart Formatting toolbars also appear when the chart is in Edit mode. They may appear on one row instead of stacked. Because only one series of bars counts the enrollments, you can describe the data with the chart title and don't need a legend.

   > **TROUBLE**
   > If you make a mistake, use the Undo button ↺ on the Chart Standard toolbar.

3. **Click the legend on the chart, then press [Delete] to remove it**

   Removing the legend provides more room for the x-axis labels.

   > **TROUBLE**
   > If you don't see the Fill Color button ▢ ▾ on the Chart Formatting toolbar, drag the left edge of the toolbars to position them on two rows to show all buttons.

4. **Click any periwinkle bar (the first color in the set of four) to select all bars of that color, click the Fill Color button arrow ▢ ▾ on the Chart Formatting toolbar, then click the Bright Green box**

   Clicking any bar selects all bars in that data series as evidenced by the sizing handle in each of the bars. The bars change to bright green in the chart placeholder.

   You also decide to shorten the department names in the database so they will better fit on the x-axis. Data changed in the database automatically updates all reports, including charts, that are based on that data.

5. **Click outside the hashed border to return to Report Design View, double-click the Employees table in the Navigation Pane, change the two instances of Information Systems to IS in the EDepartment field, then close the Employees table**

   Preview the updated chart.

   > **TROUBLE**
   > If you are prompted that the report width is greater than the page width, return to Report Design View and resize the chart and the right edge of the report to fit within a width of 8".

6. **Save the report as DepartmentChart, then display it in Print Preview**

   The final chart is shown in **FIGURE L-16**.

FIGURE L-15: Editing a chart placeholder

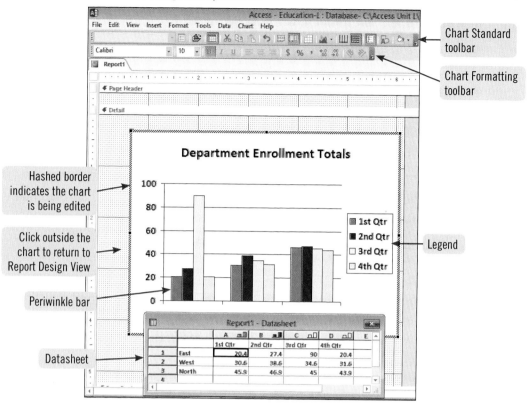

Hashed border indicates the chart is being edited

Click outside the chart to return to Report Design View

Periwinkle bar

Datasheet

Chart Standard toolbar

Chart Formatting toolbar

Legend

FIGURE L-16: Final Department Enrollment Totals column chart

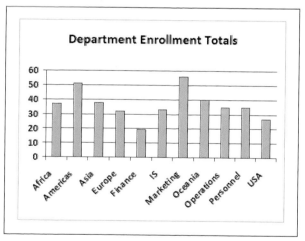

TABLE L-3: Chart areas

chart area	description
Data	Determines what field the bars (lines, wedges, etc.) on the chart represent
Axis	The x-axis (horizontal axis) or y-axis (vertical axis) on the chart
Series	Displays the legend when multiple series of data are graphed

Apply Chart Types

Learning Outcomes
• Apply different chart types
• Describe 3-D chart types

The Chart Wizard provides 20 different chart types. While column charts are the most popular, you can also use line, area, and pie charts to effectively show some types of data. Three-dimensional effects can be used to enhance the chart, but those effects can also make it difficult to compare the sizes of bars, lines, and wedges, so choose a three-dimensional effect only if it does not detract from the point of the chart. **CASE** ▶ *You change the existing column chart to other chart types and sub-types to see how the data is presented.*

STEPS

1. **Right-click the** chart, **click** Design View, **then double-click the** chart placeholder
   You must open the chart in Edit mode to change the chart type.

2. **Click** Chart **on the menu bar, then click** Chart Type
   The Chart Type dialog box opens, as shown in **FIGURE L-17**. All major chart types plus many chart sub-types are displayed. A button is available to preview any choice before applying that chart sub-type.

3. **Click the** Clustered column with a 3-D visual effect button **(second row, first column in the Chart sub-type area), click and hold the** Press and Hold to View Sample button, **click the** 3-D Column button **(third row, first column in the Chart sub-type area), then click and hold the** Press and Hold to View Sample button
   A Sample box opens, presenting a rough idea of what the final chart will look like. Although 3-D charts appear more interesting than 2-D chart types, the samples do not show the data more clearly, so you decide to preview other 2-D chart types.

4. **Click the** Bar Chart type **in the Chart type list, click and hold the** Press and Hold to View Sample button, **click the** Line Chart type **in the Chart type list, click and hold the** Press and Hold to View Sample button, **click the** Pie Chart type **in the Chart type list, click and hold the** Press and Hold to View Sample button, **click the** Default formatting check box, **then click and hold the** Press and Hold to View Sample button
   Because this chart only has one set of values that represent 100 percent of all enrollments, the data fits a pie chart.

5. **Click** OK **to accept the pie chart type, click** Chart **on the menu bar, click** Chart Options, **click the** Data Labels tab, **click the** Percentage check box, **then click** OK
   With the modifications made to change the chart into a pie chart, you view it in Print Preview to see the final result.

6. **Click outside the hashed border to return to Report Design View, click the** Label button **in the Controls group, click above the pie chart, type** Enrollment % by Department, **press [Enter], then display the report in Print Preview**
   The same departmental data, expressed as a pie chart, is shown in **FIGURE L-18**.

7. **Save and close the DepartmentChart report, close the Education-L.accdb database, then exit Access**

FIGURE L-17: Chart Type dialog box

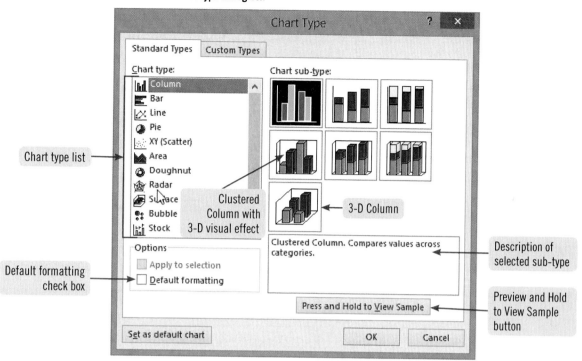

Chart type list

Default formatting
check box

Clustered
Column with
3-D visual effect

3-D Column

Description of
selected sub-type

Preview and Hold
to View Sample
button

FIGURE L-18: Department Enrollment Totals pie chart

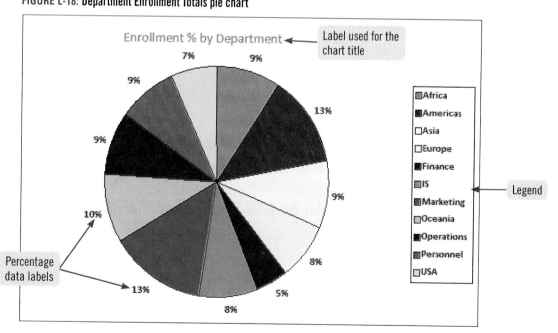

Label used for the
chart title

Legend

Percentage
data labels

Practice

Put your skills into practice with SAM! If you have a SAM account, go to www.cengage.com/sam2013 to access SAM assignments for this unit.

Concepts Review

Identify each element of Report Design View shown in FIGURE L-19.

FIGURE L-19

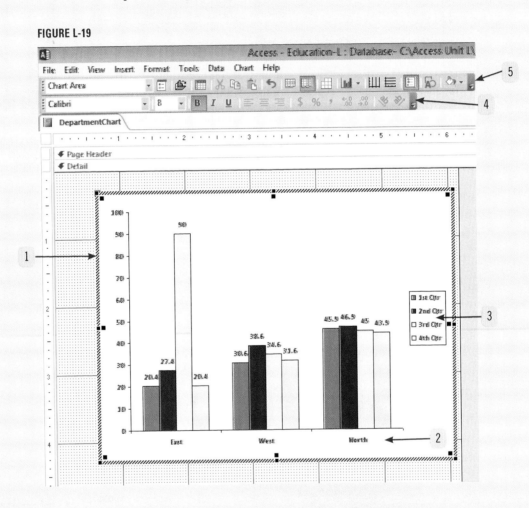

Match each term with the statement that best describes its function.

6. Table layout
7. Charts
8. Domain functions
9. Chart types
10. Data area
11. Edit mode

a. Visual representations of numeric data

b. A way of connecting controls together so that when you move or resize them in Layout or Design View, the action you take on one control applies to all controls

c. Calculate a value based on a field that is not included in the Record Source property for the form or report

d. Used to select and modify individual chart elements, such as the title, legend, bars, or axes

e. Determines what data is graphed on the chart

f. Determine the presentation of data on the chart, such as column, pie, and line

Select the best answer from the list of choices.

12. **Which button aligns the edges of two or more selected controls?**
   a. Align Right button on the ARRANGE tab
   b. Align Right button on the DESIGN tab
   c. Align button on the ARRANGE tab
   d. Align button on the DESIGN tab

13. **To set a page break before a Group Header section on a report, you would modify the properties of the:**
   a. Report.
   b. Detail section.
   c. Group Header section.
   d. Page Footer section.

14. **Which control layout is common for reports?**
   a. Stacked
   b. Datasheet
   c. Tabular
   d. Gridlines

15. **Which dialog box allows you to specify the number of columns you want to view in a report?**
   a. Print
   b. Page Setup
   c. Columns
   d. Property Sheet

16. **Which type of chart is best to show an upward sales trend over several months?**
   a. Column
   b. Line
   c. Pie
   d. Scatter

Skills Review

1. **Apply advanced formatting.**
   a. Start Access, then open the RealEstate-L.accdb database from the location where you store your Data Files. Enable content if prompted. Change the name of Sara Johnson in the Realtors table to your name, then close the table.
   b. Preview the AgencyListings report, noting the format for the SqFt and Asking fields.
   c. In Report Design View, change the Format property for the SqFt text box in the Detail section to **Standard** and change the Decimal Places property to **0**.
   d. In Report Design View, change the Format property for the Asking text box in the Detail section to **Currency** and change the Decimal Places property to **0**.
   e. Preview the report to make sure your SqFt values appear with commas, the Asking values appear with dollar signs, and no decimal places are shown.
   f. Change the top and bottom margins to **0.5"** and the left margin to **0.35"** and then save the AgencyListings report.

2. **Control layout.**
   a. Open the AgencyListings report in Design View.
   b. Open the Group, Sort, and Total pane, then open the AgencyName Footer section.
   c. Add a text box in the AgencyName Footer below the SqFt text box in the Detail section with the expression **=Sum([SqFt])**. Modify the new label to have the caption **Subtotals:**.
   d. Add a text box in the AgencyName Footer below the Asking text box in the Detail section with the expression **=Sum([Asking])**. Delete the extra label in the AgencyName Footer section.
   e. Format the =Sum([SqFt]) text box with **Standard** Format and **0** Decimals Places, format the =Sum([Asking]) text box with **Currency** Format and **0** Decimal Places, and then resize and align the text boxes under the fields they subtotal so that Print Preview looks similar to the portion of the report shown in FIGURE L-20.
   f. Insert the Page N of M page number format into the left side of the Page Footer.
   g. Print preview several pages of the report, and work in Report Design View to remove extra space so that a blank page doesn't print between pages as needed. Save the AgencyListings report.

3. **Set advanced print layout.**
   a. Open the AgencyListings report in Design View.
   b. Modify the AgencyName Footer section to force a new page after that section prints.

FIGURE L-20

Kirkpatrick	555-111-9900				
		4	Cabin	Horseshoe Bend	1,200	$150,000
		12	Ranch	Greenview	2,200	$395,613
		8	Two Story	Shell City	1,800	$138,000
		5	Ranch	Ridgedale	2,500	$199,000
		7	Two Story	Ozark Mountain	3,000	$276,000
				Subtotals:	28,115	$2,359,512

   c. Preview the report to make sure each agency prints on its own page.

   d. Close and save the AgencyListings report.

4. Create multicolumn reports.

   a. Use the Report Wizard to create a report with the AgencyName field from the Agencies table, the RFirst and RLast fields from the Realtors table, and the Type field from the Listings table. Be sure to select the fields from the table objects.

   b. View the data by Listings, add AgencyName as the grouping level, sort the records in ascending order by RLast, use a Stepped layout and a Landscape orientation, and use **Inventory** as the report title.

   c. In Report Design View, delete the RLast and RFirst labels and text boxes.

   d. Delete the page expression in the Page Footer section, delete the Type label in the Page Header section, and delete the AgencyName label in the Page Header section. Move the Type field in the Detail section to the left, just below the AgencyName text box.

   e. Add a new text box to the right of the Type control in the Detail section with the following expression: **=[RLast]&", "&[RFirst]**

   f. Delete the label for the new text box, then widen the =[RLast]&", "&[RFirst] text box in the Detail section to be about 2" wide. Drag the right edge of the report as far as you can to the left so that the report is approximately 5" wide.

   g. Preview the report, and use the Page Setup dialog box to change the Number of Columns setting to **2** and the column layout to Down, then Across. The report should look like **FIGURE L-21**.

   h. Save and close the Inventory report.

5. Use domain functions.

   a. Create a new table named **Legal** with two new fields: **LegalID** with an AutoNumber data type and **LegalText** with a Long Text data type. Make LegalID the primary key field.

   b. Add one record to the table with the following entry in the LegalText field: **The information in the listing has not been verified by an independent inspection.** Widen the column of the LegalText field as needed. Note the value of the LegalID field for the first record (probably 1), then save and close the Legal table.

FIGURE L-21

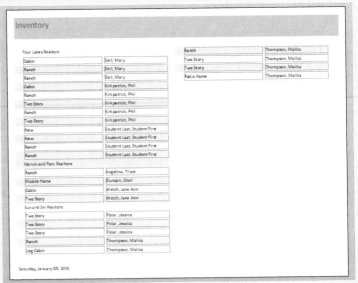

   c. Open the ListingReport in Design View, open the Report Footer section, then use a DLookup function in an expression in a text box in the Page Footer section to look up the LegalText field in the Legal table as follows: **=DLookup("[LegalText]","Legal","LegalID=1")**. Delete the accompanying label. (Note that the number in the expression must match the value of the LegalID field for the first record that you created in Step b.)

   d. Preview the report, then review the Report Footer. Switch back and forth between Report Design View and Print Preview to fix and widen the text box to be as wide as needed so that it clearly displays the entire expression, then save and close the ListingReport.

6. Create charts.

   a. Open the Inventory query in Query Design View, then add criteria to select only the **Ranch** (in the Type field) records.

   b. Save the query with a new name as **RanchHomes**, then close it.

   c. Start a new report in Report Design View.

   d. Insert a chart in the Detail section based on the RanchHomes query.

Skills Review (continued)

   e. Choose the RLast and Asking fields for the chart, choose a Column Chart, make sure the SumOfAsking field appears in the Data area, and move the RLast field from the Axis to the Series area.

   f. Title the chart **Ranch Inventory**, then preview the report to view the chart.

   g. Save the report with the name **RanchInventoryReport**.

7. Modify charts.

   a. Return to Report Design View for RanchInventoryReport, double-click the chart to open it in Edit mode.

   b. Double-click the y-axis values to open the Format Axis dialog box, click the Number tab, then choose the **Currency** format from the Category list, entering **0** for the Decimal Places.

   c. Change the color of the periwinkle bars to red.

   d. Click the By Column button on the Chart Standard toolbar to switch the position of the fields in the x-axis and legend, and then remove the legend.

   e. Return to Report Design View, then switch to Print Preview. Resize the chart as necessary so it looks like **FIGURE L-22**.

8. Apply chart types.

   a. Save and close RanchInventoryReport, then copy and paste it with the name **RanchInventoryReportBar**.

   b. Open RanchInventoryReportBar in Design View, open the chart in Edit mode, then change the chart type to a Clustered Bar.

   c. Switch between Report Design View and Print Preview, resizing the chart and changing the font sizes as needed so that all of the labels on each axis are displayed clearly.

   d. Print RanchInventoryReportBar if requested by your instructor, then save and close it.

   e. Close the RealEstate-L.accdb database, and exit Access 2013.

FIGURE L-22

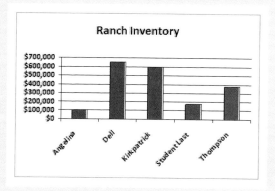

Independent Challenge 1

As the manager of a college women's basketball team, you want to enhance a form within the Basketball-L.accdb database to chart the home versus visiting team scores. You will build on your report creation skills to do so.

   a. Start Access, then open the database Basketball-L.accdb from the location where you store your Data Files. Enable content if prompted.

   b. Open and then maximize the GameInfo form. Navigate through several records as you observe the Home and Visitor scores.

   c. Open the form in Form Design View, then insert a chart on the right side of the form based on the Games table. Choose the CycloneScore and OpponentScore fields for the chart. Choose a Column Chart type.

   d. Add the OpponentScore field to the Data area so that both SumOfCycloneScore and SumOfOpponentScore appear in the Data area, double-click the SumOfCycloneScore field, select None as the summarize option, double-click the SumOfOpponentScore field, then select None as the summarize option.

   e. Click Next and choose GameNo as the Form Field and as the Chart Field so that the chart changes from record to record showing the HomeScore versus the OpponentScore in the chart.

   f. Title the chart **Scores**, and do not display a legend.

   g. Open the form in Form View, and view the record for GameNo 3, as shown in **FIGURE L-23**. If requested by your instructor, print this record. To insert your name on the printout, add it as a label to the Form Header section.

   h. Save the GameInfo form, close it, close the Basketball-L.accdb database, and exit Access 2013.

FIGURE L-23

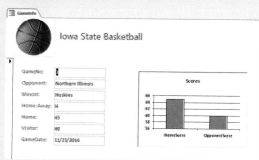

Independent Challenge 2

As the manager of a college women's basketball team, you want to build a report that shows a graph of total points per player per game.

    a. Start Access, then open the database Basketball-L.accdb from the location where you store your Data Files. Enable content if prompted.

    b. Open the PlayerStatistics report, and study the structure. Notice that this report has the total points per player in the last column. You want to graph these values for the entire season. Open the PlayerStatistics report in Report Design View.

    c. Double-click the edge of the far-right text box in the Detail section, and click the Data tab in the Property Sheet to study the Control Source property. The expression =[FT]+([FG]*2)+([3P]*3) adds one-point free throws [FT] to two-point field goals [FG] to three-point three-pointers [3P] to find the player's total contribution to the score. You will calculate the total point value in the underlying query instead of on the report to make it easier to graph.

    d. Click the report selector button, then click the Build button for the Record Source property, which currently displays the PlayerStats query. In the first blank column, add a new field with the following expression: **TotalPts:[FT]+([FG]*2)+([3P]*3)**.

    e. Save and close the PlayerStats query, then return to Design View for the PlayerStatistics report. Open the Property Sheet for the GameNo Footer section. On the Format tab, change the Force New Page property to After Section.

    f. Drag the bottom edge of the Report Footer section down so the height of the Report Footer section is about 3 inches, then insert a chart just below the existing controls in the Report Footer section.

    g. In the Chart Wizard, choose the PlayerStats query to create the chart, choose the LastName and TotalPts fields for the chart, and choose the Column Chart type.

    h. Use SumOfTotalPts in the Data area and the LastName field in the Axis area (which should be the defaults). Choose <No Field> for both the Report Fields and Chart Fields, and title the chart **Player Total Points**.

    i. Widen the chart placeholder and report to be about 6" wide in Report Design View, delete the legend, then save and preview the report. The chart should look like **FIGURE L-24**.

    j. Save the PlayerStatistics report, add your name as a label to the Report Header section, print the first and last pages if requested by your instructor, then close the report.

    k. Close the Basketball-L.accdb database, and exit Access 2013.

FIGURE L-24

Independent Challenge 3

As the manager of a college women's basketball team, you want to create a multicolumn report from the Basketball-L.accdb database to summarize total points per game per player.

    a. Start Access, then open the database Basketball-L.accdb from the location where you store your Data Files. Enable content if prompted.

    b. Open the PlayerStats query in Design View. In the first blank column, add a new field with the following expression (if it has not already been added): **TotalPts:[FT]+([FG]*2)+([3P]*3)**.

    c. Save and close the PlayerStats query.

    d. Use the Report Wizard to create a new report from the PlayerStats query with the fields **Opponent**, **GameDate, LastName**, and **TotalPts**. View the data by Games, do not add any more grouping levels, then sort the records in descending order by TotalPts.

    e. Click the Summary Options button, then click the Sum check box for the TotalPts field.

    f. Choose a Stepped layout and a Landscape orientation. Title the report **Point Production**, and preview it.

    g. Delete the long text box with the Summary expression in the GameNo Footer section. Delete the LastName and TotalPts labels from the Page Header section.

Independent Challenge 3 (continued)

h. Delete the page expression in the Page Footer section, then move the TotalPts and LastName text boxes in the Detail section to the left, just below the Opponent and GameDate text boxes in the GameNo Header section. Move any other text boxes to the left so that no control extends beyond the 4" mark on the horizontal ruler.

i. Drag the right edge of the report to the left, so that it is no wider than 4", then right-align the values within the text boxes with the subtotal for total points in the GameNo Footer and the Report Footer sections and also right-align the right edges of these two text boxes.

j. Move and right-align the Sum and Grand Total labels closer to the text boxes they describe.

k. Preview the report, and in the Page Setup dialog box, set the report to **2** columns, and specify that the column layout go down, then across.

l. In Design View, add a horizontal line across the bottom of the GameNo Footer section to separate the records from game to game.

FIGURE L-25

m. For the GameNo Footer section, change the New Row Or Col property to After Section.

n. Preview the Point Production report. It should structurally look like **FIGURE L-25**. Print the first page of the report if requested by your instructor, adding your name as a label to the Report Header section if needed for the printout.

o. Close the Point Production report, close the Basketball-L. accdb database, then exit Access.

Independent Challenge 4: Explore

In your quest to become an Access database consultant, you want to know more about the built-in Microsoft Access templates and what you can learn about report design from these samples. In this exercise, you explore the reports of the Desktop task management database.

a. Start Access 2013, then select the Desktop task management template. Name the database **TaskManagement**, save it in the location where you store your Data Files, then enable content if prompted.

b. Close the Getting Started window and expand the Navigation Pane (if it is not expanded) to review the objects in the database.

c. Open the Contacts table and add your school name in the Company field and your name in the Last Name and First Name fields. Fill in the rest of the record with fictitious but realistic data.

d. Add a second record in the Contacts table with your professor's information in the Last Name and First Name fields, using fictitious but realistic data in the rest of the record.

e. Expand the subdatasheet for your record and enter two task records with the titles **Research Paper** and **Web Site Survey**. Do not change or enter data in any of the rest of the fields, then close the Contacts table.

f. Preview each of the predeveloped reports going back and forth between Print Preview and Report Design View to study and learn about any new features or techniques these reports offer that you want to explore further.

g. Open the Contact Address Book in Print Preview and notice that the contacts are grouped by the first letter of their last name. To see how this was done, open the report in Design View and then open the Group, Sort, and Total Pane. Click the More button to reveal the characteristics of the Group on File As group. Click the list arrow for the "by first character" option to see more grouping options.

h. If requested by your instructor, print the Contact Address Book report, close the TaskManagement.accdb database, and exit Access 2013.

Visual Workshop

As the manager of a college women's basketball team, you need to create a report from the Basketball-L.accdb database that lists information about each game played and subtracts the OpponentScore from the HomeScore field to calculate the number of points by which the game was won or lost in the Win/Loss column. Use the Report Wizard to start the report. Base it on all the fields in the Games table, and sort the records in ascending order on the GameDate field. Use a Tabular layout and a Landscape orientation, and name the report **Iowa State Basketball**. Use Report Layout and Design View to move, resize, align, modify, and add controls as necessary to match FIGURE L-26. (*Hint*: You must add a text box that calculates the Win/Loss value for each game.) If requested to print the report, add your name as a label to the Report Header section before printing.

FIGURE L-26

Iowa State Basketball

GameDate	Opponent	Mascot	Home-Away	Our Score	Opponent	Win/Loss
11/13/2014	Northern Iowa	Panthers	A	81	65	16
11/16/2014	Creighton	Bluejays	H	106	60	46
11/23/2014	Northern Illinois	Huskies	H	65	60	5
11/30/2014	Louisiana Tech	Red Raiders	A	69	89	-20
12/11/2014	Drake	Bulldogs	H	80	60	20
12/19/2014	Northern Iowa	Panthers	A	38	73	-35
12/29/2014	Buffalo	Bulls	H	50	55	-5
1/1/2015	Oklahoma	Sooners	A	53	60	-7
1/4/2015	Texas	Longhorns	H	57	60	-3
1/8/2015	Kansas	Jayhawks	H	74	58	16

Creating Macros

CASE ▶ Kayla Green, the network administrator at Quest Specialty Travel, has identified several Access tasks that are repeated on a regular basis. She has asked you to help her automate these processes with macros.

Unit Objectives

After completing this unit, you will be able to:

- Understand macros
- Create a macro
- Modify actions and arguments
- Assign a macro to a command button

- Use If statements
- Work with events
- Create a data macro
- Troubleshoot macros

Files You Will Need

Technology-M.accdb
Basketball-M.accdb

Patients-M.accdb
Chocolate-M.accdb

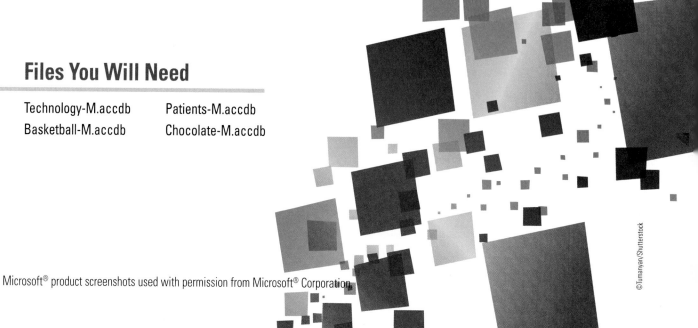

©Tiumanyan/Shutterstock

Understand Macros

Learning Outcomes
• Describe the benefits of macros
• Define macro terminology
• Describe Macro Design View components

A **macro** is a database object that stores actions to complete Access tasks. Repetitive Access tasks such as printing several reports, or opening and maximizing a form, are good candidates for a macro. Automating routine tasks by using macros builds efficiency, accuracy, and flexibility into your database. **CASE** *You decide to study the major benefits of using macros, macro terminology, and the components of the Macro Design View before building your first macro.*

DETAILS

The major benefits of using macros include the following:

- Saving time by automating routine tasks
- Increasing accuracy by ensuring that tasks are executed consistently
- Improving the functionality and ease of use of forms by using macros connected to command buttons
- Ensuring data accuracy in forms by using macros to respond to data entry errors
- Automating data transfers such as collecting data from Excel
- Helping users by responding to their interactions within a form

Macro terminology:

- A **macro** is an Access object that stores a series of actions to perform one or more tasks.
- **Macro Design View** is the window in which you create a macro. **FIGURE M-1** shows Macro Design View with an OpenForm action. See **TABLE M-1** for a description of the Macro Design View components.
- Each task that you want the macro to perform is called an **action**. A macro may contain one or more actions.
- **Arguments** are properties of an action that provide additional information on how the action should execute.
- A **conditional expression** is an expression resulting in either a true or false answer that determines whether a macro action will execute. Conditional expressions are used in If statements.
- An **event** is something that happens to a form, window, toolbar, or control—such as the click of a command button or an entry in a field—that can be used to initiate the execution of a macro.
- A **submacro** is a collection of actions within a macro object that allows you to name and create multiple, separate macros within a single macro object.

FIGURE M-1: Macro Design View with OpenForm action

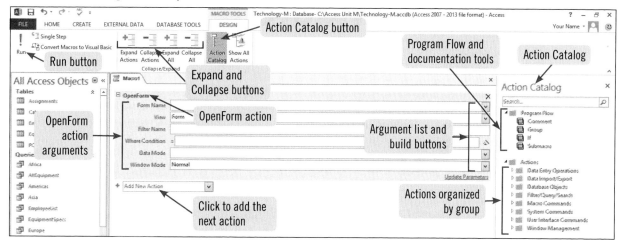

TABLE M-1: Macro Design View components

component	description
Action Catalog	Lists all available macro actions organized by category. Use the Search box to narrow the number of macro actions to a particular subject.
If statement	Contains conditional expressions that are evaluated as either true or false. If true, the macro action is executed. If false, the macro action is skipped. If statements in Access 2013 may contain Else If and Else clauses.
Comment	Allows you to document the macro with explanatory text.
Arguments	Lists required and optional arguments for the selected action.
Run button	Runs the selected macro.
Expand and Collapse buttons	Allows you to expand or collapse the macro actions to show or hide their arguments.

Create a Macro

Learning Outcomes
- Create a macro
- Describe macro actions

In Access, you create a macro by choosing a series of actions in Macro Design View that accomplishes the job you want to automate. Therefore, to become proficient with Access macros, you must be comfortable with macro actions. Some of the most common actions are listed in **TABLE M-2**. When you create a macro in other Microsoft Office products such as Word or Excel, you create Visual Basic for Applications (VBA) statements. In Access, macros do not create VBA code, though after creating a macro, you can convert it to VBA if desired. **CASE** Kayla observes that users want to open the AllEquipment report from the Employees form, so she asks you to create a macro to help automate this task.

STEPS

TROUBLE
If you do not enable content, your macros will not run.

1. **Start Access, open the Technology-M.accdb database from the location where you store your Data Files, enable content if prompted, click the CREATE tab, then click the Macro button**
   Macro Design View opens, ready for you to choose your first action.

TROUBLE
If you choose the wrong macro action, click the Delete button ✕ in the upper-right corner of the macro action block and try again.

2. **Click the Action list arrow, type op to quickly scroll to the actions that start with the letters op, then scroll and click OpenReport**
   The OpenReport action is now the first action in the macro, and the arguments that further define the OpenReport action appear in the action block. The **action block** organizes all of the arguments for a current action and is visually highlighted with a rectangle and gray background. You can expand or collapse the action block to view or hide details by clicking the Collapse/Expand button to the left of the action name or the Expand and Collapse buttons on the DESIGN tab in Macro Design View.

   The **OpenReport action** has three required arguments: Report Name, View, and Window Mode. View and Window Mode have default values, but the word *Required* is shown in the Report Name argument, indicating that you must select a choice. The Filter Name and Where Condition arguments are optional as indicated by their blank boxes.

QUICK TIP
Hover over any macro action or argument to see a ScreenTip of information about that item.

3. **Click the Report Name argument list arrow, then click AllEquipment**
   All of the report objects in the Technology-M.accdb database appear in the Report Name argument list, making it easy to choose the report you want.

4. **Click the View argument list arrow, then click Print Preview**
   Your screen should look like **FIGURE M-2**. Macros can contain one or many actions. In this case, the macro has only one action.

5. **Click the Save button 🖫 on the Quick Access toolbar, type PreviewAllEquipmentReport in the Macro Name text box, click OK, right-click the PreviewAllEquipmentReport macro tab, then click Close**
   The Navigation Pane lists the PreviewAllEquipmentReport object in the Macros group.

QUICK TIP
To print Macro Design View, click the FILE tab, click Print, click the Print button, then click OK in the Print Macro Definition dialog box.

6. **Double-click the PreviewAllEquipmentReport macro in the Navigation Pane to run the macro**
   The AllEquipment report opens in Print Preview.

7. **Close the AllEquipment report**

FIGURE M-2: Macro Design View with OpenReport action

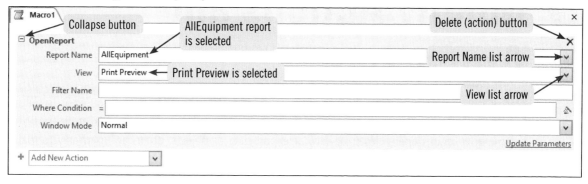

TABLE M-2: Common macro actions

subject area	macro action	description
Data Entry Operations	DeleteRecord	Deletes the current record
	SaveRecord	Saves the current record
Data Import/Export	ImportExportSpreadsheet*	Imports or exports the spreadsheet you specify
	ImportExportText*	Imports or exports the text file you specify
	EMailDatabaseObject	Sends the specified database object through Outlook with specified email settings
Database Objects	GoToControl	Moves the focus (where you are currently typing or clicking) to a specific field or control
	GoToRecord	Makes a specified record the current record
	OpenForm	Opens a form in Form View, Design View, Print Preview, or Datasheet View
	OpenReport	Opens a report in Design View or Print Preview, or prints the report
	OpenTable	Opens a table in Datasheet View, Design View, or Print Preview
	SetValue*	Sets the value of a field, control, or property
Filter/Query/Search	ApplyFilter	Restricts the number of records that appear in the resulting form or report by applying limiting criteria
	FindRecord	Finds the first record that meets the criteria
	OpenQuery	Opens a select or crosstab query; runs an action query
Macro Commands	RunCode	Runs a Visual Basic function (a series of programming statements that do a calculation or comparison and return a value)
	RunMacro	Runs a macro or attaches a macro to a custom menu command
	StopMacro	Stops the currently running macro
System Commands	Beep	Sounds a beep tone through the computer's speaker
	PrintOut*	Prints the active object, such as a datasheet, report, form, or module
	SendKeys*	Sends keystrokes directly to Microsoft Access or to an active Windows application
User Interface Commands	MessageBox	Displays a message box containing a warning or an informational message
	ShowToolbar*	Displays or hides a given toolbar
Window Management	CloseWindow	Closes a window
	MaximizeWindow	Enlarges the active window to fill the Access window

*Must click Show All Actions button on Ribbon for these actions to appear.

Access 2013

Modify Actions and Arguments

Learning
Outcomes
• Modify macro
  actions
• Modify macro
  arguments

Macros can contain as many actions as necessary to complete the process that you want to automate. Each action is evaluated in the order in which it appears in Macro Design View, starting at the top. Whereas some macro actions open, close, preview, or export data or objects, others are used only to make the database easier to use. **MessageBox** is a useful macro action because it displays an informational message to the user. **CASE** *You add a MessageBox action to the PreviewAllEquipmentReport macro to display a descriptive message in a dialog box.*

STEPS

1. **Right-click the** PreviewAllEquipmentReport macro **in the Navigation Pane, then click** Design View **on the shortcut menu**

   The PreviewAllEquipmentReport macro opens in Macro Design View.

2. **Click the** Add New Action list arrow, **type** me **to quickly scroll to the actions that start with the letters** *me*, **then click** MessageBox

   Each action has its own arguments that further clarify what the action does.

3. **Click the** Message argument text box **in the action block, then type** Click the Print button to print this report

   The Message argument determines what text appears in the message box. By default, the Beep argument is set to "Yes" and the Type argument is set to "None."

4. **Click the** Type argument list arrow **in the action block, then click** Information

   The Type argument determines which icon appears in the dialog box that is created by the MessageBox action.

5. **Click the** Title argument text box **in the action block, then type** To print this report. . .

   Your screen should look like **FIGURE M-3**. The Title argument specifies what text is displayed in the title bar of the resulting dialog box. If you leave the Title argument empty, the title bar of the resulting dialog box displays "Microsoft Access."

6. **Save the macro, then click the** Run button **in the Tools group**

   If your speakers are turned on, you should hear a beep, then the message box appears, as shown in **FIGURE M-4**.

7. **Click** OK **in the dialog box, close the AllEquipment report, then save and close Macro Design View**

FIGURE M-3: Adding the MessageBox action

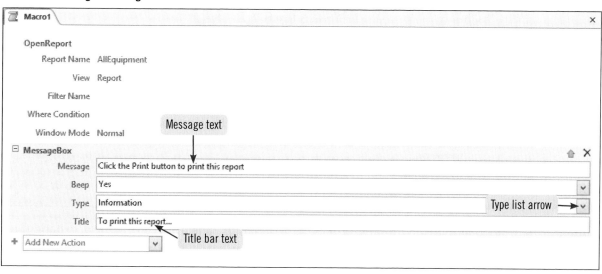

FIGURE M-4: Dialog box created by MessageBox action

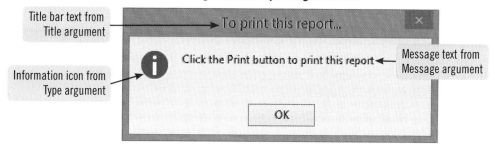

Assigning a macro to a key combination

You can assign a key combination such as [Shift][Ctrl][L] to a macro by creating a macro with the name **AutoKeys**. Enter the key combination as the submacro name. Use + for Shift, % for Alt, and ^ for Ctrl. Enclose special keys such as F3 in {curly braces}. For example, to assign a macro to [Shift][Ctrl][L], use +^L as the submacro name. To assign a macro to [Shift][F3], use +{F3} as the submacro name. Any key combination assignments you make in the AutoKeys macro override those that Access has already specified. Therefore, check the Keyboard Shortcuts information in the Microsoft Access Help system to make sure that the AutoKey assignment that you are creating doesn't override an existing Access quick keystroke that may be used for another purpose.

Learning Outcomes
- Tie a command button to a macro
- Describe trusted folders and files

Assign a Macro to a Command Button

Access provides many ways to run a macro: clicking the Run button in Macro Design View, assigning the macro to a command button, or assigning the macro to a ribbon or shortcut menu command. Assigning a macro to a command button on a form provides a very intuitive way for the user to access the macro's functionality. **CASE** ▶ *You decide to modify the Employees form to include a command button that runs the PreviewAllEquipmentReport macro.*

STEPS

QUICK TIP
Be sure the Use Control Wizards button is selected. To find it, click the More button ☰ in the Controls group on the DESIGN tab.

1. **Right-click the Employees form in the Navigation Pane, click Design View, expand the Form Footer about 0.5", click the Button button ⌧ in the Controls group, then click the left side of the Form Footer section**

   The **Command Button Wizard** starts, presenting you with 28 actions on the right organized within six categories on the left. For example, if you want the command button to open a report, you choose the OpenReport action in the Report Operations category. In this case, you want to run the PreviewAllEquipmentReport macro, which not only opens a report, but also presents a message. The Miscellaneous category contains an action that allows you to run an existing macro.

2. **Click Miscellaneous in the Categories list, click Run Macro in the Actions list, as shown in FIGURE M-5, click Next, click PreviewAllEquipmentReport, click Next, click the Text option button, select Run Macro, type All Equipment Report, then click Next**

   The Command Button Wizard asks you to give the button a meaningful name. When assigning names, a common three-character prefix for command buttons is **cmd**.

3. **Type cmdAllEquipment, click Finish, then click the Property Sheet button in the Tools group to open the Property Sheet for the command button**

   The new command button that runs a macro has been added to the Employees form in Form Design View. You work with the Property Sheet to change the text color to differentiate it from the button color as well as to examine how the macro was attached to the command button.

4. **Click the Format tab in the Property Sheet, scroll down and click the Fore Color list arrow, click Text Dark, then click the Event tab in the Property Sheet, noting that the On Click property contains [Embedded Macro]**

   The PreviewAllEquipmentReport macro was attached to the **On Click property** of this command button. In other words, the macro is run when the user clicks the command button. To make sure that the new command button works as intended, you view the form in Form View and test the command button.

5. **Close the Property Sheet, click the View button ▦ to switch to Form View, click the All Equipment Report command button in the Form Footer section, click OK in the message box, then close the AllEquipment report**

   The Employees form with the new command button should look like **FIGURE M-6**. It's common to put command buttons in the Form Footer so that users have a consistent location to find them.

6. **Save and close the Employees form**

FIGURE M-5: Adding a command button to run a macro

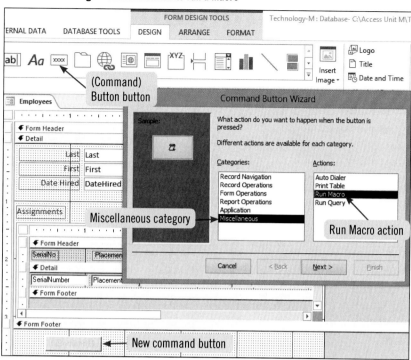

FIGURE M-6: Employees form with new command button

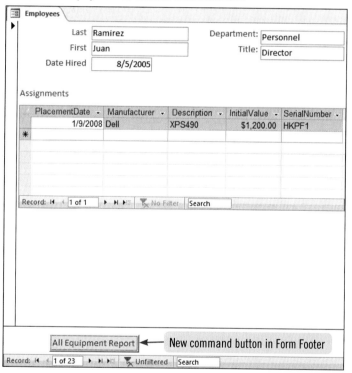

Using a trusted database and setting up a trusted folder

A **trusted database** allows you to run macros and VBA. By default, a database is not trusted. To trust a database, click the Enable Content button on the Security Warning bar each time you open a database. To permanently trust a database, store the database in a **trusted folder**. To create a trusted folder, open the Options dialog box from the FILE tab, click the Trust Center, click the Trust Center Settings button, click the Trusted Locations option, click the Add new location button, then browse to and choose the folder you want to trust.

Use If Statements

Learning
Outcomes
• Apply If state-
ments to macros
• Enter conditional
expressions

An **If statement** allows you to run macro actions based on the result of a conditional expression. A **conditional expression** is an expression such as [Price]>100 or [StateName]="MO" that results in a true or false value. If the condition evaluates true, the actions that follow the If statement are executed. If the condition evaluates false, the macro skips those actions. When building a conditional expression that refers to a value in a control on a form or report, use the following syntax: [Forms]![*formname*]![*controlname*] or [Reports]![*reportname*]![*controlname*]. Separating the object type (Forms or Reports) from the object name and from the control name by using [square brackets] and exclamation points (!) is called **bang notation**. **CASE** *At Quest Specialty Travel, everyone who has been with the company longer than five years is eligible to take their old PC equipment home as soon as it has been replaced. You use a conditional macro to help evaluate and present this information in a form.*

STEPS

1. **Click the CREATE tab, click the Macro button, click the Action Catalog button in the Show/Hide group to toggle on the Action Catalog window if it is not already visible, double-click If in the Program Flow area, then type the following in the If box:**
   [Forms]![Employees]![DateHired]<Date()-(5*365)
   The conditional expression shown in **FIGURE M-7** says, "Check the value in the DateHired control on the Employees form and evaluate true if the value is earlier than 5 years from today. Evaluate false if the value is not earlier than 5 years ago."

2. **Click the Add New Action list arrow in the If block, then scroll and click SetProperty**

   The **SetProperty** action has three arguments: Control Name, Property, and Value, which set the control, property, and value of that property.

3. **Click the Control Name argument text box in the Action Arguments pane, type LabelPCProgram, click the Property argument list arrow, click Visible, click the Value Property argument, then type True**
   Your screen should look like **FIGURE M-8**. The **Control Name** argument for the label is set to LabelPCProgram, which must match the **Name property** in the Property Sheet of the label that will be modified. The **Property argument** determines what property is being modified for the LabelPCProgram control. In this case, you are modifying the Visible property. The **Value argument** determines the value of the **Visible property**. For properties such as the Visible property that have only two choices in the Property Sheet, Yes or No, you enter a value of False for No and True for Yes.

4. **Save the macro with the name 5YearsPC, then close Macro Design View**
   Test the macro using the Employees form.

5. **In the Navigation Pane, double-click the Employees form to open it**
   The record for Juan Ramirez, hired 8/5/2005, appears. Given that Juan has worked at Quest much longer than 5 years, you anticipate that the macro will display the label when it is run.

6. **Click the DATABASE TOOLS tab, click the Run Macro button, verify that 5YearsPC is in the Macro Name text box, then click OK**
   After evaluating the DateHired field of this record and determining that this employee has been working at Quest Specialty Travel longer than five years, the LabelPCProgram label's Visible property was set to Yes, as shown in **FIGURE M-9**. The LabelPCProgram label's **Caption property** is "Eligible for PC Program!"

7. **Navigate through several records and note that the label remains visible for each employee even though the hire date may not be longer than 5 years ago**
   Because the macro only ran once, the label's Visible property remains Yes regardless of the current data in the DateHired field. You need a way to rerun or trigger the macro to evaluate the data in the DateHired field for each employee.

8. **Close the Employees form**

Creating Macros

FIGURE M-7: Using an If statement to set a control's Visible property

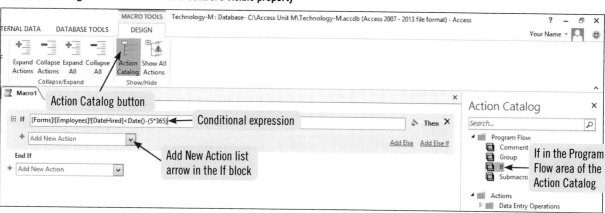

FIGURE M-8: Entering arguments for the SetProperty action

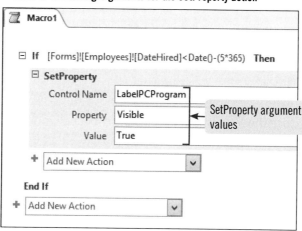

FIGURE M-9: Running the 5YearsPC macro

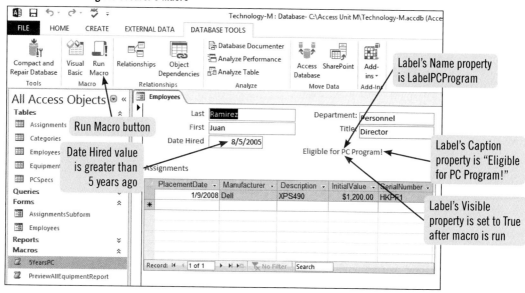

Work with Events

Learning
Outcomes
• Attach macros to
  form events

An **event** is a specific activity that occurs within the database, such as clicking a command button, moving from record to record, editing data, or opening or closing a form. Events can be triggered by the user or by the database itself. By assigning a macro to an appropriate event rather than running the macro from the DATABASE TOOLS tab or command button, you further automate and improve your database. **CASE** ▶ *You need to modify the 5YearsPC macro so that it evaluates the DateHired field to display or hide the label as you move from record to record.*

STEPS

1. **Right-click the** 5YearsPC macro **in the Navigation Pane, click** Design View **on the shortcut menu, click anywhere in the** If block **to activate it, then click the** Add Else link **in the lower-right corner of the If block**

   The **Else** portion of an If statement allows you to run a different set of macro actions if the conditional expression evaluates False. In this case, you want to set the Value of the Visible property to False if the conditional expression evaluates False (if the DateHired is less than five years from today's date) so that the label does not appear if the employee is not eligible for the PC program.

TROUBLE
If your screen doesn't match **FIGURE M-10**, use the Undo button ↩ to try again.

2. **Right-click the** SetProperty action block, **click** Copy, **right-click the** Else block, **click** Paste, **select** True **in the Value property, then type** False, **as shown in** FIGURE M-10

   With the second action edited, the macro will now turn the label's Visible property to True (Yes) *or* False (No), depending on DateHired value. To make the macro run each time you move to a new employee record, you attach the macro to the event that is triggered as you move from record to record.

3. **Save and close the** 5YearsPC macro, **right-click the** Employees form **in the Navigation Pane, click** Design View, **then click the** Property Sheet button

   All objects, sections, and controls have a variety of events to which macros can be attached. Most event names are self-explanatory, such as the **On Click event** (which occurs when that item is clicked).

TROUBLE
Be sure you are viewing the Property Sheet for the form. If not, choose Form from the Selection Type list near the top of the Property Sheet.

4. **Click the** Event tab **in the Property Sheet, click the** On Current list arrow, **then click** 5YearsPC

   Your Property Sheet should look like **FIGURE M-11**. Because the **On Current event** occurs when focus moves from one record to another, the 5YearsPC macro will automatically run each time you move from record to record in the form. Test your new macro by moving through several records in Form View.

5. **Close the** Property Sheet, **click the** View button ▦ **to switch to Form View, then click the** Next record button ▶ **in the navigation bar for the main form several times while observing the Eligible for PC Program! label**

   For every DateHired value that is earlier than five years before today's date, the Eligible for PC Program! label is visible. If the DateHired is less than five years before today's date, the label is hidden.

6. **Save and close the Employees form**

FIGURE M-10: Adding an Else portion to an If block

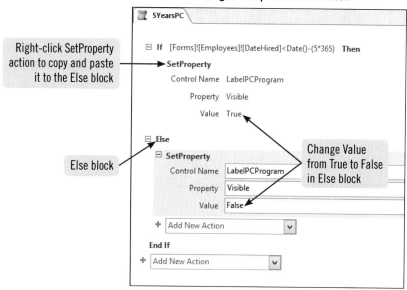

Right-click SetProperty action to copy and paste it to the Else block

Else block

Change Value from True to False in Else block

FIGURE M-11: Attaching a macro to the On Current event of the form

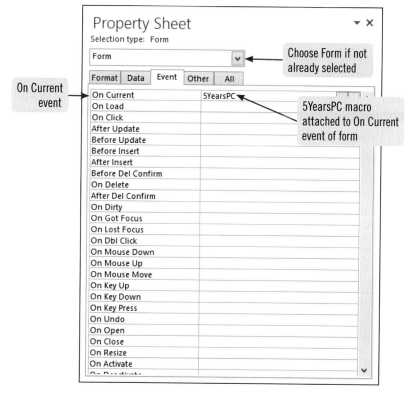

Choose Form if not already selected

On Current event

5YearsPC macro attached to On Current event of form

Create a Data Macro

A **data macro** allows you to embed macro capabilities directly in a table to add, change, or delete data based on conditions you specify. Data macros are a new feature of Access 2013. Data macros are managed directly from within tables, and do not appear in the Macros group in the Navigation Pane. You most often run a data macro based on a table event, such as modifying data or deleting a record, but you can run a data macro separately as well, similar to how you run a regular macro. **CASE** *Quest Specialty Travel grants 10 days of regular vacation to all employees except for those in the Africa and Asia departments, who receive 15 days due to the extra travel requirements of their positions. Kayla asks you to figure out an automatic way to assign each employee the correct number of vacation days based on their department. A data macro will work well for this task.*

STEPS

1. **Double-click the Employees table in the Navigation Pane, then observe the Vacation field throughout the datasheet**

   Currently, the Vacation field contains the value of 10 for each record, or each employee.

2. **Right-click the Employees table tab, click Design View on the shortcut menu, click the Create Data Macros button in the Field, Record & Table Events group, click After Insert, then click the Action Catalog button in the Show/Hide group if the Action Catalog window is not already open**

   In this case, you chose the After Insert event, which is run after a new record is entered. See **TABLE M-3** for more information on table events. Creating a data macro is very similar to creating a regular macro. You add the logic and macro actions needed to complete the task at hand.

3. **Double-click ForEachRecord in the Action Catalog to add a For Each Record In block, click the For Each Record In list arrow, click Employees in the list, click the Where Condition text box, type [Department]="Africa" or [Department]="Asia", double-click the EditRecord data block in the Action Catalog, double-click the SetField data action in the Action Catalog, click the Name box in the SetField block, type Vacation, click the Value box in the SetField block, then type 15, as shown in FIGURE M-12**

   The Default value for the Vacation field is set to 10 in Table Design View of the Employees table so all existing records should have a value of 10 in the Vacation field. Test the new data macro by adding a new record.

4. **Click the Close button, click Yes when prompted to save changes, click the View button 🔲 to display the datasheet, click Yes when prompted to save changes, click the New button in the Records group, enter the new record, as shown in FIGURE M-13, except do not enter a Vacation value, then press [Tab] to move to a new record**

   The macro is triggered by the After Insert event of the record, and the Vacation field is automatically updated to 15 for the new record and all other records with Asia or Africa in the Department field, as shown in **FIGURE M-13**.

5. **Right-click the Employees table tab, then click Close on the shortcut menu**

   Data is automatically saved when you move from record to record or close a database object.

Creating Macros

FIGURE M-12: Creating a data macro

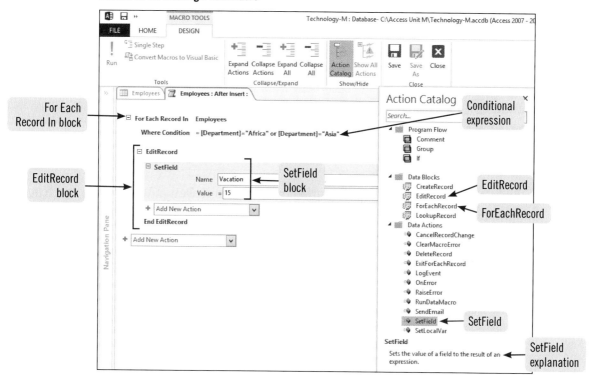

FIGURE M-13: Running a data macro

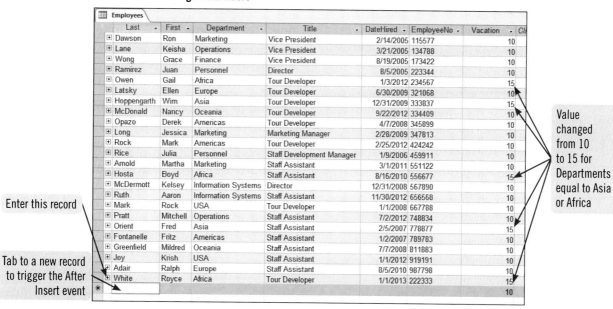

TABLE M-3: Table events

table event	runs...
After Insert	...after a new record has been inserted into the table
After Update	...after an existing record has been changed
After Delete	...after an existing record has been deleted
Before Delete	...before a record is deleted, to help the user validate or cancel the deletion
Before Change	...before a record is changed, to help the user validate or cancel the edits

Troubleshoot Macros

Learning
Outcomes
• Single step a
  macro
• Describe debugg-
  ing techniques

When macros don't run properly, Access supplies several tools to debug them. **Debugging** means determining why the macro doesn't run correctly. It usually involves breaking down a dysfunctional macro into smaller pieces that can be individually tested. For example, you can **single step** a macro, which means to run it one action at a time to observe the effect of each specific action in the Macro Single Step dialog box. **CASE** ▶ *You use the PreviewAllEquipmentReport macro to learn debugging techniques.*

STEPS

1. **Right-click the** PreviewAllEquipmentReport macro, **click** Design View **on the shortcut menu, click the** Single Step button **in the Tools group, then click the** Run button

   The screen should look like **FIGURE M-14**, with the Macro Single Step dialog box open. This dialog box displays information including the macro's name, the action's name, and the action's arguments. From the Macro Single Step dialog box, you can step into the next macro action, halt execution of the macro, or continue running the macro without single stepping.

2. **Click** Step **in the Macro Single Step dialog box**

   Stepping into the second action lets the first action run and pauses the macro at the second action. The Macro Single Step dialog box now displays information about the second action.

3. **Click** Step

   The second action, the MessageBox action, is executed, which displays the message box.

4. **Click** OK, **then close the AllEquipment report**

5. **Click the** DESIGN tab, **then click the** Single Step button **to toggle it off**

   Another technique to help troubleshoot macros is to use the built-in prompts and Help system provided by Microsoft Access. For example, you may have questions about how to use the optional Filter Name argument for the OpenReport macro action.

6. **Click the** OpenReport action block, **then point to the** Filter Name argument **to view the ScreenTip that supplies information about that argument, as shown in** FIGURE M-15

   The Access 2013 Macro Design View window has been improved with interactive prompts.

7. **Save and close the PreviewAllEquipmentReport macro, close the Technology-M.accdb database, then exit Access**

FIGURE M-14: Single stepping through a macro

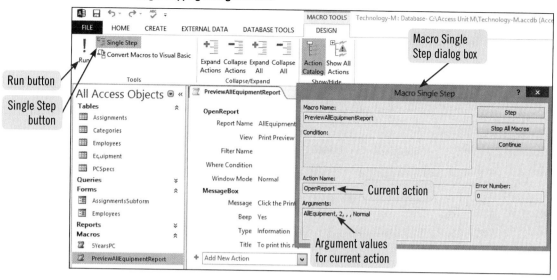

FIGURE M-15: Viewing automatic prompts

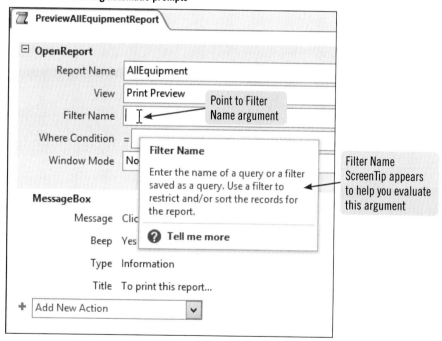

Access 2013

Practice

Put your skills into practice with SAM! If you have a SAM account, go to www.cengage.com/sam2013 to access SAM assignments for this unit.

Concepts Review

Identify each element of Macro Design View shown in FIGURE M-16.

FIGURE M-16

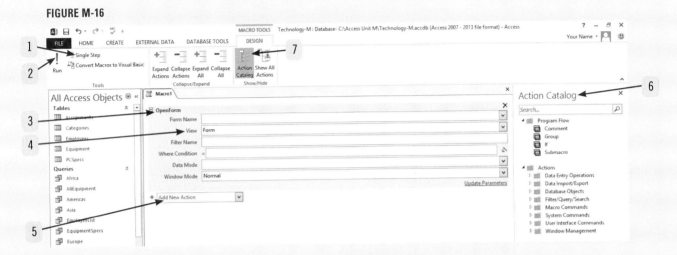

Match each term with the statement that best describes its function.

8. **Macro**
9. **Action**
10. **Argument**
11. **Event**
12. **Debugging**
13. **Conditional expression**

a. Specific action that occurs within the database, such as clicking a button or opening a form

b. Part of an If statement that evaluates as either true or false

c. Individual step that you want the Access macro to perform

d. Access object that stores one or more actions that perform one or more tasks

e. Provides additional information to define how an Access action will perform

f. Determines why a macro doesn't run properly

Select the best answer from the list of choices.

14. **Which of the following is *not* a major benefit of using a macro?**
    a. To make the database more flexible or easy to use
    b. To ensure consistency in executing routine or complex tasks
    c. To redesign the relationships among the tables of the database
    d. To save time by automating routine tasks

15. **Which of the following best describes the process of creating an Access macro?**
    a. Open Macro Design View and add actions, arguments, and If statements to accomplish the desired task.
    b. Use the single step recorder to record clicks and keystrokes as you complete a task.
    c. Use the macro recorder to record clicks and keystrokes as you complete a task.
    d. Use the Macro Wizard to determine which tasks are done most frequently.

16. **Which of the following would *not* be a way to run a macro?**
    a. Double-click a macro action within the Macro Design View window.
    b. Click the Run Macro button on the DATABASE TOOLS tab.
    c. Assign the macro to a command button on a form.
    d. Assign the macro to an event of a control on a form.

17. **Which of the following is *not* a reason to run a macro in single step mode?**
    a. You want to observe the effect of each macro action individually.
    b. You want to debug a macro that isn't working properly.
    c. You want to run only a few of the actions of a macro.
    d. You want to change the arguments of a macro while it runs.

18. **Which of the following is *not* true of conditional expressions in If statements in macros?**
    a. Macro If statements provide for Else and Else If clauses.
    b. Conditional expressions allow you to skip over actions when the expression evaluates as false.
    c. Conditional expressions give the macro more power and flexibility.
    d. More macro actions are available when you are also using conditional expressions.

19. **Which example illustrates the proper syntax to refer to a specific control on a form?**
    a. [Forms] ! [*formname*] ! [*controlname*]
    b. Forms ! formname. controlname
    c. {Forms} ! {formname} ! (controlname)
    d. (Forms) ! (formname) ! (controlname)

20. **Which event is executed every time you move from record to record in a form?**
    a. Next Record
    b. On Current
    c. New Record
    d. On Move

Skills Review

1. **Understand macros.**
   a. Start Access, then open the Basketball-M.accdb database from the location where you store your Data Files. Enable content if prompted.
   b. Open the PrintMacroGroup macro in Macro Design View, then record your answers to the following questions on a sheet of paper:
      - What is the name of the first submacro?
      - How many macro actions are in the first submacro?
      - What arguments does the first action in the first submacro contain?
      - What values were chosen for these arguments?
   c. Close Macro Design View for the PrintMacroGroup object.

2. **Create a macro.**
   a. Start a new macro in Macro Design View.
   b. Add the OpenQuery action.
   c. Select PlayerStats as the value for the Query Name argument.
   d. Select Datasheet for the View argument.
   e. Select Edit for the Data Mode argument.
   f. Save the macro with the name **ViewPlayerStats**.
   g. Run the macro to make sure it works, close the PlayerStats query, then close the ViewPlayerStats macro.

3. **Modify actions and arguments.**
   a. Open the ViewPlayerStats macro in Macro Design View.
   b. Add a MessageBox action as the second action of the query.
   c. Type **We had a great season!** for the Message argument.
   d. Select Yes for the Beep argument.
   e. Select Warning! for the Type argument.
   f. Type **Iowa State Cyclones** for the Title argument.
   g. Save the macro, then run it to make sure the MessageBox action works as intended.
   h. Click OK in the dialog box created by the MessageBox action, close the PlayerStats query, then close the ViewPlayerStats macro.
   i. Open the PrintMacroGroup macro object in Design View.
   j. Modify the View argument for the OpenReport object of the PlayerStatistics submacro from Print to **Print Preview**.

Skills Review (continued)

k. Modify the Message argument for the MessageBox object of the PlayerStatistics submacro to read **Click the Print button to send this report to the printer.**

l. Save and close the PrintMacroGroup macro.

4. Assign a macro to a command button.

a. In Design View of the PlayerEntryForm, use the Command Button Wizard to add a command button below the existing Print Current Record button. The new button should run the PlayerStatistics submacro in the PrintMacroGroup macro (PrintMacroGroup.PlayerStatistics).

b. The text on the button should read **View Player Statistics**.

c. The meaningful name for the button should be **cmdPlayerStatistics**.

d. Test the command button in Form View, click OK in the message box, then close the PlayerStats report.

e. Save and close the PlayerEntryForm.

5. Use If statements.

a. Start a new macro in Macro Design View, and open the Action Catalog window if it is not already open.

b. Double-click If in the Action Catalog window to add an If block to the macro.

c. Enter the following condition in the If box: **[Forms]![GameSummaryForm]![CycloneScore]> [OpponentScore]**.

d. Add the SetProperty action to the If block.

e. Type **VictoryLabel** in the Control Name box for the SetProperty action.

f. Select Visible for the Property argument for the SetProperty action.

g. Enter **True** for the Value argument for the SetProperty action to indicate Yes.

h. Click the Add Else link in the lower-right corner of the If block.

i. Copy the existing SetProperty action, then paste it under the Else clause.

j. Modify the Value property from True to **False** for the second SetProperty action.

k. Save the macro with the name **VictoryCalculator**, compare it with **FIGURE M-17**, make any necessary adjustments, then close Macro Design View.

6. Work with events.

a. Open the GameSummaryForm in Form Design View.

b. Open the Property Sheet for the form.

c. Assign the VictoryCalculator macro to the On Current event of the form.

d. Close the Property Sheet, save the form, then open the GameSummaryForm in Form View.

e. Navigate through the first four records. The Victory label should be visible for the first three records, but not the fourth.

f. Add your name as a label in the Form Footer section to identify your printouts, print the third and fourth records if requested by your instructor, then save and close the GameSummaryForm.

FIGURE M-17

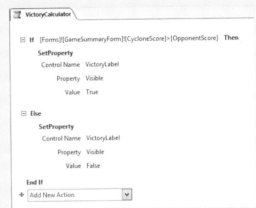

7. Create a data macro.

a. Open the Games table in Table Design View.

b. Add a field named **RoadWin** with a Yes/No data type and the following Description: **Enter Yes if the Home-Away field is Away and the CycloneScore is greater than the OpponentScore**.

c. Save the Games table and switch to Datasheet View to note that the RoadWin check box is empty (No) for every record.

d. Switch back to Table Design View, then create a data macro based on the After Insert event.

e. Insert a ForEachRecord data block, and specify **Games** for the For Each Record In argument.

f. The Where Condition should be: **[Home-Away]="A" and [CycloneScore]>[OpponentScore]**.

g. Add an EditRecord data block in the For Each Record In block, and a SetField data action. Be careful to add the EditRecord block *within* the For Each Record Block.

Skills Review (continued)

h. Enter **RoadWin** in the Name argument and **Yes** in the Value argument, as shown in **FIGURE M-18**.

i. Save and close the data macro, save the Games table, switch to Datasheet View, then test the new data macro by entering a new record in the Games table as follows:

Opponent: **Tulsa**

Mascot: **Hurricanes**

Home-Away: **A**

CycloneScore: **100**

OpponentScore: **50**

GameDate: **3/1/2015**

FIGURE M-18

j. Tab to a new record. Six records where the Home-Away field is set to "A" and the CycloneScore is greater than the OpponentScore should be checked. Close the Games table.

8. Troubleshoot macros.

a. Open the PrintMacroGroup in Macro Design View.

b. Click the Single Step button, then click the Run button.

c. Click Step twice to step through the two actions of the submacro, PlayerStatistics, then click OK in the resulting message box.

d. Close the PlayerStats report.

e. Return to Macro Design View of the PrintMacroGroup macro, and click the Single Step button on the DESIGN tab to toggle off this feature.

f. Save and close the PrintMacroGroup macro, close the Basketball-M.accdb database, then exit Access.

Independent Challenge 1

As the manager of a doctor's clinic, you have created an Access database called Patients-M.accdb to track insurance claim reimbursements. You use macros to help automate the database.

a. Start Access, then open the database Patients-M.accdb from the location where you store your Data Files. Enable content if prompted.

b. Open Macro Design View of the CPT Form Open macro. (CPT stands for Current Procedural Terminology, which is a code that describes a medical procedure.) If the Single Step button is toggled on, click it to toggle it off.

c. On a separate sheet of paper, identify the macro actions, arguments for each action, and values for each argument.

d. In two or three sentences, explain in your own words what tasks this macro automates.

e. Close the CPT Form Open macro.

f. Open the Claim Entry Form in Form Design View.

g. In the Form Footer of the Claim Entry Form are several command buttons. Open the Property Sheet of the Add CPT Code button, then click the Event tab.

h. On your paper, write the event to which the CPT Form Open macro is assigned.

i. Open the Claim Entry Form in Form View, then click the Add CPT Code button in the Form Footer.

j. On your paper, write the current record number that is displayed for you.

k. Close the Patients-M.accdb database, then exit Access.

Independent Challenge 2

As the manager of a doctor's clinic, you have created an Access database called Patients-M.accdb to track insurance claim reimbursements. You use macros to help automate the database.

a. Start Access, then open the database Patients-M.accdb from the location where you store your Data Files. Enable content if prompted.

b. Start a new macro in Macro Design View, and open the Action Catalog window if it is not already open.

Independent Challenge 2 (continued)

c. Double-click the Submacro entry in the Program Flow folder to add a submacro block.

d. Type **Preview Date of Service Denied Report** as the first submacro name, then add the OpenReport macro action.

e. Select Date of Service Report - Denied for the Report Name argument, then select Print Preview for the View argument of the OpenReport action.

f. Double-click the Submacro entry in the Program Flow folder to add another submacro block.

g. Type **Preview Date of Service Fixed Report** as a new submacro name, then add the OpenReport macro action.

h. Select Date of Service Report - Fixed for the ReportName argument, then select Print Preview for the View argument of the second OpenReport action.

i. Save the macro with the name **Preview Group**, then close Macro Design View.

j. Using the Run Macro button on the DATABASE TOOLS tab, run the Preview Group.Preview Date of Service Denied Report macro to test it, then close Print Preview.

k. Using the Run Macro button on the DATABASE TOOLS tab, run the Preview Group.Preview Date of Service Fixed Report macro to test it, then close Print Preview.

FIGURE M-19

l. Open the Preview Group macro in Macro Design View, then click the Collapse buttons to the left of the Submacro statements to collapse the two submacro blocks.

m. Create two more submacros, one that previews Monthly Claims Report - Denied and the other that previews Monthly Claims Report - Fixed. Name the two macros **Preview Monthly Denied Report** and **Preview Monthly Fixed Report**, as shown in **FIGURE M-19**.

n. Save and close the Preview Group macro.

o. In Design View of the Claim Line Items Subform, add four separate command buttons to the Form Footer to run the four submacros in the Preview Group macro. Use the captions and meaningful names of **Date Denied** and **cmdDateDenied**, **Date Fixed** and **cmdDateFixed**, **Monthly Denied** and **cmdMonthlyDenied**, and **Monthly Fixed** and **cmdMonthlyFixed** to correspond with the four submacros in the Preview Group macro.

p. Change the font color on the new command buttons to black.

q. Select all four new command buttons and use the Size/Space and Align commands on the ARRANGE tab to precisely size, align, and space the buttons equally in the Form Footer section.

FIGURE M-20

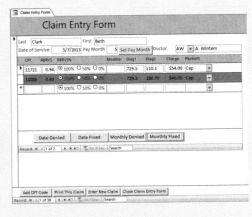

r. Save and close the Claim Line Items Subform, then open the Claim Entry Form in Form View, as shown in **FIGURE M-20**. Test each of the new command buttons to make sure it opens the correct report.

s. Close the Claim Entry Form, close the Patients-M.accdb database, then exit Access

Independent Challenge 3

As the manager of a doctor's clinic, you have created an Access database called Patients-M.accdb to track insurance claim reimbursements. You use macros to help automate the database.

a. Start Access, then open the Patients-M.accdb database from the location where you store your Data Files. Enable content if prompted.

b. Start a new macro in Macro Design View, then add an If statement.

Independent Challenge 3 (continued)

c. Enter the following in the If box: **[Forms]![CPT Form]![RBRVS]=0**.

d. Select the SetProperty action for the first action in the If block.

e. Enter the following arguments for the SetProperty action: Control Name: **ResearchLabel**, Property: **Visible**, and Value: **True**.

f. Click the Add Else link.

g. Select the SetProperty action for the first action of the Else clause.

h. Enter the following arguments for the SetProperty action: Control Name: **ResearchLabel**, Property: **Visible**, and Value: **False**.

i. Save the macro with the name **Research**, as shown in **FIGURE M-21**, then close Macro Design View.

j. Open the CPT Form in Form Design View, then open the Property Sheet for the form.

k. Assign the Research macro to the On Current event of the form.

l. Close the Property Sheet, save the form, then open the CPT Form in Form View.

m. Use the Next record button to move quickly through all 64 records in the form. Notice that the macro displays Research! only when the RBRVS value is equal to zero.

n. Save and close the CPT Form, then close the Patients-M.accdb database.

FIGURE M-21

Independent Challenge 4: Explore

You are collecting information on international chocolate factories, museums, and stores in an Access database. You tie the forms together with macros attached to command buttons.

a. Open the Chocolate-M.accdb database from the location where you store your Data Files, enable content if prompted, then open the Countries form in Form View. The database option to show overlapping windows versus tabbed documents has been set. Overlapping windows allows you to restore and size windows.

b. Click the New (blank) record button for the main form, then type **Poland** in the Country text box.

c. In the subform for the Poland record, enter **Cadbury-Wedel Polska** in the Name field, **F** in the Type field (F for factory), **Praga** in the City field, and **Lodz** in the StateProvince field. Close the Countries form. If you want the windows of this database to be maximized when you open them, you can accomplish this with a macro attached to the On Load event of the form.

d. Open Macro Design View for a new macro, then add the MaximizeWindow action. Save the macro with the name **Maximize**, then close it. The Maximize macro helps you maximize windows if a database option is set to Overlapping Windows. To see this setting, click the FILE tab, click Options, click Current Database, and then view the settings in the Document Window Options section. When Tabbed Documents is selected, the windows are automatically maximized and tabs are provided at the top of each window to help you navigate between them. When Overlapping Windows is selected, however, windows can be any size.

e. Open the Countries form in Design View, add the Maximize macro to the On Load event of the Countries form, then open the Countries form in Form View to test it.

f. Save and close the Countries form.

g. Add the Maximize macro to the On Load event of the Places of Interest report, then open the Places of Interest report in Print Preview to test it.

h. Save and close the Places of Interest report.

i. Close the Chocolate-M.accdb database, then exit Access.

Visual Workshop

As the manager of a doctor's clinic, you have created an Access database called Patients-M.accdb to track insurance claim reimbursements. Develop a new macro called **Query Group** with the actions and argument values shown in **FIGURE M-22**. Run both macros to test them by using the Run Macro button on the DATABASE TOOLS tab, and debug the macros if necessary.

FIGURE M-22

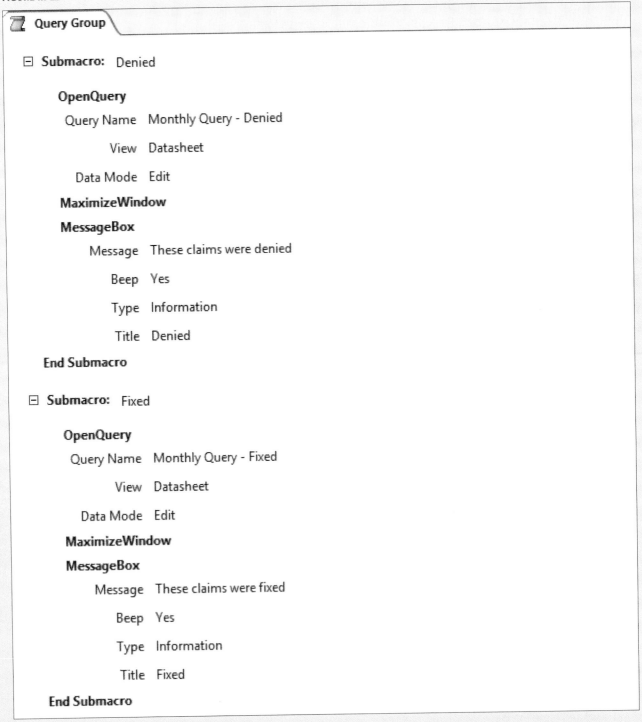

Creating Modules and VBA

CASE You want to learn about VBA and create modules to enhance the capabilities of the Technology-N database for Quest Specialty Travel.

Unit Objectives

After completing this unit, you will be able to:

- Understand modules and VBA
- Compare macros and modules
- Create functions
- Use If statements

- Document procedures
- Build class modules
- Modify sub procedures
- Troubleshoot modules

Files You Will Need

Technology-N.accdb
Baseball-N.accdb

Patients-N.accdb
Basketball-N.accdb

Understand Modules and VBA

Learning
Outcomes
• Define VBA terms
• Describe Visual
  Basic Editor
  components

Access is a robust and easy-to-use relational database program. Access provides user-friendly tools, such as wizards and Design Views, to help users quickly create reports and forms that previously took programmers hours to build. You may, however, want to automate a task or create a new function that goes beyond the capabilities of the built-in Access tools. Within each program of the Microsoft Office suite, a programming language called **Visual Basic for Applications (VBA)** is provided to help you extend the program's capabilities. In Access, VBA is stored within modules. A **module** is an Access object that stores Visual Basic for Applications (VBA) programming code. VBA is written in the **Visual Basic Editor (VBE)**, shown in FIGURE N-1. The components and text colors of the VBE are described in TABLE N-1. An Access database has two kinds of modules. **Standard modules** contain global code that can be executed from anywhere in the database. Standard modules are displayed as module objects in the Navigation Pane. **Class modules** are stored within the form or report object itself. Class modules contain VBA code used only within that particular form or report. **CASE** *Before working with modules, you ask some questions about VBA.*

DETAILS

The following questions and answers introduce the basics of Access modules:

* **What does a module contain?**

  A module contains VBA programming code organized in procedures. A procedure contains several lines of code, each of which is called a **statement**. Modules can also contain **comments**, text that helps explain and document the code.

* **What is a procedure?**

  A **procedure** is a series of VBA statements that performs an operation or calculates an answer. VBA has two types of procedures: functions and subs. **Declaration statements** precede procedure statements and help set rules for how the statements in the module are processed.

* **What is a function?**

  A **function** is a procedure that returns a value. Access supplies many built-in functions, such as Sum, Count, Pmt, and Now, that can be used in an expression in a query, form, or report to calculate a value. You might want to create a new function, however, to help perform calculations unique to your database. For example, you might create a new function called Commission to calculate the sales commission using a formula unique to your business.

* **What is a sub?**

  A **sub** (also called **sub procedure**) performs a series of VBA statements to manipulate controls and objects. Subs are generally executed when an event occurs, such as when a command button is clicked or a form is opened.

* **What are arguments?**

  Arguments are constants, variables, or expressions passed to a procedure that the procedure needs in order to execute. For example, the full syntax for the Sum function is Sum(*expr*), where *expr* represents the argument for the Sum function, the field that is being summed. In VBA, arguments are declared in the first line of the procedure. They are specified immediately after a procedure's name and are enclosed in parentheses. Multiple arguments are separated by commas.

* **What is an object?**

  In VBA, an **object** is any item that can be identified or manipulated, including the traditional Access objects (table, query, form, report, macro, and module) as well as other items that have properties, such as controls, sections, and existing procedures.

* **What is a method?**

  A **method** is an action that an object can perform. Procedures are often written to invoke methods in response to user actions. For example, you could invoke the GoToControl method to move the focus to a specific control on a form in response to the user clicking a command button.

Creating Modules and VBA

FIGURE N-1: Visual Basic Editor (VBE) window for a standard module

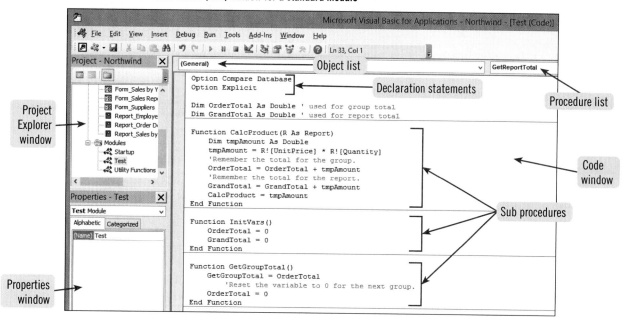

TABLE N-1: Components and text colors for the Visual Basic Editor window

component or color	description
Visual Basic Editor, VBE	Comprises the entire Microsoft Visual Basic program window that contains smaller windows, including the Code window and Project Explorer window
Code window	Contains the VBA for the project selected in the Project Explorer window
Project Explorer window	Displays a hierarchical list of the projects in the database; a **project** can be a module object or a form or report object that contains a class module
Declaration statements	Includes statements that apply to every procedure in the module, such as declarations for variables, constants, user-defined data types, and external procedures in a dynamic-link library
Object list	In a class module, lists the objects associated with the current form or report
Procedure list	In a standard module, lists the procedures in the module; in a class module, lists events (such as Click or Dblclick)
Blue	Indicates a VBA keyword; blue words are reserved by VBA and are already assigned specific meanings
Black	Indicates normal text; black words are the unique VBA code developed by the user
Red	Indicates syntax error text; a red statement indicates that it will not execute correctly because of a syntax error (perhaps a missing parenthesis or a spelling error)
Green	Indicates comment text; any text after an apostrophe is considered documentation, or a comment, and is therefore ignored in the execution of the procedure

Compare Macros and Modules

Learning
Outcomes
• Contrast macros
  and modules
• Define VBA
  keywords

Both macros and modules help run your database more efficiently and effectively. Creating a macro or a module requires some understanding of programming concepts, an ability to follow a process through its steps, and patience. Some tasks can be accomplished by using an Access macro or by writing VBA. Guidelines can help you determine which tool is best for the task. **CASE** *You compare Access macros and modules by asking more questions.*

DETAILS

The following questions and answers provide guidelines for using macros and modules:

- **For what types of tasks are macros best suited?**

  Macros are an easy way to handle common, repetitive, and simple tasks such as opening and closing forms, positioning a form to enter a new record, and printing reports.

- **Which is easier to create, a macro or a module, and why?**

  Macros are generally easier to create because Macro Design View is more structured than the VBE. The hardest part of creating a macro is choosing the correct macro action. But once the action is selected, the arguments associated with that macro action are displayed, eliminating the need to learn any special programming syntax. To create a module, however, you must know a robust programming language, VBA, as well as the correct **syntax** (rules) for each VBA statement. In a nutshell, macros are simpler to create, but VBA is more powerful.

- **When must I use a macro?**

  You must use macros to make global, shortcut key assignments. **AutoExec** is a special macro name that automatically executes when the database first opens.

- **When must I use a module?**

  1. You must use modules to create unique functions. Macros cannot create functions. For instance, you might want to create a function called Commission that calculates the appropriate commission on a sale using your company's unique commission formula.

  2. Access error messages can be confusing to the user. But using VBA procedures, you can detect the error when it occurs and display your own message.

  3. Although Access 2013 macros have been enhanced to include more powerful If-Then logic, VBA is still more robust in the area of programming flow statements with tools such as nested If statements, Case statements, and multiple looping structures. Some of the most common VBA keywords, including If...Then, are shown in **TABLE N-2**. VBA keywords appear blue in the VBE code window.

  4. VBA code may declare **variables**, which are used to store data that can be used, modified, or displayed during the execution of the procedure.

  5. VBA may be used in conjunction with SQL (Structured Query Language) to select, update, append, and delete data.

  Class modules, like the one shown in **FIGURE N-2**, are stored as part of the form or report object in which they are created. If you develop forms and reports in one database and copy them to another, the VBA class module automatically travels with the object that stores it.

Creating Modules and VBA

FIGURE N-2: Visual Basic Editor window for a class module

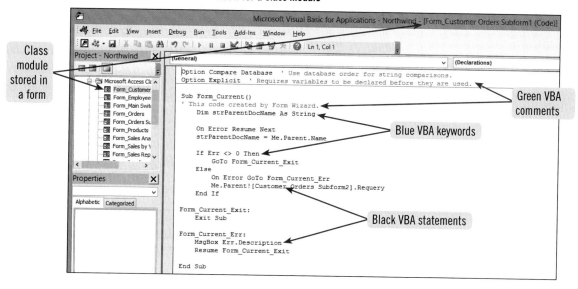

TABLE N-2: Common VBA keywords

statement	explanation
Function	Declares the name and arguments that create a new function procedure
End Function	When defining a new function, the End Function statement is required as the last statement to mark the end of the VBA code that defines the function
Sub	Declares the name for a new Sub procedure; **Private Sub** indicates that the Sub is accessible only to other procedures in the module where it is declared
End Sub	When defining a new sub, the End Sub statement is required as the last statement to mark the end of the VBA code that defines the sub
If...Then	Executes code (the code follows the Then statement) when the value of an expression is true (the expression follows the If statement)
End If	When creating an If...Then...Else clause, the End If statement is required as the last statement
Const	Declares the name and value of a **constant**, an item that retains a constant value throughout the execution of the code
Option Compare Database	A declaration statement that determines the way string values (text) will be sorted
Option Explicit	A declaration statement that specifies that you must explicitly declare all variables used in all procedures; if you attempt to use an undeclared variable name, an error occurs at **compile time**, the period during which source code is translated to executable code
Dim	Declares a **variable**, a named storage location that contains data that can be modified during program execution
On Error GoTo	Upon an error in the execution of a procedure, specifies the location (the statement) where the procedure should continue
Select Case	Executes one of several groups of statements called a **Case** depending on the value of an expression; use the Select Case statement as an alternative to using **ElseIf** in **If...Then...Else** statements when comparing one expression with several different values
End Select	When defining a new Select Case group of statements, the End Select statement is required as the last statement to mark the end of the VBA code

Create Functions

Learning Outcomes
• Create a custom function
• Use a custom function

Access supplies hundreds of functions such as Sum, Count, Ilf, First, Last, Date, and Hour. However, you might want to create a new function to calculate a value based on your company's unique business rules. You would create the new function in a standard module so that it can be used in any query, form, or report throughout the database. **CASE** ▶ *Quest Specialty Travel allows employees to purchase computer equipment when it is replaced. Equipment that is less than a year old will be sold to employees at 75 percent of its initial value, and equipment that is more than a year old will be sold at 50 percent of its initial value. Kayla Green, network administrator, asks you to create a new function called EmpPrice that determines the employee purchase price of replaced computer equipment.*

STEPS

TROUBLE
If you do not enable content, your VBA will not run.

1. **Start Access, open the Technology-N.accdb database from the location where you store your Data Files, enable content if prompted, click the CREATE tab, then click the Module button in the Macros & Code group**

   Access automatically inserts the Option Compare Database declaration statement in the Code window. You will create the new EmpPrice function one step at a time.

QUICK TIP
The Option Explicit statement appears if the Require Variable Declaration option is checked in the VBA Options dialog box. To view the default settings, click Options on the VBA Tools menu.

2. **Type Function EmpPrice(StartValue), then press [Enter]**

   This statement creates a new function named EmpPrice, and states that it contains one argument, StartValue. VBA automatically adds the blue **End Function** statement, a required statement to mark the end of the function. The insertion point is positioned between the statements so that you can enter more VBA statements to further define how the new EmpPrice function will calculate.

3. **Press [Tab], type EmpPrice = StartValue * 0.5, then press [Enter]**

   Your screen should look like **FIGURE N-3**. The EmpPrice= statement explains how the EmpPrice function will calculate. The function will return a value that is calculated by multiplying the StartValue by 0.5. It is not necessary to indent statements, but indenting code between matching Function/End Function, Sub/End Sub, or If/End If statements enhances the program's readability. When you press [Enter] at the end of a VBA statement, Access automatically adds spaces as appropriate to enhance the readability of the statement.

4. **Click the Save button [icon] on the Standard toolbar, type basFunctions in the Save As dialog box, click OK, then click the upper Close button [×] in the upper-right corner of the VBE window to close the Visual Basic Editor**

   It is common for VBA programmers to use three-character prefixes to name objects and controls. This makes it easier to identify that object or control in expressions and modules. The prefix **bas** is short for Basic and applies to global modules. Naming conventions for other objects and controls are listed in **TABLE N-3** and used throughout the Technology-N.accdb database. You can use the new function, EmpPrice, in a query, form, or report.

5. **Click the Queries bar in the Navigation Pane to expand the Queries section if it is collapsed, right-click the qryEmpPricing query in the Navigation Pane, then click Design View on the shortcut menu**

   You use the new EmpPrice function in the query to determine the employee purchase price of replaced computer equipment.

QUICK TIP
Field names used in expressions are not case sensitive, but they must exactly match the spelling of the field name as defined in Table Design View.

6. **Click the blank Field cell to the right of the InitialValue field, type Price:EmpPrice ([InitialValue]), then click the View button [icon] to switch to Datasheet View**

   Your screen should look like **FIGURE N-4**. In this query, you created a new field called Price that uses the EmpPrice function. The value in the InitialValue field is used for the StartValue argument of the new EmpPrice function. The InitialValue field is multiplied by 0.5 to create the new Price field.

7. **Save then close the qryEmpPricing query**

Creating Modules and VBA

FIGURE N-3: Creating the EmpPrice function

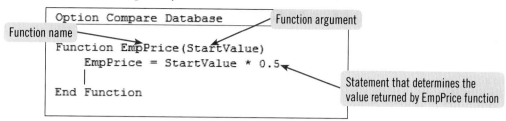

Function name → `Function EmpPrice(StartValue)` ← Function argument

`Option Compare Database`

`Function EmpPrice(StartValue)`

`    EmpPrice = StartValue * 0.5` ← Statement that determines the value returned by EmpPrice function

`End Function`

FIGURE N-4: Using the EmpPrice function in a query

ELast	Manufacture	Description	PlacementDat	InitialValue	Price
Joy	Micron	Transtrek4000	7/7/2014	$2,000.00	1000
Joy	Micron	Transtrek4000	7/7/2015	$2,000.00	1000
Dawson	Micron	Prosignet403	7/14/2014	$1,800.00	900
Rock	Micron	Prosignet403	7/30/2014	$1,800.00	900
McDermott	Micron	Prosignet403	7/30/2014	$1,800.00	900
Garmin	Micron	Prosignet403	7/30/2014	$1,800.00	900
Rice	Micron	Prosignet403	1/8/2014	$1,700.00	850
Boyd	Micron	Prosignet403	8/13/2014	$1,700.00	850
McDonald	Micron	Prosignet403	8/13/2015	$1,700.00	850
Long	Micron	Prosignet403	8/13/2014	$1,700.00	850
Orient	Compaq	Centuria9099	6/13/2015	$1,500.00	750
Greenfield	Compaq	Centuria9099	6/13/2015	$1,500.00	750

qryEmpPricing

Calculated field, Price, uses EmpPrice custom function

TABLE N-3: Three-character prefix naming conventions

object or control type	prefix	example
Table	tbl	tblProducts
Query	qry	qrySalesByRegion
Form	frm	frmProducts
Report	rpt	rptSalesByCategory
Macro	mcr	mcrCloseInventory
Module	bas	basRetirement
Label	lbl	lblFullName
Text Box	txt	txtLastName
Combo box	cbo	cboStates
Command button	cmd	cmdPrint

© 2014 Cengage Learning

Use If Statements

If...Then...Else logic allows you to test logical conditions and execute statements only if the conditions are true. If...Then...Else code can be composed of one or several statements, depending on how many conditions you want to test, how many possible answers you want to provide, and what you want the code to do based on the results of the tests. **CASE** *You need to add an If statement to the EmpPrice function to test the age of the equipment, and then calculate the answer based on that age. You want to modify the EmpPrice function so that if the equipment is less than one year old, the StartValue is multiplied by 75% (0.75) rather than by 50% (0.5).*

STEPS

1. **Scroll down the Navigation Pane, right-click the** basFunctions module, **then click Design View**

   To determine the age of the equipment, the EmpPrice function needs another argument, the purchase date of the equipment.

2. **Click just before the right parenthesis in the Function statement, type** , (a comma), **press [Spacebar], type** DateValue, **then press [↓]**

   Now that you established another argument, you can work with the argument in the definition of the function.

QUICK TIP
Indentation doesn't affect the way the function works, but does make the code easier to read.

3. **Click to the** right of the right parenthesis in the Function statement, **press [Enter], press [Tab], then type** If (Now()–DateValue) >365 Then

   The expression compares whether today's date, represented by the Access function **Now()**, minus the DateValue argument value is greater than 365 days (1 year). If true, this indicates that the equipment is older than one year.

4. **Indent and type the rest of the statements exactly as shown in** FIGURE N-5

   The **Else** statement is executed only if the expression is false (if the equipment is less than 365 days old). The **End If** statement is needed to mark the end of the If block of code.

TROUBLE
If a compile or syntax error appears, open the VBE window, compare your function with **FIGURE N-5**, then correct any errors.

5. **Click the** Save button [💾] **on the Standard toolbar, close the Visual Basic window, right-click the** qryEmpPricing query **in the Navigation Pane, then click** Design View **on the shortcut menu**

   Now that you've modified the EmpPrice function to include two arguments, you need to modify the calculated Price field expression, too.

6. **Right-click the** Price field **in the query design grid, click** Zoom **on the shortcut menu, click between the right square bracket and right parenthesis, then type** ,[PlacementDate]

   Your Zoom dialog box should look like **FIGURE N-6**. Both of the arguments used to define the EmpPrice function in the VBA code are replaced with actual field names that contain the data to be analyzed. Field names must be typed exactly as shown and surrounded by square brackets. Commas separate multiple arguments in the function.

7. **Click** OK **in the Zoom dialog box, then click the** View button [▦] **to display the datasheet**

TROUBLE
The new calculated Price field is based on the current date on your computer, so your results may vary.

8. **Click any entry in the PlacementDate field, then click the** Ascending button **in the Sort & Filter group, as shown in** FIGURE N-7

   The EmpPrice function now calculates one of two different results, depending on the age of the equipment determined by the date in the PlacementDate field.

9. **Save and then close the** qryEmpPricing query

FIGURE N-5: Using an If...Then...Else structure

```
                                                    Second argument
    Function EmpPrice(StartValue, DateValue)
If ─────→ If (Now() - DateValue) > 365 Then ←
              EmpPrice = StartValue * 0.5         Then
Else ─────→ Else
              EmpPrice = StartValue * 0.75
End If ─────→ End If

    End Function
```

FIGURE N-6: Using the Zoom dialog box for long expressions

```
┌──────────────────────────────────────────────────────────────┐
│ ≡▦                          Zoom                          ✕  │
├──────────────────────────────────────────────────────────────┤
│ Price: EmpPrice([InitialValue],[PlacementDate])        ▲     │
│                                            ┌──────────────┐   │
│                                            │      OK      │   │
│                          Second argument   └──────────────┘   │
│                          follows a comma   ┌──────────────┐   │
│                                            │   Cancel     │   │
│                                            └──────────────┘   │
└──────────────────────────────────────────────────────────────┘
```

FIGURE N-7: Price field is calculated at 50% or 75% based on the age of equipment

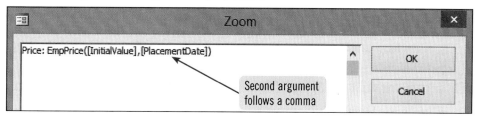

ELast	Manufacture	Description	PlacementDat	InitialValue	Price	
Ramirez	Dell	XPS490	1/9/2008	$1,200.00	600	← InitialValue * 50%
Dawson	Compaq	Deskpro99	3/13/2013	$1,800.00	1350	
Greenfield	Compaq	Deskpro89	4/8/2013	$2,200.00	1650	
Rock	Compaq	Deskpro2099	5/8/2013	$1,700.00	1275	
Joy	Dell	Inspiron609	6/8/2013	$3,200.00	2400	← InitialValue * 75%
Adair	Micron	Transtrek4000	12/30/2013	$1,900.00	1425	
Rice	Micron	Prosignet403	1/8/2014	$1,700.00	1275	
Arnold	Lexmark	Optra2000	1/13/2014	$2,000.00	1500	
Orient	Lexmark	Optra2000	1/13/2014	$2,000.00	1500	

Sort in ascending order on PlacementDate

Document Procedures

Comment lines are statements in the code that document the code; they do not affect how the code runs. At any time, if you want to read or modify existing code, you can write the modifications much more quickly if the code is properly documented. Comment lines start with an apostrophe and are green in the VBE. **CASE** *You decide to document the EmpPrice function in the basFunctions module with descriptive comments. This will make it easier for you and others to follow the purpose and logic of the function later.*

STEPS

1. **Right-click the** basFunctions module **in the Navigation Pane, then click** Design View
   The VBE window for the basFunctions module opens.

   QUICK TIP
   You can also create comments by starting the statement with the Rem statement (for remark).

2. **Click the** blank line between the Option Compare Database and Function statements, **press** [Enter], **type** 'This function is called EmpPrice and has two arguments, **then press** [Enter]
   As soon as you move to another line, the comment statement becomes green.

   TROUBLE
   Be sure to use an ' (apostrophe) and not a " (quotation mark) to begin the comment line.

3. **Type** 'Created by *Your* Name on *Today's* Date, **then press** [Enter]
   You can also place comments at the end of a line by entering an apostrophe to mark that the next part of the statement is a comment.

4. **Click to the** right of Then at the end of the If statement, **press** [Spacebar], **type** 'Now( ) returns today's date, **then press** [↓]
   This comment explains that the Now() function returns today's date. All comments are green, regardless of whether they are on their own line or at the end of an existing line.

5. **Click to the** right of 0.5, **press** [Spacebar] three times, **then type** 'If > 1 year, multiply by 50%

6. **Click to the** right of 0.75, **press** [Spacebar] twice, **type** 'If < 1 year, multiply by 75%, **then press** [↓]
   Your screen should look like **FIGURE N-8**. Each comment will turn green as soon as you move to a new statement.

7. **Click the** Save button 🖫 on the Standard toolbar, click File **on the menu bar, click** Print **if requested by your instructor, then click** OK
   TABLE N-4 provides more information about the Standard toolbar buttons in the VBE window.

8. **Click** File **on the menu bar, then click** Close and Return to Microsoft Access

FIGURE N-8: Adding comments to a module

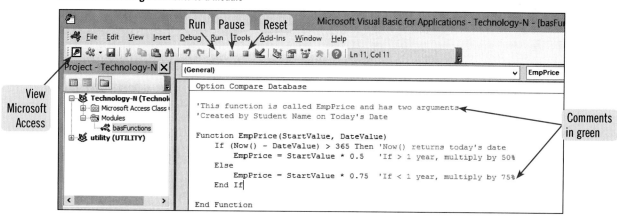

TABLE N-4: Standard toolbar buttons in the Visual Basic window

button name	button	description
View Microsoft Access		Switches from the active Visual Basic window to the Access window
Insert Module		Opens a new module or class module Code window, or inserts a new procedure in the current Code window
Run Sub/UserForm		Runs the current procedure if the insertion point is in a procedure, or runs the UserForm if it is active
Break		Stops the execution of a program while it's running and switches to Break mode, which is the temporary suspension of program execution in which you can examine, debug, reset, step through, or continue program execution
Reset		Resets the procedure
Project Explorer		Displays the Project Explorer, which displays a hierarchical list of the currently open projects (set of modules) and their contents
Object Browser		Displays the Object Browser, which lists the defined modules and procedures as well as available methods, properties, events, constants, and other items that you can use in the code

Build Class Modules

Learning Outcomes
• Build event handlers

Class modules are contained and executed within specific forms and reports. Class modules most commonly run in response to an **event**, a specific action that occurs as the result of a user action. Common events include clicking a command button, editing data, and closing a form. **CASE** *You examine an existing class module and create sub procedures connected to events that occur on the form.*

STEPS

1. **Double-click the frmEmployees form in the Navigation Pane to open it in Form View, then click the Branch of Service combo box list arrow to review the choices**

   The Branch of Service combo box provides a list of the branches of the armed services. For a choice to make sense, however, an employee would first need to be a veteran. You'll set the Visible property for the Branch of Service combo box to True if the Veteran check box is checked and False if the Veteran check box is not checked.

   TROUBLE
   If the first line of your procedure is not Private Sub chkVeteran_AfterUpdate( ), delete the stub, close the VBE, and repeat Step 2.

2. **Right-click the Employees form tab, click Design View on the shortcut menu, double-click the edge of the Veteran check box to open its Property Sheet, click the Event tab in the Property Sheet, click the After Update property, click the Build button [...], then click Code Builder and OK if the Choose Builder dialog box appears**

   The class module for the frmEmployees form opens. Because you opened the VBE window from within a specific event of a specific control on the form, the **stub**, the first and last lines of the sub procedure, were automatically created. The procedure's name in the first line, chkVeteran_AfterUpdate, contains *both* the name of the control, chkVeteran, as well as the name of the event, AfterUpdate, that triggers this procedure. (Recall that the **Name property** of a control is found on the Other tab in the control's property sheet. The **After Update property** is on the Event tab.) A sub procedure that is triggered by an event is often called an **event handler**.

3. **Enter the statements shown in FIGURE N-9**

   When you use three-character prefixes for all controls and objects in your database, it enhances the meaning and readability of your VBA. In this case, the name of the sub procedure shows that it runs on the AfterUpdate event of the chkVeteran control. (The sub runs when the Veteran check box is checked or unchecked.) The If structure contains VBA that makes the cboBranchOfService control either visible or not visible based on the value of the chkVeteran control. To test the sub procedure, you switch to Form View.

4. **Save the changes and close the VBE window, click the View button [icon] to switch to Form View, click the Veteran check box for the first record several times to observe what happens on the After Update event, then navigate through several records**

   By clicking the Veteran check box in the first record, you triggered the procedure that responds to the After Update event of the Veteran check box. However, you also want the procedure to run every time you move from record to record. The **On Current** event of the form is triggered when you navigate through records.

   TROUBLE
   If the Code window appears with a yellow line, it means the code cannot be run successfully. Click the Reset button [icon], then compare your VBA with FIGURE N-10.

5. **Right-click the Employees form tab, click Design View on the shortcut menu, click the Form Selector button [■], click the Event tab in the Property Sheet, click the On Current event property in the Property Sheet, click the Build button [...], click Code Builder and OK if the Choose Builder dialog box appears, then copy or retype the If structure from the chkVeteran_AfterUpdate sub to the Form_Current sub, as shown in FIGURE N-10**

   By copying the same If structure to a second sub procedure, you've created a second event handler. Now, the cboBranchOfService combo box will either be visible or not based on two different events: updating the chkVeteran check box or moving from record to record. To test the new sub procedure, you switch to Form View.

6. **Save the changes and close the VBE window, click [icon] to switch to Form View, then navigate to the fifth record for Gail Owen to test the new procedures**

   Now, as you move from record to record, the Branch of Service combo box should be visible for those employees with the Veteran check box selected, and not visible if the Veteran check box is not selected.

7. **Click the Branch of Service combo box list arrow, click Army, as shown in FIGURE N-11, then save and close the frmEmployees form**

Creating Modules and VBA

```
Private Sub chkVeteran_AfterUpdate()
If chkVeteran.Value = True Then
     cboBranchOfService.Visible = True
Else
     cboBranchOfService.Visible = False
End If
End Sub
```

FIGURE N-10: Copying the If structure to a new event-handler procedure

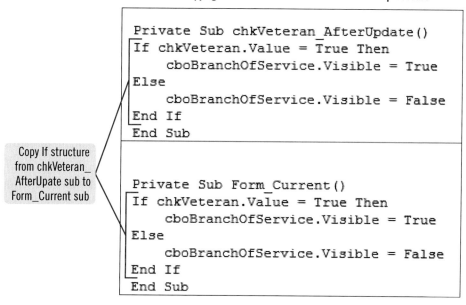

```
Private Sub chkVeteran_AfterUpdate()
If chkVeteran.Value = True Then
     cboBranchOfService.Visible = True
Else
     cboBranchOfService.Visible = False
End If
End Sub


Private Sub Form_Current()
If chkVeteran.Value = True Then
     cboBranchOfService.Visible = True
Else
     cboBranchOfService.Visible = False
End If
End Sub
```

Copy If structure from chkVeteran_AfterUpate sub to Form_Current sub

FIGURE N-11: Branch of Service combo box is visible when the Veteran check box is checked

Gail Owen record

Veteran check box is selected

Branch of Service combo box

Modify Sub Procedures

Sub procedures can be triggered on any event in the Property Sheet such as **On Got Focus** (when the control gets the focus), **After Update** (after a field is updated), or **On Dbl Click** (when the control is double-clicked). Not all items have the same set of event properties. For example, a text box control has both a Before Update and After Update event property, but neither of these events exists for a label or command button because those controls are not used to update data. **CASE** *Kayla Green asks if there is a way to require a choice in the Branch of Service combo box if the Veteran check box is checked. You use VBA sub procedures to handle this request.*

STEPS

1. **Right-click the frmEmployees form, click Design View on the shortcut menu, click the Before Update property in the Property Sheet, click the Build button [...], click Code Builder and OK if the Choose Builder dialog box appears, then enter the code in FIGURE N-12 into the Form_BeforeUpdate stub**

   Test the procedure.

2. **Close the VBE window, click the View button to switch to Form View, click the Veteran check box as needed to select it in the first record, then navigate to the second record**

   Given the chkVeteran control is selected but the cboBranchOfService combo box is null, the MsgBox statement produces the message shown in **FIGURE N-13**.

3. **Click OK, navigate back to the first record, then click the Veteran check box to uncheck it**

   The code produces the correct message, but you want the code to place the focus in the cboBranchOfService combo box to force the user to choose a branch of service when this condition occurs.

   DoCmd is a VBA object that supports many methods to run common Access commands, such as closing windows, opening forms, previewing reports, navigating records, setting focus, and setting the value of controls. As you write a VBA statement, visual aids that are part of **IntelliSense technology** help you complete it. For example, when you type the period (.) after the DoCmd object, a list of available methods appears. Watching the VBA window carefully and taking advantage of all IntelliSense clues as you complete a statement can greatly improve your accuracy and productivity in writing VBA.

4. **Right-click the Employees form tab, click Design View, click the View Code button in the Tools group, click after the MsgBox statement, press [Enter], then type DoCmd. (including the period)**

   Your sub procedure should look like **FIGURE N-14**.

5. **Type GoToControl, press the [Spacebar] noting the additional IntelliSense prompt, then type "cboBranchOfService", as shown in FIGURE N-15**

   IntelliSense helps you fill out each statement, indicating the order of arguments needed for the method to execute. If IntelliSense displays more than one argument, the current argument is listed in bold. Optional arguments are listed in [square brackets]. Test the new procedure.

6. **Close the VBE window, click the View button to switch to Form View, click the Veteran check box for the first record, then navigate to the second record**

7. **Click OK to respond to the message box, choose Navy from the Branch of Service combo box, navigate to the second record, then save and close the Employees form**

   VBA is a robust and powerful programming language. It takes years of experience to appreciate the vast number of objects, events, methods, and properties that are available. With only modest programming skills, however, you can create basic sub procedures that greatly help users work more efficiently and effectively in forms.

FIGURE N-12: Form_BeforeUpdate sub

```
Private Sub Form_BeforeUpdate(Cancel As Integer)
If chkVeteran.Value = True Then
    If IsNull(cboBranchOfService.Value) Then
        MsgBox "Please select a Branch of Service"
    End If
End If
End Sub
```

Form_BeforeUpdate sub

FIGURE N-13: Message produced by MsgBox statement

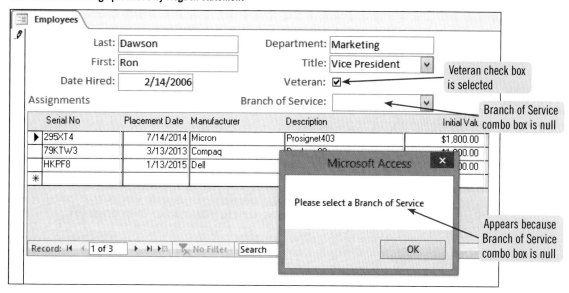

Veteran check box is selected

Branch of Service combo box is null

Appears because Branch of Service combo box is null

FIGURE N-14: IntelliSense technology prompts you as you write VBA statements

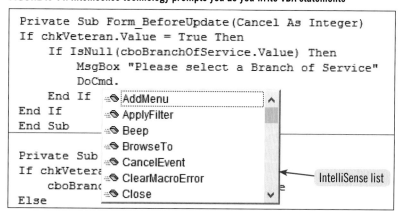

IntelliSense list

FIGURE N-15: New DoCmd statement

```
Private Sub Form_BeforeUpdate(Cancel As Integer)
If chkVeteran.Value = True Then
    If IsNull(cboBranchOfService.Value) Then
        MsgBox "Please select a Branch of Service"
        DoCmd.GoToControl "cboBranchOfService"
    End If
End If
End Sub
```

New DoCmd statement

Creating Modules and VBA

Troubleshoot Modules

Learning
Outcomes
• Set breakpoints
• Use the Immediate
  window

Access provides several techniques to help you **debug** (find and resolve) different types of VBA errors. A **syntax error** occurs immediately as you are writing a VBA statement that cannot be read by the Visual Basic Editor. This is the easiest type of error to identify because your code turns red when the syntax error occurs. **Compile-time errors** occur as a result of incorrectly constructed code and are detected as soon as you run your code or select the Compile option on the Debug menu. For example, you may have forgotten to insert an End If statement to finish an If structure. **Run-time errors** occur as incorrectly constructed code runs and include attempting an illegal operation such as dividing by zero or moving focus to a control that doesn't exist. When you encounter a run-time error, VBA will stop executing your procedure at the statement in which the error occurred and highlight the line with a yellow background in the Visual Basic Editor. **Logic errors** are the most difficult to troubleshoot because they occur when the code runs without obvious problems, but the procedure still doesn't produce the desired result. **CASE** ▶ *You study debugging techniques using the basFunctions module.*

STEPS

1. **Right-click the** basFunctions module **in the Navigation Pane, click** Design View, **click to the right of the End If statement, press the** [Spacebar], **type** *your* **name, then press** [↓]

   Because the End If *your* name statement cannot be resolved by the Visual Basic Editor, the statement immediately turns red and an error message box appears.

2. **Click** OK **in the error message box, delete** *your* **name, then press** [↓]

   Another VBA debugging tool is to set a **breakpoint**, a bookmark that suspends execution of the procedure at that statement to allow you to examine what is happening.

QUICK TIP
Click the gray bar to the left of a statement to toggle a break-point on and off.

3. **Click the** If statement line, **click** Debug **on the menu bar, then click** Toggle Breakpoint

   Your screen should look like **FIGURE N-16**.

4. **Click the** View Microsoft Access button 🖼 **on the Standard toolbar, then double-click the** qryEmpPricing query **in the Navigation Pane**

   When the qryEmpPricing query opens, it immediately runs the EmpPrice function. Because you set a breakpoint at the If statement, the statement is highlighted, indicating that the code has been suspended at that point.

QUICK TIP
Pointing to an argument in the Code window displays a ScreenTip with the argument's current value.

5. **Click** View **on the menu bar, click** Immediate Window, **type** ? DateValue, **then press** [Enter]

   Your screen should look like **FIGURE N-17**. The **Immediate window** is an area where you can determine the value of any argument at the breakpoint.

6. **Click** Debug **on the menu bar, click** Clear All Breakpoints, **click the** Continue button ▶ **on the Standard toolbar to execute the remainder of the function, then save and close the basFunctions module**

   The qryEmpPricing query's datasheet should be visible.

7. **Close the qryEmpPricing datasheet, close the Technology-N.accdb database, then exit Access**

FIGURE N-16: Setting a breakpoint

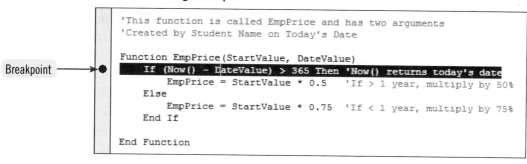

Breakpoint ●
```
'This function is called EmpPrice and has two arguments
'Created by Student Name on Today's Date

Function EmpPrice(StartValue, DateValue)
    If (Now() - DateValue) > 365 Then 'Now() returns today's date
        EmpPrice = StartValue * 0.5    'If > 1 year, multiply by 50%
    Else
        EmpPrice = StartValue * 0.75   'If < 1 year, multiply by 75%
    End If

End Function
```

FIGURE N-17: Stopping execution at a breakpoint

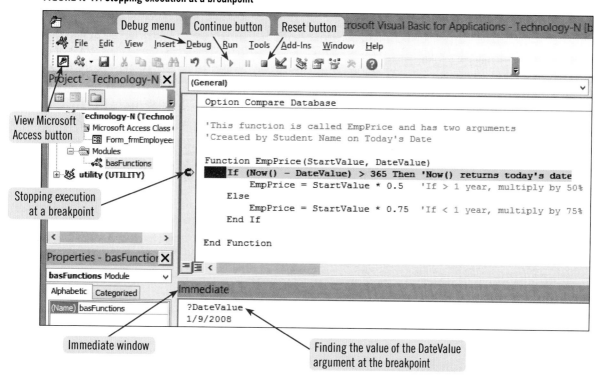

Access 2013

Practice

Concepts Review

Identify each element of the Visual Basic window shown in FIGURE N-18.

FIGURE N-18

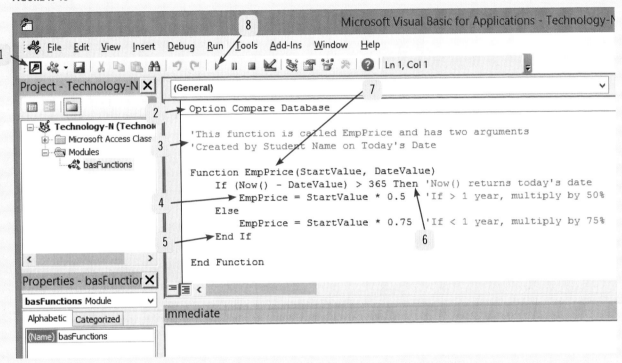

Match each term with the statement that best describes its function.

9. **Visual Basic for Applications (VBA)**
10. **Debugging**
11. **If...Then...Else statement**
12. **Class modules**
13. **Breakpoint**
14. **Function**
15. **Module**
16. **Procedure**
17. **Arguments**

a. Allows you to test a logical condition and execute commands only if the condition is true
b. The programming language used in Access modules
c. A line of code that automatically suspends execution of the procedure
d. A process to find and resolve programming errors
e. A procedure that returns a value
f. Constants, variables, or expressions passed to a procedure to further define how it should execute
g. Stored as part of the form or report object in which they are created
h. The Access object where VBA code is stored
i. A series of VBA statements that performs an operation or calculate a value

Skills Review

1. **Understand modules and VBA.**
   a. Start Access, then open the Baseball-N.accdb (not the Basketball-N.accdb) database from the location where you store your Data Files. Enable content if prompted.
   b. Open the VBE window for the basFunctions module.

Skills Review (continued)

    c. Record your answers to the following questions on a sheet of paper:

- What is the name of the function defined in this module?
- What are the names of the arguments defined in this module?
- What is the purpose of the End Function statement?
- Why is the End Function statement in blue?
- Why are some of the lines indented?

2. Compare macros and modules.

    a. If not already opened, open the VBE window for the basFunctions module.

    b. Record your answers to the following questions on a sheet of paper:

- Why was a module rather than a macro used to create this procedure?
- Why is VBA generally more difficult to create than a macro?
- Identify each of the VBA keywords or keyword phrases, and explain the purpose for each.

3. Create functions.

    a. If not already opened, open the VBE window for the basFunctions module.

    b. Create a function called **TotalBases** below the End Function statement of the BattingAverage function by typing the VBA statements shown in **FIGURE N-19**.

FIGURE N-19

```
Function TotalBases(SingleValue, DoubleValue, TripleValue, HRValue)
    TotalBases = (SingleValue + 2 * DoubleValue + 3 * TripleValue + 4 * HRValue)
End Function
```

In baseball, total bases is a popular statistic because it accounts for the power of each hit. In the TotalBases function, each hit is multiplied by the number of bases earned (1 for single, 2 for double, 3 for triple, and 4 for home run).

    c. Save the basFunctions module, then close the VBE window.

    d. Use Query Design View to create a new query using the PlayerFName and PlayerLName fields from the tblPlayers table, and the AtBats field from the tblPlayerStats table.

    e. Create a calculated field named **Batting** in the next available column by carefully typing the expression as follows: **Batting: BattingAverage([1Base],[2Base],[3Base],[4Base],[AtBats])**. (*Hint*: Use the Zoom dialog box to enter long expressions.)

    f. Create a second calculated field named **Bases** in the next available column by carefully typing the expression as follows: **Bases: TotalBases([1Base],[2Base],[3Base],[4Base])**. (*Hint*: Use the Zoom dialog box to enter long expressions.)

    g. View the datasheet, change Doug Schaller to *your* first and last name, save the query with the name **qryStats**, then close qryStats.

4. Use If statements.

    a. Open the VBE window for the basFunctions module, then modify the BattingAverage function to add the If structure shown in **FIGURE N-20**. The If structure prevents the error caused by attempting to divide by zero. The If structure checks to see if the AtBatsValue argument is equal to 0. If so, the BattingAverage function is set to 0. Else, the BattingAverage function is calculated.

FIGURE N-20

```
Function BattingAverage(SingleValue, DoubleValue, TripleValue, HRValue, AtBatsValue)
If AtBatsValue = 0 Then
    BattingAverage = 0
Else
    BattingAverage = (SingleValue + DoubleValue + TripleValue + HRValue) / AtBatsValue
End If
End Function


Function TotalBases(SingleValue, DoubleValue, TripleValue, HRValue)
    TotalBases = (SingleValue + 2 * DoubleValue + 3 * TripleValue + 4 * HRValue)
End Function
```

Skills Review (continued)

b. Save the basFunctions module, then close the VBE window.

c. Open the qryStats datasheet, then change the AtBats value to **0** for the first record and press [Tab] to test the If statement. The Batting calculated field should equal 0.

d. Close the datasheet.

5. Document procedures.

a. Open the VBE window for the basFunctions module, and add the two statements above the End Function statement for the BattingAverage function, as shown in **FIGURE N-21**. The statements use the Format function to format the calculation as a number with three digits to the right of the decimal point. The comments help clarify the statement.

b. Add a comment at the end of the VBA code that identifies *your* name and today's date, as shown in **FIGURE N-21**.

FIGURE N-21

```
Function BattingAverage(SingleValue, DoubleValue, TripleValue, HRValue, AtBatsValue)
If AtBatsValue = 0 Then
    BattingAverage = 0
Else
    BattingAverage = (SingleValue + DoubleValue + TripleValue + HRValue) / AtBatsValue
End If
'Format as a number with three digits to the right of the decimal point
BattingAverage = Format(BattingAverage, "0.000")
End Function


Function TotalBases(SingleValue, DoubleValue, TripleValue, HRValue)
    TotalBases = (SingleValue + 2 * DoubleValue + 3 * TripleValue + 4 * HRValue)
End Function

'Created by Your Name on Today's Date
```

c. Save the changes to the basFunctions module, print the module if requested by your instructor, then close the VBE window.

d. Open the qryStats query datasheet and change the AtBats value to **3** for the first record and press [Tab] to observe how the value in the Batting calculated field changes and how it is now formatted with three digits to the right of the decimal point due to the VBA statement you added to the BattingAverage function.

e. Print the qryStats datasheet if requested by your instructor, then close it.

6. Build class modules.

a. Open frmPlayerEntry in Form View, then move through several records to observe the data.

b. Switch to Design View, and on the right side of the form, select the Print Current Record button.

c. Open the Property Sheet for the button, click the Event tab, click the On Click property, then click the Build button to open the class module.

d. Add a comment to the last line to show *your* name and the current date. Save the module, print it if requested by your instructor, then close the VBE window.

7. Modify sub procedures.

a. Open the frmPlayerEntry form in Form View, move through a couple of records to observe the txtSalary text box (currently blank), then switch to Design View.

b. The base starting salary in this league is $30,000. You will add a command button with VBA to help enter the correct salary for each player. Use the Button button to add a command button below the txtSalary text box, then cancel the Command Button Wizard if it starts.

c. Open the Property Sheet for the new command button, then change the Caption property on the Format tab to **Base Salary**. Change the Name property on the Other tab to **cmdBaseSalary**.

d. On the Event tab of the Property Sheet, click the On Click property, click the Build button, then click Code Builder if prompted. The stub for the new cmdBaseSalary_Click sub is automatically created for you.

e. Enter the following statement between the Sub and End Sub statements:

txtSalary.Value = 30000

Skills Review (continued)

f. Save the changes, then close the VBE window.

g. Close the Property Sheet, then save and open the frmPlayerEntry form in Form View.

h. Click the Base Salary command button for the first player, move to the second record, then click the Base Salary command button for the second player.

i. Save, then close the frmPlayerEntry form.

8. Troubleshoot modules.

a. Open the VBE window for the basFunctions module.

b. Click anywhere in the If AtBatsValue = 0 Then statement in the BattingAverage function.

c. Click Debug on the menu bar, then click Toggle Breakpoint to set a breakpoint at this statement.

d. Save the changes, then close the VBE window and return to Microsoft Access.

e. Open the qryStats query datasheet. This action will attempt to use the BattingAverage function to calculate the value for the Batting field, which will stop and highlight the statement in the VBE window where you set a breakpoint.

f. Click View on the menu bar, click Immediate Window (if not already visible), delete any previous entries in the Immediate window, type **?AtBatsValue**, then press [Enter]. At this point in the execution of the VBA, the AtBatsValue should be 3, the value for the first record.

g. Type **?SingleValue**, then press [Enter]. At this point in the execution of the VBA code, the SingleValue should be 1, the value for the first record. (*Hint*: You can resize the Immediate window taller by dragging the top edge.)

h. Click Debug on the menu bar, click Clear All Breakpoints, then click the Continue button on the Standard toolbar. Close the VBE window.

i. Return to the qryStats query in Datasheet View.

j. Close the qryStats query, close the Baseball-N.accdb database, then exit Access.

Independent Challenge 1

As the manager of a doctor's clinic, you have created an Access database called Patients-N.accdb to track insurance claim reimbursements and general patient health. You want to modify an existing function within this database.

a. Start Access, then open the Patients-N.accdb database from the location where you store your Data Files. Enable content if prompted.

b. Open the basBodyMassIndex module in Design View, and enter the **Option Explicit** declaration statement just below the existing Option Compare Database statement.

c. Record your answers to the following questions on a sheet of paper:
- What is the name of the function in the module?
- What are the function arguments?
- What is the purpose of the Option Explicit declaration statement?

d. Edit the BMI function by adding a comment below the last line of code with *your* name and today's date.

e. Edit the BMI function by adding a comment above the Function statement with the following information: **'A healthy BMI is in the range of 21-24**.

f. Edit the BMI function by adding an If clause that checks to make sure the height argument is not equal to 0. The final BMI function code should look like **FIGURE N-22**.

g. Save the module, print it if requested by your instructor, then close the VBE window.

FIGURE N-22

```
Option Compare Database
Option Explicit

'A healthy BMI is in the range of 21-24

Function BMI(weight, height)

If height = 0 Then
    BMI = 0
Else
    BMI = (weight * 0.4536) / (height * 0.0254) ^ 2
End If


End Function

'Student Name - Today's Date
```

Independent Challenge 1 (continued)

h. Create a new query that includes the following fields from the tblPatients table: **PtLastName**, **PtFirstName**, **PtHeight**, **PtWeight**.

i. Create a calculated field with the following field name and expression: **BodyMassIndex: BMI([PtWeight], [PtHeight])**. (*Hint*: Use the Zoom dialog box for long expressions.)

j. Save the query as **qryPatientBMI**, view the qryPatientBMI query datasheet, then test the If statement by entering **0** in the PtHeight field for the first record. Press [Tab] to move to the BodyMassIndex field, which should recalculate to 0.

k. Edit the first record to contain *your* last and first names, print the datasheet if requested by your instructor, then close the qryPatientBMI query.

l. Close the Patients-N.accdb database, then exit Access.

Independent Challenge 2

As the manager of a doctor's clinic, you have created an Access database called Patients-N.accdb to track insurance claim reimbursements. You want to study the existing sub procedures stored as class modules in the Claim Entry Form.

a. Start Access, then open the Patients-N.accdb database from the location where you store your Data Files. Enable content if prompted.

b. Open frmClaimEntryForm in Form View, then switch to Design View.

c. Open the VBE window to view this class module, then record your answers to the following questions on a sheet of paper:
- What are the names of the sub procedures in this class module? (*Hint*: Be sure to scroll the window to see the complete contents.)
- What Access functions are used in the PtFirstName_AfterUpdate sub?
- How many arguments do the functions in the PtFirstName_AfterUpdate sub have?
- What do the functions in the PtFirstName_AfterUpdate sub do? (*Hint*: You may have to use the Visual Basic Help system if you are not familiar with the functions.)
- What is the purpose of the On Error command? (*Hint*: Use the Visual Basic Help system if you are not familiar with this command.)

d. Use the Property Sheet of the form to create an event-handler procedure based on the On Load property. The statement will be one line using the Maximize method of the VBA DoCmd object, which will maximize the form each time it is loaded.

e. Save the changes, close the VBE window and the Claim Entry Form, then open frmClaimEntryForm in Form View to test the new sub.

f. Close frmClaimEntryForm, close the Patients-N.accdb database, then exit Access.

Independent Challenge 3

As the manager of a doctor's clinic, you have created an Access database called Patients-N.accdb to track insurance claim reimbursements that are fixed (paid at a predetermined fixed rate) or denied (not paid by the insurance company). You want to enhance the database with a class module.

a. Start Access, then open the Patients-N.accdb database from the location where you store your Data Files. Enable content if prompted.

b. Open frmCPT in Form Design View.

c. Use the Command Button Wizard to add a command button in the Form Header section. Choose the Add New Record action from the Record Operations category.

d. Accept **Add Record** as the text on the button, then name the button **cmdAddRecord**.

Independent Challenge 3 (continued)

e. Use the Command Button Wizard to add a command button in the Form Header section to the right of the existing Add Record button. (*Hint*: Move and resize controls as necessary to put two command buttons in the Form Header section.)

f. Choose the Delete Record action from the Record Operations category.

g. Accept **Delete Record** as the text on the button, and name the button **cmdDeleteRecord**.

h. Size the two buttons to be the same height and width, and align their top edges. Move them as needed so that they do not overlap.

i. Save and view frmCPT in Form View, then click the Add Record command button.

j. Add a new record (it will be record number 65) with a CPTCode value of **999** and an RBRVS value of **1.5**.

k. To make sure that the Delete Record button works, click the record selector for the new record you just entered, click the Delete Record command button, then click Yes to confirm the deletion. Close frmCPT.

l. In Design View of the frmCPT form, open the Property Sheet for the Delete Record command button, click the Event tab, then click the Build button beside [Embedded Macro]. The Command Button Wizard created the embedded macro that deletes the current record. You can convert macro objects to VBA code to learn more about VBA. To convert an embedded macro to VBA, you must first copy and paste the embedded macro actions to a new macro object. (*Hint*: You can widen the property sheet by dragging the left edge.)

m. Press [Ctrl][A] to select all macro actions, then press [Ctrl][C] to copy all macro actions to the Clipboard.

n. Close the macro window, then save and close frmCPT.

o. On the CREATE tab, open Macro Design View, then press [Ctrl][V] to paste the macro actions to the window.

p. Click the Convert Macros to Visual Basic button, click Yes when prompted to save the macro, click Convert, then click OK when a dialog box indicates the conversion is finished.

q. Save and close all open windows with default names. Open the Converted Macro-Macro1 VBE window. Add a comment as the last line of code in the Code window with *your* name and the current date, save the module, print it if requested by your instructor, then close the VBE window.

r. Close the Patients-N.accdb database, then exit Access.

Independent Challenge 4: Explore

(*Note*: To complete this Independent Challenge, make sure you are connected to the Internet.)

Learning a programming language is sometimes compared with learning a foreign language. Imagine how it would feel to learn a new programming language if English wasn't your primary language, or if you had another type of accessibility challenge. Advances in technology are helping to break down many barriers to those with vision, hearing, mobility, cognitive, and language issues. In this challenge, you explore the Microsoft Web site for resources to address these issues.

a. Go to www.microsoft.com/enable, then print that page. Explore the Web site.

b. After exploring the Web site for products, demos, tutorials, guides, and articles, write a two-page, double-spaced paper describing five types of accessibility solutions that might make a positive impact on someone you know. Refer to your acquaintances as "my friend," "my cousin," and so forth as appropriate. Do not include real names.

c. Use bold headings for the five types of accessibility solutions to make those sections of your paper easy to find and read. Be sure to spell and grammar check your paper.

Visual Workshop

As the manager of a college basketball team, you are helping the coach build meaningful statistics to compare the relative value of the players in each game. The coach has stated that one offensive rebound is worth as much to the team as two defensive rebounds, and would like you to use this rule to develop a "rebounding impact statistic" for each game. Open the Basketball-N.accdb (not the Baseball-N.accdb) database, enable content if prompted, and use **FIGURE N-23** to develop a new function in a standard module. Name the new function **ReboundImpact** in a new module called **basFunctions** to calculate this statistic. Include *your* name and the current date as a comment in the last row of the function.

FIGURE N-23

```
Function ReboundImpact(OffenseValue As Integer, DefenseValue As Integer) As Integer
    ReboundImpact = (OffenseValue * 2) + DefenseValue
End Function

'Student Name - Today's Date
```

Create a query called **qryRebounds** with the fields shown in **FIGURE N-24**. Note that the records are sorted in ascending order on GameNo and LastName. The **ReboundPower** field is created using the following expression: **ReboundImpact([Reb-O],[Reb-D])**. Enter *your* first and last name instead of Kristen Czyenski, and print the datasheet if requested by your instructor.

FIGURE N-24

GameNo	FirstName	LastName	Reb-O	Reb-D	ReboundPower
1	Student First	Student Last	2	2	6
1	Denise	Franco	2	3	7
1	Theresa	Grant	1	3	5
1	Megan	Hile	1	2	4
1	Amy	Hodel	5	3	13
1	Ellyse	Howard	1	2	4
1	Jamie	Johnson	0	1	1
1	Lindsey	Swift	1	2	4
1	Morgan	Tyler	4	6	14
2	Student First	Student Last	3	2	8
2	Denise	Franco	5	3	13

Administering the Database

CASE ▶ Kayla Green is the network administrator at Quest corporate headquarters. You have helped Kayla develop a database to document Quest computer equipment. You use Access to create a navigation form. You also examine several administrative issues, such as setting passwords, changing startup options, and analyzing database performance to protect, improve, and enhance the database.

Unit Objectives

After completing this unit, you will be able to:

- Create a navigation form
- Compact and repair a database
- Change startup options
- Analyze database performance

- Set a database password
- Back up a database
- Convert a database
- Split a database

Files You Will Need

Technology-O.accdb
Basketball-O.accdb
Patients-O.accdb

RealEstate-O.accdb
MusicStore-O.accdb

Access 2013

UNIT O

Learning
Outcomes
• Create a navigation
  form
• Add tabs to a
  navigation form

Create a Navigation Form

A **navigation form** is a special Access form that provides an easy-to-use database interface that is also Web compatible. Being **Web compatible** means that the form can be opened and used with Internet Explorer when the database is published to a SharePoint server. A **SharePoint server** is a special type of Microsoft Web server that allows people to share and collaborate on information using only a browser such as Internet Explorer. Navigation forms can be used with any Access database, however, even if you don't publish it to a SharePoint server. **CASE** ➤ *You create a navigation form to easily access forms and reports in the Technology-O database.*

STEPS

1. **Start Access, open the Technology-O.accdb database from the location where you store your Data Files, enable content if prompted, click the CREATE tab, click the Navigation button in the Forms group, click the Horizontal Tabs option, then close the Field List window**

   The new navigation form opens in Layout View. Horizontal Tabs is a **navigation system style** that determines how the navigation buttons are displayed on the form. Other navigation system styles include vertical tabs on the left or right, or both horizontal and vertical tabs.

2. **Click the Queries collapse button ⊼ to close that section of the Navigation Pane, then drag the frmEmployees form from the Navigation Pane to the first tab, which displays [Add New]**

   The frmEmployees form is added as the first tab, as shown in **FIGURE O-1**, and a new tab with [Add New] is automatically created as well. The second and third tabs will display reports.

3. **Click the Reports expand button ⊻ to expand that section of the Navigation Pane, drag the rptAllEquipment report from the Navigation Pane to the second tab, which displays [Add New], then drag rptPCs to the third tab, which also displays [Add New]**

   With the objects in place, you rename the tabs to be less technical.

4. **Double-click the frmEmployees tab, edit it to read Employees, double-click the rptAllEquipment tab, edit it to read All Equipment, double-click the rptPCs tab, edit it to read PCs, then click the View button 📧 to display the form in Form View, as shown in FIGURE O-2**

   Test, save, and close the new navigation form.

5. **Click the All Equipment tab, click the Employees tab, click the Save button 🖫 on the Quick Access toolbar, type frmNavigation, click OK, then close frmNavigation**

FIGURE O-1: Creating a navigation form

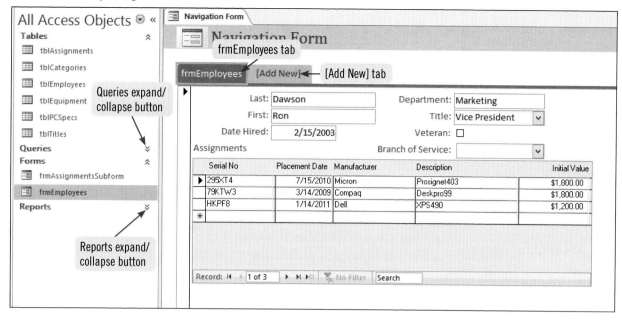

FIGURE O-2: Final navigation form in Form View

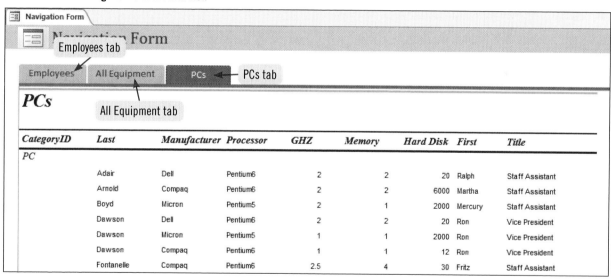

Setting navigation options

You can change the way the Navigation Pane appears by clicking the title bar of the Navigation Pane and choosing a different way to organize the objects (e.g., by Object Type, Created Date, or Custom Groups) in the upper portion of the menu. The lower portion of the menu lets you display only one object type (e.g., Tables, Queries, Forms, Reports, or All Access Objects). Right-click the Navigation Pane for more options on the shortcut menu, including Navigation Options, which allows you to create custom groups within the Navigation Pane.

Compact and Repair a Database

Learning
Outcomes
• Compact and
repair a database
• Apply Access
options

Compacting and repairing a database is a process that Access 2013 uses to reorganize the parts of a database to eliminate wasted space on the disk storage device, which also helps prevent data integrity problems. You can compact and repair a database at any time, or you can set a database option to automatically compact and repair the database when it is closed. **CASE** *You and Kayla Green decide to compact and repair the Technology database, and then learn about the option to automatically compact and repair the database when it is closed.*

STEPS

1. **Click the DATABASE TOOLS tab on the Ribbon, then click the Compact and Repair Database button**

   Access closes the database, completes the compact and repair process, and reopens the database automatically.

   Compacting and repairing a database can reduce the size of the database by 10, 50, or even 75 percent because the space occupied by deleted objects and deleted data is not reused until the database is compacted. Therefore, it's a good idea to set up a regular schedule to compact and repair a database. You decide to change Access options to automatically compact the database when it is closed.

2. **Click the FILE tab on the Ribbon, then click Options**

   The Compact on Close feature is in the Current Database category of the Access Options dialog box.

3. **Click the Current Database category, then click the Compact on Close check box**

   Your screen should look like **FIGURE O-3**. Now, every time the database is closed, Access will also compact and repair it. This helps you keep the database as small and efficient as possible and protects your database from potential corruption. The Access Options dialog box provides many important default options and techniques to customize Access, which are summarized in **TABLE O-1**.

4. **Click OK to close the Access Options dialog box, then click OK when prompted to close and reopen the current database**

Trusting a database

Trusting a database means to identify the database file as one that is safe to open. Trusted databases automatically enable all content, including all macros and VBA in modules, and, therefore, do not present the Enable Content message when they are opened. To trust a database, click the FILE tab, click Options, click Trust Center on the left, click the Trust Center Settings button, then use the Trusted Documents or Trusted Locations options to either trust an individual database file or an entire folder. To trust the folder, click Trusted Locations, click Add new location, click Browse to locate the folder to trust, select the desired folder, click the Subfolders of this location are also trusted check box to also trust subfolders, and then click OK to move through the dialog boxes and complete the process.

FIGURE O-3: Setting the Compact on Close option

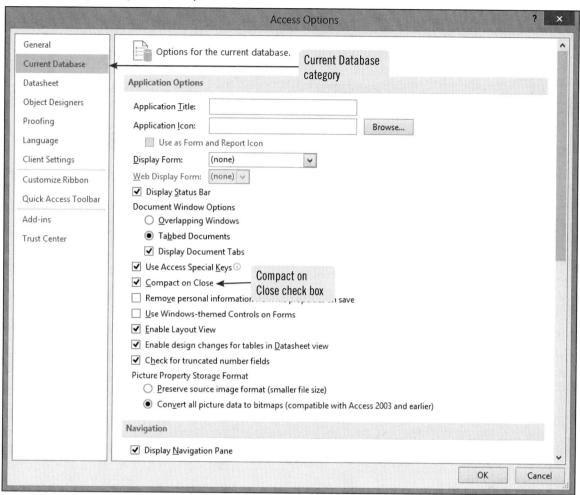

TABLE O-1: Access options

category	description
General	Sets default interface, file format, default database folder, and username options
Current Database	Provides for application changes, such as whether the windows are overlapping or tabbed, the database compacts on close, and Layout View is enabled; also provides Navigation Pane, Ribbon, toolbar, and AutoCorrect options
Datasheet	Determines the default gridlines, cell effects, and fonts of datasheets
Object Designers	Determines default Design View settings for tables, queries, forms, and reports; also provides default error-checking options
Proofing	Sets AutoCorrect and Spelling options
Language	Sets Editing, Display, and Help languages
Client Settings	Sets defaults for cursor action when editing, display elements, printing margins, date formatting, and advanced record management options
Customize Ribbon	Provides an easy-to-use interface to modify the buttons and tabs on the Ribbon
Quick Access Toolbar	Provides an easy-to-use interface to modify the buttons on the Quick Access toolbar
Add-ins	Provides a way to manage **add-ins**, software that works with Access to add or enhance functionality
Trust Center	Provides a way to manage trusted publishers, trusted locations, trusted documents, macro settings, and other privacy and security settings

Change Startup Options

Learning Outcomes

- Set the Application Title startup option
- Set the Display Form startup option
- Describe command-line options

Startup options are a series of commands that execute when the database is opened. You manage the default startup options using features in the Current Database category of the Access Options dialog box. More startup options are available through the use of **command-line options**, a special series of characters added to the end of the pathname (for example, C:\My Documents\Quest.accdb /excl), which execute a command when the file is opened. See **TABLE O-2** for information on common startup command-line options. **CASE** ▸ *You want to view and set database properties and then specify that the frmEmployees form opens when the Technology-O.accdb database is opened.*

STEPS

1. **Click the FILE tab, click Options, then click Current Database if it is not already selected**

   The startup options are in the Application Options area of the Current Database category.

2. **Click the Application Title text box, then type Quest Specialty Travel**

   The Application Title database property value appears in the title bar instead of the database filename.

QUICK TIP

The Enable Layout View check box allows or removes the ability to work with forms and reports in Layout View. Some database designers do not use this view, and therefore may decide to disable it.

3. **Click the Display Form list arrow, then click frmEmployees**

   See **FIGURE O-4**. You test the Application Title and Display Form database properties.

4. **Click OK to close the Access Options dialog box, click OK when prompted, close the Technology-O.accdb database, then reopen the Technology-O.accdb database and enable content if prompted**

   The Technology-O.accdb database opens with the new application title, followed by the frmEmployees form, as shown in **FIGURE O-5**. If you want to open an Access database and bypass startup options, press and hold [Shift] while the database opens.

5. **Close the frmEmployees form**

TABLE O-2: Startup command-line options

option	effect
/excl	Opens the database for exclusive access
/ro	Opens the database for read-only access
/pwd *password*	Opens the database using the specified *password* (applies to Access 2002–2003 and earlier version databases only)
/repair	Repairs the database (in Access 2000 and 2002, compacting the database also repairs it; if you choose the Compact on Close command, you don't need the /repair option)
/convert *target database*	Converts a previous version of a database to an Access 2000 database with the *target database* name
/x *macro*	Starts Access and runs the specified *macro*
/wrkgrp *workgroup information file*	Starts Access using the specified *workgroup information file* (applies to Access 2002–2003 and earlier version databases only)

FIGURE O-4: Setting startup options

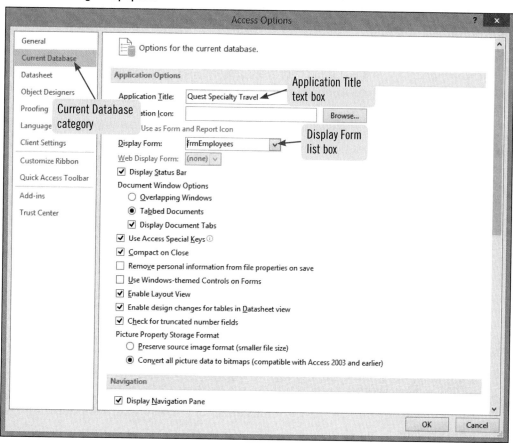

FIGURE O-5: Display Form and Application Title startup options are in effect

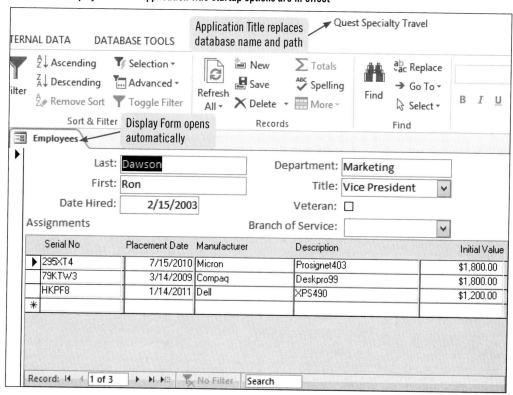

Analyze Database Performance

Access databases are typically used by multiple people and for extended periods. Therefore, spending a few hours to secure a database and improve its performance is a good investment. Access provides a tool called the **Performance Analyzer** that studies the structure and size of your database and makes a variety of recommendations on how you can improve its performance. With adequate time and Access skills, you can alleviate many performance bottlenecks by using software tools and additional programming techniques to improve database performance. You can often purchase faster processors and more memory to accomplish the same goal. See **TABLE O-3** for tips on optimizing the performance of your computer. **CASE** *You use the Performance Analyzer to see whether Access provides any recommendations on how to easily maintain peak performance of the Technology-O.accdb database.*

STEPS

1. **Click the** DATABASE TOOLS **tab, click the** Analyze Performance button **in the Analyze group, then click the** All Object Types tab

   The Performance Analyzer dialog box opens, as shown in **FIGURE O-6**. You can choose to analyze selected tables, forms, other objects, or the entire database.

2. **Click the** Select All button, **then click** OK

   The Performance Analyzer examines each object and presents the results in a dialog box, as shown in **FIGURE O-7**. The key shows that the analyzer gives four levels of advice regarding performance: recommendations, suggestions, ideas, and items that were fixed.

3. **Click** each line in the Analysis Results area, **then read each description in the Analysis Notes area**

   The lightbulb icon next to an item indicates that this is an idea. The Analysis Notes section of the Performance Analyzer dialog box gives you additional information regarding the specific item. All of the Performance Analyzer's ideas should be considered, but they are not as important as recommendations and suggestions.

4. **Click** Close **to close the Performance Analyzer dialog box**

Viewing object dependencies

Click any object in the Navigation Pane, click the DATABASE TOOLS tab, then click the Object Dependencies button in the Relationships group to view object dependencies. **Object dependencies** appear in the Object Dependencies task pane and display "Objects that depend on me" (the selected object). For example, before deleting a query you might want to select it to view its object dependencies to determine if any other queries, forms, or reports depend on that query. The Object Dependencies task pane also allows you to view "Objects that I depend on." For a selected query, this option would show you what tables are used in the query.

FIGURE O-6: Performance Analyzer dialog box

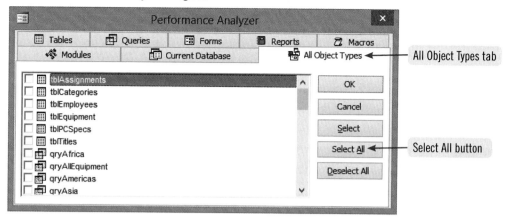

FIGURE O-7: Performance Analyzer results

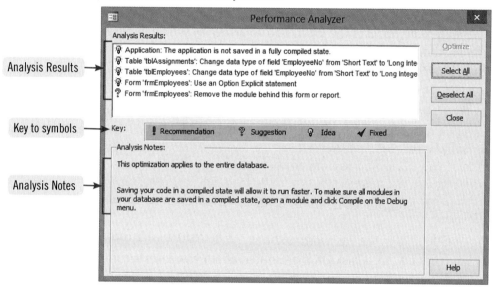

TABLE O-3: Tips for optimizing performance

degree of difficulty	tip
Easy	To free memory and other computer resources, close all applications that you don't currently need
Easy	If they can be run safely only when you need them, eliminate memory-resident programs, such as complex screen savers, email alert programs, and virus checkers
Easy	If you are the only person using a database, open it in Exclusive mode
Easy	Use the Compact on Close feature to regularly compact and repair your database
Moderate	Add more memory to your computer; once the database is open, memory is generally the single most important determinant of overall performance
Moderate	If others don't need to share the database, load it on your local hard drive instead of the network's file server (but be sure to back up local drives regularly, too)
Moderate	Split the database so that the data is stored on the file server, but other database objects are stored on your local (faster) hard drive
Moderate to difficult	If you are using disk compression software, stop doing so or move the database to an uncompressed drive
Moderate to difficult	Run Performance Analyzer on a regular basis, examining and appropriately acting on each recommendation, suggestion, and idea
Moderate to difficult	Make sure that all PCs are running the latest versions of Windows and Access; this might involve purchasing more software or upgrading hardware to properly support these robust software products

Set a Database Password

Learning Outcomes
- Open the database in Exclusive mode
- Set a password and encryption

A **password** is a combination of uppercase and lowercase letters, numbers, and symbols that the user must enter to open the database. Setting a database password means that anyone who doesn't know the password cannot open the database. Other ways to secure an Access database are listed in TABLE O-4. **CASE** ▶ *You apply a database password to the Technology-O.accdb database to secure its data.*

STEPS

1. **Click the FILE tab, then click Close**

   The Technology-O.accdb database closes, but the Access application window remains open. To set a database password, you must open the database in Exclusive mode using the Open dialog box.

TROUBLE
You cannot use the Recent list to open a database in Exclusive mode.

2. **Click Open Other Files, navigate to the location where you store your Data Files, click Technology-O.accdb, click the Open button arrow, as shown in FIGURE O-8, click Open Exclusive, then enable content if prompted**

   Exclusive mode means that you are the only person who has the database open, and others cannot open the file during this time.

   QUICK TIP
   It's always a good idea to back up a database before creating a database password.

3. **Click the FILE tab, click Info, then click the Encrypt with Password button**

   Encryption means to make the data in the database unreadable by other software. The Set Database Password dialog box opens, as shown in **FIGURE O-9**. If you lose or forget your password, it cannot be recovered. For security reasons, your password does not appear as you type; for each keystroke, an asterisk appears instead. Therefore, you must enter the same password in both the Password and Verify text boxes to make sure you haven't made a typing error. Passwords are case sensitive, so, for example, Cyclones and cyclones are different.

   QUICK TIP
   Check to make sure the Caps Lock light is not on before entering a password.

4. **Type Go!3000!ISU in the Password text box, press [Tab], type Go!3000!ISU in the Verify text box, click OK, then click OK if prompted about row-level security**

   Passwords should be easy to remember, but not as obvious as your name, the word *password*, the name of the database, or the name of your company. **Strong passwords** are longer than eight characters and use the entire keyboard, including uppercase and lowercase letters, numbers, and symbols. Microsoft provides an online tool to check the strength of your password. Go to www.microsoft.com and search for password checker.

5. **Close, then reopen Technology-O.accdb**

   The Password Required dialog box opens.

6. **Type Go!3000!ISU, then click OK**

   The Technology-O.accdb database opens, giving you full access to all of the objects. To remove a password, you must exclusively open a database, just as you did when you set the database password.

7. **Click the FILE tab, click Close, click Open Other Files, navigate to the location where you store your Data Files, click Technology-O.accdb, click the Open button arrow, click Open Exclusive, type Go!3000!ISU in the Password Required dialog box, then click OK**

8. **Click the FILE tab, click Info, click the Decrypt Database button, type Go!3000!ISU, then click OK**

FIGURE O-8: Opening a database in Exclusive mode

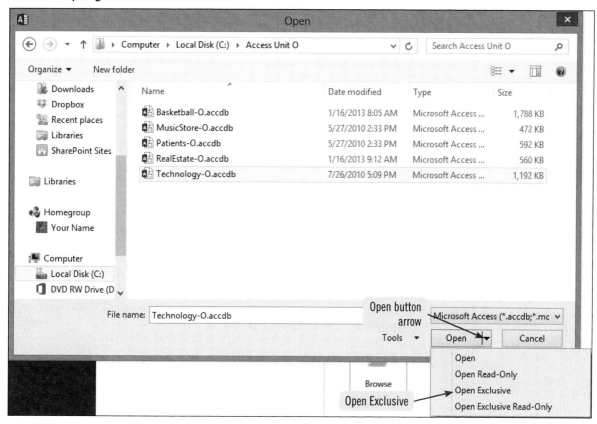

FIGURE O-9: Set Database Password dialog box

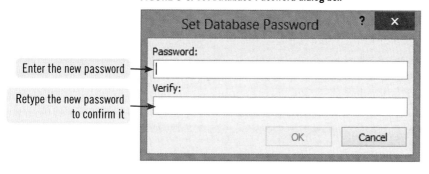

TABLE O-4: Methods to secure an Access database

method	description
Password	Restricts access to the database, and can be set at the database, workgroup, or VBA level
Encryption	Makes the data indecipherable to other programs
Startup options	Hides or disables certain functions when the database is opened
Show/hide objects	Shows or hides objects in the Navigation Pane; a simple way to prevent users from unintentionally deleting objects is to hide them in the Navigation Pane by checking the Hidden property in the object's Property Sheet
Split a database	Separates the back-end data and the front-end objects (such as forms and reports) into two databases that work together; splitting a database allows you to give each user access to only those front-end objects they need as well as add security measures to the back-end database that contains the data

Back Up a Database

Learning Outcomes
- Create a backup
- Describe portable storage media

Backing up a database refers to making a copy of it in a secure location. Backups are important to protect those who rely on a database from the problems created when the database is corrupted, stolen, or otherwise compromised. Database threats and solutions are summarized in **TABLE O-5**. Backups can be saved on an external hard drive, the hard drive of a second computer, or a Web server such as SkyDrive. Because most users are familiar with saving and copying files to hard drives, the new technology streamlines the effort of backing up a database. **CASE** ▸ *Kayla Green asks you to review the methods of backing up the database.*

STEPS

1. **Click the FILE tab, click Save As, click the Save Database As option if it is not selected, click Back Up Database, then click the Save As button, as shown in FIGURE O-10**

   The Save As dialog box is shown in **FIGURE O-11**. When using the Back Up Database option, the current date is automatically added to the database filename. However, any copy of the entire database with any filename also serves as a valid backup of the database. The **Save Database As** option saves the *entire* database, including all of its objects to a completely new database file. The **Save Object As** option saves only the *current object* (table, query, form, report, macro, or module).

   The Save As window shown in **FIGURE O-10** allows you to save the database in an older 2000 database format (.mdb file extension), a database template file (.accdt file extension), or an executable database (.accde file extension).

   The Save As dialog box shown in **FIGURE O-11** allows you to save the database to external locations such as an FTP (File Transfer Protocol) server, Dropbox folder, SkyDrive folder, or SharePoint site. Your locations will vary based on the resources available to you on the computer you are using.

2. **Navigate to the location where you store your Data Files, then click Save**

   A copy of the Technology-O.accdb database is saved in the location you selected with the name Technology-O-*currentdate*.accdb. Yet another way to make a backup copy of an Access database is to use your Windows skills to copy and paste the database file in a File Explorer or Windows Explorer window. If you choose this backup method, however, make sure the database and Access are closed before copying the database file.

   Although you can open and work in a backup database file just as you would any other file, a better way to recover data from a backup is to copy and paste the backup file to first create a production database with the name and in the location you desire, and then open and work in the copy. To copy only certain objects from a backup database to a production database, use the Access button in the Import & Link group of the EXTERNAL DATA tab to select and import specific objects from the backup database.

Using portable storage media

Technological advancements continue to make it easier and less expensive to store large files on portable storage devices. A few years ago, 3.5-inch disks with roughly 1 **MB (megabyte**, a million bytes) of storage capacity were common. Today, 3.5-inch disks have been replaced by a variety of inexpensive, high-capacity storage media that work with digital devices, such as digital cameras, cell phones, tablet computers, and personal digital assistants (PDAs). **Secure digital (SD) cards** are quarter-sized devices that slip directly into a computer and typically store around 32 **GB (gigabyte**, a million bytes or a thousand megabytes).

CompactFlash (CF) cards are slightly larger, and store more data, around 16 GB to 32 GB. **USB (Universal Serial Bus) drives** (which plug into a computer's USB port) are also popular. USB drives are also called thumb drives, flash drives, and travel drives. USB devices typically store 2 GB to 64 GB of information.

Larger still are **external hard drives**, sometimes as small as the size of a cell phone, that store anywhere from 20 GB to about 2 **TB (terabyte**, a trillion bytes or a thousand gigabytes) of information and connect to a computer using either a USB or FireWire port.

FIGURE O-10: Save As options

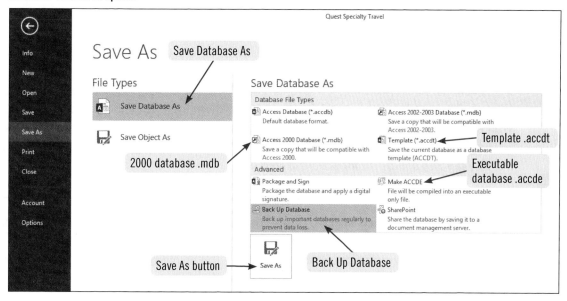

FIGURE O-11: Save As dialog box to back up a database

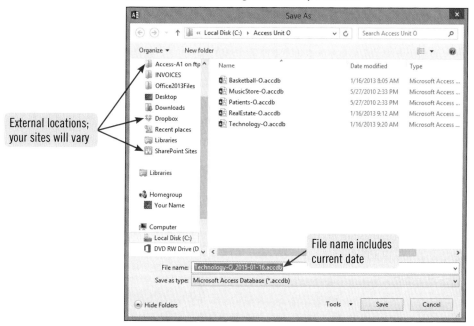

TABLE O-5: Database threats and solutions

incident	what can happen	appropriate actions
Virus	Viruses can cause a wide range of harm, from profane messages to corrupted files	Purchase the leading virus-checking software for each machine, and keep it updated
Power outage	Power problems such as construction accidents, **brownouts** (dips in power often causing lights to dim), and **spikes** (surges in power) can damage the hardware, which may render the computer useless	Purchase a **UPS** (uninterruptible power supply) to maintain constant power to the file server Purchase a **surge protector** (power strip with surge protection) for each user
Theft or intentional damage	Computer thieves or other scoundrels steal or vandalize computer equipment	Place the file server in a room that can be locked after-hours Use network drives for user data files, and back them up on a daily basis Use off-site storage for backups Set database passwords and encrypt the database so that files that are stolen cannot be used; use computer locks for equipment that is at risk, especially laptops

Convert a Database

Learning Outcomes
• Convert a database to a previous version
• Define database formats and file extensions

When you **convert** a database, you change the database file into one that can be opened in a previous version of Access. In Access 2013, the default file format is Access 2007, a database format that can be shared between users of Access 2007, 2010, or 2013. To open a current database in Access 2000, 2002 (also called Access XP), or Access 2003, however, you first need to convert it to a previous file format such as an Access 2000 database format. Access 2000 was the default file format for Access 2000, 2002, and 2003. **CASE** *The Training Department asks you to convert the Technology-O.accdb database to a version that they can open and use in early versions of Access.*

STEPS

1. **Click the FILE tab, click Save As, click Access 2000 Database, click the Save As button, then click Yes to close open objects**

   To back up or convert a database, you must make sure that no other users are currently working with it. Because you are the sole user of this database, it is safe to start the conversion process. The Save As dialog box opens, prompting you for the name of the database.

TROUBLE
If you do not see the extensions on the filenames, open Windows Explorer or File Explorer. For Windows 8, click the View tab, and click the File name extensions check box. For Windows 7, click the Organize button, click Folder and search options, click the View tab, and uncheck the Hide extensions for known file types check box.

2. **Navigate to the location where you store your Data Files, then type Technology-O-2000.mdb in the File name text box, as shown in FIGURE O-12**

   Because Access 2000, 2002, and 2003 all work with Access 2000 databases equally well, you decide to convert this database to an Access 2000 version database to allow for maximum backward compatibility. Recall that Access 2013 databases have an **.accdb** file extension, but Access 2000 and 2002–2003 databases have the **.mdb** file extension.

   You may occasionally see two other database extensions, .ldb for older databases and .laccdb for newer databases. The **.ldb** and **.laccdb** files are temporary files that keep track of record-locking information when the database is open. They help coordinate the multiuser capabilities of an Access database so that several people can read and update the same database at the same time.

3. **Click Save, then click OK**

   A copy of the database with the name Technology-O-2000.mdb is saved to the location you specified and is opened in the Access window. You can open and use Access 2000 and 2002–2003 databases in Access 2013 just as you would open and use an Access 2007 database. Each database version has its advantages, however, which are summarized in **TABLE O-6**.

4. **Close the database**

FIGURE O-12: Save As dialog box for Access 2000 file format

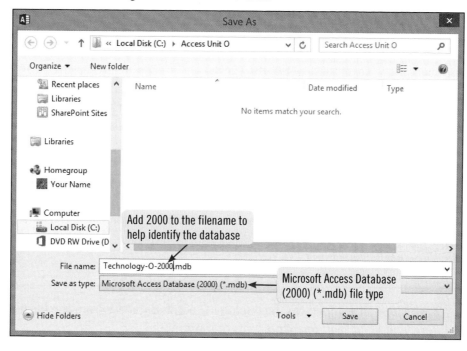

TABLE O-6: Differences between database file formats

database file format	file extension	Access version(s) that can read this file	benefits
2000	.mdb	2000, 2002, 2003, 2007, 2010, and 2013	Most versatile if working in an environment where multiple versions of Access are still in use
2002–2003	.mdb	2002, 2003, 2007, 2010, and 2013	Provides some advanced technical advantages for large databases over the Access 2000 file format
2007	.accdb	2007, 2010, and 2013	Supports the Attachment data type Supports multivalued fields Provides excellent integration with SharePoint and Outlook Provides more robust encryption

Access 2013

Split a Database

As your database grows, more people will want to use it, which creates the need for higher levels of database connectivity. **Local area networks (LANs)** are installed to link multiple PCs so they can share hardware and software resources. After a LAN is installed, a shared database is generally stored on a **file server**, a centrally located computer from which every user can access the database via the network. To improve the performance of a database shared among several users, you might **split** the database into two database files: the **back-end database**, which contains the actual table objects and is stored on the file server, and the **front-end database**, which contains the other database objects (forms and reports, for example). The front-end database is stored on each user's computer and links to the back-end database tables. You can also customize the objects contained in each front-end database. Therefore, front-end databases not only improve performance, but also add a level of customization and security. **CASE** ▶ *You split the Technology-O.accdb database into two databases in preparation for the new LAN being installed in the Information Systems Department.*

STEPS

1. **Start Access, then open the** Technology-O.accdb database **from the location where you store your Data Files, enabling content if prompted**

2. **Close the frmEmployees form, click the** DATABASE TOOLS **tab, click the** Access Database button **in the Move Data group, read the dialog box, then click** Split Database

   Access suggests the name of Technology-O_be.accdb for the back-end database in the Create Back-end Database dialog box.

3. **Navigate to the location where you store your Data Files, click** Split, **then click** OK

   Technology-O.accdb has now become the front-end database, which contains all of the Access objects except for the tables, as shown in **FIGURE O-13**. The tables have been replaced with links to the physical tables in the back-end database.

4. **Point to several linked** table icons **to read the path to the back-end database, right-click any of the** linked table icons, **then click** Linked Table Manager

   The Linked Table Manager dialog box opens, as shown in **FIGURE O-14**. This allows you to select and manually update tables. This is useful if the path to the back-end database changes and you need to reconnect the front-end and back-end database.

5. **Click** Cancel

   Linked tables work just like regular physical tables, even though the data is physically stored in another database.

6. **Close the Technology-O.accdb database and exit Access**

FIGURE O-13: Front-end database with linked tables

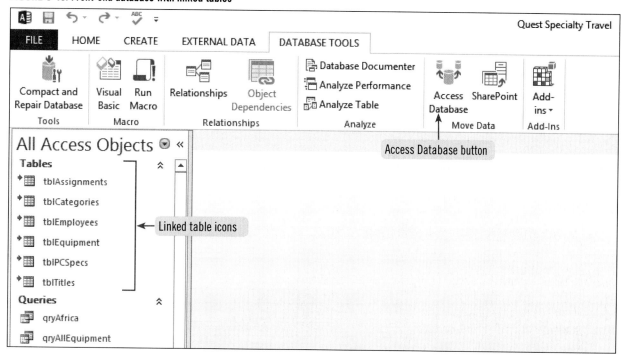

FIGURE O-14: Linked Table Manager dialog box

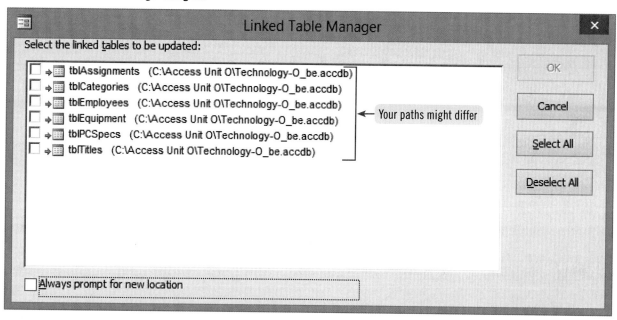

Databases and client/server computing

Splitting a database into a front-end and back-end database that work together is an excellent example of client/server computing. **Client/server computing** can be defined as two or more information systems cooperatively processing to solve a problem. In most implementations, the **client** is defined as the user's PC and the **server** is defined as the shared file server, minicomputer, or mainframe computer. The server usually handles corporate-wide computing activities, such as data storage and management, security, and connectivity to other networks. Within Access, client computers generally handle those tasks specific to each user, such as storing all of the queries, forms, and reports used by a particular user. Effectively managing a client/server network in which many front-end databases link to a single back-end database is a tremendous task, but the performance and security benefits are worth the effort.

Practice

Concepts Review

Identify each element of the Access Options dialog box in FIGURE O-15.

FIGURE O-15

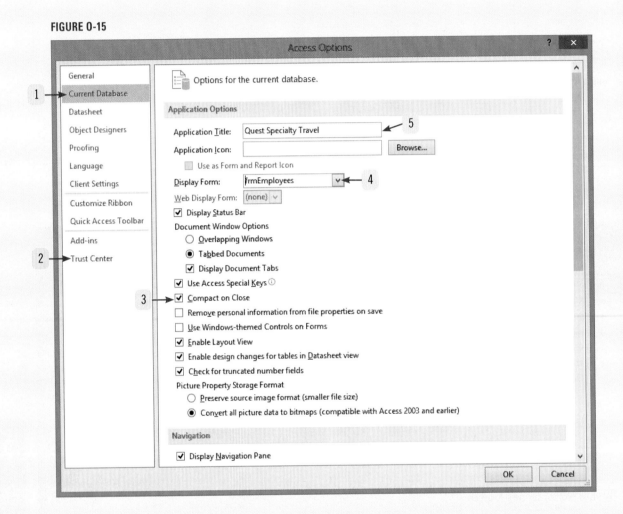

Match each term with the statement that best describes its function.

6. **Exclusive mode**
7. **Back-end database**
8. **Encrypting**
9. **Performance Analyzer**
10. **Navigation form**

a. Scrambles data so that it is indecipherable when opened by another program

b. Studies the structure and size of your database, and makes a variety of recommendations on how you can improve its speed

c. Contains database tables

d. Provides an easy-to-use database interface

e. Means that no other users can have access to the database file while it's open

Select the best answer from the list of choices.

11. **Changing a database file so that a previous version of Access can open it is called:**
    a. Splitting.
    b. Analyzing.
    c. Converting.
    d. Encrypting.

12. **Which is *not* a strong password?**
    a. 1234$College=6789
    b. password
    c. 5Matthew14?
    d. Lip44Balm*!

13. **Power outages can be caused by which of the following?**
    a. Surges
    b. Spikes
    c. Construction accidents
    d. All of the above

14. **Which character precedes a command-line option?**
    a. ^
    b. /
    c. @
    d. !

15. **Client/server computing is defined as:**
    a. Analyzing the performance of the database.
    b. Two or more information systems cooperatively processing to solve a problem.
    c. Creating an easy-to-use interface for a database application.
    d. Making sure that the database is encrypted and secure.

16. **Compacting and repairing a database does *not* help with which issue?**
    a. Eliminating wasted space
    b. Preventing data integrity problems
    c. Making the database as small as possible
    d. Identifying unused database objects

17. **Which of the following is *not* an item that you can "trust"?**
    a. Database table
    b. Database file
    c. Folder that stores the database
    d. You can trust all of the above.

18. **Which of the following is *not* a reason to create a backup?**
    a. Improve performance of the database
    b. Safeguard information should a natural disaster destroy the database
    c. Minimize damage caused by an incident that corrupts data
    d. Protect against theft

19. **Why might you split a database?**
    a. To make access to the database more secure
    b. To customize the front-end databases
    c. To improve performance
    d. All of the above

20. Which phrase best defines a SharePoint server?

  a. A special type of Microsoft Web server

  b. An online learning management system

  c. An academic wiki Web site

  d. A UNIX-based Web server

Skills Review

1. Create a navigation form.

  a. Start Access, open the Basketball-O.accdb database from the location where you store your Data Files, and enable content if prompted.

  b. Create a navigation form using the Vertical Tabs, Left style.

  c. Close the Field List.

  d. Add the frmGameInfo form, the frmGameSummaryForm, and the frmPlayerInformationForm to the tabs.

  e. Rename the tabs **Game Info**, **Game Summary**, and **Player Information**.

  f. Display the form in Form View, then test each tab.

  g. Save the form with the name **frmNavigation**, then close it.

2. Compact and repair a database.

  a. Compact and repair the database using an option on the DATABASE TOOLS tab.

  b. Open the Access Options dialog box, and check the Compact on Close option in the Current Database category.

3. Change startup options.

  a. Open the Access Options dialog box.

  b. Type **Iowa State Cyclones** in the Application Title text box, click the Display Form list arrow, click the frmNavigation form, then apply the changes.

  c. Close the Basketball-O.accdb database, then reopen it to check the startup options. Notice the change in the Access title bar.

  d. Close the frmNavigation form that automatically opened when the database was opened.

4. Analyze database performance.

  a. On the DATABASE TOOLS tab, click the Analyze Performance button.

  b. On the All Object Types tab, select all objects, then click OK.

  c. Read each of the ideas and descriptions, then close the Performance Analyzer and the database.

5. Set a database password.

  a. Open the Basketball-O.accdb database in Exclusive mode.

  b. Set the database password to **b*i*g*1*2**. (*Hint*: Check to make sure the Caps Lock light is not on because passwords are case sensitive.) Click OK if prompted about row level locking.

  c. Close the Basketball-O.accdb database, but leave Access open.

  d. Reopen the Basketball-O.accdb database to test the password. Close the Basketball-O.accdb database.

  e. Reopen the Basketball-O.accdb database in Exclusive mode. Type **b*i*g*1*2** as the password.

  f. Unset the database password.

  g. Close the frmNavigation form.

6. Back up a database.

  a. Click the FILE tab, click Save As, then use the Back Up Database option to save a database backup with the name **Basketball-O-*currentdate*.accdb** in the location where you store your Data Files.

Skills Review (continued)

7. Convert a database.

  a. Click the FILE tab, click Save As, and save the database backup as an Access 2000 database with the name **Basketball-O-2000.mdb** in the location where you store your Data Files.

  b. Notice that the frmNavigation no longer works correctly because the navigation form is a feature that is only compatible with Access 2007 database file formats. Close frmNavigation.

  c. Open the Access Options dialog box.

  d. Click the Display Form list arrow, select (none), then apply the changes.

  e. If the Navigation Pane displays only Tables, click the arrow to the right of Tables in the Navigation Pane title bar, and then click All Access Objects.

  f. Close the Basketball-O-2000.mdb database and click OK if prompted about a collating sequence.

8. Split a database.

  a. Start Access, open the Basketball-O.accdb database from the location where you store your Data Files, and enable content if prompted.

  b. Close frmNavigation.

  c. On the DATABASE TOOLS tab, click the Access Database button and split the database.

  d. Name the back-end database with the default name, **Basketball-O_be.accdb**, and save it in the location where you store your Data Files.

  e. Point to the linked table icons to observe the path to the back-end database.

  f. Close the Basketball-O.accdb database and exit Access.

Independent Challenge 1

As the manager of a doctor's clinic, you have created an Access database called Patients-O.accdb to track insurance claims. You want to set a database password and encrypt the database, as well as set options to automatically compact the database when it is closed.

  a. Start Access. Open Patients-O.accdb in Exclusive mode from the location where you store your Data Files. Enable content if prompted.

  b. Encrypt the database with a password.

  c. Enter **4-your-health** in the Password text box and the Verify text box, then click OK. Click OK if prompted about row level locking.

  d. Close the Patients-O.accdb database, but leave Access running.

  e. Reopen the Patients-O.accdb database, enter **4-your-health** as the password, then click OK.

  f. In the Access Options dialog box, check the Compact on Close option.

  g. Close the database and Access.

Independent Challenge 2

As the manager of a doctor's clinic, you have created an Access database called Patients-O.accdb to track insurance claims. You want to analyze database performance.

  a. Open the Patients-O.accdb database from the location where you store your Data Files, and enable content if prompted.

  b. Enter **4-your-health** as the password if prompted.

  c. Use the Analyze Performance tool on the DATABASE TOOLS tab to analyze all objects.

  d. Click each item in the Performance Analyzer results window, and read the Analysis Notes in the Performance Analyzer dialog box.

Independent Challenge 2 (continued)

e. Click Close in the Performance Analyzer dialog box and apply the first suggestion by double-clicking the basBodyMassIndex module. Choose Debug on the menu bar, then Compile. Save and close the VBE and run the Performance Analyzer again.

f. Click each item in the Performance Analyzer results window, and read the Analysis Notes in the Performance Analyzer dialog box.

g. Click Close in the Performance Analyzer dialog box and apply the third suggestion by double-clicking the basBodyMassIndex module. Enter **Option Explicit** as the second declaration statement, just below the Option Compare Database statement. Save and close the VBE and run the Performance Analyzer again.

h. Click each item in the Performance Analyzer results window, and read the Analysis Notes in the Performance Analyzer dialog box.

i. Click Close in the Performance Analyzer dialog box and consider the second suggestion by opening the tblClaimLineItems table in Datasheet View. The suggestion was to change the Data Type of the Diag1 field from Short Text to Number with a Field Size property value of Double. Given those values represent codes and not quantities, Short Text is a better description of the data and you will not implement this suggestion. Close the tblClaimLineItems table.

j. Run the Performance Analyzer for all objects again. To implement the first suggestion, close the Performance Analyzer dialog box, click the FILE tab, click Save As, click Make ACCDE, then click the Save As button. Save the Patients-O.accde file to the location where you save your Data Files. An accde file is a database file that can be used just like an accdb file, but many of the objects cannot be modified in Design View.

k. Close the Patients-O.accde database, then close Access.

Independent Challenge 3

As the manager of a residential real estate listing service, you have created an Access database called RealEstate-O.accdb to track properties that are for sale. You want to analyze how the compact and repair feature affects a database.

a. Open File Explorer (Windows 8) or Windows Explorer (Windows 7), then open the folder that contains your Data Files.

b. Change the view to Details. (In Windows 8, click the Details button on the right side of the status bar. In Windows 7, click the More Options button in the upper-right corner of the window, then click Details. Record the Size value for the RealEstate-O.accdb database.

c. Double-click RealEstate-O.accdb to open it, right-click the frmListingsEntryForm, and then click Delete.

d. Close the RealEstate-O.accdb database and return to File Explorer or Windows Explorer. Record the Size value for the RealEstate-O.accdb database.

e. Double-click RealEstate-O.accdb to open it, click the DATABASE TOOLS tab, then click the Compact and Repair Database button.

f. Close the RealEstate-O.accdb database and return to File Explorer or Windows Explorer. Record the Size value for the RealEstate-O.accdb database.

Independent Challenge 4: Explore

Microsoft provides extra information, templates, files, and ideas at a Web site called Tools on the Web. You have been given an opportunity to intern with an Access consultant and are considering this type of work for your career. As such, you know that you need to be familiar with all of the resources on the Web that Microsoft provides to help you work with Access. In this exercise, you explore the Tools on the Web services.

a. Start Access, but do not open any databases.

b. Click the Microsoft Access Help button.

c. Click the What's new in Access link to open a page similar to the one shown in **FIGURE O-16**.

d. Click the link to watch the video about What's New in Access 2013.

e. After the video is finished, scroll through the Access Help window to read the article.

f. In a Word document, create a one-page, double-spaced article to summarize your understanding of an Access app. Include an example of where, how, and why you would apply an Access app in the real world.

g. Close Access and any open Access Help windows.

FIGURE O-16

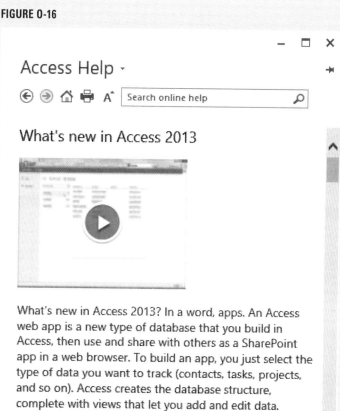

Visual Workshop

As the manager of a music store, you have created an Access database called MusicStore-O.accdb that tracks musical instrument rentals to schoolchildren. Use the Performance Analyzer to generate the results shown in **FIGURE O-17** by analyzing all object types. Save the database as an ACCDE file, but do not implement the other ideas. In a Word document, explain why implementing the last three ideas might not be appropriate.

FIGURE O-17

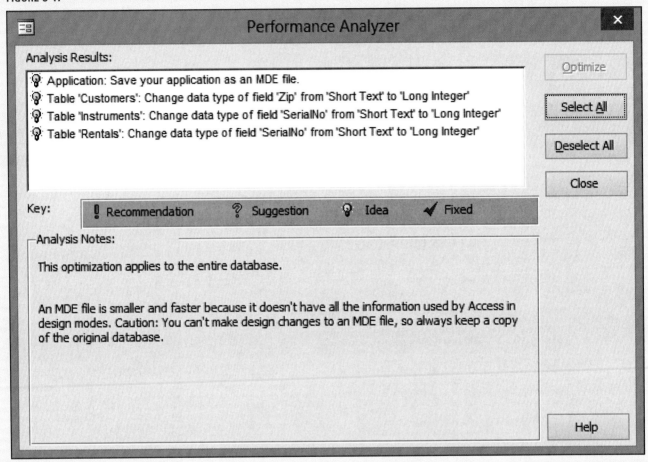

Access and the Web

Unit Objectives

After completing this unit, you will be able to:

- Create a hyperlink field
- Create a hyperlink control
- Use HTML tags to format text
- Export to HTML and XML
- Import from HTML and XML
- Save and share a database with SkyDrive
- Understand Access Web apps
- Create an Access Web app

Files You Will Need

QuestTravel-P.accdb
Vail.docx
Newsletter.docx
NewCustomers.html
NewTours.xml
NewTours.xsd
Basketball-P.accdb
Cavalier.png

NextSeason.html
NewPlayers.xml
NewPlayers.xsd
Unit P Skills Review
Question 7.docx
Patients-P.accdb
MusicStore-P.accdb

Create a Hyperlink Field

Learning Outcomes
• Create a hyperlink field
• Enter hyperlink data for a Web page or file

A **hyperlink field** is a field with the **Hyperlink** data type. Use the Hyperlink data type when you want to store a link to a Web page or file. The file can be located on the Internet, on your company's local area network, or on your own computer. **CASE** ▸ *You create two hyperlink fields to store linked information about each tour record in the Tours table. The first hyperlink field will link to a Web page that provides information about the tour location. The second hyperlink field will link to a Word document that contains a tour flyer.*

STEPS

1. **Start Access, open the QuestTravel-P.accdb database from the location where you store your Data Files, enable content if prompted, then double-click the Tours table to open it in Datasheet View**

   You can add new fields in either Datasheet View or Design View.

2. **Click the *Click to Add* placeholder to the right of the Price field, click Hyperlink in the drop-down list, type WebPage as the new field name, then press [Enter]**

   The new WebPage field will store a hyperlink to the Web page address for that tour. Before you enter those values, you will create another hyperlink field to link to a local Word document that contains a flyer for the tour.

3. **Click the *Click to Add* placeholder to the right of the WebPage field if the placeholder is not selected, click Hyperlink, type Flyer, press [Enter], then click the WebPage field for the first record**

   The Tours datasheet should look like **FIGURE P-1**. With the new hyperlink fields in place, you'll use them to further describe the Vail Biking Tour record. Hyperlink values such as Web page addresses may be typed directly in the field.

4. **Click the WebPage field for the Vail Biking Tour record (TourNo 5), type www.vail.com, then press [Enter]**

   To store the link to a local Word document, you browse for the file.

TROUBLE
If you do not see the Hyperlink option on the shortcut menu, click in the Flyer field to switch to Edit mode (you will see the blinking insertion point in the field), then redo Step 5.

5. **Right-click the Flyer field for the Vail Biking Tour record (TourNo 5), click Hyperlink, click Edit Hyperlink, browse for the Vail.docx file in the location where you store your Data Files, click the Vail.docx file, as shown in FIGURE P-2, then click OK in the Edit Hyperlink dialog box**

   The Edit Hyperlink dialog box lets you link to an existing file, Web page, or email address. Test your hyperlinks.

6. **Click the www.vail.com hyperlink, close the browser to return to Access, click the Vail.docx hyperlink, click Yes if prompted about a security concern, then close Word to return to Access**

   Note that your mouse pointer becomes a **hyperlink pointer** ⬚ and displays the path to the resource when you hover over a hyperlink. Also note that the hyperlink changes colors, from blue to purple, once the hyperlink has been visited, as shown in **FIGURE P-3**.

7. **Right-click the Tours table tab, then click Close**

   Hyperlink fields store paths to files and Web pages, not the files or Web pages themselves. If the location of the hyperlink file or database changes, the Hyperlink value must be changed in the Edit Hyperlink dialog box to reflect the new path as well.

FIGURE P-1: Creating hyperlink fields

	TourNc	TourName	TourStartDate	Duration	City	State	Category	Price	WebPage	Flyer	Click to Add
⊞	1	Stanley Bay Shelling	07/06/2014	3	Captiva	FL	Adventure	$750			
⊞	2	Red Reef Scuba	07/06/2014	3	Islamadora	FL	Adventure	$1,500			
⊞	3	Ames Ski Club	01/02/2015	7	Breckenridge	CO	Adventure	$850			
⊞	4	Boy Scout Jamboree	01/13/2015	7	Vail	CO	Adventure	$1,900			
⊞	5	Vail Biking Tour	02/15/2015	10	Vail	CO	Adventure	$1,200			
⊞	6	Franklin Family Reunion	03/11/2015	3	Breckenridge	CO	Family	$700			
⊞	7	Spare Tire Ski Club	03/13/2015	7	Monmouth	WA	Adventure	$600			

New WebPage field   New Flyer field

FIGURE P-2: Edit Hyperlink dialog box

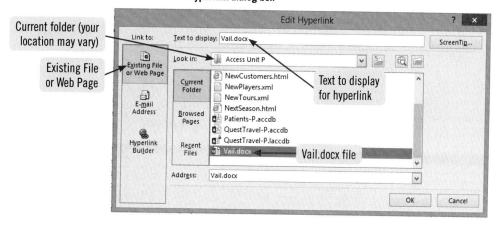

Current folder (your location may vary)

Existing File or Web Page

Text to display for hyperlink

Vail.docx file

FIGURE P-3: Tours datasheet with visited hyperlinks

Visited hyperlinks change from blue to purple

	TourNc	TourName	TourStartDate	Duration	City	State	Category	Price	WebPage	Flyer	Click to Add
⊞	1	Stanley Bay Shelling	07/06/2014	3	Captiva	FL	Adventure	$750			
⊞	2	Red Reef Scuba	07/06/2014	3	Islamadora	FL	Adventure	$1,500			
⊞	3	Ames Ski Club	01/02/2015	7	Breckenridge	CO	Adventure	$850			
⊞	4	Boy Scout Jamboree	01/13/2015	7	Vail	CO	Adventure	$1,900			
⊞	5	Vail Biking Tour	02/15/2015	10	Vail	CO	Adventure	$1,200	www.vail.com	Vail.docx	
⊞	6	Franklin Family Reunion	03/11/2015	3	Breckenridge	CO	Family	$700			
⊞	7	Spare Tire Ski Club	03/13/2015	7	Monmouth	WA	Adventure	$600			
⊞	8	Eagan Family Reunion	06/12/2015	7	Osage Beach	MO	Family	$500			

ScreenTip with path to the hyperlink resource

Hyperlink mouse pointer

http://www.vail.com

Create a Hyperlink Control

Learning Outcomes
• Modify a command button to be a hyperlink
• Modify a label to be a hyperlink

A **hyperlink control** is a control on a form that when clicked, works like a hyperlink to redirect the user to a Web page or file. You can convert a label control into a hyperlink label by modifying the label's **Hyperlink Address property**. Command button and image controls can also be used as hyperlinks. **CASE** ▶ *Kayla asks you to create hyperlinks to quickly open the QST newsletter (a Word document) as well as the www.mapquest.com Web site from the Tour Entry form. You will create a hyperlink command button for each link.*

STEPS

1. **Right-click the** TourEntry form **in the Navigation Pane, then click** Design View
   You will add two new hyperlink controls in the Form Header, just to the left of the existing command buttons.

2. **Click the** Button button ⌧ **in the Controls group, click at about the 4.5" mark on the horizontal ruler in the Form Header section, then click** Cancel **to close the Command Button Wizard**
   You work with the command button's Property Sheet to modify it into a hyperlink control.

TROUBLE
The default Caption might be Command19 or display another number depending on the previous activity in the form.

3. **Click the** Property Sheet button **to toggle open the Property Sheet if it is closed, click the** Format tab **in the Property Sheet if it is not already selected, select** Command19 **in the Caption property, type** Mapquest, **click the** Hyperlink Address property, **type** http://www.mapquest.com, **then press** [Enter]
   The command button's Property Sheet should look like **FIGURE P-4**. Now you will add another command button hyperlink for the newsletter.

4. **Click the** Button button ⌧ **in the Controls group, click at about the 3" mark on the horizontal ruler in the Form Header section, then click** Cancel **to close the Command Button Wizard**

QUICK TIP
You can also use the Build button ⋯ to enter the Hyperlink Address property.

5. **In the Property Sheet for the new command button, select** Command20 **in the Caption property, type** Newsletter, **click the** Hyperlink Address property, **type** newsletter.docx, **then press** [Enter]
   With the new hyperlink command buttons in place, you will align them for a more professional look.

QUICK TIP
You can also use [Shift]+click to add more controls to a selection.

6. **Click the** Property Sheet button **to close the Property Sheet, drag a selection box through all four command buttons in the Form Header section, click the** ARRANGE tab **on the Ribbon, click the** Align button, **then click** Top **to align the top edges of the four buttons, as shown in FIGURE P-5**
   Test the hyperlinks in Form View.

7. **Right-click the** TourEntry form tab, **click** Form View, **click the** Newsletter link, **click** Yes **if prompted about unsafe content, close Word to return to Access, click the** Mapquest link, **close your browser to return to Access, as shown in FIGURE P-6, close the** TourEntry form, **then click** Yes **when prompted to save it**

FIGURE P-4: Property Sheet for hyperlink command button

Property Sheet for Command Button control

Format tab

Caption property

Hyperlink Address property

FIGURE P-5: Aligning new command buttons

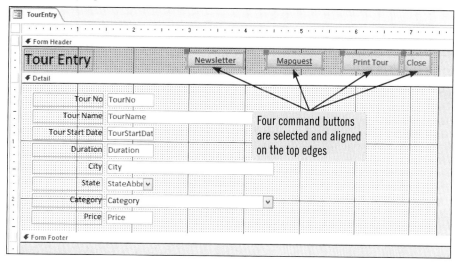

Four command buttons are selected and aligned on the top edges

FIGURE P-6: TourEntry form with hyperlink command buttons

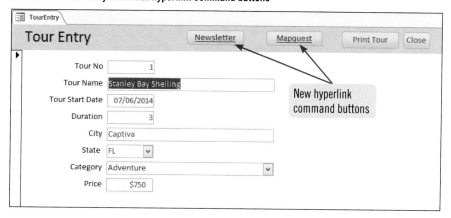

New hyperlink command buttons

Access 2013

Use HTML Tags to Format Text

Learning
Outcomes
• Apply the Rich
  Text format
• Apply HTML
  formatting tags
• Apply HTML line
  break tags

HTML is the language used to describe content in a traditional Web page. HTML stands for **Hypertext Markup Language**. HTML **tags** are the codes used to identify or "mark up" the content in the page. Tags are entered into an HTML file in <angle brackets> and many HTML tags are used in pairs to mark the beginning and end of the content they identify. For example, you would use the <b> tag to mark where bold starts. The same tag with a slash, </b>, marks where bold ends. See **TABLE P-1** for more examples of common HTML tags you can use with the Rich Text format. **Rich Text** is a Text Format property that allows you to mix formatting of text displayed by a text box on a form or a report. With a little bit of HTML knowledge, you can transform a large block of text on a report into a paragraph with multiple formatting embellishments. **CASE** *Kayla has asked you to review the CustomerInvoice report. She wants you to format the payment disclaimer paragraph so it is more readable. You will use HTML tags to format the text.*

STEPS

1. **Double-click the** Switchboard form **to open it in Form View, click the** FIND Customer Invoice combo box arrow, **click the** Alman, Jacob entry, **click the** Preview Invoice command button **to open the Customer Invoice report in Print Preview, then click the report to zoom in on it**

   You want to better format the sentences in the large text box that starts with "Thank you for your order."

2. **Right-click the** CustomerInvoice tab, **then click** Design View **to open the report in Design View**

   The first step in formatting text in a text box is to change the Text Format property to Rich Text.

QUICK TIP
HTML tags are more
precisely called HTML
elements by Web
page developers.

3. **Click the** large text box **in the Detail section to select it, click the** Property Sheet button **to open the Property Sheet for the text box if it is not already visible, click the** Data tab **in the Property Sheet if it is not already selected, click the** Text Format property, **click the** Text Format list arrow, **then click** Rich Text

   With the Text Format property set to Rich Text, you can mark up the text with HTML tags.

4. **Edit the text box entry, as shown in** FIGURE P-7

   Note that all HTML tags are surrounded by <angle brackets>. The beginning of the text to be formatted is marked with an **opening tag** such as <b> for start bold. The end of the text to be formatted is marked with a **closing tag**, which is identified with a forward slash such as </b> for end bold. **Empty tags**, those that are a single tag and not paired, end with a forward slash such as <br/> for line break.

5. **Save and close the CustomerInvoice report**

   Test the new Rich Text box with HTML formatting tags.

TROUBLE
If you encounter an
error message, switch
to Design View and
double-check the
HTML tags, as shown
in FIGURE P-7.

6. **On the Switchboard form, click the** FIND Customer Invoice combo box arrow, **click the** Alman, Jacob entry, **click the** Preview Invoice command button **to open the** CustomerInvoice report in Print Preview, **then click the report to zoom in**

   The final report should look like **FIGURE P-8**.

7. **Close the CustomerInvoice report, and then close the Switchboard form**

FIGURE P-7: Using HTML tags to format Rich Text

="<font size=6>Thank you for your order.</font>

Payment Notes: 10% deposit is due at time of booking.

50%, nonrefundable deposit is due two weeks prior to departure date.

 <font color=red>The full balance is due 2 days prior to departure date.</font>"

HTML tags must be entered precisely as shown

FIGURE P-8: Formatted CustomerInvoice report

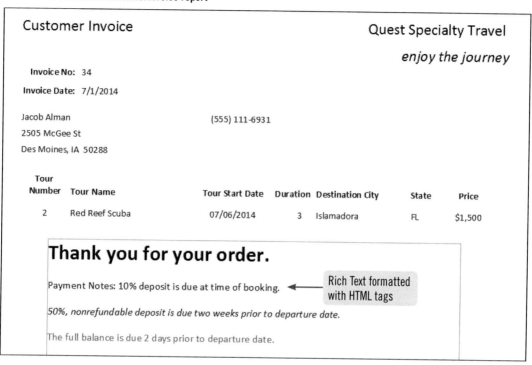

Customer Invoice

Quest Specialty Travel

enjoy the journey

Invoice No: 34

Invoice Date: 7/1/2014

Jacob Alman
2505 McGee St
Des Moines, IA 50288

(555) 111-6931

Tour Number	Tour Name	Tour Start Date	Duration	Destination City	State	Price
2	Red Reef Scuba	07/06/2014	3	Islamadora	FL	$1,500

Thank you for your order.

Payment Notes: 10% deposit is due at time of booking.

Rich Text formatted with HTML tags

50%, nonrefundable deposit is due two weeks prior to departure date.

The full balance is due 2 days prior to departure date.

TABLE P-1: Common HTML tags

HTML tag	description	example
p	paragraph	<p>The p tag marks the beginning and ending of a paragraph of text. </p>
br	Marks a line break	 (*Note*: The br tag is not a paired tag. One single tag creates the line break. Non-paired tags are also called empty tags.)
b	Marks the beginning and end of **bold** text	We **appreciate** your business.
i	Marks the beginning and end of *italic* text	Product may be returned for a full refund <i>*within 30 days.*</i>
code	Marks the beginning and end of monospaced text	<code>Terms and Conditions</code>
font	Identifies the color, font face, and size of the marked content	<font color=red>Merry Christmas!</font> <font font_family=Arial>Purchase Order</font> <font size=16>Inventory Report</font>

HTML 5

HTML 5 is the latest version of HTML as defined by the leading international standards committee on fundamental Web technologies, the **W3C**, or **World Wide Web Consortium**, at www.w3c.org. HTML 5 has **deprecated** (retired due to new, better technologies) the HTML font tag in favor of a much more powerful, flexible, and productive way to define Web page formatting and presentation called **CSS, Cascading Style Sheets**. Therefore, it would not be appropriate or professional to use the HTML font tag in traditional Web page development. Given there is no current way to apply CSS technology to a Rich Text control in an Access form or report, however, the HTML formatting tags such as the font tag still have a meaningful role for this situation.

Export to HTML and XML

Given the widespread use of the Web to share information, you may want to export Access data to a format that works well with existing Web technologies. For example, you might want to view data stored in an Access database using a common browser such as Internet Explorer. Access allows you to export data to two common Web-related formats: HTML and XML. Recall that HTML files are Web pages that use HTML tags to mark up content stored in the file. **XML**, short for **Extensible Markup Language**, is a language used to mark up structured data so that the data can be more easily shared between different computer programs. The process of exporting a report to an HTML or XML file is very similar. **CASE** ➤ *You use Access export features to export data to both an HTML file as well as an XML file to compare and better understand them.*

STEPS

1. **Click the** Customers table **in the Navigation pane, click the** EXTERNAL DATA tab, **click the** More button **in the Export group, then click** HTML Document

   The Export - HTML Document dialog box opens, prompting you for a name and location of the HTML file it is about to create, as shown in **FIGURE P-9**.

2. **Click the** Export data with formatting and layout check box, **click the** Open the destination file after the export option is complete check box, **click** Browse, **navigate to the location where you store your Data Files, click** Save **in the File Save dialog box, click** OK **in the Export - HTML Document dialog box, click** OK **in the HTML Output Options dialog box, then click** Close **if prompted**

   The Web page created by the export process automatically opens in the program that is associated with the HTML file extension, which is probably your default browser, such as Internet Explorer or Firefox. If you were to look at the HTML in this Web page, you would see a mixture of tags used to structure as well as format this data. Although mixing structure and formatting works well if you need to distribute the Web page for people to read, it creates problems when you want to pass the data to another program. XML files address this issue by separating the data from the presentation (formatting) of the data.

3. **Close the window with the Customers.html file to return to Access, click** Close **in the Export - HTML Document dialog box if it is not already closed, click the** Tours table **if it is not already selected, click the** XML File button **in the Export group, click** Browse, **navigate to the location where you store your Data Files, click** Save **in the File Save dialog box, click** OK, **click** OK **in the Export XML dialog box, then click** Close **in the Export - XML File dialog box**

   The Export - XML File dialog box doesn't have an option to automatically open the exported XML file, but you can find and double-click the Tours.xml to review its contents.

4. **Start** File Explorer, **navigate to the location where you store your Data Files, then double-click the** Tours.xml file **to open it**

   Tours.xml opens in the program associated with the .xml file extension, which is probably Notepad, as shown in **FIGURE P-10**. Note that the XML file uses markup tags to identify content similarly to how an HTML file uses markup tags. An XML file, therefore, is often a better choice when your goal is to share structured data because it separates the raw data into one file (**XML**), a description of the data's characteristics into another file (**XSD**), and a description of how the data should be formatted into a third file (**XSL**).

5. **Close the Tours.xml file and return to Access**

   The decision on which file format to choose when exporting Access data is dictated by the needs of the person or program that is receiving the file. Simply realize that you can export Access data just as easily to an HTML or XML file format as you previously experienced with other common file formats, such as Excel and PDF in Unit I.

FIGURE P-9: Export - HTML Document dialog box

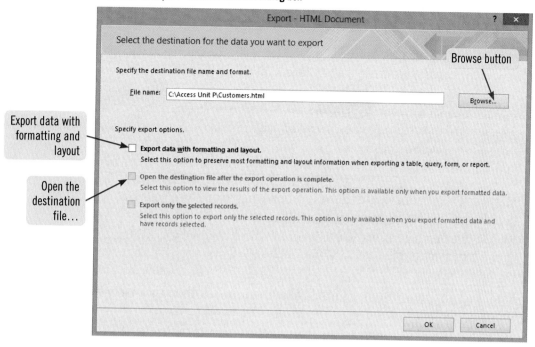

Export data with formatting and layout

Open the destination file...

Browse button

FIGURE P-10: Tours.xml file

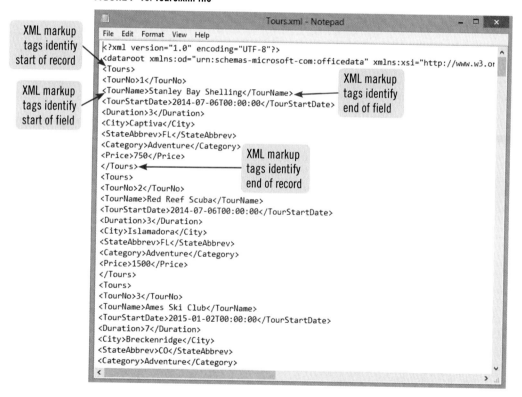

XML markup tags identify start of record

XML markup tags identify start of field

XML markup tags identify end of field

XML markup tags identify end of record

XML, XSD, and XSL files

When you export data as an XML file, you are prompted to export two helper files, XSD and XSL. The **XSD** file stores the schema of data stored in the XML file. The **schema** of the data is a description of the fields and their properties. The **XSL** file describes how to display an XML file. Therefore, if you're using the XML file to pass data from one computer application to another, the XSD file provides information about the data types and properties that can be used to describe and ensure the integrity of the data. The XSL file isn't used to pass data from one computer to another, but if you want a human to open and be able to easily read an XML file, include an XSL file in the export.

Import from HTML and XML

Importing brings data into the database from an external file. You can import data directly from an HTML file provided the data is structured in the HTML file with HTML table tags so that Access knows where each field and record starts and stops. If the data is stored in an XML file, it is by definition already structured into fields and records with XML tags. **CASE** *You use Access import features to import new customer data from an HTML file that the Marketing Department created. You also import new tour data from an XML file that the Information Systems Department created.*

STEPS

1. **Start File Explorer, navigate to the location where you store your Data Files, then double-click the NewCustomers.html file to open it**

   The NewCustomers.html file opens in the program associated with viewing HTML files, which is probably a browser such as Internet Explorer, as shown in **FIGURE P-11**. View the HTML stored in the page to see how the data is structured.

   > **TROUBLE**
   > The View source option in Internet Explorer is named View Page Source in Firefox.

2. **Right-click the NewCustomers.html file in the browser, then click View source on the shortcut menu**

   The NewCustomers.html file opens in the program associated with creating and editing HTML files, which may be a text editor program such as Notepad or the Original Source window, as shown in **FIGURE P-12**. Note that HTML table tags separate the data using HTML **tr** tags to separate the records and **td** tags to separate each field. HTML table tags are further described in **TABLE P-2**.

   > **TROUBLE**
   > Be sure to click the More button in the *Import & Link* group on the Ribbon and not the *Export* group.

3. **Close all windows that display the NewCustomers.html file to return to Access, click the EXTERNAL DATA tab on the Ribbon, click the More button in the Import & Link group, click HTML Document, click Browse, navigate to the location of your Data Files, click NewCustomers.html, click Open, click OK in the Get External Data - HTML Document dialog box, click the First Row Contains Column Headings check box, click Next, click Next to accept the default field options for each field, click the No primary key option button, click Next, type NewCustomers, click Finish, then click Close if prompted**

   The records in the NewCustomers.html file are imported to a new Access table named NewCustomers. That gives you the ability to view the imported data in Access to make sure the import was successful and then use an Append query to combine the records from the imported table to an existing table.

4. **Double-click the NewCustomers table to make sure the import process was successful, then right-click the NewCustomers tab and click Close to close the table**

   Confident that the data in the HTML file was successfully imported into the Access database as a new table, you import the XML file.

   > **TROUBLE**
   > Be sure to click the XML File button in the *Import & Link* group on the Ribbon and not the *Export* group.

5. **Click the XML File button in the Import & Link group, click Browse, navigate to the location of your Data Files, click NewTours.xml, click Open, click OK in the Get External Data – XML File dialog box, click OK in the Import XML dialog box, click Close in the Get External Data - XML File dialog box, then double-click the NewTours table to make sure that the data imported successfully**

   The NewTours.xml data imported successfully. Switch to Design View to see more information about each field.

6. **Right-click the NewTours tab, then click Design View**

   The TourNo and Duration fields are identified as Number fields, the NewTourStartDate field with a Date/Time data type, and the Price field has a Currency data type. The import process made these intelligent choices because of the information about the fields stored in the schema file, the XSD file.

7. **Right-click the NewTours tab, then click Close**

FIGURE P-11: NewCustomers.html file opened in a browser

Customers							
FName	LName	Street	City	State	Zip	Phone	FirstContact
Marcus	Welby	39411 Oakmont Rd	Texarama City	TX	84144	(333) 444-1934	List
Todd	Grant	9303 Monrovia St	Fisher	IA	30988	(333) 111-8931	List
Stan	Lovelace	3900 Meriam St	Austin	TX	84103	(333) 111-3081	List
Fritz	Arnold	55 Main Dr	Lemonwood	OK	88914	(333) 999-9101	List
Stewart	Baker	10 Cherry St	Overton	OK	88031	(333) 999-7009	List
Kelly	Sanders	500 W 10th St	Oklahoma City	OK	84103	(333) 999-3809	List
Tom	Cardwell	222 W 20th St	Oklahoma City	OK	84103	(333) 999-3809	List
Samuel	Adams	88 8th St	Wellman	OK	88910	(333) 999-8409	List
Harrison	Barnes	33 W. 303 Ter	Stillwater	OK	88913	(333) 333-9871	List
Boo	Palo	11 Memory Lane	Texarcana	TX	84143	(333) 333-0401	List

← HTML table

FIGURE P-12: NewCustomers.html tags

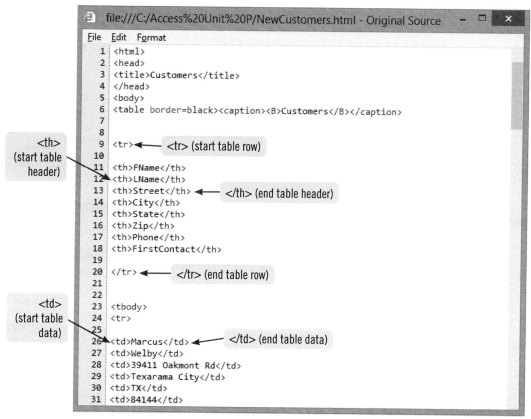

<th> (start table header)

<tr> (start table row)

</th> (end table header)

</tr> (end table row)

<td> (start table data)

</td> (end table data)

```
1  <html>
2  <head>
3  <title>Customers</title>
4  </head>
5  <body>
6  <table border=black><caption><B>Customers</B></caption>
7
8
9  <tr>
10
11 <th>FName</th>
12 <th>LName</th>
13 <th>Street</th>
14 <th>City</th>
15 <th>State</th>
16 <th>Zip</th>
17 <th>Phone</th>
18 <th>FirstContact</th>
19
20 </tr>
21
22
23 <tbody>
24 <tr>
25
26 <td>Marcus</td>
27 <td>Welby</td>
28 <td>39411 Oakmont Rd</td>
29 <td>Texarama City</td>
30 <td>TX</td>
31 <td>84144</td>
```

file:///C:/Access%20Unit%20P/NewCustomers.html - Original Source

File   Edit   Format

TABLE P-2: HTML table tags

tag	description
`<table> </table>`	Marks the beginning and end of the entire table
`<tr> </tr>`	Marks the beginning and end of a table row (a table row in HTML becomes a table record in Access)
`<th> </th>`	Marks the beginning and end of a table header entry (a table header entry in HTML becomes a field name in Access)
`<td> </td>`	Marks the beginning and end of a table data entry (a table data entry in HTML becomes a field value in Access)

Access 2013

Save and Share a Database with SkyDrive

Learning Outcomes
• Create a SkyDrive folder
• Save a database to SkyDrive
• Share a database from SkyDrive

SkyDrive is a cloud-based storage and file-sharing service provided by Microsoft. Saving files to SkyDrive means that you can access those files from any computer connected to the Internet. You can also share the file with other people or create **shared folders** in your SkyDrive to organize shared files. SkyDrive is particularly helpful to students who work on many different computers. The shared file and folder feature is very useful to anyone who works on group projects where the same file or files need to be constantly accessible to several team members. **CASE** ▶ *Kayla Green asks you to create a folder on your SkyDrive to save and share the QuestTravel-P database.*

STEPS

1. **Click the FILE tab on the Ribbon, click** Save As, **click the** Save As button, **click** SkyDrive **in your Favorites section or navigate to your SkyDrive, and then click** Save

   A copy of the QuestTravel-P.accdb database can be saved to your personal SkyDrive if it is available in the Save As dialog box. The SkyDrive works just like your hard drive but is available to you on any computer connected to the Internet.

2. **Close the QuestTravel-P database and Access 2013, start** Internet Explorer **or another browser, type** skydrive.com **in the Address box, then press** [Enter]

   The contents of your SkyDrive appear. From here, you can upload, delete, move, download, or copy files, similarly to how you work with files on your local computer. You want to share the QuestTravel-P database with your instructor. You decide to first create a folder for the database. That way, your SkyDrive will stay more organized.

3. **Click the** Create button, **click** Folder, **type** Quest Shared Files **as the new folder name, then press** [Enter] **to create the folder, as shown in** FIGURE P-13

   Now you're ready to open the Quest Shared Files folder, then upload the QuestTravel-P database file into it.

4. **Click the** Quest Shared Files folder **to open it, click the** Upload button, **navigate to the location where you store your Data Files, click** QuestTravel-P.accdb, **then click** Open **in the Choose File to Upload dialog box**

   See **FIGURE P-14**. With the QuestTravel-P database stored in an appropriate folder on the SkyDrive, you're now ready to invite your instructor to share it.

5. **Click the** Sharing button, **enter the** email address of your instructor, **enter** Quest Unit P **as the personal message, click** Share, **then click** Done **or** Close

   To review the share permissions, right-click the QuestTravel-P tile and click Sharing on the shortcut menu. A list of the individuals who have permission to view and or edit the file is listed on the left, and you can modify the permissions or delete people from the list. You can also share the entire folder, which automatically shares all files stored in that folder.

6. **Close the skydrive.com browser window**

FIGURE P-13: Creating a Quest Shared Files folder

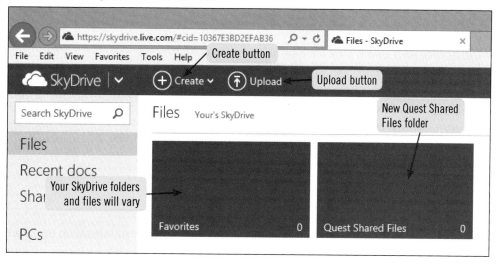

FIGURE P-14: SkyDrive with new file and folder

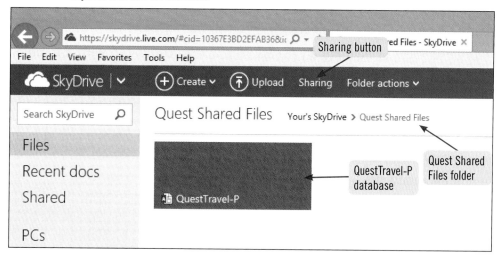

Understand Access Web Apps

Learning
Outcomes
• Describe the
advantages and
disadvantages of
an Access Web app
• Define the software
requirements for
an Access Web app

An **Access Web app** is a special type of Access database that is stored on a SharePoint 2013 server and allows users to enter and edit data using a common browser. An Access Web app is saved with the extension of **.accdw**. See **TABLE P-3** for a description of the software requirements to create and use an Access Web app, which include SharePoint 2013, SQL Server 2012, Access 2013, and a browser. **FIGURE P-15** shows how those software tools are used to develop and use an Access Web app. **CASE** ▶ *Kayla Green asks you review the benefits of and requirements for an Access Web app.*

DETAILS

Advantages **of building an Access Web app over a traditional desktop application include the following:**

- **Access is not required for the user**

  A copy of Microsoft Access on each client computer is no longer required for each user. An Access Web app is available to any user with a current browser.

- **A local connection to the database is not required for each user**

  An Access Web app is available to any user with an Internet connection.

- **Access Web app data is stored in a back-end SQL Server database**

  Storing data in SQL Server tables versus embedded Access tables provides these benefits:

  - **User-level security**: The data is more secure because it can be password protected at a user level.
  - **Scalabilility**: Much larger amounts of data can be stored and managed.
  - **Performance**: More people can be reliably working with the application with very fast response times.

Disadvantages **of building an Access Web app as compared with a traditional desktop application include the following:**

- **Complexity**

  Access Web apps require several technical prerequisites. See **TABLE P-3** for a listing of the software requirements to create, modify, and use an Access Web app. See **TABLE P-4** for a short listing of helpful Access Web app resources.

- **Less robust development tools**

  The tools used to develop Access Web apps are not as mature as those you use to create traditional desktop applications. For example, the objects in an Access Web app do not provide a full set of development tools in Design View as compared with their desktop counterparts. Also, VBA, Visual Basic for Applications, is not available to extend or enhance an Access Web app.

- **Traditional desktop databases cannot be easily upgraded to Access Web apps**

  Although the data from a traditional Access database can be easily imported into an SQL Server database, other objects such as forms and reports cannot be transferred from traditional databases to Web app applications.

  In conclusion, Access Web apps are a powerful new tool to deploy Access database applications across the Internet. By marrying the fast, easy application developments of Microsoft Access with the power, speed, and ubiquity of SQL Server and the Internet, Access Web apps provide a fast way to deploy secure relational database applications across the Internet.

FIGURE P-15: Software required to develop and use an Access Web app

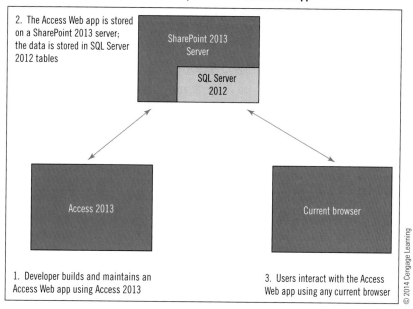

2. The Access Web app is stored on a SharePoint 2013 server; the data is stored in SQL Server 2012 tables

SharePoint 2013 Server

SQL Server 2012

Access 2013

Current browser

1. Developer builds and maintains an Access Web app using Access 2013

3. Users interact with the Access Web app using any current browser

© 2014 Cengage Learning

TABLE P-3: Software required to create, modify, and use an Access Web app

software	description
SharePoint 2013	An Access Web app is deployed to a file server loaded with SharePoint 2013. **SharePoint** is a Microsoft software product that is loaded on a file server to help a company organize and share files and data across its business. SharePoint 2013 can be purchased separately and is also included in the Microsoft Office 365 Small Business Premium and Office 365 Enterprise plans.
SQL Server 2012	**SQL Server** is a Microsoft software product used to store and manage a relational database. All Access Web apps use SQL Server 2012 to manage the data. No tables are created or managed by Access.
Access 2013	Access is required to make modifications to Access Web apps.
Web browser	A browser is required for users to view and enter data into an Access Web app.
Other	See the white paper article titled "Office 2013 - Access Services Setup for an On-Premises Installation" found at www.microsoft.com/en-us/download/details.aspx?id=30445 (or search for *Access Services Setup* on microsoft.com) for a full description of the software requirements for Access Web apps.

© 2014 Cengage Learning

TABLE P-4: Reference material for Access Web apps

type of resource	title	author	location
Article	How to: Create and Customize a Web App in Access 2013	Microsoft	http://msdn.microsoft.com/en-us/library/office/jj249372.aspx or search for this article by title on microsoft.com
YouTube, Article, and Blog	Get Started with Access 2013 Web Apps	Microsoft	http://blogs.office.com/b/microsoft-access/archive/2012/07/30/get-started-with-access-2013.aspx or search for this article by title on microsoft.com
YouTube, Article, and Blog	4 Ways to Create Business Apps with Access 2013	Microsoft	http://blogs.office.com/b/microsoft-access/archive/2012/08/20/4-ways-to-create-access-apps.aspx or search for this article by title on microsoft.com
Article	What's New for Access 2013 Developers	Microsoft	http://msdn.microsoft.com/en-us/library/office/jj250134.aspx or search for this article by title on microsoft.com
YouTube	Creating and Using an Access Web App	Lisa Friedrichsen	Search for this Lisa Friedrichsen video on YouTube
YouTube	Modify an Access Web App	Lisa Friedrichsen	Search for this Lisa Friedrichsen video on YouTube

© 2014 Cengage Learning

Create an Access Web App

Learning Outcomes
• Create an Access Web app

If you have access to a SharePoint 2013 server that is configured to support Access Web apps, you can quickly create an Access Web app using Access 2013. Setup issues require that you have a SharePoint 2013 server location (a Web address) where you will store the Access Web app, and a username and password that has already been given permission to save files on the SharePoint server. **CASE** ▶ *Kayla asks you to explore the possibility of using an Access Web app to allow employees to track customer comments, concerns, and issues. You explore how this would be started using Access 2013, and then read the rest of the process from the Microsoft Web site.*

STEPS

QUICK TIP
Notice that the icons for Access Web app templates display a globe.

1. **Start Access 2013, click the** Issue tracking database template, **then click OK if prompted with an error message about not being able to connect to a server**

   The Issue tracking Web app template information window opens, as shown in **FIGURE P-16**, to provide a quick preview of what types of tables the template will create (Issues, Customers, and Employees) and what the List View for the Issues table will look like. Note that SharePoint is required and that you can customize the Web app after it is created. You are also prompted for an App Name and Web Location.

TROUBLE
If you do not have access to a SharePoint 2013 server, close the Issue tracking window and continue to Step 5.

2. **Type** Customer Feedback **as the App Name, enter the** Web location of your SharePoint 2013 server **in the Web Location box, click** Create, **then enter** *your* **username and password when prompted**

   Access and SharePoint work together to create the Web app. Three tables—Issues, Customers, and Employees—are created automatically. Two **views** (called forms in a traditional desktop database) of each table, named **List** and **Datasheet**, are also automatically created to give you a fast way to quickly enter and edit data.

3. **Close Access 2013, open** Internet Explorer **or another browser, enter the** Web location **for your new Access Web app, then enter** *your* **username and** password **when prompted**

4. **Click the** Customers table **in the left panel, enter** *your* **name and fictitious but realistic data for the rest of the record, click the** Save button, **then click the** Datasheet button **to observe your new record in that view**

   At this point, you could continue to enter data into one of the three tables using either the List or Datasheet views created by the Issue tracking Web app template. To modify the interface (the views), however, you have to download the Web app and open it in Access 2013.

5. **Go to** http://msdn.microsoft.com/en-us/library/office/jj249372.aspx **or go to** www.microsoft.com **and search for** how to create a web app in Access 2013

6. **Read the Microsoft article about how to create and customize an Access Web app, as shown in** FIGURE P-17

7. **Close your browser, then close Access 2013**

FIGURE P-16: Issue tracking Web app template information window

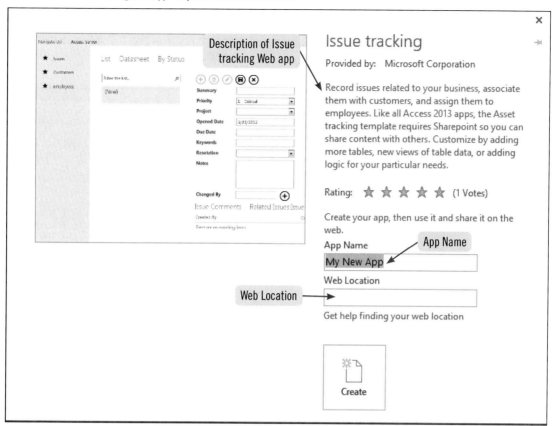

FIGURE P-17: How to: Create and Customize a Web App in Access 2013 article

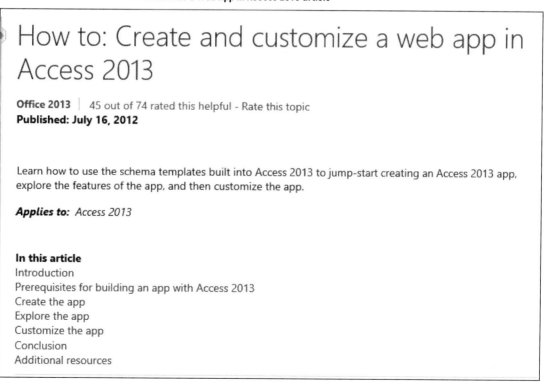

Practice

Concepts Review

Identify each element of Form Design View in FIGURE P-18.

FIGURE P-18

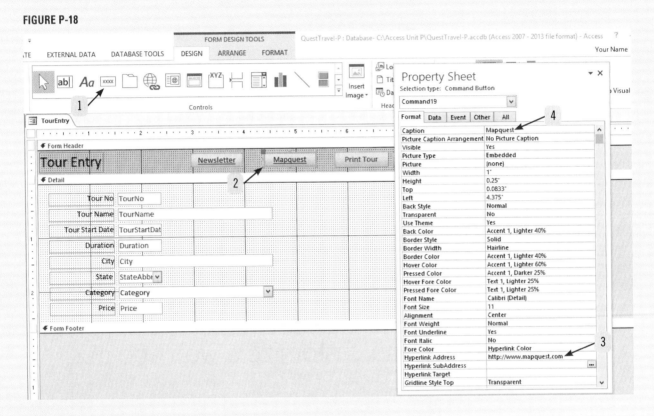

Match each term with the statement that best describes its function.

5. SQL Server
6. Hyperlink data type
7. Access Web app
8. HTML
9. XML
10. SkyDrive

a. The language used to describe content in a traditional Web page
b. A cloud-based storage and file-sharing service
c. Used to store a link to a Web page or file
d. A language used to mark up structured data
e. A Microsoft relational database management program
f. A special type of Access database that is stored on a SharePoint 2013 server

Select the best answer from the list of choices.

11. **If you wanted to create a field that stored email addresses, which data type would work best?**
    a. Short Text
    b. Long Text
    c. Hyperlink
    d. Memo

12. **Which of the following is *not* used to work with Access Web apps?**
    a. SharePoint Server 2013
    b. SQL Server 2012
    c. Access 2013
    d. All are used.

13. **Where is an Access Web app stored?**
    a. On a SharePoint server
    b. In the Data Files folder on your local hard drive
    c. In a SkyDrive folder
    d. In the Downloads folder on your local hard drive

14. **What is the purpose of an .accdw file?**
    a. To help you connect an Access Web app to your SkyDrive
    b. To allow you to modify the Access Web app in Access 2013
    c. To store Access Web app data in Access tables
    d. To sync your local hard drive to a shared SkyDrive

15. **Which HTML tags would you use to identify the start and end of a paragraph?**
    a. <p> </p>
    b.
    c.
    d. <start text> </end text>

16. **Which of the following form controls is *not* a common candidate for a hyperlink?**
    a. Combo box
    b. Label
    c. Command button
    d. Image

17. **What are forms called in an Access Web app?**
    a. Tables
    b. Reports
    c. Layouts
    d. Views

18. **Where is data stored in an Access Web app?**
    a. Access tables
    b. SQL Server tables
    c. SkyDrive folders
    d. XML files

19. **Which of the following is *not* a reason to use SkyDrive?**
    a. To access to your files from any computer connected to the Internet
    b. To share files with others
    c. To deploy an Access Web app
    d. To eliminate the problems associated with losing a flash drive

20. **HTML tags are also called:**
    a. Elements.
    b. Properties.
    c. Selectors.
    d. Attributes.

Skills Review

1. **Create a hyperlink field.**
   a. Start Access, open the Basketball-P.accdb database from the location where you store your Data Files, and enable content if prompted.
   b. Open the tblGames table and add two fields each with a Hyperlink data type, **SchoolWebSite** and **Logo**.
   c. Save the tblGames table and switch to Datasheet View. Enter a new record with *your* school name in the Opponent field and **Cavaliers** in the Mascot field. Enter the Web page address for *your* school's home page in the SchoolWebSite field. Browse for the file named **Cavalier.png** in the location where you store your Data Files, then insert it in the Logo field.
   d. Click both hyperlinks to test that they locate and display the desired resource. The SchoolWebSite hyperlink should open a browser that takes you to the home page for your school. The Cavalier.png hyperlink should display the Cavalier.png image.
   e. Close the tblGames table.

2. **Create a hyperlink control.**
   a. Open the frmPlayerInformation form in Form Design View, then open the Form Header section by dragging the top edge of the Detail section down about 0.5".
   b. Add a command button to the left side of the Form Header section, then cancel the Command Button Wizard.

Skills Review (continued)

   c. Open the Property Sheet for the new command button and make these property modifications:

      Caption: **NCAA**

      Hyperlink Address: **http://www.ncaa.org**

   d. Add a second command button to the right side of the Form Header section, then cancel the Command Button Wizard.

   e. In the Property Sheet for the new command button, make these property modifications:

      Caption: **Player Statistics**

      Hyperlink Address: Click the Build button, click Object in This Database on the left, expand the Reports section on the right, click rptPlayerStatistics, then click OK. (*Note:* You can also directly type **Report rptPlayerStatistics** in the Hyperlink SubAddress property.)

   f. Save the frmPlayerInformation form, test both of the new command buttons in Form View, close the NCAA Web page, close the rptPlayerStatistics report, then close the frmPlayerInformation form.

3. Use HTML tags to format text.

   a. Right-click the rptCodeOfConduct report, then click Print Preview to review the Player Code of Conduct. Although this is an unbound report (it does not display data from the database and the Record Source property is blank), you want to keep the information in the Basketball-P database.

   b. Switch to Report Design View, select the text box that contains the code of conduct text, then change the Text Format property to **Rich Text**.

   c. Use HTML tags to format the report as follows:

- Increase the size of the Player Code of Conduct title with the font tag: **<font size=8>**Player Code of Conduct**</font>**
- Increase the size of four introductory phrases with the font tags:
  - **<font size=6>** As a college player, I recognize that: **</font>**
  - **<font size=6>** I therefore pledge that: **</font>**
  - **<font size=6>** I understand that: **</font>**
  - **<font size=6>** The consequences for any such behavior could be: **</font>**
- Add two line breaks to create spaces between the lines with two line break tags at the end of every line: **

**
  - Format Player Name in red, bold text with the font tags: **<font color=red>**Player Name**</font>**

   d. Save and preview the rptCodeOfConduct report, as shown in **FIGURE P-19**.

   e. Close the rptCodeOfConduct report.

4. Export to HTML and XML.

   a. Select the tblPlayers table in the Navigation Pane, then export it to an HTML document named **Players.html** in the location where you store your Data Files.

   b. Select the qryFieldGoalStats query, then export it to an XML document named **FieldGoals.xml** in the location where you store your Data Files. Export both the XML and XSD files.

5. Import from HTML and XML.

   a. Import the NextSeason.html file into the database. The first row does not contain column headings.

   b. In the Import HTML Wizard, use the Field Name box in the Field Options area to rename Field1 through Field4: **Opponent**, **Mascot**, **HomeOrAway**, and **GameDate**. Let Access add the primary key, then import the data to a new table named **tblNextSeason**.

   c. Import the NewPlayers.xml file into the database.

   d. After Access imports the data into a table named tblPlayers1, rename the tblPlayers1 table to **tblNewPlayers**.

FIGURE P-19

rptCodeOfConduct

Player Code of Conduct

As a college player, I recognize that:

- It is my obligation to conduct myself in a manner that brings honor and distinction to my sport, my team, my school, my community, myself, and my family.

I therefore pledge that:

- I will strive to be a model citizen, and so help create goodwill and a positive perception of my team, my school, and my community.

I understand that:

- The coaches have no tolerance for behavior that casts my team, my sport, or my community in a negative way.

The consequences for any such behavior could be:

- Release from the team
- Notification to parents

Player Name _____

Player Signature: _____

Skills Review (continued)

6. **Save and share a database with SkyDrive.**

   a. Save the Basketball-P.accdb database to your SkyDrive using the Save As option on the FILE tab, or going directly to the SkyDrive through a browser (see Step b).

   b. Open Internet Explorer or another browser, then go to **www.skydrive.com**.

   c. Create a new folder named **UnitP** on your SkyDrive, then upload the Basketball-P.accdb database to the Basketball folder.

   d. Share the UnitP folder with your instructor using your instructor's email address. Type **Unit P Exercises** for the message.

   e. Close the browser, close the Basketball-P.accdb database, then exit Access 2013.

7. **Understand Access Web apps.**

   a. Start Word 2013 and open the Unit P Skills Review Question 7.docx document from the location where you store your Data Files.

   b. Complete the header information to identify your name, the current date, the class, and the instructor's name.

   c. Respond to the following three instructions in the document using complete sentences, proper grammar, and spelling.

      1. Briefly describe the difference between the purpose for an Access Web app and an Access traditional desktop database.

      2. Briefly describe the different software requirements for an Access Web app and an Access traditional desktop database.

      3. Why do you think Microsoft uses the word desktop to describe traditional Access databases?

   d. Save the document, close it, then close Word 2013.

8. **Create an Access Web app.**

   a. Start Access 2013 and click the Contacts Access Web App template. (*Note*: If you do not have access to a SharePoint server, watch a video that demonstrates Step 8 by going to www.youtube.com or www.microsoft.com and searching for a video that shows how to create an Access Web app.)

   b. Enter **Alumni Contacts** as the App Name, enter your SharePoint server Web location, then click Create.

   c. Enter *your* username and password as prompted.

   d. Click the Contacts table icon on the left, click the Navigation Pane button, then double-click the Contacts table.

   e. Add a field named **Pledge** with a Currency data type to the end of the field list, then save and close the table.

   f. Click the Launch App button to view the Access Web app in your browser. Enter *your* information in the First Name, Last Name, and Email fields. Enter realistic but fictitious information in the other fields. Enter **5000** in the Pledge field, then click the Save button.

   g. Close the browser, then close Access 2013.

Independent Challenge 1

As the manager of a doctor's clinic, you have created an Access database called Patients-P.accdb to track patient visits. You need to create two hyperlink fields to reference the patient's employer and insurance company. You also want to add some hyperlink command buttons to a form to link the form to medical reference guides on the Web.

   a. Start Access 2013, then open the Patients-P.accdb database from the location where you store your Data Files. Enable content if prompted.

   b. Open the tblPatients table in Design View. Add the following two new fields at the bottom of the list, each with the Hyperlink data type: **Employer**, **Insurance**.

   c. Save the tblPatients table, then switch to Datasheet View. Enter **www.iastate.edu** for the Employer field in the first record for PatientSequence 20. Enter **www.welmark.com** for the Insurance field for PatientSequence 20.

   d. Enter *your* school's Web site address in the Employer field for the second record for PatientSequence 21. Research and enter the Web site address for a common health insurance company in your state in the Insurance field.

   e. Test all four hyperlinks to make sure they work correctly, close all browser windows to return to Access, then save and close the tblPatients table.

Independent Challenge 1 (continued)

f. Open frmClaimEntryForm in Design View, then add a command button to the upper-right corner of the Form Header. The Hyperlink Address property for the button should match the value of the Web Page address value in the Insurance field for the first record you previously entered in the tblPatients table. Be sure to include http:// as the first part of the Hyperlink Address property for the button. The Caption property should be **Welmark**.

g. Add a second command button to the upper-right corner of the Form Header section. The Hyperlink Address property for the button should match the value of the Web Page address value in the Insurance field for the second record you previously entered in the tblPatients table. The Caption property should refer to the name of the company that the Web address references. Be sure to include http:// as the first part of the Hyperlink Address property for the button. **FIGURE P-20** shows how the command buttons look for the Welmark and Blue KC insurance companies. The Caption for your second command button will vary based on the insurance company you chose in Step d.

h. Save frmClaimEntryForm, then test both of your new hyperlink command buttons.

i. Close all browser windows and return to Access, close the Patients-P database, then close Access 2013.

FIGURE P-20

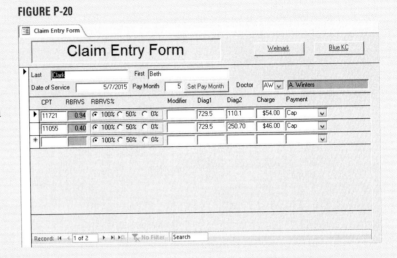

Independent Challenge 2

As the manager of a doctor's clinic, you have created an Access database called Patients-P.accdb. You are in the process of expanding the database to include information about employees. One of the first documents a new employee must read and sign is the Employee Pledge, which you have partially completed and stored as an Access report. Your employer wants you to format certain words with red and bold text. You use a Rich Text format and HTML tags to format the pledge.

a. Open the Patients-P.accdb database from the location where you store your Data Files, then enable content if prompted.

b. In the Navigation Pane, double-click the rptPledge report to open it in Report View. Open the rptPledge report in Report Design View, select the large text box in the Detail section, open the Property Sheet, then change the Text Format property on the Data tab to **Rich Text**.

c. Use HTML tags as follows to format and space the following phrases with red, bold text and line breaks:

To the best of my ability, I pledge to:**\
\
**

arrive and begin work **\<font color=red>**on time**\</font>\
\
**

focus on my work and the **\<font color=red>**patients**\</font>** while on the job**\
\
**

maintain a **\<font color=red>**positive attitude**\</font>\
\
**

continue to **\<font color=red>**learn and improve**\</font>\
\
**

be **\<font color=red>**honest and trustworthy **\</font>\
\
**

treat everyone with **\<font color=red>**respect

**\</font>\
\
**

limit all personal communication to a minimum while on the job**\
\
**

follow the law and regulations**\
\
**

**** not complain about the job I agreed to take

**\\
\
**

Signature: _____ **\
\
**

Independent Challenge 2 (continued)

d. Save and preview the rptPledge report, as shown in **FIGURE P-21**. Switch between Report Design View and Print Preview as needed to perfect the report.

e. Close the rptPledge report, close the Patients-P database, then close Access 2013.

Independent Challenge 3

In this exercise, you will create a SkyDrive folder and share all of the databases you used to complete the end-of-unit exercises for Unit P with your instructor.

a. Open File Explorer, then open the folder that contains your completed Data Files to review them.

b. Open a browser window, then open your SkyDrive folder by going to **www.skydrive.com**.

c. If you completed all steps of the Skills Review, you have already created a SkyDrive folder named UnitP and shared it with your instructor. If that is the case, add the Patients-P.accdb database to the shared UnitP folder.

d. If you have not completed all of the steps of the Skills Review, complete Skills Review Step 6 to create the shared SkyDrive UnitP folder with the Basketball-P.accdb database. After you have completed Independent Challenges 1 and 2, add the Patients-P.accdb database to the shared UnitP folder.

e. After you have completed Independent Challenge 4, add the Web Based Benefits document to the shared UnitP folder.

f. After you have completed the Visual Workshop, add the MusicStore-P.accdb file to the shared UnitP folder.

g. Close File Explorer and the browser window that displays your SkyDrive.

FIGURE P-21

rptPledge

Employee Pledge

To the best of my ability, I pledge to:

· arrive and begin work on time

· focus on my work and the patients while on the job

· maintain a positive attitude

· continue to learn and improve

· be honest and trustworthy

· treat everyone with respect

· limit all personal communication to a minimum while on the job

· follow the law and regulations

· **not complain about the job I agreed to take**

Signature:_____

Date:_____

Independent Challenge 4: Explore

Developing software solutions in a proprietary technology such as Microsoft Access is a simpler, faster solution for the developer because he or she only has to work with one software product for both developing and using the application Access. As soon as an application is deployed to the Internet, the work becomes more difficult because multiple software products are typically involved. To create and deploy an Access Web app, for example, the developer needs Access 2013, SharePoint 2013, SQL Server 2012, and a Web browser. However, there are also many benefits to making your application Web accessible. In this exercise, you'll research the Web to document five benefits of Web-based applications.

a. Using a browser and your favorite search engine, search for **benefits of Web-based applications**.

b. In a Word document, create a table with *your* name and the current date on the first line. Below your name, create a table with three columns and six rows. Enter these column headings in the first row: **Benefit**, **Description**, **Source**.

c. Complete the table with five more rows that identify and describe five benefits of a Web-based application over a traditional desktop Access database application. In the first column, identify the benefit. In the second column, briefly describe the benefit using one to two sentences. In the third column, copy and paste the Web address of the source you are citing for that benefit. The five benefits should reference at least three different sources.

d. Save your document with the name **Web Based Benefits** to the location where you save your Data Files, and then close Word.

Visual Workshop

As the manager of a music store, you have created an Access database called MusicStore-P.accdb, which tracks musical instrument rentals to schoolchildren. You need to provide parents a list of current rentals posted as a Web page, a portion of which is shown in FIGURE P-22. To create this page, create a query using all four tables in the database to select the fields in the order shown in the Web page. Note that the records are sorted by SchoolName and then by LastName. Save the query with the name **CurrentRentals**. Export the CurrentRentals query with the name **CurrentRentals.html** to the location where you store your Data Files. Do not select the Export data with formatting and layout check box. Open the CurrentRentals.html file in a browser to make sure that the export was successful.

FIGURE P-22

CurrentRentals			
Blackbob School Elementary	Eagan	7714	Clarinet
Blackbob School Elementary	Eagan	55442	Viola
Blackbob School Elementary	Eagan	7715	Clarinet
Blackbob School Elementary	Eagan	90	Bass
Blackbob School Elementary	Jupiter	89	Bass
Blackbob School Elementary	Jupiter	12999	Trumpet
Blackbob School Elementary	Shering	12997	Trumpet
Blackbob School Elementary	Shering	1234570	Cello
Blue Eye Elementary	Andrews	9988776	Violin
Blue Eye Elementary	Scott	12998	Trumpet
Blue Eye Elementary	Scott	55443	Viola
Blue Eye Elementary	Thompson	1234569	Cello
Blue Eye Elementary	Thompson	1234567	Cello
Blue Eye Elementary	Thompson	888335	Saxophone
Naish Middle School	Douglas	888334	Saxophone
Naish Middle School	Douglas	9988775	Violin
Naish Middle School	Friend	7713	Clarinet

Glossary

.accdb The file extension that usually means the database is an Access 2007 format database.

.accdw The file extension for an Access Web App file.

Access Web App A special type of Access database that is stored on a SharePoint 2013 server and allows users to enter and edit data using a common browser.

Action Each task that you want a macro to perform.

Action block In Macro Design View, the area of the window that organizes all of the arguments for a current action.

Action query A query that changes all of the selected records when it is run. Access provides four types of action queries: Delete, Update, Append, and Make Table.

Add-in An extra program, such as Solver and the Analysis ToolPak, that provides optional Excel features. To activate an add-in, click the File tab, click Options, click Add-Ins, then select or deselect add-ins from the list.

Add-in Software that works with Access to add or enhance functionality.

Adobe Reader software A software program provided free of charge by Adobe Systems for reading PDF files.

After Update A property that specifies an action to perform after an object or control is updated.

Alias A property that renames a field list in Query Design View.

Allow Multiple Values property A field property that allows you to store multiple values in one field.

Allow Zero Length A field property that does not allow zero-length strings (""), which are intentional "nothing" entries, such as a blank Phone Number field for an employee who does not provide a home phone number.

Alternative text A text description of a picture or any non-text object that is read by a screen reader for people who are visually impaired.

Append To add records to an existing table.

Append Only A field property available for Memo or Long Text fields in Access 2007 databases. When enabled, the property allows users to add data to a Memo or Long Text field, but not change or remove existing data.

Append query An action query that adds selected records to an existing table, and works like an export feature because the records are copied from one location and a duplicate set is pasted within the target table.

Append To row When creating an Append query, a row that appears in the query design grid to show how the fields in the query match fields in the target table.

Application Part An object template that creates objects such as tables and forms.

Apply (a template) To open a document based on an Excel template.

Argument Information that a function uses to create the final answer. Multiple arguments in a function are separated by commas. All of the arguments for a function are surrounded by a single set of parentheses. For example, the Ilf function has three arguments: IIf(logical test, value if true, value if false). In a macro, an argument provides additional information on how to carry out an action. In VBA, a constant, variable, or expression passed to a procedure that the procedure needs in order to execute. *See also* Main procedure.

ASCII file A text file that contains data but no formatting; instead of being divided into columns, ASCII file data are separated, or delimited, by tabs or commas.

Attributes Styling characteristics such as bold, italic, and underlining that you can apply to change the way text and numbers look in a worksheet or chart. In XML, the components that provides information about the document's elements.

Auditing An Excel feature that helps track errors and check worksheet logic.

AutoComplete In the Visual Basic for Applications (VBA) programming language, a list of words that appears as you enter code; helps you automatically enter elements with the correct syntax.

AutoExec A special macro name that automatically executes when a database opens.

AutoKeys A macro designed to be assigned a key combination (such as [Shift][Ctrl][L]).

Back up (*verb*) To create a duplicate copy of a database that is stored in a secure location.

Back-end database Part of a split database that contains the table objects and is stored on a file server that all users can access.

Backsolving A problem-solving method in which you specify a solution and then find the input value that produces the answer you want; sometimes described as a what-if analysis in reverse. In Excel, the Goal Seek feature performs backsolving.

Backup A copy of the database.

Bang notation A format that separates the object type from an object name and from a control name by using [square brackets] and exclamation points (!).

Between...and Criteria that selects all records between the two dates, including the two dates. Between...and criteria work the same way as the >= and <= operators.

Bibliography A list of sources that you consulted or cited while creating a document.

Bookmark Text that identifies a location, such as the beginning of a paragraph or a selection of text in a document.

Border Style A form property that determines the appearance of the outside border of the form.

Breakpoint A VBA debugging tool that works like a bookmark to suspend execution of the procedure at that statement so you can examine what is happening.

Brown-out A power problem caused by a dip in power, often making the lights dim.

Bug In programming, an error that causes a procedure to run incorrectly.

Call statement A Visual Basic statement that retrieves a procedure that you want to run, using the syntax Call *procedurename*.

Caption (Access) A field property that determines the default field name at the top of the field column in datasheets as well as in labels on forms and reports.

Caption (Word) Text that is attached to a figure and provides a title or a brief explanation of the figure.

Caption property A property that specifies the text to display in place of the value of the Name property for an object, control, or field.

Cascade Delete Related Records A relationship option that means that if a record in the "one" side of a one-to-many relationship is deleted, all related records in the "many" table are also deleted.

Cascade Update Related Fields A relationship option that means that if a value in the primary key field (the field on the "one" side of a one-to-many relationship) is modified, all values in the foreign key field (the field on the "many" side of a one-to-many relationship) are automatically updated as well.

Cascading Style Sheets (CSS) A powerful, flexible, and productive way to define web page formatting and layout.

Case In VBA, a programming structure that executes one of several groups of statements depending on the value of an expression.

Category axis Horizontal axis of a chart, usually containing the names of data groups; in a 2-dimensional chart, also known as the x-axis.

CCur function A built-in Access function used to convert an expression to Currency.

Cell comments Notes you've written about a workbook that appear when you place the pointer over a cell.

Change history A worksheet containing a list of changes made to a shared workbook.

Changing cells In what-if analysis, cells that contain the values that change in order to produce multiple sets of results.

Character style A named set of character format settings that can be applied to text to format it all at once; you use a character style to apply format settings only to select text within a paragraph.

Chart A visual representation of numeric data that helps users see comparisons, patterns, and trends in data. Also called a graph.

Chart animation The movement of a chart element after the relevant worksheet data changes.

Chart elements Parts of a chart, such as its title or its legend, which you can add, remove, or modify.

Chart type A category of chart layouts that determines the presentation of data on the chart such as column, pie, and line.

Chart Wizard A wizard that guides you through the steps of creating a chart in Access.

Check Box content control A content control that inserts a check box. You click a Check Box content control to insert a symbol, such as an "X" or a check mark.

Child record A record contained in the "many" table in a one-to-many relationship.

Citation A parenthetical reference in the document text that gives credit to the source for a quotation or other information used in a document.

Class module An Access module that is contained and executed within specific forms and reports.

Client In client/server computing, the user's PC.

Client/server computing Two or more information systems cooperatively processing to solve a problem.

Closing tag In HTML, the tag used to mark the end of text to be identified or formatted, such as </b> for end bold.

cmd The common three-character prefix for command buttons.

Code *See* Program code.

Code window (Access) Contains the VBA for the project selected in the Project Explorer window.

Code window (Excel) In the Visual Basic Editor, the window that displays the selected module's procedures, written in the Visual Basic programming language.

Combination chart A chart that combines two or more chart types in a single chart.

Combo Box content control One of the two Drop-Down content controls. To use a Combo Box content control, you select an item from a list of choices or type in a new item.

Comma-separated values (CSV) A text file where fields are delimited, or separated, by commas.

Command Button Wizard A wizard that organizes 28 of the most common command button actions within six categories.

Command-line option A special series of characters added to the end of the path to the file (for example, C:\Quest.accdb /excl), and execute a special command when the file is opened.

Comment (Word) An embedded note or annotation that an author or a reviewer adds to a document; appears in a comment balloon, usually to the right of the document text.

Comment (Access) Text in a module that helps explain and document the code.

Comment line In VBA, a statement in the code that documents the code; it does not affect how the code runs.

Comments In a Visual Basic procedure, notes that explain the purpose of the macro or procedure; they are preceded by a single apostrophe and appear in green. *See also* Cell comments.

Compact and repair To reorganize the pieces of the database to eliminate wasted space on the disk storage device, which also helps prevent data integrity problems.

Compact Flash (CF) card A card about the size of a matchbook that you can plug into your computer to store data. Current compact flash cards store anywhere from 128MB to about 4GB of data.

Compatible The capability of different programs to work together and exchange data.

Compile time The period during which source code is translated to executable code.

Compile-time error In VBA, an error that occurs as a result of incorrectly constructed code and is detected as soon as you run your code or select the Compile option on the Debug menu.

Conditional expression An expression resulting in either a true or false answer that determines whether a macro action will execute. Conditional expressions are used in VBA If statements.

Constant In VBA, an value that doesn't change throughout the execution of the code.

Constraints Limitations or restrictions on input data in what-if analysis.

Control Box A form property that determines whether a control box (which provides access to menu commands that let you close or minimize a form, for example) are displayed in a form.

Control Name A property that specifies the name of a control on a form or report.

Convert To change the database file into one that can be opened in another version of Access.

Crop To trim away part of a graphic. The act of making a picture smaller by taking away parts of the top, bottom, and sides.

Cross-reference Text that electronically refers the reader to another part of the document; you click a cross-reference to move directly to a specific location in the document.

CSV *See* comma-separated values.

Currency A number format provided by the Format property that displays numbers with a currency symbol.

Custom chart type A specially formatted Excel chart.

Data area When creating a chart, the area in the Chart Wizard that determines what data the chart graphs.

Data label Descriptive text that appears above a data marker in a chart.

Data macro A type of macro that allows you to embed macro capabilities directly in a table to add, change, or delete data based on conditions you specify.

Data series A column or row in a datasheet. Also, the selected range in a worksheet that Excel converts into a chart.

Data source (Word) In mail merge, the file with the unique data for individual people or items; the data merged with a main document to produce multiple versions.

Data source (Excel) Worksheet data used to create a chart or a PivotTable.

Data table A range of cells that shows the resulting values when one or more input values are varied in a formula; when one input value is changed, the table is called a one-input data table, and when two input values are changed, it is called a two-input data table. In a chart, it is a grid containing the chart data.

Data validation A feature that allows you to specify what data is allowable (valid) for a range of cells.

Database An organized collection of related information. In Excel, a database is called a table.

Database administration The task of making a database faster, easier, more secure, and more reliable.

Database Documenter A feature on the DATABASE TOOLS tab that helps you create reports containing information about the database.

Database program An application, such as Microsoft Access, that lets you manage large amounts of data organized in tables.

Database table A set of data organized using columns and rows that is created in a database program.

Database template A tool that can be used to quickly create a new database based on a particular subject such as assets, contacts, events, or projects.

Date Picker content control A content control that provides you with a calendar you can use to select a specific date.

Debug To determine why a macro or program doesn't run correctly.

Declaration statement A type of VBA statement that precedes procedure statements and helps set rules for how the statements in the module are processed.

Declare In the Visual Basic programming language, to assign a type, such as numeric or text, to a variable.

Delete query An action query that deletes selected records from one or more tables.

Delete row When creating a Delete query, a row that appears in the query design grid to specify criteria for deleting records.

Delimited text file A text file that typically stores one record on each line, with the field values separated by a common character such as a comma, tab, or dash.

Delimiter (Access) A common character, such as a comma, tab, or dash.

Delimiter (Excel) A separator such as a space, comma, or semicolon between elements in imported data.

Dependent cell A cell, usually containing a formula, whose value changes depending on the values in the input cells. For example, a payment formula or function that depends on an input cell containing changing interest rates is a dependent cell.

Deprecate To retire the usage of some type of technology in the current standard. For example the font tag has been deprecated in the latest HTML standards.

Description A query property that allows you to better document the purpose or author of a query.

Desktop database A traditional Access database available to users who work with Access on their computers over a local area network. Desktop database templates are identified by the word *desktop* in the template name.

Destination file The file to which data is copied.

Destination program The program to which data is copied.

Dialog box In Access, a special form used to display information or prompt a user for a choice. In Windows, a window with controls that lets you tell Windows how you want to complete an application program's (app's) command.

Digital signature An electronic stamp attached to a document to authenticate the document.

Dim A VBA keyword that declares a variable.

DLookup A domain function that returns, or "looks up," a value from a specified table or query.

DoCmd A VBA object that supports many methods to run common Access commands such as closing windows, opening forms, previewing reports, navigating records, and setting the value of controls.

Document To make notes about basic worksheet assumptions, complex formulas, or questionable data. In a macro, to insert comments that explain the Visual Basic code.

Domain The recordset (table or query) that contains the field used in a domain function calculation.

Domain function A function used in an expression to calculate a value based on a field that is not included in the Record Source property for a form or report. Also called domain aggregate function.

Drop-Down Form Field control A content control that provides users with a list of choices. Two drop-down content controls are available: the Drop-Down List content control and the Combo Box content control.

Drop-Down List content control One of the two Drop-Down content controls. To use a Drop-Down List content control, you select an item from a list of choices.

Dynaset A property value for the Recordset Type query property that allows updates to data in a recordset.

E

dit Link A link to a workbook on a SkyDrive that can be edited by users.

Edit mode When working with Access records, the mode in which Access assumes you are trying to edit a particular field, so keystrokes such as [Ctrl][End], [Ctrl][Home], [←], and [→] move the insertion point within the field. When working with charts, a mode that lets you select and modify individual chart elements such as the title, legend, bars, or axes.

Element An XML component that defines the document content.

Else The part of an If statement that allows you to run a different set of actions if the conditional expression evaluates False.

ElseIf In VBA, a keyword that executes a statement depending on the value of an expression.

Embed To insert a copy of data into a destination document; you can double-click the embedded object to modify it using the tools of the source program.

Embedded chart A chart displayed as an object in a worksheet.

Embedded object An object contained in a source file and inserted into a destination file; an embedded object becomes part of the destination file and it is no longer linked to the source file.

Empty tag In HTML, a single, unpaired tag that ends with a forward slash, such as <br/> for line break.

Encrypted data Data protected by use of a password, which encodes it in a form that only authorized people with a password can decode.

Encryption To make the data in the database unreadable by tools other than opening the Access database itself, which is protected by a password.

End Function In VBA, a required statement to mark the end of the code that defines the new function.

End If In VBA, a statement needed to mark the end of the If block of code.

End Select When defining a new Select Case group of VBA statements, the End Select statement is required as the last statement to mark the end of the VBA code.

End Sub When defining a new sub in VBA, the End Sub statement is required as the last statement to mark the end of the VBA code that defines the sub.

Endnotes Text that provides additional information or acknowledges sources for text in a document and that appears at the end of a document.

Event A specific activity that happens in a database, such as the click of a command button or an entry in a field, that can be used to initiate the execution of a macro or VBA procedure.

Event handler A procedure that is triggered by an event. Also called an event procedure.

Exclusive mode A mode indicating that you are the only person who has the database open, and others cannot open the file during this time.

Export To copy Access information to another database, spreadsheet, or file format.

Expression Builder A dialog box that helps you evaluate and create expressions.

Extensible Markup Language (XML) A programming language used to mark up structured data so that the data can be more easily shared between different computer programs.

External hard drive A device that plugs into a computer using either a USB or FireWire port and stores anywhere from 20 to 200 GB of information.

External reference indicator In a macro name, and exclamation point (!) that indicates that a macro is outside the active workbook.

Field (Excel) In a table (an Excel database) or PivotTable, a column that describes a characteristic about records, such as first name or city. In a PivotTable, drag field names to PivotTable row, column, data, or report filter areas to explore data relationships.

field (Access) A code that serves as a placeholder for data that changes in a document, such as a page number.

Field property A property that helps define a field.

Figure Any object such as a chart, a picture, an equation, or an embedded object to which a caption can be added.

Find Duplications Query Wizard A wizard that guides you through the steps of creating a query that finds duplicate values in a field, which can help you find and correct data-entry errors.

Find Unmatched Query Wizard A wizard that guides you through the steps of creating a query that finds records in one table that do not have matching records in a related table.

First normal form (1NF) The first degree of normalization, in which a table has rows and columns with no repeating groups.

Footnotes Text that provides additional information or acknowledges sources for text in a document and that appears at the bottom of the page on which the note reference mark appears.

form A structured document with spaces reserved for entering information.

Form control (Excel) An object that can be added to a worksheet to help users enter data. An example is a list box form control.

Form control (Word) A field into which users type information.

Form template A file that contains the structure of a form. You create new forms from a form template. Changes made to new forms based on a form template, such as changing labels, do not affect the structure of the form template file.

Format A property that provides ways to format text, dates, and numbers.

Front-end database Part of a split database that contains the database objects other than tables (queries, forms, reports, macros, and modules), and which links to the back-end database tables.

Function (Access) A special, predefined formula that provides a shortcut way to make a calculation. Sum, Count, and IIF are examples of built-in Access functions. You can create custom functions using VBA.

Function (Excel) A built-in formula that includes the information necessary to calculate an answer; for example, SUM (for calculating a sum) or FV (for calculating the future value of an investment) (Visual Basic) In the Visual Basic for Applications (VBA) programming language, a predefined procedure that returns a value, such as the InputBox function that prompts the user to enter information.

Get External Data – Excel Spreadsheet A dialog box used to import data from an external file into an Access database.

Gigabyte (GB or G) One billion bytes (or one thousand megabytes).

Goal cell In backsolving, a cell containing a formula in which you can substitute values to find a specific value, or goal.

Goal Seek A problem-solving method in which you specify a solution and then find the input value that produces the answer you want; sometimes described as a what-if analysis in reverse; also called backsolving.

Hidden A property you can apply to an object to hide the object in the Navigation Pane.

HTML 5 the latest version of HTML as defined by the leading international standards committee on fundamental Web technologies, the W3C, www.w3c.org.

Hyperlink Address property A control property that allows the control to behave like a hyperlink.

Hyperlink control A control on a form that when clicked, works like a hyperlink to redirect the user to a web page or file.

Hyperlink data type A data type for fields that store a link to a web page, file, or email address.

Hyperlink field A field with the Hyperlink data type.

Hyperlink pointer A mouse pointer that looks like a pointing hand when it is positioned over a hyperlink.

Hypertext Markup Language (HTML) The language used to describe content in a traditional web page.

If statement A statement in a macro that allows you to run macro actions based on the result of a conditional expression.

If...Then In VBA, a logical structure that executes code (the code that follows the Then statement) when the value of an expression is true (the expression follows the If statement).

If...Then...Else (Access) In VBA, a logical structure that allows you to test logical conditions and execute statements only if the conditions are true. If...Then...Else code can be composed of one or several statements, depending on how many conditions you want to test, how many possible answers you want to provide, and what you want the code to do based on the results of the tests.

If...Then...Else statement (Excel) In the Visual Basic programming language, a conditional statement that directs Excel to perform specified actions under certain conditions; its syntax is "If *condition* Then *statements* Else [*elsestatements*]."

Immediate window In the Visual Basic Editor, a pane where you can determine the value of any argument at the breakpoint.

Import Spreadsheet Wizard A wizard that guides you through the steps of importing data from Excel into an Access database.

Import To quickly convert data from an external file into an Access database. You can import data from one Access database to another—or from many other data sources such as files created by Excel, SharePoint, Outlook, or text files in an HTML, XML, or delimited text file format.

Index (Access) A field property that keeps track of the order of the values in the indexed field as data is being entered and edited. Therefore, if you often sort on a field, the Index property should be set to Yes as this theoretically speeds up the presentation of the sorted data later (because the index has already been created).

Index (Word) Text, usually appearing at the end of a document, that lists terms and topics in a document that you have marked for inclusion, along with the pages on which they appear.

Indexed property A field property used to improve database performance when a field is often used for sorting.

Inner join A type of relationship in which a query displays only records where joined fields from *both* tables are equal. This means that if a parent table has any records for which there are no matching records in the child table, those records do not appear in the resulting datasheet.

Input cells Spreadsheet cells that contain data instead of formulas and that act as input to a what-if analysis; input values often change to produce different results. Examples include interest rates, prices, or other data.

Input values In a data table, the variable values that are substi-tuted in the table's formula to obtain varying results, such as interest rates.

Integration A process in which data is exchanged among Excel and other Windows programs; can include pasting, importing, exporting, embedding, and linking.

IntelliSense technology In VBA, visual aids that appear as you write a VBA statement to help you complete it.

Is Not Null An operator you use to query for any value other than a null value.

Is Null An operator you use to query for null values.

Junction table The intermediate table used to join two other tables in a many-to-many relationship.

Keyword (Excel) Terms added to a workbook's Document Properties that help locate the file in a search. (Macros) In a macro procedure, a word that is recognized as part of the Visual Basic programming language.

Label (form) A word or phrase such as "Date" or "Location" that tells you the kind of information required for a given area in a form.

.laccdb The file extension for a temporary file that keeps track of record-locking information when a .accdb database is open. It helps coordinate the multiuser capabilities of an Access database so that several people can read and update the same database at the same time.

Layout The general arrangement in which a form displays the fields in the underlying recordset. Layout types include Columnar, Tabular, and Datasheet. Columnar is most popular for a form, and Datasheet is most popular for a subform. In Windows, an arrangement of files or folders in a window, such as Large icons or Details. There are eight layouts available.

.ldb The file extension for a temporary file that keeps track of record-locking information when a .mdb database is open. It helps coordinate the multiuser capabilities of an Access database so that several people can read and update the same database at the same time.

Left outer join A type of relationship in which a query displays all of the records in the "one" table, regardless of whether they have matching records in the "many" table. Also called a left join.

Legacy Tools controls Form controls used when the form designer requires more control over the type of content entered into the form than is available with content controls. Legacy Tools controls include Text form field controls and Check Box form field controls.

Linear trendline In an Excel chart, a straight line representing an overall trend in a data series.

Link (Access) To connect an Access database to data in an external file such as another Access database; an Excel or other type of spreadsheet; a text file; an HTML file; or an XML file. In Windows, text or an image that you click to display another location, such as a Help topic, a Web site, or a device.

Link (Excel) To insert an object into a destination program; the information you insert will be updated automatically when the data in the source document changes.

Link Spreadsheet Wizard A wizard that guides you through the steps of linking to a spreadsheet.

Linked object An object created in a source file and inserted into a destination file that maintains a connection between the two files; changes made to the data in the source file are reflected in the destination file.

Linked style A named set of format settings that are applied either to characters within a paragraph or to the entire paragraph, depending on whether the entire paragraph or specific text is selected.

List style A named set of format settings, such as indent and outline numbering, that you can apply to a list to format it all at once.

Local area network (LAN) A type of network installed to link multiple PCs together so they can share hardware and software resources.

Logic error In VBA, an error that occurs when the code runs without obvious problems, but the procedure still doesn't produce the desired result.

Long Date A date format provided by the Format property that displays dates in the following format: Friday, June 19, 2016.

Lookup table A table that contains one record for each field value and supplies the values for a foreign key field in another table.

Macro A named set of instructions, written in the Visual Basic programming language, that performs tasks automatically in a specified order.

Macro Series of Word commands and instructions grouped together as a single command to accomplish a task automatically.

Macro Design View An Access window in which you create and modify macros.

Mail merge A way to export Access data by merging it to a Word document. Data from an Access table or query is combined into a Word form letter, label, or envelope to create mass mailing documents.

Main document In a mail merge, the document used to determine how the letter and Access data are combined. This is the standard text that will be consistent for each letter created in the mail merge process.

Main procedure A macro procedure containing several macros that run sequentially.

Make Table query An action query that creates a new table of data for a selected datasheet. The location of the new table can be the current database or another Access database.

Manual calculation An option that turns off automatic calculation of worksheet formulas, allowing you to selectively determine if and when you want Excel to perform calculations.

Many-to-many relationship A relationship that exists when two tables are related to the same intermediate table with one-to-many relationships.

Map An XML schema that is attached to a workbook.

Map an XML element A process in which XML element names are placed on an Excel worksheet in specific locations.

.mdb The file extension for Access 2000 and 2002–2003 databases.

Medium Date A date format provided by the Format property that displays dates in the dd-Mmm-yy format, such as 19-Jun-16.

Megabyte (MB or M) One million bytes (or one thousand kilobytes).

Merge field A code in the main document of a mail merge that is replaced with the values in the field that the code represents when the mail merge is processed.

Message Box A macro action that displays an informational message to the user.

Method An action that an object can perform. Procedures are often written to invoke methods in response to user actions.

Microsoft Excel The spreadsheet program in the Microsoft Office suite.

Microsoft Word The word-processing program in the Microsoft Office suite.

Microsoft Word Mail Merge Wizard A wizard that guides you through the steps of preparing to merge Access data with a Word document.

Min Max Buttons A form property that determines whether Minimize and Maximize buttons are displayed in a form.

Mode In dialog boxes, a state that offers a limited set of possible choices.

Model A worksheet used to produce a what-if analysis that acts as the basis for multiple outcomes.

Modeless Describes dialog boxes that, when opened, allow you to select other elements on a chart or worksheet to change the dialog box options and format, or otherwise alter the selected elements.

Module In Visual Basic, a module is stored in a workbook and contains macro procedures.

Multicolumn report A report that repeats the same information in more than one column on the page.

Multifield primary key A primary key that is composed of two or more fields. For example, an OrderID value can be listed multiple times in the Order Details table, and a ProductID value can be listed multiple times in the Order Details table. But the combination of a particular OrderID value plus a ProductID value should be unique for each record.

Name property The property that determines that name of a control or object that is used when you want to work with that control or object in VBA.

Navigation Buttons A form property that determines whether a navigation bar is displayed in a form.

Navigation form A special Access form that provides an easy-to-use database interface to navigate between the objects of the database.

Navigation pane A pane showing the headings and subheadings as entries that you can click to move directly to a specific heading anywhere in a document. The Navigation pane opens along the left side of the document window.

Navigation system style In a navigation form, a style that determines how the navigation buttons will be displayed on the form.

Normal template The paragraph style that is used by default to format text typed in a blank Word document.

Normalize To structure data for a relational database.

Northwind.mdb A fully developed relational database in an Access 2000 file format that illustrates many advanced database techniques you can apply to your own development needs.

Note reference mark A mark (such as a letter or a number) that appears next to text to indicate that additional information is offered in a footnote or endnote.

Now() An Access function that displays today's date.

Null A field value that means that a value has not been entered for the field.

Object (Excel) A chart or graphic image that can be moved and resized and contains handles when selected. In object linking and embedding (OLE), the data to be exchanged between another document or program. In Visual Basic, every Excel element, including ranges.

Object (Access) A table, query, form, report, macro, or module in a database. In VBA, any item that can be identified or manipulated is an objective, including the traditional Access objects (table, query, form, report, macro, module) as well as other items that have properties such as controls, sections, and existing procedures.

Object (Word) Self-contained information that can be in the form of text, spreadsheet data, graphics, charts, tables, or sound and video clips.

Object dependency Indicates whether an object depends on the selected object or whether the selected object depends on other objects and displayed in the Object Dependencies task pane.

Object Linking and Embedding (OLE) A Microsoft Windows technology that allows you to transfer data from one document and program to another using embedding or linking.

Object list In a VBA class module, lists the objects associated with the current form or report.

Objective *See* Target cell

ODBC *See* open database connectivity

Office App Applications that can be added to a worksheet to help manage and personalize the data. Examples are maps, dictionaries, and calendars.

OLE *See* Object Linking and Embedding.

On Click A property of a control such as a command button that triggers an event when the control is clicked.

On Current An event that occurs when focus moves from one record to another in a form.

On Dbl Click An Access event that is triggered by a double-click.

On Error GoTo Upon an error in the execution of a procedure, the On Error GoTo statement specifies the location (the statement) where the procedure should continue.

On Got Focus An Access event that is triggered when a specified control gets the focus.

One-input data table A range of cells that shows resulting values when one input value in a formula is changed.

Open database connectivity (ODBC) A collection of standards that govern how Access connects to other sources of data.

Opening tag In HTML, the tag used to mark the beginning of text to be identified or formatted, such as <b> for start bold.

OpenReport action A macro action that opens a specified report.

Option Compare Database A VBA declaration statement that determines the way string values (text) will be sorted.

Option Explicit A VBA declaration statement that specifies that you must explicitly declare all variables used in all procedures; if you attempt to use an undeclared variable name, an error occurs at compile time.

Outline symbols In outline view, the buttons that, when clicked, change the amount of detail in the outlined worksheet.

Output values In a data table, the calculated results that appear in the body of the table.

Page border A graphical line or series of small graphics that encloses one or more pages of a document.

Paragraph style A named set of paragraph and character format settings that can be applied to a paragraph to format it all at once.

Parameter query A query that displays a dialog box to prompt users for field criteria. The entry in the dialog box determines which records appear on the final datasheet, similar to criteria entered directly in the query design grid.

Parent record A record contained in the "one" table in a one-to-many relationship.

Password A combination of uppercase and lowercase letters, numbers, and symbols that when entered correctly, allow you to open a database (Access) or a user account (Windows).

Percent A number format provided by the Format property that displays numbers with a percent symbol.

Performance Analyzer An Access tool that studies the structure and size of your database and makes a variety of recommendations on how you can improve its performance.

Personal macro workbook A workbook that can contain macros that are available to any open workbook. By default, the personal macro workbook is hidden.

Picture A form and report property that determines which image is displayed in the form or report (if any).

Picture content control A content control used in forms that provides a placeholder for a picture; you can insert a picture in a Picture content control in a form.

PivotChart report An Excel feature that lets you summarize worksheet data in the form of a chart in which you can rearrange, or "pivot," parts of the chart structure to explore new data relationships.

PivotTable Interactive table format that lets you summarize worksheet data.

PivotTable Field List A window containing fields that can be used to create or modify a PivotTable.

PivotTable Report An Excel feature that allows you to summarize worksheet data in the form of a table in which you can rearrange, or "pivot," parts of the table structure to explore new data relationships; also called a PivotTable.

Plain Text content control A form control used when you do not need formatting applied to text when users complete a form and enter text in the form control. You can also specify that a style be applied to text entered in a Plain Text content control when form users enter text in the form.

Plot area In a chart, the area inside the horizontal and vertical axes.

Plot The Excel process that converts numerical information into data points on a chart.

Populate The process of importing an XML file and filling the mapped elements on the worksheet with data from the XML file. Also the process of adding data or fields to a table, PivotTable, or a worksheet.

Portable Document Format (PDF) A file format developed by Adobe Systems that has become the standard format for exchanging documents.

Presentation graphics program A program such as Microsoft PowerPoint that you can use to create slide show presentations.

Primary key The field in a database that contains unique information for each record.

Private Sub A statement that indicates that a sub procedure is accessible only to other procedures in the module where it is declared.

Procedure (Access) A series of VBA statements that performs an operation or calculates an answer. VBA has two types of procedures: functions and subs.

Procedure (Excel) A sequence of Visual Basic statements contained in a macro that accomplishes a specific task.

Procedure footer In Visual Basic, the last line of a Sub procedure.

Procedure header The first line in a Visual Basic procedure, it defines the procedure type, name, and arguments.

Procedure list In a VBA standard module, lists the procedures in the module; in a class module, lists events (such as Click or Dblclick).

Program code Macro instructions, written in the Visual Basic for Applications (VBA) programming language.

Project (Access) In VBA, a module object or a form or report object that contains a class module.

Project (Excel) In the Visual Basic Editor, the equivalent of a workbook; a project contains Visual Basic modules.

Project Explorer In the Visual Basic Editor, a window that lists all open projects (or workbooks) and the worksheets and modules they contain.

Project Explorer window In the Visual Basic Editor, a window you use to switch between objects that can contain VBA code.

Properties window In the Visual Basic Editor, the window that displays a list of characteristics, or properties, associated with a module.

Property (Access) A characteristic that defines the appearance and behavior of items in the database such as objects, fields, sections, and controls. You can view the properties for an item by opening its Property Sheet. In a macro, an argument that determines what property is being modified.

Property (Excel) In Visual Basic, an attribute of an object that describes its character or behavior.

Range object In Visual Basic, an object that represents a cell or a range of cells.

Record Selectors A form property that determines whether record selectors are displayed in a form.

Recordset Type A property that determines if and how records displayed by a query are locked. The Recordset Type settings are Snapshot and Dynaset.

Refresh To update a PivotTable so it reflects changes to the underlying data.

Regression analysis A way of representing data with a mathematically-calculated trendline showing the overall trend represented by the data.

Repeating Section content control Permits users to add additional content controls such as additional table rows containing form controls or additional picture content controls.

Report filter A feature that allows you to specify the ranges you want summarized in a PivotTable.

Revisions pane Used to view comments.

Rich Text A Text Format property that allows you to mix formatting of text displayed by a text box on a form or a report.

Rich Text content control A form control used when you want the content entered in the Rich Text content control by a user to be formatted with specific font and paragraph formats. You can also specify that a style be applied to text when form users enter text in the Rich Text content control.

Rich Text Format (.rtf) A file type used when you want to limit the size of a document and share it with users who may not have access to Word.

Right outer join A type of relationship in which a query selects all records in the "many" table even if there are no matches in the "one" table. Also called a right join.

RTF *See* Rich Text Format.

Run To play, as a macro.

Run-time error In VBA, an error that occurs as incorrectly constructed code runs and includes attempting an illegal operation such as dividing by zero or moving focus to a control that doesn't exist. When you encounter a run-time error, VBA will stop executing your procedure at the statement in which the error occurred and highlight the line with a yellow background in the Visual Basic Editor.

Save Database As An Access command that saves an entire database including all of its objects to a completely new database file.

Save Object As An Access command that allows you to save the current object, such as a table, query, form, report, macro, or module with a new name.

Saved Exports An option provided in Access that lets you quickly repeat the export process by saving the export steps.

Saved Imports An option provided in Access that lets you quickly repeat the import process by saving the import steps.

Scenario A set of values you use to forecast results; the Excel Scenario Manager lets you store and manage different scenarios.

Scenario summary An Excel table that compiles data from various scenarios so that you can view the scenario results next to each other for easy comparison.

Schema In an XML document, a list of the fields, called elements or attributes, and their properties.

Screenshot Used to take a snapshot of another active window. The snapshot image is inserted in the current document as a graphic object that you can size and position.

Scroll Bars A form property that determines whether vertical, horizontal, or both scroll bars are displayed in a form.

Second normal form (2NF) The second degree of normalization, in which redundant data from an original table is extracted, placed in a new table, and related to the original table.

Secure digital (SD) card A small device that slips directly into a computer, and typically stores around 256 MB.

SELECT A SQL keyword that used to create select queries.

Select Case In VBA, executes one of several groups of Case statements depending on the value of an expression.

Select query A query that selects fields and records matching specific criteria and displays them in a datasheet.

Selection pane Shows the objects on the current page and their stacking order; the picture at the top of the Selection pane is the picture on top.

Server In client/server computing, the shared file server, mini, or mainframe computer. The server usually handles corporate-wide computing activities such as data storage and management, security, and connectivity to other networks.

SetProperty A macro action that allows you to manipulate the property value of any control on a form.

Share *See* Shared workbook.

Shared folder A folder created online, such as on SkyDrive, which you allow others to open and access.

Shared workbook An Excel workbook that several users can open and modify.

SharePoint server A server computer that runs Microsoft SharePoint, software that allows an organization to host Web pages on an intranet.

Short Date A date format provided by the Format property that displays dates in the mm/dd/yyyy format, such as 6/19/2016.

Single step To run a macro one line (one action) at a time to observe the effect of each specific action in the Macro Single Step dialog box.

SkyDrive A cloud-based storage and file-sharing service provided by Microsoft. Saving files to SkyDrive means that you can access those files from any computer connected to the Internet.

Slicer A graphic object used to filter a PivotTable.

SmartArt graphic A diagram, list, organizational chart, or other graphic created using the SmartArt command and used to provide a visual representation of data. Eight predesigned layout categories of SmartArt graphics are available: List, Picture, Process, Cycle, Hierarchy, Relationship, Matrix, and Pyramid.

Snapshot A property value for the Recordset Type query property that locks the recordset (which prevents it from being updated).

Source file The file in which data is originally created and saved.

Source program The program in which data is originally created.

Sparklines Miniature charts that show data trends in a worksheet range, such as increases or decreases.

Spike A surge in power, which can cause damage to the hardware.

Splash screen A special form used to announce information. A splash screen is often set to automatically appear when you open a database.

Split To separate the tables into one database and the other database objects into another.

SQL Server A Microsoft software product used to store and manage a relational database. All Access Web apps use SQL Server 2012 to manage the data.

Standard A number format provided by the Format property that displays numbers with no symbols or decimal places.

Standard module A type of Access module that contains global code that can be executed from anywhere in the database. Standard modules are displayed as module objects in the Navigation Pane.

Startup option One of a series of commands that execute when the database is opened.

Statement A single line of code within a VBA procedure.

Strong password A password that is difficult to guess and that helps to protect your workbooks from security threats; has at least 14 characters that are a mix of upper- and lowercase letters, numbers, and special characters.

Stub In the Visual Basic window, the first and last lines of an event handler procedure.

Style A named collection of character and paragraph formats that are stored together and can be applied to text to format it quickly.

Style Set A named set of format settings that can be applied to a document to format it all at once. The Style Set includes both font and paragraph settings.

Styles gallery Location where all the styles associated with a Style Set are stored; you access the Style Gallery by clicking the More button in the Styles group on the Home tab.

Styles task pane Contains all the styles available to the current document and the buttons to access the Style Inspector, the Reveal Formatting task pane, and the Manage Styles dialog box.

Sub (sub procedure) A procedure that performs a series of VBA statements, but it does not return a value and cannot be used in an expression like a function procedure. You use subs to manipulate controls and objects. They are generally executed when an event occurs, such as when a command button is clicked or a form is opened.

Select query A query that selects fields and records matching specific criteria and displays them in a datasheet.

Subentry Text included under a main entry in an index.

Submacro A collection of actions within a macro object that allows you to name and create multiple, separate macros within a single macro object.

Subquery A query based on another query's field list.

Summary function In a PivotTable, a function that determines the type of calculation applied to the PivotTable data, such as SUM or COUNT.

Surge protector A power strip with surge protection.

Switchboard A special Access form that provides command buttons to help users navigate throughout a database.

Syntax Rules that govern how to write programming statements so that they execute properly.

Syntax error In VBA, an error that occurs immediately as you are writing a VBA statement that cannot be read by the Visual Basic Editor. Syntax errors are displayed in a red text color.

Table layout A way of connecting controls together so that when you move or resize them in Layout or Design View, the action you take on one control applies to all the controls in the layout.

Table of figures A list of all the figures used in a document.

Table style A named set of table format settings that can be applied to a table to format it all at once. The Table style includes settings for both the table grid and the table text.

Tag In HTML, the codes used to identify or "mark up" the content in a web page. Also called an HTML element.

Target cell In what-if analysis (specifically, in Excel Solver), the cell containing the formula. Also called objective.

Target table The table to which an Append query adds records.

td An HTML table data tag that separates each field of data in a table.

Template (Excel) A file whose content or formatting serves as the basis for a new workbook; Excel template files have the file extension .xltx. the macro will run correctly.

Template (Word) A formatted document that contains placeholder text you can replace with new text. A file that contains the basic structure of a document including headers and footers, styles, and graphical elements.

Terabyte (TB) One trillion bytes (or one thousand gigabytes).

Text control A Legacy Tool used when the form developer requires more control over how the content control is configured than is possible when using a Rich Text content control or a Plain Text content control. A Text Form Field control is inserted using the Legacy Tools command in the Controls group on the developer tab.

Text file *See* ASCII file.

Text Form Field control A Legacy Tool used when the form developer requires more control over how the content control is configured than is possible when using a Rich Text content control or a Plain Text content control. A Text Form Field control is inserted using the Legacy Tools command in the Controls group on the Developer tab.

Third normal form (3NF) The third degree of normalization, in which calculated fields (also called derived fields) such as totals or taxes are removed. Strive to create databases that adhere to the rules of third normal form.

Toggle A button with two settings, on and off.

Top Values A feature in Query Design View that lets you specify a number or percentage of sorted records that you want to display in the query's datasheet.

tr An HTML table row tag that separates each record in a table.

Tracer arrows In Excel worksheet auditing, arrows that point from cells that might have caused an error to the active cell containing an error.

Track To identify and keep a record of who makes which changes to a workbook.

Trendline A series of data points on a line that shows data values that represent the general direction in a series of data.

Trusted database A database that allows you to run macros and VBA.

Trusted folder A folder specified as a trusted location for storing files.

Two-input data table A range of cells that shows resulting values when two input values in a formula are changed.

Update query An action query that updates the values in a field.

Update To row When creating an Update query, a row that appears in the query design grid to specify criteria or an expression for updating records.

UPS (Uninterruptible Power Supply) A device that provides constant power to other devices, including computers.

USB (Universal Serial Bus) drive A device that plugs into a computer's USB port to store data. USB drives are also called thumb drives, flash drives, and travel drives. USB devices typically store 1 GB to 10 GB of information.

Username The name that appears in the User name text box of the Excel Options dialog box. This name is displayed at the beginning of comments added to a worksheet.

Utility project A VBA project containing code that helps Access with certain activities such as presenting the Zoom dialog box. It automatically appears in the Project Explorer window when you use the Access features that use this code.

Validate A process in which an xml schema makes sure the xml data follows the rules outlined in the schema.

Validation *See* Data Validation.

Value argument In a macro, the argument that determines the value of a property or field.

Value axis In a chart, vertical axis that contains numerical values; in a 2-dimensional chart, also known as the y-axis.

Variable (Excel) In the Visual Basic programming language, an area in memory in which you can temporarily store an item of information; variables are often declared in Dim statements such as *DimNameAsString*. In an Excel scenario or what-if analysis, a changing input value, such as price or interest rate, that affects a calculated result.

Variable (Access) In VBA, a named location that stores data that can be used, modified, or displayed during the execution of the procedure.

VBA *See* Visual Basic for Applications.

VBE *See* Visual Basic Editor.

View In an Access Web App, the equivalent to a form in a traditional desktop database.

View Link A link to a workbook on a SkyDrive that can be viewed by users.

Virus Destructive software that can damage your computer files.

Visible property A property that determines whether a control such as a label is visible in a form or report.

Visual Basic for Applications (VBA) A programming language used to create macros in Excel.

Visual Basic Editor (VBE) Comprises the entire Microsoft Visual Basic program window that contains smaller windows, including the Code window and Project Explorer window. Lets you display and edit macro code.

Visual Basic for Applications (VBA) A programming language provided within each program of the Microsoft Office suite to help you extend the program's capabilities. In Access, VBA code is stored within modules.

Watermark (Access) A background picture applied to a form or report.

Watermark (Word) A picture or other type of graphics object that appears lightly shaded behind text in a document.

Web app An Access database published to a SharePoint server and which is available to users to interact with using a Web browser.

Web query An Excel feature that lets you obtain data from a Web, Internet, or intranet site and places it in an Excel workbook for analysis.

What-if analysis A decision-making tool in which data is changed and formulas are recalculated in order to predict various possible outcomes.

Word wrap A feature in word processing programs that determines when a line of text extends into the right margin of the page and automatically forces the text to the next line without you needing to press Enter.

WordArt Specially formatted text, created using the WordArt button on the Drawing toolbar.

Works cited A list of sources that you cited while creating a document.

World Wide Web Consortium (W3C) The leading international standards committee on fundamental Web technologies.

Write access The ability to make changes to a workbook; with read access, a user can only read the workbook contents and cannot make changes.

XE (index entry) Field code inserted next to text marked for inclusion in an index.

XML Short for Extensible Markup Language, a language used to mark up structured data so that the data can be more easily shared between different computer programs.

XML file A text file containing XML tags that identify field names and data. *See also* Extensible Markup Language (XML).

XPS file A structured XML file that can be exchanged and read with Word, similar to a PDF file.

XSD A file that stores the schema of data stored in an XML file.

XSL A file that describes how to display the data in an XML file.

Zero-length string A deliberate entry that contains no characters. You enter a zero-length string by typing two quotation marks ("") with no space between them.

Index

S